Pacific Basin Industries in Distress

The Pacific Basin Studies Program
Studies of the East Asian Institute, Columbia University

PACIFIC BASIN INDUSTRIES IN DISTRESS

Structural Adjustment and Trade Policy in
the Nine Industrialized Economies

Edited by
HUGH PATRICK

With
LARRY MEISSNER

Columbia University Press   New York

Columbia University Press
New York   Oxford

Library of Congress Cataloging-in-Publication Data
Pacific Basin industries in distress : structural adjustment and trade
   policy in the nine industrialized economies / edited by Hugh Patrick:
   with Larry Meissner.
        p.   cm. — (Studies of the East Asian Institute)
   Includes bibliographical references.
   ISBN 0-231-07570-7
      1. Pacific Area—Industries—Case studies—Congresses.   2. Pacific
   Area—Foreign economic relations—Case studies—Congresses.
   3. Pacific Area—Economic policy—Case studies—Congresses.
   I. Patrick, Hugh T.   II. Meissner, Larry.   III. Series.
   HC681.P2829   1991
   338.99—dc20   91-15740
                                                                     CIP

Printed in the United States of America

c 10 9 8 7 6 5 4 3 2 1
p 10 9 8 7 6 5 4 3 2 1

The Pacific Basin Studies Program
Columbia University

The Pacific Basin Studies Program is jointly administered by the East Asian Institute and the Center on Japanese Economy and Business. The East Asian Institute is Columbia University's central institution for research, publication, and teaching on modern East Asia. The Studies of the East Asian Institute were inaugurated in 1962 to bring to a wider public the results of significant new research on modern and contemporary East Asia.

A Study of the East Asian Institute

CONTENTS

Data series in the tables are indexed; bibliographies follow each chapter.

PREFACE

Pacific Basin Industries in Distress analyzes nine of the region's most important and dynamic economies for insights into how to deal with one consequence of economic growth: decline. Changes in comparative advantage mean changes in what countries an industry is most competitively based, and some industries face globally shrinking markets.

We believe this book will be of value to policy makers, specialists, and a generally informed audience alike. The country analyses are pursued in considerably more depth and at greater length than is usually the case. This study is also distinctive in explicitly linking trade policy and structural adjustment by distressed industries, as well as in its comparative focus on the Pacific Basin—the most dynamic economic region in the world.

In chapters on Canada, the United States, New Zealand, Australia, Singapore, Hong Kong, Taiwan, Korea, and Japan, each author provides case studies of distressed industries in his country, in the context of a macroeconomic overview, and also comments on government adjustment policy—past and prospective—and its impact on trade policy.

A great deal of structural adjustment has taken place in all nine countries, primarily through the market. But solely market-determined outcomes are simply not politically acceptable in all cases: every government, except Hong Kong's, has intervened to assist certain distressed industries. The issues have been ones of degree, type of policy instrument used, and who is helped. These issues are taken up for each country both in general discussion and in case studies of specific industries.

Thus, this book will be of particular use to those interested in studies of industrial structure and its relationship to trade policy, and to those interested in comparative analyses of the advanced and newly industrial Pacific Basin economies.

When I began planning this project in 1987, under the auspices of the Pacific Basin Studies Program at Columbia University, I rapidly realized the depth of knowledge required about each country was outside the capabilities of any single individual. Accordingly, our strategy was to assemble a team of research economists who could provide the necessary expertise. We worked together closely, devising a common framework and general outline for each country study, and meeting in two workshops (in July 1988 and January 1989) to consider drafts. At the same time, each author as an experienced scholar retained autonomy in determining the central thrust of his argument and in selecting the particular industry cases for his country. Much of 1989 was devoted to further refining the various chapters.

My greatest debt is thus to the colleagues who have authored these studies. They labored far beyond the call of duty. My second greatest debt is to my friend and colleague Larry Meissner, who as a perfectionist worked assiduously to enhance the substance, style, and lucidity of each of the chapters, especially my own. We have learned over the years to work well together; we each learn from our collaborative efforts, and I am happy to acknowledge how much this book owes to his efforts.

We all benefited immensely from constructive criticism and insights from fellow participants in our two workshop meetings: Professor Edward English (Carleton University, Ottawa), Dr. Sahathavan Meyanathan (Economic Development Institute, World Bank), Dr. Wisarn Pupphavesa (National Institute of Development Administration, Bangkok), and Professor Michael Young (Columbia University, New York) at both workshops; Professor Lawrence Krause (University of California, San Diego) at the first meeting, and Dr. William James (East-West Center, Honolulu) at the second.

In the organization and handling of this project, I was assisted by three Columbia PhD students in sequence: Robert Uriu, who worked with me from the beginning and ably served as rapporteur for the two workshops; Taka Suzuki, who took charge of the middle phase when Bob went off to Japan for dissertation research; and Anthony Iaquinto, who oversaw the final phase after Taka went to Japan for dissertation research. We all owe a special debt to Susan Thau, who typed and proofread the manuscript with energy, intelligence, and goodwill. Ann K. Fuller read the evolving manuscript as a representative of the "informed citizen" segment of the audience for whom this book is intended. I appreciate the efforts of Kate Wittenberg and Leslie Bialler of Columbia University Press, who shepherded the manuscript through the publication process. Larry Meissner and I are especially indebted to Sheri Ranis, Associate Director of the Center on Japanese Economy and Business, who, with great care, competence, and timeliness, took care of the myriad of detail the publication process somehow entailed.

I acknowledge a special intellectual debt to Professor Barbara Ruch, my wife, whose broad vision, high scholarly and intellectual standards, and own hard work are both a guide and a gentle goad. I am fortunate to have such a role model.

Deep appreciation is also due the funders that have made possible this and related projects of Columbia University's Pacific Basin Studies Program: the Ford Foundation, the Luce Foundation, the Rockefeller Brothers Fund, Nissho-Iwai and Nissho-Iwai America Corporations, Toyota Motor Company, Tokyo Electric Power Company, Tokyo Gas Company, Kansai Electric Power Company, and Dengen Kaihatsu Corporation.

Hugh Patrick

CONTRIBUTORS

ALAN E. BOLLARD is Director of the New Zealand Institute of Economic Research, Wellington, a specialist in industrial economics, and serves as a lay member of the High Court of New Zealand. He has written widely on the program of economic liberalization and structural reform that New Zealand has undergone since the early 1980s, as well as on related topics. His books include *Small Businesses in New Zealand, Liberalisation of the New Zealand Economy, New Zealand / East Asian Economic Relations, The Economics of the New Zealand Commerce Act, Meeting the East Asian Challenge,* and *Turning It Around: Closure and Revitalization in New Zealand Industry.*

PETER M. CORNELL is a former Director of the Economic Council of Canada and is now an economic consultant. Following reception of an economics Ph.D. from Harvard University, he worked in various capacities at the Bank of Canada and the Economic Council of Canada for 30 years; a career which culminated in his appointment as Director of the Economic Council in 1981. He has made numerous public appearances in more recent years throughout Canada and the United States, speaking on topics in economic policy. Publications include an article in *The Canadian Business Review* (Spring 1978), entitled "Trade Liberalization: How Far? How Fast?"

PAUL K. GORECKI is a senior economist at the Economic Council of Canada, Ottawa, where he has helped prepare or direct three Council reports: on regulation; on trade, technology and income growth; and on adjustment policies for trade-sensitive industries. He is currently on secondment to Statistics Canada conducting research on the dynamics of the competitive process.

ROBERT G. GREGORY is chairman of the Economics and Politics Division, Research School of Social Sciences, Australia National University, Canberra, and a member of the Board of the Reserve Bank of Australia and of the Australian Science and Technology Council. He has written extensively, including an early development of the effects of a booming export sector on structural change (*Australian Journal of Agricultural Economics*, 1976 Aug) and on hysteresis on the Australian labor market (*Economica*, 1986 supl).

YIN-PING HO is a lecturer at the Department of Economics at the Chinese University of Hong Kong. He is the author of "Hong Kong's Trade and Industry: Changing Patterns and Prospects," in Joseph Y. S. Cheng, editor, *Hong Kong in Transition* (Oxford University Press, 1986) and co-author with Tzong-biau Lin and Victor Mok of *Manufactured Exports and Employment in Hong Kong* (Chinese University Press, 1980).

GARY C. HUFBAUER is Marcus Wallenberg Professor at the School of Foreign Service, Georgetown University, and a Visiting Fellow at the Institute for International Economics, both in Washington DC. His recent works include (as editor) *Europe 1992: An American Perspective* (The Brookings Institution, 1990).

JI-HONG KIM is an economist fellow at at the Korea Development Institute, Seoul. A University of California PhD, with Masters degrees from Harvard and Seoul National University, he has taught at Berkeley, Korea University, and Soogang University. His areas of ongoing research include trade policy, the effect of industry structure on trade and social welfare, and industrial policy's impact on technological innovation.

TZONG-BIAU LIN is Chair Professor of the Department of Economics at the Chinese University of Hong Kong. His publications include (with Victor Mok) "Trade, Foreign Investment, and Development in Hong Kong," in Walter Galenson, editor, *Foreign Trade and Investment: Economic Development in the Newly Industrializing Countries* (University of Wisconsin Press, 1985); "Trade Structure and Economic Growth in Hong Kong," in M. H. Hsing and A. King, editors, *The Development Experience of Hong Kong* (Chinese University Press, 1985); and, also with Victor Mok, *Trade Barriers and the Promotion of Hong Kong Exports* (Chinese University Press, 1980).

LARRY MEISSNER is an economist and portfolio manager. He has participated in a number of other studies of Pacific Basin economies. The resulting publications include (with Hugh Patrick as principal editor)

Japanese Industrialization and its Social Consequences (University of California Press, 1976) and *Japan's High Technology Industries* (University of Washington Press, 1986), as well as (with Kazushi Ohkawa and Gustav Ranis as principal editors) *Japan and the Developing Countries* (Basil Blackwell, 1985).

PANG ENG FONG is associate professor, Department of Business Policy, National University of Singapore (NUS). Previous appointments include visiting professor at the University of Michigan and director of NUS' Economic Research Centre. Recent publications include (with Linda Y C Lim) *Industrial Restructuring and Foreign Investment in Malaysia, Singapore, Taiwan and Thailand* (OECD Development Centre, 1990) and (as editor) *Labour Market Developments and Structural Change: the Experience of ASEAN and Australia* (Singapore University Press, 1988).

HUGH PATRICK is R. D. Calkins Professor of International Business, Director of the Center on Japanese Economy and Business, and Co-director of the Pacific Basin Studies Program at Columbia University's Graduate School of Business, New York. He has served widely in an advisory capacity to government and business and in professional organizations, including as chairman of the International Steering Committee of the Pacific Trade and Development conference series. Among his many publications are (as editor, with Henry Rosovsky) *Asia's New Giant: How the Japanese Economy Works* (The Brookings Institution, 1976).

SUEO SEKIGUCHI is professor of economics at Seikei University, Tokyo. His publications in English include (as editor) *ASEAN-Japan Relations: Investment* (ISEAS Singapore 1983) and, with Lawrence B. Krause, *Economic Interaction in the Pacific Basin* (The Brookings Institution, 1980). He also authored with Toshihiro Horiuchi a chapter on trade and adjustment assistance in Ryutaro Komiya et al editors, *Industrial Policy of Japan* (Academic Press, 1984).

RONG-I WU is professor of economics at National Chung Hsing University, Taipei, where he previously served as director of the Institute of Economics. He is a consultant to several government agencies and a part-time senior research fellow at the Taiwan Institute of Economic Research. He has published some 60 books and papers, including *The Strategy of Economic Development: a Case Study of Taiwan*, the *Impact of US Investment on the Taiwan Economy*, and *Economic Infrastructure in Taiwan*.

Pacific Basin Industries in Distress

CONCEPTS, ISSUES, AND SELECTED FINDINGS

Hugh Patrick

Profound change in industrial structure is inherent in economic growth and development. This means while some industries grow, others find themselves in distress. Technological innovation, demand shifts, and changes in the availability of capital, labor, and raw materials bring about losses in cost competitiveness, either for some sustained period or permanently, as comparative advantage changes to disadvantage. How industries and governments handle problems related to the distress resulting from structural adjustment, and the implications of this for trade policy, are the central concerns of these essays.

The spread of industrialization from the economically advanced countries to the newly industrialized economies (NIEs) has generated in its wake severe problems as specific industries have become distressed not just in high-income countries, but increasingly in NIEs as well. Ultimately, adjustment is a micro phenomenon of individual firms and workers; it goes on all the time. But where major industries are involved, the problems have significant policy implications. How adjustment is handled, how inefficiencies are dealt with, and how resources are reallocated are important domestic economic and political concerns in every country. Moreover, they have equally important implications for the relationships of these countries with each other, in trade flows and

The author is indebted to the colleagues, anonymous referees, and especially Robert Uriu, who provided comments on an earlier draft of this chapter.

particularly in the rules and practices of the international trading system itself.

Virtually all industrially advanced countries used import restrictions in the 1980s to help distressed industries (OECD 1987). Indeed, one of the issues in the Tokyo and Uruguay Rounds of GATT negotiations was whether and how to apply safeguards when an industry is in distress. GATT Article 19 provides a mechanism for a finite time period when a domestic industry can prove serious injury from imports, but it requires compensation to trading partners who have made reciprocal concessions under GATT; thus it has not been used extensively (Kelly et al 1988, p 36). In the absence of effective multilateral rules, each of the countries studied here has in effect developed its own approaches and procedures.

In the following sections I discuss the concepts of declining and troubled industries, the importance of the macroeconomic environment for the adjustment process, and some of the specifics of why and how governments intervene. Because of their importance to trade and development, textiles, apparel, and automobiles are dealt with by many of the authors, and I discuss these industries. From this, and the rich findings in each chapter, I draw some general comparative conclusions. In the final section, I speculate on the implications for structural adjustment policies and practices and for the international trading system in the 1990s.

The Pacific Basin, led by Japan and the four newly industrialized economies (NIEs), is the most rapidly growing region in the world. Ranging from the world's two largest economies through the medium-sized to the region's two city-states, the region's five advanced nations—Canada, the United States, New Zealand, Australia, Japan—and the NIEs—the so-called four tigers of Singapore, Hong Kong, Taiwan, Korea—are our focus, with a chapter for each. These nine economies, plus China and the South East Asian developing nations, engage in about the same share of world trade as the European Community (some 40% each); and their trade with each other, at 56% of their total trade, is greater than European Community members' trade with each other (about 50%). Table 1 provides basic data on the nine economies. [1]

While there are comparative studies of structural adjustment for specific industries, and for the OECD (predominantly Western European) advanced industrial countries, there is a paucity of comparative studies in a Pacific Basin regional context. Yet these nine economies well illus-

1. Following an International Monetary Fund convention (Kelly et al 1988, p 6 note 18) "country" is used to include territorial entities, such as Hong Kong and Taiwan, that pursue independent economic and trade policies, practices, and statistical reporting, as distinct from a "territorial entity that is a state as understood by international law and practice." In this book, country and economy are used interchangeably.

Table 1. A Comparison of the Countries Studied, 1987

(in millions)		*Manufacturing*		*Trade in Manufactures*			
		% of			*(in billion US$)*		*Country*
Popu-	*Labor*	*Labor*	*% of*	*% of*			*(in Chapter*
lation	*Force*	*Force*	*GDP*	*GDP*	*Exports*	*Imports*	*Sequence)*
26	13.4	14	19	36	57	78	Canada
248	121.6	16	20	12	198	328	United States
3	1.6	20	21	24	2	6	New Zealand
16	7.7	16	17	17	6	25	Australia
3	1.2	26	29	215	20	22	Singapore
6	2.6	35	22	185	45	40	Hong Kong
20	8.0	35	40	80	53	28	Taiwan
43	16.9	27	30	57	46	25	Korea
123	60.3	24	29	12	223	57	Japan

Population (1989 July estimates) and labor force data are from the respective country pages of the *World Factbook 1989* (US Central Intelligence Agency) except US and Japan labor force data are from their respective *1987/88 OECD Economic Surveys*, p 115 and p 19.

Manufacturing as a percentage of GDP is for 1987 as reported in the *World Development Report 1989*, p 169 table 3 (World Bank). GDP is at producer prices for Canada and Hong Kong, at purchaser values (market prices) for other countries.

Manufacturing trade as a percentage of GDP is computed by adding exports and imports (see source below) and dividing it by GDP (see source above). Hong Kong and Singapore do a tremendous amount of re-exporting, which accounts for the very large percentages.

Exports are FOB and imports are CIF, on a customs basis, 1987 estimates, as reported on the respective country pages of the *World Tables 1988–89* (World Bank).

Taiwan data are from the *Taiwan Statistical Data Book* 1989, except GDP is from (Taiwan) *National Income* 1988 (table 1).

trate the spectrum of adjustment mechanisms utilized in market economies. Also, Pacific Basin economic cooperation—a form of open regionalism with full commitment to the GATT-based multilateral system (Drysdale 1988)—exemplifies a more organic, less structured, and more outward-looking approach to economic integration than the European Community model.

The countries studied here represent a diversity of typologies beyond the standard (but decreasingly relevant) division between earlier developers and newly industrialized. This led to spirited discussion as to how to group the chapters. The result is a simple geographic clockwise progression from Canada around the Pacific Basin to Japan. Coincidentally, this grouped the four English-speaking advanced economies, and the four NIE tigers, and ends the book on the important case of Japan.

The focus is on manufacturing in the 1980s, in a somewhat longer historical context and with explicit speculation about future policy and its effectiveness, in keeping with the fact problems of structural adjustment are inherently long-run. Each chapter considers first the country's overall economic performance, then identifies those industries in distress, uses case studies of the mechanisms of adjustment to illuminate the respective role and importance of the market and various types of government policy, and examines the relationship between structural adjustment policies and trade policy.

The analysis is that of an industry, at some degree of disaggregation, though considerable regional and firm-level evidence is utilized where available and relevant. Agriculture is not treated: we deemed the problems of its structural adjustment and trade sufficiently different and complex to merit separate study. Defense industries are also excluded: they have their own national security rationale whether or not they are efficient. The industries treated explicitly in each country study are listed in Table 2.

Losses of competitiveness in specific industries across countries have been stressed. This is appropriate because most of the reductions in demand for an industry's products in a particular country are due to decreases in exports or increases in import competition. And most of the industry demands for government assistance are based on the threat of foreign competition. However, most changes in demand for particular products at a highly disaggregated level are due to changes in technology —new products make older ones less attractive—and changes in tastes. The process of change and adjustment is continuous, and the foreign element is only one of many factors simultaneously at work.

Some industries are declining absolutely, both globally and nationally. Most, however, are relocating geographically across national boundaries, growing in one country while shrinking in another. These are the

Table 2. Case Studies, by Country (in Chapter Sequence)

CANADA	shipbuilding, pulp, automobiles, textiles and apparel
USA	steel, automobiles, textiles and apparel
NEW ZEALAND	oil refining, flour milling, meat packing, automobiles, and textiles
AUSTRALIA	footwear, automobiles, textiles and apparel
SINGAPORE	shipbuilding, oil refining, textiles and apparel
HONG KONG	plastic goods, electronics, wigs, textiles and apparel
TAIWAN	plywood, canned food, and automobiles
KOREA	shipbuilding, coal mining, textiles and apparel
JAPAN	shipbuilding, and paper

categories of principal concern here. Relative decline—substantially slower growth in output or employment than for manufacturing as a whole— is a relevant concept primarily when it is a leading indicator of future absolute declines, though in some countries it does evoke national policy discussion.

DISTRESSED INDUSTRIES

"Adjustment policy" and "structural adjustment" generally conjure up concern with what are variously called dying, sunset, and declining industries. The original working title for this project used the term "declining industries." However, a decline can be secular and permanent; or the result of sustained but presumably transitory unfavorable conditions in a longer run sense; or cyclical. Hence, in this introduction "distressed industries" is used as an umbrella term for "declining" and "troubled"—the former having secular problems, the latter having sustained but not enduring ones—and this distinction is made in all the essays.

The problems pertain to competitiveness. The important criteria for being a distressed industry are absolute declines in output, employment, and profitability, or the presence of government intervention—such as protection or subsidy—intended to prevent such declines. Of the first three, employment is the most clear-cut; data are available and much of the stated concern about the social costs of adjustment relate to the distress of those made unemployed. Profitability is a good measure, but the data are less accurate. Output is in some ways ambiguous, as it may rise even as employment declines because of increasing labor productivity. Thus, a distressed industry has excess capacity, unemployment, or produces inefficiently for a sustained period.

A domestic price substantially higher than the world price is an indicator of an industry's uncompetitiveness; by efficiency criteria, such an industry should decline. In practice the authors found few industries so highly protected from import competition that there were no absolute declines in employment over time. The exceptions are automobile assembly in Australia and Taiwan, and both face reduced protection and probable employment reductions in the 1990s.

Declining industries are those that have lost the ability to compete over the longer run. A troubled industry has not lost its potential to compete in the long run or under normal circumstances. In principle, a troubled industry faces problems that transcend the ordinary business cycle, though in practice cyclical conditions muddy identification. A declining industry should be downsized until it becomes competitive, with resources allocated away from it to other activities. A troubled industry merits continued resource input. Because the problems to be solved are different, so too are the appropriate responses, in capital and labor markets and in government policy.

The distinction between a troubled and a declining industry is important. Unfortunately, it is difficult in practice to distinguish. Some segments of an industry may be troubled while others truly are declining. It is of course politically much more attractive for representatives to portray their industry as troubled rather than declining in order to justify government assistance as only a "temporary" measure.

In all nine countries there have been substantial declines in employment in specific manufacturing sectors; this is the single most important measure of a declining industry. Employment decreases and capacity scrapping have been substantially greater in the five advanced industrial countries, reflecting greater loss of competitiveness. In the NIEs, the main problems have arisen in troubled industries.

A troubled industry's difficulties may come from a sudden decline in world demand despite basic competitiveness—such as shipbuilding in Japan, Korea, and Singapore in the early to mid 1980s (but not in the uncompetitive United States or Canada). Or they may be the consequence of an over-valued exchange rate for a sustained period—such as Canadian pulp and paper in the mid 1970s and a wide variety of US industries during 1981–85. Or it may reflect the impact of other countries' policies—such as the European Community restricting agricultural imports while dumping its excess production abroad, leading the US to retaliate with export subsidies, to the detriment of Australia and New Zealand.

Troubled industries have also emerged as the direct consequence of earlier government policies to create new industries. While some industrial policy choices have been successful, others have been mistakes in timing or extent of expansion, if not in selection. Indeed, inefficient, high-cost troubled industries are a frequent consequence of the import-substituting industrial development strategy pursued by a number of developing economies. In Korea, for instance, the government aggressively promoted heavy and chemical industries in the mid to late 1970s in order to move up the ladders of capital, technology, and skill intensity. Pohang Steel has been a success. Even while expansion was under way, shipbuilding could be seen as at least a timing mistake, and aluminum as a selection mistake.

For declining industries, the loss of competitiveness is typically a consequence of a rise in the relative cost of the factor of production most intensively used in the production process. Historically, the factor pricing an industry out of its market has been labor, so that as incomes have risen, labor-intensive industries have shifted to countries with lower labor costs. However, when labor productivity can be increased as fast or faster than wages, an industry need not decline in output terms—or even in employment if demand is still growing.

Textiles and apparel are the prototypical cases. As the country studies stress, they have been increasingly uncompetitive and declining in all the advanced Pacific Basin countries since the 1970s or earlier. Indeed, the early economic success of Singapore, Hong Kong, Taiwan, and Korea was based in substantial part on their ability to produce and export textiles and garments to the higher-income countries. By the 1980s, their continual successful economic development had brought about sustained rises in real wages and a loss of competitiveness to lower-income countries in Asia and elsewhere. In all these countries, textiles and, more recently, apparel were entering incipient or actual decline.

Declining industries broadly defined, even textiles and apparel, cannot be considered dying or likely to lose competitiveness altogether, even in high-income countries. Aggregation, especially at the two-digit SIC level typical of much analysis, masks very different degrees of competitiveness at the three-, four-, or five-digit industry levels, and even more at the level of individual firms. Some segments are capital- and technology-intensive (eg, synthetic fibers), some have achieved labor-saving innovations (such as weaving), while yet others have developed niches based on quality, design skills, flexible and quick responses to changes in tastes, and nearness to market. (See Wilson 1989 on the theory of firm entry, survival, and exit.)

The greater the disaggregation of industrial classification, the larger the number the cases of decline, but the smaller the number of firms and workers involved. At this level, firms and workers often shift to new products (and sub-industry categories) so that decline in one segment is offset by increase in another. For example, the Canadian and Australian studies show a considerable degree of labor mobility within the textile and apparel industries. Perhaps the most spectacular example is the rise and abrupt decline of wig making in Hong Kong, as Ho and Lin demonstrate, and in Korea. Thus, broadly defined industry categories mask a tremendous amount of market-generated micro adjustment by individual firms and workers. In general, once a declining industry completes its process of structural downsizing, competitive and profitable firms will persist in particular segments and niches. (See Harrigan 1980 and 1988 for strategies on how to be the profitable surviving firm in a declining industry.)

MACROECONOMIC CONTEXT

The single most important contributor to successful structural adjustment of distressed industries is good, stable, sustained economic growth. Growth creates new investment opportunities. Growth creates jobs that absorb unemployed workers and new entrants; it sucks workers out of low-wage jobs. These country studies make clear that new job creation as a consequence of good macroeconomic performance has mitigated many of the reasons governments otherwise intervene to protect jobs.

While successful growth performance over time makes structural adjustment easier, it also makes it more necessary. By the early 1980s rapid growth had sufficiently increased the demand for industrial labor (and in Taiwan and Korea, abolished the rural surplus) that wages began a rapid rise. It is not by chance that the industries in decline in Korea, Taiwan, Hong Kong, and Singapore are labor-intensive: their most immediate problem is that they can no longer compete in domestic labor markets. In a broad social sense as well as for affected workers, this market-based adjustment is highly beneficial and desirable.

Less rapid overall growth means a less easy path to effective industrial restructuring. So, too, does a high level of development. The United States, Japan, Canada, and Australia are more or less at the technological frontiers. Their growth rates are constrained over the longer run by the rate of technological innovation. In the medium term, a good domestic saving performance is important to finance the investment that expands capacity and raises productivity (Hatsopoulos et al 1988) even with the possibility of substantial capital inflows in any increasingly perfect global capital market. In the short run, macroeconomic policy packages to stimulate saving and investment, maintain price stability, and achieve full employment levels are important, though not always easy to implement.

Exchange Rates

In general, a "high" exchange rate for a sustained period both exacerbates the cost-price problems of an uncompetitive industry already in decline and turns reasonably competitive industries into troubled ones. Conversely, a "low" exchange rate enhances price competitiveness and ameliorates or retards the process of structural adjustment. There are various criteria for evaluating the underlying economic conditions to determine in what sense the actual market rate is not an equilibrium rate. Let us consider three cases that have been of particular importance for structural adjustment processes and policies on the Pacific Basin.

The effect of changing commodity terms of trade on the exchange rate is taken up first. This has been dubbed the Gregory effect, following his seminal analysis (1976) of the macro-structural consequences of a minerals boom in Australia. Consider a country with comparative advantage in some capital-intensive, natural-resource-based export that also both produces and imports manufactured goods. An externally induced boom in the prices of its export goods results in rising export earnings, GNP growth, and higher domestic incomes, but also leads to a rising exchange rate, a less competitive domestic manufacturing sector, and increased inflows of competitive imports.

If this change in the terms of trade is permanent, the domestic industries brought into distress should indeed decline. However, if the change is temporary, domestic manufacturing has not lost long-run competitiveness (aside from the problems of hysteresis, to the extent they exist). Such cases present a plausible argument for government assistance. Indeed, much of the story in the chapter on Australia is the way real exchange rate movements have affected government policies, both to protect highly uncompetitive quota industries and to reduce that protection and orchestrate orderly decline.

A second case is where a high exchange rate is the consequence of a domestic fiscal or monetary policy that results in high nominal and real interest rates. Such countries attract inflows of foreign capital, which bid up the exchange rate. Imports, now more competitive, flow in and exports are retarded. This is the common view of US policy from 1982 until 1986 (and until 1990, in the view of many).

A smaller country that pegs its exchange rate to the currency of a large country is the third case. In the 1980s, Singapore, Hong Kong, Taiwan, and Korea pegged, more or less tightly, to the US dollar. During this period their economies experienced export-based (US-import-based) development. When the dollar was high (until 1985), their exports were relatively less competitive in non-US markets, but burgeoning US demand made that a non-issue. When the dollar declined, competitiveness was lost in the US market but gained elsewhere—notably, in Japan and the European Community.

The exchange rate effect on specific industries has to be analyzed carefully at a more micro level. For example, an industry relying heavily on imported inputs benefits from their lower prices, relative to other domestic industries. Exports, or imports of specific final products in competition with domestic production, may involve countries whose own exchange rates have risen. Average exchange rate movements mask these specific country-currency effects for particular inputs and products. These industry-specific exchange rate effects apparently have been significant for New Zealand, for instance.

Trade Imbalances

One of the major surprises of the 1980s was the emergence of huge national trade imbalances, particularly those of the United States and Japan. These were so important because of the dominant role of both nations in the world economy, and their sheer size and rapidity of emergence. The policy responses have had domestic, bilateral, and third-party repercussions (Cline 1989).

The US deficit and the Japanese surplus of the 1980s were primarily the consequence of the same domestic forces that resulted in an over-valued dollar and an under-valued yen. Although a substantial portion of the US deficit was reflected directly in Japan's surplus, the causes were not mirror images of each other. As Hufbauer demonstrates in his essay, the major culprits in the US were both its large federal budget deficit—the component of GNP most susceptible to policy—and the decline in the private saving rate. In Japan there was a surplus of private saving over investment, which flowed overseas in search of higher returns than those available domestically.

These imbalances have been important factors in shaping both trade and adjustment policies in the United States and Japan. The rising, then persisting US trade deficit substantially strengthened protectionist forces in the United States. It helped legitimize the efforts of the automobile and steel industries to obtain special import protection, and it was a major factor contributing to support for restrictive trade bills that resulted in the 1988 Omnibus Trade and Competitiveness Act.

Despite the deficits, much of the American trade policy effort was not to close its markets, though that was the threat and at times the reality for certain products, but to pressure others to open their markets further. From autumn 1985 it did so through an activist trade policy based primarily on bilateral negotiations outside the GATT (General Agreement on Tariffs and Trade) framework. Several of the country chapters, Hong Kong in particular, stress anxieties about US protectionist actions, threats, and the bullying nature of US negotiations and style. (For further discussion see Bhagwati and Patrick 1990.)

Japan has been under persistent pressure since the mid 1960s to liberalize its imports and otherwise open its markets to foreigners. By the mid 1980s tariffs and quotas on manufactured imports were on average very low—comparable to those in the United States and European Community. Even before the emergence of the 1980s current account surpluses, it would have been difficult in terms of foreign relations for Japan to impose new, explicit import barriers to assist an industry in secular decline or even in trouble. As Sekiguchi discusses, help for the distressed has involved domestically oriented measures rather than import restrictions.

A current account deficit is not necessarily bad, even over the longer run. When investment opportunities outstrip domestic savings, the net inflow of resources adds to a country's rate of economic growth. Similarly, a surplus makes sense for a country with a high saving rate and lower investment opportunities; in what is essentially a capital-short world, these additional (Japanese, Taiwanese, and other) savings are a benefit to the world economy. Both Canada and Australia, as resource-rich economies, have had net resource inflows (current account deficits) for most of their economic history. Australia's rising current account deficits and debt balances did attract concern in the late 1980s, but this has not been the problem for the international economic system the way US deficits have. Indeed, in order to reduce its current account deficit, Australia's exchange rate is likely to depreciate which, on Gregory's analysis, means the government's policies to reduce official quota and tariff protection are more likely to stay in place.

MARKET ADJUSTMENT AND GOVERNMENT POLICY

In terms of a nation's economic welfare, the ultimate objective is to have a distressed industry, or what remains of it, become internationally competitive. This means obsolete capacity has to be scrapped (as excess in declining industries, to be replaced or upgraded with superior technologies in troubled ones) and the industry's labor force reduced (usually sharply in declining industries). Countries can, and frequently do, simply leave the adjustment process to market forces. In most cases, reliance on the market process of adjustment is the preferred policy choice. Firms upgrade products, shift to new product lines, develop or acquire new technologies and capital, and otherwise cut costs. Workers learn new skills, or seek new opportunities. Extensive intra-industry and inter-industry labor mobility in all these economies is indicative of the market process at work.

However, the presumption that market-based adjustment is the optimal mechanism in practice and in theory is certainly not held by all policy makers and politicians. Prospects of a painful process of adjustment bring powerful social and political as well as economic forces into play, so pressure for government intervention in the market process can become severe.

Albeit to differing degrees, all nine countries in this study subscribe to the concept of free trade and free markets. At the same time, the governments of all but Hong Kong have policies intended to directly affect adjustment. Thus, the important issues relate to the interaction between market mechanisms and government policies: for which industries does the government becomes involved, at what stage, to what degree, and for what purposes.

Belief in the efficacy of free markets is most strongly voiced in Hong Kong, the United States, Canada, and (since 1985) New Zealand, though actual behavior deviates somewhat from the ideals of ideology. Hong Kong is the world's purest example of a free trade, laissez-faire economy; its intervention is the most limited—essentially, determining exchange rate policy. But, as Ho and Lin point out, even it is increasing its indirect involvement through land use and education policies. In Japan, Korea, Taiwan, Singapore, and Australia, the governments seem more willing to assume market imperfections or failure in one form or another. In these five and (prior to 1985) in New Zealand, government micro intervention has been taken for granted as an inevitable element of an explicit or implicit industrial strategy. The 1970s and '80s have seen a shift away from intervention in the western Pacific, though probably for reasons of self-interest.

Economic size counts. The huge domestic markets, diversity of absolutely large industries, and smaller share of foreign trade in GNP in the United States and Japan mean they can support industries in distress at less cost relative to GNP. For Hong Kong, Singapore, and New Zealand, very small size argues for minimal government intervention in product markets as the pragmatic policy. This has been the case for Hong Kong and Singapore, but in New Zealand exploitation of vast land resources made possible a policy of protecting a very inefficient manufacturing sector. New Zealand has paid a price for this: the slowest growth rate from the 1960s to '80s of the nine countries considered here—and in 1985 made major policy changes away from intervention.

RATIONALES FOR INTERVENTION

Three sorts of grounds are advanced for intervention: economic, moral, and political. (For a nice summary of the extensive theoretical and empirical literature, see Trebliock 1986, ch 1.) Politicians have to evaluate and balance trade-offs among economic efficiency, social costs, and political efficacy. Economic rationales are cast in terms of market imperfections, market failures, and (without irony) failure of other government policies. Even on economic grounds, temporary intervention to smooth adjustment can be justified, and this is routinely exploited by those seeking help. Thus, the publicly stated objective of intervention is virtually always to smooth out the process in order to ameliorate its costs. The principal moral argument relates to the appropriate sharing of social costs among a country's citizens. A major moral underpinning for intervention is that the beneficiaries of economic change and open trade—society as a whole—should compensate those who bear the direct costs. This is an aspect of the judgment that the income distribution consequences of the operations of the market are not always socially optimal, and up to a point the distribution can and should be altered. The plight of unemployment elicits a greater social concern than the plight of investors, who after all are supposed to be risk-takers.

The political grounds arise from the fact that the costs of structural adjustment are concentrated, while the even greater benefits typically are dispersed widely, with each member of society receiving only modest improvement in welfare. Thus, not surprisingly, producer interest groups —owners, managers, workers, and their trade associations and unions —are better organized, and are thereby better able to mobilize the political system to their benefit than is the general public of consumers and taxpayers. The politically more powerful the producer interest—in votes, money, or appeal to public sympathy—the greater the ability to obtain government assistance. There are, however, countervailing pressure groups: export industries which fear retaliation and support an open trading system; industrial purchasers and users of the distressed industry's products; and foreign trading partners.

The political rationale for government intervention is often the most powerful in practice and in the extreme is a travesty of the moral argument as specific interest groups seek intervention to force others to absorb the costs of adjustment that otherwise would fall on them. Some governments partially insulate themselves from such political pressures through mechanisms that use more objective criteria in determining whether to apply import-restrictive measures; examples include the US International Trade Commission and the Industries Assistance Commission in Australia.

In Canada and the United States, where intervention is considered at least theoretically undesirable, interventionist political rhetoric tends to focus on unemployed workers and social costs, although the importance of the industry to national well-being and security are also often argued. Hence the emphasis there, as well as in New Zealand, Australia, and Japan, on at least lip service to programs for unemployment compensation, retraining, and enhanced labor mobility. Social concern for displaced workers is greater in high-income countries for a variety of reasons, including greater specificity of labor skills, slower GNP growth and hence smaller increases in employment opportunities, and a greater political role of workers and unions.

INTERVENTION FOR WHOM?

The economic rationale for government intervention is market failure. However, the case has to be obvious to policy makers—politicians or bureaucrats—before market failure is likely to be invoked and intervention pursued. Typically the industry must be large to attract attention. While there are exceptions, industries with a small share of total manufacturing employment and output are not well able to escape or ameliorate the test of the marketplace by obtaining special government assistance. However, where a small industry is geographically concentrated and an important contributor to regional employment and economic performance, it may be able to obtain government support. In geographically smaller countries, displaced workers can more readily find alternative jobs without moving than is the case in larger countries.

Organized labor has been an important player in Canada, the United States, New Zealand, and Australia. The Australian and New Zealand cases are remarkable in that powerful labor interests have gone along with Labour Governments' market-oriented reform programs.

In virtually all countries the rhetoric justifying intervention is to help displaced workers. In practice the benefits of government assistance accrue substantially to the owners, managers, and creditors of firms, particularly banks. Japan and Korea are cases where these were at least the implicit targets of government assistance. This is true more for large firms than small; small manufacturing owner-operators often are left to fend for themselves.

Changes in domestic demand are regarded as one of the inevitable uncertainties of the market, and the governments in these nine countries typically have not been willing to provide direct assistance in such cases. Similarly, the loss of export markets only infrequently occasions intervention and this is only in part because of possible retaliation. Shipbuilding and repair in Japan, Korea, and Singapore are exceptions discussed in their respective chapters.

Japan is an exception to these generalizations. In Japan the focal point of government policy has been excess capacity and declines in production, whether cyclical, sustained, or indeed secular, or whether the sources of difficulties are domestic or international—hence the support of cyclical anti-recession cartels prominent in the 1960s and '70s and the structurally depressed industries policies of the 1970s and '80s. In textiles and apparel, government assistance from the 1970s was in response to decreases in exports as markets were lost to lower wage countries (Dore 1986a and 1986b). On the whole, the government was relatively willing to intervene, with little concern as to whether import competition was a special problem. The government has operated in a democratic environment in which interest group politics is very important, and, since the mid 1970s, in an international policy environment in which any increases in import protection were unacceptable.

In general, the major locus of government structural adjustment intervention is in industries facing severe import competition. Conceptually the social costs and problems of resource reallocation may be no different for import-competing industries than for domestic or export industries. But as a policy matter this is where governments have been most likely to intervene. In part this is because loss of competitiveness is typically more apparent. Perhaps most important, governments can provide assistance at minimal budgetary costs simply by imposing import restrictions. Protection does not have to be the policy instrument; indeed, it is likely to be less effective in bringing about structural adjustment and resource reallocation than more direct means of government assistance that are more efficient (less costly) and more transparent (hence politically less attractive).

POLICY APPROACHES TO INTERVENTION

The political and administrative requirements of a comprehensive, successful distressed industry policy are substantial. An effective policy requires a clear identification of objectives, analysis of the causes and alternative solutions to the problem, establishment of operational targets with credible time limits, the choice of appropriate policy instruments, and a political and bureaucratic willingness to keep intervention from becoming open ended and ongoing. The implementation of policy requires substantial bureaucratic capacity, the ability to attach and enforce performance conditions, focused mechanisms, and prevention of politicization of the process.

In practice, the policy determination and implementation process is quite messy. Often there is no clear political consensus; specific actions are ad hoc, fragmented, and thus frequently inconsistent with each other, if not with the objectives. Those directly affected seek to maximize the benefits government offers while evading restrictions and conditions. This applies not just to firms and workers, but to politicians and government bureaucrats as well. Political variables explain the nature, pattern, and form of government intervention better than do economic variables.

Governments have three general approaches to intervention: anticipative (picking losers), facilitative (the OECD's positive adjustment policies), and defensive (including protection).

Identifying industries that have not yet declined but are very likely to in the future, then providing incentives not only for rationalization but early transfer of resources into other, more promising sectors is the anticipative approach. But, as Cornell and Gorecki note in their essay, picking losers can be as difficult as picking winners. It is politically difficult to take anticipatory policies: if nothing else, the demonstration effect of being labeled expendable can make the decline less orderly than if the industry had been left alone. Firms routinely anticipate on their own. There are virtually no instances of government anticipatory intervention.

Smoothing, easing, and even accelerating the adjustment process through government policies to reduce the costs of transferring resources of the declining industry—in economic terminology, reducing the costs of market failure—is the facilitative approach. This involves such things as retraining and relocating workers and, in some instances, offering incentives to scrap capacity. The OECD adopted guidelines for a package of such "positive adjustment policies" in June 1978. Under the guidelines, policies (1) should increase efficiency and preserve market competition so that prices become world competitive, (2) be for a specified limited period (5–10 years) during which assistance is progressively reduced, (3) be transparent (that is, the social costs and benefits should be specified and the methods and processes of achieving adjustment be clear), and (4) speed up, not retard, adjustment.

Governments that have accepted the OECD guidelines in principle have done little in practice to accelerate the process of adjustment. Rather, they have accepted as politically and socially necessary a slower pace of change to smooth and ease the consequences of adjustment.

Slowing the process of adjustment by providing firms and workers support while they otherwise solve their own problems and again become competitive is the third, essentially defensive, general approach. In many circumstances this can be viewed as market-oriented: the government simply provides direct subsidies (unusual) or protection from imports (typical) for a stipulated period. Firms can become more efficient and workers are displaced in a more orderly way. This is successful sometimes. But in most cases the expectation is that the period of support will be extended, everyone becomes more complacent, and frequently less adjustment takes place than had been anticipated, and it occurs less rapidly.

The speed of adjustment, in the absence of government intervention, depends on domestic and international demand and supply factors. Adjustment is eased where domestic demand grows more rapidly and foreign supply is siphoned off into burgeoning markets elsewhere. Supply is crucially affected by the specificity and durability of an industry's assets; the more specific and durable they are, the less the ability to shift them efficiently to other uses and hence the greater the economic benefit of generating cash flow by continuing production. As Bollard notes in his essay, there has been a marked contrast in New Zealand in the rapid adjustment of industries such as banking, with little in the way of specific durable assets, and the slow adjustment (up to 10 years) in meat processing, with its large plants not suitable for alternative uses.

Thus, there is no a priori reason as to whether adjustment should proceed in declining industries faster, slower, or at the same rate as the economy as a whole. Given the sector-specific nature of interventions, this more macro question typically is not raised as a policy issue. I find it very interesting that the rate of adjustment in Canada's declining industries is about the same as for all manufacturing. This is a result, not an explicit objective. Cornell and Gorecki conclude government policy did not help much in the adjustment process, with the exception of footwear (where there was a comprehensive, focused program for a small industry). The counter-factual hypothesis—that government policy somehow was effective in ensuring a common rate of adjustment, so that factors of production in declining industries were not disadvantaged by a faster rate of adjustment—cannot be tested readily, but seems unlikely.

Policy Options

The form intervention takes matters. The options range from import protection to positive domestic programs that shift resources away from inefficient activities, or to domestic defensive programs to slow adjustment. Typically, the stated objective of protection is to buy time for adjustment to take place through domestic market mechanisms; this has been the principal approach pursued by Canada, the United States, New Zealand, and Australia. Positive domestic programs include providing incentives for labor retraining and mobility, orderly scrapping of excess capacity, and restructuring and upgrading of remaining capacity. This alternative in practice generally involves direct government assistance to firms and workers; it has been the approach of Japan and, in a much more limited way, Singapore.

Defensive programs usually eschew direct subsidy payments, which both industries and policy makers dislike as being too obvious. Instead, there are less transparent subsidies, such as loan guarantees, preferential loans at below-market interest rates (a favorite instrument), special tax treatment, subsidized input costs, special unemployment compensation programs, and regional development programs. In addition, joint marketing agreements or other forms of cartel-like behavior, are allowed, if not encouraged.

All of the options are open to abuse—retarding adjustment and increasing its costs—protection more so than the others, although incentives can end up being ongoing subsidies. Whether abuse occurs depends in part on what the objectives really are. Although the stated objective is almost always to allow adjustment to take place albeit over a longer time period than if there were no intervention, in many instances—particularly with politically powerful industries—the actual objective is to maintain the industry for an indefinite period.

That protection is a crude, blunt, economically costly and inefficient policy instrument which in practice tends to be self-defeating is well known and well documented both in these case studies and in the theoretical and empirical literature (see, eg, Bhagwati 1988, Kelly et al 1988, OECD 1985 and 1987, Trebliock 1986). However, it is also politically attractive, and thus import restrictions are the main instrument used to protect distressed industries in most of the countries studied.

The costs of protection are off-budget; while immense, they are widely diffused, thus typically small for individuals; the benefits are focused and direct; there is a nationalistic appeal to shifting some of the perceived costs to foreigners; and import protection may be easier and less costly to administer than domestically oriented programs.

The United States in particular has imposed new import restrictions to help industries deemed worthy of protection, and import restrictions have been a major instrument in Canada. Australia, and to a lesser degree Korea, Taiwan, and New Zealand have retained quotas and high tariffs in some sectors even while significantly lowering them for most manufacturing. Japan's reduction of formal import barriers has shifted attention to its non-governmental barriers.

Import restrictions may not be optimally efficient, but adjustment has taken place. There are, however, two serious problems. First, as Cornell and Gorecki argue for Canada and Hufbauer for the United States, perhaps without protection the same adjustment could have taken place at lower cost to the economy, and without the often inequitable redistribution of income to workers, managers, owners, and creditors of protected industries. Second, for the politically powerful, there are no effective time limits to protection: it has been renewed time and time again. Adjustment continues, but at an inadequate rate, so the industry remains inefficient and in decline for far longer than the initial commitment of government assistance.

Japan's program of negotiated, orderly capacity reduction has been effective, particularly in industries with a relatively small number of large firms, as is discussed below.

Given that there will be intervention and its resulting economic costs, which is more efficient, effective, and less costly: import restriction with market-based adjustment or government-supported orderly capacity reduction? Is one better at resolving the political difficulties of the adjustment process? In my judgment, the orderly capacity reduction model has been more effective, at least in Japan, because it set the adjustment process in motion, and set and achieved a reduction in industrial capacity without great social cost.

Nonetheless, there are two important caveats. First, Japanese policy makers might well have preferred protection instead of or in addition to capacity reduction. That option was not available, however, because of foreign, particularly United States, pressures on Japan to open its markets, not to restrict access to them. Second, and more important, when adjustment becomes an issue of government intervention, it is a matter more of political economy, government-business relationships, and bureaucratic administrative capacity than of economic efficiency. Policy choice is much conditioned by environment. The orderly capacity reduction without import restrictions of the Japanese model probably will not work in Canada or the United States. (For more on the transportability and lessons of industrial policy, see Patrick 1986, particularly the Eads and Nelson essay, and Okimoto 1989.)

Voluntary Restraints on Exports

Voluntary restraints by the governments of exporting countries instead of the imposition of tariffs or, more likely, quotas by importing countries initially seemed attractive for their flexibility, presumed temporary nature, and political acceptability to both. VERs (voluntary export restraint agreements, also called VRAs—voluntary restraint agreements) have become, in my judgment, one of the most pernicious instruments of import restriction.

Like other quota systems, they result in higher prices to consumers, and rents go not only to domestic producers but also to foreign exporters

—which dilutes the purpose of restricting imports to facilitate adjustment. Thus, the profits Japanese automakers gained from VERs were reinvested in further competitive advantage—and specifically to attack the mid-size car market that has been the mainstay of the US industry. It is unfortunate the sharing of VER rents seems so attractive not just to diplomats engaged in bilateral trade negotiations but also to domestic politicians who receive campaign contributions not only from domestic producers but from lobbyists representing foreign interests as well (Hillman and Ursprung 1988).

VERs have other disadvantages. As is well known, quantitative restrictions generally result in less efficient resource allocation than tariffs that would achieve the equivalent initial level of protection. Japan, as the major new and highly competitive entrant into world export markets, has been the major user of VERs. While each VER has been a specific pragmatic, ad hoc decision, the cumulative effect is that Japan has made popular an import-restrictive instrument that has particularly high costs and inefficiencies. And the United States has willingly pressured Japan (and Taiwan, Korea, and Hong Kong, among others) into applying VERs in a variety of industries.

Perhaps the highest costs of the widespread use of VERs are borne by the GATT multilateral trading system. VERs are bilateral, outside GATT. They undermine the multilateral approach to trade policy, and provide an existential basis for selective and discriminatory "safeguards" as proposed by the European Community—import restrictions overtly aimed at export industries in Japan, Korea, Taiwan, Singapore, and a few other countries.

PATTERNS OF GOVERNMENT ASSISTANCE

Government intervention policies reflect a mixture of concerns with efficiency in resource allocation, social objectives, and interest group politics. Applications of measures to protect industries from strong import competition depend greatly on a country's general trade policies and practices as well as domestic macroeconomic performance and the external conditions it faces. There are several patterns, as the country studies elaborate. Hong Kong and Singapore maintain free trade policies; Singapore's assistance has been directly to the industry in trouble when it has chosen to intervene (which is seldom). The United States and Canada, generally open economies, have used import restrictions (typically quantitative quotas in one form or another) to help politically powerful industries. Australia maintained protection of "quota industries" even as it lowered import barriers for manufactures in general.

New Zealand, which industrialized behind high protectionist barriers, since 1985 has undertaken a comprehensive and dramatic program of micro-market-oriented reform, including general import liberalization (though remaining tariffs are still well above OECD averages).

Korea and Taiwan have had high levels of import protection even though they were not necessary for their labor-intensive manufacturing sectors. From the mid 1980s they began to reduce barriers substantially. In the 1990s, when their labor-intensive industries may no longer be fully competitive even in domestic markets, import barriers are projected to be low. It will be interesting to see how the industries are affected and the governments respond.

When governments intervene, it is primarily to assist industries rather than targeted individual firms. Korea is an exception, reflecting the history of government involvement and the importance of large conglomerates (*chaebol*) in the country's economy. But, with its imperfect capital markets, this has been primarily in financing; the government has not been much involved in the process of capacity reduction. In the United States there have been the Chrysler and Lockheed bailouts, but they were exceptional. In New Zealand the oil refining industry is one firm.

The two Pacific Basin industrial leaders, the United States and Japan, pursued quite different policy approaches in the 1980s regarding government assistance to industries in distress. Because of their importance, each is worth elaborating on.

Japan

Since the 1960s Japan has been successively reducing its high tariff and quota barriers, reaching very low levels for manufactures by the mid 1980s. Unlike the United States, with limited exceptions Japan in the 1980s did not impose new protectionist measures to implement structural adjustment. This was probably not because its policy makers deliberately rejected such measures as inefficient. It is simply that they had no choice. From the early 1970s, the strong and rising foreign pressure on Japan to open its markets and liberalize imports, intensified by the huge trade and current account surpluses of the 1980s, has made it politically impossible for Japan to use import-restricting measures in support of domestic structural adjustment.

Two points should be made, however. Import competition, actual or potential, was not a major factor in most of Japan's structurally depressed industries, though it was in aluminum, coal, low-value-added textiles, lumber, and plywood. And Japan's economic growth performance throughout has been very good, with full employment and new job creation the norm.

The exceptions in a way demonstrate Japanese practices. Japanese aluminum represents probably the most extreme case of rapid industrial decline in the world. The government provided discriminatorily favorable tariff treatment to the imports of domestic producers for several years, but foreign pressure forced its termination. Japan is the only major industrial nation not imposing quotas on textiles and apparel under the Multi-Fiber Arrangement. It did, however, in the late 1980s, arrange limited bilateral VERs (voluntary export restraints) on silk from Bangladesh, China, and Korea, and on knitwear from Korea—all countries reliant on Japanese trade and investment.

During the 1970s and '80s the Japanese government pursued its own types of policies to help structurally declining industries, providing direct incentives to firms and workers, as Sekiguchi discusses. In my judgment, the Japanese government has pursued on the whole an effective set of policies towards its declining industries. It has provided modest financial and tax incentives and mechanisms for firms, particularly large firms in oligopolistic declining industries, to scrap capacity and rationalize on an orderly, cooperative basis without going through the trauma of bankruptcy.

While it is not clear this pattern has been more efficient than simply allowing the market to achieve similar downsizing, at least that result was achieved. The industries probably had too much political power to allow themselves to be subjected to purely market solutions. Given that government would intervene, orderly capacity reduction was surely more effective and efficient than the alternative of import protection. On the other hand, there is some evidence of ongoing collusive market-sharing in a few highly concentrated industrial products, which the government has yet to challenge. The more overt form is in government sanctioned joint distribution arrangements, as discussed by Sekiguchi. Given the salience of Japan, it is not surprising the United States has pressed Japan for stronger, more rigorously enforced antitrust laws.

As I read the evidence, Japanese government programs in the 1980s to assist workers and small enterprises in depressed industries and regions have been on the whole highly market-reliant in practice, though supportive in principle. Programs have been devised to help firms and workers, yet the funding involved and the impact have been limited. In the 1980s, programs for retraining and relocating workers were expanded, but funding and the number of workers actually helped remain modest.

Apparently the government has succeeded in getting across its basic message to small business: the government will try to help, but ultimately adjustment is the responsibility of the individual worker and the (small) individual firm. (For a fuller statement of the message, see Dore 1986a and 1986b, p 150.) The main objective seems to have been social and political rather than more efficient utilization of workers made unemployed by decline in their industry.

The United States

Protection of distressed industries in the United States has not been done lightly. Import restrictions have been imposed only after foreign penetration of the American market was substantial—typically 20% or more. Each major intervention—textiles, apparel, steel, automobiles—ultimately reflects the political power of the industry in distress and its advocates. Restrictions have been quantitative quotas rather than tariff increases—frequently so-called voluntary restraints. Presented as ad hoc, flexible, and limited in time, they have been bilaterally negotiated outside of GATT.

Comprehensive, or even focused, domestic policies to help distressed industries have been unattractive because of lack of administrative capability and budget, as well as from rejection of industrial policy per se. As noted in my comments on voluntary restraints, the results have been particularly sub-optimal. In a sense, the United States has been hoisted on its own petard. The consistent US policy objective has been to reduce world tariffs, quotas, and other official trade barriers; accordingly, it cannot justify increasing tariffs to assist distressed industries, as that would contravene GATT and send the wrong signal to others. Domestically, for practical and ideological reasons, the US has rejected comprehensive industrial policy. It is not surprising VERs, orderly marketing arrangements, and the like have been perceived as a solution.

HELPING WORKERS

Much of the stated rationale for intervention is to help reduce costs to displaced workers. Many countries have experimented with job retraining, relocation, and placement programs for workers made unemployed by structural change. The United States and Japan have had labor adjustment programs over the years, with spotty success. Nowhere, however, have programs been applied comprehensively and broadly, or with sufficient resources to solve the particular problems of unemployed workers in distressed industries. The reasons are complex.

Part of the reason for the limited commitment is that programs are usually aimed at workers affected by import competition, yet most unemployment and worker turnover is a consequence of a myriad of other factors. Moreover, labor markets do work pretty well; most displaced workers simply relocate or find new jobs on their own.

Retraining and related programs often become primarily income support measures, and thus can be said to retard adjustment. Nonetheless, Aho and Bayard (1984) found that in the United States, the costs of trade-related worker assistance programs were much less than the welfare benefits from expanded trade, and thus are a relatively inexpensive price to pay to prevent import restriction or to handle the political costs of trade liberalization (also see Tan 1989). Japanese programs have the same political rationale, and as such have been quite successful. The reluctance to undertake more comprehensive labor adjustment reflects faith in the market, fear of budgetary costs, and skepticism of the capability of bureaucrats to administer programs effectively.

Among the essays, Cornell and Gorecki (Canada) and Sekiguchi (Japan) look most closely at labor-related issues. One point emerging from Cornell and Gorecki's analysis warrants greater consideration by unions, firms, and government policy makers than it has received; it relates to the issue of who loses their job when an industry declines or when a troubled industry seeks to regain competitiveness—and thus health in production and profitability terms—by reducing employment. To the extent retraining is unlikely or difficult, it is probably better to keep the older workers and let the younger ones seek new careers. This is not quite the same as the traditional seniority system. Frequently, "older" workers—often people still in their 50s—are given "early retirement" so that younger workers can keep the then-remaining jobs, even when those jobs may well last no longer than the remaining usual working career of those laid off. Rather than being moved out of dead-end jobs sooner, the younger workers are moved later, when it is undoubtedly harder for them to make the adjustment.

Helping Non-Native Workers

In several countries, non-native workers—immigrants or guest workers—constitute a special factor in policy choice. Canada, the United States, and Australia all justify protection of apparel production in part on the grounds it provides entry-level jobs for unskilled female immigrants. A similar rationale has been used for male workers in South Australia's auto industry. In contrast, Singapore intends to reduce the role of labor-intensive manufacturing and to this end has constrained the apparel and other labor-intensive industries by limiting the percentage of foreign workers on temporary contracts.

In all countries, some firms in most declining industries have sought to regain cost competitiveness by shifting their labor-intensive processes or components production to lower-wage countries through direct foreign investment and offshore procurement. Singapore has been a major beneficiary; indeed, most of its manufacturing activity is done by American, Japanese, or other foreign firms.

In a few instances, governments have provided some incentives for firms to invest abroad: Taiwan (plywood), Korea (textiles), and Japan (aluminum) are examples. It appears the purpose of this is mainly ameliorative and political, to help the domestic owners and managers by keeping firms alive. To the extent firms invest abroad and also import to their home market, utilizing their existing distribution system, it undermines the ability of firms in the industry to unite to seek government protection from imports.

TEXTILES, APPAREL, AND AUTOMOBILES

Textiles and apparel are industries in which trade patterns and comparative advantage have been shifting globally for decades. In the postwar period, comparative advantage has moved inexorably from high-wage economically advanced countries to low-wage industrializing ones, making them the classic cases of trade-related declining industry within a country. Automobiles have also seen comparative advantage shift geographically, but production scale and domestic market size are important. Country-specific automobile production is an excellent illustration of both broad types of troubled industry—those facing temporary loss of competitiveness and those government-supported at high cost in the face of major inefficiencies. At the same time, all three industries, as broadly defined, reflect the heterogeneity of products and of efficient modes of production.

Textiles and Apparel

Textiles and apparel are major industries in every economy, certainly in the nine countries studied here. They comprise almost one-tenth of the world trade in manufactures, yet are the world's most protected manufacturing industries, with relatively high tariffs and, more importantly, quotas. The Multi-Fiber Arrangement, involving some 54 countries, enforces a system of bilateral quota restrictions on exports from developing economies to advanced industrial countries. As the case studies here attest, the cost of this protection is high in Canada, the United States, New Zealand, and Australia. And the opportunities for even deeper specialization have been restricted in the three major NIE suppliers—Hong Kong, Taiwan, and Korea. Singapore and Japan represent ongoing loss of advantage as wages rise, but from positions of initially highly competitive industries. [2]

Employment in textiles has declined in all nine countries, even when output has increased, as it has in many cases. Technological innovation and labor-saving investment have been the major causes of this. So too have new, low-cost sources of supply: capital-intensive synthetic fibers exported by the United States and Japan, among others, and labor-intensive cotton yarn and cloth in especially low-wage countries being examples. Hong Kong now imports much of the cloth used in its apparel industry.

In Singapore, Hong Kong, Taiwan, and Korea, workers displaced in textiles have been readily absorbed elsewhere in the economy without resort to government intervention. In fact, workers apparently were pulled out of low-wage textile production by market demand for labor. The common complaint of textile producers in these countries, especially Singapore, is that they cannot compete because they cannot hire workers. This contrasts with Canada, the United States, and Australia, where domestic producers protest rising imports.

Apparel is generally more labor-intensive than textiles, so comparative advantage has shifted even more to low-wage economies. Employment has decreased in Canada, the United States, and Australia—but at substantially slower rates than if there had been no protection. Yet imports have also risen, both absolutely and as a share of domestic markets. Sometime in the 1990s, Singapore will no longer be able to compete widely in apparel production.

Hong Kong, Taiwan, and Korea are more complex cases. As wages have risen, they have succeeded in upgrading quality and value-added production. Still, employment in apparel may have peaked by the end of the 1980s, if not earlier. This may be due to increasingly severe import barriers in foreign markets, but more likely it is rising labor costs, a

---

2. Cline (1987) and Hamilton (1990) provide more detail on the industries' trade and development. "Textiles and apparel" is used in this book for (using US SIC numbers) two major groups, textile mill products (22) and apparel (23), plus the synthetic fiber industry group (282, from the chemicals major group). The apparel group covers principally the "cut up and needle" trades. Knit goods that are essentially made directly from yarn into garments are actually textile mill products (industry group 225). Hosiery and certain types of underwear comprise the bulk of such knit goods, although some night and outerwear (gloves, sweaters) are also covered.

general reduction in competitiveness relative to low-wage countries, and greater specialization.

Automobiles

Technological, design, and production management innovations are critical to ongoing success, but automaking is nonetheless mostly a medium-technology industry in terms of production labor skills. These characteristics also make it a prototypical troubled industry in a number of countries. It also is heterogeneous—covering a wide range of finished-product niches (from sports cars to stretch limos to subcompacts) and levels of technological sophistication needed to build various of the myriad parts and components—some 20,000 in any specific vehicle.

Assembly exhibits major economies of scale and scope in production and marketing. It thus is relatively concentrated, with product differentiation, brand names, imperfect competition, and price leadership being the name of the game. Production conditions for components and parts vary substantially. In some, such as engines or transmissions, economies of scale are important. For many other items, small-scale, labor-intensive methods are efficient. For parts, there is both an original equipment and a replacement market.

The major global transformation in the industry during the 1970s and '80s has been the rise of Japanese producers challenging the dominance of General Motors, Ford, and Chrysler in their home North American market. A later phenomenon has been the largely unanticipated emergence to competitiveness of Korean small-car suppliers. Even allowing for the 1973 and 1979 oil shocks, the rise of Japanese producers in North America is a story not only of Japanese success but also of American failure. And although the American industry in the 1980s was troubled by an over-valued dollar, this only exacerbated factors endogenous to the domestic industry, such as a failure to control labor costs or to respond adequately to shifts in demand related to quality as well as to fuel economy or price. The industry will persist in North America, but more of it is in Japanese-owned factories, following the dramatic rise in Japanese direct investment in the 1980s.

There has been a proclivity for smaller countries to establish domestic assembly and some parts production for their home market, inevitably behind highly protective import restrictions. These, too, are troubled industries, exemplifying the government-created variety. The intentions were good: the linkage effects of an automobile industry in terms of both upgrading the technological level of development and in providing a service (internal transportation) needed in tying a country together politically and economically make it an attractive target for planners and politicians. However, as has been well-documented, the linkages that made the industry attractive proved too complex to create quickly and from scratch, particularly on a competitive scale. (For a discussion in a broader Asian context, including countries not covered here, see Odaka, Ono, and Adachi 1988 and the works cited there.)

Only Hong Kong among the countries here has never had an assembly industry. Singapore initially did, but it quickly disappeared when the government wisely abandoned intervention to maintain it. In contrast, New Zealand, Australia, and Taiwan have had very small, highly protected, multi-producer, multi-model, very inefficient domestic assembly industries. In all three, import barriers are being reduced. As that occurs, the industry will decline, at least to the extent their governments allow it to. In a complete free trade regime it seems possible their car assembly industries would wither away, depending on the sourcing strategies of Japanese and American multinationals. Taiwan already has a competitive export industry for simple replacement parts for older American and Japanese cars. Selected, specialized components production for new vehicles may become efficient in all these countries.

Indeed, global sourcing through the market may in the 1990s provide many of the development benefits governments sought in the 1970s and '80s. Efficient diversified assembly industries are improbable in most countries that do not already have them, and in most of the smaller countries that do. But, as a local market grows, it certainly can be efficient to build parts and perhaps even assemble some niche models locally if a substantial part of the output can be exported as part of a global trade in vehicles. There are indications the major Japanese, European, and American assemblers and parts suppliers will continue to implement such a situation if given the opportunity. Lower-wage countries are already becoming a source of labor-intensive components, and workers with no particular initial technical skills seem able to assemble cars, for example, in Mexico.

THOUGHTS ABOUT THE FUTURE

In light of the structural adjustment experience of these nine Pacific Basin countries, what can we say about the 1990s and beyond? Four basic conclusions serve as premises for thinking about the future and drawing policy conclusions. (These reflect my own judgment; while they may agree with me, the authors each derive their own conclusions in the country studies.)

First, some industries will become distressed; the question is what is done about it. The adjustment process inevitably carries with it social and political, as well as economic, costs. Experience in all nine countries suggests it is generally less costly to have the process of adjustment take place sooner rather than—as generally occurs—later. Otherwise, inefficiencies accumulate and costs to consumers rise not only from the delay but from ever-widening protectionist barriers or other forms of government support.

Second, some industries are so important and powerful they will succeed in obtaining government support in times of distress. This is a fundamental political reality in almost all countries. The policy conclusion is that decisions on the nature and form of intervention need to be guided by objectives of economic efficiency and consumer welfare. It is the task of economists and other advisers to make the economic choices and associated costs clear, especially to the political leaders who have the ultimate decision-making authority regarding intervention.

Third, macroeconomic performance—domestically and globally—is probably the single most important determinant of the costs of structural adjustment. This is a direct effect, as expanding industries pull workers and other resources out of distressed industries, and an indirect one, because workers and resources pushed out of a distressed industry are less likely to seek (or obtain) government intervention when they can readily and quickly go to work elsewhere. The policy conclusions are obvious: governments have to get their macroeconomic policies right, including basic fiscal and monetary responsibility. This includes both aggregate demand policy—the appropriate degree and mix of fiscal and monetary ease or restraint—and policies shaping the growth of aggregate supply capability—research and development, savings, and capital formation, as well as education. Also, the policy mix has to result in an exchange rate consistent with a desired balance of payments equilibrium. The government helps most when it provides a rules-of-the-game framework for all players rather than simply support or coddling.

Fourth, the international trade regime, international economic system, and foreign pressures are important in determining whether governments intervene by means of positive domestic policies or import restrictions and, if with restrictions, by what mechanism. Is the approach bilateral or multilateral; "voluntary" or formally imposed; quotas or tariffs; sanctioned by, outside of, or in violation of GATT rules. The policy conclusion is that if the world is to have an effective, comprehensive, open multilateral trading system, GATT must be strengthened or replaced by a much stronger world trade organization. GATT needs a more powerful set of institutional structures, powers, and procedures both to monitor and to judge individual country trade policy performance. The time has come for it to condemn discriminatory safeguards under whatever guise (including "voluntary" systems and orderly marketing arrangements) and press for domestically based positive policies of adjustment.

These policy prescriptions are feasible but require considerable political will, domestically and internationally, which means strong leadership will need to be exercised by the United States, Japan, and members of the European Community working together. But globalism and multilateralism do not have the constituencies they once did—despite their benefits, past, present, and prospective. The world political environment has changed dramatically as a result of the decrease in US-Soviet tension, Central Europe's rejection of its Communist leaders, German reunification, and increasing European Community integration as symbolized by 1992. It is unclear whether the international economic system can be recrafted in the 1990s to increase global well-being and economic efficiency. The minimal reasonable projection is that the system and its leaders will muddle along as they have in the past.

I am optimistic things at least will not get worse and are likely to improve somewhat. However, it does not appear likely the Uruguay Round alone will resolve many of the outstanding issues. For the pessimist, there is the possibility the trading system will deteriorate into several competitive, regionally based blocs (dependent in substantial part on European Community policies and behavior in the 1990s) as well as the danger there will be a widening in the scope of managed trade on a sector basis, particularly for powerful distressed industries.

Textiles and apparel are a major test in the early 1990s of how countries will deal with structural adjustment. In April 1989, Uruguay Round negotiators agreed to phase out the current Multi-Fiber Arrangement, due to expire in mid 1991, and to reintegrate textile and apparel trade into GATT. Whatever the outcome, it is necessary to overcome the formidable political obstacles of vested interest groups who benefit, in exporting as well as in importing countries, from the present system. Indeed, there is the danger GATT will become contaminated by the introduction of some of the MFA's most pernicious aspects into GATT. In any case, it is probably unrealistic as a political matter to expect free trade in textiles and apparel by the end of this century. (See Hamilton 1990, especially chapters 1 and 9 through 12 for insightful consideration of possible outcomes.)

Structural adjustment problems from industries in distress will persist in Canada, the United States, New Zealand, and Australia, and import-restricting measures will continue as the main instrument of intervention. Whether Australia will continue this approach is somewhat less clear. A comprehensive report to the Australian government articulates a clarion call to end all industrial protection by 2000, to expand economic relations with North East Asia and other Pacific Basin countries, and to carry out significant domestic reforms in transport, education, and migration policy (Garnaut 1989).

Japan will be a pivotal case. As in the other four advanced countries, considerable adjustment has taken place. But manufactured imports as a share of domestic consumption is still low, and if it rises rapidly, as I anticipate, the real test of Japan's structural adjustment capabilities is yet to come. Textiles, and particularly apparel, as well as other labor-intensive manufacturers, will be subject to considerable dislocation and decline.

As Taiwan and Korea integrate their domestic markets into the international trading system through further reductions in tariffs and quotas, there are likely to be a number of troubled industries. Given American pressure on their import policies, they likely will use the Japanese model of domestic adjustment. This is congenial, as they have intervened in the past, particularly in Korea, mainly through preferential access to cheap loans.

Change cannot be stopped; at most, it can be delayed, usually at great cost. Markets have demonstrably done the best job accommodating change. Societies normally choose to ameliorate the burdens of those significantly negatively affected, and this can be done in ways that do not reduce overall efficiency or impose other costs that lead to an actual reduction of overall well-being. The goal, then, is to accept change while seeking ways to minimize its social, economic, and political costs, and the costs of those ameliorative actions. To achieve this means to fight against the additional costs that self-serving interest groups attempt to impose on society for their own gain.

BIBLIOGRAPHY

Aho, Michael C. and Thomas O. Bayard. 1984. "Costs and Benefits of Trade Adjustment Assistance." In Robert E. Baldwin and Anne O. Krueger, editors, *The Structure and Evolution of Recent US Trade Policy*. University of Chicago Press.

Bhagwati, Jagdish. 1988. *Protectionism*. Cambridge MA: MIT Press.

—— and Hugh Patrick. 1990. *Aggressive Unilateralism: American's 301 Trade Policy and the World Trading System*. University of Michigan Press.

Cline, William R. 1987. *The Future of World Trade in Textiles and Apparel*. Washington DC: Institute for International Economics.

——. 1989. *American Trade Adjustment: The Global Impact*. Washington DC: Institute for International Economics.

Dore, Ronald P. 1986a. *Flexible Rigidities: Industrial Policy and Structural Adjustment in the Japanese Economy, 1970–1980*. Stanford University Press.

——. 1986b. *Structural Adjustment in Japan, 1970–1982.* Geneva: International Labour Office.

Drysdale, Peter. 1988. *International Economic Pluralism: Economic Policy in East Asia and the Pacific.* Columbia University Press.

Garnaut, Ross. 1989. *Australia and the Northeast Asian Ascendancy: Report to the Prime Minister and the Minister of Foreign Affairs and Trade, 1989 October.* Canberra: Australian Government Publishing Service.

Gregory, Robert G. 1976. "Some Implications of the Growth of the Mining Sector." *Australian Journal of Agricultural Economics* 29(2): 71–91 (Aug).

Hamilton, Carl B., editor. 1990. *Textiles Trade and the Developing Countries: Eliminating the Multifibre Arrangement in the 1990s.* Washington DC: World Bank.

Harrigan, Kathryn Rudie. 1980. *Strategies for Declining Industries.* Lexington MA: DC Heath.

——. 1988. *Managing Maturing Businesses: Restructuring Declining Industries and Revitalizing Troubled Operations.* Lexington MA: DC Heath.

Hatsopoulos, George N., Paul R. Krugman, and Lawrence H. Summers. 1988. "US Competitiveness: Beyond the Trade Deficit." *Science* 241: 299–307 (Jul 15).

Hillman, Arye L. and Heinrich W. Ursprung. 1988. "Domestic Politics, Foreign Interests, and International Trade Policy." *American Economic Review* 78: 729–44 (Sep).

Kelly, Margaret et al. 1988 Dec. *Issues and Developments in International Trade Policy.* International Monetary Fund Occasional Paper # 63. Washington DC: IMF.

Odaka, Konosuke, Keinosuke Ono, and Fumihiko Adachi. 1988. *The Automobile Industry in Japan: A Study of Ancillary Firm Development.* Tokyo: Kinokuniya, and Oxford University Press.

OECD = Organization for Economic Cooperation and Development. 1985. *Cost and Benefit of Protection.* Paris: OECD.

——. 1987. *Structural Adjustment and Economic Performance.*

Okimoto, Daniel I. 1989. *Between MITI and the Market.* Stanford University Press.

Patrick, Hugh, editor, with the assistance of Larry Meissner. 1986. *Japan's High Technology Industries: Lessons and Limitations of Industrial Policy.* University of Washington Press.

Tan, Hong W. 1989 Mar. "Policies towards Troubled Industries in the United States: An Overview." Paper prepared for the RAND-JCER Conference on Restructuring Troubled Industries.

Trebliock, Michael J. 1986. *The Political Economy of Economic Assistance: The Case of Declining Sectors.* V 8 in the series The Collected Research Studies (Royal Commission on the Economic Union and Development Prospects for Canada). University of Toronto Press.

Wilson, Robert. 1989. "Entry and Exit." In George R. Feiwel, editor, *The Economics of Imperfect Competition and Employment.* Macmillan.

1

CANADA
Adjustment Despite Deficiencies in Program Design and Execution

Peter M. Cornell and Paul K. Gorecki

Canada, like other countries, is facing rapid changes in its domestic and international economic environment. Its growth and prosperity demand structural adjustments in response to those changes—a continuous reallocation of resources to pursuits where they will be most productive.

Canada's standard of living is, of course, already highly dependent on foreign trade. Implementation of the Canada-US Free Trade Agreement between 1989 and 1998, and even partial success in the Uruguay Round of Multilateral Trade Negotiations under the General Agreement on Tariffs and Trade (GATT) by 1991 will see that dependence become even greater. The importance of rapid adjustment to trade and trade policy changes will thus increase correspondingly.

In fact, Canadian industry and the particular focus of this essay—those trade-sensitive manufacturing industries facing competition from

This paper has benefited considerably from the comments of the participants in the Declining Industries Structural Adjustment and Trade Policy Implications project, particularly Hugh Patrick's. Dorothy Barette and Micheline St-Cyr conducted valuable data collection tasks, and Lorraine Milobar and the Council's Text Processing Unit ably typed the manuscript under tight deadlines. The usual disclaimer applies. The paper draws upon and extends Economic Council of Canada (1988a, 1988b).

imports—have undergone a good deal of structural adjustment in response to a variety of internal and external shocks. That adjustment has taken place within an environment conditioned both by market forces and by government policies, some of a general, framework nature, others of a more selective nature, targeted at individual groups and industries.

For the most part, however, adjustment in the trade-sensitive industries seems to have taken place despite rather than because of the selective measures. Although the stated goal of those policies was almost invariably one of positive adjustment, their actual implementation, with the exception of those for Canada's footwear industry, seems to have impeded the adjustment process.

This fact has important implications for Canada's own trade policy, which has favored "an open, multilateral trading system" (Canada DEA 1983a, p iv), and for trade negotiations in general. Delay in positive adjustment measures is likely to increase the eventual costs of adjustment and resistance to trade policy changes. Moreover, it means that Canada, a nation with a very strong stake in expanding international trade, has in fact contributed to the recent proliferation of non-tariff barriers to trade which threaten and complicate trade negotiations.

The Environment for Adjustment

Few periods can compare with the last 15 years or so for the variety and intensity of changes bearing on the structural adjustment process. The challenge of international competition for Canadian industry has increased enormously. So too has pressure for adjustment from other sources including technological change. The ability of Canadian governments to deal with such pressures has been conditioned by a wide range of factors, some adverse, some favorable.

The rise of the newly industrialized economies (NIEs) as well as the continued growth of the Japanese economy has resulted in severe pressure on a relatively small number of manufacturing industries in many developed countries, including Canada, since the early 1960s. This pressure was enhanced by a number of factors: tariff reductions under the Kennedy (1966–70) and Tokyo (1979–87) Rounds; declining transport costs; and the growth in developed countries of multinational corporations and large, knowledgeable buyers, such as retail chains, who could quickly take advantage of supply opportunities in the NIEs and Japan. With the prospect of further trade liberalization and the recent emergence of the next-tier NIEs, including the ASEAN countries and China, these pressures are unlikely to abate in the future.[1]

These trade and trade policy changes, which are part of the central focus of this chapter, must, however, be viewed in the context of a much wider range of changes that affect the adjustment process. Indeed, it seems likely they are not the dominant sources of change affecting the industrial economies. Rapid technological advance, especially the influence of microelectronics and the Information Revolution, and shifts in demand, have also brought great pressure for change and major concerns about employment.

Whatever the source of change, the ability of an economy to adjust will depend to a considerable extent on its overall macroeconomic performance. Other things equal, a thriving, growing economy will be more likely to create an environment in which resources flow unimpeded from one industry, region, or occupation to another. Jobs will be easier to come by and workers more willing to move in such an atmosphere of economic security. Furthermore, with strong overall economic growth, domestic production in trade-sensitive industries may increase absolutely even while imports are increasing in relative importance. In such circumstances, adjustment is likely to take the form of new entrants to the labor force or the corporate universe moving to the growing segments, rather than via the more difficult route of existing firms and workers being forced to change job, location, or industry.

In contrast, with sluggish or negative growth, new job opportunities are reduced, general economic uncertainty increased, and workers will be less willing to move to new occupations, regions, or industries. Such conditions also provide a fertile ground for the formation of coalitions of businessmen, workers and regional representatives to seek ameliorative intervention by the state.

This more pessimistic picture is the one that most closely fits Canada —and many other OECD countries—over much of the last two decades, especially during the latter half of the 1970s and early '80s. Such conditions led the OECD (1979) to advocate as an appropriate policy response the goal of "positive adjustment"—that is, policies should aim

---

1. For a fuller account of Canada's trade policy, see Canada, Department of External Affairs 1983b, p 3–10; Hart 1986; and Stone 1984. For a case study of trade-policy making see Protheroe 1980.

The NIEs are, according to the OECD (1988), South Korea, Taiwan, Singapore, Hong Kong, Mexico, and Brazil. The Association of South East Asian Nations (ASEAN) is made up of Malaysia, Thailand, the Philippines, Singapore, Brunei, and Indonesia. Note Singapore is both in ASEAN and an NIE.

to encourage and facilitate the movement of resources in the direction indicated by the market.

Table 1.1 presents several indicators that show the Canadian economy performed much worse in the period after the first OPEC oil price shock of 1973–74 than during the 1960s and early '70s: overall economic growth and productivity declined while unemployment, inflation, and interest rates increased.

The situation was exacerbated by the recession of the early 1980s, for Canada the deepest since the 1930s. Inflation peaked in late 1981 and unemployment reached extremely high levels by historical standards, in excess of 11% for each year from 1982 to 1984. Despite a reasonably strong economic recovery, output took some time to surpass its pre-recession level and it remained below capacity until the second half of the decade. Unemployment averaged close to 10% in the period 1980–87, and it fell below the 9–10% range only in 1987.

It is not only the overall rate of growth of the economy that must be taken into account in considering the environment for change. The

Table 1.1. Indicators of Macroeconomic Performance, 1962–87 (percent; growth rates are annual averages)

	Growth Rate of		Unemployment Level[3]	Inflation	Short-term Interest[4]	Federal Goverment as a Percentage of GDP[5]		
	GDP[1]	Productivity[2]				Expenditures	Revenues	Debt
1962–64	6.3	—	—	1.6	3.8	15.6	15.4	38.8
1965–69	5.4	1.9[a]	4.0[b]	3.7	5.4	15.1	15.9	29.6
1970–74	5.2	2.1	5.8	5.9	5.3	17.5	17.9	23.8
1975–79	4.2	1.5	7.6	8.9	8.8	19.5	16.7	20.6
1980–84	2.3	1.1	9.8	8.7	12.9	21.7	17.1	26.1
1985–87	3.9	1.1	9.7	4.2	8.8	22.6	17.5	38.0

1. Measured in constant 1981 dollars
2. Measured as real GDP per employed person, in constant 1981 dollars
3. Persons aged 15 and over
4. Three-month Treasury Bill rate
5. All measured in current dollars
a. Data for 1967–69
b. Data for 1966–69

For further details on Canada's macroeconomic performance see Economic Council of Canada 1983a and 1988c; Canada, Department of Finance 1987, and various issues of the Bank of Canada Review, a monthly publication that often carries policy statements by Canada's central bank.

Source: Economic Council of Canada, Chart Book Data Bank Series

composition of that growth may also be important. By contrast with the earlier post-World War II years when a major transfer of resources out of Canadian agriculture was accomplished without too much resistance because of rapid growth in other sectors of the economy, the major growth in employment in recent years has been in the service sector (Table 1.2). The fear of manufacturing jobs being replaced by lower-wage employment in services has created an additional obstacle to adjustment.

On the policy side, the problems of macroeconomic demand management were underscored by increasing inflation in the face of little or no economic growth in the latter 1970s and early '80s, then by high unemployment in the face of renewed growth after 1981–82. Fiscal policy remained basically expansionary from the early 1970s to the mid '80s, while monetary policy became increasingly restrictive, especially in the period 1979–82. With the federal government running a persistent deficit after 1975, there has also been a substantial increase in the national debt and in the proportion of federal revenues required for interest. For example, in 1987 the debt constituted almost 40% of GDP, and 28% of

Table 1.2. Employment Distribution and Change, by Industry, 1946–87 (in percents)

1946	1963	1987	Change 1946–87	
60.2	45.3	29.2	24	goods-producing industries
29.4	12.9	6.4	−44	primary
30.8	32.4	22.8	89	secondary[1]
39.8	54.7	70.8	355	service industries
8.1	8.5	7.6	140	regulated services[2]
12.3	16.0	17.7	269	trade
2.7	4.0	5.8	460	finance, insurance, and real estate
16.8	26.2	39.7	506	other services[3]
4,666	6,365	11,955	7,289	total employment, in thousands, a 156% increase during 1946–87

The figures for 1946 and 1963 include 14–year-olds, whereas those for 1987 do not. Newfoundland is not included in the data for 1946.
1. Includes manufacturing and construction
2. Includes transportation, communications, and public utilities
3. Includes community, business, and personal services; and public administration
Source: Economic Council of Canada (1988c, p 5 Table 1–2) based on Economic Council of Canada, 1964; *Economic Goals for Canada* to 1970, First Annual Review; and Statistics Canada, *The Labour Force,* catalog # 71–001, 1987 Dec.

federal revenues were required for interest charges. This overhang of debt reduces the scope for compensatory fiscal action in the event of any renewed slowdown in growth.

Nevertheless, the environment for adjustment has experienced some favorable features. The decline of the foreign exchange value of the Canadian dollar after 1976 was one factor that provided a breathing space for reallocation of resources. That has been reinforced since 1985 by the fact Canada has registered one of the strongest growth rates of all the industrial countries. Moreover, labor force growth has slowed.

On the policy side, too, there have been developments that have helped to cushion the effects of adverse economic conditions on the adjustment process. One was the introduction or expansion in the 1960s and early '70s of a variety of universal publicly funded programs socializing some of the more important risks associated with change. These programs included unemployment insurance, the Canada and Quebec pension plans, and health care. In addition, federal equalization payments to the provinces were set up to provide higher basic standards of government services across the nation.

Moreover, since 1982 Canadian governments have also moved to introduce policies that place greater emphasis on market forces; forces that seem more likely to facilitate change than the interventionist actions they supplant. These market orientated policies include privatization, deregulation, tax reform, repeal of the National Energy Policy, and a considerable reduction in the screening and monitoring of foreign direct investment in Canada. All of these favorable features, along with the absence of at least some of the severe international shocks that characterized the 1970s and early '80s, provide grounds for cautious optimism that the socioeconomic environment will be more conducive to facilitating change.

Canada's Manufacturing Sector

Manufacturing is an important sector of the Canadian economy. In the postwar period it has accounted for approximately one-fifth of Canada's output of goods and services. In contrast, the sector's relative importance in terms of employment and capital stock has declined. These divergent trends reflect the increase in manufacturing productivity that has enabled resources to be released to other sectors of the economy, particularly the service sector. (Similar patterns have been observed in a number of other industrialized countries by Charette et al 1986; on the shift to service sector in Canada, see Picot 1986.)

In terms of the number of workers, the capital stock, and the volume of total output (particularly the latter two), the Canadian manufacturing sector has increased in absolute size since 1971. Thus, resource reallocation has meant that growth of resource use in the manufacturing sector has been slower than in the economy as a whole. Table 1.3 provides data on the relative and absolute size of Canadian manufacturing.

The manufacturing sector is of substantial and growing importance in accounting for Canada's overall levels of exports and imports (Table 1.4). For example, 65% of Canada's exports of goods and services in 1985 were manufactured goods, up from 55% in 1950; the correspond-

Table 1.3. Relative Importance and Growth of Manufacturing, 1961–87 (percents)

	Manufacturing's Share of			Indices of		
	Real Domestic Product[1]	Person-Hours Worked	Net Capital Stock[2]	Real Domestic Product[1]	Employ-ment[3]	Net Capital Stock[2]
1961	19.6	21.6	17.4	—	—	—
1965	21.7	22.9	16.8	—	—	—
1971	20.9	21.5	16.8	72.7	100.0	100.0
1975	20.0	20.0	16.3	83.7	106.9	118.2
1977	20.4	19.3	15.9	93.1	104.7	127.0
1979	20.6	19.3	15.4	101.0	113.9	133.8
1981	19.3	18.3	15.2	100.0	113.9	144.6
1982	17.4	17.3	15.2	87.1	105.0	150.3
1983	18.0	17.1	14.9	92.7	103.0	152.5
1984	19.2	17.4	14.6	104.7	106.2	152.7
1985	19.3	17.1	14.3	110.6	108.9	153.9
1986	19.2	—	14.3	113.5	110.1	157.0
1987	19.4	—	14.3	119.6	—	161.2

1. In 1981 dollars
2. In 1971 dollars, mid-year net stock
3. Defined as the combined total of production and non-production workers; the figure for 1986 is preliminary.

By 1986 employment had, according to this table's source, yet to recover to the level reached prior to the severe recession of the early 1980s. Another source, which contains information for 1987 but is not directly comparable, shows employment in 1987 in manufacturing to be at a level slightly above the peak experienced during 1979–81. In contrast, in other goods producing industries there has been a decline in employment. If goods producing industries are divided into secondary (manufacturing and construction) and primary (agricultural, mining, logging) then, over the period 1946 to 1987, secondary industries increased their employment level by 89% but primary declined by 44%. See Table 1.2 for details.

Source: Based on data from Statistics Canada.

Table 1.4. The Importance of Manufactured Imports and Exports in Canada's Trade, 1950–85

| | Percentage of Total Trade in Goods and Services Accounted for by: | | | | Manufactured Goods as a Percentage of All Goods | | Motor Vehicles and Parts Share of Manufactured Goods | |
| | All Goods | | Manufactured Goods | | | | | |
	Imports	Exports	Imports	Exports	Imports	Exports	Imports	Exports
1950	70.7	75.6	45.1	54.9	65.7	72.6	12.7	1.9
1955	72.3	75.3	53.1	54.3	76.1	72.1	11.3	1.6
1960	68.1	76.9	50.5	51.8	77.5	67.3	13.7	2.1
1965	70.2	78.4	53.7	51.9	81.0	66.3	16.0	6.0
1970	69.6	79.5	57.2	59.2	85.2	74.5	27.1	26.8
1975	76.4	82.5	58.9	55.0	79.4	66.6	29.2	28.4
1980	74.2	83.7	56.1	61.2	78.3	73.2	25.1	19.4
1985	72.6	84.0	62.0	65.0	88.2	77.4	34.6	36.0

Based on current-dollar values of imports and exports
Source: Economic Council of Canada (1988b, p 7 Table 1–1) based on Economic Council of Canada, CANDIDE database, derived from Statistics Canada data

ing numbers for manufactured imports were 62 and 45. An important factor in both of these increases was the signing of the 1965 Canada-US Auto Pact, which allowed duty free trade in automobiles and parts, at least on the production side, provided certain conditions were fulfilled. (For a discussion of the Auto Pact see, eg, Beigie 1970 and Wonnacott 1987.)

Trade in manufactures has also increased in relation to the size of the manufacturing sector. Manufactured exports (in relation to domestic production of manufactured goods) and manufactured imports (in relation to Canadian domestic consumption of manufactured goods) have both grown substantially in the period 1966–87 (Table 1.5). By the end of the period, exports accounted for 36% of domestic production; imports, 37% of domestic consumption. (See Table 1.8 for the corresponding ratios for 20 manufacturing industries.)

While a number of factors, including the Auto Pact, are responsible for these increases in trade of manufactured goods, falling multilateral tariffs are undoubtedly important. Table 1.6 presents details of Canada's tariffs on manufactured goods, using a variety of indicators. All show substantial reduction in protection between 1971 and 1985: the nominal tariff on all imports fell from 7.1% to 4.2%; while duty free imports rose from 54% of all imports in 1971 to 63% in 1985.

The growth of the manufacturing sector measured in terms of im-

Table 1.5. The importance of manufactured exports and imports, 1966–87

	Percentage of Manufactured Goods	
	Exports, in Production	Imports, in Consumption[1]
1966	18.8	21.0
1968	23.4	24.0
1970	26.2	25.5
1972	25.8	27.6
1974	25.0	29.1
1975	23.9	28.8
1976	26.2	29.2
1977	28.5	30.6
1978	30.4	31.6
1979	30.3	32.6
1980	30.6	31.3
1981	29.6	31.3
1982	30.2	28.8
1983	31.7	31.5
1984	35.8	35.8
1985	34.7	35.6
1986	37.0	37.9
1987	35.9	37.0

The 1966 to 1984 data are based on the 1970 Standard Industrial Classification; the 1985, 1986, and 1987 data use the 1980 SIC. A comparison of the import and export ratios for the years 1981 to 1984 —when they were available using both the 1970 and 1980 SIC definitions of manufacturing —indicates differences ranging between 0.2 and 0.5 of a percentage point.

1. consumption = domestic production + imports—exports

Source: Canada, Department of Regional Industrial Expansion, *Manufacturing Trade and Measures,* various issues.

ports, exports, and openness to trade provides the background for our examination of the processes and mechanisms of adjustment within manufacturing to the challenges and opportunities offered in the international marketplace.

IDENTIFICATION OF TRADE-SENSITIVE MANUFACTURING INDUSTRIES

Canada, like most other industrialized countries, has a number of industries that are experiencing problems in the international marketplace. But whether such problems are permanent—thus calling for re-

Table 1.6. Level of Nominal Tariff Protection in Manufacturing, 1971–85

	Nominal Tariff Level on		Percentage of Imports not Dutiable
	All Imports[1]	Dutiable Imports[2]	
1971	7.1	15.4	54.0
1972	7.3	15.5	52.9
1973	6.9	15.3	55.0
1974	7.1	15.0	52.9
1975	6.7	15.1	55.9
1976	6.4	15.1	57.4
1977	6.0	14.7	58.8
1978	5.9	14.4	59.3
1979	5.6	14.2	60.6
1980	5.4	13.8	60.6
1981	5.4	13.2	59.4
1982	5.1	12.9	60.1
1983	4.9	12.5	60.9
1984	4.5	11.6	61.6
1985	4.2	11.2	62.8

1. Total duties collected, divided by total value of all imports, excluding duties
2. Total duties collected, divided by total value of dutiable imports, excluding duties
3. Percentage of all imports (excluding duties) that entered Canada duty free
Source: Economic Council of Canada (1988b, p 142 Table A-10) based on special tabulations provided by the International Trade Division of Statistics Canada

sources to be reallocated to other industries or sectors of the economy — or temporary, is not always easy to specify in advance. Picking losers can be as difficult as picking winners.

In recognition of this difficulty we tried to use a systematic approach to choosing an appropriate sample of industries. That involved assessment of a number of "problem" industries on the basis of four criteria. Did the industry actually decline in size? Were there any indications of a loss of comparative advantage? What happened to the tariff levels affecting the industry? Were sector-specific government policies to assist the industry to adjust to the realities of the international market actually introduced? Such an approach should ensure the sample's representativeness and provide more confidence in the use of the results as a basis for policy.

Industry Size

Industry size can be measured in several ways. Here we have chosen to focus on labor inputs or, more specifically, the number of people employed. A decline in employment may be either absolute or relative. Resources will likely be reallocated when the level of industry employment actually contracts. On the other hand, existing labor resources are less likely to be reallocated if an industry only suffers a decline in employment relative to total manufacturing—as new workers enter the labor force, they are more likely to enter the growing industries whose share of manufacturing sector employment is increasing. To the extent that decline is gradual, no labor may be "forced" to reallocate if quits and other forms of attrition are sufficiently large to cover any decline. (This discussion draws upon and extends Baldwin and Gorecki 1990, ch 2.)

In Table 1.7 we present, for various periods between 1951 and 1983, the sign of changes in absolute employment for an industry classification

Table 1.7. Sign of Changes in the Level of Industry Employment in Manufacturing, 1951–83

1951–58	1958–63	1963–67	1967–72	1972–79	1979–83	
+	+	+	+	+	−	food and beverages
+	−	0	−	−	0	tobacco
+	+	+	+	+	0	rubber and plastics
0	+	−	−	−	−	leather
−	+	+	+	−	−	textiles
−	+	+	+	+	−	knitting mills and clothing
+	+	−	+	+	−	wood
+	+	+	+	+	−	furniture and fixtures
+	+	+	+	+	−	paper and allied products
+	+	+	+	+	+	printing and publishing
−	+	+	+	+	−	primary metals
+	+	+	+	+	−	metal fabricating
−	+	+	+	+	−	machinery
+	−	+	+	+	−	transportation equipment
+	+	+	0	+	−	electrical products
+	+	+	+	+	−	non-metallic mineral products
+	−	+	+	+	+	petroleum and coal
+	+	+	0	+	+	chemicals
+	+	+	+	+	−	miscellaneous

The use of a broad classification system rather than a narrower industry definition reflects two factors. First, an implicit assumption that adjustment is easier within rather than between broad industry categories. Use of a narrower or finer classification system would thus overstate adjustment problems. Second, the longer the time span for comparison, the more aggregative tend to be the available data. Because our interest lies in structural, not transitory or cyclical, changes, the longer time span is preferred.

Source: Based on Economic Council of Canada, CANDIDE database.

system that divides manufacturing into 19 industries. In view of our discussion of Table 1.3, we would expect more consistently positive than negative signs. However, only one industry demonstrated a continuous trend up (or down)—printing and publishing—reflecting, in part, the recession of the early 1980s. If attention is confined to the periods prior to 1979, 6 more industries exhibit continuous positive signs for all periods; no additional industries exhibit consistent negative signs. If 1979–84 is used instead of 1979–83, 5 more industries exhibit a positive rather than negative employment change: primary metals; electrical products; tobacco; rubber and plastics; and paper and allied industries.

Because a sign change may not be sufficient to reverse a trend, the level of industry employment was regressed on a time trend. Virtually all of the industries exhibited a consistent significant (at the 5% level) increase in employment; only leather had a negative and significant sign; while tobacco, textiles, and knitting mills and clothing all had no trend, either up or down, over the period 1951–83.

A similar exercise on the sign of relative share of manufacturing employment shows only two industries exhibit continuous relative growth or decline. Rubber and plastics moved up steadily; leather moved down in every period. In all other cases there are sign reversals. (See Baldwin and Gorecki 1990, p 18 table 2–2.) Again, because sign changes may not reverse a trend, the shares for each industry were regressed on a time trend. On this basis, in addition to leather, three other industries—tobacco, textiles, and knitting mills and clothing—stand out as having a significant negative trend at the 5% level of significance. Transportation equipment, printing and publishing, and rubber and plastics show an upward trend. Transportation equipment reflects the influence of the 1965 Canada-US Auto Pact. However, using annual data from 1961 to 1985 it appears shipbuilding recorded significant declines in relative and absolute employment levels.

The absolute level of employment in the four industries that experienced a relative decline in importance either fell or remained essentially unchanged. On the other hand, most of those industries showing a significant increase in employment demonstrated no discernible trend in relative importance.

Comparative Advantage

There are several possible measures of how well particular industries do in terms of importing and exporting, and thus of their ability to compete in the international market place. Table 1.8 presents such measures for 1971, 1978, and 1982: an index of comparative advantage;

imports as a proportion of domestic disappearance; exports as a percentage of domestic production; and an index of intra-industry trade. Each reveals a different facet of the trade picture of an industry.

Of the measures, perhaps the most revealing in terms of selecting industries suffering potential problems of foreign competition is the index of comparative advantage. The lower the value of the index, the less the ability of the Canadian industry to compete with imports, or the greater the loss in comparative advantage. The index varies between 0 (imports, no exports) and 2 (exports, no imports).

The measure can be used to divide industries by whether gains or losses in comparative advantage are experienced. Only 3 industries of the 20 in the table have successively lower values of the index: leather, knitting mills, and clothing. By 1982 these 3 recorded the lowest values of the comparative advantage index in the manufacturing sector. Successively higher values of the index appear for 9 industries: rubber and plastic products, textiles, printing and publishing, primary metals, metal fabricating, machinery, nonmetallic mineral products, petroleum and coal products, and chemicals and chemical products. These industries included both those with high values of the index in 1982 (eg, primary metals) and those with low values (eg, textiles). The 8 remaining industries showed no consistent trend, up or down, using the three data points 1971, 1978, and 1982.

Tariffs

Tariffs have been reduced in the successive rounds of the Multilateral Trade Negotiations under GATT since 1947. In industries that had or expected to have the greatest difficulty in competing with offshore competition, one would expect tariffs would not only remain high but also fall more slowly; in industries where Canada expected to be able to compete, tariffs would be much more likely to fall to low levels. (For further discussion on this for Canada, see Baldwin and Gorecki 1985.)

To capture the impact of the Tokyo Round of tariff cuts, our focus is on the period 1978 to 1985. The 5 industries showing the smallest decline in tariffs were food and beverages (where tariff protection actually increased), leather, textiles, knitting mills, and clothing. The last 4 had the highest levels of tariff protection in Canada's manufacturing sector apart from furniture and fixtures. In 1985 duties as a percentage of imports (net of duties) ranged from 11 to 22% for these 4; only furniture and fixtures exceeded 11% among the 20 industries listed in Table 1.8. The average for all manufacturing was 4.2%. The 5 industries with the largest decline in tariffs were paper and allied industries, print-

Table 1.8. Significance of Imports, Exports, and Intra-industry Trade in Manufacturing, 1971, 1978, and 1982

Comparative Advantage[1]			Imports as a Percentage of Disappearance[2]			Exports as a Percentage of Production[3]			Index of Intra-industry Trade[4]			
1971	1978	1982	1971	1978	1982	1971	1978	1982	1971	1978	1982	
71	66	78	18	23	21	12	14	14	45	46	44	food and beverages
58	50	51	2	2	3	1	1	1	58	50	51	tobacco products
31	53	85	19	25	23	4	12	20	31	53	85	rubber and plastic products
32	31	29	25	36	36	6	9	9	32	30	29	leather
27	27	38	27	34	32	6	8	12	27	26	37	textiles
12	7	7	32	34	33	3	2	2	12	7	7	knitting mills
64	33	28	10	15	18	4	3	4	60	29	23	clothing
144	154	162	11	19	18	39	51	55	55	41	35	wood
86	49	82	6	15	12	5	6	10	78	41	61	furniture and fixtures
132	130	132	9	13	13	43	44	45	25	26	29	paper and allied products
21	30	34	27	20	21	3	4	4	21	30	34	printing and publishing

primary metals	110	124	128	35	30	30	38	40	43	72	73	67
metal fabricating	51	56	58	22	29	29	10	14	14	48	55	55
machinery	47	52	54	70	75	76	44	55	58	47	52	54
transportation equipment	94	90	92	76	86	90	78	87	91	76	75	67
electrical products	49	45	59	33	50	47	14	26	27	48	45	59
nonmetallic mineral products	34	51	52	36	40	43	11	16	18	26	41	43
petroleum and coal products	50	100	115	25	46	—	17	42	86	50	52	76
chemicals & chemical products	59	63	78	40	52	35	26	31	28	44	48	60
miscellaneous	37	33	42	57	62	70	27	30	48	37	33	42

For each major group, each of the four indices is the weighted average for the four-digit industries into which the industry is divided. The weights used are each industry's total imports in the year for which the variable was estimated. All 167 four-digit manufacturing industries were used.

1. Measured as 100 times [(exports minus imports) divided by (exports plus imports)] plus 1. The index varies between 0 and 200; the greater the importance of exports relative to imports, the closer the index is to its upper limit.

2. Domestic disappearance = domestic production + imports − exports. If there are no imports, the index is equal to 0; if imports supply the entire demand of the Canadian market, the index is equal to 100.

3. If there are no exports, this index equals 0; if all domestic production is exported, the index will equal 100.

4. Measured as 100 times [(exports plus imports) minus (the absolute value of exports minus imports)] divided by (exports plus imports). This index varies between 0 and 100. When the values of imports and exports are the same, the index is equal to 100; when trade consists of either only imports or exports, the index is equal to 0. The closer the value of the index to 100, the greater the importance of intra-industry trade.

Source: Economic Council of Canada (1988b, p 19 Table 2–2) based on special tabulations prepared by the International Trade Division of Statistics Canada.

ing and publishing, electrical products, petroleum and coal products, and miscellaneous manufacturing. These industries all had nominal tariff protection of 6.7% or less in 1985, some 3 percentage points below their 1978 levels.[2]

Sector-Specific Policies

The final criteria for selecting industries experiencing difficulties competing with imports is the provision by government of sector-specific policy assistance. In effect, these industries have identified themselves as experiencing trade-related adjustment problems.

In providing assistance targeted selectively at an individual industry, governments can choose from a wide array of instruments. Three have been of particular importance in Canada: quantitative restrictions on imports; modernization and output subsidies (in contrast to some other countries, such as Japan, subsidies to reduce capacity have not been used); and labor adjustment programs. Each of these is discussed below. The industries assisted, and in some cases continuing to be assisted, are: clothing, knitting mills, textiles, leather (footwear); paper and allied industries (pulp and paper mills); and transportation equipment (automobiles and shipbuilding).

Industries Likely to Experience Adjustment Problems

We have used four criteria to identify a sample of industries suffering competitive problems. Use of the criteria to determine the sample of

2. See Economic Council of Canada 1988b, p 133 table A-1, for more complete data.

Tobacco should be included on the list of smallest declines as it experienced the lowest decline of all the industries between 1978 and 1985—actually an increase of 20%. However, in view of the very high tariff levels, it was decided to omit it from consideration. Furthermore, there is a problem in interpreting nominal tariffs for tobacco as an indicator of the percentage by which domestic prices can be raised, because of the large difference between the imported price and the domestic Canadian selling price, which reflects the imposition of various excise taxes, not typical of most industries.

An alternative measure of tariff protection is the effective rate of protection. This is defined as the decline in value added that may occur if nominal tariff protection is removed on both inputs and outputs. More formally, it is $(V'-V)/V'$, where $V' =$ value added per unit of output under protection, $V =$ value added per unit of output after protection has been removed, and "value added" is defined as the return to the primary factors of production, labor, and capital. Unfortunately data exist only after protection has been imposed and thus certain assumptions are necessary to derive the no-protection case, V. Since the validity of these assumptions may vary over time with the possibility that the trend will be affected, it was decided to use nominal tariff rates. For further discussion and some results—which demonstrate that the level of effective tariffs exceed the level of nominal tariffs—see Economic Council of Canada 1983b, p 112 table 9–2, and 1988b, p 134 table A–2; and Wilkinson and Norrie 1975.

trade-sensitive industries is not without a certain ambiguity, since some of the industries have had gains in one or another of the criteria. Also, the results across these criteria are not wholly comparable for a number of reasons, including different time periods, industry classification, and statistical techniques used. Despite these shortcomings, some reasonably concrete conclusions do emerge as to an appropriate sample for a study of policies, processes, and mechanisms for resource reallocation.

To resolve the issue of industries that have had gains in one or another of the criteria, we have divided the trade-sensitive industries into two groups, each of which, as we shall see later, relate to the cause of their adjustment problems. First are industries that appear to be suffering longer term structural decline in relative if not absolute terms usually, in part at least, because of a loss of comparative advantage. These industries—textiles, clothing, knitting mills, footwear (part of leather), and shipbuilding (part of transportation equipment)—have also received sector-specific assistance. A question mark is perhaps in order for textiles because, although the industry is declining in relative importance, the measure of comparative advantage suggests its ability to meet international competition has increased.

A second group includes industries that appear to be experiencing temporary, cyclical, or transitory downside adjustment problems—automobiles (part of transportation equipment), and pulp and paper (part of paper and allied industries). These two industries appear only because they are in receipt of sector-specific policy assistance. Indeed transportation equipment has positive trends for both absolute and relative share employment indicators, and paper and allied products has a positive trend in absolute employment and had significant tariff reduction in the 1978–85 period.

The ambiguity in the appropriate designation illustrates the problems of determining ex ante whether an industry is experiencing a long-term structural loss of competitiveness or a short-term transitory problem. In the early 1980s it looked as though the North American automobile industry belonged in the first category. Now with the rise in the value of the Japanese yen as well as some improvement in the performance of the North American industry the transitory designation seems more appropriate. Hence, the distinctions between transitory and permanent should be viewed with some caution.

In any case, we have five broad industries in our sample of trade-sensitive industries: paper and allied products (narrowed to pulp and paper mills where possible), leather, textiles, knitting mills and clothing, and transportation equipment. At times in the discussion that follows the last of these is separated into shipbuilding and automobiles, and knitting mills and clothing are treated separately, giving us seven industries. [3]

ADJUSTMENT IN TRADE-SENSITIVE MANUFACTURING INDUSTRIES

Adjustment by workers and firms to changes in supply and demand is an ongoing part of the working of the market economy. Workers change regions, occupations, or employers for a better match of their skills and satisfaction of various preferences. Firms not only attempt to hire workers who will best meet their requirements, but they also experiment with new products and production processes, some of which will be successful, others less so. This ongoing dynamic of the market results in worker layoffs, instituted by firms, and quits by workers, new firm creation and failure, as well as in expansion and contraction of existing producers. (This section draws on Economic Council of Canada 1988b, ch 3 p 21–35.)

In considering the adjustment process in trade-sensitive industries, a benchmark of comparison is needed to gauge whether their ongoing adjustment is such as to suggest there are prima facie grounds for introducing sector-specific policies to supplement general or framework policies such as unemployment insurance and medicare. Are rates of firm failure, permanent layoffs and indicators of occupation and interindustry mobility much lower in those industries? Is the work force composed disproportionately of older workers who are likely to experience particularly difficult adjustment problems? The benchmark selected is the record of total manufacturing. This is taken as the "norm" or "average" adjustment that can be and is accommodated. In some sense then, it can be taken as a level acceptable to society.

Worker Turnover

The first indicator of adjustment looks directly at the number of workers who leave their employer. These separations can be either temporary—if the worker returns to the same employer—or permanent. In the administrative data source used here, a two-year period is used to determine whether a layoff is permanent or temporary.

3. Two industries that might have been are not included in the sample. Tobacco is not included because although it experienced a relative decline, it received no sector-specific assistance and, judging from Table 1.8, little import penetration. If time and resources had permitted, it might have been useful to compare this industry's adjustment experience with the others. Also not included is food and beverages, which has had increased tariff protection, but does not meet the criteria that it declined in size.

"Worker separations" are divided into two different but related components—displacements and attrition. Data on the two components for various trade-sensitive industries and manufacturing are presented in Table 1.9.

Displacements are firm-initiated and refer to those worker separations resulting from layoffs caused by lack of work. The permanent layoff rate indicates the degree to which workers are required or forced to find work elsewhere because of firm activity. In contrast, the temporary layoff rate reflects such factors as the seasonal or cyclical nature of the industry. Hence, our attention will be on the permanent layoff component of displacements.

Over the period 1975–83 the average annual number of permanent layoffs in manufacturing as a whole was 11.6% of the labor force. All of the trade-sensitive industries had permanent layoff rates at or slightly below the manufacturing average. Hence, it would appear that in terms

Table 1.9. Separation Rates in Selected Trade-Sensitive Manufacturing Industries, 1975–83 (annual averages, in percents)

Displacements		Attritions		
Permanent	*Return*[1]	*Quits*	*Others*[2]	
11.4	13.4	10.8	14.0	leather
11.1	14.9	9.8	14.4	textiles
11.6	11.9	9.6	16.0	knitting mills and clothing
11.0	18.6	6.6	16.7	paper and allied products[3]
11.5	42.0	8.1	37.5	transportation equipment[4]
11.6	12.9	9.5	14.2	all industries mean[5]
1.1	2.1	0.5	1.4	standard error of the mean

Separation rates are as a percentage of employment, defined as all workers for whom an employer filed at least one T4s income tax return in a year and whose income is largely from work in a manufacturing industry.

Due to data problems, 1980 is excluded from the averages.

1. Workers returning to the same employer within 2 years of being laid off

2. Includes the following reasons for separation: labor dispute; return to school; illness or injury; pregnancy; and early retirement

3. Pulp and paper represented 69% of the 1971 labor force in paper and allied products, and 68% in 1981.

4. Shipbuilding had 8% of the 1971 transportation equipment labor force, motor vehicles (which includes manufacturing, parts, and accessories) had 55%. In 1981 the shares were 8% and 53%.

5. The industry classification system divides manufacturing into the same 19 industries as Table 1.7.

Source: Robertson 1987, Tables A-26 to A-33; and additional data supplied by Robertson

of the costs imposed on workers forced to find another employer because of a layoff, trade-sensitive industries appear to impose less, not more, costs on workers.

Attritions, on the other hand, are worker-initiated, although they may sometimes be caused indirectly by the decline of a firm, if it leads workers to anticipate a layoff and thus leave their jobs. Attritions are divided into several categories for administrative purposes: quits, labor dispute, return to school, illness or injury, pregnancy, early retirement, and "other." On an annual basis, "quits" was the primary cause of attrition over the period 1974–83, accounting, on average, for about 40% of all attritions.

Quits in the trade-sensitive industries were quite similar to those for the manufacturing sector, with the exception of paper and allied products and transportation equipment. It is not clear why these two industries have a lower quit rate. It may be because their wage rates are much higher than the other trade-sensitive industries. Transportation equipment has, inexplicably, a rate of "attrition for other reasons" markedly higher than the manufacturing average, but the other four industries are fairly close to it. Thus, there is considerable ongoing adjustment in trade-sensitive industries because of attritions.

Permanent layoffs, quits, and other reasons typically do not differ markedly between trade-sensitive industries and the total manufacturing sector. Thus, suggestions that these industries are bearing undue costs of adjustment or that there is a smaller margin for adjustment are not supported by this evidence.

The data on displacements and attritions are a useful starting point in examining worker adjustment. However, it is only a starting point. If workers leave one employer to move to another offering work in a closely related occupation in the same industry, it may be difficult for them to adjust should that industry undergo a long-term decline in activity as a result of structural change in the economy. On the other hand, if workers move to other industries or occupations relatively frequently, we can expect adjustment to be less painful and a wider margin of adjustment to exist. The degree of labor mobility thus provides indirect evidence of the adaptability of the labor force.

Employer and Occupational Mobility

In any given year, separations in the Canadian economy are equal to about one-third of the labor force. About one-half of all these workers simply change employers, while the other half draws unemployment insurance. Employer and occupational mobility rates have been calculated for a sample of those in the manufacturing sector who drew unemployment insurance; the results are summarized in Table 1.10.

The data suggest there is greater occupational mobility in trade-sensitive industries than across all manufacturing industries. This conclusion holds irrespective of whether the worker changed employer or not. Thus, in terms of occupational mobility, trade-sensitive industries do not appear to suffer any particular problems or to have a narrower margin for adjustment, should the industry suffer long-term decline.

Interindustry Movements of Workers

The evidence on the degree of movement between occupations, whether or not accompanied by a change in employer, does not by itself adequately reveal the degree of adjustment, since it does not show whether those workers who change employers move only a short distance to other employers in the same industry or in closely related industries. The greater the ongoing movement of workers between industries, the easier it will be for them to find alternative employment in other industries should their present industry of employment undergo structural change. The indices available on inter-industry movement of workers are mostly of the case study type. Usually there is little in the way of a benchmark such as an average of all manufacturing, thus making comparisons and inferences difficult.

In an early attempt to examine the impact of textile and clothing plant closures in the mid 1970s, surveys were conducted of workers who had been laid off because of plant closures and cutbacks. The results indicated a substantial degree of inter-industry relocation by workers. The proportions of laid-off workers who subsequently found work in the same industry were only 10% for textiles and 37% for clothing. The proportions of those who found work in other manufacturing industries were 39 and 24% respectively; in each case, the remainder went to services and other industries.

Subsequent studies of interindustry mobility using various administrative records of the federal government provide a more detailed view of the data. They look not only at the destination of workers but also at their origin. Such studies have been conducted for several trade-sensitive industries identified above: footwear (Alam 1985), shipbuilding (Henderson 1987), automobiles (Automotive Industry Human Resources Task Force 1986). All demonstrate considerable worker mobility across industries.[4]

4. Adjustment to increased trade flows can either be intra- or inter-industry. In the former case what is relevant is the ability of workers to move within an industry, perhaps

Table 1.10. Employer and Occupational Mobility in Manufacturing, 1987–82 (percents)

Re-Employed Workers Changing					
	Occupation			Additional	
Em-			And Em-	Mobility	
ployer[1]	Total[2]	Only[3]	ployer[4]	(ratio)[5]	
68	56	40	64	1.6	food & beverages
60	—	—	—	—	tobacco products
77	56	32	63	2.0	rubber & plastic products
71	53	62	50	0.8	leather
66	64	62	65	1.1	textiles
74	63	56	65	1.2	knitting mills
67	56	43	63	1.5	clothing
72	58	53	60	1.1	wood
72	56	38	63	1.7	furniture & fixtures
50	49	40	58	1.5	paper & allied products
72	44	30	49	1.7	printing & publishing
45	40	30	53	1.8	primary metals
72	51	33	58	1.8	metal fabricating
58	49	41	55	1.3	machinery
36	62	63	60	1.0	transportation equipment
64	43	28	52	1.9	electrical products
68	52	38	59	1.6	nonmetallic mineral products
64	22	17	25	1.5	petroleum & coal products
68	39	13	51	3.9	chemicals & chemical products
72	48	29	56	1.9	miscellaneous
65	50	39	56	1.6	average

Mobility is calculated by comparing the status in 1978 and 1982 of workers who claimed unemployment insurance benefits at least twice during the intervening period. The data are drawn from Employment and Immigration Canada's operational (longitudinal) data, based on a sample of 17,216 individuals.

1. Re-employed workers changing employer as a percentage of all those re-employed.

2. Re-employed workers changing occupation as a percentage of all those re-employed.

3. Workers re-employed by their previous employer but changing occupation, as a percentage of those re-employed by their previous employer. This can be thought of as the probability that a worker who remained with the same employer changed occupation.

4. Re-employed workers changing *both* employer and occupation, as a percentage of those changing employer. This can be thought of as the probability that a worker who changed employers changed occupation.

5. This column is intended to estimate the additional occupational mobility of workers who changed employers. The ratios are obtained by dividing column 4 by column 3. When the ratio is 1, workers who changed employers showed no greater inclination to change occupations than those who returned to their previous employer. The greater the ratio, the more likely changing employers is to result in a change in occupation.

Source: Grey 1985, p 11 and 20, plus revisions supplied by Grey and authors' calculations.

Mobility By Age Group

Age is an important factor in determining the ease with which workers can adjust to long-term industry decline. Using a number of indicators including changes in rates of pay, the time needed to find another job, and the duration of any subsequent job, the evidence suggests that older workers, particularly those 55 or older, had more adjustment problems than younger workers. Thus there may be a rationale for some form of government assistance to older workers, particularly those who have exhausted their unemployment insurance benefits and have little prospect of re-employment, even with training.

If the proportion of older workers in the labor force is significantly higher in trade-sensitive industries than in all manufacturing, it would suggest particularly difficult adjustment problems in these industries. The relevant data are provided in Table 1.11, at the level of industry classification most closely approximating the industries receiving assistance. Concentrating only on workers aged 55 to 64, the data suggest that in 1971 three of the seven trade-sensitive industries—shipbuilding, pulp and paper mills, and motor vehicles—differed substantially (2 percentage points or more) from all manufacturing, while the others were within 1 point. By 1981, older workers accounted for a smaller proportion of the labor force in all but two of the industries, even though such workers were a larger part of the total manufacturing labor force. Only shipbuilding had a higher than average proportion of older workers. Thus, by 1981 the trade-sensitive industries did not, on the whole, have older worker forces.

Firm Turnover

The focus of attention now moves from workers to the behavior of firms. In this context we mean the degree to which firms enter and exit an industry. Trade-sensitive industries may, for example, be characterized by much lower levels of firm turnover, suggesting excessive rigidity.

In order to address these issues we analyzed firm data for two years,

---

between different firms or regions; in the latter case what is relevant is the ability to move between industries. An indicator of whether trade is primarily intra- rather than inter-industry is to be found in Table 1.8. This suggests that, by and large, for the trade-sensitive industries selected for study, the primary adjustment process would be inter- rather than intra-industry (ie, a low value of the intra-industry trade index). Thus, to some extent, the record of worker mobility across industries in trade-sensitive industries will reflect the importance of this mechanism.

Table 1.11. Importance of Older Workers in Selected Trade-Sensitive Industries, 1971 and 1981 (in thousands and percents)

| | All Ages | | Age 45–54 | | | | Age 55–64 | | | |
	1971 No.	1981 No.	1971 No.	1971 %[1]	1981 No.	1981 %[1]	1971 No.	1971 %[1]	1981 No.	1981 %[1]
shoe factories	18	20	2.7	15	2.9	14	1.9	11	1.8	9
textiles	69	83	12.1	18	13.7	16	7.7	11	9.3	11
knitting mills	18	23	2.8	16	3.8	17	2.0	11	2.1	9
clothing	95	130	16.5	17	23.5	18	11.2	12	12.5	10
motor vehicles	90	110	16.9	19	21.8	20	7.5	8	10.6	10
shipbuilding and repair	13	17	3.1	24	2.7	16	2.7	20	2.7	16
pulp and paper mills	85	99	17.6	21	18.2	18	11.6	14	13.0	13
all manufacturing	1,707	2,279	315.0	18	375.4	16	186.8	11	238.6	14

1. Percentage of the industry's labor force accounted for by workers in the specified age group.
Source: Statistics Canada, Census of Canada for 1971 and 1981.

1970 and 1979. Firms in each industry were divided into two categories: new firms, or "births" (existed in the industry in 1979 but not in 1970); and exiting firms or "deaths" (existed in the industry in 1970 but not 1979). A birth can occur in two ways: the firm can build a new plant, or it can acquire an existing plant. Similarly, death can occur in two ways: a firm can close a plant or it can sell it. Table 1.12 presents data on the degree of firm entry and exit.

The critical question with respect to the data is whether the behavior of firm entry and exit differs so significantly between total manufacturing and the trade-sensitive industries as to suggest the latter may have particular adjustment problems. There are clearly differences between individual trade-sensitive industries and the overall pattern of change at the manufacturing level. Nevertheless, in one very important sense, the patterns of change for manufacturing and the trade-sensitive industries show substantial agreement: there is considerable underlying firm turnover because of entry and exit. Thus, there is little evidence that Canada's trade-sensitive industries face an adjustment problem because of an unduly rigid industrial structure.

Table 1.12. Firm Entry and Exit in Selected Trade-Sensitive Manufacturing Industries, 1970–79 (percentages of the number of firms in the industry in 1970)

Exit[1]	Entry[2]	
33	18	shoe factories
46	34	textiles
39	26	clothing
45	26	knitting mills
24	25	pulp and paper
47	35	motor vehicles
50	57	shipbuilding and repair
43	36	manufacturing

The data on firm entry and exit were estimated at the 4–digit level, which divides manufacturing into 167 industries. For the 2–digit classification and the manufacturing sector data, unweighted averages of the relevant set of 4–digit industries were used.

1. Firm exit via plant closure or divestiture in the given industry. An exit is defined as a firm that owned at least one plant in the industry in 1970 but not in 1979.

2. Firm entry via plant opening or acquisition in the given industry. An entrant is defined as a firm that owned at least one plant in the industry in 1979 but not in 1970.

Source: Special tabulations provided by Business and Labour Market Analysis, Statistical Canada

Conclusion

In considering adjustment in Canada's trade-sensitive industries we have used a variety of indicators of firm and worker behavior to determine whether:

• the structure of these industries is excessively rigid;
• there is a smaller margin for adjustment; and
• labor market behavior suggests higher costs of labor adjustment.

On the basis of the evidence—albeit limited—the most appropriate conclusion is that trade-sensitive industries do not seem to differ from manufacturing in general in ways that would suggest greater structural rigidities, a smaller margin for adjustment, or higher labor market adjustment costs.

One implication of these results is that the levels of skill specificity and sunk capital do not differ significantly between trade-sensitive industries and all manufacturing. Some preliminary work was undertaken on the importance of sunk capital—measured very crudely as capital stock per employe—in trade-sensitive industries. With the exception of paper and allied industries, capital stock was not more important in trade-sensitive industries compared to all manufacturing.[5]

The similarities that appear when the observed adjustment patterns in trade-sensitive industries are compared to those in all manufacturing may reflect structural traits characterizing the large majority of Canadian manufacturing industries. But they could also reflect successful sector-specific government intervention designed to ensure trade-sensitive industries should not have to adjust any more than the manufacturing average. To address this issue fully requires a suitable counterfactual —what would have happened without sector-specific government intervention—which could then be compared with the adjustment record. Unfortunately, such an exercise has not been undertaken. Instead, limited information is available on the impact of sector-specific policies.

This research suggests that impact of the sector-specific policies (discussed below) was limited. The subsidy programs, for example, appear to have had little incremental impact on investment (and thus employment). Quantitative restrictions on imports of clothing accounted for

5. Capital is measured as mid-year gross stock in 1971 dollars, while employment includes both production and non-production employees. Such data were used to estimate capital stock per employe for the years 1971, 1978, 1982, and 1985, and were only available at the 2-digit level of industry aggregation (eg, leather rather than shoe factories, paper and allied industries rather than pulp and paper mills). The data source was various Statistics Canada publications (Catalog # 13–568 and 13–211).

only an estimated 9% of the industry's employment in 1979. In contrast, tariffs protected 12%. Hence, while sector-specific policies had an impact, they would not seem powerful enough to explain the similarity between the observed patterns of adjustment in trade-sensitive industries and all manufacturing. This is not altogether surprising in view of all of the other changes—macroeconomic conditions, demand, technology—that are also taking place. Indeed, decomposition studies, which attempt to separate the reasons for industry employment change, usually find—even for trade-sensitive industries—that changes in domestic demand are the most important cause of employment change. (See Economic Council of Canada 1988b, p 13, and references cited therein for further details.)

MECHANISMS OF ADJUSTMENT

Earlier we divided our sample of seven trade-sensitive industries into two groups: those that appear to be suffering transitory or cyclical adjustment problems, and those apparently facing a long-term structural loss in comparative advantage likely to lead to a decline in relative if not absolute output and employment. According to a variety of indicators, the first group seems able to compete on the world stage, but nonetheless, have received sector-specific assistance in one form or another. There are some similarities between the two groups for at least some industries, and the distinctions are to some extent arbitrary. (It is difficult to specify in advance the cause of a loss in comparative advantage and whether it is permanent or temporary. Indeed, some of the distinctions we have made may prove erroneous in a few years.) Still, each group is treated separately.

Adjustment in Industries Experiencing Cyclical or Transitory Change

Two industries—pulp and paper, and automobiles—fall in the group appearing to suffer a cyclical or transitory loss of comparative advantage. While this was clearly the case for the pulp and paper industry in the mid 1970s it was not quite such a cut and dried distinction for the automobile industry in the 1980s. Both industries appear to be in reasonably sound health by some criteria, but due to such factors as unfavorable movements in exchange rates, a lag in introducing innovations, or competition from a better quality product, they have experienced competitive problems and difficulties. Because they have few common characteristics, we will consider these two industries—and the salient characteristics that have resulted in their competitive difficulties—separately.

For any commentator familiar with Canadian manufacturing, the perennial problem is small market size in relation to available scale economies (Eastman and Stykolt 1967; Gorecki 1976). Hence, suboptimal plant sizes and short production runs cause problems when such industries are called on to compete in the world market. However, this does not appear to be a major cause of the problems of the trade-sensitive industries studied here. For the automobile industry, this was the case until 1965, but with the advent of the Canada-US Auto Pact, the Canadian industry gained access to the US market, and the large US producers, who had plants in both countries, rationalized their production by, for example, greater plant specialization.

The automotive industry in Canada is dominated by the three major US automakers—Ford, Chrysler, and GM. Through the 1965 Canada-US Auto Pact, production in North America became fully integrated and rationalized. Thus, with some differences, the competitive difficulties experienced by US automakers in the US are likely to be similar to those experienced in Canada.

There are three separate but related factors affecting the automobile industry that resulted in adjustment problems in the late 1970s and '80s: market structure; a change in the relative price of oil; and competition from Japan. For much of the postwar period the oligopolistic market structure of the North American automobile industry combined with the production of relatively large automobiles—reflecting high income, inexpensive gasoline, and a good road system—meant little import competition occurred. However, the rise in the price of gasoline because of the 1973–74 and 1978–79 oil shocks brought a marked increase in the demand for smaller, fuel-efficient cars. Although North American manufacturers attempted to meet this demand, there was strong competition from Japan, which was able to provide a product not only price competitive but of substantially better quality. Indeed, there are reasons to doubt whether the North American automakers found it profitable to produce small cars in North America. When combined with the effects of the severe recession of 1981–82, these factors led to substantial pressure on the industry's profitability and wage levels.

The pulp and paper industry is one in which Canada is considered to have a comparative advantage (see de Silva 1988a). This is consistent with the index of comparative advantage presented in Table 1.8, which shows paper and allied industries had the second highest value of the index, after wood, another forest products industry. Despite this record, the industry experienced difficulties in competing in its major market, the US, in the early and mid 1970s. This reflected the fact there was no offsetting change in the exchange rate to compensate for the much more rapid increase in the Canadian industry's unit labor costs relative to either those in the Canadian manufacturing sector or (measured in own-country currencies) in the corresponding US industry. The increase in unit labor costs reflected both slower productivity growth in Canada and an increase in wage rates greater than that in both the US industry and the Canadian manufacturing sector as a whole.

The adjustment experience of pulp and paper and automobiles has been quite different. If the cyclical or transitory designation is correct, any adjustment problems should be relatively short-lived. The transitory description certainly fits pulp and paper: in 1977–78 the change in the value of the Canadian dollar vis-à-vis the US dollar went a long way toward restoring competitiveness. However, this is much less true of the automobile industry. According to some reports, the late 1980s appreciation of the Japanese yen certainly made US automobiles competitively priced with Japanese imports, although Japanese quality and productivity still seem to be higher.

In some important respects the small car segment of the automobile market has come to take on the characteristics of an industry facing a long-term structural loss in comparative advantage. Production has spread from Japan to the NIEs (South Korea, in particular, but also Taiwan) and at least one ASEAN country (Thailand). In North America, production of such cars has been considerably reduced by US-based automakers, which have formed joint ventures with Japanese firms and imported small cars under their own marque. Captive imports account, according to one recent estimate, for 20% of all Canadian automobile imports from Japan.

The implications for North American automobile manufacturers of the Japanese challenge, however, go far beyond the small car segment of the market. The Japanese have been able to produce better quality automobiles than their US counterparts, and with greater labor productivity. Hence, in the 1980s the North American automobile manufacturers introduced programs and policies, including joint ventures, to copy the best experience of the Japanese. If these are not successful then as the Japanese move up market and increasingly locate plants in North America, particularly Canada, US ownership of Canada's auto industry will likely decline.

Our discussion of the reaction of the automobile industry to the Japanese challenge so far suggests essentially that it has followed a policy of revitalization. However, the protectionist option has also been favored by the manufacturers and their unions. A similar situation obtained in the 1970s with respect to pulp and paper, although in a somewhat different guise.

Adjustment in Industries Experiencing Structural Change

Footwear, textiles, knitting mills, clothing, and shipbuilding have (or had) characteristics suggesting comparative advantage does not reside with developed countries such as Canada, at least for some of the industry's output. These characteristics, which have been summarized by the OECD (1985, p 107) in reference to textiles and clothing, are:

- Limited product differentiability, so that competition occurs primarily on a cost basis
- A cost structure heavily dominated by labor costs, giving a major and durable competitive advantage to low wage countries
- Weak barriers to entry and exit, reflected in a fragmented industry structure, high rates of firm turnover, and the virtual absence of supranormal profits
- Wholesalers, retailers, and some producers are highly sensitive to new sourcing opportunities

To these can be added the rapid diffusion of new technology across international borders. Of course, there are variations in the degree to which these stylized facts apply to the industries experiencing structural change. Textiles, for example, are reasonably capital intensive, while the reference to wholesalers and retailers is not wholly appropriate in the case of shipbuilding. Nevertheless, as a broad brush approach they will suffice for the purposes at hand.

The competition into the Canadian market has, initially at least, usually come from Japan (Italy in the case of footwear), followed by several of the NIEs and, more recently, the next-tier NIEs and China.

Faced with foreign competition, producers have three broad sets of options: exit; revitalization—the restoration of the industry's international competitiveness; and protection. The rise of competitors combined with the characteristics of the industry may be taken as a signal by firms and workers that the industry has permanently lost its competitive edge and resources should be moved out of the industry. Alternatively, the challenge of foreign competitors might spur efforts to revitalize by such methods as: introduction of new products, carving out specialist niches, reducing the compensation to employees, substituting capital for labor, and, if the stages of production are separable, locating offshore some intermediary steps. The final option is to petition the relevant political and legal authorities to provide protective measures, including subsidies and quantitative restraints on imports to stem or reverse the flow of imports.

The strategies of exit, revitalization, and protection are not necessarily mutually exclusive. Government may grant a period of import relief during which the industry can become smaller or revitalize itself or both. Different firms may have different expectations about the future and their competitive abilities vis-à-vis other domestic producers and off-shore producers. This may lead to exit or to attempts to meet the competition.

Exit. Our earlier discussion treats exit strategy at two levels: that of the individual worker or firm, and that of the industry. The data on worker attritions and displacements and firm closure suggest for indus-tries facing a long-term structural loss in comparative advantage there has been considerable use of the exit option. However, the evidence also suggests this is not markedly different from the overall performance of the manufacturing sector, except perhaps in shipbuilding.

Casual empiricism suggests there are no particularly important bar-riers to exit in these industries, such as considerable sunk capital or general laws such as those relating to bankruptcy or competition. In-deed, with respect to Canada's competition law there is specific provi-sion for: (1) specialization agreements to permit firms, in concert, to exit certain product lines and concentrate on others, and (2) in the determi-nation of whether a merger is likely to lessen competition substantially, taking into account the fact a firm may fail.

Whether there is a reduction in employment at the level of the indus-try depends upon more than attrition, displacements, and firm closures. It also depends upon firm entry, as well as the expansion and contraction of continuing or surviving firms. Definitionally, all five industries in this group can be classified as in relative decline. However, only in the cases of leather (footwear) and shipbuilding has a long-term absolute decline been observed. Hence, resources are being reallocated away from these five trade-sensitive industries but, this is achieved mainly by slower growth in employment rather than actual decline. [6]

6. For reasons outlined in the notes to Table 1.7, much of the discussion involved in identifying Canada's trade-sensitive industries was conducted at a fairly aggregative level of industry classification. Nevertheless, some limited work was undertaken to determine if, at a finer level of classification, there were absolute declines in employment of some seriousness. Applying a definition of "employment decline of some seriousness" as in-stances where 1979 industry employment was 80% or less of 1970 employment to a classification that divides the manufacturing sector into 167 industries yields 17 industries. Of these, 12 were part of one of the 4 broad industry groups that suffered relative

Table 1.13. Production Worker Average Hourly Wage in Selected Trade-Sensitive Manufacturing Industries, 1971–85 (Index, Manufacturing = 100)

1971	1978	1982	1985	
65.2	67.1	61.1	63.7	shoe factories
79.3	79.1	76.7	75.4	textiles
58.6	67.1	62.5	58.4	clothing
63.0	65.9	60.7	—	knitting mills
131.0	137.0	135.8	142.9	pulp and paper
140.1	125.3	124.5	127.4	motor vehicles
115.0	129.6	130.9	128.3	shipbuilding and repair

Includes overtime, paid leave, bonuses, and so on. Remuneration to outside pieceworkers is not included. (It is included in the cost of materials in the Census of Manufactures data.)

Source: Based on data from Statistics Canada.

Revitalization. Several strategies could be followed by firms and workers opting to stay in an industry in the face of import competition. One strategy, given that the cost structure of this group of industries is heavily dominated by labor costs, is to seek a reduction in the compensation paid to managers and workers. Table 1.13 presents data on the average hourly wage levels in the Canadian manufacturing sector for the trade-sensitive industries under consideration. The manufacturing sector is used as a benchmark of comparison to see whether wage rates have fallen or risen.

The data indicate little change in the relative position of the wage rates in the five trade-sensitive industries in the first group in the period 1971–85. The only exceptions are textiles, in which relative wage rates have moved downward in every successive year, and shipbuilding, in which they increased between 1971 and 1978 and then remained at much the same level. Clothing, for example, is consistently at the bottom, while pulp and paper is most frequently at the top.

One caveat concerns clothing. This industry's employment is largely accounted for by women, many of whom speak neither of Canada's official languages. This feature, combined with the relatively low levels

employment declines in the 1951–83 period (tobacco plus 3 in our sample: leather, textiles, and knitting mills and clothing). Each of the 5 remaining industries were drawn from a separate one of the 19 industries listed in Table 1.7. The industry with the greatest decline, over half, was household radio and TV receivers; import competition was a major factor accounting for its decline. For details see Jenkins et al (1986).

of education of clothing workers, helps explain the low wage. Further-more, in the early 1980s the industrial production system changed. There was a pronounced rise in the importance of homeworkers, some of whom appear to go unrecorded and who possibly work at wage rates below those indicated in the table. Hence, in clothing at least, the recent period may have seen a drop in relative wage rates that the data in the table understate. (The number of homeworkers in the clothing labor force is estimated at 27% [Canada, Department of Finance 1988b]. On immigrant women, with some discussion of the clothing industry, see Seward and McDade 1988.)

Another possible strategy is the substitution of capital for labor so as to nullify the labor cost advantage of the NIEs and other such nations. The feasibility of this strategy depends upon the degree to which the production process can be mechanized (as well as, of course, on the cost of capital in Canada compared to the NIEs). The evidence on this varies considerably. In the case of textiles and knitting mills there has been a concerted effort at increased mechanization and capital intensity. In contrast, in footwear and, even more, in clothing, the opportunity for substitution of capital for labor has been much lower, so this strategy is not as important.

The ability to introduce new products and product designs and to carve out product niches such that a firm is able to differentiate its products from those of its rivals depends in part on the innovativeness of the entrepreneurs and partly on the scope for such product differentia-tion. In the industries studied here, we see some evidence of differentia-tion in textiles, clothing, and shoes; but, given the limited scope, such a strategy cannot work for the whole industry.

The final strategy refers to vertical disintegration combined with lo-cation of certain stages of production offshore. If labor intensive produc-tion in particular can be located offshore and then imported to Canada, the advantage of the new competitors may be nullified. We see little evidence of this, but there has been a limited attempt to take advantage of the availability of low-cost offshore supplies. In the case of shirts, the Canadian government has offered producers the right to import one duty-free shirt for every additional shirt produced in Canada above some base level. In 1988 announcements were made that new duty remission schemes would be introduced for some fabrics and clothing items. (For full details, see Canada, Department of Finance 1988b.) However, these would appear to be relatively minor in the overall scheme of things, with the maximum duty remission for the new and existing programs totaling $50 million.

Protectionism. In all five industries experiencing structural change, firms (either individually or through an industry-wide trade association) and workers (through their unions) have petitioned governments for import relief (in the form of direct controls over imports) or financial assistance to help the industry better compete with imports, if not both. These appeals have all been successful to varying degrees. The next section discusses whether the granting of such relief is consistent with the protectionist sentiment from which it frequently flows or the provision of a breathing space during which revitalization or exit is designed to take place.

GOVERNMENT POLICY OVERVIEW

Unquestionably there has been a good deal of structural adjustment and reallocation of resources in Canada's manufacturing industries, including those we have identified as being "trade-sensitive." What may be surprising at first glance, however, is that by and large the pace of adjustment in the trade-sensitive industries has differed very little from the average for the manufacturing sector. Yet as other writers have pointed out, trade shocks represent "an incremental addition to much greater pressure for adjustment from other sources" (Salembier et al 1987, p 148).

In these circumstances, one is tempted to conclude that adjustment in the trade-sensitive industries has in fact been slower than it might have been if left solely to market forces. Such a view would undoubtedly be overly simplistic since the pace of adjustment was affected by a variety of factors. Nevertheless, detailed examination of Canadian adjustment assistance policies does suggest that with the exception of the measures applied in the footwear industry, Canada has used sector-specific policies that have tended to impede rather than facilitate adjustment.

The problem does not seem to stem from a definition of goals. Indeed, without exception, the stated goal of the various adjustment assistance policies and programs Canada has adopted has been to facilitate positive adjustment. But translating general goals into the achievement of more specific objectives is something else. That requires a combination of factors: a thorough analysis of the problem, its causes and solutions; the appropriate machinery and the political will to use it; the setting of operational targets, especially creditable time limits; and the choice of the appropriate policy instruments. In Canada, this combination has typically been lacking.

Framework vs Sector-Specific Policies

Canadian governments have used a variety of policies and programs to respond to the changing domestic and international environment. These have included framework policies at both the national and international levels. At the national level these policies include macroeconomic policy and the universal publicly funded social policies as well as competition policy, bankruptcy legislation, and so on. At the international level, GATT is particularly relevant to the adjustment issue. These and other framework policies set the rules within which the market system works, and they can be of great assistance in redirecting resources to their most productive uses through market decisions by providing an environment conducive to accommodating change.

In addition, from time to time, because framework policies in conjunction with market forces have been perceived as working too slowly or as yielding unacceptably harsh results, governments have intervened at the behest of individual unions, trade associations, and regions to provide sector-specific policies aimed at industries adversely affected by change. There are, of course, links between framework and sector-specific policies. The better and more successful framework policies are, the less need for sector-specific policies. On the other hand, if sector-specific policies introduce rigidities in individual markets, this may make macroeconomic policy less effective as well as throwing the burden of adjustment on fewer sectors. The remainder of the discussion of government policy is confined to such sector-specific policies.

SECTOR-SPECIFIC GOVERNMENT POLICIES

The selective measures used by Canada have been of three major types:

1. Special import restrictions: quantitative limitations on the volume of goods that could be imported into Canada from all countries (global quotas) or from selected countries (bilateral restraints or voluntary export restraints)
2. Firm and industry subsidies, usually aimed at modernizing an industry's capital equipment so producers might better compete with foreign firms
3. Labor adjustment measures which attempted to encourage the reemployment of workers by providing financial assistance for retraining and mobility or to maintain the income of older workers who

had exhausted their unemployment insurance and had little prospect for re-employment

Special import measures and firm and industry subsidies have been used as sector-specific policy instruments to a much greater extent than labor adjustment measures. Although it is somewhat judgmental, trade restrictions have been more important and durable than capital subsidies. Sectoral policies have usually been justified on the basis of efficiency and equity objectives, but political objectives have also been important.

Since Canada has well-functioning capital markets, support to firms is much more difficult to justify on efficiency grounds than support to workers. Workers cannot easily diversify risks, they have less information on new opportunities than firms, and they would face much more difficulty in borrowing funds for (say) retraining than would firms wishing to undertake new investment.

The equity rationale is of special importance in Canada, with its federal structure, widely dispersed population, and history of sharing by, for example, equalizing standards of government service across the country through redistribution of income. The gains from reductions in trade barriers tend to be widely shared across the country while the burden of adjustment tends to be concentrated in certain distressed regions and localities. Compensation to such areas or particular groups can be justified since they have to bear the burden of adjustment, while all of society benefits. Such compensation appeals to society's sense of "fairness" or "justice." Again, however, this rationale is likely to apply with more force to assistance for workers than to firms.

In the absence of any economic rationale, governments may also intervene for largely political reasons, responding to the demands of certain groups of voters such as workers, firms, and regional representatives. These demands may succeed despite opposing forces (some of which, such as consumers, may be poorly organized) and general government philosophy in favor of an open multilateral trading system. It is naive to expect politics will not motivate intervention. The danger is where political objectives are dominant. Then the selective measures used are likely to last for a long time, delaying the adjustment process and incurring the risk that the ultimate adjustment will be even greater.

Stated Goals

In all cases the stated goals of Canada's sector-specific measures are at the positive adjustment end of the policy spectrum—that is to say, they are policies designed to promote, encourage, and facilitate the movement of resources presaged by import competition and changing comparative advantage. Impressive as these statements of goals might sound, however, the programs frequently fell short when it came to implementation. In some cases, there were conflicts built into the goals. In the case of subsidies, for example, the emphasis on new capital would run counter to attempts to maintain employment. Equally important, there was sometimes a failure to lay the groundwork for achieving specific objectives, because of lack of adequate institutional machinery or establishment of effective time horizons. We turn now to such matters.

Legislative and Administrative Framework

When one realizes the rather bewildering array of legislative and administrative arrangements behind them, it is perhaps not surprising that implementation of these assistance measures lacked consistency and coherence. In fact, the responsibility for Canada's assistance "system" is spread among a complex of federal departments and agencies, and in some cases it is shared with the provinces. Moreover, it usually depends upon a variety of national or international legislation, and in one instance there was no legislation empowering the government to adopt the chosen sectoral policy.

The measures used for shipbuilding, autos, and pulp and paper were administered directly by governments. Shipbuilding assistance was run through the federal Department of Regional Industrial Expansion while pulp and paper assistance was based on a cost-sharing arrangement with the provinces and administered in each province concerned by a committee of officials from both levels of government. Under both subsidy programs, virtually all applications were approved, although each program gave officials the power to reject the applications. VERs (voluntary export restraints) for autos were based directly on annually negotiated arrangements between the governments of Canada and Japan, with no built-in machinery for analysis to address such issues as the necessity, duration, level, and cost of such arrangements.

The various labor adjustment programs were administered in large part by government departments with responsibility for employment and labor policies. The criteria and procedures needed for a worker to obtain a benefit were explicit in terms (say) of age and the number of years of employment in a particular industry required before income maintenance was provided. In some instances these procedures were administered, in part at least, by an outside body. The net result of these arrangements was that sectoral labor policy probably involved less discretion in its implementation and administration than the subsidies for pulp and paper and shipbuilding or the VERs in automobiles. This applies particularly when comparing the criteria a worker had to satisfy to receive a benefit compared to those that a firm had to meet in order to receive a subsidy.

Special import measures for textiles, clothing, and footwear came under somewhat different arrangements. Eligibility for import restrictions was established on the basis of recommendations by the Canadian Import Tribunal (CIT) or the Textile and Clothing Board (TCB). The government of the day then decided if and how to implement the recommendations.

Both of the agencies were administrative tribunals set up by the Parliament of Canada. The CIT, which goes back to 1969, has responsibility for not only inquiring into antidumping and countervailing, but also safeguard cases, of which footwear was one. It can only start a safeguard investigation after a reference by the government. This has been done by the government on only a few occasions: for mushrooms in 1973, and for footwear in 1971, 1977, 1980, and 1984. The TCB's mandate has, since its creation in 1971, been to conduct inquiries and render advice to governments on trade matters with respect to the textile and clothing industries. Such inquiries can be started either by the Minister, the Board itself, or a producer.

An interesting experiment in sector-specific policies occurred with the Canadian Industrial Renewal Program (CIRP), a comprehensive five-year (1981–86) adjustment package for the textile, clothing, and footwear industries. Linked to abolition of special import measures, it offered an aid package to communities and regions relying heavily on these industries by encouraging diversification of the industrial base, assisting workers to find new jobs, and modernization grants to the three industries.

CIRP, which became the focal point for all except labor market measures, was run by the Canadian Industrial Renewal Board (CIRB), made up of directors from the private sector responsible to the Minister of Regional Industrial Expansion. This novel feature marked quite a shift from the administrative arrangements used for subsidy in shipbuilding and pulp and paper. In part because of this, CIRB actually rejected a sizable proportion of loan applicants. Nevertheless, CIRB was less than completely successful: apart from footwear, special import measures were not reduced and grants continued to be administered by government directly when CIRP/CIRB stopped in 1986.

Like the administrative machinery, the legislative background for the various measure also has varied widely. The automobile arrangements, for example, were imposed outside of GATT and with no basis in domestic legislation. Pulp and paper and shipbuilding subsidies were administered pursuant to very general domestic legislation. In the case of pulp and paper the Law Reform Commission of Canada felt the legislation had an "extremely vague" objective which provided "little direction as to what is and is not eligible under the program" (1986, p 46). Pulp and paper was restricted to purchasing Canadian equipment, which would appear to contravene Canada's national treatment obligations under GATT. (For a case with strong parallels, Italian tractors, see Jackson and Davey 1986, p 486–91.)

The international framework for textile and clothing measures came primarily from the Multi-Fiber Arrangement (MFA), an international agreement under GATT. The domestic framework was supplied by the Textile Policy of 1970 and the Textile and Clothing Board Act, passed the following year. Footwear measures were based on Canada's legislation, the Special Import Measures Act, passed pursuant to Article 19 of GATT. Quantitative restraints in both cases were implemented under the *Export and Import Permits Act.*

Implementation

With such a widely differing background of administrative machinery and legislation, there were bound to be considerable differences in the interpretation of goals, the specification of objectives, analysis of the problems, and appropriate solutions and implementation generally. In what follows we look at these aspects of each of the three main types of selective measures.

Special Import Measures. Canada has imposed or negotiated quantitative import restraints on several products.

• Textiles and clothing, usually between Canada and a non-OECD country such as Hong Kong or Korea. The major exception was global quotas on clothing between 1976 and 1978. The MFA restraints also covered mainly clothing.
• Automobiles, with Japan.
• Footwear, globally, but Italy, Korea and Taiwan have been particularly affected.

In general, the objective of the restraint was to provide a short period during which the industry could adjust to the competition via exit or revitalization.

The potential for a successful *textile and clothing* restraint program certainly seemed possible with the advent of the government Textile Policy of 1970, the cornerstone of subsequent policy in this area. Following the 1970 Policy Statement, in 1971 the Textile and Clothing Board Act passed and the Board was set up. The Act provided, for example, that special measures of protection "are not to be implemented for the purpose of encouraging the maintenance of lines of production that have no prospects of becoming competitive with foreign goods" in the Canadian market "if the only protection to be provided" is that of the tariff. The Minister of the day could refer issues to the TCB (Textile and Clothing Board), while the Board could examine critically the plans of firms designed to meet the import threat in investigating the complaints of firms. All of this was consistent with the 1970 Policy.

The record of the implementation of textile and clothing special import measures legislation suggests the policy fell well short of its original goals. The right issues were typically not raised by the TCB. They should have included questions concerning such issues as: who gained and who lost from the policy, the prospects of the product lines under investigation becoming competitive; and also alternative adjustment policies such as job retraining and early retirement, the cost per job saved, and alternative mechanisms to the MFA. (The cost of protectionism was addressed in the Board's 1985 report: TCB 1985, v 1 p 87–91. However, this would appear to be largely a defensive reaction to earlier work, such as that of Jenkins 1985.)

There was also little political leadership in providing terms of reference to the Board that would encourage positive adjustment. These factors, combined with the fact the Board oversaw only one industry sector, seem to have resulted in what is referred to in the regulation literature as industry capture.

Bilateral restraints affected the pattern of adjustment, particularly in the case of clothing. On the one hand, bilateral restraints under the MFA meant the benefits of restraints accrued to a large extent to foreign producers, who hold the quota entitlement. Since the restraints were fixed in volume terms and aimed at the most efficient producing countries, they resulted in these producers moving up the value-added chain, putting greater pressure on their Canadian counterparts. Of course, special import measures in textiles and clothing imposed costs on the Canadian consumer. One widely quoted estimate of the cost of bilateral clothing quotas set the cost in 1979 as $327 million to consumers, saving 9,231 jobs at $35,457 per job (Jenkins 1985) when the average clothing worker earned about $10,000 a year.

Despite the original emphasis on the temporary nature of restrictions on textiles and clothing, they are now more comprehensive than when initiated under the first MFA in 1974. The 5 bilateral restraint agreements under MFA I rose to 25 under MFA IV. Indeed, over 86% of clothing imports were subject to restraint in 1982–86, compared with 69% in 1974–77, and restraints are expected to continue until 1991. In contrast, only 7% of textile imports were subject to bilateral restraints in 1982–86. In brief, no creditable timetable for restraints was established.

The development of the application of VERs (voluntary export restraints) for *automobiles* was quite different than the textiles and clothing bilateral restraints. There was a lack of a legislative or administrative framework and little opportunity for parliamentary or public review and analysis prior to the imposition of such restraints. In fact, one of the major analyses was carried out by a task force consisting of representatives of the North American industry, with no consumer or other interest represented. Neither the length of the "breathing space" nor the level of the VERs was specified in the report. There was no investigation of "serious injury"—the criteria needed to be met under Article 19 of GATT. The major recommendation of the report, that Japanese exporters to Canada be required to meet certain local content rules, was, in many ways, the antithesis of positive adjustment.

The benefits of the restrictions on automobiles from Japan accrued to both domestic and foreign manufacturers. The strategies for revitalization adopted by the North American automobile industry met with some success, but it is not at all clear if this was related to VERs. However, the cost to consumers per job retained was very high. For example, it has been estimated that the cost per job saved in 1985 was between $179,000 and $226,000, while the average earnings in the industry varied between $29,000 (parts) and $35,000 (assembly). The number of jobs saved by VERs was quite small (Hazledine and Wigington 1987; Coopers and Lybrand 1986). Furthermore, the VERs were of limited effectiveness as Japanese producers upgraded their products faster than they otherwise would have and a low-priced entrant—Hyundai of Korea—moved into the market gap at the low end of the market in the 1983–85 period. Although the formal arrangement has been discontinued, officials in both Japan and Canada "monitor" export levels.

The *footwear industry* provides a marked contrast. There was a good deal of restructuring over the period 1978–83, though not so much by downsizing through exit of firms as via modernization, re-equipment, product rationalization, and employment declines for existing firms. The use of global quotas between 1977 and 1985 resulted in little upgrading by exporters. Most of the direct benefits of the restraints accrued to Canadian importers rather than manufacturers because of the way the quotas were administered. Moreover, the costs to consumers (in 1978 dollars) per job saved were very high—between $53,668 (in 1982) and $69,460 (in 1979); the average annual earnings of a footwear worker were, in contrast, slightly above $7,000 in 1978. The jobs saved varied between 2.1 and 4.4% of industry employment in the period. But in other ways the system worked well (Canadian Import Tribunal 1985; Moroz and Salembier 1985.)

The Canadian Import Tribunal (CIT, previously called the Anti-dumping Tribunal) was responsible for recommendations on footwear restraints. It had a stronger mandate than the Textile and Clothing Board, and the 1984 mandate given the CIT by the government was intended to lead to the elimination of the quota. The CIT laid down its own strict interpretation of "serious injury," linked it with imports, and carried out a thorough analysis, with the results being directly reflected in its shifting conclusions on the industry's need for protective measures. (Anti-dumping Tribunal 1973, p 103–06, contains the most extensive discussion by the Tribunal on the concept of "serious injury.") Its frequent reports made for a good deal of public awareness. And, perhaps most important, the CIT's strong mandate was combined with a creditable timetable for phasing-out the restraints. By 1985 the Tribunal found that successful adjustment had in fact taken place and all footwear quotas were abolished except for those on women's and girls' products. These were phased out over the period 1985–88.

Firm and Industry Subsidies. Canada employed sector-specific subsidies for pulp and paper (the Pulp and Paper Modernization Program (PPMP) set up in 1979), shipbuilding (the Shipbuilding Industry Assistance Program (SIAP) set up in 1975 to integrate two existing subsidy programs) and (under the Canadian Industrial Renewal Program (CIRP) introduced in 1981) for textile, clothing and footwear. (For more details on these programs see Ahmad 1988, and de Silva 1988a and 1988b.) With the possible exception of certain parts of CIRP, these programs were not successful in achieving their stated objectives. Their components are outlined in Table 1.14.

Both PPMP and SIAP were aimed at making the affected industries more competitive and, in the latter case, at stabilizing employment. SIAP followed both a strategy of capital and output subsidies, while PPMP used only the former. But neither policy set out a valid economic rationale in terms of efficiency or equity. There was no evidence of capital market failure, so the use of subsidies as the policy instrument was questionable. In each case, too little attention was paid to the need for incrementality of investment as a program criterion.

Table 1.14. Firm and Industry Subsidies

Footwear, Textiles, and Clothing
The Canadian Industrial Renewal Program (CIRP) was introduced by the federal government in 1981 and terminated in 1986. Administered (apart from the labor program) by an arm's-length agency, the Canadian Industrial Renewal Board, CIRP had three main components: the Business and Industrial Development Program (BIDP), the Labour Adjustment Program (LAP), and the Sector Firms Program (SFP). CIRP was designed (1) to create new employment in communities affected by industrial adjustment (BIDP), (2) to help displaced workers take advantage of new employment opportunities (LAP), (3) to assist the modernization of viable firms in textiles and clothing (SFP) and (4), at its conclusion, to encourage a reduction of reliance on quantitative import barriers.

Over the period 1981–86, CIRP spent about $364 million, mostly on BIDP and SFP; labor assistance was handled primarily under other existing, nonspecific government programs. Some firms applying for CIRP grants were rejected: 57% of the applications under the modernization and restructuring part of the program.

Pulp and Paper
The Pulp and Paper Modernization Program (PPMP) was a subsidy program administered jointly by the Department of Regional Industrial Expansion and the provincial governments. It was designed primarily to encourage the modernization of mills in eastern Canada. The PPMP funded only a proportion of the eligible modernization expenditures a mill made, but essentially all those applying received funding. The mills receiving assistance accounted for about 80% of capacity in eastern Canada. Government funds expended totaled $542 million over the period 1979–84.

The program contained provisions to ensure the funds were expended on Canadian supplies. Consequently, among the principal beneficiaries were pulp and paper machinery and equipment makers.

Shipbuilding
The Shipbuilding Industry Assistance Program (SIAP) was introduced in 1975 by the federal government to encourage the industry to become more competitive and thus promote stable employment. It was administered through the Department of Regional Industrial Expansion. SIAP consisted of two parts: a subsidy for new vessel construction, and a subsidy for yard modernization that was related directly to the construction subsidy. In both cases only a portion of the eligible costs were subsidized. There was a Canadian-content requirement.

Over the period 1975–85, approximately $480 million was spent, $426 million being directed to vessel construction. The program originally was intended to reduce the vessel subsidy gradually, but this was not achieved. Virtually all applicants received the new-vessel subsidy.

Prior to SIAP, the industry had, since 1961, benefitted from two sector-specific subsidy programs. Although the program ended in 1985, unused modernization credits remain to be spent. The industry still receives special assistance via an increase in tariff levels in 1983 and via government procurement, which now accounts for a very significant share of new ship construction.

At least in part because of the administrative framework for each of them, there was little or no analysis of the problems or provision for public scrutiny. Moreover, in both cases no creditable timetable for the elimination of government financial assistance was established. Although both programs were terminated—in 1984 for PPMP and 1985 for SIAP —assistance is still available to the industries under other government programs.

CIRP (the Canadian Industrial Renewal Program) sounded more promising. For a start, it had a better organizational structure. Certainly, too, the program envisaged a reduction in reliance on quantitative barriers for the industries concerned after the program ended. And at least part of the program had a number of other favorable attributes. Its main components were the Business and Industrial Development Program (BIDP), Sector Firms Program (SFP), and the Labor Adjustment Program (LAP).

By contrast with the shipbuilding and pulp and paper programs, a valid economic rationale was established for the BIDP and LAP components: the provision of new employment opportunities and help for displaced workers, both of which conform to the equity and efficiency rationales for government intervention. And, in implementing the BIDP, a good deal of importance was pinned on incrementality criterion. However, both the economic rationale and, to a considerable extent, the incremental criterion were absent in the case of the subsidy to modernize plant and equipment, SFP, and that was the component of CIRP that ultimately came in for the lion's share of funding. Moreover, both BIDP and SFP relied on an inappropriate instrument—capital and output subsidies—reflecting once again a failure to analyze the problems properly. In the end, however, import controls (apart from footwear) were not removed and assistance continues.

Labor Adjustment Measures. Canada has provided a wide variety of programs to assist in labor market adjustment. For the period that is the focus of this discussion, major universal framework programs—especially unemployment insurance and training assistance—were in effect. The vast majority of expenditure went toward unemployment insurance rather than training or mobility programs. Such programs provided a cushion for loss of jobs or skills and in some cases (eg, unemployment insurance), they also promoted planning for change. These programs were made available whether the reason for job loss was import competition or some other factors such as technological change.

The universal programs were also supplemented with measures targeted at workers in specific trade-sensitive industries: textile and clothing workers from 1971 to 1986, and footwear and tanning workers from 1978 to 1986. In addition, during 1981–86, the labor adjustment programs available to these specific industries were also provided communities experiencing dislocation because of dependence upon a small number of industries undergoing structural change. The programs were not limited to dealing with the effects of import competition, but several of the community and industry designations did in fact involve just such industries (eg, shipbuilding, pulp and paper, and automobiles). The financial cost of these sector-specific programs were quite small compared to the framework unemployment insurance and training programs.

The targeted labor programs made available were of two kinds: those providing early retirement benefits for older workers, sometimes referred to as pre-retirement; and re-employment measures designed to encourage job mobility, relocation, and retraining. Re-employment opportunities were essentially enhanced benefits of the existing labor adjustment programs. The level of income maintenance was linked to years of service and hours worked per year. There was a rationale for both types of programs. Both were subject to policy reviews in which many of the right questions were asked (see Task Force on Program Review 1985 and Labor Canada 1985) and appropriate action was taken to address some of the problems identified. The 1981–86 programs were subject to specified time limits. Thus, designation as a community eligible for the programs could last for a maximum of two years.

True, there were some important deficiencies. In particular, in the period prior to 1982 there were quite sensible, but tight, eligibility requirements for the early retirement benefits program. The worker had to meet several criteria, including: 54 to 65 years of age; involuntarily unemployed; considerable job tenure with the designated trade-sensitive industry; exhausted unemployment insurance; and little prospect of employment.

Such workers were likely to have acquired industry-specific human capital with little application to other areas of endeavor so that they would be more prone to particularly difficult adjustment problems. However, the criteria were—inappropriately in our view—relaxed in 1982, perhaps because of the recession. One change was abolition of the involuntarily unemployed requirement. Under the revised rules, an older worker could "volunteer" for unemployment and still be eligible for benefits (unemployment insurance payments until age 65). In other words, if the employer had to reduce his labor force by x workers he could ask older workers if any would like to accept voluntary unemployment. Normally, of course, because of seniority, older workers would be the last laid off. In a trade-sensitive or declining industry it seems sensible to encourage younger, more mobile workers to leave and retain older workers whose output is thus not lost to society forever. The revised 1982 rules created, of course, precisely the opposite incentive. Another change: prior to 1982 layoffs had to be trade-related; after this date, no such link was required.

Program utilization and expenditures grew substantially. For example, active claims increased from 531 in fiscal 1981 (ends March 31) to 6,947 in fiscal 1986; expenditure went from $3.8 million to $59.7 million over the same period. The Program for Older Workers announced in 1988 is designed to make involuntary unemployment a condition of receiving any benefit.

Ultimately, however, the removal of special protection in most of the industries concerned did not take place. In part because of this, labor policies were not heavily utilized until the 1980s, and then the causes were the relaxation of criteria and the recession rather than trade liberalization. Thus, these programs, although part of a concerted adjustment package to reduce protection, have not been successful in this endeavor.

ASSESSMENT OF GOVERNMENT POLICY AND CURRENT POLICY DEVELOPMENTS

The discussion of sector-specific policies suggests there is a large gap between the reality of policy implementation and the rhetoric of policy goals. This is explained by a number of factors:

- lack of an appropriate equity or efficiency rationale
- inadequate program design
- lack of a creditable timetable to phase out the sector-specific policy
- use of the wrong policy, even when there may have been a justification for government intervention
- the presence of strong forces demanding protection

Nevertheless, footwear was an exception. The policy process *appears* to have worked well in this case. "Appears" because Korea and Taiwan have, since 1986 and 1987, respectively, moderated their exports to Canada of footwear not covered by global quota. Spain and Italy rejected such export restraints. (See GATT 1988, p 142, and Kelly et al 1988, p 85, for details.) It is not clear what the present situation is although Canadian government officials do state that they consult with exporting nations and suggest a "gradual and prudent" approach to footwear exports (ie, no surges).

The footwear case can be explained by a number of factors. There was a political will to work at the positive adjustment end of the policy spectrum. It was expressed through the terms of reference given the Canadian Import Tribunal, which produced a series of thoughtful reports. There were other factors too. One of the countries affected by global quotas, Italy, sought and obtained compensation from Canada for the imposition of quotas and thus raised the cost to Canada of restricting imports. Furthermore, there is evidence that in 1982 South Korea and Taiwan refused to agree to footwear VERs. Hence, the successful adjustment in footwear was a confluence of good intentions, use of appropriate administrative machinery, and external pressures from the principal footwear exporters to Canada.

There are many possible ways of moving adjustment policy toward the positive adjustment end of the spectrum. In terms of trade policy instruments, suggestions have included: greater reliance on labor adjustment programs; cessation of capital and output subsidies; global quotas rather than selective restraints negotiated outside the GATT framework; and auctioning of quotas. (For further discussion see, for example, Economic Council of Canada 1988b, and Trebliock et al 1988.)

Labor policies aimed at facilitating adjustment should apply to all older workers or immigrant women experiencing labor market problems, not just those in trade-sensitive industries. This approach reflects a number of factors: a perceived failure of past sector- and cause-specific policies; the practical difficulty of separating trade from other displaced workers; and, on equity grounds, the unfairness to non-trade displaced workers who, in comparable situations, receive no special sectoral assistance.

To improve procedure and administration, greater transparency with respect to identification of the beneficiaries of a policy, its costs to the consumer and society, and the way in which the policy will achieve its objectives, would all be helpful. In other words, good analysis and wide dissemination of the results of the policy are needed. Transparency could also be improved by the creation of one agency covering virtually all economic activity, in place of sector-specific boards such as the Textile and Clothing Board (TCB). Such measures would make it much easier for the political process to make decisions compatible with the positive adjustment rhetoric of policy objectives and the liberal trading philosophy underlying Canadian trade policies.

There is some evidence of movement towards an agency to increase transparency in this field. The Canadian International Trade Tribunal, which was formed in 1988, combines all of the country's administrative trade bodies, including the TCB and the Canadian Import Tribunal (CIT), into a single unit. One of the first references directed at the new

Tribunal from the Minister of Finance was to examine how best to reduce textile tariffs from twice that of other industrialized nations to the average of such nations. (See Canada, Department of Finance 1988b. This move was motivated in part by the competitive disadvantage such high tariffs placed on clothing and furniture producers.)

There has been less success with respect to the auctioning of quotas. The Canadian government commissioned a report by Deloitte Haskins and Sells (an international accounting and consulting firm) that concluded, on the basis of a number of administrative, equity, and efficiency criteria, that auctions were the preferred method of allocating quotas. Nevertheless, the government chose to ignore the report's recommendations, primarily because quota holders and affected industries could not agree to the preferred method.

Most of the global quotas referred to a small number of agricultural commodities—broilers, eggs, turkeys, dairy products—as well as footwear. Global quotas on agricultural products are part of the supply management schemes that restrict domestic production and raise prices as much as 30% above levels in the US. A number of bodies have called for the relaxation of such restrictive arrangements (eg, Economic Council of Canada 1981, p 51–68). Although supply management is left unaffected by the Canada-US Free Trade Agreement, tariffs will fall on further processed products, such as frozen pizzas and chicken TV dinners, made from supply-managed commodities. This will lead to pressure from these processors for lower input costs. The Advisory Council on Adjustment (1989, p 113–24) recommended a two-price system under which further processors of poultry, meat and milk pay the same price for these inputs as their US competitors. All other purchasers would pay the typically higher price determined by the cost-of-production formula.

TRADE POLICY IMPLICATIONS

Special protection for troubled traditional industries has become the most significant source of trade barriers in industrial countries. Canada is no exception. Special import measures along with other forms of sector-specific programs have been used ostensibly to promote positive adjustment in a variety of industries including textiles and clothing, footwear, and automobiles. (Much of this section is based on Cornell 1987.)

With some notable exceptions, these measures have tended instead to impede adjustment to the realities of the international economic situation. They have proven to be costly, even ineffective, ways of maintaining jobs. When they have been trade-related, they have blocked up adjustment to other, perhaps more important, sources of change such as technological advance. They have tended to dominate the effects of more promising approaches to adjustment such as labor market assistance.

Such restrictions inhibit the growth of developing countries and their ability to repay debt. Yet they not only endure in Canada and other industrial countries, they have expanded in scope, either outside the discipline of GATT (eg, VERs) or contrary to the original principles of GATT (eg, the Multi-Fibre Arrangement). The need to bring such measures under better international discipline or control—to phase out existing measures of special protection and to promote orderly adjustment for new relief applicants—is close to the top of negotiating priorities for many countries in the upcoming round of multilateral trade negotiations. Indeed, many developing countries feel that such legacies of the past must be resolved before negotiations are undertaken in new areas such as the treatment of services.

It is difficult to see a final successful outcome for the Uruguay Round of trade negotiations unless a good deal of progress is made on the adjustment issue. Moreover, in Canada's case the perceived inadequacy of the adjustment assistance system proved to be one of the major stumbling blocks in reducing resistance from labor and other groups to the establishment of a Canada-US Free Trade Agreement. This was the case despite a number of studies and analyses suggesting overall economic gain from the Agreement, equal to about one year's economic growth (Economic Council of Canada 1988d; Canada, Department of Regional Industrial Expansion 1988; Canada, Department of Finance 1988a).

Even in the small number of instances in the Canadian economy where employment declines are expected the magnitude is "low": between 0.3 and 3.4% of 1988 industry employment spread over 10 years. (Several of the industries expected to experience employment declines are discussed in this paper: leather, textiles, and knitting mills.) The perceived inadequacy of the adjustment system may be changing with the publication of the report of the Advisory Council on Adjustment (1989), which is generally optimistic about the Canadian economy's ability to adjust. The thrust of the report is on how adjustment policy could be designed to better equip Canada to face the challenges of the international marketplace, an issue for which the Canada-US Free Trade Agreement has provided a focus. The Council, which had representatives from both business and labor, seemed to be of the view that Canada had adjusted well in the past and, with the right policies, had the capability to do so in the future.[7]

Clearly, it is in Canada's interest to promote greater agreement on the use of alternatives to long-term special protection. That will not be easy. (For a somewhat more optimistic view see Bhagwati 1988.) Certainly, there will continue to be a strong need for measures that will allow the attainment of the potential gains from trade liberalization—whether bilateral or multilateral (indeed more in the latter case)—while minimizing the possible transitional costs in terms of employment and income for particular groups or regions. And it would be naive to expect in the circumstances that this would not include strong pressures for trade-related measures including some special protection. In fact, it is highly unlikely a complete set of alternatives to such protection can be designed.

There are several reasons for this. For one, in the industrial countries there appears to be much more acceptance of adaptation to non-trade than trade changes. Perhaps this is because the "trade culprits" can be more easily identified. Second, there will always be some cases where sector-specific intervention can be justified on economic grounds. Many economists would, of course, favor subsidies rather than trade restrictions to promote adjustment. But much remains to be done to define acceptable subsidies in the international trading environment. Indeed, GATT itself may have generated a built-in bias towards the use of trade restrictions since it does define certain circumstances under which they can be used, while it has had little to say about other methods. Nor has it developed a monitoring capability. Moreover, the use of trade restric-

---

7. Employment decline estimates are from Economic Council of Canada (1988d, p 22 table 2) using SIM.2, which includes the effects of the removal of trade barriers and productivity gains. For further details on adjustment, also see the views of the Advisory Council's chairman, A Jean de Grandpré (Canada, Senate of, 1988). In general, specific adjustment policies aimed at sectors likely to be adversely affected by the Canada-US Free Trade Agreement were not recommended by the Council, both on grounds of practicality and equity (for details see Advisory Council of Adjustment 1989, p 111–27). Nevertheless, in a small number of instances, in agriculture and food processing, "which could face extraordinary challenges—circumstances that go beyond the normal competitive challenges of the market place" (p 111), the Council did make some recommendations to allow Canadian food processors to compete on equal terms with their US counterparts. The Council's broad-ranging recommendations emphasized the importance of worker training as opposed to expenditures on income maintenance, the necessity of increasing Canada's level of R&D, the need to reduce interprovincial barriers to the flow of goods, professionals, and tradesmen within Canada, and that the governments should provide a stable framework of laws and tax policies within which business can plan and make investment decisions.

tions can generate the revenues needed to implement adjustment, an attractive feature for countries with large budgetary deficits.

The trick will be to create an environment in which those measures will be kept to a minimum and, if they are used as a last resort, to implement them in ways that are more effective than has been the case in recent years. That implies among other things better use of macroeconomic and other framework policies, including more emphasis on nationwide labor adjustment measures. (It is worth noting that trade measures assist both labor and firms so a greater emphasis on labor adjustment would automatically throw more weight on universal approaches). And when import restrictions are used they should lean much more to the Article 19 approach with its emphasis on their temporary nature than to long-term protection.

All of this adds up to the need for a concerted effort, in which Canada's self-interest as well as some of its shared interests with developing countries (eg, as an important exporter of primary and semifabricated goods) should lead to Canada playing a leading role to strengthen GATT as an institution. That would involve support for improving GATT's surveillance capabilities and better definition of acceptable subsidies. More generally, it would require bringing GATT's supervisory capabilities up to the levels of the other "regulators" of international economic life—the International Monetary Fund and the World Bank—and strengthening the links between these institutions. Canadian support for such changes will be highly desirable—even more so with the passage of the Canada-US Free Trade Agreement—as a route towards offsetting the fears of both Canadians and their overseas trading partners of a US-dominated "Fortress North America."

BIBLIOGRAPHY

Advisory Council on Adjustment. 1989. *Adjusting to Win*. Ottawa: Supply and Services Canada.

Ahmad, Jaleel. 1988. "Trade-related, Sector-specific Industrial Adjustment Policies in Canada: An Analysis of Textile, Clothing and Footwear Industries." Economic Council of Canada Discussion Paper 45. Ottawa: Economic Council of Canada.

Alam, Jahangir. 1985. "Cost of Dislocation: An Investigation into the Nature and Magnitude of Labour Adjustment Problems in the Canadian Footwear Industry." Ottawa: Canada Employment and Immigration Commission. Unpublished paper.

Anti-dumping Tribunal. 1973. *Report Respecting the Effects of Footwear Imports on Canadian Production of Like Goods.* Ottawa: Information Canada.

Automotive Industry Human Resources Task Force. 1986. *Report.* Ottawa: Supply and Services Canada.

Baldwin, John R., and Paul K. Gorecki. 1985. "The Determinants of the Canadian Tariff Structure Before and After the Kennedy Round: 1966, 1970." Economic Council of Canada Discussion Paper 280. Ottawa: Economic Council of Canada.

———. 1990. *Structural Change and the Adjustment Process: Perspectives on Firm Growth and Worker Turnover.* Ottawa: Economic Council of Canada.

Beigie, Carl E. 1970. *The Canada-U.S. Automotive Agreement: An Evaluation.* Montreal and Washington: Private Planning Association of Canada and National Planning Association.

Bhagwati, Jagdish. 1988. *Protectionism.* Cambridge, MA: MIT Press.

Canada DEA = Department of External Affairs. 1983a. "Canadian Trade in the 1980s," a discussion paper. Ottawa: Supply and Services Canada.

———. 1983b. *A Review of Canadian Trade Policy.* Ottawa: Supply and Services Canada.

Canada. Department of Finance. 1987. "Annual Reference Tables." *Quarterly Economic Review,* Jun.

———. 1988a. *The Canada-US Free Trade Agreement, An Economic Assessment.* Ottawa: The Department.

———. 1988b. "Tariff Relief for the Textile and Apparel Industries." Information Release 88–29 (Mar 22). Ottawa: The Department.

Canada. Department of Regional Industrial Expansion. 1988. *The Canada-US Free Trade Agreement and Industry, An Assessment.* Ottawa: The Department.

Canada. Senate of Canada. Standing Committee on Foreign Affairs. 1988. *Proceedings on Bill C-2, An Act to Implement the Free Trade Agreement Between Canada and the United States of America.* Issue 3: 53–77 (Dec 29). Ottawa: Supply and Services Canada.

Canadian Import Tribunal. 1985. *Report Respecting the Canadian Footwear Industry.* Ottawa: Supply and Services Canada.

Charette, Michael F., Robert P. Henry, and Barry Kaufmann. 1986. "The Evolution of the Canadian Industrial Structure: An international perspective." In Donald G. McFetridge, editor, *Canadian Industry in Transition,* p 61–133. University of Toronto Press.

Coopers and Lybrand Consulting Group. 1986. *Five Years since the Introduction of the Voluntary Export Restraints Quotas on the Importation of Japanese Cars into Canada.* Willowdale, Ontario: Canadian Association of Japanese Automobile Dealers.

Cornell, Peter M. 1987. "The Reduction of Trade Restrictions on Traditional Manufactures." Paper prepared for the Trade Policy Studies Program of the Pacific Economic Co-operation Conference. Ottawa.

Deloitte Haskins and Sells Associates. 1986. "Allocations of Global Import

Quotas to Importers: Assessment of Current System and Alternatives." Ottawa: Department of External Affairs. Unpublished paper.

de Silva, K. E. Arnold. 1988a. "The Pulp and Paper Modernization Grants Program: An assessment." Economic Council of Canada Discussion Paper 350. Ottawa: Economic Council of Canada.

———. 1988b. "An Economic Analysis of the Shipbuilding Industry Assistance Program." Economic Council of Canada Discussion Paper 351. Ottawa: Economic Council of Canada.

Eastman, Harry C. and Stefan Stykolt. 1967. *The Tariff and Competition in Canada*. Toronto: Macmillan.

Economic Council of Canada. 1981. *Reforming Regulation*. Ottawa: Supply and Services Canada.

———. 1983a. *On the Mend*. Economic Council of Canada, Twentieth Annual Review. Ottawa: Supply and Services Canada.

———. 1983b. *The Bottom Line, Technology, Trade and Economic Growth*. Ottawa: Supply and Services Canada.

———. 1988a. *Managing Adjustment, a Statement by the Economic Council*. Ottawa: Supply and Services Canada.

———. 1988b. *Adjustment Policies for Trade-Sensitive Industries, a Research Report Prepared for the Economic Council of Canada*. Ottawa: Supply and Services Canada.

———. 1988c. *Back to Basics*. Economic Council of Canada, Twenty-fifth Annual Review. Ottawa: Supply and Services Canada.

———. 1988d. *Venturing Forth, An Assessment of the Canada-US Trade Agreement*. Ottawa: Supply and Services Canada.

General Agreement of Tariffs and Trade. 1988. *Review of Developments in the Trading System*, Apr-Sep.

Gorecki, Paul K. 1976. *Economics of Scale and Efficient Plant Size in Canadian Manufacturing Industries*. Ottawa: Consumer and Corporate Affairs.

Grey, Alex. 1985. "Aspects of Labour Flexibility in Canada: Patterns of Regional, Inter-firm and Occupational Mobility." Ottawa: Labour Market Studies Division, Strategic Policy and Planning, Department of Employment and Immigration. Unpublished paper.

Hart, Michael M. 1986. *Canadian Economic Development and the International Trading System*. University of Toronto Press.

Hazledine, Tim and Ian Wigington. 1987. "Protection in the Canadian Automobile Market: Costs, Benefits and Implications for Industrial Structure and Adjustment." In Organization for Economic Cooperation and Development, editor, *The Costs of Restricting Imports: The Automobile Industry*.

Henderson, Richard. 1987. "The Adjustment Experience of Workers Separated from the Shipbuilding Industry." Ottawa: Canada Employment and Immigration Commission. Unpublished draft.

Jackson, John H. and William J. Davey. 1986. *Legal Problems of International Economic Relations, Cases, Materials and Text*, 2d ed. St Paul MN: West Publishing Company.

Jenkins, Glenn P. 1985. *The Costs and Consequences of the New Protectionism: The Case of Canada's Clothing Sector*, 2d ed. Ottawa: North-South Institute.

——, Gary C. Sawchuk, and Gloria Webster. 1986 Sep. "Trade, Protection, and Industrial Adjustment: The Consumer Electronics Industry in North America." Paper prepared for the NSI-ISEAS Project on Trade, Protectionism and Industrial Adjustment.

Kelly, Margaret, Naheed Kirmani, Miranda Xafa, Clemens Boonekamp, and Peter Winglee. 1988 Dec. *Issues and Developments in International Trade Policy*. International Monetary Fund Occasional Paper 63. Washington DC: IMF.

Labour Canada. 1985. "Labour Adjustment Benefits Policy Review." Ottawa: Labour Canada. Unpublished paper.

Law Reform Commission of Canada. 1986. *Policy Implementation, Compliance and Administrative Law*. Working Paper 51. Ottawa: The Commission.

Moroz, Andrew R. and Gerry E. Salembier. 1985. "A Quantitative Assessment of the Costs and Benefits of the Footwear Import Quota." Discussion Papers in International Economics 8506. Ottawa: Institute for Research on Public Policy.

OECD = Organization for Economic Cooperation and Development. 1979. *The Case for Positive Adjustment Policies*.

——. 1985. *Costs and Benefits of Protection*.

——. 1988. *The Newly Industrializing Countries: Challenge and Opportunities for OECD Industries*.

Picot, W. Garnett. 1986. *Canada's Industries: Growth in Jobs over Three Decades, A Review of the Changing Industrial Mix of Employment, 1951–1984*. Statistics Canada, Catalog # 89–507E. Ottawa: Supply and Services Canada.

Protheroe, David R. 1980. *Imports and Politics*. Montreal: Institute for Research on Public Policy.

Robertson, Matthew. 1987. "Perspectives on Labour Adjustment in the Canadian Economy." Ottawa: Department of Employment and Immigration. Unpublished paper.

Salembier, Gerry E., Andrew R. Moroz, and Frank Stone. 1987. *The Canadian Import File: Trade, Protection and Adjustment*. Montreal: Institute for Research on Public Policy.

Seward, Shirley B. and Kathryn McDade. 1988. "Immigrant Women in Canada: A Policy Perspective." Background paper. Canadian Advisory Council on the Status of Women, Ottawa.

Stone, Frank. 1984. *Canada, the GATT and the International Trading System*. Montreal: The Institute for Research on Public Policy.

Task Force on Program Review. 1985. *Job Creation, Training and Employment Services*. Ottawa: Supply and Services Canada.

TCB = Textile and Clothing Board. 1985. *Textile and Clothing Inquiry*. Ottawa: The Board.

Trebliock, Michael J., Marsha Chandler, and Robert Howse with Peter A. Simm.

1988. "Adjusting to Trade: A Comparative Perspective." Economic Council of Canada Discussion Paper 358. Ottawa: Economic Council of Canada.

Wilkinson, Bruce W. and Kenneth Norrie. 1975. *Effective Protection and the Return to Capital.* Ottawa: Information Canada.

Wonnacott, Paul. 1987. *US and Canadian Auto Policies in a Changing World Environment.* Toronto: C. D. Howe Institute and Washington DC: National Planning Association.

2

UNITED STATES
Adjustment Through Import Restriction

Gary C. Hufbauer

The 1970s and '80s were decades of seeming decline in US manufacturing prowess. The mood of industrial decline was created by three features of the economic landscape:

1. Slow manufacturing productivity growth in the 1970s, followed by numerous instances where US firms were surpassed by their Japanese competitors in the 1980s
2. Declining manufacturing employment and flat real wages in the 1980s
3. Rapidly rising merchandise trade deficits in the 1980s, concentrated in manufactured goods

Nestled within the broad story of sagging US manufacturing capability were several industries in genuine long-term decline—industries beset by slow demand growth at home and dwindling comparative advantage in world markets. The main concern in this chapter is the experience of such industries. The problems confronting those industries were accentuated by the broader economic context of the 1970s and '80s, and these are outlined in the first section. The second section provides an overview of policy toward declining industries, and looks closely at trade policies. Trade policy and adjustment in four industries—textiles, apparel, carbon steel, and automobiles—are analyzed in the third section. Means of unwinding sector arrangements are taken up in the concluding section.

Eduardo Maldonado, now an attorney in Washington DC, assisted in writing this chapter.

THE STATE OF MANUFACTURING

Slower productivity, lagging innovation, declining manufacturing employment, and flat real wages have been characteristics of most of the 1970s and '80s. In addition, the 1980s have witnessed a spectacular deficit in the US trade balance. This section analyzes these to provide a context for the four case studies, and also looks at the prospects for the 1990s.

Productivity and Innovation

US productivity growth was at a low during the 1973–79 period. In the manufacturing sector, labor productivity grew by a respectable 3% in the 1950s and '60s; plunged to 1.1% in the 1973–79 period; and recovered in the 1980s, to about 3.5%. The abrupt decline in US manufacturing productivity in the 1970s was confined to a relatively brief period and could be explained by dramatically higher energy prices. In any event, manufacturing productivity growth has consistently exceeded productivity growth in the private economy at large, mainly because service sector productivity gains have been so meager.

Even though US productivity is performing at trend rates, it is nothing to brag about compared to other industrial countries (see Table 2.1). The main reason why, over long periods, the United States has done poorly relative to its industrial competitors is that the net national savings rate, and correspondingly the rate of net investment in plant and equipment, are relatively low in the United States. For the period 1962–85, average

Table 2.1. International Comparisons of Productivity Growth by Sectors, 1960–85 (average annual percentage growth over periods shown)

Agriculture		Manufacturing		Services		
1960 –73	1973 –85	1960 –73	1973 –85	1960 –73	1973 –85	
6.2	0.7	4.1	1.2	1.2	1.6	Canada
7.7	2.0	9.5	5.7	6.3	0.8	Japan
4.1	2.7	3.4	1.2	1.6	0.3	United States
6.1	4.6	5.3	2.8	3.0	1.0	European Community
6.2	4.9	6.4	3.3	3.3	1.1	France
6.3	4.2	4.6	2.8	3.0	1.7	Germany
6.1	4.6	3.6	2.2	2.5	1.1	United Kingdom

Source: Morici 1988, p 15

annual manufacturing productivity growth correlates well with net national savings as a percentage of GNP for the five principal western economies. The US and the UK are close together at the lower left end, France and West Germany cluster in the middle, and Japan is at the upper right end of the regression line. (See Hatsopoulos et al 1988, p 304.)

Viewing the problem through another lens, the cost of capital in the United States has been persistently higher than in Japan by 3 to 4 or more percentage points in the 1979–86 period, and this has discouraged capital formation in America by comparison with Japan (Dornbusch et al 1988, p 15).

The significant productivity story is not the blip decline in the 1970s, but rather the persistent last-place showing of the United States relative to other industrial nations. This handicap in turn reflects a deep-seated national preference to consume rather than to save and invest.

Taking this handicap one step further than the broad productivity statistics, there are painful instances where specific US firms have been surpassed by their foreign competitors. Many examples can be given of industries where the United States was once the world's technical leader and now has either lost leadership or must share its position with other nations. Affected sectors include high performance ceramics, semiconductors, biotechnology, and robotics. Lagging US technology has become a central issue of the late 1980s in assessing US competitiveness, with articles appearing in the press almost weekly. For example, in 1988: "The Global Biotechnology Race," *New York Times*, July 13, p D1; "US Lags in Television Research," *Journal of Commerce*, October 27, p 5A; "Experts Warn of US Lag in Vital Chip Technology," *New York Times*, December 12, p 1. Reflecting such episodes, US trade structure is decidedly less high-tech today than it was in 1970; Germany, France and the United Kingdom have all drawn even with the United States; and Japan is well ahead (see Morici 1988, p 104).

Employment and Wages

It is well known that US manufacturing employment is declining: from a peak of 21.0 million in 1979, the number of manufacturing employes dropped to 19.0 million in 1986, but recovered to about 19.6 million in 1988. As long as productivity growth exceeds demand growth for manufactured products, the number of employes will continue to decline. Conceivably the manufacturing employment figure could fall to 16 or 17 million, some 10% of the labor force, by 2010—compared with a peak of 30% in the early 1950s. In terms of long-term employment decline, manufacturing in the late 20th century resembles agriculture in the late 19th century.

Equally alarming, to those concerned about manufacturing strength, is the behavior of real wages. At one time, blue-collar workers in the bastions of industrial America were the princes of labor. But those days have faded; meanwhile, the compensation of manufacturing workers in other industrial countries has significantly gained on the United States (see Table 2.2).

The twin facts of declining employment and flat real wages are not necessarily associated with a shrinking share of manufacturing in the national economic pie. According to official statistics, the manufacturing share of GNP has merely fluctuated between 20 and 22% of GNP since 1975 (Economic Report of the President 1988, p 261; recent revisions, however, indicate the share figure could be as low as 19 to 20%). (*New York Times*, 1988 November 28, p D1.) Automation is gradually replacing labor, while the quantity of goods shipped is more or less growing at the same rate as real GNP. If the US manufacturing sector does become more competitive, these trends could be accentuated: the manufacturing share of GNP could marginally rise, even as the number of workers declines and their pay gains merely match the service sector.

Spectacular Trade Deficit

The most powerful force acting on trade and adjustment policy in the 1980s has been the spectacular trade deficit. In the popular mind, huge trade deficits are the mirror image of industrial decline. Over the 1980s,

Table 2.2. International Comparisons of Compensation per hour in Manufacturing, 1950–87 (index, with US = 100 in each year)

1950	1960	1970	1980	1985	1987	
63	77	79	85	85	89	Canada
26	29	39	91	60	92	France
21	30	55	125	75	125	Germany
7	10	23	57	50	84	Japan
26	29	32	72	48	67	United Kingdom
—	—	—	15	14	18	Hong Kong
—	—	—	10	10	13	Korea
—	—	—	15	19	18	Singapore
—	—	—	10	11	17	Taiwan

Source: Morici 1988, p 16.

the US trade deficit worsened with every major country and area partner except OPEC. Likewise, the trade deficit worsened in every major product category except mineral fuels. The deterioration was especially spectacular in non-high-technology manufactured goods. Table 2.3 gives details of merchandise trade by product group.

On a balance of payments basis, the overall US merchandise trade deficit increased by $101 billion between 1980 and 1988, starting the period with a trade deficit of $26 billion and ending at $127 billion. The remainder of this section is an attempt to quantify the causes of this deterioration. The results are summarized in Table 2.4.

According to a line of thinking that is popular in the United States, a good part of the rising US trade deficit can be attributed to microeconomic factors: lagging US technology, poor quality US products, and foreign unfair trade practices. One plausible estimate suggests lagging technology and poor quality, that is, explanations emphasizing indus-

Table 2.3. US Merchandise Trade by Major Product Groups, 1980–87 ($ Billions)

	Total	Agri-culture	Mineral fuels	Manufactured Goods[1]		
				Hi-Tech[2]	Non-Hi-Tech	Other
Exports						
1980	225.7	41.8	8.2	54.7	106.0	15.1
1981	238.7	43.8	10.3	60.4	111.4	12.8
1982	216.4	37.0	12.8	58.1	97.2	11.4
1983	205.6	36.5	9.6	60.2	88.3	11.1
1984	224.0	30.2	9.5	65.5	98.1	12.7
1985	218.8	29.6	8.2	72.5	107.4	12.1
1986	226.8	26.6	8.2	72.5	107.4	12.1
1987	252.9	29.1	7.8	84.1	116.0	15.9
Imports						
1980	257.0	18.9	82.4	28.0	110.8	17.0
1981	273.4	18.8	84.4	33.8	122.6	13.7
1982	254.9	17.3	67.7	34.6	123.5	11.9
1983	269.9	18.1	60.2	41.4	137.1	13.1
1984	346.4	21.6	63.3	59.5	182.4	19.7
1985	352.5	22.0	55.8	64.8	204.7	15.2
1986	383.0	23.1	39.8	75.1	233.8	11.1
1987	424.1	22.6	46.7	83.5	254.3	17.0

| | | | Manufactured Goods[1] | | |
	Total	Agri-culture	Mineral fuels	Hi-Tech[2]	Non-Hi-Tech	Other
Balance						
1980	− 31.3	22.9	− 74.2	26.7	− 4.7	− 1.9
1981	− 34.7	25.0	− 74.1	26.6	− 11.2	− 0.9
1982	− 38.4	19.7	− 54.9	23.6	− 26.3	− 0.5
1983	− 64.2	18.4	− 50.6	18.8	− 48.7	− 2.0
1984	− 122.4	16.6	− 53.8	6.0	− 84.3	− 7.0
1985	− 133.6	7.6	− 45.7	3.6	− 105.2	− 4.0
1986	− 156.1	3.5	− 31.7	− 2.6	− 126.3	0.9
1987	− 171.2	6.4	− 38.9	0.6	− 138.3	− 1.1

1. Domestic and foreign exports are valued FAS (free along side); general imports are valued CIF. The merchandise trade figures in the balance of payments are valued somewhat differently; in particular, imports are valued FOB.

2. High technology products are listed below with 1987 export and import figures in millions of dollars (from USTR 1987, Table 15):

exports	imports	
84,071	83,481	total high-technology
848	48	guided missiles, spacecraft
17,758	36,340	communications equipment and electronic components
20,968	5,825	aircraft and parts
19,586	17,918	office, computing, accounting machines
654	381	ordinance and accessories
3,258	2,877	drugs and medicine
3,641	2,959	industrial inorganic chemicals
8,681	11,538	precision and scientific instruments
3,024	3,739	engines, turbines, parts
5,654	1,856	plastics and resins

Source: USTR 1987, Tables 4 and 14

trial decline, might have increased the deficit by $26 billion, thus accounting for about 26% of its net increase.

As regards trade barriers, the United States was the biggest user, among industrial nations, of new non-tariff measures during the 1980s, as shown in Table 2.5. Thus rising US non-tariff measures (largely in response to the problems of declining industries) more than offset the export loss inflicted on the United States by rising foreign barriers, so that, overall, unfair trade practices reduced the deficit some $11 billion.

Moreover, in the 1980s the United States enjoyed progressively lower petroleum prices. In sum, microeconomic causes actually reduced the deficit by $20 billion.

Overall, the spiraling US trade deficit primarily reflects a confluence of macroeconomic forces. First there was the rise in the value of the

Table 2.4. Causes of the Worsening US Merchandise Trade Deficit, 1980–88
($ billions)

The $101 billion deterioration in the merchandise trade deficit between 1980
and 1988 can be explained as follows (minus numbers reduce the deficit).

Microeconomic Explanations (reduced the deficit by $20)

	"industrial decline"
20	lagging US technology
6	poor US product quality
	unfair trade practices (NTM = non-tariff measures)
6	new NTMs by industrial countries against US exports
− 17	new NTMs by the United States against US imports
− 35	lower petroleum prices

Macroeconomic Explanations (increased the deficit by $114)

	dollar exchange rate
120	rise of 40 index points between 1980 and 1985
− 110	fall of 43 index points between 1985 and 1988
25	government deficit: increase in unified federal budget deficit from average of $57 (2.2% of GNP) in FY 1979 and FY 1980 to average of $153 (3.2% of GNP) in FY 1987 and FY 1988
58	private savings: decrease in personal savings from 4.9% of GNP in 1979 and 1980 to 2.6% of GNP in 1987 and 1988
	growth gap
9	lag in ROECD growth of 1% per year
12	decline in US exports to Western Hemisphere developing countries

---

Unexplained residual deterioration increased the deficit by $7
Source: Hufbauer 1989

dollar from late 1980 to early 1985, prompted in the early 1980s both
by the Federal Reserve's tight monetary policy and the Administration's
tax incentives for investment. The anti-inflationary monetary policy pushed
real short-term interest rates from -0.4% in 1980 to 6.1% in 1984.
Meanwhile, new tax depreciation schedules made investment projects
more attractive. The result was a tremendous rush of foreign capital to
the United States and a huge appreciation of the dollar. The sustained
overvaluation of the dollar enabled foreign firms to capture market share
in the United States. Hence, as a result of the overvaluation episode,

Table 2.5. Industrial Country Imports Subject to "Hard-Core" Non-Tariff Measures (NTMs), 1981–86 (in percents)

Source of Imports						
Industrial Countries		Developing Countries		All Countries[1]		
1981	1986	1981	1986	1981	1986	Importer
10	13	22	23	12	15	European Community
29	29	22	22	25	25	Japan
9	15	14	17	11	16	United States
13	16	19	21	15	18	all industrial countries

"Hard-core" NTMs represent a subgroup of all possible NTMs. They are the ones most likely to have significant restrictive effects. Hard-core NTMs include import prohibitions, quantitative restrictions, voluntary export restraints, variable levies, MFA restrictions, and non-automatic licensing. Examples of NTMs that are not considered hard core include technical barriers (health and safety restrictions and standards), minimum pricing regulations, the use of price investigations (eg, for countervailing and antidumping purposes) and price surveillance. The percentage of imports subject to NTMs measures the sum of the value of a country's import group affected by NTMs, divided by the total value of its imports of that group. The figures here differ from my 23% estimate in the text because the latter is for 1988 and has somewhat different coverage; it is an update of Hufbauer and Rosen 1986, table 2–4.

1. The figures for "all countries" are calculated as weighted averages (1986 weights) of imports originating in industrial and developing countries, respectively. For this calculation, the Eastern trading area is grouped with the developing countries.

Sources: World Bank 1987, Table 8.3; GATT 1987, Tables A3 to A7.

these foreign firms are in a better competitive position than they would have been if the exchange rate had not appreciated.

If the dollar had remained at its lofty 1985 heights, it might have caused an extra $110 billion deterioration in the trade deficit between 1980 and 1988. After 1985, however, the finance ministers and central bankers of the major nations began to focus on exchange rates: initially to lower the dollar (the Plaza Accord), and then, in 1987, to stabilize exchange rates among key currencies (the Louvre Accord). The Louvre Accord was the work of the Group of Seven (G-7) nations: Canada, France, Germany, Italy, Japan, the United Kingdom, and the United States. Thus the dollar has retraced all its pre-1985 rise, and the overall adverse effect on the trade balance in the 1980–88 period has perhaps dwindled to about $11 billion.

Exchange rate movements in the early 1980s were the immediate reason for the reduced competitiveness of American industry. The burden on mature industries, some of which became troubled industries, was particularly acute (see Branson and Love 1988, table 9.5). US unit labor costs in manufacturing increased 24% from 1979 to 1985. In the same period, measured in US dollars, Japan's costs dropped 14%, and Germany's dropped 27%. With the realignment of exchange rates after the Plaza Accord, the United States regained its cost position by comparison with Japan, but not with Germany.

The second cause of the huge trade deficit was the rising budget deficit prompted by the Reagan Administration's twin policies—implemented with a big assist from Congressional Democrats—of cutting taxes (sharply in 1981, followed by slow backtracking in 1982, 1983, and 1984) and increasing military expenditures.

Some of the President's outspoken advisers hoped that lower tax rates would actually increase tax revenues (the Laffer curve argument), but this belief was not ratified by ensuing events. Meanwhile, from 1980 to 1985, government expenditure rose as a share of GNP. Defense spending grew from 5.5% of GNP in fiscal 1981 to 6.5% in fiscal 1985; entitlement expenditure also increased; and interest payments, propelled by the deficit, surged from 2.4% of GNP in 1981 to 3.2% in 1985. After the Balanced Budget and Emergency Control Act of 1985 (the Gramm-Rudman-Hollings Act), the growth of federal spending declined substantially. Outlays dropped from 24.0% of GNP in fiscal 1985 to 22.8% in 1987.

During the 1980s, the net effect of fiscal expansion on the manufacturing sector was approximately a wash because of two offsetting forces. On the one hand, demand for manufactures was stimulated by the US defense buildup. Between 1980 and 1986, when total manufacturing employment contracted by 1.29 million, defense-related employment increased by 0.74 million jobs (Dornbusch et al 1988, p 11). On the other hand, the larger budget deficits probably worsened the trade balance by about $25 billion. This is based on a rough estimate that, in the late 1980s, the US trade deficit worsens approximately $25 billion for each 1% of GNP increase in the fiscal deficit, with a lag of three to five years (Bryant 1988, Simulation C). In the 1980s the budget deficit worsened about 1% of GNP—going from an average of $57 billion in FY 1979 and FY 1980 taken together (2.2% of GNP) to an average of $153 billion in FY 1987 and FY 1988 (3.2% of GNP).

In the mid-1980s, each billion dollars of manufactured exports was associated with about 30,000 jobs, so the budget deficit might have slashed manufacturing employment by 750,000 on account of the deteriorating trade balance.

The third macroeconomic cause of the rising trade deficit was the falling rate of private savings. Just when government deficits were rising, private savings were falling. It is not clear why US household savings fell so much, but several hypotheses have been offered:

- Rising stock exchange and real estate prices have created the same gains in private wealth that more private savings would, so households ask "why save from income?"
- Improvements in Social Security, Medicare, and private health and pension plans have eroded household incentives to save.
- Meanwhile, high interest rates have enabled private pension plans to meet their financial targets with lower current contributions.
- Despite the cut in marginal tax rates, and despite high real interest rates, the tax structure still favors current consumption.

Whatever its origins, the falling savings rate made a major contribution to the worsening trade balance. The lower the rate of private savings, the greater the trade deficit, for any given amount of investment. Accounting definitions teach us that a nation's current account deficit equals its public sector financial deficit (government spending minus government revenue) plus its private sector financial deficit (private investment minus private savings). In the 1980s, a decline in the household savings rate of 1% of GNP probably caused a $25 billion increase in the trade deficit. Thus, the decline in personal savings from an average of 4.9% of GNP in 1979–80 to an average of 2.6% of GNP in 1987–88 was possibly responsible for a $58 billion worsening of the trade deficit account. (Data on personal savings are reported in the Economic Report of the President 1988, Table 828; and the *Survey of Current Business* of 1988 September, p 9. The coefficient of $25 billion per 1% of GNP change in household savings is based on Bryant 1988, Simulation C.)

The fourth and final macroeconomic cause of the rising US trade deficit can be found in the slow growth in other OECD nations and the collapsing fortunes of developing countries during the 1980s. In the 1970s, the OECD nations apart from the United States (ROECD) grew at an average rate of 3.7%, while the United States grew at an average rate of 2.8%. In the 1980s, ROECD growth fell to 2.8% (*OECD Economic Outlook* 1988, Tables 1 and R1). The slowdown in ROECD growth of about 0.9% per year can be attributed with increasing the US trade deficit by about $9 billion annually. This calculation assumes 1% faster growth in the ROECD nations improves the US trade balance by $10 billion (Bryant 1988, Simulation G). Other estimates find a much bigger impact from faster ROECD growth. For example, Bergsten (1988, table 1.3) assumes 1% faster ROECD demand growth improves the US current account by about $50 billion per year in 1992.

The troubles of the developing world are well known. The most pointed case, from the standpoint of US exports, concerns the developing countries of the Western Hemisphere. If the Western Hemisphere had not been visited by the debt crisis and deteriorating terms of trade, US exports in 1987 to that region might have been $12 billion higher. In 1980, when world merchandise imports were $1,928 billion, imports by Western Hemisphere developing countries were $111 billion. In 1987, when world imports were $2,418 billion, imports by Western Hemisphere developing countries were only $110 billion. If the Western Hemisphere developing countries had maintained their share of world merchandise imports, their imports would have been $29 billion higher, and US exports to the region would plausibly have increased by $12 billion (40% of the counterfactual increase). (Data are from IMF 1986 and 1988.)

Outlook for the 1990s

Just as the story of the 1980s was sagging industry, the story of the 1990s could well be surging industry. But the surge, if it comes, will likely stress volume gains, rather than a catch-up in productivity or innovation by US firms.

The good news is that most of the macroeconomic features that provoked a rising trade deficit in the 1980s are being slowly reversed. By the end of 1987 the exchange rate for the dollar was back to its 1980 level, and could well be nudged lower in 1990. The government deficit has gradually shrunk as a percentage of GNP, and should shrink further as the collective minds of the Administration and Congress are focused on fiscal austerity (assisted by the mechanical targets of the Gramm-Rudman-Hollings Act). Household savings could well rise, as the euphoria of the 1980s yields to the realism of the 1990s. Led by Japan and Germany, the other OECD nations could turn in a sparkling economic performance; and developing countries are likely to pay more attention to the politics of growth than the demands of foreign bankers.

The bad news is that nothing indicates that private savings in the United States will undergo the fundamental transformation that would propel the United States from the bottom of the OECD savings league to the top. Nor can signs be found of a renaissance in technical education, a boom in research and development, a surge in plant and equipment investment, or the embrace of long planning horizons by corporate leaders. Looking forward to the 1990s, it seems likely that many American high-tech firms will find themselves jostling to catch up with European or Japanese industrial leaders. Meanwhile, the industries in genuine decline will find temporary respite in the warmer macroeconomic climate of the 1990s; but their long-term adjustment problems will likely persist into the next century.

POLICY TOWARD DECLINING INDUSTRIES: AN OVERVIEW

The cutting edge of US policy towards declining industries is trade policy. How is it that the United States has come to use trade policy as the almost-exclusive vehicle for addressing the problems of troubled industries? Three reasons explain this state of affairs. (This section draws heavily from Hufbauer, Berliner, and Elliot 1986; and Hufbauer and Rosen 1986.)

The first reason is the fact that non-intervention is the prevailing American ideology. According to this ideology, if firms get in trouble, that is their own fault and their own worry. The ideology of non-intervention has been significantly and persistently breached in only four major sectors: banking; agriculture; the regulated utilities; and high-tech military. Domestic policy tools are seldom deployed to address the problems of troubled firms in other sectors. For example, little was done through domestic remedies to ease the difficulties visited on the automobile industry or the steel industry in the early 1980s.

The second reason is that the ideology of free markets has never gained the same acceptance in the sphere of international trade as in the sphere of domestic trade. The Smoot-Hawley Tariff of 1930 climaxed a long period of US economic policy that revolved around periodic tariff adjustments. To be sure, beginning in 1934, the fabric of the Reciprocal Trade Agreements Acts, the General Agreement on Tariffs and Trade (GATT), and the Trade Expansion Act of 1962 and its successors gave an internationalist overlay to the preceding century of American tariff history. But the overlay was always thin. It worked best so long as America enjoyed technical superiority in most industries and kept a healthy merchandise trade surplus. In recent years, those conditions have faded, and the internationalist overlay has worn through. The third reason, of more recent vintage, is the political arithmetic of the federal budget. The squeeze between tax politics and expenditure politics means that very few large on-budget programs can be added to the federal domain. By implication, most new programs will necessarily take an off-budget form—exemplified by trade restrictions.

All these forces combined to make trade policy the high-profile industrial policy of the 1980s, a role that could possibly extend into the 1990s. It is worth noting that trade policy played a similar role from 1830 until 1930. In fact, even during the liberal era of trade policy—the first four decades after World War II—the United States pursued a two-track policy. On one track, the United States championed free trade and took the lead in eight rounds of GATT negotiations. On the other track, the United States adopted numerous special measures to protect problem industries—dairy, orange juice, beef, textiles and apparel, automobiles, carbon steel, semiconductors, and others. The Reagan Administration, faced with strong pressure from the Democratic Congress, allowed this sort of "special protection" to soar from a coverage of some 12% of imports in 1980 to some 23% of imports in 1988. ("Special protection" refers to protection for a significant industry that exceeds an ad valorem tariff equivalent of about 12%.)

By traditional measures, the gains from special protection were nearly always outweighed by the costs. For example, in 1988 special protection inflicted an estimated $80 billion cost on US consumers per year. Of this amount, domestic producers gained about $50 billion, about $9 billion was collected in tariffs, and about $11 billion went to foreign producers in the form of quota rents. The remaining $10 billion represented a straightforward efficiency loss. Quite commonly, the cost to consumers exceeded $100,000 per year per job "saved" in the protected industry—and in some cases (specialty steel and benzenoid chemicals) the cost has been $1 million per job. (For more examples, see Hufbauer et al 1986, table 1.2.)

Many thousands of workers are locked into jobs that are sometimes well-paying but often unproductive in terms of the national economy. Moreover, as a consequence of protection, jobs were lost in industries that buy inputs from the protected industries. In recent years, this has become especially noticeable in the case of steel users (for example, Caterpillar) and computer manufactures that require sophisticated semi-conductors (for example, Hewlett-Packard).

Special protection might have had a counter-cyclical logic in the years between 1982 and 1985, when the US economy was handicapped by a badly overvalued exchange rate and unemployed resources. But those economic factors are now reversed. At the end of the 1980s the foreign exchange value of the dollar had returned to its 1980 levels and the US unemployment rate had declined to 5%. Capacity has been strained in many industries and labor shortages have been evident on both the East and West coasts. Since 1986, certainly, the main task has been to use American resources more efficiently, not to put idle factories and idle men back to work, nor to revive depressed regions.

Why, then, has the United States engaged in the politics of protection with greater gusto than any time since the 1930s? Why is it that President Bush promised in the 1988 campaign to renew the carbon steel import restraints? Why is it all but inevitable that textile and apparel restraints will continue beyond the expiration of the fourth Multi-Fiber Arrangement in 1991? There are three reasons for these phenomena: a transient reason; an "old" fundamental reason; and a "new" fundamental reason.

The transient reason is that the string of outsized merchandise trade deficits of the 1980s have badly sapped the political vitality of the free trade camp. Coinciding with deeper concerns about an ascendant Japan and a second-rate America, merchandise trade deficits exceeding $100 billion seem to demonstrate that liberal trade policies are, at best, naive.

The "old" fundamental reason is that protection is a politician's delight. Protectionist policies provide a ready answer to the woes of troubled industries: they deliver visible and concentrated benefits to chosen firms while imposing hidden and diffuse costs on other industries. Unfortunately, once adopted, protectionist policies tend to spread: by protecting the steel industry, for example, the government points itself in the direction of protecting other industries that either use steel or can draw on the political example of steel (such as automobiles and machine tools).

The "new" fundamental reason finds its roots in the industrial policy debate associated with such names as Laura Tyson, Robert Kuttner, Lester Thurow, and Clyde Prestowitz. According to their argument, comparative advantage in the manufacturing sector no longer stems, in textbook fashion, from resource endowments; rather it is created by government policies across a broad front, including trade policy. If America is to hold its own place in the emerging industries of the 21st century, it must nourish those industries with protection today, using all the weapons that Japan and Europe are said to deploy. (For a survey of these ideas see Hale 1988.)

To be sure, this "new" fundamental reason has little logical connection with the problems of mature, declining industries. But when the analysis of the Berkeley Roundtable is picked up by the popular media, it is quickly turned into a generalized argument for protecting all kinds of manufacturing activity.

Yet the negative implications of prolonged protection for mature industries are severe. Protective policies essentially tax the emerging industries that industrial policy advocates would like to nourish. Meanwhile, protection enables foreign producers to strengthen their own competitive position, because restrictive actions create a more lucrative US market. Foreign firms thereby earn larger profits, which they can spend to improve their plant and equipment and to introduce new and more sophisticated products.

Application of Trade Policy to Declining Industries

The US Constitution assigns roles to both the President and the Congress in formulating international trade policy. This division of power creates tension when a constituent-minded Congress pushes a globally minded President to impose import restraints. The result has been the creation of five distinct legal paths to special protection for declining industries. The key difference between the five paths is the distinction between more congressional control and more presidential control. Each of these is discussed below.

High Tariffs. In the 1920s and '30s, high tariffs were the main answer —designed by the Congress and accepted by the President—to troublesome competition from foreign quarters. The high tariffs remaining today are largely a legacy from the Fordney-McCumber Tariff of 1922 and the Smoot-Hawley Tariff of 1930, retained by industries with sufficient political strength to guard their ancestral ramparts against the erosion of seven tariff-cutting rounds conducted under GATT. Prior to each round, certain industries have managed to persuade Congress, and through Congress the White House, that they cannot survive without their accustomed tariffs.

The average US tariff on dutiable imports has now dwindled to about 5%. By contrast, tariffs imposed in instances of special protection are about 15% and higher. The most important case is textiles and apparel; other US industries still protected by high tariffs include benzenoid chemicals, rubber footwear, ceramic articles and tiles, glassware, canned tuna, and orange juice.

Escape Clause Relief. In theory, the "escape clause" was meant to provide the major route to special protection. In practice, it has become a secondary road. The broad contours of escape clause relief are laid down in Article 19 of the GATT; the governing US provisions are set out in Section 201 of the Trade Act of 1974.[1]

1. Section 201 of the Trade Act of 1974 followed several other versions of an escape clause: an industry consultation provision in the Reciprocal Trade Agreements Act of 1934; a formal "escape clause" in the 1942 bilateral trade agreement with Mexico; Executive Order 9832 of 1945 in which President Truman required that an escape clause be included in all future trade agreements; a legislative escape clause in Section 7 of the Trade Agreements Extension Act of 1951; and a revised escape clause in Section 301 of the Trade Expansion Act of 1962. The 1962 Act required that trade concessions be the major cause of increased imports and that rising imports be a major factor in causing or threatening injury; the 1974 Act dropped the linkage to trade concessions and relaxed the causation test to "substantial cause." The Omnibus Trade and Competitiveness Act of

Under US law, award of escape clause relief is highly discretionary (the President plays a decisive role). Moreover, the escape clause contains features that are disagreeable to industry: it contemplates declining protection from year to year, and corresponding adjustment of the petitioning industry to the realities of international competition.

Between 1975 and 1988, some 55 escape clause petitions were brought to the US International Trade Commission. A majority of the ITC recommended trade relief in 30 instances; and on 3 cases the Commission was evenly split. Of these 33 cases (30 plus 3), the President granted trade relief in only 14. However, in those 14 cases—generally covering small industries with limited political clout—there have been significant success stories in the realm of adjustment. The outstanding example was the revival of motorcycle producer Harley-Davidson. Another small industry that looks set on the path to recovery is cedar shakes and shingles.

Presidential Powers. The President may use his inherent responsibility for the conduct of foreign policy to persuade a foreign government to limit its exports to the United States. This low-visibility, high-flexibility form of protection has become a favored Executive branch means of helping large troubled industries. The President can claim credit both for defending the principles of free trade (against more protective Congressional or ITC solutions) and for defending the domestic industry. Moreover, the President can usually conceal the cost of protection from the public (economists are still debating the cost of the 1981 restraints on automotive imports from Japan). Finally, the President can more easily relax or remove the restraints once political attitudes or economic fortunes change.

An early example of the use of inherent presidential powers was President Johnson's steel restraints. Recent examples include President Reagan's use of voluntary restraint agreements to limit carbon steel shipments from practically all significant suppliers and to limit machinery imports from Japan, Switzerland, Taiwan, and West Germany.

Discretionary Protection Within a Statutory Framework. Some statutory frameworks give the President considerable latitude in deciding how to answer the trade problems of affected industries. In practice, that

---

1988 made three main changes to the 1974 legislation. First, it encouraged petitioners to submit an adjustment plan to show how import relief would help them to adjust; second, if an injury determination is made the United States International Trade Commission (USITC) must consider the submitted plan when making its remedy recommendations; finally, the number of Presidential relief options was increased. See USITC 1982, p 1–4; Metzger 1971, p 319–21; Baldwin 1984, ch 3; US Chamber of Commerce 1988, ch 5.

latitude may be narrowed by Congressional surveillance. Examples are Section 204 of the Agricultural Act of 1956, used as the statutory vehicle for placing quantitative restraints on textile and apparel imports, and Section 22 of the Agricultural Adjustment Act of 1933 (1935 amendment), currently used to limit dairy, peanut, cotton, and sugar imports. In deploying both these statutes, the President must pay close attention to Congressional sentiment.

Unusual relief (including quantitative restraints) in countervailing duty and antidumping duty cases provide the latest example of special protection applied within a statutory framework. This twist was inaugurated in 1978 by the trigger price mechanism in steel; it was followed in the settlement of both antidumping and subsidy petitions against European steel in 1982; and it was used to settle subsidy complaints against Chinese textiles in 1983.

Statutory Quotas. Statutory quotas represent the most decisive exercise of congressional power. Each such law strictly limits foreign entry, and only allows presidential discretion as to details of implementation. They often set a rigid limit on imports, expressed as a percentage of domestic consumption or as a residual between domestic consumption and domestic production, or they altogether bar foreign suppliers from the US market. Examples of the first include the Meat Act and the Magnuson Fisheries Act. The 1920 Jones Act exemplifies the second: it continues a ban on coastal shipping (cabotage) that dates to the First Congress.

Characteristics of Special Protection

Special protection has several characteristics: the widespread use of quantitative restraints; the duration and review of protection; the costs to consumers and the efficiency loss to the nation; and the extent of adjustment during the life of trade restraints. (Tables 1.1 and 1.2 of Hufbauer et al 1986 summarize several of these features for 31 industries.)

Quantitative Restraints. Unilateral quantitative restrictions made a modern appearance as early as 1463 when England imposed a zero quota on a range of manufactured articles. By contrast "voluntary" restraints on exports, negotiated between governments and implemented by the supplying country, date from US policy initiatives in the 1930s first spawned by the National Industrial Recovery Act. (See Metzger 1971, p 167–70.) In the postwar period for the United States, special protection has usually entailed quantitative restraints (QRs), ranging from voluntary restraint agreements (VRAs) in which the restraints are self-imposed by the foreign country, to orderly marketing agreements (OMAs) in which restraints are monitored by the United States, to global and bilateral quotas in which the US Customs Service allows only fixed quantities to enter the United States.

The use of QRs rather than high tariffs, countervailing duties, or anti-dumping duties, answers a strong preference of both domestic producers and foreign exporters. Domestic producers prefer QRs for three reasons: first, their share of the domestic market is more certain; second, domestic prices are less variable since fluctuations in foreign supply conditions have almost no effect on quantities offered for sale in the US market; third, for a given degree of political clout, the domestic industry can secure more protection through quantitative restraints than through tariffs, since the American public usually understands the price-raising impact of tariffs but often believes that QRs have little effect on prices.

Foreign exporters prefer quantitative restraints for somewhat different reasons, which vary depending on whether they are traditional suppliers or new entrants to the US market. In the postwar period, most QRs have been selectively applied. Exempt from control are "well-behaved" exporting countries that are not considered to be disrupting the domestic US market. For this reason, traditional suppliers prefer QRs both because they do not need to cut back their own export levels and because restrictions on third-country competitors may increase price levels in the US market.

Moreover, foreign exports that are affected—usually the "aggressive" new entrants—prefer QRs to tariffs because QRs are customarily implemented in a way that confers valuable quota rents on the restrained exporters. Quota rents result from the reduced supply of imported goods and the subsequent higher prices. Quota rents are captured by exporters because quotas are allocated to foreign governments which in turn distribute the export rights to established firms. The United States almost never auctions quota rights and seldom allocates them to US importers or producers—two methods of distribution that would deprive foreign suppliers of the scarcity rents. New Zealand and the United Kingdom have experimented with these alternative approaches.

Duration and Review. Cases of special protection vary widely in terms of the duration of protection and the frequency of review. At one extreme are instances of short-term relief lasting five years or less. In these instances, usually associated with use of the escape clause, relief was designed and implemented to provide "breathing room" for an adjusting industry.

At the other extreme are protective measures designed to insulate the domestic industry from foreign competition for an extended period. "Indefinite protection" describes most of the high tariffs still standing from the Tariff Acts of 1922 and 1930. Other examples are the maritime laws (dating from 1789), and the Magnuson Fisheries Act (dating from 1977).

Between these two extremes are cases in which Presidential review is permitted by statute but constrained by custom. For example, Section 204 of the Agricultural Act of 1956 nominally allows the President great flexibility in setting textile and apparel quotas, but in reality every Presidential decision is carefully monitored by Congress and the business community.

In terms of endgames, the cases of special protection can be divided into three broad categories. The first and largest category includes cases that were ongoing in 1988, often because earlier episodes of protection had been rolled over into new phases of protection (for example, textile, apparel, and carbon steel). The second category includes cases where special protection was terminated because of a cyclical revival in demand and an upsurge in product prices (examples include ball bearings and petroleum). The third category, which is small in terms of trade volumes, includes cases where protection was terminated after the industry had adjusted through a combination of downsizing, product shifts, and modernization (examples are the bicycle, motorcycle, and CB radio industries).

This categorization of cases suggests that, while adjustment may point to the end of special protection, in more cases protection endures indefinitely, or is brought to an end by the happenstance of cyclical revival.

Adjustment During Special Protection. Despite the long duration of most instances of special protection, a great deal of adjustment takes place in most episodes. In terms of labor force adjustment, production jobs almost always drop. At the same time, the import share of the domestic market is usually allowed to rise, but at constrained rates. Typically, the rise in the import share of the domestic market ranges from 0.5 to as many as 3.0 percentage points annually.

Why does the US government not do more for displaced workers than the standard fare of 26 weeks of unemployment insurance? The reasons are many and varied, but they come down to four arguments against generous relief. First is the argument that the government should foster adjustment of the work force to economic change across-the-board, whether the impetus comes from inside or outside the borders. It would be inequitable, so the argument runs, to do more for workers displaced by imports than workers laid off, for example, in the wake of leveraged buy-outs. Second, comprehensive adjustment policies would be tremendously expensive—a cost the deficit-ridden federal government simply cannot afford. Third, generous programs run the risk of malingering: if the United States emulated German retraining and unemployment benefits, so the argument goes, the United States would also acquire the German 9% unemployment rate. Fourth, none of the targeted adjustment programs has been terribly successful. Right on point, the Trade Adjustment Assistance Program (created in the Trade Expansion Act of 1962) acquired a notorious reputation for mismanagement and ineffectiveness. Nor have other programs (such as the Jobs Training Partnership Act) done much better in terms of speeding the return of workers to "good jobs at good wages."

Special protection as practiced in the United States cannot, for the most part, be faulted for freezing the status quo. Instead, it should be criticized for imposing huge costs on consumers while providing rather little assistance to workers and firms that depart the troubled industry. Moreover, the system of special protection creates widespread opposition to trade liberalization. On the one hand, workers expelled from the industry blame imports for their misfortune—misfortune that was inadequately mitigated by retraining, relocation, or make-up wage allowances. On the other hand, the firms and workers remaining in the industry cling with great tenacity to trade protection, however prosperous the industry may have become.

EXPERIENCE IN FOUR INDUSTRIES

In recent years, four mature US industries—textiles, apparel, steel, and automobiles—have received extensive protection from foreign competition. In each case, from the beginning, protection was rationalized by the argument that it would permit the domestic industry to adjust and once again become competitive with foreign producers. In the pages that follow, the section on each industry first outlines the trade policy history and then evaluates the success of adjustment during the 1980s. (The trade policy histories that begin each subsection below draw heavily from Hufbauer, Berliner, and Elliot 1986.)

Textiles

The postwar history of textile and apparel protection started with President Eisenhower's bilateral agreement with Japan in 1957. Japan agreed to limit certain cotton textile exports to the United States for five years; and in 1959 bilateral agreements were initiated by the United Kingdom with Hong Kong, India, and Pakistan. These arrangements paved the way for the so-called short-term arrangement (STA). The 1961 STA allowed the importing country to ask the exporting country to limit its exports if there was the existence or threat of "market disruption." A long-term arrangement (LTA) followed in 1962. It embedded the terms of the STA, but allowed quotas to grow 5% annually under "normal" circumstances. The LTA was renewed in 1967 and again in 1970 at the insistence of the United States.

In 1974 the first Multi-Fiber Arrangement (MFA) was signed. It added to the provisions of the long-term arrangement, and allowed import quotas on man-made fibers and wool products. However, the "normal" quota growth rate was increased to 6% annually. In 1977 the second Multi-Fiber Arrangement was negotiated with provisions allowing for "reasonable departures" from the framework of the first MFA. The second MFA was inherited by the Reagan Administration when it took office in January 1981.

Table 2.6. US Textile Industry, 1980–87

1980	1982	1984	1986	1987	
					production, in billion dollars[1]
44.7	44.9	52.3	52.3	54.1	current value
49.4	44.9	50.1	50.1	51.2	constant value (1982 dollars)
90	100	103	103	105	producer price index[2]
					net profit after taxes[3]
977	851	1,635	1,706	1,828	in million dollars
2.2	2.1	3.2	3.7	3.8	as a percentage of sales
					capital expenditures,
1,540	1,460	1,920	1,670	1,950	in million dollars[4]
					trade, in million dollars[5]
2,676	3,000	4,874	6,151	6,918	imports
3,632	2,784	2,382	2,570	2,900	exports
					trade, percentages
6.1	6.7	8.9	11.1	11.9	imports, of consumption
8.1	6.2	4.6	5.0	5.4	exports, of production
2.1	(0.4)	(4.8)	(6.9)	(7.4)	trade balance relative to consumption[6]

1980	1982	1984	1986	1987	
848	750	746	703	725	employment, in thousands[7]
					labor productivity, 1980 = 100
100	107	114	124	123	textiles index[8]
100	99	99	95	92	relative to all manufacturing[9]
					textile wages as a percentage of
70	69	70	71	72	all-manufacturing wages[10]

Notes and Sources

Except as noted, data are from the American Textile Manufacturers Institute's *Textile Hi-Lights* 1988 Sep issue (abbreviated ATMI) or Cline (1987, p 27 table 2.1, which provides annual data for 1960–86 for production, investment and employment, drawing primarily from the *US Industrial Outlook* for various years).

1. Product data for SIC 22 (textile mill products), which excludes synthetic fibers (SIC 2823 and 2824), taken from Cline for 1980–84; and the *1989 US Industrial Outlook,* p 40–1, for 1986–87.

2. The 1980 entry is the index for all textile products and apparel from the *Statistical Abstract of the US 1988* table 736; other entries are for textiles only from ATMI p 18.

3. ATMI p 13 for 1986–87; the 1987 Dec issue, p 13, was used for 1980–84.

4. Includes replacement outlays. ATMI p 21. These data differ from those in Cline because of differences in coverage.

5. Values are CIF. ATMI p 24.

6. Computed as (exports minus imports) divided by production.

7. ATMI p 22. These data are higher than those in Cline and the *US Industrial Outlook* (eg, 1989, p 40–1) because of differences in coverage.

8. Output per hour of all employes in cotton and synthetic broad woven fabrics; 1987 estimated on the basis of constant value of production and employment data in the source, which is the Bureau of Labor Statistics' *Productivity Measures for Selected Industries and Government Services* (1988 Feb, Bulletin 2296, Table 65).

9. Calculated as the index of labor productivity in textiles divided by the index of labor productivity in all manufacturing (from the *Monthly Labor Review,* 1988 Nov, p 90).

10. ATMI p 23 for 1986–87; the 1987 Dec issue, p 23, was used for 1980–84.

In December 1981, at the urging of the European Community, the 1981 Protocol to the Multi-Fiber Arrangement was negotiated (this is known as the third MFA). The 1981 Protocol incorporated several restrictive approaches to textiles initially built into President Carter's White Paper on Trade, which was issued in 1979 as part of the legislative bargain that surrounded the Tokyo Round of Multilateral Trade Agreements under GATT. In the event of market disruption, the "normal" minimum import growth rate of 6% in volume terms would be eliminated for "dominant suppliers" (eg, Hong Kong, Taiwan, Korea, and Macao). Further, "market disruption" was redefined to refer to the overall growth of the market for the product in the importing country, and thus would take into account any decline in growth resulting from shifting patterns of demand. An "anti-surge" clause was drafted to preclude full utilization of previously unused quotas.

The net result of these three changes was that import growth both from the major suppliers and in "sensitive categories" was often limited, through bilateral agreements, to the same rate as domestic consumption growth. Between 1982 and 1987, for example, the US-Hong Kong bilateral agreement limited export growth to between 0.5 and 1.5% per year for 26 restricted categories covering 60% of Hong Kong textile exports to the United States.

Despite such restrictions, under the third MFA the rate of growth of US imports was 15.1% annually, substantially higher than the 1.4% rate of growth of domestic consumption. This was mainly due to exporters circumventing quota restrictions by increasing exports in non-restricted categories and transhipping through countries with unused quotas. Both practices were identified as "loopholes" when it came time to draft the fourth MFA.

Meanwhile, the People's Republic of China was emerging as a major new supplier of textiles and apparel. In January 1983 the United States and China reached an impasse in negotiating the renewal of their bilateral export restraint agreement. The Reagan Administration imposed quotas unilaterally and China retaliated against US agricultural products. Farm groups pressed the Administration to soften its position, and a new bilateral agreement was reached in July 1983. Although denounced as a "disaster" by the textile camp, the bilateral agreement nevertheless contained tighter limits on Chinese export growth to the United States than the one it replaced. At the end of 1987, the US-China bilateral textile agreement was renegotiated. The new agreement, set to run to the end of 1991, is somewhat more liberal than agreements with Hong Kong, Korea and Taiwan.

Early in 1985, Representative Ed Jenkins (D-GA) introduced a textile bill that would have substantially cut textile and apparel imports (which expanded very rapidly after 1980). Jenkins' complaint was that the textile restraint system still allowed for rapid import growth, as new suppliers and new products found loopholes in a less-than-comprehensive program. His answer was to deal with the "problem" once and for all by applying global quotas to all textile and apparel imports, even from Canada and Europe, a sharp departure from past practice in which only imports from developing countries and Japan had been restricted. The bill passed both houses of Congress, but was predictably vetoed by President Reagan. However, Congress scheduled the override vote to take place after the negotiations on the fourth renewal of the MFA. The textile industry kept pressure on negotiators and was able to get bilateral agreements with Hong Kong, Korea, and Taiwan that cut growth rates of their exports to the United States to a mere 1% per year.

In 1986 the MFA was renewed for five years extending through 1991 July 31. Among new restrictions, the fourth MFA provides that an initial quota freezing the level of imports may be extended for a second year, and, in the case of major suppliers, the freeze may be extended indefinitely.

Even bilateral quotas negotiated under the restrictive fourth MFA were not sufficiently tight to satisfy the domestic industry. Thus, in early 1987, members of Congress from South Carolina proposed the Textile and Apparel Trade Act of 1987. The bill provided for comprehensive global quotas on textiles and apparel, based on actual 1986 import volume. The level of quotas would be constrained to grow at only 1% per year. Like the 1985 bill, the 1987 bill proposed to cover all sources of imports, including imports from Canada and Europe. The 1987 bill sought to deal with the risk of foreign retaliation by providing that suppliers would be provided compensation in the form of reduced tariff levels on textile and apparel imports, and by giving extra quotas to countries that buy more US farm goods. This bill passed the House in 1987 and the Senate in 1988. Like its 1985 predecessor, it was vetoed by President Reagan.

The next major round of textile policy will evolve in the context of the Uruguay Round and the 1991 MFA renewal. The challenge facing President Bush will be to resist industry pressures to tighten the regime and, instead, to inaugurate a framework of gradual relaxation, even extended over a period of 10 to 15 years. In fact, the April 1989 GATT review held in Geneva points the way towards gradual elimination of MFA restrictions.

By 1986 the MFA system had created a tariff equivalent of protection of 28% on textiles. This trade protection costs US consumers at least $2.8 billion annually. The benefit to US producers is about $1.5 billion per year (about the same as industry profits). The difference between consumer costs and producer benefits, about $1.3 billion annually, is accounted for by tariff revenues ($0.5 billion), quota rents to foreign producers ($0.6 billion) and efficiency loss ($0.2 billion). (Cline 1987, p 191. The consumer cost figure is measured at the wholesale level.)

Adjustment. The adjustment to new conditions in an industry normally occurs in four areas: output, finance, trade, and labor. The textile industry has responded to its protected environment in all four. The story is told in Table 2.6.

Since the third MFA in 1981, the textile industry has prospered:

production rose, industry profits blossomed, and import penetration remained tolerable. There was some international adjustment in the form of a rising import share, and some domestic adjustment in the form of a smaller labor force. Production rose during the Reagan Administration, notably after the 1981–82 recession. The constant dollar value of US textile production increased 14% from 1982 to 1987, while physical volume went from 9.4 to 13.0 billion pounds.

During the same period, the textile industry enjoyed remarkable financial health. Following the 1981–82 recession, net profits after taxes had risen 115% by 1987, and profit margins expanded almost 80% to 3.4% of sales. But if trade protection were suddenly removed, it is likely that profits would drop sharply.

As it happened, financial prosperity, buttressed by trade protection, prompted new capital expenditures by the textile industry; in turn, the ensuing labor savings and product improvements contributed to the industry's financial health. Annual investment (including replacement) during 1984–87 has averaged more than a sixth higher than in 1980–83; the cumulative total for the eight years is over $13.5 billion. Much of this investment has gone into technologically sophisticated labor-saving machinery. Even so, the industry is less competitive today, in relative wage and relative productivity terms, than it was in 1980.

Despite the MFA regime, textile trade responded to the realities of world competition. Trade flows in the 1980s were, of course, influenced by the roller coaster rise and fall of the dollar, but the deeper underlying force was the comparative disadvantage of the US industry. Imports almost doubled their share of consumption between 1980 and 1987. In contrast, exports declined as a percentage of production. The trade balance, expressed as a percentage of production, declined almost steadily, swinging 9.5 percentage points from a 2.1% surplus in 1980 to a 7.4% deficit in 1987.

The surface statistics tell a relatively good story of labor adjustment; but the underlying statistics are not so bright. To begin with the good news (seen from an adjustment perspective): textile employment declined by about 123,000 workers between 1980 and 1987, and the combination of labor attrition, structural changes, and new equipment increased the output of textiles per worker from about 13,200 pounds in 1980 to about 17,900 pounds per worker in 1987.

The underlying data do not tell such a good story. Labor productivity growth rates in textiles were faster than the national manufacturing average from 1981 until 1983, thanks to very substantial labor layoffs. Since 1983, however, labor productivity growth has slowed in textiles as continuing improvement has come to depend on new investment.

Long-term progress in reducing an industry's comparative disadvantage depends not only on the productivity of labor in that industry relative to the manufacturing average but also on the cost of labor in that industry relative to the manufacturing average. The textile industry has not managed to compensate for its below-average labor productivity growth since 1983. To do that, it would have had to reduce its growth of labor costs relative to the manufacturing average. Instead, wages per worker in the textile industry, expressed as a percent of the manufacturing average, have increased slightly, from 69% in 1981 to 72% in 1987. Consequently, the ratio of relative textile wages to relative textile productivity increased from an index of 95 in 1983 to 112 in 1987 (1980 = 100).

To summarize: the textile industry was operating at a greater comparative disadvantage in 1987 than it was in 1980. This is true despite a trade regime that ensured rising output, high profits, and substantial capital investment. Of course, a full picture of the industry's position would require information on productivity and wage changes abroad, both in textiles and in other industries. However, it seems likely that textile productivity and wages in countries such as Taiwan and Korea would reinforce the story told on the basis of US statistics.

Apparel

To a large extent the trade policy story for apparel parallels that for textiles. This account focuses on the differences. During the 1980s, as the bilateral apparel agreements between the United States and 25 of its trading partners came up for sequential renewal, they were replaced by multiyear agreements with more extensive product coverage and less flexibility. For example, in 1983 the United States renegotiated a multiyear agreement with China, implementing the spirit of trade restriction by establishing quotas on twice as many products as the old agreement. In September 1984, tighter "rules of origin" were established for apparel imported into the United States.

In July 1986 more than 50 trading nations negotiated the fourth MFA. The fourth MFA amended many terms of the third MFA, strengthened anti-fraud and circumvention provisions, and extended coverage to products of exotic fibers, such as ramie, linen, and silk blends, that were not previously included.

By 1986 restrictions on apparel trade had created a tariff equivalent of about 53%. This protection costs US consumers at least $17.6 billion annually. Of this, the benefit to producers was about $8.0 billion, more than twice the industry's profits. The difference between consumer costs

Table 2.7. US Apparel Industry, 1980–87

1980	1982	1984	1986	1987	
					production, in billion dollars[1]
40.3	46.7	50.7	51.5	53.2	current value
45.7	46.7	49.2	48.9	49.7	constant value (1982 dollars)
90	100	104	106	108	producer price index[2]
4.6	4.2	5.5	5.5	5.5	net profit as a percentage of sales for public companies[3]
608	654	na	na	na	capital expenditures, in million dollars[4]
					trade, in million dollars[5]
6,849	8,703	14,513	18,554	21,960	imports
1,202	953	807	900	1,132	exports
					trade, percentages
14.9	16.0	22.5	26.1	28.6	imports, of consumption
3.0	2.0	1.6	1.7	2.0	exports, of production
(14.0)	(16.6)	(27.0)	(33.1)	(37.3)	trade balance relative to consumption[6]
1,307	1,189	1,142	1,016	1,045	employment, in thousands[7]
					labor productivity, 1980 = 100
100	109	122	136	143	apparel index[8]
100	105	105	108	110	relative to all manufacturing[9]
63	61	60	60	60	apparel wages as a percentage of all-manufacturing wages[10]

Notes and Sources
Except as noted, data are from the American Textile Manufacturers Institute's *Textile Hi-Lights* 1988 Sep issue (abbreviated ATMI) or Cline (1987, p 27 table 2.1, which provides annual data for 1960–86 for production, investment and employment, drawing primarily from the *US Industrial Outlook* for various years).

1. Product data for SIC 23 (apparel and other mill products) taken from Cline for 1980–84; and the *1989 US Industrial Outlook*, p 41–1, for 1986–87.
2. The 1980 entry is the index for all textile products and apparel from the *Statistical Abstract of the US 1988*, table 736. Other entries are for apparel only from ATMI p 18.
3. Data are for the apparel companies followed by the Value Line Investment Survey. In 1987 they accounted for $9.2 billion, about 17%, of total industry sales.
4. Cline.
5. Values are CIF. ATMI p 24.
6. Computed as (exports minus imports) divided by production.
7. Cline for 1980–84; *1989 US Industrial Outlook*, p 41–1, for 1986–87.
8. Output per hour of all persons; 1987 estimated on the basis of constant value of production and employment data in the source, which is the Bureau of Labor Statistics' *Productivity Measures for Selected Industries and Government Services* (1988 Feb, Bulletin 2296, Table 268).
9. Calculated as the index of labor productivity in apparel divided by the index of labor productivity in all manufacturing (from the *Monthly Labor Review*, 1988 Nov, p 90).
10. ATMI p 23 for 1986–87; the 1987 Dec issue, p 23, was used for 1980–84.

and producer benefits, about $9.6 billion annually, is accounted for by tariff revenues ($4.0 billion), quota rents to foreign producers ($2.4 billion), and efficiency losses ($3.1 billion). (Cline 1987, p 191.)

Adjustment. The adjustment story for apparel is told in Table 2.7. By comparison with textiles, the broad story is less prosperity and much more adjustment. Production has risen slowly; profits have begun rising in dollar terms, though they remain flat as a percentage of sales. Meanwhile, import penetration has grown rapidly and the labor force has declined sharply. On the whole, the data suggest firms did relatively well, but the workers did not. Employment declined sharply and relative wages did not rise. It would appear the firms were able to capture all the gains in relative productivity growth.

From 1980 to 1982 US apparel production measured at constant prices was almost flat, in 1983 it rose almost 5% to $48.9 billion, and fluctuated around that level in 1984–87. Based on financial reports of publicly owned apparel companies (which account for less than 20% of industry sales), the industry neither experienced a bust nor enjoyed a boom in the 1980s. Expressed as a percentage of sales, net profits ranged from a low of 4.1% in 1981 to a plateau of 5.5% in most years since 1983. Judging from very partial data, industry capital expenditures have probably stagnated at between $600 million and $800 million per year (data after 1982 are not available).

The adjustment of the apparel industry to the realities of international competition is evident in the import penetration figures. From 1980 through 1987 imports almost doubled their share of US consumption, to 29%; and the trade deficit in apparel (as a percentage of production) increased substantially, spectacularly in 1984.

Labor adjustment has been pronounced. Employment declined by over 260,000 workers between 1980 and 1987. Largely as a result, labor productivity growth exceeded the national average for all manufacturing. During these eight years, wages in the apparel industry, expressed as a percentage of the manufacturing average, fell slightly. The combination of faster than average productivity growth and slower than average wage growth conveys a picture of an industry combating its comparative disadvantage. Indeed, the ratio of relative apparel wages to relative apparel productivity decreased from an index level of 100 in 1980 to a level of 87 in 1987.

Yet the outlook for apparel is not particularly bright. Apparel productivity growth is probably much higher in the NIEs and the emerging NIEs than in the United States. Also, absolute labor costs are much lower in the NIEs. At best, the US apparel industry faces more years of difficult labor adjustment.

Carbon Steel

Special protection for the carbon steel industry started in 1969. From 1969 to 1974, Japanese and European Community steel exports to the United States were limited to 5.75 million tons from each supplier. These voluntary restraint agreements (VRAs) were allowed to expire in December 1974, within the context of strong demand for steel products.

In 1978, responding to an overwhelming number of antidumping petitions, the Carter Administration established the trigger price mechanism (TPM). The TPM established "fair value" import reference prices for steel products, constructed on the basis of Japanese average unit

Table 2.8. US Carbon Steel Industry, 1980–87

1980	1982	1984	1986	1987	
					production, in billion dollars[1]
60.2	46.0	50.5	44.1	49.1	current value
69.3	46.0	48.3	44.2	47.5	constant value (1982 dollars)
84	62	74	70	77	production, in million tons[2]
90	100	105	101	102	producer price index[3]
					net profits after taxes[4]
681	(3,384)	(31)	(4,150)	1,017	in million dollars
1.8	(12.0)	(0.1)	(16.7)	3.8	as a percentage of sales
2,651	2,258	1,203	862	1,160	capital expenditures, in million dollars[5]
					trade, in million dollars[6]
6,612	8,869	10,102	7,887	8,030	imports
2,507	1,587	880	713	857	exports
					trade, tons[7]
15.5	16.7	26.2	20.7	20.4	imports
4.1	1.8	1.0	0.9	1.1	exports
					trade, percentages[7]
16.3	21.8	26.4	23.0	21.3	imports, of consumption
4.9	1.6	1.3	1.3	1.5	exports, of production
(13.6)	(24.1)	(34.1)	(28.1)	(25.2)	trade balance relative to consumption[7]

1980	1982	1984	1986	1987	
					trade, dollars per ton[8]
426	531	386	381	394	imports
611	882	880	792	779	exports
481	360	308	249	237	employment, in thousands[9]
					labor productivity, 1980 = 100
100	88	128	138	145	steel index[10]
100	85	110	110	112	relative to all manufacturing
163	164	147	149	147	steel wages as a percentage of all-manufacturing wages[11]

Notes and Sources
Data are from the American Iron & Steel Institute's 1987 *Annual Statistical Report* (abbreviated AISI) except as noted.

1. Industry value of shipments data for SIC 3312 and 3315–17 from the *US Industrial Outlook*, 1987, p 19, for 1980–82; 1988, p 20–2, for 1984; and 1989, p 17–1, for 1986–87.

2. Net shipments of steel mill products as reported by AISI, Table 1A.

3. *Statistical Abstract of the US 1988*, table 736, for 1980–86; Bureau of Labor Statistics, *Supplement to Producer Price Indexes: Data for 1987*.

4. AISI, table 1C.

5. Includes replacement outlays. AISI, table 1D.

6. *1988 US Industrial Outlook*, p 20–2 and 20–5.

7. Volume of steel mill products from AISI, table 1A, so all share data relate to volumes. Trade balance relative to consumption is (exports minus imports) divided by production.

8. Calculated by dividing the value by the volume data in this table.

9. *1988 US Industrial Outlook*, p 20–2 and 20–5.

10. AISI, table 7, using Bureau of Labor Statistics data.

11. Index of steel payroll costs per hour from AISI, table 5, relative to hourly gross earnings in all manufacturing from the American Textile Manufacturers Institute's *Textile Hi-Lights* (1988 Sep, p 23, and 1987 Dec, p 23).

costs of production, plus an arbitrary margin for general and administrative expenses and another margin for profits, plus the cost of transportation. Steel imported below the trigger price was presumed to be dumped and was automatically subject to an administrative investigation. In return for the TPM system, the US steel industry withdrew antidumping complaints against Japanese and European producers.

The system worked nicely from the viewpoint of the domestic industry in the 1978–79 period when the dollar weakened and reference prices for Japanese steel correspondingly rose. But as the dollar began to strengthen, even before its big surge in the 1980s, the industry suddenly was hoisted with a macroeconomic petard. A stronger dollar meant that Japanese steel prices, expressed in dollar terms, began to decline. As a result, the TPM no longer satisfied the industry's drive for trade protection. In March 1980 the United States Steel Corporation filed a number of new antidumping and countervailing duty petitions; in response, the Carter Administration suspended the TPM. After protracted litigation, the Department of Commerce and the US International Trade Commission (ITC) ruled in favor of domestic steel producers in their petitions against 41 suppliers of 9 steel products from 11 countries.

The stage was now set for a new trade regime, one more to the liking of the US steel industry. In October 1982 the United States negotiated a VRA with the European Community, limiting EC exports of carbon steel to the United States. The VRA offered a diplomatic escape hatch from the prospect of imposing countervailing and antidumping duties that would have differentiated between members of the Common Market. Moreover, the VRA left the quota rents emanating from a controlled US market in the pockets of European steel producers.

The VRA, which had a stated lifetime of 1982 November 1 to 1985 December 31, required the EC to limit exports of 11 carbon steel products to 5.5% of the projected US market, with subceilings for individual products. To reinforce the effectiveness of the VRA, the United States agreed to initiate talks with third-country suppliers intended to limit the growth of their share of the US market. Since 1969, Japan had informally limited its steel shipments to the United States to between 5 and 6.5% of the US market. Thus, possible additional Japanese exports in the wake of the VRA with the European Community did not present a problem. However, other suppliers did pose a threat and VRAs were negotiated with many of them.

Before the various VRAs expired, the ITC determined, in June 1984, that five segments of the carbon steel industry, accounting for 74% of domestic shipments, were injured by imports and were eligible for escape clause relief under Section 201 of the Trade Act of 1974. The ITC recommended President Reagan impose a mixture of tariffs and quotas on 70% of US steel imports for five years.

The President declined to follow the statutory path. Instead, in September 1984, President Reagan directed the US Trade Representative (USTR) to seek voluntary export restraints for a period of five years (1984 October 1 through 1989 September 30). The measures were expected to reduce the share of carbon steel imports (excluding semifinished steel) in the US market to approximately 18.5%. In addition, imports of semifinished steel would be limited to 1.7 million tons per year. As a quid pro quo for protection, the ITC was called upon to monitor steel industry modernization: the goal was to encourage firms to reinvest their steel profits in refurbishing steel plants, and it was largely achieved. As a further measure of assistance, bankrupt firms in the steel industry were relieved of several hundred million dollars of unfunded pension liabilities through a federal pension guarantee program.

To assure that the total level of finished and unfinished steel imports would be limited to about 20.2% of the total US steel market, the USTR eventually established VRAs with 19 countries plus the European Community (then 10 countries) covering some 30 to 40 products. The agreements took the form of market share arrangements and tonnage quotas. They were tailored to each country, with considerable variation in the number of individual product categories subject to limitations. No formal VRA was negotiated with Canada, but an informal understanding was reached to the effect that Canadian producers would not "take advantage" of the situation. The effect of such informal limits was not addressed in the US-Canada Free Trade Agreement.

Overall, the coverage reached 80% of imports to the US market. Parallel formal and informal trade restraints were implemented by the European Community, Japan, and other countries to protect their home markets. By the late 1980s, world steel trade was truly managed.

Just before the November 1988 election, Bush promised to renew the VRA system in 1989. As justification, Bush said, "A comprehensive VRA program has proven to be more effective in offsetting unfair trade practices than trying to counter these practices on a case-by-case basis." In July 1989, after heated debate between steel users and steel producers, the Bush Administration extended the VRA system for a further 2½ years, pledged to seek an end to foreign subsidy and dumping practices, and liberalized imports of steel products in short supply.

The initial result of the VRA system was the creation of tariff equivalent protection on carbon steel imports of approximately 30%, costing US consumers about $6.8 billion annually in 1985. The benefit to US producers was about $3.8 billion annually. The difference between consumer costs and producer benefits, about $3.0 billion annually, is accounted for by tariff revenues ($0.6 billion), quota rents to foreign producers ($2.0 billion), and efficiency losses ($0.4 billion). (Hufbauer 1986, p 179.)

With the significant drop in the value of the dollar between 1985 and 1988, and the general tightening of world steel markets, the tariff equivalent protection probably dropped to 5 to 10% and the cost to US consumers probably declined to $1 to $3 billion annually. The dramatic change in tariff equivalent protection over the space of a few years illustrates a key feature of all quantitative restraint systems: the extent of protection varies enormously, depending on exchange rates and world demand conditions.

Adjustment. Since the Reagan Administration established voluntary export restraints on carbon steel imports in 1982, the US steel industry has adjusted in significant ways. Production levels have remained approximately constant, import shares have risen, and trade deficits have gotten larger. Financial losses were the rule between 1982 and 1986; however the industry returned to profitability in 1987, and earned about $2 billion in 1988. The story is told in Table 2.8.

The volume of steel produced in the United States, expressed on a net shipments basis, rose to 88.5 million tons in 1981, over 5% above the 1980 level. But then the 1981–82 recession and the shift to substitute materials devastated the industry. Steel production fell 30% in 1982 and has since fluctuated between 65 and 75 million tons. Yet, because antique capacity was retired on a large scale, capacity utilization levels significantly improved, going from 56% in 1983 to 80% in 1987. In 1988, many mills were running at 90% of capacity.

Between 1982 and 1986 the industry lost nearly $12 billion (after taxes). Not surprisingly, capital expenditures have remained stuck at under $2 billion per year since 1982. However, with the much lower dollar in 1987 and 1988, and a worldwide surge in steel demand, the industry enjoyed considerable prosperity and capital expenditures rebounded some in the late 1980s, though they have remained below the level of the early 1980s. In any event, the industry has embraced highly efficient continuous casting (60% of production in 1987, versus 32% in 1982); it has forged extensive management and technology links with Japanese firms; and flexible minimills now account for some 20% of US carbon steel production.

Despite the protective regime, considerable adjustment has also occurred in trade. The import share of the domestic market was allowed to rise from 16% in 1980 to about 26% in 1984, before being suppressed by the VRAs to about 21% in 1987.

The area in which adjustment is clearest is labor. Employment in 1987 is less than half its 1980 level, representing some 245,000 jobs. About 45% of the decline came in 1982. At the same time, labor productivity has surged, from an index of 100 in 1980 to 109 in 1981 then, after a drop in 1982, to 114 in 1983 and 145 in 1987. Relative to the manufacturing average, productivity in making steel improved by about 10% from 1980 to 1984, and has kept pace since.

The steel industry further improved its competitive position by squeezing labor costs. Wages per worker as a percentage of the manufacturing average fell from around 164% in the early 1980s to 152% in 1983 and were around 147% in 1984–87. As a result, the ratio of relative wages to relative productivity declined from an index level of 100 in 1980 to

90 in 1983 and was in the low 80s in 1984–87. The steel industry is thus operating at a far less severe comparative disadvantage today than it was in 1980. In fact, at exchange rates prevailing in 1988, the United States is now one of the world's lower cost steel producers. (*Wall Street Journal,* 1988 November 18, p A8; *Forbes,* 1988 November 28, p 41.)

In terms of regaining comparative advantage, the steel industry was an outstanding performer during the 1980s; but, as the trade policy review indicated, successful adjustment has not slaked the industry's appetite for continuing protection. Moreover, looking past the boom conditions of 1987–89, it seems likely the industry will again feel competitive pressure from Korea, Canada, and even Britain in the 1990s, especially if the VRA system is finally scrapped in 1992.

Automobiles

In June 1980 the Ford Motor Company and the United Auto Workers filed a joint petition with the US International Trade Commission for relief from imports under the "escape clause," Section 201 of the Trade Act of 1974. In November 1980 the Commission determined by a 3–2 vote that imports of passenger cars were not a substantial cause of serious injury or threat of serious injury to the domestic automobile industry. The Commissioners cited the domestic recession and downsizing as more important causes for the difficulties of the US automobile industry. Thus, the Reagan Administration inherited a situation where normal escape clause relief was denied to a powerful and restive industry.

By early 1981, legislation to restrict Japanese car imports was advancing in Congress. The President stated it would be difficult to veto such a bill. In the context of tax legislation and other Administration priorities, President Reagan simply did not want to spend valuable political chips fighting the auto industry.

Consequently, in May 1981 the Japanese Ministry of International Trade and Industry (MITI) concluded a VRA on Japanese auto exports to the United States, cutting projected exports by about 8% from their 1980 levels. The VRA restrained exports to 1.68 million units for the 1981 Japanese fiscal year (1981 April 1 through 1982 March 31). Later, the Japanese announced exports to the United States of four-wheel-drive station wagons and "Jeep"-type vehicles would be limited to 82,500 units for the United States and 70,000 for Puerto Rico. Thus, total Japanese exports of autos and "off-road" vehicles were set at 1,832,500 units. These "voluntary" restraint levels were continued into fiscal 1982 and 1983.

In November 1983 the Japanese government announced it would increase its voluntary export limit from 1.68 to 1.85 million automobiles during fiscal 1984. In addition, it announced that the four-wheel-drive vehicle and "Jeep"-type vehicle limit would be increased to 90,848 units and exports to Puerto Rico would rise to 77,083 units. The total number of Japanese automobiles exported to the United States during fiscal 1984 was to increase to 2,017,931, 10.1% above the previous three years.

In January 1985, MITI disclosed Japan's voluntary ceiling on automobile exports would not be renewed when it expired on 1985 March 31. However, in a distinction without a difference, MITI officials announced, in March 1985, that Japan would hold auto exports to the United States at 2.3 million units in 1985. Since 1985, the VRA on Japanese automobiles has remained at 2.3 million units. In fact, with the sharp decline in the dollar and the locating of Japanese plants in the United States, the VRA limits have not been reached since 1986. There

Table 2.9. US Automobile Industry, 1980–87

1980	1982	1984	1986	1987	
					production, in billion dollars[1]
66.3	70.7	118.1	125.9	127.1	current value
76.4	70.7	112.4	112.9	109.2	constant value (1982 dollars)
6,375	5,073	7,773	7,829	7,099	production, in thousand units[2]
87	100	105	111	114	producer price index[3]
9.0	7.8	11.2	14.0	11.9	capital expenditures, in million dollars[4]
					trade, in million dollars[5]
27.9	34.1	56.6	78.1	85.2	imports
17.5	17.4	22.5	24.9	26.3	exports
					trade, in thousand units
2,398	2,223	2,439	3,245	3,197	imports[6]
559	353	591	648	599	exports[7]
					trade, percentages
26.7	27.9	23.5	28.3	31.1	imports, of consumption[6]
8.8	7.0	7.6	8.3	8.4	exports, of production[7]
(28.9)	(36.9)	(23.8)	(33.2)	(36.6)	trade balance relative to consumption[8]
789	699	862	872	865	employment, in thousands[9]

1980	*1982*	*1984*	*1986*	*1987*	
					labor productivity, 1980 = 100
100	107	128	136	155	auto index[10]
100	103	110	108	119	relative to all manufacturing
135	137	139	138	137	auto wages as a percentage of all-manufacturing wages[11]

Notes and Sources
Except as noted, data are from the Motor Vehicle Manufacturers Association (abbreviated MVMA), principally *MVMA Motor Vehicles Facts and Figures (MVFF)*, a yearbook, and *Economic Indicators (EI)*, a quarterly.

1. Industry value of shipment data for SIC 3711, which includes motor vehicles and car bodies, taken from the *US Industrial Outlook* 1988, p 38–2, for 1980–84; 1989, p 34–2, for 1986–87.

2. Includes passenger cars only. *MVFF 1988*, p 6.

3. *Statistical Abstract of the US 1988*, table 736, for 1980–86; Bureau of Labor Statistics, *Supplement to Producer Price Indexes: Data for 1987*.

4. Includes replacement outlays. *EI 1988 Third Quarter*, table 15.

5. Includes all motor vehicles and parts. *EI 1988 Third Quarter*, table 18.

6. Passenger cars only; share data are for number of units. *EI 1988 Third Quarter*, table 4.

7. Passenger cars only, including exports to Canada; share data are for number of units. *MVFF 1985*, p 11, for 1980–82; *MVFF 1988*, p 11, for 1984–87.

8. Trade balance relative to consumption is for passenger car volumes, computed as (exports minus imports) divided by production.

9. Includes all motor vehicle and equipment manufacturing employment. *EI 1988 Third Quarter*, table 13.

10. Output per hour for all employes in motor vehicles and equipment; 1987 estimated on the basis of constant value of production and employment data in the source, which is the Bureau of Labor Statistics' *Productivity Measures for Selected Industries and Government Services* (1988 Feb, Bulletin 2296, table 244).

11. Average hourly earnings for production workers in motor vehicles and equipment from *MVFF 1988*, p 70, relative to hourly gross earnings in all manufacturing from the American Textile Manufacturers Institute's *Textile Hi-Lights* (1988 Sep, p 23, and 1987 Dec, p 23).

can be little doubt, however, that the history of VRA restraints still casts a shadow over the industry, and foreign producers are well aware the VRAs could spring to life if US producers are financially threatened by a future recession, or if aggressive imports find their way to the US market from Korea or elsewhere.

When it had its greatest impact, in 1984 and 1985, the VRA imposed a tariff equivalent rate on automobiles of about 11% and cost US consumers about $5.8 billion per year. The benefit to US producers was $2.6 billion annually, about one fourth of industry profits. The difference between consumer costs and producers benefits, about $3.2 billion annually at that time, was accounted for by tariff revenue ($0.8 billion), quota rents to foreign producers ($2.2 billion), and efficiency losses ($0.2 billion). (Hufbauer 1986, p 257.)

Adjustment. The automobile adjustment story is told in Table 2.9. Of the industries surveyed, the automobile industry adjusted the best. Production rose on a cyclical basis; the industry managed to turn losses into profits; and labor productivity increased relative to other manufacturing.

The US market for passenger cars exemplifies a mature, cyclical industry. Production of passenger cars in the United States dropped from 6.4 million in 1980 to 5.1 million in 1982, rose to 8.2 million in 1985, and declined to 7.1 million in 1987. However, the value of the motor vehicle industry's production (measured in constant dollars) showed more growth and less fluctuation, as the industry diversified into other product areas and made more expensive autos.

During this period, the automobile industry enjoyed a dramatic improvement in its financial health. Chrysler, Ford, and General Motors moved from a combined $4 billion loss in 1981 to $11 billion in profits in 1988, though this includes their non-automotive activities as well. Financial prosperity, coupled with the entry of Japanese firms, prompted rising capital expenditure, from $9 billion in 1980 to $12 billion in 1987.

Automobile trade has largely adjusted to the realities of world competition. Import penetration in the sensitive passenger car market rose modestly, mostly after 1985, when the level was 25.7% (of units sold). Many of the imports are "sponsored" by US automobile manufacturers. For example, in 1987 the then-four US auto producers sponsored imports of 927,000 passenger cars from Canada and 348,000 from other countries, nearly 40% of total imports that year.

Employment in the automobile industry has been cyclical, with a modest upward drift. In 1978 employment reached its peak of 1,005,000. There was a cyclical decline in the 1981–82 recession, but between 1980 and 1987 about 76,000 workers were added to the payroll over the entire eight years. Meanwhile, the industry's labor productivity has grown faster than the national manufacturing average, though much of this has been in spurts. Wages in the industry remained at about 135 to 140% of the national manufacturing average throughout the period. Overall, the ratio of relative wages to relative productivity fell from an index level of 100 in 1980 to 85 in 1987, although for most of the period it was in the mid 90s.

To summarize: based on these statistics, the industry improved its competitive position significantly between 1980 and 1987. The automobile industry is a case where special protection, coupled with a more realistic exchange rate, paid off in terms of rising output, higher returns to capital, substantial capital investment, dramatic improvement in relative labor productivity, and a return to freer markets.

While the auto industry did not renounce VRAs for all time, after 1985 the industry no longer publicly pressured the Administration to continue the system. Even so, the Japanese have continued to announce limits on automotive exports.

The behavior of the US auto industry in allowing a semi-retirement of the VRA system stands in marked contrast to the steel industry. There are two main reasons for the differing attitudes of these giant industries toward special protection. First, the steel industry is far less confident of its long-term competitive position than the automobile industry. Second, the automobile industry is characterized by multinational firms whose operations may be hindered by trade restraints; by contrast, the steel industry is dominated by strictly national firms which have no organizational stake in open markets.

CONCLUSION: UNWINDING SECTOR ARRANGEMENTS

A decade ago, French leaders advocated "organized free trade" as a recipe for addressing the difficult problems of troubled industries. At the time, the very phrase was derided as an oxymoron. But "organized free trade" has increasingly become the policy style for dealing with troubled industries, not only of Europe and Japan but also of the United States. The product coverage is impressive: starting with selected agricultural products in the 1950s; reaching textiles and apparel in the early 1960s; extending to carbon steel in the late 1960s; encompassing automobiles and semiconductors in the 1980s. (This section draws on Hufbauer 1989.)

Two notable sector agreements paved the way for broad free trade arrangements: the European Coal and Steel Community of the 1950s and the US-Canada Automobile Agreement of the 1960s. But these two agreements were created in a spirit of eliminating trade barriers. By contrast, most sector agreements embody large elements of special protection and have quite different purposes and results. They are noteworthy for four characteristics:

1. The industry in question is plagued by low demand growth and excess capacity
2. Comparative advantage is usually shifting to countries that have acquired a good command of production technology; in the 1960s this was Japan, in the 1980s the newcomers are Korea, Taiwan, and Brazil
3. Sector arrangements serve to mute competition by allocating market

shares, both between exporting and importing countries, and among exporters

4. In the process, the management of sector arrangements is captured by producers; established firms at home and abroad benefit from the arrangement; while new exporting firms and new exporting countries find their growth curtailed

Few would deny a beleaguered sector temporary protection to adjust —to revive if it can, to downsize if it must. But how long should "temporary" protection last? Is the point of a sector arrangement to provide the domestic industry a chance to compete or to ensure the domestic industry always retains a certain market share?

On these fundamental questions, the evidence strongly points to restrictive tendencies: sector arrangements tend to persist for long periods, to encompass an ever wider range of products with ever higher restrictions, to freeze market shares, and to bilateralize trade flows. In this survey, the only notable exception is automobiles; and it can reasonably be feared that automobile VRAs will spring to life in the next recession.

Sector arrangements cannot be wished away. Whatever happens in the Uruguay Round of multilateral trade negotiations, the United States and other industrial nations will continue to rely on special protection to assist troubled industries; consequently, deals will continue to be struck along sectoral lines between major trading countries. In 1989 the carbon steel "voluntary" restraint agreement was renegotiated even as the industry enjoyed a worldwide boom; in 1991 the Multi-Fiber Arrangement may yield to less comprehensive, but still formidable, restraints. Beyond these arrangements, new deals could be struck in automobiles, especially as the European Community consolidates its member-country quotas with a view toward completion of the internal market by 1992.

In short, sector arrangements will not disappear during the 1990s. Those that protect older industries, where comparative advantage has migrated to developing nations, will be kept to slow the inevitable transition. Those that bolster emerging high-tech industries, such as semiconductors, will be kept to provide an auxiliary off-budget stimulant. Accepting these facts of political and economic life, the major trading nations should announce, in the Uruguay Round and other forums, two principles that will gradually enable a more liberal trading system to emerge in the early years of the next century.

First, quantitative restraints should be converted, at the margin, to tariffs or auctioned quotas. This eliminates some of the quota rent that serves as the political glue for the perpetuation of trade restrictions.

Moreover, in mature low-tech industries, such as textiles, apparel, and carbon steel, the revenues should be devoted to making adjustment a more humane process. Within the United States these industries have significantly cut their work forces. But the expulsion of large numbers of workers, with no golden parachutes, has left an enduring residue of resentment against the international economy.

Second, all countries that participate in sector agreements should commit to liberalizing their imports. In mature sectors, this obligation should extend to Mexico and China, as well as to the United States and Europe. As a reasonable target, imports should be allowed to increase share of a domestic market by 1 percentage point annually until complete liberalization is achieved. Such targets should be accepted not only by countries that use "voluntary" restraint agreements and outright quotas to limit imports (such as the United States, Brazil, and India) but also by nations that rely on vertical integration and closed distribution systems to limit imports (such as Japan).

The application of these two principles to the carbon steel VRAs, over the period 1989 to 1992, and the Multi-Fiber Arrangement when it is reviewed in 1991, could set the stage for the gradual unwinding of special protection as the almost exclusive means of addressing the problems of troubled industries.

BIBLIOGRAPHY

Baldwin, Robert E. 1984. *The Political Economy of US Import Policy*. University of Wisconsin.

Branson, William H., and James P. Love. 1988. "US Manufacturing and the Real Exchange Rate." In Richard C. Marston, editor, *Misalignment of Exchange Rates*. University of Chicago Press for the National Bureau of Economic Research.

Bergsten, C. Fred. 1975. "Economic Adjustment to Liberal Trade: A New Approach." In C. Fred Bergsten, editor, *Toward a New World Trade Policy: The Maidenhead Papers*. Lexington MA: Lexington Books.

——. 1988. *America in the World Economy: A Strategy for the 1990s*. Washington DC: Institute for International Economics.

—— et al. 1987 Sep. "Auction Quotas and United States Trade Policy." Washington DC: Institute for International Economics. Processed.

Bryant, Ralph C. 1988. *Empirical Macroeconomics for Interdependent Economies*. Washington DC: The Brookings Institution.

Cline, William R. 1987. *The Future of World Trade in Textiles and Apparel*. Washington DC: Institute for International Economics.

Dornbusch, Rudiger, James Poterba, and Lawrence Summers. 1988. *The Case for Manufacturing in America's Future*. Rochester NY: Eastman Kodak Company. (There are two versions of this; citations are to the full essay rather than to the pamphlet.)

GATT = General Agreement on Tariffs and Trade. 1987. *International Trade 1986–87*. Geneva.

Hale, David. 1988. "The Post Chicago Era in American Economic Policy." *Wallenberg Papers in International Finance*, v 2 # 3. Washington DC: International Law Institute.

Hatsopoulos, George N., Paul R. Krugman, Lawrence H. Summers. 1988. "US Competitiveness: Beyond the Trade Deficit." *Science* 241: 299–307 (Jul 15).

Hufbauer, Gary C. 1989. "U.S. Trade Policy: Guideposts for the Bush Administration." Unpublished study for the Twentieth Century Fund, New York.

——, Diane T. Berliner, and Kimberly A. Elliott. 1986. *Trade Protection in the United States: 31 Case Studies*. Washington DC: Institute for International Economics.

—— and Howard F. Rosen. 1986. *Trade Policy for Troubled Industries*. Washington DC: Institute for International Economics.

IMF = International Monetary Fund. 1986 and 1988. *Direction of Trade Statistics, Yearbook*.

Metzger, Stanley D. 1971 Jul. "Injury and Market Disruption From Imports." In *President's Commission on International Trade and Investment Policy, United States International Economic Policy in an Interdependent World: Compendium of Papers*, v 1. Washington DC.

Morici, Peter. 1988. *Reassessing American Competitiveness*. Washington: National Planning Association.

US Chamber of Commerce. 1988. *The Omnibus Trade and Competitiveness Act of 1988*, ch 5. Washington DC.

USITC = US International Trade Commission. 1982 Mar. *The Effectiveness of Escape Clause Relief in Promoting Adjustment to Import Competition*. USITC Publication 1229.

USTR = United States Trade Representative. 1987. *United States Trade Performance in 1987*. Washington DC.

World Bank. 1987. *World Development Report*. Washington DC.

3

NEW ZEALAND
Radical Market-Oriented Reform

Alan E. Bollard

Refrigerated New Zealand meat first reached England in 1882, ushering in both a long period of prosperity for the export-oriented meat and dairy products industries and a growing dichotomy between the economy's traded and non-traded sectors including manufactures. The traded sectors are dominated by agricultural production—sheep meats, beef, cross-bred wools, horticultural products, and dairy products (especially casein, milk powder, butter and hard cheese). A high proportion of output is exported, mainly in unprocessed or semi-processed forms, marketed by producer boards. The major traditional market was the UK. Production and processing have always been technologically advanced, with long runs and high levels of efficiency. In contrast, manufacturing output is generally untraded and has traditionally been highly protected and supported, developing behind a shield of import controls, price controls, and regulation. Manufacturing is the focus of this paper.

More specifically, this chapter reviews declining and troubled industries in New Zealand and analyzes the patterns of adjustment. The first section outlines the postwar experience of the New Zealand economy

I wish to thank those who helped with this chapter, particularly Hugh Patrick, other participants in the Declining Industries project, and colleagues at the New Zealand Institute of Economic Research. My thanks also to Larry Meissner for very comprehensive editing. Financial support for the case studies came from the NZ Department of Trade and Industry.

leading up to the end of the 1970s, by which time a number of structural problems had become evident in a range of New Zealand industries. Characteristics of these structurally troubled industries are reviewed in the second section, while the third looks at the government's policy on adjustment, documenting the reversal of interventionist policies, the deregulation of the 1980s, and the intellectual basis for this switch.

The new policy stance rejects direct intervention in favor of market mechanisms for adjustment, and in the fourth section these market signals are analyzed. Most of these policies apply broadly to all production sectors rather than being industry-specific; the response to them is detailed in the fifth section. The sixth looks in more detail at several structurally troubled industries. Trade policy implications of restructuring are examined in the seventh section, while the last section speculates about future policy direction. Table 3.1 provides an overview of the economy.

BACKGROUND

New Zealand has a small local market (1988 population: 3.35 million) and is geographically very isolated from major world markets (Auckland-Sydney is over 2100 kms, or about the distance from Moscow to Amsterdam). Resulting high external transport costs—due to long distances, small loadings, and inefficient transport industries—have provided a high degree of natural protection against imports. In addition, internal transport costs are high, due to sparse population, the country's length (over 1600 kms), and its terrain. Consequently, there has always been a significant degree of regional and national self-sufficiency.

The population, British and Polynesian in origin, is relatively conformist and egalitarian. In 1893 New Zealand became the first country to enfranchise women. Unionization was compulsory between 1936 and 1961; in 1988, about 62% of the labor force was unionized. Government traditionally has had a major role, especially in the provision of social services (the public sector accounts for 25% of GDP). Free compulsory primary education for all was one of the first acts of the central government after moving to Wellington in 1876. New Zealand was on the cutting edge of the welfare state from the 1890s, when Prime Minister Richard J. Seddon introduced old-age pensions, as well as such labor reforms as shorter working hours, compulsory arbitration of disputes, and accident compensation.

Significant British settlement began in the 1840s, and many who came for the gold rushes of the early 1860s stayed as pastoralists or farmers,

Table 3.1. Distribution of GDP by Kind of Economic Activity

1970	1974	1980	1984	1987	
14.3	13.9	12.9	9.5	9.1	primary sector
26.6	21.3	22.6	22.9	21.0	manufacturing
6.1	6.2	4.9	5.4	5.0	construction
2.9	1.9	3.3	3.1	3.5	utilities
6.4	6.1	5.7	5.6	4.8	transport & storage
2.1	1.9	2.6	3.0	2.9	communications
35.1	36.1	32.7	36.4	35.6	services, ex public
9.4	10.0	12.6	12.2	11.8	government services

Columns do not add to 100 because of omitted items (bank service charges, imputed rent, import taxes, indirect taxation, etc)

Principal Components of Primary Sector (percentage of GDP)

12.6	12.4	10.9	7.0	5.9	agriculture
1.0	0.9	1.0	1.3	1.9	forestry

Principal Manufacturing Industries (percentage of GDP)

8.5	5.0	5.4	6.9	6.0	food, beverages, tobacco
2.9	2.5	2.7	2.1	1.9	textiles, apparel, leather
3.0	2.4	2.7	2.5	2.4	paper, printing, publishing
2.4	1.9	2.5	2.0	2.4	chemicals, petroleum,
5.9	5.7	5.7	5.6	4.8	plastics machinery and metal products

Principal Services (percentage of GDP)

22.2	22.6	17.6	20.6	17.7	trade, restaurants, hotels
9.8	9.2	10.3	11.3	13.5	finance, insurance, etc

Data are for fiscal years ending March of year shown.
Sources: Original absolute data are from various issues of the Monthly Abstract of Statistics. For 1980-87, they are in the OECD Economic Survey, New Zealand, 1989 Jul (p 130). The table here reflects some revisions and a correction of a typo in the OECD table.

particularly in the South Island, which had the larger share of the population until the 20th century but now has only a quarter. Trade disruptions in the 1930s encouraged formation of light manufacturing companies, and worldwide growth in the 1950s saw a wave of new industries and firms. Many companies are still managed by their founders. There is a high proportion of small private firms (90% of manufacturing firms employ fewer than 20 workers). Use of home-grown technologies is fairly widespread. The work force is relatively mobile and flexible, possessing good general skills but with limited specialization.

New Zealand has a long history of import controls, although not particularly for industrial assistance reasons. Until the 1920s, the average tariff rate was around 20%, covering a wide range of industrial goods. The Ottawa Agreement of 1932 established the principle of British Preference in exchange for free access to the UK for New Zealand exports. Following a foreign exchange crisis in 1938, widespread import controls were introduced to discourage imports and revive the balance of payments. In the postwar years, many categories of imports remained subject to licensing despite several attempts to liberalize.

By the 1960s import licensing had been whittled down to only those goods competing with New Zealand production; by this time it was seen mainly as a cushioning device allowing local industry a prolonged breathing space to develop. Underlaying import controls has been a system of tariffs, generally of increasing magnitude the more finished the import, but with widely dispersed rates. The original rationale of the tariff system was to raise revenue. By 1976 the World Bank calculated New Zealand manufacturing had an overall average rate of protection in the 60 to 70% range (Wooding 1987). Wooding concludes: "The resulting protection system provided a highly uneven pattern of effective subsidy to economic activities, an average level of protection high by comparison with OECD countries and a high degree of dependence on import licensing which made estimating the levels of protection very difficult. It was also a fiscally expensive system, dependent on costly subsidies but giving away import licenses and yielding little tariff revenue" (p 90).

In addition to the above controls, industry grew up with a wide range of regulation affecting entry, operations, use of inputs, and quality of output. The most important of these has been industry licensing, particularly in the service sector, restricting entry to transport industries, financial services, distributive trades, and other parts of the economy. There has been considerable occupational licensing, a raft of labor laws, tight zoning, and land use regulation. A study of economic regulation in New Zealand (New Zealand Planning Council 1985) found 400 Acts of Parliament and 1000 associated regulations with potentially significant economic effects. To generalize, the effects of this regulatory structure have been to create a protected trading environment with a high degree of stability, cushioned from international market forces and with a low level of internal competition in many industries, where existing firms could enjoy economic rents with resulting inefficiencies, and would-be new firms encounter barriers to entry.

Several studies of scale in New Zealand manufacturing (Bollard and Daly 1984, Pickford 1984) conclude that in many industries, plants operate considerably below minimum efficient scale. A consequence has been low levels of productivity and high production costs. In addition the low level of competition has encouraged poorly directed investment, cost-plus pricing, a low degree of consumer sovereignty, a tendency to produce non-differentiated products of variable quality, unadventurous and inefficient management, and a low level of company exit, takeover, or restructuring. It should be noted that these generalizations apply more particularly to import-substituting industries than to primary-processing ones.

From the 1960s pressures began to mount to liberalize sectors and engender a more outward-looking economy (Wooding 1987, Rayner and Lattimore 1987). These pressures originated from international sources such as the OECD, and from domestic sources such as frustrated would-be entrants. In the 1960s a number of manufacturing export incentive programs were put into place, and in 1966 a very limited free trade area (NAFTA) was signed with Australia to promote trans-Tasman exports. (The Tasman Sea separates the two countries, named for the Dutch navigator who named New Zealand.)

A major impetus for reform was the entry of Britain into the EEC in 1973 and the subsequent tightening of the British market to New Zealand produce. New Zealand had relied heavily on imports from and exports to the UK. In 1950 Britain took two-thirds of New Zealand's exports and in the 1960s still over a half. The pattern changed very rapidly after 1973, so that by 1988 Britain took only 8.5% of exports. Barriers to importing New Zealand goods to the EEC, and the effects of the EEC Common Agricultural Policy on third markets remain major problems for New Zealand traders.

A fall in the agricultural terms of trade from the early 1960s has meant a more difficult trading regime for agricultural produce more generally. The New Zealand dollar had been fixed against sterling until 1971. By 1973 it had broken the sterling and dollar links and was fixed to a trade-weighted basket of currencies. The New Zealand dollar has been freely floating since 1985 and in 1988 averaged approximately US$0.65. New Zealand's standard of living began to drop in relative (though not absolute) terms. In 1953 New Zealand had the third highest per capita GNP in the world; in 1965 it was the eighth; by 1978 it had dropped to the twenty-second (though in purchasing power parity terms this may overstate the drop).

These changes were magnified by the OPEC oil crises of 1974 and 1979 and the ensuing world inflation and recession. New Zealand suffered from a severely falling terms of trade index, which dropped from 119 in 1957 to 78 in 1975, with consequent balance of payments problems. The government response was to encourage and invest in what were called "Think Big" energy projects in which a series of 16 very large-scale energy-based plants were set up or expanded to produce fuels, manufacture petrochemicals, and carry out energy-intensive industrial processing, most under direct or joint government ownership. The scale of these projects was much bigger than any previous industrial development in New Zealand, with a total capital cost of around $NZ7.5 billion dollars. These projects were responsible for a large increase in New Zealand's overseas debt.

Since the 1960s, New Zealand's trading patterns have changed to include many more non-traditional countries. In 1960 nearly 75% of imports came from the UK, Australia, and the US. By 1985 this was only 40%. Similarly, export markets have become more diversified. Despite the more outward looking policy stance adopted during this period, domestic regulation and import control remained in place. The effect was to prolong inappropriate and ultimately unsustainable price signals to industry, dissuading firms from responding to external competitive pressures.

CHARACTERISTICS OF DECLINING INDUSTRIES

Industrial decline in New Zealand is likely to reflect poorly invested and overly protected capital responding to the wrong signals rather than old and immobile capital. This is somewhat different from the experience of Northern Hemisphere countries. This section reviews the industrial development that has taken place in New Zealand's regulated and protected environment, and examines the nature of industries that may be thought of as declining or troubled.

In line with other studies in this book I use the term "declining" to mean an industry where the long-term prospects are so bad as to imply exit or major restructuring. A declining industry exhibits an inadequate performance in terms of some indicator such as output, employment, efficiency, productivity, competitiveness, or profitability in the face of changing structural pressures, particularly competition from overseas firms that may be lower cost, technologically more sophisticated, more efficient, or more subsidized.

In contrast, a "troubled" industry is one in difficulty for some length of time (typically longer than the business cycle), but where there is a prospect of regaining competitiveness. The distinction is one made by economists with hindsight, but policy makers and business people cannot necessarily distinguish between the two states at the time.

About 10% of New Zealand's labor force works in agriculture and 21% in manufacturing. In contrast to most OECD countries, New Zealand did not suffer the decline in manufacturing employment felt by many countries up to 1980. Manufacturing output continued to expand in postwar years both in absolute terms and (until 1986) in its share of GDP.

The most important sectors of New Zealand manufacturing have always been those that processed local crops and animal products: food, wool, textiles, fish, wood, and paper products. Since the war these sectors have accounted for around 60% of New Zealand's manufacturing value added. They are predominantly export ones, and in organization and performance are to be distinguished from the other industrial sectors, which have traditionally been for the domestic market.

As these figures may indicate, New Zealand's experiences of deindustrialization have occurred rather later than has been felt by many industrial countries. Manufacturing employment reached a peak of 328,000 in early 1986 and has been declining ever since (264,000 at September 1988). While certain industries have felt competitive pressures for some time, either they remained protected until the radical liberalization of the 1980s or their demise was balanced against the expansion of other industries.

Table 3.2 compares manufacturing sectors at the three-digit level in fiscal 1974/75 and 1985/86. In terms of employment, the beverages industry, textiles, clothing and footwear, industrial chemicals, rubber products, non-metallic mineral products, electrical machinery, and other manufacturing all declined over this period. The paper and paper products industry, chemicals, petroleum refining, basic metal industry, and transport equipment also declined in terms of profitability.

There are several ways in which industrial decline becomes evident. Firstly, there may be increased competition in export markets from local producers there who operate with the advantage of import barriers or industrial assistance. This does not necessarily imply the exporting industry has performed badly: the opposite may in fact be the case. A second problem for exporters is competition from overseas producers in third markets. This may be because these producers are lower cost, more technologically sophisticated, more efficient, or again because they are more subsidized. Thirdly, industry decline may result from competition from overseas producers in local markets, either due to sudden easing of access or to a gradual loss of competitiveness.

It should be noted that because an industry is in decline does not per se indicate it is inefficient, but rather that it has lost competitiveness,

Table 3.2. Real Output and Employment in Manufacturing

NZSIC		1974/5				1985/6				Percentage Change 1974/5–1985/6			
		a	b	c	d	a	b	c	d	a	b	c	d
311–12	food	1121	62.6	7402	350	1649	69.5	8196	559	47	11	11	60
313–14	beverages	144	5.7	661	98	163	4.3	936	109	13	−25	42	12
321	textiles	370	18.7	1475	150	664	13.9	1415	107	79	−25	−4	−28
322–24	clothing & footwear	1000	29.8	1297	129	1300	24.9	1399	143	30	−16	8	11
331–32	wood & its products	1318	22.9	1941	232	2271	23.6	2071	233	72	3	7	0
341	paper & its products	106	9.7	1521	259	162	13.0	1831	165	53	35	20	−36
342	printing & publishing	559	18.1	1003	125	1052	17.7	1478	208	88	−2	47	66
351	industrial chemicals	117	5.3	1018	138	198	4.9	1145	120	69	−7	12	−13
352	other chemicals	187	7.2	792	123	366	7.2	1127	111	96	0	42	−9
353	petroleum refining	12	0.3	132	25	17	1.1	204	−71	42	237	54	−381
354	petrol & coal prod.	27	0.4	51	8	34	0.4	71	5	26	−2	39	−30
355	rubber products	108	4.9	372	31	130	3.8	329	47	20	−22	−11	54
356	plastic products	192	5.0	469	44	400	7.9	830	98	108	58	77	123

												Code	Category
497	10.8	1065	134	839	9.3	1154	149	69	−14	8	11	361–69	non-metallic minerals
126	6.2	1124	157	157	7.1	1181	118	25	16	5	−25	371–72	basic metal
1124	23.0	1963	231	2167	26.1	2545	264	93	14	30	14	381	fabricated metals
810	14.2	1221	148	1984	18.7	1565	167	145	31	28	13	382	machinery
307	18.0	1445	170	614	15.0	1404	94	100	−17	−3	−44	383	electrical machinery
347	19.5	1712	157	738	22.2	2030	110	113	14	19	−30	384	transport equipment
42	0.8	57	8	87	1.2	114	16	107	48	97	104	385	professional equip.
255	4.2	253	30	620	3.9	280	652	143	−8	11	2077	390	other

Fiscal years, ending in March

a. Units: 1974/5 data are establishments; 1985/6 data are activity units (a unit carrying out a single activity at one location). The latter may have wider coverage of 1- and 2-person units.

b. Employes, in thousands: full-time and working proprietors, plus half of part-time workers.

c. Total revenue, in millions of 1985/6 $NZ

d. Operating surplus, in millions of 1985/6 $NZ

Sources: 1974/5 Census of Manufacturing; 1985/6 Enterprise Survey

which is not the same thing. A loss in competitiveness may stem from factors internal to the firm (innovation, productivity, X-efficiency), macroeconomic variables (inflation, exchange rates, cost of capital), or exogenous factors (eg, protection by other countries).

This suggests two rather different types of declining New Zealand industry: first, the traditional export industry that has lost access or competitiveness. This is a problem for New Zealand agriculture, less so for manufacturing. Second is the traditional import-substituting industry that is exposed to foreign competition. Most declining manufacturing industries in New Zealand fall into this latter category.

In order to investigate the process of decline and resulting adjustment in more depth, five industries in various states of decline are examined. They have been picked to demonstrate a variety of troubled-industry problems, and as such do not represent a statistically valid cross-section of New Zealand manufacturing. The industries are:

1. Flour milling, which was heavily regulated in New Zealand to protect New Zealand wheat production and has since been deregulated with a consequent impact on the location and closure of mills.
2. Automobile assembly, an industry nursed through a period of some restructuring by public policy but now more likely to be left to market forces and rationalization from abroad, resulting in a much smaller sector.
3. Oil refining, a product of New Zealand's "Think Big" era with highly capital intensive public sector investment; complete deregulation of this sector has not proved possible, and the government has sought a compromise.
4. Wool textiles, a traditional export industry with declining competitiveness, which has undergone two contracting periods of restructuring; the carpet subsector is taken up in some detail.
5. Meat processing for export, which used to be licensed and has since seen considerable rationalization, but where overcapacity and inefficiencies continue.

ADJUSTMENT POLICY

In the early 1980s government industry policy changed abruptly from one based on protection, regulation, and industrial assistance to radical deregulation of entry and operating conditions in industry and trade liberalization. Although the groundwork had been laid for some years, the catalyst was the election of a Labour Government in 1984. (The National Party had been in power since 1975; it is a more traditional coalition of farmers, industrialists, and broader interests.)

The Labour Party is the traditional party of the Left in New Zealand, and on the surface their policies of deregulation were hard to understand, cutting across their traditional support base. However, the radical changes that eventuated can be seen as the general reaction of the electorate to many years of economic protection and distortion. The fact it was the Labour Party that brought such change is perhaps surprising —many of the policies of protection were originated by the first Labour Government of 1935. On the other hand, the Labour Party is the party of reform in New Zealand, and came into office with considerable popular support, not beholden to the traditional supporters of the status quo—manufacturing groups, farmers, exporters.

The radical policy switch, though not completely anticipated by the business sector, represented a planned and relatively consistent policy, developed through a close intellectual relationship between the Minister of Finance and the Treasury Department, backed by a few other central ministers and key departments. Many senior civil servants, painfully aware of the expensive failures of earlier industrial interventions, have independently formed the view that their most positive contribution would be to minimize their involvement in private investment, and they have supported the reform.

In its first few years of office, the Labour Government presented a tight united front, with deregulation as a top priority. It was felt that the most urgent policy moves had the potential to improve efficiency and, by moving the economy outwards towards the production possibility curve, simultaneously to improve income distribution. In 1987 the Labour Party was returned to Government with a sizable majority, indicating reasonably broad popular support for their policies. However, since 1987 this united front has weakened, with a reformist center-right wing arguing against a center-left wing more concerned with equity objectives.

The intellectual origins of the reformist thinking are a mixture of Chicago/Austria/supply-sider/libertarian philosophies. In a 1988 conference on the influence of US economic thinking on New Zealand policy, most commentators pointed to the influence of Chicago/Rochester teachings, though in contrast to similar influences on the Southern Cone reforms of the 1970s, the focus in New Zealand has been primarily microeconomic. In addition there have been important liberalizing influences from the OECD, IMF, and the UK Government experience.

The government saw its role as freeing up product and factor markets to allow unimpeded price signals to guide investment decisions against the backdrop of a neutral policy environment for business. It was not intended that this imply no government role; however the role of the state in the production sector was expected to be much reduced, and traditional public interventions in economic allocation could no longer be anticipated as automatic.

Traditional arguments for intervention based on market failure or public goods claims were viewed with extreme distrust; they were usually seen as excuses for inadequate private performance or attempts at regulatory or subsidy capture. Instead Treasury thinking tended towards a property rights/transactions cost approach based on Coase, Demsetz, and Williamson. This viewed the government's role as defining and enforcing property rights in order to minimize the traditional allocation problems of appropriability, indivisibility, measurability, and asymmetric information. Where these problems still remain, the government looks to the existence of a range of other governance mechanisms: vertical integration, bilateral contracts, or third-party mechanisms, all of which offer non-market ways of allocating resources that may be efficient depending on the circumstances.

Only after reviewing all of these mechanisms would the government consider traditional market failure arguments. The argument as applied to government's role in R&D policy is outlined in Bollard and Harper (1987). Relatively little attention was paid to the macroeconomic issues accompanying this microeconomic reform, and in retrospect this has presented a major problem, as discussed below.

Considering New Zealand's limited domestic markets, relatively few domestic producers, and large traded sector, international economic forces will always be seen as playing a large part in its liberalization process, although these forces were intended to be microeconomic not macroeconomic in nature. Contestability theories gained considerable force in policy circles, although strictly speaking policy makers have misapplied the true theoretical results of the model. The theory was popularly thought to imply that in any industry with relatively few incumbents, the removal of entry barriers would bring an improvement in welfare. (However, the [laboratory] evidence on whether this relationship holds in non-polar form is unclear.) As a generalization it was felt removal of barriers to overseas investment and to foreign imports would increase contestability in the New Zealand economy, and this was a good thing. (Greer [1989a] argues that the theory is inappropriate for New Zealand, and has been badly misapplied.)

The distributive consequences of these policies were not clearly worked through. It was generally assumed that consumers had suffered from previous policies, and therefore that a redistribution from producer to consumer would be a good thing; that deregulation should first address the more purely economic markets (product markets, factor markets excluding labor, and the markets for corporate control) and leave the more difficult social markets (labor, education, health, social welfare) to later; that the policies should first concentrate on efficiency objectives rather than equity objectives, the latter to be addressed by a Royal Commission on Social Policy; and that while the two were not inseparable it might be possible to increase both equity and efficiency by the same policy deregulation, at least in the early stage (Hawke 1987, Pinfield 1987).

Critics of the policy (eg, Easton 1988) have argued it was naive to present this as an efficiency-enhancing policy without recognizing the value judgments about distribution policy that were being implicitly made. Policies were designed to signal the need for adjustment to industry and have them bear the costs of the adjustment. In fact the burden has fallen on others as well, as is shown below.

These policies were first signaled in the 1984 Post Election Treasury Briefing to the incoming Government. A succinct survey of the principles of New Zealand's industrial reform was outlined by the OECD in its 1986–87 New Zealand Economic Survey.

Their new policy approach is based on the following principles:

(a) optimal use of resources is best promoted by allowing economic agents to pursue opportunities within a competitive environment subject to government intervention to secure rights, assign costs (in the case of market failure), and reduce transactions costs;

(b) such a competitive environment can be best promoted by contestability of product and factor markets through removal of unnecessary impediments to market entry and by ensuring that government interventions are as neutral as possible, given the objective of the intervention;

(c) intervention can improve equity by increasing access to markets and by targeting assistance to disadvantaged individuals and groups.

(d) However, all intervention will need to be assessed to ensure that the gains outweigh the costs, based on a realistic appraisal of their effects, taking into account the difficulty of achieving appropriate incentives and accountability, particularly in the public sector.

The program of deregulation to date is outlined in Table 3.3. It was always intended to be neutral in its impact, with a rejection of policies that pick winners or cushion losers and (with minor exceptions) a rejection of targeting in general. As can be seen from the dates, it involves radical and comprehensive change and was intended to be accomplished in a short period of time. What has been the net cost of this program? It has not been possible to measure. The government has been inclined to view the cost in purely fiscal terms.

Table 3.4 indicates the fiscal outcome. Government spending on in-

Table 3.3. List of Economic Liberalization Measures

1983–	Establishment of Closer Economic Relations with Australia
1983–88	Deregulation of the transport sector
1984	Removal of foreign exchange controls
1984–	Deregulation of entry licensing in industry
1984–	Removal of other operating barriers in industry
1984–	Removal of concessions for favored investment (eg, R&D)
1984–	Removal of concessions for favored sectors (agriculture, export sectors)
1984–86	Removal of financial controls (interest rate ceiling, reserve ratio requirements, priorities for various sectors)
1984–88	Removal of price control
1984–88	Removal of import licensing
1985	Liberalization of foreign direct investment
1985	Floating of the exchange rate
1985–	Partial deregulation of occupational licensing
1985–92	Significant decrease in import tariffs
1986	Partial deregulation of labor market
1986	Deregulation of financial services sector
1986–	Partial deregulation of energy sector
1986–	Corporatization of state trading activities
1986–	Removal of monopoly rights on state trading
1986–88	Reform of corporate, personal and indirect taxation
1986–89	Review of competition regulation (Commerce Act, Bank Act, Securities Act, Companies Act)
1987	Revision of town and country planning
1987	Abolition of many quasi-government organizations and quangos (quasi non-governmental organizations)
1987–	Reorganization of core government departments
1987–	Revision of role of producer marketing boards
1987	Program of sale of state assets
1988–	Review of education and health provision
1989	Deregulation of wharves and shipping
1989–	Reform of local government
1990–	Resource management law enforced

dustrial development assistance programs and regional development fell in real terms in the six years through fiscal 1988/89 (ended 1989 March), as did the revenue earned from the sale of import licenses. It should be noted that these decreases took place despite pressures for further spending to cushion the transitional influence of adjustment.

The complication is that this microeconomic reform program has had to take place against a difficult macroeconomic setting. At the start of

Table 3.4. Government Industrial Assistance: Revenue and Expenditure
($NZ million at 1988 prices)

1982/3	1983/4	1984/5	1985/6	1986/7	1987/8	1988/9	
891.5	1021.5	1149.3	994.5	994.5	894.6	507.5	revenue[1]
							expenditure for:
22.9	24.8	24.3	23.3	16.7	11.3	4.6	industrial development
50.6	49.6	42.2	30.2	14.4	13.0	4.2	regional development

Fiscal years, ending in March
1. Includes tariffs, import licenses, etc
Source: Estimates of Expenditure, The Budget, Government of New Zealand

the period, in 1984, New Zealand had an inflation rate of 9% (to rise to 18% within two years exacerbated by the introduction of a value-added tax in 1986), an unimpressive and fluctuating record of growth, a budget deficit of 7% of GDP, a current account deficit of 6%, and an external debt of 50% of GDP (partly due to the financing requirements of the previous Government's "Think Big" investment program). This constrained the government's policy options severely. At the same time, the program of deregulation further limited government options by removing the use of selective taxes, subsidy, or direct intervention as policy instruments, generally blunting the effectiveness of fiscal policy, and ensuring that industry policy would not be used as a stabilization tool. Despite the reductions in industry spending, and a general austerity program, other items of public expenditure have remained very high or increased.

Monetary policy has been targeted at reducing inflation. Tight money has meant a high interest rate exacerbated by the need to finance the budget deficit. This has attracted capital inflows which in turn have exerted pressure to increase the exchange rate against trading partners, maintaining it at high levels throughout the period of reform.

ADJUSTMENT SIGNALS

Investment signals in the 1960s and '70s relied heavily on direct government regulation, exhortation, guidance, and quantity controls resulting in rationing (of credit and import licenses) and ceilings on prices (eg, price control). In contrast, the signals of the 1980s deregulation are provided by market prices. They have acted mainly through the factor, financial, and foreign exchange markets, rather than through final goods markets. Most of them are economy-wide signals rather than being specific to industries or firms.

Although the business sector was not initially prepared for the severity of the reforms, the government rapidly established credibility as to its determination to carry out the program. Buckle (1988) considers this was crucial in its success in disinflation (the rate of increase in the consumer price index fell from 17% in 1985 to 4% by 1989); the same credibility has been important in industry policy.

Most radical has been price signaling through deregulation of capital markets. This has been signaled by the end of credit rationing, the removal of favored categories for investment, competition for borrowers, and a range of new financial instruments especially for corporate customers. Despite these reforms, real interest rates have remained high, partly in response to the considerable public sector demand for funds for restructuring and to finance the deficit. The overall signal is clear: funds are available but expensive and therefore need to be well targeted. In addition, interest rates are likely to be more volatile.

Other factor markets, including energy, materials, machinery, and transport, have been substantially liberalized. Removal of entry and pricing restrictions in the energy and freight transport industries have generally resulted in cheaper and more differentiated service and price schedules (Culy and Gale 1987, Guria 1987).

Weak signals have been transmitted through limited labor market deregulation. It has become easier to negotiate plant and region-specific agreements on wages and working conditions rather than relying on national awards, and the latter are now more closely tied to the rate of inflation, to productivity gains, and to profitability. Skill shortages are now more easily reflected in wage agreements. However these changes are all gradual and taking some years to have effect. It is in labor market deregulation that the Labour Party has felt most constrained by its traditional ties. It has been criticized for failing to ensure faster wage adjustment and greater wage dispersion, and hence for disadvantaging labor-intensive industry.

Selective assistance for investment has been reduced with the removal of accelerated tax write-offs available on industrial machinery and a number of agricultural investments, and the withdrawal of incentives for R&D. (The argument has been that even with "good" investments such as R&D, the private investor reacting to unfettered market returns is generally in the best position to make an optimal investment decision.) In addition, most regional development incentives have been removed. The price signals on investment have been strongest in the traded sector:

removal of import licenses, reduction of tariffs, and the high exchange rate have made imports of materials and technology more easily available and cheaper.

Product markets have been less important as a signaling device. The removal of all items from price control has affected profitability in several key industries. A few industries that relied on output subsidies (agriculture and certain energy industries) have lost them. While some product price pressure has been felt in a number of industries, these have been the result either of cyclical downturn rather than deregulation, or of overseas prices (which affect a high proportion of New Zealand output).

The reduction in import barriers involved firstly the almost complete removal of the system of import licensing, exposing a rather high set of tariffs, which are subsequently being reduced to nominal rates of around 10–20% by the end of March 1992. There have been significant reductions in protection for most industries, as shown by data on effective rates of assistance in Table 3.5.

Because this liberalization took effect during a recession, it has not led to the flood of imports feared by manufacturers. Certainly however, the threat and availability of imports has had an effect on pricing, and most noticeably on the structure of the distribution industry. There has been a general increase in competitive pressures in most markets, reinforced by sterner provisions relating to restrictive trade practices in the

Table 3.5. Effective Rate of Assistance by Industry (percents)

1981/2	1985/6	1987/8	NZSIC	*Industry*
11	9	6	31	food, beverage, and tobacco manufacturing
37	60	29	32	textile, wearing apparel, leather
24	14	11	33	wood and wood products, including furniture
18	14	12	34	paper & its products; printing & publishing
17	17	14	35	chemicals and petroleum; coal; rubber and plastic products
12	12	11	36	non-metallic mineral products (not in SIC 35)
7	7	6	37	basic metal industries
31	28	25	38	fabricated metal products; machinery and equipment
31	31	24	39	other manufacturing industries

The effective rate of assistance is measured as (gross subsidy equivalent minus gross tax equivalent plus subsidy on value-adding factors) as a proportion of unassisted value added.

Protection levels have continued to fall since this table was compiled.

Source: Syntec Economic Services 1988

1986 Commerce Act; again, the stronger price signals have been in traded goods where the high value of the New Zealand dollar has meant strong competition and declining competitiveness on export markets.

Markets for corporate control have been the subject of intense interest. The 1986 Commerce Act enacted new legislation on mergers, acquisitions, and buyouts. It is based on US and Australian legislation. As of early 1989 only 8 of about 900 merger applications had been turned down. It is a mark of the attitude of New Zealand industry that it has nevertheless been accused of being too restrictive. Securities and company legislation has been struggling to keep up with the high level of corporate takeover, and is now under review. These are all examples of regulations felt to be necessary to allow more general deregulation to take place.

The ability to merge, acquire, and buy out has been reinforced by new financial instruments and access to debt and equity financing through the newly deregulated financial sector. Credit is no longer rationed, and there are many new financial institutions. Stock markets were very active until the October 1987 crash. Both in their rises and falls, the stock markets have sent up very strong signals relating to the profitability of corporate reorganization. Incidentally, it was also the crash in stock market prices that transmitted disinvestment signals strongly through to the non-traded sector, particularly construction and services.

How clear and consistent have these signals been? A serious confusion has arisen in the tension between the microeconomic price signals of liberalization and macroeconomic signals (exchange rates, rates of interest), which relates to the underlying state of the economy at the time of liberalization. A high exchange rate and interest rate have the potentially dangerous effects of reducing competitiveness and discouraging investment with a consequent reduction in capacity just at the time when restructuring requires reinvestment. It is further possible that the disinvestment taking place will not be matched by symmetrical reinvestment in the future, that is, the hysteresis effect (see Savage 1986). The industry case studies below investigate this possibility further. Of course the micro and macro tensions are not completely independent of one another.

An additional tension arises in the differential impact of signals on the traded and non-traded sectors via the high and potentially volatile exchange rate. Importers and exporters have felt much stronger pressures to adjust than have domestic traders. Despite a considerable deficit on the balance of payments, the value of the New Zealand dollar has remained high. This signals importers to expand and exporters to invest elsewhere. The consequent danger is a "de-industrialization" of the traded (manufacturing and agricultural) sectors as happened in the UK in the early 1980s.

In a study of competitiveness by sector, Williams (1988) found that after some fluctuation over the period 1978–84, the period 1985–88 has been marked by a significant decline in the international competitiveness of domestic manufacturers. This has mainly been due to the strong exchange rate, to some extent offset by cheaper imports of intermediate goods.

The increasing exchange rate has been associated with a rapid increase in relative costs (measured as the ratio of non-tradeable to tradeable input prices). That is, costs for non-tradeables have risen much faster than for tradeables. The implication is that manufacturers have recovered some proportion of the value added lost on export markets by raising prices on the domestic market. The overall conclusion was that export competitiveness had fallen considerably, largely due to exchange rate movements.

The sequencing of reforms has affected the efficiency of the signals. New Zealand faces the now-standard criticisms of IMF-type liberalizations: capital and exchange markets were opened up without trade liberalization and while the government was still running a budget deficit, thus inviting capital inflows and exchange rate appreciation (Spencer and Carey 1988, Rayner and Lattimore 1987, Krueger 1985, Buckle 1987, Savage 1986).

In addition, labor market flexibility has received little attention, leading to an inflexible adjustment response in labor-intensive traded industries. This argument is well known, but the sequencing of reform in New Zealand was guided by political reality rather than economic theory and in retrospect it is hard to see that there was much alternative at the time. The Labour Government came to power during a financial crisis in 1984, and rather than following the recommended deregulation sequence of factor markets first, then domestic capital markets, followed by international capital markets, they seized the opportunity to liberalize capital markets completely.

The Government has also been criticized for taking an over-simplified comparative static view of two economic states, one pre- and one post-deregulation. The assumption was that the act of deregulation achieved the second desired state, without addressing the real dynamic issues of adjustment paths, lags, sunk costs, and the process of rationalization in a realistic way.

Hunn, Mayes, and Vandersyp (1987) in a study of the financial effects of macroeconomic deregulation, report the same general problems in

New Zealand as occurred with Latin American and British liberalization, with the real sector being unable to adjust quickly enough to price signals, resulting in excessive reactions in the financial sector, which can adjust more speedily; this in turn causes a more costly real sector adjustment than might otherwise have been experienced.

A major influence on the strength of market signals has been the state of the business cycle and the strength of demand. Reform was commenced during a relatively strong stage of the business cycle, though the agricultural and allied sector was weak (1984); it continued during a substantial downturn (1987–88). Not surprisingly, adjustment has generally been easier for industries experiencing strong demand (finance sector, air transport); however price signals have been more distinct for industries facing weaker demand (freight transport, meat processing).

THE ADJUSTMENT RESPONSE

The response of industries to adjustment policies is viewed in this paper in a traditional structure-conduct-performance framework. This approach views government intervention as potentially falling in any of three areas: market structure (via entry regulation, restrictions on labor or land use, safety and health, and quality requirements); conduct (price controls); or performance (profit, rate of return restrictions on monopolies). Any sort of intervention is likely to have an impact in turn on the conduct of firms, in particular their production, pricing, and competitive strategies, which will then affect their performance (output, profitability, efficiency).

The usual criticisms of this approach are that the process of regulatory change is oversimplified, that lines of causation should not be one-way, that the explanation is only a partially equilibrium one, and that it ignores the possibilities for integration or other internal responses.

An important recent addition to the regulatory literature has been the emergence of contestability theory. This argues that what is important is not so much the level of competition in a market, but the level of contestability: for example, markets with only one incumbent may still be effectively regulated by the threat of other potential entrants without overt government intervention. Contestability theory has been particularly useful in dealing with regulation in New Zealand industry, which is characterized by markets of a limited size with declining cost curves, monopolistic or oligopolistic structures, and multi-product firms.

The early response of New Zealand industry to deregulation and liberalization has been documented in a number of studies. Of most general interest are two Department of Trade and Industry surveys which, though limited by their small sample size (30 firms) provide a useful taxonomy for varying types of response (see Galt 1986). The most noteworthy responses of management to structural changes were to reduce staff numbers, drop product lines, make new investments, increase importing (as opposed to manufacturing), develop new products, and rationalize the corporate structure. The results from the initial survey are shown in Table 3.6.

A follow-up of the same firms two years later brought a broadly similar response with some noteworthy exceptions. The economy was now entering a recessionary phase, there had been some additional reforms, and a high exchange rate had become a dominant feature of corporate concern. More attention was being paid to financial management as a consequence of high interest rates, exchange rate risk manage-

Table 3.6. Responses to Adjustment Pressure

"Which of the following responses has your industry made to adjust, and of those, which do you consider important?"

Yes, and Important	Yes[1]	No	No Reply	Response
4	11	2	1	drop products
3	8	4	2	switch to importing
0	4	8	2	switch to exporting
3	7	6	1	new products
1	8	3	3	better marketing
3	8	6	0	new investment
2	7	6	1	change technology
0	5	4	5	more R&D or quality control
0	5	6	3	relocate operations within New Zealand
2	2	12	0	investment abroad
1	7	4	3	corporate rationalization
0	3	6	5	change management
1	2	7	5	change labor or wage practices
5	12	0	2	reduce staff
	8	5	1	less lobbying than before
	8	1	5	complete closure of plants or companies
	10	1	3	rationalization was likely without a plan

The 14 industries covered are shipbuilding, general rubber, ceramics, glass, electric motors, motor vehicle parts, motor vehicle assembly, carpets, plastic (partial), footwear, textiles (not including apparel), and writing instruments.
   1. "Yes" includes those considering the response important (first column).
Source: Galt 1986, p 49

ment had been increased, there had been a tendency towards labor-substituting investment, towards further processing of products, and towards producing higher quality products that compete less directly with imports. Companies noted a greater tendency to try to absorb cost increases rather than automatically pass them on, and increased use of outside expertise. In addition, one-third of the original companies had been involved in ownership changes in part or all of their operations, indicating quite significant corporate restructuring.

There have been a number of other studies of the industrial reform process concentrating on particular aspects of change. These are briefly summarized below.

Campbell et al (1989) and Orr (1989) have attempted to trace the effects of deregulation on industrial productivity. They found that at a macro level it does not appear possible to trace an effect as unequivocally attributed to the reforms. At a micro level, however, a survey of firms found most reported they had been significantly affected by government policy changes: they paid much more attention to quality and productivity strategies.

Bollard and Easton (1985) examined the effects of deregulation on pricing and adjustment in six industries. They found there was generally pressure to contain consumer prices following deregulation (though in occasional cases pressures to contain cross subsidization in fact led to price rises on certain lines). As a general rule there was a move toward product differentiation and the growth of "boutique" rather than "supermarket" production. Producers were able to cut prices because of increased managerial efficiency (meat processing, brewing, baking), increased factor efficiency (meat processing), increased efficiency due to changing technologies (freight transport), declining profitability (brewing), lower returns to other factors (brewing, meat processing, freight transport), reduced cross-subsidization (the foreign exchange industry), and declining costs through not having to meet the administrative expenses of intervention (baking, cement).

There have been a number of studies on the response of infrastructure service industries to deregulation. While a long-term assessment is not yet possible, studies of the financial services sector (Harper 1986, Harper and Karacaoglu 1987), land transport (Bollard and Easton 1985, Guria 1987), energy industries (Culy and Gale 1987, Clough 1989), and the distributive trades (Ayto and Bollard 1987) all noted a number of common outcomes: reasonably speedy initial adjustment, some increased investment, downward pressure on prices, a wider range of differentiated services, a reduction in cross-subsidization, increased competition, and in some cases exit.

A further question concerns the path of adjustment. In general, industries have been given little warning of regulatory and fiscal change, minimal consultation opportunities and little time to comply, with few transitional measures to cushion them during the interim. (The reason for this speed is the Government's feeling it needed to act before forces opposed to change had organized themselves.) The main exception to this would be trade liberalization, where the reduction of frontier protection has been the result of a longer program of consultation, with certain industries continuing to receive transitional protection.

The speed of response has varied considerably, depending on the type of signal, the asset structure of the industry involved, and the state of demand in the industry. Adjustment has been faster in expanding industries, and slower in depressed ones. The main reason is that it is easier to invest than disinvest. This also accounts for differences in the rate of responses between different industries. Those with a highly specific asset base are likely to have considerable sunk costs and consequently be more reluctant to retire capital in response to some price signal (Hazledine and Savage 1988). The existence of sunk and other fixed costs is important because it determines how long a firm will continue its current operations and when it will be forced to restructure.

The contrasting response to entry deregulation of the meat processing industry with its highly specific technology and depressed demand on the one hand, and the financial services industry with its non-specific assets and buoyant demand on the other, illustrates the point. The former has been gradually adjusting through exit or contraction of firms for some years; the latter trebled its number of participants in a year.

Faced with a deregulation like removal of entry licensing, a number of industries have seen new entrants joining rapidly, producing an initial oversupply, only later to face a shakeout of firms and products. This oscillating reaction, which represents learning about new opportunities, was observed following the deregulation of the financial services, freight transport, and brewing industries (Bollard and Easton 1985).

Following regulatory change, many firms have found themselves subject to increased competition, and ultimately become non-viable. They face a choice of restructuring or exit. Most have attempted the former. A survey quoted in Campbell-Hunt et al (1989) showed 44% of New Zealand firms had undergone a significant change in ownership over the previous few years. There have also been many firms closing down. No comprehensive data on this is available, but in the late 1980s bankruptcies were at record levels, with the engineering, textiles, tourist, financial, and agricultural-related sectors particularly badly hit.

Unemployment had risen to a record post-1930s level of 7.1% of the labor force in early 1990. Some of this comes from closures, but the indications are that the majority is from company contractions. A study by Savage (1988) of the electrical and electronics assembly industries found that following trade liberalization the initial reaction by employers was to avoid firing workers, and to use internal labor market forms of flexibility (reducing basic hours, bonuses, allowances, basic wages, and the retirement age, plus making temporary layoffs, in order of importance), especially for more highly skilled workers. (The unemployment rate is as measured from the Household Labour Force Survey and is broadly comparable internationally. The level may not appear high by Western standards, but New Zealand has traditionally maintained high levels of employment.)

It is too early to gauge the impact of trade liberalization on import penetration. To date foreign imports do not appear to have grown rapidly in competition to declining industries. In part this is because the 1986–88 recession depressed consumption and imports.

After a few years of regulatory change, firms recognized the need for harder decisions, and laid off workers permanently. The lead was given by the newly corporatized state-owned enterprises. New Zealand Railways for example has reduced its staff from 23,000 to 9,000 in six years without significantly reducing services. Redundancy payments have in many cases been reasonably large, and all of the redundancies in the earlier years of reform were voluntary ones.

There does not seem to be a clear pattern as to where these excess workers have gone: some have found jobs within the industry, some have moved outside, some have set up their own small firms (new firm formation and growth of self-employment are currently high), and others have followed the New Zealand tradition of cyclical emigration to Australia. The latter has been an important safety valve, particularly for construction-sector trades-people and semi-skilled workers.

The state provides a comprehensive safety net of reasonably liberal unemployment benefits and retraining assistance. There have been claims by pressure groups that these, minimum wage legislation, and compulsory unionism are a disincentive to work effort. The Labour Government does not take these claims seriously.

There is little data on the costs of adjustment and how they have been borne. Clearly both transitional and longer term structural costs have been substantial. There have been regional disparities in the burden of deregulation, with rural regions, small towns, and the south being most badly hit (Ministry of Works and Development 1986). Consumers, as a class, have probably benefited most from the changes. Employees and owners of capital have both suffered, especially in the traded sectors, and most concern has been expressed for farmers, a number of whom have been bankrupted and evicted (40% of agricultural land is leased from the Crown). In some industries the laid-off work force has included a disproportionate number of Maoris, who already suffer from high unemployment rates. Snively (1989) argues that disparities go deeper than this, with the whole focus of New Zealand fiscal policy slanted in favor of higher income groups.

In the first few years of reform, the Government did not concern itself much with resulting equity questions, promising a Royal Commission on Social Policy to consider them. This Commission reported in 1988 in highly critical terms, claiming the need for a "broader and more sensitive framework for both choosing and implementing economic and social goals." This has provoked a political split in Government between supporters of continued reform and those more concerned with its costs to specific groups. Of course it could be argued that the long-term costs of not reforming would also have been substantial.

CASE STUDIES OF ADJUSTMENT IN TROUBLED INDUSTRIES

Flour Milling

Many small flour mills grew up in New Zealand during the late 19th and early 20th centuries serving local communities. Government policy was to encourage them in order to ensure self-sufficiency in basic foods, despite the fact wheat does not grow as well in New Zealand as in some countries and, in particular, hard wheats yielding good quality flour are difficult to grow. (This section draws heavily on a report by Miller 1989. Here and in subsequent sections, $ means $NZ and tonnes are metric.)

Most flour mills were sited in the South Island, which is the traditional area of wheat production (90% of some 92,000 hectares of land and 380,000 tonnes of wheat in 1986). However, 75% of consumers reside in the North Island, and transport costs are high. Table 3.7 provides an overview of the industry.

The baking industry, also originally located in the South, began to rationalize much faster without being hindered by the regulation and licensing that characterized the milling industry.

Wheat and milling were highly regulated. Since the 1930s, the Wheat Board, after discussion with millers and farmers, would set up a quota system determining quantities of wheat to be grown and where it was to be milled. All New Zealand wheat growers had to offer their wheat for sale to the Wheat Board, which was in turn obligated to purchase all wheat of milling quality. Further, the Board purchased all flour produced

Table 3.7. Flour Milling Industry, 1978–88

1978/79	1983/84	1988	
23	26	30	plants[1]
927	864	644	employment[2]
40	33	21	employment per plant
146	246	159*	output (million $NZ at 1988 prices)
158	284	247*	output per employee (thousand $NZ)

Data are year end (fiscal years end in March)
* Output data are for 1987.
1. Number of establishments ('78/79) but activity units ('83/84 and '88); the latter has wider coverage of 1- and 2-person units. For this reason, the apparent increase in the number of plants between 1983/84 and 1988 is misleading.
2. Full-time employes, working proprietors, and half of part-time workers.
Sources: NZ Census of Manufacturing 1978/79 and 1983/84; NZ Business Patterns 1988 (Department of Statistics). Covers NZSIC 31161.

by the mills, under flour quotas assigned by the Wheat Board, then resold it to bakeries and to retailers for direct sale. In addition, the Board controlled the total importation of wheat and flour. It also had responsibility for storage and transportation of wheat and flour; these services were carried out by farmers, transport operators, and others, working as agents on contract to the Wheat Board.

The national pricing formula used by the Wheat Board in purchasing from farmers was based on a three-year moving average of Australian wheat prices. The price at which flour was purchased back from each mill covered the cost of wheat (set equal for each mill), the actual cost of milling incurred in each mill, and a return of 15% on the mill's assets. To complete this chain of price control, the Board resold the flour to bakers at controlled prices, and the retail price of bread was fixed by the government.

Clearly, for 50 years there was no inducement for efficiency. Old mills with inefficient machinery or poor management could sell at high prices to recoup their inefficiencies: their output was guaranteed and their returns assured. Despite considerable over-capacity, there was no incentive to rationalize. In addition, the quality of wheat produced often failed to meet bakers' requirements: quality incentives for growers were inadequate. Further, differing transport costs in different locations were not reflected in prices paid, subsidizing distant growers.

The dangers of this regulation had been apparent for some time. A 1982 report by two academics (Borrell and Zwart) concluded policy constraints were insulating the market from underlying economic forces, including economies of scale in milling and transport, and the possibilities of inter-regional competition, resulting in a fragmented and dispersed market structure. This was supported by a government report (Durbin and Hall 1982) which calculated that transportation and milling costs could only be reduced with rationalization.

Also, for some time pressure to deregulate the system had been mounting, even within the industry. North Island milling plants, besides being closer to markets, have been, in general, larger scale, more modern, and thereby more likely to be profitable than South Island mills. Thus, North Island millers were early proponents of deregulation, using threats to import more Australian wheat as part of their advocacy. Bakers were unhappy with the quality and price of their flours and so sought ways to get better quality, cheaper wheat in the North Island, as well as increased import of quality flour from Australia.

In 1984 the Government announced full deregulation of the milling industry would take place in 1987. Amendment to the Wheat Board Act completely removed controls over flour milling after a transitional period, abolished the flour quota system, liberalized global import licenses, ended control of flour and bread prices, and promised to review the very existence of the Wheat Board. In announcing the plan, the reason given by the Minister of Agriculture was that the system could not survive, given New Zealand's requirements to liberalize trade with Australia under the Closer Economic Relations Agreement. The tariff on wheat imports has dropped to zero for Australian wheat and 24% for Canadian and LDC imports. Deregulation of transport has also meant lower transport costs, and it is now cheaper to move bulk wheat than flour. Table 3.8 shows the milling industry's pre- and post-deregulation structure.

Table 3.8. Flour Milling Industry Structure: Pre- and Post-Deregulation (capacity in thousand tonnes)

1986		1988		
Mills	Capacity	Mills	Capacity	
4	101	5	177	Goodman Group[1]
4	132			Watties
4	97	3	82	Ireland/Defiance
—	—	2	61	Allied
6	76	6	na	independents

1. Includes Watties in 1988
The independents' plant is generally older, smaller and less economic.
Source: Miller 1989

Some wheat farmers, primarily in South Island, opposed deregulation, expecting to be offered lower prices, with millers preferring to import Australian wheat. They met under a Federated Farmers banner to negotiate contracts with the Wheat Board and expressed concern about dumping and damage to the industry. They appear to have been justified in their fears, as significant regional effects from the change are under way. South Island farmers now receive far less for their product and in the long term look likely to move out of wheat. In the three years 1985–88, shipments of flour from South Island farmers to North Island mills decreased from 40,000 to 16,000 tonnes. In the same period, imports of Australian wheat have risen from 65,000 to 133,000 tonnes; imports of flour from 570 to 2400 tonnes. Meanwhile, North Island wheat plantings have expanded considerably, particularly close to the Auckland market, which houses almost one-third of the country's population.

The Government did seek to mitigate somewhat the initial impact. In the first year following deregulation, a one-time grant was made to wheat growers of $27.50 per tonne for wheat produced, to compensate for lost income, assist farmers to adjust, and cushion the ending of dumping duty actions against Australian wheat (Crump 1988). The impact has been worsened by a low price for grain (since risen somewhat) and a high average level of farm debt, with a consequent farm crisis.

The baking industry, also originally located in the South, has faced less regulation than the milling industry. Bakers had themselves begun to rationalize and amalgamate their industry before deregulation was announced. In the five years leading up to deregulation, three baking companies, sensing strategic change, began to buy into milling, so that by 1987 they owned 12 of the 18 mills then operating (82% of capacity). The other 6 mills were small independents (some operated by farmers cooperatives) and not affiliated with bakers.

The arrival of deregulation brought further considerable amalgamation. The two largest companies, the Goodman Group and Watties, in 1987 announced plans to merge. This caused considerable concern in a prolonged hearing before the New Zealand Commerce Commission due to the dominance of the two companies in milling, their forward integration in baking, and their wide interests in many other food industries. The merger was eventually allowed with conditions. The new firm, Goodman Fielder Wattie (GFW), accounted for around 70% of milling production and 60% of capacity at the time of the merger, which became effective in November 1987.

Goodman Fielder Wattie moved offshore to domicile itself in Australia shortly after its creation. GFW moved partly to facilitate expansion in Australia: it has become the largest food company in both Australia and New Zealand, and in 1988 attempted to take over one of the UK's largest food groups, Ranks Hovis McDougall. There is considerable New Zealand ownership of GFW's stock, which trades locally.

From December 1987, the third biggest baking-milling group was sold to Defiance Mills, an Australian company. Another Australian firm, Allied Mills, bought the two largest independent mills. Thus, within the space of a few years, New Zealand flour milling has moved from a regulated industry with many small independents and total domestic ownership to a deregulated industry with three foreign companies owning 80% of capacity and about 90% of production. In addition, they account for 80% of baking production. Interestingly, this concentration has yet to arouse any public criticism.

Perhaps this is because consumers have noticed the changes primarily by receiving better quality fancy breads. Still-independent bakers report they are getting better quality flours, a wide range of types, all at very competitive prices. An attempt to estimate the effect of price decontrol on retail bread prices was unable to reach a conclusion due to the effects of price freezes and restructuring (Hunn and Easton 1985). Millers claim there has been significant price cutting, and more price flexibility is also likely. Interestingly, the rationalized but now highly amalgamated bakery industry is currently reporting very high profits, and the implication is that rents previously enjoyed by millers may now have been transferred at least temporarily to bakers.

Accompanying changes in ownership has been an increase in the importation of Australian wheat, which is now shipped in large consignments. The Goodman Fielder Wattie mills are well equipped to handle this, being relatively large (average 35,000 tonnes capacity, much larger than the industry average). A study by Miller (1989) concludes there is considerable integration within these three large firms between milling and baking, with cutthroat competition amongst the remaining six independent millers for contracts with the independent bakers. The price paid farmers for wheat has become much more responsive to weather conditions, world prices, etc, and has generally reduced.

Milling suffers considerable excess capacity. The problem is not new: mills have quit in large numbers—at least 40 since 1935—but further rationalization is under way. The Wheat Board certainly slowed this process by guaranteeing mill returns since the mid 1960s. In at least one case it also had the perverse effect of encouraging overinvestment in new facilities. The pressure to restructure is being given by new price signals and competition for bakery contracts.

Most small mills have been operating on one shift, though the marginal costs of two- or three-shift production are very low. Attempts to change this situation are being obstructed by old machinery and limited market demand, not by work-force resistance. Many small independent mills are making a very low or zero return on capital. Several are farmers cooperatives, and their criteria for continued operation has not been any target return on capital, but simply a non-negative cash flow. The remaining independents are also plagued by very high transport costs, being mainly sited far from population centers. Deregulation of the inland transport industry has cut truck and rail costs considerably, but port and shipping costs remain very high.

A strong desire for survival amongst the independents has slowed their exit from the industry. However, there have been three further closures during 1988 and another mill has shifted out of flour production. Several more closures are considered likely, and eventually only one (a Goodman Fielder Wattie mill) may survive in the South Island. The Wheat Board is likely to be disbanded, and the Wheat Research Institute (an independent tasting and research facility) may not survive. This would further jeopardize the independents.

Thus extremely tight regulation inhibited the natural development of the milling until pressure from Australian imports forced the industry to restructure. Government industry policy amounted to wholesale deregulation after a three-year transition period, without any other assistance, relying on the industry to rationalize on its own. This seems to have occurred at the cost of considerable concentration in the milling industry, and a number of mill closures. The main costs are being borne by southern independent mill owners and their (small) work forces and South Island farmers, all of whom had earned some economic rents under regulation.

Automobile Assembly Industry

Since 1926 New Zealand has had its own motor assembly industry, and since the 1930s there have been at least four assemblers active. Initially they were protected by a high tariff structure with a considerable degree of British and, later, Commonwealth preference. During the 1960s the industry began to expand in this protected environment and several new assembly plants were set up, assembling Japanese and European cars. The number of plants reached a peak of 16 in the 1970s and output grew from 50,000 to 90,000 units per year. During the 1970s the principal source of vehicles shifted from the UK and Australia to Japan, despite the tariff differentials applying to that country. Table 3.9 pro-

Table 3.9. Automobile Assembly 1978–88

1978/79	1983/84	1988	
24	23	28	plants
6646	5786	4359	employment
277	252	156	employment per plant
1243	1254	1118	output (million $NZ at 1988 prices)
186	217	256	output per employe (thousand $NZ)
8.7*	16.4	18.9	cars per employe[1]

* Data are for 1975/6
Notes and Sources: Same as Table 3.7. Covers NZSIC 38431. Cars assembled per full-time employe are from Savage (1989).

vides an overview of the industry. (This section draws heavily on a recent study by Greer 1989b.)

The industry has long been protected by a high level of import barriers. Tariffs are highest for non-Commonwealth countries and are considerably higher on CBU (completely built up) units compared to CKD (completely knocked down). Tariffs on Japanese cars in the 1970s, for example, ranged from 45 to 55%. More importantly, imported units required licenses. These have traditionally been limited for balance of payments reasons, being made available only to a limited number of assemblers and contingent on the inclusion of as high a proportion as possible of local content.

This has led to considerable inefficiencies, especially in componentry. It has been impossible to import many components where substitutes are locally available, despite the fact these have generally been produced in very small runs at high unit cost. Thus, for example, CKD units have been imported with spark plugs already installed in engines; assemblers have then been required to remove and destroy these spark plugs and replace them with inferior local substitutes. The rationing of import licenses led to a regime where for many years consumers had to queue for new cars. In addition to this import protection, the government levied a high sales tax. The result of this pricing structure has been very high local retail prices for new cars, unsatisfied demand, high second-hand prices, and a very high average age for the car population.

By 1985, 14 major assembly plants employed 6,000 employees. Table 3.10 shows the distribution of plants. The industry as a whole, including componentry and retail, employed ten times this number. Labor has been organized along traditional British lines, with productivity hampered by the multiplicity of unions on a single work site. Most assembly

Table 3.10. Motor Vehicle Assembly Plants in New Zealand

| 1985 | | 1988 | |
Capacity	Plants	Plants	
20,000	2	1	Ford Motors
18,000	1	1	General Motors
2,760	1	1*	Mazda Motors
9,200	2	—	Motor Holdings
15,000	2	1	NZMC/Honda
10,900	2	1	Nissan
2,990	1	—	Suzuki
24,000	1	1	Todd Motors/Mitsubishi
20,000	2	2	Toyota
122,850	14	8	total

* Mazda and Ford now operate their plants jointly.
Sources: Witt 1986 and industry data.

plants had seven or eight unions with separate individual agreements. The Engineers Union has been a progressive one. Management relations with other unions have been less positive.

A very large number of products was produced: 50 models were available in 259 variants in 1985, 183 of which were locally assembled. This is in a small market, buying only 80,000 new cars per year, which means very low production runs, difficulties in running inventory and spare parts efficiently, and high unit costs. A study by Witt (1986) found New Zealand plants had developed their own small batch-production techniques, far removed from Detroit-style mass production, but nevertheless capable of producing runs as small as a few hundred units. In addition, contract assembly in competitors' plants was common, especially for the smaller firms.

Despite reasonable competition, the tiny size of the market and high import protection has meant very high unit costs and a high retail price. It was this high price and its contrast with car prices in other developed countries that provoked the most pressure for reform of the industry. In 1981 the government referred the industry to the Industries Development Commission to develop a motor vehicle plan with the objectives of retaining an assembly and a componentry industry while improving efficiency in the face of "the chill of international competition."[1]

1. The Industries Development Commission was set up by the National Government to act as a restructuring body. A number of industries were referred to it in the late 1970s and early '80s. In consultation with industry parties, the IDC would draw up a report with

This plan was instituted in 1984 and involved the gradual liberalization of the industry by progressively opening up import licensing, reducing tariffs, and liberalizing importation of componentry. It was stipulated that the plan be revised four years later. Subject to this, the Closer Economic Relations Agreement with Australia temporarily excluded the freeing of trade in motor vehicles and components. The fear of New Zealand manufacturers was that they could be swamped by a flood of built-up cars from Australia, even though the industry there was itself high cost and fragmented.

It should be noted that this rationalization represented a very traditional industry policy approach and this sat uneasily with the new Labour Government, which looked to treat the automotive industry the same as any other, but was aware of the reasons for its long treatment as a special industry. Consequently it used the 1988 review of the motor vehicle industry plan to accelerate tariff reductions radically, lower sales taxes, terminate import licensing, and end the distinction in treatment between CKD and CBU units. The Government appears to hope that by 1992, when a further review is planned, they may be able to treat the auto industry on the same basis as any other.

The revised plan has been enshrined in the Closer Economic Relations Agreement with Australia, and consequently New Zealand cannot alter the plan without consulting that country. The New Zealand Government has seen the CER Agreement as a useful lever on industries such as motor vehicle assembly. They have indicated that if the assembly industry appeared in danger of collapse, the plan might be reexamined, but that the closure of one of the major assemblers is unlikely to be viewed as "collapse." The Government's announcement of possible changes in domestic content rules for protection has raised concern among assemblers. The present (1989) requirement is 25%. A rise to 50% as hinted could probably not be met by assemblers, given the decline in the local component industry. Without the 35% (global) tariff protection, the local industry could not survive.

The implications of these policy changes for assemblers is considerable. The whole structure of production costs and incentive to assemble locally is being changed. The freedom in importing CBUs, CKDs, and components has meant local assembly is being concentrated on getting longer runs of popular models. There has been some investment in modern technologies in assembly (electrostatic paint processes, just in time inventories, etc). However given the state of the industry this has

recommendations for rationalization, liberalization or continued protection oriented to "needs-based assistance." The Labour Government abolished the body.

not been major. Robotics are used in only one plant (a Ford-Mazda joint venture), and in many firms there has been disinvestment not investment.

The effect of reduced protection has been very noticeable. In 1984, 93% of additions to the stock of cars were local assemblies. By 1988 local assembly had dropped to 65%, new CBU imports had risen to 13%, and, astonishingly, imports of used cars had jumped to 23%. The last are mainly from Japan, acquired very cheaply because of Japan's tax on used cars and strong Japanese consumer preference for new cars. New Zealand is one of very few left-hand drive countries without tariff barriers or quantity constraints on used imports. New Zealand assemblers claim to be seriously hurt by these imports.

In addition, there has been a wide range of built-up luxury European cars imported. Built-up Korean (Hyundai and Daewoo/Pontiac) cars are becoming more common, and the Malaysian Proton has also been launched on the local market. Exchange rate movements have made larger Australian cars more attractive and Japanese cars less so (though they continue to dominate the market).

The New Zealand assembly industry is generally depressed, and is aware the future of local assembling is limited. There has been considerable company and plant rationalization. Of the 14 plants existing in 1985, 5 had closed by 1989. Of these, Subaru is the only manufacturer to completely withdraw from domestic production. Daihatsu, which had plans to build its own plant, scrapped them. Ford has closed 1 plant and established a joint venture assembly operation with Mazda. New Zealand Motor Corporation (Honda), Motor Holdings Ltd, and Nissan have all closed 1 of their 2 plants. Closure of 2 other plants appears likely, possibly during 1990. Firms ceasing assembly would probably keep a market presence by importing.

The tariff of 35% represents a trade-off between the two (incompatible) goals of reasonable consumer cost and a viable domestic assembly industry. At this tariff it is felt the cut-off for viable operation is 7–10 thousand units per year. Only the three largest Japanese assembly operations would continue on this basis.

One move has been vertical integration by Japanese suppliers, previously content to use local assemblers. In the last few years Toyota, Nissan, Mitsubishi, and Honda have all bought out their assemblers. They appear more likely to take major rationalization decisions. GM-Holden and Toyota have announced plans to merge interests, and Nissan appears to be developing a new truck with Ford.

There has been considerable layoff of employees in the auto industry. Companies are also using the depressed situation to reach flexible work agreements with unions, aided by the 1987 Labour Act. Nissan has been the leader, achieving an all-union "Nissan Way" agreement in its plant based on much more flexible work practices and pay rates.

The auto parts industry appears to be even more badly hit. It has long been hopelessly inefficient, due to the wide range of products required and tiny production runs. This has been reflected in the history of protection. In the short run, liberalization of sourcing componentry means cheaper (and sometimes better quality) cars. In the long run, a collapsed local parts industry reduces incentives to assemble locally, and makes it more difficult to achieve the required local content (at least 50% of ex-factory price) to allow preferential treatment on market access to Australia under CER.

In the longer term, it is the Australian connection that is most important. The inclusion of the auto industry in a revised CER Agreement means Australian-sourced cars have an advantage over others in return for access there. The Australian Motor Vehicle Industry Plan appears to encourage a strong local car industry using Australian materials and design, with some economies of scale, fewer producers involved, and incentives to increase annual production to at least 20,000 units per model. The feeling is that the market cannot sort these decisions out unaided.

In practice the New Zealand industry is likely to become more of an offshoot of the Australian one, with head offices in Tokyo and elsewhere directing Australian subsidiaries to treat the Australasian market as one. This could mean further disinvestment in New Zealand. There is the likelihood that a few New Zealand plants may concentrate on single-model runs for export to Australia. However the major flow of built-up cars will be from Australia to New Zealand (although this is limited by high trans-Tasman freight rates).

The general impression in 1989 is that the New Zealand assembly industry is probably as efficient as it could be, in the narrow sense of producing output at lowest input cost. However it can never be regarded as efficient in an allocative sense.

Greer (1989b) stresses that auto assembly in New Zealand is entirely artificial, a creation of the state. The cost of landing a fully assembled new car on the dock in Auckland is essentially the same as the cost of the unassembled knocked down kit. Thus it is inconsistent to say (as was said in the 1984 industry plan) that despite greatly reduced protection, it is the government's intent to retain the assembly sector of the industry but to have it efficient.

In summary, the auto assembly industry in New Zealand grew up under a protective umbrella, with local assembly encouraged. However, it has proved unable to achieve the technical efficiencies available in larger countries. The National Government instituted a traditional rationalization scheme in 1984. This has been taken over by the Labour Government and accelerated, at the cost of local component production, and resulting in a much smaller assembly industry being rationalized by its foreign owners and more closely integrated with Australia.

Oil Refining

New Zealand has since 1964 been served by one oil refinery (at Marsden Point, near Whangarei, 150 km north of Auckland), plus direct imports of refined petrol. Following the two OPEC crises in the 1970s there were concerted government efforts to increase fuel self-sufficiency. This resulted in the "Think Big" program of public sector investment in energy exploration, extraction and distribution industries, petrochemicals, and other downstream energy-using industries. A number of gas fields were exploited, resulting in synthetic fuels production and some crude oil discoveries. (This section draws heavily on reports by Clough 1989 and Miller 1989).

Part of the "Think Big" investment program involved the expansion of Marsden Point, including new processing units, a new control system, a new tank farm, the building of a hydrocracker, and a high-capacity distribution pipeline. The cost was $1.65 billion (at 1983/84 prices), and the project was completed by 1986, increasing capacity to 3.4 million tonnes per annum (about 68,000 barrels per day). Feedstocks are crude oil and condensate, which are refined to produce a wide range of industrial and domestic fuels and sulphur. Most of the feedstock is imported; some 40% comes from local onshore oil wells (crude oil) and offshore gas fields (condensate). In addition, synthetic petrol is produced from natural gas at Motunui in the central North Island, then leaded and blended at Marsden Point. Motunui is owned 75% by the Government, 25% by Mobil. The result is around 50% self-sufficiency for New Zealand in liquid transport fuels.

The refinery is run by the New Zealand Refining Company, 66% owned by four major multinationals (British Petroleum, Shell, Mobil, and Caltex), 20% by the New Zealand Government and 11% by Petrocorp, a government-owned exploration company until privatized in 1988. In contrast with other energy industries such as gas, coal, and electricity, the oil sector in New Zealand has considerable private ownership and for that reason has been tightly regulated. The refinery operates as a tolling operation, with a guaranteed unit return to its shareholders. Historically, to induce the oil companies to undertake the upgrading of the refinery, the government of the day guaranteed repayment of the cost through a levy on petrol sales and allowed no refined motor spirits to be imported except through the refinery. For their part, the four companies agreed to use the refinery in preference to direct imports. The agreements amongst the wholesalers for the use of the refinery meant all knew one another's costs reasonably well. They also had been encouraged to co-operate over coastal shipping and tankage (storage). This meant in the past tacit collusion was possible.

A number of forces put pressure on the viability of the oil refinery industry in the mid 1980s. There has been considerable overcapacity, with 80–90 refineries closing worldwide in the mid 1980s. This reflected downward pressure on the prices of refined products as those remaining sought to utilize their plant.

The small size of the New Zealand market means at most one refinery can be considered viable. Total oil consumption is around 60,000 barrels per day (3 million tonnes annually), approximately the capacity of Marsden Point. The refinery has been designed to produce a wide range of fuels in small quantities and its 1986 upgrade has kept it technically very advanced. In comparison with the nearest exporting refineries (Singapore), Marsden Point has a much greater ability to upgrade crude. However, its unit costs are relatively high by world standards, in large part because of its flexibility, its range of product, and the small size of any given product run. Costs depend crucially on throughput: breakeven is at least 80% of capacity, below 70% Marsden becomes uncompetitive.[2]

The economic assumptions behind refurbishment and expansion of Marsden Point were proving mistaken even as work got under way. When the Labour Government came in, it was immediately faced with the question of what to do with the refinery. Had New Zealand not had any developed domestic oil and gas reserves, a decision might have been easier. The Government, basically committed to deregulating the petroleum industry from refining through retail, was in a quandary because, although the refinery may be too small to be efficient, local feedstock production cannot be used without it. There was a willingness to pay some price for the security of complete domestic integration. Still, the Government suspected capture by the oil companies and resented its

2. Refined petroleum products are generally grouped in five major categories broadly based on use. These are gasolines (automobile transport), kerosenes (including jet fuels), distillates (including diesel and space-heating fuel), residuals (burned for steam, including electrical power generation and bunkers for ships), and lubricants. In New Zealand the first three categories are often grouped as "white oil products." Because of the wide range of possible inputs and outputs, "capacity" is a tricky concept in refining. A good account of what is involved in refining is British Petroleum (1977).

inability to withdraw from responsibility for protecting the refinery, leaving the outcome to the market.

The oil companies argued that in an otherwise deregulated environment, Marsden Point would still need considerable protection from imported refined products, or else they and new entrants would bypass the refinery and import directly, sabotaging the processing of locally extracted fuels. (Local feedstock is provided from joint ventures of the large oil companies with some New Zealand local partners.)

On top of this, the refinery had huge debts—over $2 billion—from its expansions and upgradings. Disposition of the refinery's debt held up the whole issue of oil sector deregulation for several years. Had the issue not had implications for the viability of local oil and gas extraction, it seems likely the Government would simply have regarded the $2 billion as a sunk cost and allowed NZ Refining to close Marsden Point if it wished. Forced to the painful conclusion that intervention was necessary, the Government considered the possibility of imposing import licensing of refined petrol, erecting a tariff, or making a bounty payment. In the end, the Government took responsibility for the debt as part of NZ Refining's financial restructuring, raising its own funds to pay it off. The Government also agreed to a direct payment to the company of $85 million over three years (beginning in August 1988) in return for a guarantee the plant would remain open. This was seen as the most transparent and non-distortionary method.

Finally, in May 1988, the downstream oil industry was radically deregulated by the Petroleum Sector Reform Act. Until then, distribution had been tightly regulated, with wholesalers requiring licenses. The conditions for licenses involved participation in price-smoothing pool accounts, charging a uniform price, divorcement from retailing, and agreement to use the refinery to the maximum extent possible. Under such conditions, each company had an incentive to hold down its costs, since they could not be passed on to the consumer in full, thus maximizing production efficiency. However, since margin and price control prevented individual firms from engaging in price competition, the incentive for allocative efficiency and the degree of competition had been blunted. The final retail price was controlled by the government.

Deregulation has meant the illegality of collusion, removal of requirements for divorcement of wholesaling and retailing, the end of entry licenses, and the end of price control. In addition, there are no import restrictions or customs tariffs on imports, merely a flat rate of excise duty on motor spirits. Thus the oil refinery, having received its bounty payment and debt restructuring, must compete without protection in the world market.

The initial effects of industry restructuring have been dominated by downstream deregulation. Considerable change came quickly, with wholesalers buying into service stations, increased price competition, differentiation of services, restructuring, and exit. However, the oil companies' joint ownership and operation of the refinery still gives them certain information on their relative costs and throughput, which may be blunting the competitive response at the retail level. Table 3.11 provides an overview of oil-related industries.

It is as yet difficult to assess long-term changes to the refinery operation. The emergence of new wholesalers was hoped for by the Government, and looked like occurring. But instead, within months of deregulation, oil companies bought up the two independent chains and new entry appears less likely. Consequently there are no operators in the industry, outside the big four companies, with the incentive or ability to directly import refined petrol in competition with the refinery.

In late 1988, six months after deregulation, the refinery was understood to be making good profits, and the retail price of petrol showed some price discounting and regional variation. However, overall, retailers' margins appear to have remained stable, and wholesalers' margins have actually increased. This maintenance of profits at every stage of the operation has occurred despite low local demand and low international prices; it causes the Government some concern, but under a deregulated system of its own design, there is little the Government can do about it. (The Commerce Act still gives the Government the power to reimpose price regulation on any industry, but to use this power would be an admission of deregulatory failure.)

To summarize, this industry enjoyed considerable public sector involvement and protection in order to promote energy self-sufficiency.

Table 3.11. Oil Refining Industry, 1978–88

1978/79	1983/84	1988	
13	19	16	plants
464	787	1001	employment
36	41	62	employment per plant
180	238	752*	output (million $NZ at 1988 prices)
387	302	747*	output per employe (thousand $NZ)

* Data are for 1986/87.
Notes and Sources: Same as table 3.7. Covers NZSIC 35300, which contains, in addition to the major refinery, a number of other very small operations, mainly carrying out the re-refining of used oils.

The industry was put under pressure by low international oil prices and downstream oil deregulation. Without government intervention, the refinery may have closed. Despite its disinclination to intervene, the Labour Government has felt it necessary to restructure the debt of the refinery and provide a direct subsidy to ensure it continues; the belief is that its operation will be increasingly market disciplined in the future.

Export Meat Processing

Since the turn of the century New Zealand has had a number of meat works licensed to process its large stock of cattle and sheep for export. While some rationalization occurred over this long period, by 1980 there were still 35 licensed export slaughter houses. Ownership was divided amongst farmer cooperatives, overseas companies, large diversified New Zealand companies and small specialized New Zealand firms. They were located throughout New Zealand, generally in stock-growing areas. (Beef and dairy cattle are mostly in the North Island; sheep are everywhere—over 65 million head in 1985.)

This is in the nature of a service industry. Slaughterers do not buy stock but provide the service of processing live animals into carcasses which the farmer then sells to a meat exporter; for this service they levy a slaughtering charge. In practice the slaughterer is often also the processor and exporter. Meat exports have provided about 20% of New Zealand's export receipts for many years. Half are lamb, the rest beef, mutton, and, increasingly, exotic meats such as venison.

The establishment and operation of export slaughter houses traditionally has been regulated by the Meat Act, and since 1932 the Meat Producers Board has had wide powers to control and coordinate New Zealand's meat export trade. This includes meat grading, storage, shipping, export licensing, market research, and promotion. Licenses to set up were issued subject to whether it was felt there was an economic need for a facility and whether it would have an effect on the viability of other operators. Clearly this system had important consequences for competitive efficiency: the result was a high-cost industry, with unions in a particularly strong position due to their ability to withhold labor at crucial times. The high costs got passed on in high slaughtering charges. While this annoyed farmers, it was tolerated because of high export prices.

Most New Zealand meat exports went to the UK until its entry to the EEC in 1973 forced New Zealand away from such single-country dependence. For the first time the industry had to worry about market access.

Also during the 1970s, the EEC and the United States demanded very high hygiene standards, requiring refitting of most existing plants.

In 1976 the licensing system was liberalized slightly and several new slaughtering lines (called chains, and effectively a production line) were approved, but other proposals got turned down. In the late 1970s real prices for meat fell and this instituted pressure for change.

The Meat Act was repealed in 1980, removing discretionary government licensing and leaving only hygiene requirements to be satisfied for entry. There was no longer an incentive to keep works open simply to transfer licenses because the rent accruing to license holders was effectively eliminated. The effect of partial deregulation initially was to increase entry and investment in the industry. This was true even though plants had become increasingly capital intensive to build and high cost to operate. For example, a new plant with 5 or 6 chains, capable of processing 15–20 thousand animals a day cost about $40 million in 1983. During the 1970s only 5 new licenses had been approved; between 1980 and 1984, 11 new licenses were approved, 19 chains expanded or opened up, and a similar number closed. Table 3.12 provides an overview.

Pricing traditionally has been relatively uniform, with firms following a bench market-price leader in setting slaughter charges. There was a large increase in charges in real terms up to 1982, when they reached half the price paid for a carcass for export. Between 1982 and 1984 slaughtering charges were fixed by the wage and price freeze of the period.

In 1984 the incoming Government removed price subsidies, which sparked off a severe farm crisis, resulting in considerable agricultural disinvestment. This initially meant more stock available for the works.

Table 3.12. Meat Export Works, 1978–88

1978/79	1983/84	1988	
44	44	46	plants
31,327	32,168	25,732	employment
731	731	560	employment per plant
2,322	2,468	2,658	output (million $NZ at 1988 prices)
74	77	100	output per employe (thousand $NZ)
22.5*	24.4	30.4	tonnes exported per employe

* Data are for 1975

Notes and Sources: Same as Table 3.7. Covers NZSIC 31111. Exports per employe from Savage 1989.

However reduced stock numbers soon led farmers to put considerable pressure on processors to reduce charges. At the same time, live sheep exports to the Middle East began, further reducing stock available to slaughter.

From 1985 onwards, with stock intakes and profits dropping markedly, the industry increasingly realized something had to be done. There were a plethora of reports on rationalization strategies, although it proved difficult to carry most of the plans to fruition. The effect of partial deregulation initially was to increase entry and investment in the industry. During the 1970s only 5 new licenses had been approved, but between 1980 and 1984, 11 new licenses were approved, 19 chains expanded or opened up, and a similar number closed.

Overcapacity in 1988 was estimated at 10–40% (depending on product and region). There have been many closures to reduce this: 8 works have closed permanently (all relatively old large plants); a further 5 have reduced capacity, and several others "temporarily" closed. This has been achieved by internal rationalization, takeover/merger, and firms going into receivership. Somewhat surprisingly, at the same time, 26 new plants have been established: 15 involve new entrants and 10 former local abattoirs have upgraded to export status. Almost all new plants are small (frequently single-chain) operations exploiting latest technologies.

In a breakthrough from traditional labor relations a number of plants are operating double shifts and employing workers from outside the Meat Workers Union. One plant is shifting to 24–hour operation. Because of these new entrants, over-capacity continues at high levels. Yet there are plans afoot for a number of new independent plants. Certainly these new entrants have the advantage of better capacity utilization, economies of specialization, modern technology, and new, more flexible work practices. The better profitability of these new entrants has generally allowed them to offer wages as good as older plants, but in exchange for greater labor productivity.

The remaining established firms have been through a complex series of ownership changes and internal restructuring. This has included mergers, joint ventures, and increased vertical integration. Several producer cooperatives remain strong in the industry. There has been integration into export markets; for example one small freezing company supplies an American fast food chain directly.

New technologies have included pelting machines, automatic slaughtering techniques, computer-controlled grading, movement, and staff control. The other major change has been to increase value added via further processing and product lines more closely oriented to customer needs. From 1980 to 1986 the percentage of exports in carcass form fell from 85% to 65% (lamb) and 30% (mutton). There has been consequent better use of animal by-products.

Since 1984, processing charges have stabilized and decreased in real terms in 1978–88, reflecting some improved efficiencies and greater competitive pressures. There has also been some divergence, something not previously common.

The rationalization process has been slowed by several institutional and economic obstacles. The role of the Meat Producers Board, its monopoly control over developing markets, and its equity shares in some processing firms with a view to aiding industry rationalization in some unspecified way, have all been criticized by the industry.

Attempts by firms to reach agreement among themselves regarding closures and rationalization have brought investigations by the Commerce Commission, New Zealand's antitrust regulator. Eventually these agreements were ruled as anticompetitive but allowable due to the efficiency gains resulting in net public benefit.

Labor productivity traditionally has been low in New Zealand plants, with highly seasonal production, resistance to new automated technologies, no use of double shifts, high labor costs, and a high strike rate. Labor was slow to share the industry's reduced prosperity. Employment has decreased since 1980. The downturn since 1985 has resulted in layoffs and the first use of double shifts in processing (after considerable disputes). There has been some lengthening of the seasonal kill, using price incentives for farmers.

In 1986 the Labour Relations Act promoted partial labor deregulation, encouraging the formation of "on site" agreements and plant-level awards with considerable repercussions for the industry. Still, prevailing labor market regulations are cited by the industry as a constraint to change. The sector has a notoriously bad industrial relations record. The number of stoppages has declined from very high levels in the 1970s, although it is still the most strike-prone industry in New Zealand. The Labour Relations Act allows for some increased flexibility, but the requirement for compulsory membership remains.

The major economic obstacle to rationalization is the high level of sunk costs in the industry. Established freezing plants contain highly durable and specialized capital and labor investment. Plant closure implies a large capital write-off since resale value is usually very low and chains cannot easily be moved. Redundancy payments are likely to be sizable—around $20 million in some late 1980s closures.

In contrast to these exit barriers, new technology and other changing aspects of the industry mean barriers to entry are relatively low—a new single-chain plant (with simplified slaughtering chain design) may be built for as little as $4–5 million. The final constraint is psychological. A long history of a profitable regulated industry with government support has left the industry ill-equipped to adjust to changed economic circumstances.

In summary, this traditional New Zealand industry survived for many years protected by local regulation and with buoyant export markets. The end of this regime has forced considerable reduction of capacity with further rationalization yet to come. These changes have been catalyzed by new, more efficient entrants to the industry.

Wool Textiles

Wool scouring, spinning, weaving, knitting, and carpetmaking make up the wool textiles industry. These are traditional industries in New Zealand, using abundant local wools. Due to the dominance of crossbred sheep, carpetmaking is of particular importance. The industry grew up with small textile mills in almost every town, especially in the South Island. It was relatively slow to modernize and has had various government measures to protect it since the 1930s. However small uneconomic plants gradually have been closed or absorbed, leading in the 1970s to dominance by a few big firms. Despite this, financial returns were estimated to be poor, and there was excess capacity and a high level of duplication. (This section is based on a study by Savage and Greer in Savage 1989.)

The wool textile industry was one of the first to be studied by the Industries Development Commission, an official body for industry rationalization in the late 1970s. A 1979 review suggested a major rationalization. It foresaw considerable growth of wool-based yarns, fabrics, and carpets. However the industry continued to be fragmented and came under increasing pressure from synthetics.

In 1980 a major company collapse sparked off the closure of a number of plants. A joint government/industry committee funded by the Development Finance Corporation was set up to recommend rationalization of the whole industry. Alliance, the largest surviving firm, was chosen as the principal vehicle for change. A plan was agreed to reduce total industry capacity, and this involved relocation of plant so that remaining mills could specialize. Government loans, a $5 million relocation grant with investment allowances, tax concessions, and a bounty for woven production were made available. Table 3.13 provides an overview of the industry.

Alliance bought up a number of large plants from other firms, then began to reduce total capacity by closing specified plants, eliminating duplication, and restructuring establishments from their traditionally

Table 3.13. Wool Textile Production, 1978–88

1978/79	1983/84	1988	
405	608	829	plants
15,972	14,974	12,999	employment
39	22	19	employment per plant
1,697	1,706	1,629	output (million $NZ at 1988 prices)
106	114	125	output per employe (thousand $NZ)

Notes and Sources: Same as Table 3.7. Covers NZSIC 321.

vertically integrated nature to make each unit a specialized one. This company is now dominant in markets for knitting, woven fabrics, jersey fabrics, and suit making. Plants now specialize in one product range such as worsted fabric, hand knitting yarns, blanketing and apparel fabric, and upholstery fabric.

Wool based textiles have long been protected from imports (though acrylic mix substitutes have not). The Closer Economic Relationship Agreement with Australia spelled the end of this. In 1984 import licensing for textiles was liberalized: by 1986 imports from Australia were duty free while imports from LDCs were subject to a 12% tariff and those from developed countries, 25%. It has been estimated that the effective rate of protection in the industry is in the region of 45%.

In the carpetmaking subsector this put New Zealand producers under some pressure, initially in competition with some Australian exporters that were receiving bounties for their production. The main New Zealand carpet producers began to invest in production facilities in Australia from 1980, as protection against exchange rate fluctuations and to circumvent quota and subsidy problems.

The rising value of the New Zealand dollar in 1986 and high interest rates put local industry under further pressure, with a number of plants closing. This time the Labour Government showed itself unwilling to take the lead in company rationalization, as had occurred previously, and its only role has been to accelerate the progress of import liberalization.

In carpet-making, this left three major local producers (UEB, Feltex, and Cavalier) accounting for 75% of production. Each was left to work out its own rationalization strategies. UEB's profitability was badly hit and, having closed several plants, in 1988 it exited the industry completely, selling its remaining plants to the other two producers. Feltex, a long-established company, was bought by an investment company in 1984 (as were many New Zealand manufacturers in this period) and when the latter went into receivership in 1988–89 (as did many New

Zealand investment companies at this time) was sold to an Australian company. In the process, Feltex has closed five plants, placed more emphasis on marketing and product style variations, and cut costs. Cavalier was established by an ex-UEB employee in 1972, and has grown rapidly by concentrating on export market development. In particular it has established a chain of retail operations in the US selling mainly synthetic carpet.

New Zealand carpet producers for some years had a gentlemen's agreement to produce only all-wool carpets. Certainly New Zealand has a comparative advantage in wool, and this has directed development to the top end of the market; however it has also meant that synthetic-mixes have remained less developed, and New Zealand consumers have had less access to cheap synthetic product. Several smaller firms that are now growing rapidly are concentrating on synthetic blends (though they are reluctant to be precise about this because it is still regarded as "unpatriotic" in the industry). Several of these smaller firms are Australian-owned, and synthetic yarns are sourced from Australia. New Zealand's market is currently 20% synthetic (compared to 70% in Australia and 98% in the US).

In addition these smaller companies are specializing in relatively few lines and styles which lengthens production runs and substantially reduces idle set-up time. In the larger firms, for example, tufting machines may be idle as much as half the time due to setting-up requirements, constituting a major industry cost. Further efficiencies have been obtained from more flexible work practices. For these reasons these smaller firms appear to be relatively profitable and growing.

Protection for New Zealand carpetmakers has dropped significantly. All Australian imports are now tariff and quota free. Most global carpet imports face a 40% tariff (22.5–27% for developing countries). Carpets imported (except from Australia) with over 20% synthetic content still face licensing, though this was being reviewed during 1989.

Carpet production slumped from a peak of 15 million square meters in 1985 to 9 million in 1988, with a further reduction in the proportion exported. It now appears market-led rationalization has proceeded satisfactorily, and that production will stabilize at this level with prospects for improved profitability.

In summary, the carpet industry in New Zealand has been through two contrasting periods of decline and restructuring. In the first, the 1970s, the government took a very active role in directing rationalization. In the second, the 1980s, the signal to rationalize was import liberalization, but in other respects the government followed a strictly hands-off policy. To some extent the experience of carpet manufacturing reflects developments in the wool textiles industry generally.

TRADE POLICY IMPLICATIONS

New Zealand trade policy plays a markedly different role than in many Pacific Basin countries. In New Zealand it is being used as a deliberate and unilateral instrument for liberalization of the domestic economy rather than being seen as an objective of policy. In brief, trade policy is seen as an input into reform and a mechanism of adjustment, rather than being viewed as an outcome of reform. The theoretical underpinning to this is the fact that New Zealand has a high degree of natural monopoly with decreasing average cost curves due to its small markets. Both the theoretical conclusions of contestability theory, and more intuitive observations on barriers to entry point to the role imports and foreign investment can play in such a small economy in terms of providing competition to stimulate innovation, give scope for product specialization, reduce prices, and drive out excess profits.

New Zealand trade policy needs to be understood against a backdrop of Northern Hemisphere agricultural protection. Since the United Kingdom, New Zealand's traditional market, joined the EEC, New Zealand has encountered great difficulty selling its efficient agricultural produce into high-income Northern markets. This is one reason why resources have been diverted into higher cost domestic manufacturing. The agricultural trade barriers faced include access to EEC markets, EEC agricultural export subsidies into third-country markets, quarantine and distributive barriers in Japan, complete prohibition of some imports into Korea, political and religious restrictions in Middle East markets, and quotas in the US. In most cases these restrictions stem from strong political pressures by domestic farmers in potential markets. In addition, the US (unsuccessfully) used threats of trade restrictions to dissuade New Zealand from its policy barring nuclear ships.

There are two arms to New Zealand trade policy: firstly, the liberalization of global imports and foreign direct investment into New Zealand; secondly, and rather more pragmatically, the creation of a trans-Tasman free trade area, which is particularly important because Australia is a major destination for manufactured exports and the most likely source of potential competition.

Keen argument has raged over whether, faced by foreign governments that do not liberalize, it is still rational for New Zealand to do so. The new trade models of imperfect competition suggest there may be a number of circumstances in which it is optimal for a government to retaliate to trade barriers for both static and dynamic reasons. (See Thompson and Tomkinson 1987 for a survey and applications to New Zealand.) The opposite view is that tariffs represent a tax on local consumers and should be eliminated. If a foreign country distorts trade patterns by erecting market barriers or production subsidies, this means a transfer from their consumers to their producers; for New Zealand to retaliate might level the playing field for New Zealand producers, but at the cost of local consumers.

This latter view has been adopted by the New Zealand Government. The argument has taken place in the context of the 1987/88 Tariff Review Working Party, in which the manufacturers and the unions united to oppose liberalization. However, they were eventually induced to agree to a resolution to cut most tariffs in half over a four-year period from 1988. Using the Swiss formula where the biggest cuts are in the highest tariffs, a present rate of 50% will drop to 20.5% by 1992 and one of 5% will drop to 4%. Nominal tariffs will average 10–20% by 1991/92. Any remaining import duties are to convert to tariffs.

Recent estimates of industrial protection and assistance to New Zealand manufacturing suggest the effective rate of assistance has declined from 39% in 1981/82 to 26% in 1987/88 (Syntec Economic Services 1988). The present Developing Country Preference Scheme is to be reviewed. Under that scheme, countries pay only 80% of the normal tariff. However, a dozen countries with exports to New Zealand exceeding $100,000 and 25% of imports in each category have recently lost that status. This mainly includes NIEs. Any industries on special plans continue until the plan review, at which time they are subject to the above reform program.

The New Zealand Government would of course like to see other countries liberalizing, for two reasons: one is to improve New Zealand market access, and the other is to vindicate it in the view that liberalizing is the right approach. However, when this does not happen (as in the case of international air passenger transport), the Government has shown it is prepared to forgo bilateral bargaining advantages in order to continue its internal liberalization process.

New Zealand has been pursuing this line at international economic forums. At the 1988 Pacific Basin Economic Council meeting it noted that its own adjustment would be made much easier if other countries were to liberalize on a similar path, and induced the meeting to recommend the Council pursue deregulation as a high priority.

In terms of Pacific trade policy options, New Zealand is supporting broad liberalization under the Uruguay Round of GATT. As an active member of the Cairns Group, New Zealand's primary objective has been to attack what has been seen as the country's major postwar constraint to expansion: agricultural protection in Northern Hemisphere industrial markets, especially for highly processed primary products. These barriers have long determined New Zealand trade patterns, slowed down development of primary processing, and indirectly encouraged New

Zealand (as a specialist agricultural producer) to invest in manufacturing. The initial official New Zealand view on GATT was that "progress on outstanding 'hard core' issues should not be frustrated or delayed by the pace of negotiations on new issues," that is, New Zealand would not support developed countries' attempts to liberalize services until there was agreement on liberalization of agriculture.

Since then the official view has changed (Tyndall 1988). The feeling now is that progress on liberalizing trade in services would be beneficial to New Zealand, even in the absence of any reciprocal agricultural concessions. The Government is therefore arguing for a legally binding Framework Agreement without permanent or sectoral exclusions based on transparency and non-discriminatory GATT principles, to apply to all new regulations relating to trade in services, and to provide a mechanism to free up the existing services market.

New Zealand was pleased that the US put agriculture at the top of the GATT agenda. However, the apparent lack of progress in the Uruguay Round has alerted the Government to the fact there is unlikely to be a swift resolution of agricultural protectionism.

The other arm of trade policy is to pursue more deliberate forms of economic integration. To date this has meant a limited access agreement for countries of the South Pacific (SPARTECA). The SPARTEC Agreement allows duty-free imports of industrial goods into New Zealand from Pacific Forum countries. Its main effect has been that a number of ailing labor-intensive New Zealand firms in industries such as clothing have relocated in Fiji and other islands.

The Closer Economic Relations (CER) agreement with Australia is much more important. Signed in 1983, and reviewed after five years of operation, this agreement has had a significant effect in increasing trans-Tasman trade and investment. During this period Australia has become the major destination for New Zealand exports and one of the major sources of imports; in particular, intra-industry trade between the countries has grown markedly in the period. Direct investment flows in both directions have increased significantly. For New Zealand, Australia remains an important safety valve. (For further details see Bollard and Thompson 1987, Holmes 1987.)

CER was renegotiated in 1988. This involved widening it to include all manufactured products and some agricultural items, speeding up the timetable for removal of trade barriers (to be completed by 1990), the inclusion of services (with a number of exceptions noted by Australia), and the harmonization of many business practices. New Zealand's attempts to include an investment agreement were unsuccessful. CER does not attempt to erect a common external tariff.

The Closer Economic Relationship is felt to have been largely successful by both countries, although clearly of more importance to New Zealand. Emboldened by this, New Zealand has been investigating the possibilities of extending it to third countries in the Pacific Basin. A study of Australian-New Zealand-Canadian trade relations has outlined this as a possibility (Holmes 1988). One potential attraction of this is the Canadian-US Trade Agreement.

New Zealand has also responded with cautious interest to other regional initiatives on possible plurilateral trade groupings. In particular the ramifications of the various Japanese initiatives on Pacific Basin economic integration are being explored. Also the Government has backed Australia's proposal for a new Asia-Pacific economic organization but stressed it must include the US and Canada. Though the Government has not officially admitted it, this interest in regional trade groupings is somewhat at odds with the official policy of unilateral trade liberalization, and represents a rare example of second-best realpolitik.

THE FUTURE

New Zealand's industry policy for declining industry involves a severe and austere program of comprehensive deregulation to allow market forces to signal the need for exit or rationalization. This raises a number of questions for the future.

Will the program work? One school of thinking on the New Zealand economy is that due to its small and open nature, exogenous international economic forces are the primary influence on the economy, and that government policy is therefore severely limited in its scope (Easton 1987). It is far too soon to reach a conclusion on the outcome of deregulation. After five years it is clearly having a positive effect on restructuring, though with considerable costs being felt. The full effects will not be known for another decade, by which time they will not be measurable.

Will the program continue? By the beginning of 1989 the Minister of Finance had been deposed, and a significant anti-reform lobby was growing within the Government. The pace of reform slowed, though it still continued. In particular, the privatization process ran into political and administrative problems, and the capping of Government spending turned out to be a long process. More sensitivity was being shown to the social and political costs of structural change. Moreover, it should be noted that the original program of reform was not yet complete.

In October 1990 the Labour Government was removed from office and replaced by a national Government with a very large majority vote, which largely reflected public dissatisfaction at the failure of the reform process to yield immediate improvements in economic growth. This effectively marks the end of the chapter of radical economic reform begun in 1984.

Will the reforms be undone? In general this seems unlikely even with the change of Government. Some of the first moves in the program of deregulation removed discretionary powers from Ministers to impose regulations such as price control. Import protection is unlikely to be raised. Industry controls are unlikely to be reinstated, with the possible exception of prudential and ethical requirements. What is possible, however, is the renewal of selective industry assistance and a more active Government role in trade and industry policy.

Will declining manufacturing industries survive? Many individual firms have not, and there has been a significant shift in New Zealand's pattern of industrial activity. New Zealand's manufacturing sector as a whole, however, should survive, albeit in slimmed-down form. In any event, the main determinant of survival continues to be macroeconomic conditions rather than microeconomic reform.

By late 1990 the economy had not yet achieved a satisfactory performance. Significant deflation had been achieved, with increases in the consumers' price index falling from 18 to 5% annually (although interest rates remain high). There had been substantial improvements in labor productivity and trade competitiveness. The government's financial budget deficit was reduced from 7 to 3% of GDP. Against this, however, growth rates were flat or negative during 1987–90, and the prospects for future growth were disappointing. With unemployment sticking at a postwar high of 7%, there was widespread dissatisfaction with the results achieved from deregulation.

The future of many of the troubled and declining industries described in this chapter depends on whether growth can be achieved. The danger is that the Government's failure to achieve satisfactory fiscal policy reform may be interpreted as a failure in microeconomic regulatory reform.

BIBLIOGRAPHY

Ayto, Jonathan and Alan E. Bollard. 1987. *New Zealand Distributive Trades: Pricing, Regulation and Structural Change*. NZ Institute of Economic Research, Research Paper 34. Wellington.

Bollard, Alan E. and Anne Daly. 1984. "A Comparison of Plant Sizes in Australia and New Zealand Manufacturing." *New Zealand Economic Papers*, v 18.

—— and Brian Easton, editors. 1985. *Markets, Regulation and Pricing: Six Case Studies.* NZ Institute of Economic Research, Research Paper 31. Wellington.

—— and David Harper. 1987. *Research and Development in New Zealand: A Public Policy Framework.* NZ Institute of Economic Research, Research Monograph 39. Wellington.

—— and Mary Anne Thompson, editors. 1987. *Trans-Tasman Trade and Investment.* NZ Institute of Economic Research / Institute of Policy Studies, Research Monograph 38. Wellington.

Borrell, Brent and Anthony Zwart. 1982. *The New Zealand Wheat and Flour Industry: Market Structure and Policy Implications.* Lincoln College, Agricultural Economics Research Unit, Research Report 124. Christchurch.

British Petroleum. 1977. *Our Industry: Petroleum.* London.

Buckle, Robert A. 1987. "Sequencing and the Role of Foreign Exchange Markets." In Alan E. Bollard and Robert A. Buckle, editors, *Economic Liberalisation in New Zealand,* ch 11. Wellington: Allen & Unwin.

——. 1988. *Expectations and Credibility in the Disinflation Process.* NZ Institute of Economic Research, Discussion Paper 33. Wellington.

Campbell-Hunt, Colin A., Alan E. Bollard, and John Savage. 1989. *Productivity and Quality in New Zealand Firms: Effects of Deregulation.* NZ Institute of Economic Research, Research Monograph 46. Wellington.

Clough, Peter J. 1989. *Issues in Oil Sector Deregulation.* NZ Institute of Economic Research, Research Monograph 43. Wellington.

Crump, Donald K. 1988. "Adjustment in the Wheat and Flour Industry." Paper presented at a Conference of the New Zealand Branch of the Australian Agricultural Economics Society, Blenheim.

Culy, John and Stephen Gale. 1987. "Regulatory Change in the Energy Sector." In Alan E. Bollard and Robert A. Buckle, editors, *Economic Liberalisation in New Zealand,* ch 7. Wellington: Allen & Unwin.

Durbin, Sydney and Kevin R. Hall. 1982. *Analysis of Distribution and Milling in the Wheat Industry: Costs and Policies, Economics Division.* Wellington: Ministry of Agriculture and Fisheries.

Easton, Brian H. 1987. *How Bad is New Zealand's Economic Performance and Why?* University of Melbourne, Department of Economics, Research Paper 176.

——. 1988. "The Distributional Consequences of Policy Changes." Paper presented at a Conference on Social Policy, New Zealand Planning Council, Wellington.

Economic Monitoring Group. 1985. *The Regulated Economy, Monitoring Report.* Wellington: New Zealand Planning Council.

Galt, David. 1986. "Adjustment to Change in New Zealand Manufacturing." In T. Lindop, editor, *Liberalising the New Zealand Economy.* Fourth National Business Conference. Dunedin: University of Otago.

——. 1988. *Industry and Trade Policies.* Wellington: Department of Trade and Industry. Processed.

Greer, Douglas F. 1989a. "Contestability in Competition Policy: Replacement, Supplement or Impediment?" In *The Influence of US Economics on New Zealand*. NZ Institute of Economic Research / NZ-US Educational Foundation, Research Monograph 42. Wellington.

—— 1989b. "Automobile Assembly." In John Savage, editor, *Industry Rationalisation: Strategies and Constraints*. NZ Institute of Economic Research, Research Report. Wellington.

Grimmond, David. 1985. "Delicensing in the Meat Industry." In Alan E. Bollard and Bruce Easton, editors, *Markets, Regulation and Pricing: Six Case Studies*. NZ Institute of Economic Research, Research Paper 31. Wellington.

Guria, Jagdish C. 1987. "Regulatory Change in the Transport Sector." In Alan E. Bollard and Robert A. Buckle, editors, *Economic Liberalisation in New Zealand*, ch 4. Wellington: Allen & Unwin.

Harper, David. 1986. *The Financial Services Industry: Effects of Regulatory Reform*. NZ Institute of Economic Research, Research Monograph 35. Wellington.

—— and Girol Karacaoglu. 1987. "Financial Policy Reform in New Zealand." In Alan E. Bollard and Robert A. Buckle, editors, *Economic Liberalisation in New Zealand*, ch 10. Wellington: Allen & Unwin.

Hawke, Gary. 1987 Jun. "New Initiatives for the New Zealand Economy." *Quarterly Predictions*.

Hazledine, Timothy and John Savage. 1988. *Disinvestment in New Zealand Manufacturing*. NZ Institute of Economic Research, Research Report. Wellington.

Holmes, Sir Frank H. 1987. *Closer Economic Relations with Australia: Agenda for Progress*. Wellington: Institute of Policy Studies.

—— 1988. *Directions in Foreign Exchange Earnings: Partners in the Pacific*. Wellington: New Zealand Trade Development Board.

Hunn, Nicola and Brian Easton. 1985. "Bread Controls and the Bread Market." In Alan E. Bollard and Robert A. Buckle, editors, *Markets, Regulation and Pricing: Six Case Studies*. NZ Institute of Economic Research, Research Paper 31. Wellington.

——, David Mayes and C. J. (Stan) Vandersyp. 1987. *The Macroeconomic Effects of Financial Deregulation*. NZ Institute of Economic Research, Research Report. Wellington.

Krueger, Anne. 1985. *Economic Liberalisation Experiences: The Costs and Benefits*. Wellington: The Treasury.

Miller, Richard A. 1989. *Price Setting and Deregulation*. NZ Institute of Economic Research, Research Monograph 49. Wellington.

Ministry of Works and Development. 1986. *Mid-Year Development Review*.

Orr, Adrian. 1989. *Productivity Trends in New Zealand: A Sectoral and Cyclical Analysis: 1961/87*. NZ Institute of Economic Research, Research Monograph 48. Wellington.

Pickford, Michael. 1984. "Estimating Economies of Plant Scale in New Zealand

Manufacturing Industries Using Census Data." *New Zealand Economic Papers*, v 18.

Pinfield, Christopher. 1987. *Equity and Economic Policy*. Wellington: The Treasury. Processed.

Rayner, Tony and Ralph Lattimore. 1987. *The Timing and Sequencing of a Trade Liberalisation Policy: The Case of New Zealand*. Christchurch: Lincoln College.

Royal Commission on Social Policy. 1988. *Towards a Fair and Just Society*. Wellington: Government Printer.

Savage, John. 1986. *Economic Liberalisation and the Outlook for Manufacturing*. NZ Institute of Economic Research, Working Paper 86/33. Wellington.

——. 1988. *Internal Labour Markets and Adjustment: Labour Adjustment Within Firms*. NZ Institute of Economic Research, Research Monograph 45. Wellington.

——, editor. 1989. *Industry Rationalisation: Strategies and Constraints*. NZ Institute of Economic Research, Research Report. Wellington.

Snively, Suzanne. 1989. "Labour Markets and Social Policy: Reversing the Roles." In *The Influence of US Economics on New Zealand*. NZ Institute of Economic Research / NZ-US Educational Foundation, Research Monograph 42. Wellington.

Spencer, Grant and David Carey. 1988. *Financial Policy Reform: The New Zealand Experience 1984–87*. Reserve Bank of New Zealand, Discussion Paper G88/1. Wellington.

Staley, Heather. 1988. *Follow-up Survey of Manufacturers' Responses to Economic Policy Changes Following the 1984 General Election*. Department of Trade and Industry, Working Paper 7. Wellington.

Syntec Economic Services. 1988. *Industry Assistance Reform in NZ*. Institute of Economic Research, Report for the Ministry of Agriculture and Fisheries. Wellington.

Thompson, Mary Anne and Paul Tompkinson. 1987. *Tax Burden on New Zealand Exports Relative to Trading Partners*. NZ Institute of Economic Research, Research Report. Wellington.

Tyndall, Jo. 1988. "New Zealand's Objectives in the MTNs." Paper presented at a Trade In Services Conference, Department of Trade and Industry. Auckland.

Williams, Neil. 1988. *Some Sectoral Aspects of Disinflation in New Zealand with Particular Emphasis on Manufacturing*. NZ Institute of Economic Research, Research Report. Wellington.

Witt, Daniel. 1986. *The New Zealand Motor Car Industry After the Plan*. NZ Institute of Economic Research, Research Monograph 32. Wellington.

Wooding, Paul. 1987. "Liberalising the International Trade Regime." In Alan Bollard and Robert Buckle, editors, *Economic Liberalisation in New Zealand*, ch 5. Wellington: Allen & Unwin.

4

AUSTRALIA
Exchange Rate Variability and
Permanent Protection

Robert G. Gregory

The economic development and growth of Australia has been conditioned, more than for most countries, by its geography and natural
resource base. The vast land and mineral resources, exploited by capital-
intensive technologies, have provided the basis for the earlier and continuing prosperity of Australia's relatively small population of 16.5 million.
Immense distance and transport costs have been a natural barrier, and
historically Australia developed a large and diversified industrial structure to supply what is a predominantly urban populace. It then pursued
policies both to support and to adjust that industrial structure as ongoing reductions in transport and communications costs and the rise of
new nodes of industrial activity in the Pacific Basin have created new
opportunities and pressures for greater economic specialization.

Steady structural change and strong growth characterized the Australian economy during the 1950s and '60s. Employment growth averaged
2.5% per annum and unemployment rarely exceeded 2%. As the labor
force steadily moved out of rural employment into the service sector,
manufacturing maintained a 28% share of total employment. The 1970s
and early '80s were not so vigorous: employment growth in the '70s was
the lowest for any decade since the depression of the '30s, with manufacturing experiencing absolute declines in employment. The shift from

rural activities continued, however. Unemployment peaked at 10.3% in August 1983, and since then there are signs the economy may be returning to the pattern of structural change and faster growth of the '50s and '60s. The decline in manufacturing employment slowed, and unemployment began to fall—to around 6% in 1989. Tables 4.1 and 4.2 provide an overview; employment data are in Table 4.3.

Government sectoral policies have contributed and responded to these structural changes. In addition, Australia has a number of declining agricultural and secondary industries that have attracted intense policy

Table 4.1. Macroeconomic Overview

1967	1972	1977	1982	1984	1986	1987	
12	13	14	15	15	16	16	population (millions)
(billions of 1980 Australian dollars)							
69	94	107	120	127	137	142	real GDP at factor cost
(billions of current Australian dollars)							
24	42	91	164	202	246	277	GDP (gross domestic product)
3.5	6.2	14	24	30	39	45	exports[1]
4.0	5.0	15	30	35	46	49	imports[1]
(billions of current US dollars)							
3.4	6.3	13	21	23	22	25	exports[2]
3.9	5.0	13	27	26	26	29	imports[2]
112	116	115	110	91	70	66	US cents per $A[3]

1. Goods and non-factor services only. (See source, p 7.)
2. Customs basis; exports are FOB, imports are CIF. (See source, p 9.)
3. Annual average.
Source: The World Bank: World Tables, 1988–89, p 108–11.

Table 4.2. Selected Economic Indicators (percents)

1950s	1960s	1970s	1980s	Annual Average Rates of
5.0	6.7	3.9	3.6	real GDP growth
1.9	3.0	1.4	3.0	employment growth
2.0	1.6	3.7	6.7	unemployment
6.5	2.5	9.8	8.3	inflation

Decades are of fiscal years beginning July 1. Thus the 1950s is from 1949 July 1 through 1959 June 30. Data for the 1980s are the 9 years through 1988 June 30.
Source: Economic Round-up, 1989 October (Canberra: The Treasury).

Table 4.3. Labor Force and Employment (thousands and percents)

1970	1976	1980	1984	1987	1989	
5,608	5,889	6,676	7,067	7,675	8,197	labor force
60.0	61.6	61.0	59.9	61.4	62.7	participation rate (%)
93	106	394	505	602	469	unemployment
1.7	1.8	5.9	8.6	7.8	5.7	unemployment rate (%)
						major sectors
502	496	492	493	504	511	primary sector
1,364	1,382	1,240	1,141	1,151	1,236	manufacturing
470	503	486	423	486	601	construction
3,180	3,402	4,064	4,404	4,933	5,079	services
						selected industries
201	215	181	185	187	192	food, beverages, tobacco
57	58	38	38	37	34	textiles
118	114	87	84	83	88	garments, leather
84	91	90	92	95	109	wood, furniture
107	102	113	120	129	134	paper, printing
71	72	70	55	56	60	chemicals, petrochemicals
60	61	55	51	48	49	rubber, non-metals
104	98	98	80	79	76	base metals
127	126	108	108	116	128	fabricated metal products
199	183	182	141	141	150	other machinery & equipment
162	157	146	421	116	131	transport equipment

Sources: Australian Bureau of Statistics: *Labour Force Australia, Historical Summary 1966–1984* (1986, ABS Cat # 6204.0) and various subsequent issues of *Labour Force Australia* (ABS Cat # 6203.0).

interest. There are significant differences between the two groups. The adjustment problems of agricultural industries relate primarily to self-employed small-scale farmers whereas those for secondary industries relate more to potential job losses among wage and salary earners in urban conurbations. As rural sector employment declined, a number of industries attracted government assistance: dairying, sugar, apples, dried fruits (see IAC 1984–85 Annual Report). Something similar occurred when manufacturing began to decline. In this chapter, attention is confined to secondary industries as these are the largest beneficiaries of government assistance and the most vulnerable to import competition.

Although the government had begun to move towards lower tariffs during the early 1970s, this policy was reversed to some extent in 1975 when, in response to increased unemployment and imports of manufactured goods, import quotas were introduced in an attempt to protect employment in footwear, textiles, clothing, and motor vehicles. With the exception of motor vehicles, quotas are still in place. Protection for these quota industries has increased quite considerably, although general protection levels for secondary industry have fallen. Import quotas may have arrested some of the decline, but employment has continued to fall in quota industries and in all instances in 1989 was below 1973 levels.

In the first section, I describe the change in development policy from a protectionist strategy for secondary industry to a policy of lower tariffs. The change, which occurred within a few years in the early 1970s, has met with mixed success. The most obvious features have been uneven reductions of industry assistance and division of the manufacturing sector into two groups: those industries protected by tariffs and those protected by quotas. The tariff (non-quota) industries, which account for 80% of sectoral value added, have been subject to large tariff reductions without exceptional disruption of economic activity. The quota industries have experienced large increases in assistance and in this sense the policy to reduce protection throughout manufacturing and to create a more efficient and outward looking sector has failed. As a result, the dispersion of industry assistance has widened as successive governments have come to accept lower tariff benchmarks for tariff industries and higher benchmarks for quota industries.

In recognition of the quota industries' inability to compete against imports, Industry Plans have been developed to facilitate structural adjustment and a move towards lower assistance levels. They have not been a great success. The current Plans are designed to achieve by 1995 a tariff of 55% for clothing, 45% for footwear, and 35% for motor vehicles. These tariffs are high by OECD standards. The development, strengths, and weaknesses of the Plans are discussed in the second section.

Exchange rate and industry policy interrelationships are explored in the third section. To understand fully variations in industry assistance and the motivation for policy changes, it is important to appreciate the links between the import-competing manufacturing sector and the primary- producing export sector. Large export price changes generate considerable swings in the real exchange rate, so that the import-competing manufacturing sector loses competitiveness when export prices increase and the exchange rate appreciates, and gains competitiveness when export prices fall and the exchange rate devalues.

The exchange rate and competitiveness cycle has been an important factor in determining the short-run economic health of the manufacturing sector, the short-run level of industry assistance, the timing of policy changes, and the long-run target assistance levels. The manufacturing

Table 4.4. Distribution of Merchandise Trade (percents)

1967	1974	1981	1986	(Fiscal Years Ended June 30)
Exports				
67	51	46	39	rural products
6	13	32	39	metal ores and minerals
14	17	14	13	metal manufacturers, machinery
13	19	8	9	other
Imports				
38	38	35	26	food, fuels, basic materials, chemicals, textiles
43	41	44	50	metals and machinery
18	21	20	24	other

Source: Australian Bureau of Statistics: *Balance of Payments* (Cat # 5303.0), various issues.

sector has been subject to periods of deep pessimism each time the exchange rate appreciates substantially. This was especially so over the 1975–84 period, but following large devaluations during 1985 and 1986 a degree of optimism returned, only to be moderated by appreciations in the late '80s. To some extent other countries, such as the UK and US, have become aware much later than Australia of the impact large exchange rate changes have on manufacturing. The fourth section discusses adjustment and the labor market and concluding remarks are grouped together in the fifth section.[1]

THE EVOLUTION OF INDUSTRY POLICY

Australia is a relatively closed economy. Imports have varied between 10 and 18% of Gross Domestic Expenditure since the early 1960s. This is greater than for the US, but very much smaller than individual countries of Western Europe. Despite the relatively closed nature of the economy, trade policy has been of central concern throughout Australia's history, and foreign trade shocks have been the major source of economic instability.

In very broad terms the structure of international trade has not changed much this century (Table 4.4). Exports have been dominated by rural and mineral products. The manufacturing sector has always struggled

1. Overviews and histories of the Australian economy include Maddock and McLean (1987), Caves and Krause (1984), and Arndt and Corden (1963).

against foreign competition and 90% of imports are manufactured goods. With a relatively small population and without large export markets, the small domestic economy prevents achievement of manufacturing scale economies. The development of manufactured exports has been difficult because dominance of rural and mineral exports leads to cost structures that disadvantage manufacturing. (For the development of this argument, see Gregory 1976.)

Australia's great rural and mineral export industries—wool, gold, wheat and, since the 1960s, beef, coal, bauxite, and iron ore—have created considerable wealth and income. It has been estimated that at the beginning of this century Australian living standards were the highest in the world, 10 to 40% above the US and UK (Anderson and Garnaut 1987). Despite this success there has been a general desire on the part of Federal governments since 1901 to change the economic structure away from primary industries towards manufacturing. During the 1950s and '60s, for example, the usual policy was to respond positively to all protection requests and, by the late 1960s, the average nominal tariff was 24%. With the exception of the mid 1950s, when import quotas were widespread, this was the peak of industry protection, enabling Anderson and Garnaut (1987, p 6) to state, "by 1970 Australia was rivalled only by New Zealand as having the highest manufacturing tariffs among the industrial countries."

The desire to encourage manufacturing with tariffs and quotas can be traced to policy objectives that have always been thought to be important: the need to diversify exports, the need for population growth through immigration, and the desirability of a more equal distribution of income. It was believed by successive governments that industries protected against imports would grow, prosper, and export, giving rise to a strong and diversified economy with less reliance on primary products with volatile prices. Because Australian traditional export industries were increasingly becoming a small employer of labor, a larger manufacturing sector was seen as providing employment opportunities for immigrants. Finally, manufacturing protected by tariffs could pay high wages for unskilled labor and redistribute income away from large-scale primary producers.

These ideas, which have a long history in Australia, were widely accepted in policy-making circles and were rarely questioned. They were articulated most clearly in the 1965 "Report of the Committee of Economic Enquiry" (The Vernon Committee), which fully supported the policy of protecting manufacturing industry, subject to a more uniform distribution of industry assistance and reductions in very high tariffs. It said, in commenting on the Report of the Brigden Committee of 1929, which was concerned with similar issues:

The war of 1939–45 confirmed industry as an objective to be supported by appropriate policies and led to immigration as an unchallenged national policy. Therefore it is probably rather easier for us than for the Brigden Committee to dismiss free trade with no measures substituted for tariff protection as a thinkable alternative.

Time has simply pointed to the truth of one of the Brigden Committee conclusions, namely that expansion of rural enterprises under free trade, along with no change in policies designed to give the equivalent effect of tariff protection, would not have provided employment for a rapidly increasing population. (p 357)

The diversification of Australian industry in the senses of both an expanded manufacturing sector in relation to other sectors and of the addition of new industries to the manufacturing sector has been rapid in the past 30 years. We consider that the Tariff has been an important factor in this development. . . . [R]egardless of whether protection results in more or less income than might have been the case under a different system, most people will risk receiving less in order to enjoy the general social benefits of diversity. (p 361)

The Vernon Committee recommended that manufacturing be supported by a fairly uniform tariff of about 20 to 30%.

Just after the report was completed, the attitudes linking tariff protection and manufacturing development as essential ingredients in the processes of economic growth, export diversity, and income redistribution began to be modified. Firstly, there was some downgrading of the traditional policy objectives. The rapid growth of mineral exports during the late 1960s, and expected growth rates over the next decade, appeared to relieve the perennial balance of payments problems that had worried the Vernon Committee. (For an account of mining's development in the 1960s and early '70s, see Smith 1978.) The need to diversify the economy and encourage manufactured exports seemed less urgent. With the rapid growth of the service sector, it also appeared manufacturing jobs were no longer quite as necessary to maintain immigration. In addition, distributing income away from the agrarian sector had become less of an issue as its national income share fell after World War II.

Secondly, it was also being questioned whether manufacturing development behind tariffs and quotas would meet the traditional objectives. In the late 1960s the Tariff Board began to produce estimates of the average tariff level by industry and argued that the traditional development policy had failed. In its view, the Vernon Committee suggestion that "most people will risk receiving less in order to enjoy the general social benefits of diversity" understated the cost and overstated the benefits of the policy to encourage manufacturing.

The costs of protection did seem excessive. This can be illustrated by calculating the net subsidy equivalent of the tariff, which is the amount necessary to provide industry with the same assistance by subsidy as is provided by the effective tariff rate. For some industries, such as Clothing and Footwear, and Fabricated Metal products, the net subsidy equivalent in fiscal 1969 (ended June 30) was 81 and 91% of the average wage paid. If the only purpose was to provide a tariff to maintain employment in these industries, the subsidy required was very high, almost equal to the total wage bill.

It was also clear the old policy failed to generate large increases in manufactured exports, which were less than 7% of manufacturing turnover for fiscal 1969, and largely confined to the processing of foodstuffs and basic minerals. As was intended, the policy had probably created a larger and more diversified manufacturing sector than the free-trade alternative and, as a result, it was a larger employer of unskilled labor, but it had become excessively inward looking and fragmented with many small-scale plants. The gaps between Australian productivity levels and best practice overseas were not narrowing and many parts of manufacturing seemed to need ever-increasing levels of assistance.

In response to attitude changes and new mineral exports, which were generating considerable balance of payment surpluses and a strongly appreciating currency in the early 1970s, Australia seemed set for a new industry policy of lower tariffs. Reductions in protection had begun in an ad hoc way in the early '70s, and in July 1973 all tariffs were reduced by 25%. The policy change occurred quickly and by late 1973 the only outstanding issues were whether to pursue a target tariff level and over what period tariff reductions should be phased in. (The history of policy change is more complex than the brief outline given here; for fuller description, see Glezer 1982 and Anderson and Garnaut 1986.) There was little support for complete free trade and the new Labour Government seemed to be favoring tariff reductions to a benchmark of 25%. Table 4.5 provides data on the level of assistance provided by tariffs and quotas.

The new policy had two objectives. One was new, to lower the cost of protection by reducing high levels of industry assistance; and the other was old, to create a more outward looking manufacturing sector that could export and compete against imports. It was argued that lower tariffs would set resources free from inefficient industries so they could flow to efficient export industries that did not need protection. The

Table 4.5. Average Rates of Assistance, Manufacturing (percents)

1969	1974	1977	1981	1988	ASIC	Industry
Effective Rates						
16	18	16	9	5	21	food, beverages, and tobacco
43	35	51	54	68	23	textiles
97	64	138	204	183	24	clothing and footwear
26	16	18	14	18	25	wood, wood products, and furniture
52	38	30	26	16	26	paper & paper products, printing & publishing
31	25	22	14	12	27	chemical, petroleum & coal products
15	11	7	4	4	28	non-metallic mineral products
31	22	15	11	9	29	basic metal products
61	44	34	31	23	31	fabricated metal products
50	39	57	71	44	32	transport equipment
52	38	67	108	86		motor vehicles
43	29	22	21	23	33	other machinery & equipment
34	24	25	27	28	34	miscellaneous manufacturing
36	27	27	25	19		total manufacturing
Nominal Rates						
14	8	7	6	8	21	food, beverages, and tobacco
25	19	24	26	22	23	textiles
53	36	62	82	66	24	clothing and footwear
22	14	13	11	14	25	wood, wood products, and furniture
29	21	17	14	12	26	paper & paper products, printing & publishing
21	16	8	9	4	27	chemical, petroleum & coal products
12	8	5	4	3	28	non-metallic mineral products
14	10	7	6	5	29	basic metal products
38	27	22	19	16	31	fabricated metal products
34	26	30	45	22	32	transport equipment
35	26	32	54	33		motor vehicles
34	23	19	14	16	33	other machinery & equipment
30	21	20	20	19	34	miscellaneous manufacturing
24	17	15	16	11		total manufacturing

Includes tariffs and other forms of assistance such as the tariff-equivalent of any applicable quota. Data are for fiscal years ending June 30. For 1969–77, 1969 production weights are used; for 1977, 1975 weights; for 1988, 1987 weights.

ASIC is the Australian Standard Industrial Classification number.

Source: IAC 1985b and IAC *Annual Report* for 1978–79 and 1987–88.

Industries Assistance Commission (IAC) in its first Annual Report (1973) stated:

The approach which the Commission has proposed will involve a gradual reduction of levels of assistance which are relatively high. . . . The industries which will be encouraged by the approach to industry development as outlined are those with low levels of assistance, or no assistance at all. They will gain because the costs of some of their inputs will fall, their competitive position in the markets for labor and capital and their ability to export will improve. (p 22)

An Assessment of the New Industry Policy

The old policy had been successful in meeting some objectives. From World War II until the late 1960s manufacturing grew in relative terms and in fiscal 1969 it accounted for 27% of GDP and 28% of employment. The policy had created a large and diversified sector which was a substantial employer of unskilled immigrant labor. Furthermore, unskilled workers were better paid relative to average weekly earnings than their US and UK counterparts (Gregory, Anstie, and Klug 1987). The policy failures were that assistance costs seemed excessive, manufacturing exports had not done well, and there was little evidence industry would develop sufficiently to enable tariff reductions without considerable disruption.

The new policy has had some success but its impact on manufacturing has been disappointing. On the positive side the average of tariff rates has been about halved. On the negative side is a long list of disappointments, three of which warrant particular comment.

First, the manufacturing sector has not prospered. Its share of GDP and employment has shrunk to 17% and manufacturing employs onefifth fewer workers than wholesale and retail trade. Most OECD countries have experienced similar changes in manufacturing, but Australia is among those with the greatest decline. Of course, many economists have long argued there should be no target for the manufacturing share of GDP and, because the sector required high levels of industry assistance, the decline should be seen as a success. Nevertheless, when the new policy emerged, many had hoped manufacturing would do better.

Second, as might be expected in response to substantial tariff reductions, the decline has been associated with increased import competition. But the share of manufactured goods in total exports has not changed substantially and Australia has not shared the experience common among

OECD countries of import and export shares increasing for each manufacturing industry. The new policy of low tariffs has been as unsuccessful at generating manufacturing exports as the old policy of high tariffs was.

The third disappointment is that policy has become bifurcated, with the low-tariff strategy having been abandoned for a significant segment of manufacturing. During late 1974 imports increased rapidly, encouraged by the 25% tariff reduction, a strongly growing economy with excess demand, and an appreciated exchange rate. Unemployment moved sharply upwards and in early 1975 import quotas were put in place for industries troubled by foreign competition: textiles, clothing and footwear, and motor vehicles. As noted above, these are called quota industries. Table 4.6 compares the characteristics of quota and non-quota (or tariff) industries.

It was argued at the time that quotas were temporary. However, they remained until 1988 for Motor Vehicles and are still in place for Textiles, Clothing, and Footwear. For almost a decade, import shares of domestic consumption were kept constant and, as competitiveness deteriorated, the tariff equivalent of quotas increased in a spectacular fashion. The high point occurred around the mid-1980s when effective rates of protection (tariff equivalent) exceeded 200%. In the late 1980s, following large depreciations of the Australian dollar, quota values have fallen but many effective rates remain between 70 and 200%.

The uncompetitive nature of quota industries can also be illustrated by data other than high levels of industry assistance. Table 4.7 presents an international comparison of these industries' export-import ratios. Australian ratios are the lowest, indicating, among other things, the high level of Australian costs relative to other countries.

As a result of these disappointments, successive governments have come to accept long-run protection levels for quota industries greater than those prevailing at the beginning of the 1970s. One good point, however, is that quota industries have steadily declined. Despite the fact the net subsidy equivalent of most quotas now exceeds the average wage, employment has continued to fall. In the late 1960s quota industries accounted for 6% of GDP; in 1988, 3%. Consequently, the macro adjustment from further contraction should be small.

Outcomes for tariff industries, which now account for 84% of manufacturing value added, have been similar with one important and positive exception: the average effective tariff rate has been reduced from 34% in fiscal 1969 to 15% in fiscal 1988. Over the five years 1988–92 there are to be further reforms as high nominal tariffs on specific products are reduced to 15% in five equal steps, and tariffs greater than 10

Table 4.6. Characteristics of Quota and Non-Quota Industries
(percents, except as noted)

1969	1974	1977	1981	1987	
					imports as a percentage of market supply
23	29	32	33	41	quota
14	16	19	20	24	non-quota
					dutiable imports as a percentage of market supply[1]
11	16	20	18	na	quota
7	7	7	6	na	non-quota
					nominal tariff rate[2]
37	27	39	51	40	quota
24	16	13	11	11	non-quota
					effective rate of protection
63	46	85	122	167	quota
34	25	21	17	15	non-quota
					share of manufacturing value added
21	19	19	16	na	quota
79	81	81	84	na	non-quota
					employment index
100	99	82	75	68	quota
100	108	97	97	89	non-quota

Data are for fiscal years ending June 30 and, except for tariffs, are arithmetic averages of ASIC two-digit industries (listed in Table 4.5). Quota industries are Textiles (ASIC 23), Clothing and Footwear (24), and Motor Vehicles (3231), but except for tariffs, all of Transport Equipment (32) is included in quota-industry data because of aggregation in the sources.

1. Many items have no import duty because there is no domestic source or Australian producers are considered competitive enough not to have tariff protection. The presence of a tariff is thus a convenient proxy for an industry that would have trouble facing competition from duty-free imports.

2. Tariff rates are weighted by Australian production levels within ASIC two-digit industries.

na not available

Sources: IAC 1985a and IAC *Annual Report* for various years.

but less than 15% will be reduced to 10%. The first reductions took effect on 1 July 1988.[2]

The increase in import share for tariff industries during the 1970s and '80s has been substantial, rising from 14 to 24%, a relative increase almost the same as for quota industries. There has been an absolute fall

2. These tariff reductions should not pose any particular structural adjustment problems. First, the reductions are quite small relative to the large changes that have occurred

Table 4.7. Exports as a Percentage of Imports for Selected Countries

Textiles in 1982	Clothing in 1982	Passenger Vehicles in 1979	
14	2	5	Australia
78	70	395	France
114	38	328	West Germany
190	649	103	Italy
318	30	477	Japan
48	19	289	Sweden
61	56	40	United Kingdom
97	11	26	United States

Sources: clothing: IAC 1986 v 2; passenger vehicles: IAC 1981.

in employment of 11% over the period 1969–87. Yet the tariff reductions, increased import shares, and reduced employment have not been accompanied by the same lobbying intensity by tariff industries that successively increased assistance for quota industries.

Why has the government adhered to its policy for one group of industries, and is planning further tariff reductions, but has quickly abandoned the policy for the other? These are not easy questions to answer; the degree of unionization is similar across these industries and there is no systematic industry distribution across electorates that might fully explain exceptional lobbying power. (See Anderson and Garnaut 1987, p 93–97.)

I conjecture there are three possible answers, which are complementary. First, quota industries have always had a close connection with governments because they need assistance more and, as a result, have developed well-organized and adept lobby structures. The quota industries dominated the assistance process when it was accepted policy to give high tariff protection. For the Textile, Clothing, and Footwear industries there have been some 500 different reports on government assistance since the 1920s. For Motor Vehicles an efficient lobby structure developed in connection with local content schemes introduced in

---

in relative costs in response to exchange rate variations (which have not led to severe adjustment problems). Second, at the two-digit industrial classification level only 2 of 9 non-quota industries are protected by an average nominal tariff in excess of 15%. At the four-digit level, a classification which contains 146 industries, the only industries with nominal tariffs in excess of 25% (excluding various foodstuffs and the quota industries) are Beer (36%), Furniture (25%), and Batteries (30%).

the 1960s, which required close government and industry involvement and a myriad of continually changing regulations.

Second, increased imports directly and obviously reduce domestic sales for quota industries, as there is a high degree of substitution between imports and domestic products. For tariff industries, the relationship between import competition and domestic production is less direct. Many imports categorized as non-quota industries do not have close substitutes produced in Australia and are therefore not subject to a tariff. As a result, it is always more difficult for tariff industries to argue direct harm from increased imports.

Some evidence for the different substitutability between imports and domestic production for the two industry groups can be found in Table 4.6's data on dutiable imports as a percentage of market supply. Presence of a tariff can be used as a proxy for an industry that would have trouble facing competition from duty-free imports. For non-quota industries, import market share rose substantially—by 6 percentage points between 1969 and 1981 and a further 4 points in 1987—while there was essentially no change for those subject to tariff duties. All such duty-free imports can be regarded as not competing with domestic production.

Third, quota industries obtained increased assistance when governments were very concerned about unemployment increases and thus were more ready to agree to protection requests. (There was, until the late 1980s, a tradition in Australia of responding to imported unemployment—and all economic cycles are considered imported—by reducing import flows.) Furthermore, reliance on quotas has enabled assistance to increase without an explicit decision being taken. As argued earlier, attitudes seem to have changed and it is more difficult to obtain increased protection today. Despite protectionist pressure, since 1975 there have been no significant increases in assistance outside the quota industries.

THE INDUSTRY PLANS

Within a short time after 1975 it became obvious quotas could not be removed without considerable disruption to protected industries. In response, Industry Plans were developed after full consultation with industry and union representatives. The Plans usually involved immediate short-run increases in assistance, but the long-run objective was to improve industry performance and achieve lower assistance levels. The policy instruments for import restrictions were: quotas on specified imports at a base tariff rate; the allocation of some quotas by tender auction, resulting in a tariff payment in addition to the base rate; and additional imports, out of quota, at a very high tariff rate.

A full discussion of the Plans can be found in the 1987–88 Annual Report of the Industries Assistance Commission. Here I discuss the two major Plans—Clothing and Footwear, and Motor Vehicles—and focus on two aspects of their role in structural adjustment: strategies for trade liberalization, and interrelationships between trade liberalization and exchange rate changes.

The Clothing and Footwear Plan

Over the period fiscal 1969–75, the new industry policy allowed the import share to increase from 7.5% to 20.5%. Then, in response to the general employment downturn of 1975, quotas were introduced and they remain in place. The quotas consisted of a specified import volume and a base tariff—usually 50% for Clothing and 40% for Footwear. Most items also have specific duties, usually prohibitive, for out-of-quota imports. For the first five years, quotas were allocated free of charge and adjusted on an ad hoc basis every six months or so. Those who received free allocations could sell their quotas to other importers. Then, to enable the government to share in the profits created by the trade restriction, the Plans were amended so that an increasing share of the quotas were offered for sale by tender. Potential buyers bid for a one-year quota entitlement in terms of a tariff premium on top of the base tariff rate. The Plans provide that by 1992 all quotas will be sold.

For seven years (1975–81) the import share increased only marginally. In August 1980 the government announced the first seven-year plan, which was to apply from January 1982. The stated policy was to increase quotas so that all domestic market growth would be met by imports. There was no provision to reduce prohibitive out-of-quota duties. In June 1987, the 1989 Plan was announced. It reduced assistance by two mechanisms. First, quotas would continue to expand. Second, total duties on out-of-quota imports were set at around 134% and reduced in annual steps to a base tariff of 60% for Clothing and 50% for Footwear by 1996. The intention was to increase the import share by controlled quota growth, as in the past, but also to increase the proportion of imports paying out-of-quota duties. The latter adjustment mechanism is a very important change with significant implications for whether the Plan will survive intact. In May 1988 the Plan was revised to reach lower target tariffs of 55 and 45% in 1995.

Failure to increase the import share significantly for the first seven years, and strictly controlled import growth under the first Plan (1982–

88), resulted in quotas increasing in value. The extent became evident as soon as quotas were sold on a tender basis. In 1982, for example, quotas for Shirts and Blouses were sold at a premium of 36%, increasing the total tariff to 86%. By 1985, and despite import share increases, the premium increased to 105%, giving a total tariff of 155%. For Other Footwear in 1982 the tariff premium for a quota purchased by tender was 50% and the total tariff was 90%. By 1985, and despite import growth, the premium had increased to 126%, giving a total tariff of 166%. Large increases were quite general and by 1985 quotas for many items carried tariff premiums greater than the base tariff. After 1986, following a large exchange rate devaluation of 30%, many premiums fell to zero, indicating the role of exchange rate changes in determining quota values. Table 4.8 shows the base duty and tender sale premiums during 1982–89 for most of the items with quotas.

The 1989 Plan's provisions were developed in the two years after the large exchange rate devaluations of 1985 and 1986. It is readily apparent that quota removal and tariff levels of 45 to 55% by 1995 imply a different size industry depending on whether the real average exchange rate over the period approximates that before 1985 or the lower value of subsequent years. If exchange rate levels similar to 1982–85 prevail then, as the out-of-quota tariff is reduced, there is likely to be an import flood and very rapid rates of structural change of the local industry.

In recognition of this possibility the 1989 Plan includes safety net provisions. The Textile, Clothing and Footwear Development Authority is to review the operation of the Plan before 1992 and if, in its judgment, there is likely to be substantial and widespread contraction of industry production, it may suspend the Plan for up to 12 months. The government would regard an industry contraction of 15% value added over the period 1986 to 1995 as an unreasonable adjustment rate. This is only the same amount of decline as actually occurred in the shorter first Plan period (1982–88).

It seems very likely the 1989 Plan will not remain in place unless there are further large exchange rate devaluations, and the Textile, Clothing and Footwear Development Authority will probably intervene. A downsizing of the industry of only 15% along with planned reductions in tariffs from 134% to 45 and 55% seems incompatible unless the exchange rate is lower. If this judgment is correct then the key issue will be the speed at which the Authority acts and whether it will allow import quotas to be set at new, higher levels.

Table 4.8. Tender Sale Premiums for Quota Entitlements in
Textile, Clothing, and Footwear, 1982–89 (percents)

1982	1985	1987	1989	
				50% base duty rate categories
34	85	21	18	knitted or crocheted coats, jumpers, cardigans, sweaters, and the like; tube tops
36	105	97	na	shirts and blouses; knitted or crocheted tops
20	50	5	20	trousers, jeans, overalls
12	50	0	22	shorts and male swimwear
5	25	0	35	leather coats and jackets
25	83	20	0	women's, girls', and infants' swimwear
34	90	81	31	brassieres; corsets, girdles, etc
21	100	0	2	certain children's wear
10	32	2	0	garments of plastic material, rubber, etc
20	20	60	77	tights and pantyhose <4.4 tex
26	33	6	0	socks etc; tights and pantyhose >4.4 tex
40	32	65	31	other undergarments (all sexes and ages)
31	41	30	25	terry toweling, towels, babies' napkins, etc
				40% base duty rate categories
31	78	31	45	footwear with leather uppers or having a customs value over $11 per pair
50	126	30	20	other footwear
15	51	51	13	parts of footwear
20	16	20	22	bed linen, including quilt covers and ruffles
8	15	20	20	fabric suitable for use as bed sheeting and the like, or in the making up of bed linen[1]
30	56	23	40	woven fabrics of synthetic fibres

Items are arranged by tender category number (not shown) within base duty rate groupings. The tender premium is in addition to the base duty rate. Duty rate category numbers (not shown) are different than the tender category numbers.

1. Base duty rate is as low as 0% for some items in this tender category.

na not available

Sources: IAC *Annual Report* for 1986–87 and 1987–88, plus various Customs Notices and other information supplied by the Customs Service.

The Motor Vehicle Plan

Since World War II the Motor Vehicle industry has played a special part in Australia's development strategy. It has been seen as an engine for growth and a significant employer of immigrant labor. Industry plans have been designed to foster its development, to restrict imports, and to produce vehicles with high local content. The following short history is very simplified but it nevertheless illustrates the complex nature and many changes in the Plans. (For a fuller discussion see Gregory 1988.)

Successive Plans have been associated with a deterioration of efficiency. In 1960 the Australian tariff was 35%, not dissimilar to France, Japan and the United Kingdom. By 1988 other countries had reduced their tariff two-thirds or more. In Australia, industry assistance peaked in fiscal 1984 at about three times the 1960 tariff level. In 1988 the tariff stood at 45%, still above that of the early 1960s. (See Table 4.5 for the effective rate of assistance since 1969.)

From the late 1950s to the mid '60s the tariff was 35%, increasing to 45% in 1966 when the import share exceeded 7.5%. In July 1973 the tariff was reduced to 33.75% only to increase again to 45% in August 1974. In 1975 quotas were introduced to reduce the import share of the domestic market to 20%. Over the next 12 years the industry's competitive position deteriorated and the tariff equivalent of quotas increased in a spectacular fashion. In 1978 the base tariff paid on quota imports increased from 45% to 57.5%. Then, in November 1979, part of the quota allocation was sold by tender at an additional tariff of 50.5% giving a total duty of 95.5% (for quotas that were sold, the base tariff was 45%). In March 1980 another quota allocation was sold by tender at an additional tariff of 86.5%, making a total duty of 131.5%. In December 1980, perhaps embarrassed by the prices paid, the government announced quotas would no longer be sold but allocated by administrative rule and quota holders would pay a 57.5% tariff.

In December 1981, following two years of appreciating exchange rates, the Liberal Government announced an eight-year adjustment plan to begin in 1984. The key assistance measure was a tariff quota system with an out-of-quota tariff of 150% to be reduced in annual steps to reach 125% in 1991. The quota was fixed at 20% of the market. Thus, from 1973 to 1984 the tariff increased from 33.5 to 150% and government was prepared to accept a long-run tariff of 125%.

In May 1984 the new Labour Government announced a preliminary version of its Plan: quota imports were limited to 20% of the market and the out-of-quota tariff was set at 100% phased down to 57.5% by 1992. The long-run tariff was 67.5 percentage points less than that announced by the Liberal government three years earlier. In December 1984, some quotas were again subject to tender, leading to a total tariff of 94.5%, suggesting the tariff quotas of 125–150% favored by the previous Liberal Government were prohibitive but that a long-run tariff of 57.5% announced by the Labour Government would probably involve substantial import increases.

Circumstances changed during 1985, with the Australian dollar devaluing 30%. Because the yen had been appreciating, the devaluation against Japan was more substantial: 46% over the period June 1984 to June 1986. Motor vehicle sales had been depressed for a number of years and suddenly quotas were unfilled and high rates of assistance were not needed. For fiscal 1987 imports supplied 13% of the market, a low fraction for an OECD country.

In May 1988 the Labour Government announced another Plan: a tariff of 45% reducing to 35% by 1992, and all import quotas to be abolished immediately. The change over the 1982–88 period is extraordinary. In 1982 there were permanent quotas to keep imports to 20% of the market and a planned long-run out-of-quota tariff of 125%. Then suddenly in May 1988 it was announced, and agreed to by the industry, that major elements of the protection regime will be much weaker and indeed similar to that of two and a half decades earlier, before Japanese imports and before the industry began to experience difficult times. What led to these dramatic changes? Has the industry improved its efficiency?

At the beginning of the 1970s there were four major vehicle manufacturers. In 1989 there were five—Nissan, AMI (Toyota), Mitsubishi, Ford, and General Motors Holden (an affiliate of General Motors). In an industry where economies of scale are important, five producers sharing a market one-twentieth of the US must involve higher costs. The total Australian market is about 600,000 units per annum and the largest model production run is about 70,000. The minimum efficient scale of plant is usually estimated to be somewhere between 200 and 400 thousand.

Successive governments have always recognized the importance of scale economies but found it too difficult to create circumstances under which some manufacturers would leave. Indeed, major decisions to encourage Japanese companies in 1976 and 1980 to produce in Australia, and thus increase the number of producers, ensured that the situation would get worse. The 1988 Plan is a major breakthrough in that it attempts to tackle the problem of a lack of scale economies.

The Plan calls for amalgamations so that there are no more than three "manufacturing groups." If this is not achieved by 1992, the government will deny industry assistance to some manufacturers. In response, each manufacturer has increased investment, indicating their intention of not withdrawing. General Motors Holden and AMI (Toyota) have formed a joint venture to share all models, while Ford and Nissan have announced plans that include sharing production of a medium-sized vehicle.

In addition, following world trends, there have been moves towards sharing of facilities, commonality of components, and badge engineering (selling each other's models under a different name and with minor changes in body styling). The Plan also calls for producers to cease low-volume production of individual models and to produce fewer than six models in aggregate by 1992. Five low-volume models were scheduled to cease production by the end of 1989 and it appears amalgamations and model rationalization are proceeding.

Besides small production runs, another factor increasing production costs is a local content scheme. Imported components are subject to an average tariff of 25%, but during the late 1960s manufacturers agreed to source 95% of vehicle value from local component suppliers in return either for duty-free import of the remaining 5% of components or the equivalent value of vehicles. The local content protection offered to marginal components was very high. For example, in 1979 domestic components for a Toyota Corolla manufactured in Australia at 85% local content were between 1.5 and 6 times as costly as their Japanese counterparts, representing a price disadvantage ranging between 50 and 500% (IAC 1981). The inefficient production of components has led to higher tariffs for vehicle manufacturers.

Abolition of the local content scheme is a precondition for an efficient industry but successive governments have been reluctant to act. However, in response to the dramatic deterioration of competitiveness between 1975 and 1985 a series of adjustments have begun. The first local content liberalization occurred in 1975, going from 95% on a model basis to 85% defined on a company basis, thus enabling a range of local content for different vehicles and a further 10% of components to be sourced overseas.

The second change occurred in 1982 and linked local content reductions to scale economies. An export facilitation scheme was introduced allowing manufacturers to substitute export value for a further 7.5% local content or to import the equivalent in additional motor vehicles duty free. These provisions can improve competitiveness by scale economies as exports are added to production for the home market, by additional duty concessions if motor vehicles are imported duty free, or by cost reductions from substituting cheaper foreign components for high cost local equivalents. Of course, some of the improvement will be dissipated as Australian cost levels are generally above those of foreign competitors and unsubsidized exports would involve a loss.

The potential gains to firms from export facilitation may be quite considerable at the margin. For example, in December 1984 quotas were sold for a tariff equivalent of 94.5%. An export credit used to import a vehicle duty free under these circumstances could involve an export subsidy well over 50%. Furthermore, export facilitation has been recently extended to 17.5%, thus reducing the minimum local content to 67.5%.

Could it be argued that as a result of amalgamation, model rationalization, and local content changes, five producers will be able to operate efficiently in the small Australian market at a long-run tariff of 35%? The improvements at the margin may be significant but I very much doubt whether in aggregate they will be sufficient to offset the cost disadvantages of small-scale production. In almost every year since the advent of imported Japanese motor vehicles in the 1960s, either the import share or industry assistance has increased. The domestic industry has not yet improved its competitive position against other Australian industries. Relative to manufacturing as a whole, average wages in the industry remain in much the same relationship (higher) and current productivity levels are marginally lower than a decade and a half earlier.

It might be suggested, correctly, that the benefits from the 1988 Plan will accrue in the future. Furthermore, some encouragement might be drawn from the fact vehicle exports increased six-fold between 1984 and 1987 (rising from 0.4 to 3.0% of production) and imports fell to about half their earlier level. Over the first six months of 1989, however, circumstances have changed; exports were down (to 0.7% of production), imports were supplying 28% of the local market, the most popular imported model was Korean, and there had been considerable imports of second-hand Japanese vehicles, undercutting local Japanese producers. Although excess demand has contributed to these outcomes, industry competitiveness is deteriorating again and Korea may well be poised to destabilize the 1988 Plan, playing much the same role as Japanese producers in the early 1970s.

The improvement during 1985–88 and the 1989 deterioration in competitiveness are not the result of efficiency changes relative to other Australian industries, or changes in industry plans and government assistance. The changing circumstances are predominantly the result of exchange rate changes. The 1988 Plan was announced after three years of the lowest real exchange rate since quotas were introduced. The real effective exchange rate during May 1988 was at least 50% lower than the 1982 level when the Liberal government announced a long-run tariff of 125%, and 25% lower than in May 1984 when the Labour Government announced a long-run tariff of 57.5%. The exchange rate will be the key to the future and will determine whether the 1988 Plan remains in place.

Importance of the Exchange Rate

The key role of the exchange rate is supported in part by the fact that the histories of both Plan industries are so similar. Quotas were imposed at the same time, and the tariff equivalences increased to about 200% in fiscal 1984. The Industry Plans of 1982 reflect deteriorating competitiveness for both industries. Vehicle imports are restricted to 20% of the market by a combination of quotas and prohibitive out-of-quota tariffs of between 125 and 150%. Clothing and Footwear imports are also controlled by quotas and prohibitive out-of-quota tariffs. Then, following the large devaluations of 1985, both Plans are liberalized with the objective of achieving long-run tariff levels equal to or marginally above those prevailing before quotas were imposed in 1975. Quotas have been abolished for Motor Vehicle imports, and quotas for Clothing and Footwear will phase out by 1994. The common factor leading to these parallel variations in assistance and Industry Plans is real exchange rate changes.

EXCHANGE RATES AND INSTABILITY OF INDUSTRY PLANS

Over the last decade Australians have become increasingly conscious of the relationship between exchange rate changes and industry development. In the short run, exchange rate appreciations lead to lower import prices and increased import flows in much the same way as tariff reductions. Depreciations lead to higher import prices and reduced import flows in much the same way as tariff increases. Relative to the situation before floating exchange rates, tariffs do not provide stable short-run protection. If, for example, the tariff is 50%, then a 20% appreciation is equivalent, in terms of its immediate impact on import prices, to a 60% tariff reduction. If the tariff is 20%, a 20% appreciation is equivalent to tariff removal. In the longer term these equivalences would not apply, as exchange rate changes are likely to have a greater effect on the overall domestic price and cost level than a tariff change, but in the short run there is close association between tariff and exchange rate changes. (For a fuller discussion see Gregory and Martin 1976.)

Figure 4.1 plots the real effective exchange rate calculated as trade-weighted exchange rates adjusted for Australian and trading partner price levels. Real effective exchange rate variations are predominantly determined by nominal exchange rate changes and devaluations and appreciations consequently affect competitiveness. If the real effective exchange rate movements are representative of those faced by a typical

Figure 1. Indexes of Trade-Weighted Exchange Rates

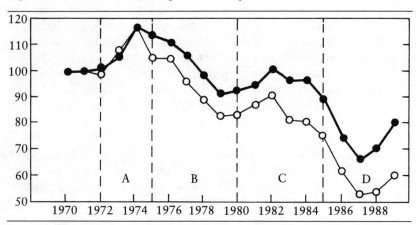

o   nominal rate   ● rate adjusted for consumer price index 1970 = 100. Annual data; 1989 data are through May.
Source: Economic Round-up, various issues (Canberra: The Treasury).

manufacturing industry, then long periods of high or low real exchange rates—relative to trend—will have a significant impact on industry structure. Relative to trend, periods A and C were times of high exchange rates, cheaper imports, and increased pressure on the import competing sector. B and D were periods of low exchange rates, more expensive imports, and reduced pressure on the import-competing sector.

It might be expected in periods such as A and C, when exchange rates are high and imports are increasing, that governments may react to industry pressure and increase assistance. Conversely, governments may seize the opportunity for tariff reductions in periods such as B and D when the exchange rate is low and import pressure on industry is abated. This behavior would suggest tariff policy has an important short-run component. Furthermore, where the long-run goal is to reduce tariffs, exchange rate variations may influence the speed and timing of reductions.

Although by no means exact, there has been a systematic relationship between exchange rate and tariff changes in Australia with the exception of the beginning of period A (1972–75). In these years, tariffs were reduced during a period of high exchange rates for reasons of internal economic management, as the new Labour Government attempted to increase market supplies to finance additional expenditure and moderate inflation. Then, in mid 1975 at the end of period A, just after the real effective exchange rate peaked, imports increased to record levels, and policy was reversed. Quotas were placed on Clothing, Footwear and Motor Vehicle imports, and tariff reductions for non-quota industries ceased. Protection increased during a period of high exchange rates.

Period B (1975–79) was a time of relatively low exchange rates and reduced pressure on import-competing industries. Widespread tariff reductions were adopted for non-quota industries in January 1977, following the 17.5% devaluation of November 1976. Period C (1980–85) had high exchange rates, the tariff equivalences of quotas increased and high long-run tariffs were announced for the quota industries. Period D (1985–88) saw the lowest exchange rates yet; vehicle quotas have been abolished, and the government announced a timetable for phasing out clothing and footwear quotas. In addition, a five-year plan to reduce tariffs to 10 and 15% was introduced for non-quota imports.

Will the historical relationship between assistance and exchange rate variations be maintained? Now that tariffs for non-quota industries are quite low, further tariff reductions will probably continue irrespective of exchange rate changes. However, my view for quota industries is that the close association between assistance and exchange rate changes will continue. It is very unlikely quota industries can significantly improve their performance against imports unless there is a substantial devaluation of the exchange rate. Relative price trends have been against quota industries over the last two decades and these trends are likely to continue. Consequently if the real exchange rate does not devalue there must be some doubt whether current Industry Plans can be maintained. Under these circumstances there will be large increases in imports and accelerated and perhaps politically unacceptable rates of structural change.

To illustrate this point further and document the relationship between competitiveness and exchange rates, I have analyzed domestic and import price data for quota industries for the period September 1981 to December 1988.

For Motor Vehicles between September 1981 and March 1985 there was little change in the relationship between the price series. This was the period when quotas were purchased at tariff rates of 94.5% and the Liberal Government announced a long-run out-of-quota tariff of 125%. Then, between mid-1985 and early 1986 large devaluations led to a more rapid rise in import prices relative to domestic prices, which meant competitive pressures eased, quotas lost value and were eventually removed. The largest gap between the two price series occurred in the fourth quarter of 1986. However, throughout 1987 domestic industry prices continued to rise while import prices fell, but the domestic advantage remained large. In May 1988, in response to the improved position of the industries over the previous three years, the tariff was reduced from 57.5% to 45%, import quotas were removed, and a long-run tariff of 35% announced.

Almost immediately after the May announcement, competitiveness changed as the exchange rate began to appreciate. According to my estimates, competitiveness at the end of 1988 is only marginally better than when quotas were sold at a premium tariff of 94.5%, yet the tariff is 45%. In the absence of significant devaluations, the speed and extent of adjustment required will be much greater than anticipated when the 1988 Plan was announced. The industry has yet to experience the full implications of these relative prices because of the import lag behind relative price changes and the current state of excess demand in the economy.

The Clothing and Footwear history is similar. The exchange rate devaluations of 1985 and 1986 increased import prices, but this advantage has now virtually disappeared. In 1987 the out-of-quota tariff of 134% provided protection similar to the quotas of fiscal 1985, but exchange rate and domestic price changes since then suggest a 134% tariff level, to be phased down to 45–55%, will be insufficient to prevent a large increase in imports at current exchange rates.

These data illustrate that general factors—those influencing the real exchange rate—play an important part in determining the short-run economic health of quota industries and it is variations in the exchange rate that has led to the cyclical variation in assistance needed to prevent imports increasing quickly.

An important contributor to exchange rate variations and therefore changes in assistance is the terms of trade. Australia is an exporter of primary products, basic metals, and fuels. As the price of these commodities varies over the world economic cycle, Australia's national income and exchange rate move in a parallel fashion. The cycle in the terms of trade generates a cycle in the exchange rate. Other factors are important —different stances of monetary policy and differential rates of growth of economic activity in Australia and abroad—but the association between the terms of trade and the exchange rate is close.

Consequently, the future outlook for import-competing manufacturing depends to a large extent on the terms of trade outlook. If the terms of trade improve further, this implies a marked exchange rate appreciation and increased pressure on quota industries. If they deteriorate, the exchange rate will devalue and import pressure on quota industries will ease. During the first half of 1989 the terms of trade were higher than at any other time since the mid 1970s. If current levels are maintained, and in the absence of a change in attitudes as to an acceptable rate of industry decline, it seems inevitable that the Industry Plans will be changed again.

There is greater optimism as to the long-run outlook for the terms of trade than a few years ago, the exchange rate is higher, and, as a corollary, there is greater pessimism as to the future of the quota industries. In 1988 and '89 the Australian economy experienced boom economic conditions and the impact of greater import flows on the quota industries is yet to be felt.

In the past it has been usual to focus on the close relationship between terms of trade and exchange rates. There is, however, a new feature of the economy that is beginning to emerge—a rapid increase in overseas debt. The overseas debt to GDP ratio for 1989 is just above 30% and it may rise to over 40% by 1991. Whether this will lead to large exchange rate devaluations in order to service that debt and improved opportunities for import-competing manufacturing remains to be seen.

ADJUSTMENT AND THE LABOR MARKET

Would lower tariffs, increased imports, and a substantial decline in quota industries present any special problems for the economy? Probably not. The industries have already been subject to considerable adjustment. During the 1968–88 period, employment increased 50% for the economy as a whole whereas quota industry employment fell 30%. Their employment share going from 6.3 to 3.0% suggests a further employment phasedown may not present any particular labor market problems. In each of the years 1984–88, the economy generated more new jobs than total employment in quota industries.

There are some features of the quota industries labor force that may add to adjustment costs, however. The Clothing and Footwear labor force is largely female, although it was only 3.5% of total female employment in fiscal 1988 (down from 4.2% in 1981). As a proportion of female full-time employment, the ratios are higher. In addition, manufacturing in general and quota industries in particular are large employers of low-skill immigrant labor, and the foreign born are concentrated in quota industries. Among Australian-born full-time employees in 1981, 24% of males and 14% of females were employed in manufacturing. But among Southern European born, the proportions were 49% of males and 61% of females. Table 4.9 shows the percentage of major ethnic groups in manufacturing and in footwear and clothing.

However, in terms of other labor market characteristics, the quota industries seem fairly typical. Employment is predominantly in the large cities. Job tenure (Table 4.10) is similar to the national average; and

Table 4.9. Distribution of Ethnic Groups by Industry Categories, 1981 (percentage of group's labor force employed in category)

Males		Females		
Clothing and Footwear	*All Manu- facturing*	*Clothing and Footwear*	*All Manu- facturing*	*Birthplace*
0.6	34	3.4	20	UK and Ireland
1.4	49	22.7	61	Southern Europe
1.1	40	10.7	34	rest of Europe
1.5	43	10.6	39	Asia
0.5	31	2.7	18	other
0.9	39	9.5	33	all overseas born
0.3	24	2.4	14	Australia
0.5	28	4.2	18	entire labour force

Source: Australia Census for 1981

Table 4.10. Distribution of Duration of Current Job, by Industry, 1985 (percents)

Less Than 1 Year			1–5 Years			More Than 5 Years			*Industry of Current Job*
M	F	All	M	F	All	M	F	All	
19	27	25	32	41	38	49	32	37	textiles, clothing, footwear
12	21	13	35	37	35	53	41	52	motor vehicles
18	27	20	35	40	36	47	34	44	manufacturing
21	26	23	37	43	39	43	31	38	all industries

Source: Australian Bureau of Statistics 1985 and unpublished data supplied by the ABS from its survey of labor mobility.

turnover is higher for women than men, suggesting that the concentration of female jobs in Clothing and Footwear may not be a particular problem. Greater labor mobility reduces the adjustment problem. The high degree of labor mobility in these industries is not confined to job changes within the industry.

Table 4.11 classifies those employed in their current job for less than 12 months by their previous labor market status. Approximately half were drawn from outside the labor force or from the unemployed, and half of the remaining half were previously employed in another industry.

Table 4.11. Persons Employed in Textiles, Clothing and Footwear for Less Than 12 Months, by Industry of Previous Employment

| | Industry of Previous Employment | | | Previously | |
Year[1]	TCF	Other	Total	not Employed	Total
1976	5,528	13,495	19,023	18,373	37,396
1981	6,626	9,715	16,341	11,155	27,496
1985	6,607	5,553	12,160	18,626	30,786

TCF = textiles, clothing, and footwear
1. Year ending in February
Source: IAC 1986

These data, which are typical of manufacturing as a whole, indicate quota industries have a high degree of labor turnover and, consequently, labor market adjustment should not be serious.

To ease any special problems that may arise, the Clothing and Footwear Plan contains adjustment measures to assist displaced workers who have been employed for 24 of the last 36 months. They are entitled to: income support of $100 per week for up to 12 months while they undertake vocational training (the average weekly male wage is around $500), wage subsidies for the first six months in full-time employment, and generous relocation assistance. To date, the scheme, which is available to men and women, is largely unused, an outcome quite common for retraining programs in Australia (as well as in the United States and in Europe other than Scandinavia).

CONCLUDING REMARKS

It is important to divide Australian manufacturing into two segments: quota industries—Clothing, Footwear and Motor Vehicles—and the remainder, which I have called tariff industries. The assistance regimes, policy stance, and recent history are very different for each segment.

For tariff industries the average tariff was halved between 1968 and 1988, and further reductions have been announced that will reduce the average to 5 or 6% by 1994. The reductions should be accomplished without too much difficulty and the policy should stay in place, irrespective of the economic environment. The GDP share for tariff industries has fallen from 21% in fiscal 1969 to 13% in fiscal 1988. The decline is likely to continue, but at a slower rate. If the real exchange rate falls, it is possible that GDP share will marginally increase and these industries may develop an export base.

For quota industries the assistance history has been quite different. During 1974–85 the assistance level at least doubled, as quotas imposed in 1975 increased in value. Following the large exchange rate devaluations of 1985 and 1986 the government adopted new Industry Plans. The 1988 Footwear and Clothing Plan involves quotas allocating all market growth to imports and reducing out-of-quota tariffs to levels that prevailed two decades earlier. Although long-run tariffs of 45 and 55% for Footwear and Clothing will be high by international standards, they are low relative to the early 1980s when tariff equivalences of quotas were probably of the order of 125–150%. The 1988 Motor Vehicle Plan replaces quotas by a 45% tariff, to be reduced to 35%. Again, although high by OECD standards, the tariff is low relative to the early 1980s when quotas were sold for tariff premiums of 95–125%.

If these Plans are realized, assistance levels will be more than halved relative to the average protection of 1975–84 and by 1994 they should be close to early 1970 levels when the new policy began, but with a substantially increased share of imports in domestic consumption. Although imports have increased market share in the 1970s and '80s, and therefore the social cost and inefficiency of resource allocation are less than they otherwise would be, no progress has been made in reducing high tariffs from the early 1970s base. Furthermore, assistance dispersion across manufacturing will have increased considerably. In fiscal 1969 the average tariff for quota industries was half-again the industry average, but the 1994 tariffs planned for quota industries will be around six or more times the manufacturing average.

Since 1975 quotas have protected the Clothing and Footwear, and Motor Vehicle Industries from large exchange rate and relative cost fluctuations. As a result, adjustments to exchange rate changes have been felt through variations in quota values, the tariff equivalent of quotas increasing when the exchange rate appreciates and decreasing when it devalues. The recent move away from quotas towards tariffs will change this situation and economic activity will become more responsive to exchange rate variations. The economic fortunes of these industries will be more variable as protection against imports will no longer automatically offset changes in relative costs. In addition, long-run tariffs announced in the 1988 Plans were decided during a period of exceptionally low exchange rates. It is likely therefore that governments will be subject to considerable pressure to increase assistance if real exchange rates appreciate and the import flows increase more than anticipated. As improved competitiveness from the 1985 devaluation is eroded, a choice will need to be made; either the industries will need to adapt to a faster rate of decline than originally envisaged or, if this is to

Table 4.12. Subsidy Equivalent of Industry Protection as a Percentage of the
Wage Bill

1969	1974	1977	1981	1987	
76	62	90	97	130	clothing and footwear
58	41	63	64	88	motor vehicles

Source: IAC 1985a, 1985b, and 1987–88 Annual Report.

be avoided, there will be a move back to quotas. In the absence of new
and large exchange rate devaluations, the choice of faster adjustment or
increased protection may be faced quite soon.

The government is prepared to allow further slow scaling down of
the Clothing and Footwear industries. This has been announced policy
since the early 1980s and some down-sizing has occurred. But the adjustment rate specified in the 1988 Plan is quite slow, no more than a
15% reduction of production over the 1986–95 period. Moreover, thus
far there has been no public recognition of the large reduction in the size
of the motor vehicle industry that may be implied by current assistance
levels. There is still some optimism that the industry can develop exports
and achieve economies of scale. Even with model rationalization, export
subsidies, a liberalized local content scheme, and amalgamations among
five producers, it seems to me that a 35% tariff is not compatible with a
local motor vehicle industry of the present size.

The cost of protecting these industries is very high. For example, the
protection offered the quota industries over the period fiscal 1977–88,
expressed in terms of net subsidy equivalent, has varied between 41 and
130% of the wage bill and is increasing for both industries (Table 4.12).
Given that not all jobs depend on tariff assistance, the protection offered
the extra employment by this subsidy is very much higher. These jobs
appear to have no special characteristics; the tariff is a high price to pay
for them.

BIBLIOGRAPHY

Anderson, Kym and Ross Garnaut. 1986. "The Political Economy of Manufac-
    turing Protection in Australia." In Christopher Findlay and Ross Garnaut,
    editors, The Political Economy of Manufacturing Protection: Experiences of
    ASEAN and Australia. Sydney: Allen & Unwin.
——. 1987. Australian Protectionism. Sydney: Allen & Unwin.
Arndt, HW and WM Corden, editors. 1963. The Australian Economy: A Vol-
    ume of Readings. Melbourne: Chesire.

Australian Bureau of Statistics. 1985. *Labour Mobility* (catalog # 6209.0). Canberra.

Automotive Industry Authority. 1987. *Report on the State of the Automotive Industry*. Canberra: Australian Government Publishing Service.

Brigden, J. B., D. B. Copeland, E. C. Dyason, J. F. Giblin, and C. H. Wickens. 1929. *The Australian Tariff: An Economic Inquiry*. Melbourne University Press.

Caves, Richard E. and Lawrence B. Krause, editors. 1984. *The Australian Economy, A View from the North*. Washington DC: The Brookings Institution.

GATT = General Agreement on Trade and Tariff. 1985. *International Trade 1984/85*. Geneva.

Glezer, Leon. 1982. *Tariff Politics: Australian Policy Making 1960–1980*. Melbourne University Press.

Gregory, Robert G. 1976. "Some Implications of the Growth of the Mining Sector." *Australian Journal of Agricultural Economics* 20(2): 71–79 (Aug).

——. 1988. "A Sad and Sorry Story: Industry Policy for the Australian Motor Vehicle Industry." In A. Michael Spencer and Heather A. Hazard, editors, *International Competitiveness*. Cambridge MA: Balinger.

—— and L.D. Martin. 1976. "An Analysis of Recent Relationships between Import Flows and Import Prices." *Economic Record* 52(137): 1–25 (Mar).

——, R. Anstie, and E. Klug. 1987. "Why Are Low Skilled Immigrants in the US Poorly Paid Relative to Their Australian Counterparts? Some of the Issues in the Context of the Australian Footwear, Clothing and Textile Industries." Processed.

IAC = Industries Assistance Commission. Publisher is Canberra: Australian Government Publishing Service.

—— . *Annual Report* for various years.

——. 1981. *Passenger Motor Vehicles and Components—Post-1984 Assistance Arrangements*. Report 267.

——. 1985a Mar. *Australian Trade Classified by Industry: 1968–69 to 1981–82*. Working Paper.

——. 1985b May. *Assistance to Manufacturing Industries in Australia, 1977–78 to 1982–83*.

——. 1986. *The Textile, Clothing and Footwear Industries*. Report 386.

Maddock, Rodney and Ian W. McLean, editors. 1987. *The Australian Economy in the Long Run*. Cambridge University Press.

Smith, Ben. 1978. "Australia's Minerals Production and Trade: Case Study of a Resource-Rich Developed Country." In Lawrence B. Krause and Hugh Patrick, editors, *Mineral Resources in the Pacific Area*. Papers and Proceedings of the Ninth Pacific Trade and Development Conference. Federal Reserve Bank of San Francisco.

Vernon, J., J. G. Crawford, P. H. Karmel, D. G. Molesworth, and K. B. Meyer. 1965. *Report of the Committee of Economic Enquiry*. Canberra: Commonwealth Government Printing Office.

5

SINGAPORE
Market-Led Adjustment in an Interventionist State

Pang Eng Fong

Since independence in 1965, Singapore has evolved rapidly from a regional entrepôt into a globally oriented manufacturing-service city-economy. Rapid economic growth has created new industries such as electronics, computers, and petrochemicals, and transformed old ones such as shipbuilding and repairing, financial services and communications. This chapter analyzes how changing internal and external conditions have affected the growth and adjustment of three important manufacturing industries—oil refining, shipbuilding and repair, and textiles and garments. It discusses the problems these three industries have faced, especially since the late 1970s, and how government trade and development policies have influenced their ability to deal with these problems.

The next section provides an overview of the development and structural change in Singapore's economy since 1960. This is followed by a discussion of the historical and policy context—including trade and

Participants of the Hong Kong and Honolulu Workshops on Structural Adjustment and Declining Industries, particularly Edward English, Paul Gorecki, Sahathavan Meyanathan, and Tzong-Biau Lin gave helpful comments on drafts of this chapter. The author is indebted most of all to Hugh Patrick, whose detailed and incisive comments he found invaluable in revising and expanding this paper. Cheong Boo Chin, Maria Tan, Phang Yew Huat, Geraldine Chen helped in collecting research and statistical materials.

exchange rate policy, government development strategies, and the role of the state. The third section introduces the three case studies, and their adjustment experience is compared in the seventh section. The chapter concludes with a discussion of the prospects and trade policy implications of Singapore's adjustment.

DEVELOPMENT AND STRUCTURAL CHANGE

Singapore's impressive economic achievements since 1960 are evident from Table 5.1. Singapore's GDP expanded by 9% a year in the 1960s and '70s, and 6% a year in the 1980s, despite two world recessions and a domestic recession in 1985–86. Domestic export growth of over 25% a year powered the economy's expansion. From 1960 to 1988, per capita GNP increased thirteen-fold—six-fold in real terms—to almost US$9,000. Except in 1974–75 and 1985–86, two periods of slow growth, full employment has prevailed since 1970. Sustained growth accompanied by low inflation contributed to a healthy balance of payments, while high savings (averaging over 30% of GNP) have boosted foreign reserves from S$3 billion in 1970 to S$33.3 billion in 1988. Singapore has only a small external debt because it relies on domestic savings and foreign direct investments, and not external loans, to finance domestic capital formation.

Structural change in the economy has accompanied rapid growth. As Table 5.2 shows, there was a diversification in the 1960s away from commerce (mostly entrepôt trade) and other services (largely personal and low value-added) into manufacturing. In the 1970s and '80s, the economy diversified further, with the expansion of financial and business services, and transport and communications. In 1988 financial and business services was the second largest sector after manufacturing. Commerce, the largest sector in 1960 with an almost one-third share of GDP, ranked a distant third in 1988.

Employment patterns reflect the sectoral composition of output (Table 5.3). Manufacturing is the largest employer, accounting for nearly a quarter of the work force. Though it ranks third in output, commerce is the second largest employer, with about a fifth of total employment. In 1973–80, employment expanded faster than did domestic labor force growth. Employment expansion during the period was fastest in financial and business services (13.6% a year). Since 1980, employment growth has moderated, partly because of slower economic growth and partly because rising wage costs have encouraged a more efficient use of labor.

Dramatic changes have occurred also within the manufacturing sector

Table 5.1. Selected Economic Indicators (in percents except as indicated)

1960	1970	1980	1985	1987	1988[a]	
1646	2074	2414	2558	2613	2647	population (000)
2.4	1.5	1.2	1.1	1.2	1.5	growth rate[1]
na	693	1116	1204	1252	1281	total labor force (000)
na	4.4	5.5	−8.1	5.7	5.4	employment growth rate[1]
4.9[b]	6.5	3.0	4.1	4.7	3.3	unemployment rate
na	57.7	62.7	62.2	62.7	62.9	labor force participation
1330	2825	9941	14828	15869	17673	per capital GNP ($S)
8.7	9.4	9.7	−1.6	8.8	11.0	GDP real growth rate[1]
na	4.3	5.7	3.6	4.5	4.4	productivity growth[1]
9	32	42	41	35	34	investment rate[2]
na	174	937	596	303	241	external public debt (in $S million)
						gross national saving
−52	1130	8282	16543	17605	20927	in $S million
na	19	34	41	40	42	as a percentage of GNP
na	60	81	101	116	122	as a percentage of gross fixed capital formation
1.2	5.6	8.5	0.5	0.5	1.5	change in consumer price index[1]
na	na	13.6	7.2	6.1	6.1	short term interest rate
						balance of payments (in $S million)
−244	−1751	−3346	−8	1163	3340	current account
140	565	1444	2942	2328	3344	overall balance
						growth rates of[1]
4.2	20.2	34.0	−4.0	23.1	30.0	total merchandise trade
4.8	19.9	33.9	−5.4	23.2	29.0	imports
3.5	20.6	34.0	−2.3	23.0	31.2	total exports
25.5	26.9	41.8	−1.4	21.9	26.8	domestic exports
−0.7	15.3	22.8	−3.7	25.2	39.2	re-exports
na	3.1	13.8	27.1	30.4	33.3	official foreign reserves (in $S billion)
na	3.09	2.14	2.20	2.11	2.01	$S per US$

1. Rates in the 1960s and '70s columns are annual averages for the decade; 1980–88 are year over year changes.
2. The investment rate is gross fixed capital formation as a percentage of GNP.
a. Data for 1988 are preliminary.
b. Data are for 1957.
Sources: Economic and Social Statistics of Singapore 1960–82; Singapore Yearbook of Statistics (various years); Economic Survey of Singapore (various years).

Table 5.2. Distribution of GDP by Industry
(at current market prices, in percents)

1960	1970	1973	1980	1985	1988[a]	
3.5	2.4	2.1	1.3	0.8	0.4	agriculture
0.3	0.3	0.3	0.3	0.3	0.1	quarrying
11.6	20.5	23.8	29.1	23.6	30.2	manufacturing
3.4	6.8	7.1	6.4	10.8	5.7	construction
2.3	6.8	2.1	2.2	2.0	2.4	utilities
33.5	28.3	27.2	21.7	17.0	18.4	commerce
13.6	10.8	11.1	14.0	13.4	13.8	transport & communications
11.5	14.3	15.1	19.6	27.1	27.3	financial & business services
17.5	13.3	11.0	9.3	12.0	10.9	other services
1.5	1.9	2.1	5.6	8.2	10.4	less imputed bank service charge
4.3	2.5	2.3	1.7	1.2	1.2	plus import duties
2150	5805	10205	25091	38924	48046	GDP (in S$ million)

a. Data for 1988 are preliminary.
Sources: Same as Table 5.1.

(Table 5.4). In the 1960s, most manufacturing firms produced for the domestic and regional markets, and the key industries were petroleum refining, food and beverage, and printing and publishing. In 1970 the three largest industries were petroleum and petroleum products (with 20% of manufacturing value-added), electrical machinery and electronic products (11%), and transport equipment (mostly shipbuilding and repair, 15%). In the 1970s and '80s, many industries, including wearing apparel, metal products, chemicals, electrical machinery, and electronics products, expanded rapidly, creating a more diversified manufacturing sector. The electronics industry expanded fastest, its growth sustained in the 1980s by the influx of computer and disk drive manufacturing firms. By 1986 it had become the largest industry, with a 32% share of manufacturing value-added, compared with 9% for transport equipment, the second largest industry, and 7% for petroleum and petroleum products. In 1988 the manufacturing sector exported over three-fifths of its output of S$55.4 billion.

There have also been significant changes in the pattern of manufacturing employment since 1970. All industries, except textiles and beverage, have increased their work force, though at vastly different rates. The electrical and electronics industry, the largest in terms of employment,

Table 5.3. Size and Growth of Employment by Industry

	Annual Growth (%)			Number of Workers (in thousands)				
	1973–80	1980–84	1985–88	1969	1973	1980	1985	1988[a]
agriculture	-2.8	-12.3	-9.6	2.4	21.4	17.0	8.1	5.4
quarrying	—	11.6	-24.0	1.7	1.1	1.1	2.4	0.8
manufacturing	6.9	-0.1	4.7	110.0	189.9	324.1	293.8	352.6
construction	4.3	6.7	-5.1	21.2	51.5	72.3	102.8	83.3
utilities	-3.4	1.6	0.3	13.1	11.2	8.5	7.7	7.8
commerce	2.0	2.9	1.1	89.3	196.1	229.8	271.1	283.6
transport and communications	3.1	0.4	0.7	38.2	93.7	119.9	117.0	120.2
financial & business services	13.6	4.9	2.6	na	28.7	79.4	100.7	111.4
other services	1.1	1.5	2.3	123.6[b]	205.8	224.6	248.3	271.6
not included elsewhere				—	0.2	0.4	2.4	1.8
total employment	3.8	1.8	1.8	399.5	799.6	1077.1	1154.3	1238.5

a. Data for 1988 are preliminary.
b. Other services includes financial and business services in 1969.
Sources: Same as Table 5.1

expanded its work force 530% in 1970–86 compared with less than 6% for food.

Singapore's export growth was led by foreign firms. Wholly owned foreign firms dominate Singapore's manufacturing sector. In 1986 they employed two-fifths of all manufacturing workers and accounted for two-thirds of Singapore's manufacturing exports. Wholly owned local firms employed one-third of all manufacturing workers but their share of manufacturing exports was only 11% (Table 5.5).

HISTORICAL AND POLICY CONTEXT

The transformation of Singapore's economy took place within a specific historical and policy context. Since 1959, Singapore's trade and development policies have changed in response to new conditions. So has the role of the government in the economy. An understanding of these changes is important for an analysis of the adjustment problems faced by the three industries that are the focus of this paper.

Trade Policy

Unlike many developing countries, Singapore has a long history of practicing free trade. Established by the British as a free port in 1819, it remained a classical laissez-faire economy with no protective trade barriers until 1959. In that year the free trade regime was modified when the first representative government under the People's Action Party came to power and began to pursue an industrialization strategy based on promoting import-substituting industries for a Malaysian common market. This strategy required infant industry tariff protection, which a UN Industrial Survey Mission recommended should be applied selectively so as not to damage Singapore's entrepôt trade.

In the first half of the 1960s, while Singapore awaited the formation of a customs union or common market with Malaysia, protective duties were imposed on only two product groups, soaps and detergents, and paints. It was only after separation from Malaysia in August 1965 that tariff and quota protection was rapidly extended to a large number of items. At its peak in 1969, protection covered over 300 items (Tay 1986, p 140). The rise in protection in the years immediately after independence was not a response to political or industry-group pressures but was an attempt to expand employment in local industries.

Because of Singapore's small domestic market, the government itself recognized that protection of local industries could not be a long-term solution to the island's serious economic problems of high unemployment and a stagnating entrepôt. From 1966 onwards, it encouraged the influx of labor-intensive manufacturing firms. This strategy was highly successful in expanding exports and creating new employment opportunities. From 1969 onwards, the government began removing protective tariffs. Because the protective tariffs had been low, no strong interest groups emerged to resist the shift to an export-oriented development strategy or the removal of tariffs. By 1980 all protection tariffs had been scrapped.

Preferences for locally assembled automobiles were also lifted. As a result, the tiny automobile assembly plant, which was first established in

Table 5.4. Major Manufacturing Industries, Selected Characteristics

IC[1]	Employment (thousands)				Value Added ($S million)			
	1970	1973	1980	1986	1970	1973	1980	1986
	140.5	198.6	285.3	246.7	1094	2541	8522	11900
311–12	9.1	9.4	10.1	9.6	76	128	262	408
313	2.3	2.7	2.7	2.3	35	38	109	190
321	7.1	14.1	9.7	2.7	24	122	158	78
322	10.0	20.9	27.2	24.8	24	82	266	362
341	2.6	3.4	4.3	3.2	12	32	94	188
342	7.0	7.7	12.1	13.1	51	93	278	536
351	0.8	1.3	2.1	3.1	16	51	109	504
352	3.1	3.4	4.3	4.3	34	89	304	764
353–54	2.2	3.1	3.3	3.4	210	363	1470	780
357	2.2	4.8	9.2	7.8	12	41	174	227
381	8.7	10.2	17.7	18.3	72	125	416	695
382	3.8	10.9	20.2	17.7	28	146	745	754
383	13.6[a]	14.9	15.9	14.8	127[a]	132	357	480
384	[a]	29.5	71.7	70.9	[a]	351	1669	3781
385	16.2	22.1	27.4	16.9	159	297	1060	1008

1. Singapore Industrial Codes
2. except footwear
3. and other chemical products
4. except machinery and equipment

the 1920s and at its peak produced fewer than 50 cars a day, could no longer compete with imports and had to close. Singapore thus became one of the few countries in the Asia-Pacific region without a protected automobile industry.

The importance of trade to Singapore's economy is clear from Table 5.6. The volume of total trade is greater than Singapore's GDP. In 1969 the ratio was 2.1 to 1. In the 1970s trade expanded faster than GDP, with the result that by 1980 the ratio stood at 3.8, one of the highest in the world. In the period 1969–88, total trade multiplied more than 16 times. Imports exceed exports, giving Singapore a merchandise

Output ($S million)				Direct Exports ($S million)				
1970	1973	1980	1986	1970	1973	1980	1986	
3891	7938	31658	37259	1523	4270	19173	24387	total
551	715	1662	2204	186	229	872	1424	food
66	80	249	365	13	21	56	61	beverage
84	314	489	239	40	206	238	82	textiles
86	289	848	1244	56	557	602	994	apparel[2]
36	85	273	427	6	12	24	159	paper and its products
98	168	550	971	13	33	99	193	printing and publishing
35	109	346	1506	5	28	179	867	industrial chemicals and gases
78	184	583	1299	22	90	353	985	paints, pharmaceuticals[3]
1222	1968	11520	6990	580	1244	7619	4539	petroleum and its products
35	108	498	591	10	25	107	94	plastic products
218	341	1235	1844	51	72	355	542	fabricated metal products[4]
75	338	1663	1683	17	199	1086	1023	non-electrical machinery
283[a]	333	974	1334	212[a]	242	585	950	electrical machinery
[a]	906	5344	11493	[a]	892	4508	10149	electronic products
330	636	2043	1794	98	221	969	1079	transport equipment

a. For 1970, electrical machinery (383) included electronic products
Sources: Singapore, Department of Statistics, *Report on the Census of Industrial Production* (1979 and 1980); and Economic Development Board, *Report on the Census of Industrial Production* (1986).

trade deficit. (This deficit is, however, more than offset by exports of services, with the result that Singapore has enjoyed balance of payments surpluses in most years since the early 1970s).

Exchange Rate Policy

At independence in 1965, Singapore adopted a fixed exchange rate system, pegging its currency to pound sterling because of historical ties to Britain. In 1967, when the pound sterling was devalued, the peg was changed to gold and the US dollar. But the fixed exchange rate system was maintained. In 1972, when sterling floated, the intervention currency was changed from pound sterling to the US dollar. In June 1973 the Monetary Authority of Singapore (MAS), the country's quasi-central bank, floated the Singapore dollar against an undisclosed trade-weighted basket of currencies. The shift to a managed floating system resulted in the appreciation of the Singapore dollar against many currencies because of Singapore's strong economic performance. However, this appreciation did not erode Singapore's international competitiveness in the 1970s because domestic operating costs, particularly wage costs, remained low.

Up to 1981 the exchange rate policy of MAS was to maintain a strong Singapore dollar, while ensuring sufficient liquidity to meet the needs of economic growth (MAS 1982, p 4). This meant attention was given mainly to meeting interest rate and money growth targets. In 1982 the MAS shifted from interest rate targeting to exchange rate targeting. The

Table 5.5. Manufacturing Sector Statistics, by Percentage of Local Ownership (in S$ millions except as noted)

	Local Ownership Percentage				
Total	100%	50–99%	1–49%	0%	
3449	2406	342	201	500	number of establishments
247	81	31	28	106	employment (thousands)
37259	7508	3936	5541	20274	output
11900	2486	1571	1090	6753	value added
37578	7583	3912	5530	20553	total sales
24387	2641	1930	3693	16123	direct exports
1746	289	113	176	1168	capital expenditures

Rubber processing and granite quarrying are excluded.
Source: Report on the Census of Industrial Production 1986, p 4 and 9 (Tables 4 and 9)

Table 5.6. External Trade (at current market prices, in S$ billions)

1969	1973	1980	1985	1986	1987	1988	
11.0	21.4	92.8	108.0	104.5	128.7	167.3	total trade
							exports
4.7	8.9	41.5	50.2	49.0	60.3	79.1	total
2.0	3.1	14.5	16.5	12.4	12.2	na	oil
2.7	5.9	26.9	33.7	36.6	48.1	na	non-oil
	4.4	25.8	32.6	32.1	39.1	49.6	domestic
	1.3	14.2	15.8	12.0	11.8	11.3	oil
	3.1	11.6	16.7	20.1	27.3	38.2	non-oil
	4.5	15.6	17.6	16.9	21.2	29.5	re-export
							imports
6.2	12.5	51.3	57.8	55.6	68.4	88.2	total
2.2	3.8	14.9	17.0	11.0	12.5	na	oil
4.0	8.7	36.5	40.8	44.6	55.9	na	non-oil
							ratio to GDP of
0.9	0.9	1.7	1.3	1.3	1.4	1.6	exports
1.2	1.2	2.1	1.5	1.5	1.6	1.8	imports

Sources: Singapore Yearbook of Statistics, 1987; Economic Survey of Singapore, various years.

shift resulted in a greater emphasis on the goal of price stability, a goal the government felt was crucial to the economic restructuring strategy it was pursuing. Since 1983 the thrust of exchange rate policy has been to balance the objective of domestic price stability with that of export competitiveness. Stable growth did not enter explicitly into the determination of the policy.

In 1980–85, the Singapore dollar appreciated 27.9% against an export-weighted basket of currencies. This appreciation eroded the international competitiveness of Singapore's exports and contributed, together with other external and internal factors, to the swift downturn of the economy in 1985. The Singapore dollar appreciated about 15% against the US dollar in 1985–89. But it has depreciated against the Japanese yen, Taiwan dollar, and Korean won. In consequence, Singapore's competitiveness against the other Asian newly industrializing economies (NIEs) has strengthened. In 1988, for example, manufacturing unit labor costs in US dollars rose by 11% compared with 16% in other Asian NIEs.

Development Strategies

Singapore's development strategies since 1959 may be divided into four distinct periods. In the inward-looking first period from 1959 to 1965, the emphasis was on the domestic market and on industries that could capitalize on Singapore's location and abundant labor. Shipbuilding and repairing and oil refining were among the industries the government (with the assistance of a United Nations team) singled out for special attention. During this phase, industrial progress was slow due to labor unrest and political uncertainty, but some diversification did occur. Besides the establishment of refineries, there was a flow of clothing firms from Hong Kong and Taiwan into Singapore. Also, the foundations were laid for an efficient public bureaucracy to implement the government's development policies.

In the second period, from 1966 to 1978, the government's overriding objective was to promote export manufacturing to diversify the economy and create employment opportunities. Its development strategy was to invite foreign firms to participate in the Singapore economy. This strategy succeeded because the government was able to ensure political stability and low labor costs at home, and because of favorable conditions abroad. During this period, manufacturing grew fastest, its annual output growth exceeding 20% in most years. In keeping with the rest of the manufacturing sector, oil refining, shipbuilding and repairing, and textiles and garments also enjoyed high growth rates.

The success of labor-intensive export industrialization and the appearance of full employment in the early 1970s led the government to promote higher value-added and less labor-intensive activities. But this upgrading policy was not followed through because of the 1974–75 worldwide recession, which slowed growth in Singapore and refocused policy attention on employment creation.

From 1974 to 1978, government policies were aimed at maintaining a high level of economic growth and full employment. Industrial restructuring was not the overriding policy objective. During this period, the economy continued to diversify with the expansion of the traded services sectors including transport and communications, finance and business services, and tourism. But dependence on foreign labor increased rapidly and productivity growth slowed.

The third period began in 1979 when the government, recognizing the need for industrial restructuring, introduced new policies to accelerate the island's transformation into a broad-based industrialized, high-income economy. Both internal and external factors made restructuring an urgent task. Internally, labor shortages were widespread and becoming more severe because of the diminishing pool of new labor force entrants. At the same time, there was a need to create more skilled (and better paying) jobs to meet the changing expectations of workers whose education and skill levels were rising. Externally, Singapore faced the threat of growing protectionism in developed countries and increasing supply-side competition from lower-cost producers.

Four major policies were introduced to restructure the economy. A wage correction policy was adopted to encourage employers to use labor more efficiently and introduce labor-saving equipment. The assumption underlying this policy was that wages had been over-restrained in the 1970s, leading to an under-pricing of labor and excessive demand for unskilled labor and increasing dependence on unskilled foreign labor. Skilled and professional foreign labor would continue to be welcomed, as it has been since the early 1960s.

New investment incentives for priority industries were introduced. Training and educational facilities for new labor force entrants and workers in industry were greatly expanded. And a vigorous program of investment promotion to attract high value-added industries were instituted. Of the four policies, only the wage correction (high wage) policy was really new. Its introduction reflected the heavy hand of the government in the labor market.

The wage correction policy was designed to restore wages to market-clearing levels, and was implemented by the National Wages Council, an influential tripartite body set up by the government in 1972 to recommend non-mandatory annual wage guidelines. It resulted in labor cost increases of about 20% a year in 1979–81. The policy achieved some of its objectives—employment growth slowed and productivity gains doubled to 5% annually compared to 2–3% in the 1970s (Pang 1988, p 213). But it was also a "blunt instrument" in that the recommended wage guidelines were not flexibly implemented to take account of industry and company differences in profitability and productivity (Lee 1987b, p 196; Pang 1988, p 211). Across-the-board application of the wage guidelines meant less profitable industries had to pay wage increases similar to those of more profitable industries. Shipbuilding and repairing and textiles and garments—two highly labor-intensive industries that faced strong international competition—were badly hurt. Oil refining was also affected, but to a much lesser extent because labor costs formed only a small proportion of total costs.

Though the wage correction policy ended in 1981, wages continued to rise strongly from 1982 to 1984 because of the tight labor market. They increased an average of 11% a year in 1982–84, nearly 3 percentage points above the average recommended wage guidelines for the same period. It could therefore be argued that it was excess labor demand aggravated by a policy of reducing the importation of unskilled foreign workers in 1982–83, not government-approved wage guidelines, that led wages to rise faster than productivity. Expectations of high wage increases generated during the wage correction period also made it difficult for employers to resist pressures for high wage increases in 1983–84.

The fourth and current phase of Singapore's development strategy began in 1985 when the economy plunged into an unexpectedly severe recession. Both external and internal factors contributed to the recession, which was deeper than the slowdown that affected other newly industrializing Asian economies. Externally, there was worldwide excess capacity in shipbuilding and a slump in the electronics—industries that account for a significant share of Singapore's manufacturing exports. The collapse in oil prices hurt regional oil-producing economies, which reduced their imports of Singapore's goods and services. It also had a serious impact on Singapore's large petroleum industry and reduced greatly the demand for oil rigs produced by Singapore's shipyards.

By itself weak external demand would have slowed Singapore's growth; combined with a number of internal factors, it triggered a sharp recession. Internal factors included the end of a construction boom (which had quickened growth in the early 1980s but led to excess supplies of all types of properties by the mid-1980s); a rising savings rate unmatched by a rise in productive investment (much of the savings went into property investment rather than into investment in machinery and equipment); and labor cost increases (which outpaced productivity gains, resulting in significant increases in unit labor cost) (Krause 1987a, p 10–14). More controversially, a tight monetary policy that squeezed liquidity and deterred consumption and domestic investment as well as the relative appreciation of the Singapore dollar (especially against the currencies of Singapore's competitors) may have made the recession worse than it otherwise would have been (Lee 1987a, p 155–61).

In 1985–86 the government introduced a package of cost-cutting measures to revive the economy and identified new directions for the economy. The policy changes to restore the economy's international competitiveness included a wage restraint policy (relaxed only in 1988), a 15 percentage point cut (from 25%) in the contribution of employers to the Central Provident Fund (a forced savings scheme), and reductions in fees charged by quasi-government bodies. (The CPF contribution of employes, also set at 25% in 1985, was not reduced because such a move, by raising domestic demand, would increase imports but would not make Singapore's exports more competitive.)

The recovery that followed the cost-cutting measures and policy changes in 1986 was patchy and uneven, with commerce, construction, and many manufacturing industries including oil refining and shipbuilding and repairing still weak. In 1987 the recovery became stronger and more broad-based because of robust external demand and rising domestic investments by local and foreign firms. In 1988, thanks to strong internal and external demand, GDP rose by 11.0% compared with 8.8% in 1987, 1.8% in 1986, and a negative 1.6% in 1985. Shipbuilding and repairing, and the garment industry registered strong growth rates, but not the petroleum industry, which contracted in 1987 because of weak demand for spot and contract oil processing arising from a narrowing price differential between crude oil and refined products. In 1988 the number of foreign workers, which had fallen to less than 100,000 in 1986, rose to 150,000 or 12% of the work force. All sectors, except construction, were buoyant.

Role of the State in the Economy

The government plays a highly interventionist role in Singapore's polity and economy. The People's Action Party, in power since self-rule began in 1959, wields complete political control through its near-exclusive representation in Parliament (it won all but one seat in the 1988 general elections), and its de facto control of the government bureaucracy, the labor movement (through the National Trades Union Congress, whose secretary-general is also a deputy prime minister), and local community organization. (For a detailed analysis of the role of the state in the economy, see Lim 1983, Lim and Pang 1986, p 75–85, and Lim and Associates 1987, p 59–67.)

From the beginning, and especially since 1965, the government has emphasized the importance of private enterprise and foreign investment to Singapore's industrial development. It affirmed the philosophy of economic freedom established in the colonial period but added selective and powerful state controls to guide the economy and society. There are only a few import tariffs, and most of these are aimed at deterring consumption of "luxury" items such as cigarettes, alcohol, and automobiles.

There are no officially designated protective duties on consumer or industrial goods. But there remains a 5% duty on garments imported from outside the ASEAN region. The duty, first imposed in the early 1960s, has been retained not to protect the local garment industry but so that Singapore can offer its ASEAN partners a preferential rate of 3.25%. There are few controls on private investment or enterprise, no anti-monopoly laws, no technology transfer controls, or compulsory registration of contracts. Firms do not have to meet minimum local content requirements, and they are free to import capital, remit profits, and repatriate capital.

The absence of regulation on the flow of capital and goods does not make Singapore a laissez-faire economy. The government participates in the economy through its ownership, control, or investments in 450 companies (excluding the subsidiaries of statutory boards), of which 65 are in the manufacturing sector (Krause 1987b, p 118). In 1984 government-associated companies employed 5% of the labor force. The government expects them to operate on a commercial basis: that is, to be efficient and make profits. Most do.

The government became involved in a wide range of manufacturing and service industries including oil refining, shipbuilding and repairing, and even textiles and garments, in the early 1960s. It felt involvement was vital in getting the industrialization process going. This view that it must play a catalytic and pivotal role in the economy held sway through the years of rapid growth until the recession of 1985–86 when for the first time the dominant and positive economic role of the state was seriously challenged. Since then, the government's revised view is that the private sector should become the engine for economic development (Ministry of Trade and Industry 1986, p 17).

The government has announced plans to divest itself of companies in which it has a minority share and does not need to be effectively in control. But it will continue to maintain a controlling interest in companies considered vital to the national interest, and also to invest in priority industries where private entrepreneurs do not have the will or capital to enter. The new strategy suggests that, while the government will try to encroach less on the private sector, it will continue to be heavily involved in the economy, particularly in providing the infrastructure and manpower needed to sustain the restructuring drive. So far, the government has divested part of its equity in only a small number of companies. It has no immediate plans to sell off any of its equity stake in the major shipyards (which are all listed on the Singapore Stock Exchange) or petroleum and petrochemical companies. Even if it does, the effect on the operations or future of these companies is likely to be small because they have always been run by professional managers.

State involvement in the economy is not limited to government-owned enterprises and statutory boards. The state exercises considerable leverage on the rest of the economy through its monetary, fiscal, exchange rate, wage and manpower policies as well as through its extensive and selective interventions in various factor markets, interventions that affect the performance and productivity of various industries in different ways. The government dominates the land market because it owns about two-thirds of all land in the country and houses over four-fifths of the population. Its periodic land sales influence the supply of land. As the major holder of domestic savings—channeled through the Central Provident Fund, Post Office Saving Bank, and DBS Bank (a large government-owned bank)—the government strongly influences developments in the domestic capital market.

Government intervention is particularly visible in the labor market.[1] In addition to regulations on labor organization and labor immigration (which affects the supply of labor available to industries), the government also influences wage changes in both the private and public sectors through the National Wages Council, a tripartite body set up in 1972 with representatives from employers, unions, and the public sector. Up to 1979, the Council recommended moderate wage increases, which were followed closely by most large employers. The guidelines facilitated wage negotiations and contributed to industrial peace. In the 1972–79 period, actual wage increases averaging 9.6% a year were close to the recommended annual wage increases of 9.1% (Lee 1987b, p 181).

From 1979 to 1984, wage increases were high because of reduced imports of unskilled foreign workers and strong labor demand aggravated by high wage expectations developed during the three years of wage correction policy (1979–81). In 1985 a wage restraint policy was implemented to restore the competitiveness of Singapore industry. This policy was discontinued only in 1988 when the economy had fully recovered from the recession. Since 1986, the government has also encouraged wage reform to increase wage and labor market flexibility. In 1988 the Council did not recommend quantitative wage guidelines, only that wage increases should be moderate, lag behind productivity gains, and take account of specific industry and company conditions.

Compared to its interventions in factor markets, government interventions in product markets are minimal. There are no direct controls

---

1. According to Brigadier-General Lee Hsien Loong, Singapore's Trade and Industry Minister and first son of Prime Minister Lee Kuan Yew, "because the market is imperfect, the Government cannot take a totally hands-off policy, passively accepting whatever the market settles to be the optimum wage level. It has the responsibility to try to look ahead, to influence expectations of both employers and unions, and to make provisions for future downturns which the market may on its own neglect" (*Straits Times*, 1988 November 25). In other words, the government must continue to be deeply involved in the wage determination process.

on private sector production. Restrictions on investment in the services sector are not to protect local firms, but for social, strategic, and other reasons.

ADJUSTMENT EXPERIENCES OF THREE INDUSTRIES

Of the three industries reviewed in this chapter, oil refining is the largest in terms of output and is the most capital-intensive. It expanded in the early 1960s when multinational oil firms began commissioning regional refineries to serve new growth markets. Singapore was chosen to serve the growing South East Asian market because of its strategic location and efficient port facilities. In contrast to oil refining, shipbuilding and repairing is a much older industry, with roots going back to the last century, and so has a long history of adjusting to changes in local and international conditions. A land- and labor-intensive industry, its comparative advantage, like that of oil refining, derives from Singapore's geography.

These two adjuncts of Singapore's historic entrepôt role were outward-looking from the beginning. In contrast, textiles and garments started as a domestically oriented industry, becoming export-oriented only after Hong Kong and Taiwanese firms came to Singapore to circumvent quota restrictions imposed on their home countries. Today, perhaps as much as half the output of the industry is produced by firms that are majority or wholly foreign-owned. Textiles and garments is an internationally regulated industry. International and bilateral negotiations under the Multi-Fiber Arrangement (MFA) determine the market access of Singapore firms to industrial countries.

In the 1960s and '70s, all three industries expanded rapidly, oil refining because of the fast-growing South East Asian region, shipbuilding and repairing in part because of the boom in tanker trade and the rising worldwide demand for oil rigs, and textiles and garments because of expanding market access to industrial countries except Japan (which, until 1987 when a strong yen led Japan to greatly increase its imports from developing Asia, was a difficult market for Singapore as well as other countries to penetrate). In the early 1980s, however, all three industries began, for different reasons, to encounter serious problems. Weakening external demand—the result of low oil prices and increasing competition from new refineries in Indonesia and Malaysia—created excess capacity in oil refining. High domestic costs and a strong Singapore dollar blunted the international competitiveness of shipbuilding and repairing at a time when the industry all over the world was suffering from excess capacity.

In the case of textiles and garments, there was no sudden decline in external demand, but export growth slowed because of high operating costs in Singapore and growing competition from new and low-cost suppliers including China and Thailand. By 1985, the year Singapore's economy contracted for the first time in two decades, all three industries were in deep trouble as output, exports, and employment fell to their lowest levels since 1979. With the recovery of the economy since mid-1986—a recovery that owes as much to domestic cost-cutting measures as to improving world and regional economic conditions—all three industries have increased their international competitiveness, though to different degrees. Their swift recovery suggests some of their problems are cyclical in origin. In the context of this book, textiles and garments, and shipbuilding and oil rigs, share many characteristics of declining industries. Ship repair and oil refining are merely troubled.

TEXTILES AND GARMENTS

Textiles and garments have different characteristics, market performance, and adjustment experiences. Nonetheless, they are generally treated together, and I do so here. The more capital-intensive segment, textiles, peaked in 1980 when it had 99 firms and an output of S$488 million (Table 5.7). In 1980–84, textile output shrank by an average of 9.2% a year, in contrast to the 1970s when it expanded by 20.5% a year. It fell further in 1985 (to S$193 million) before recovering in 1986 (to S$239 million, still below the pre-recession 1984 level and only half the peak output in 1980). Despite some improvement since 1986, textiles remains a problem industry with an uncertain future. (This section uses materials from Pang 1986; statistics are from Singapore's Census of Industrial Production.)

In contrast to textiles, garment firms are more labor-intensive and have performed much better (Table 5.8). Output increased by 25.9% annually in the 1970s and continued to grow in 1980–84, but at a much slower pace (8.3% a year). Output shrank slightly in 1985 due to weak external demand and declining competitiveness. In 1986 it recovered strongly, reaching an all-time high of S$1.3 billion. Rising demand in major industrial-country markets and an improvement in the industry's competitiveness due to cost-cutting measures and the depreciation of the Singapore dollar against major currencies were the key factors behind the recovery. After declining steadily since 1982, the number of garment firms jumped in 1986 to an all-time high of 447. This contrasts with textiles, which saw an increase of only three firms in 1986.

The relative position of textiles and garments has changed over time.

Table 5.7. Textile Industry, 1975–86

1970	1973	1978	1980	1983	1986	
49	68	80	99	87	65	number of firms
84	314	353	489	272	239	output (S$ million)
24	122	115	158	94	78	value added (S$ million)
						employment
7.1	14.1	9.8	9.7	4.6	2.3	total (thousands)
144	207	122	98	53	35	per firm
						per worker (S$ thousand)
1.9	3.1	5.5	6.3	10.6	12.3	remuneration
3.3	8.6	11.8	16.2	20.3	29.2	value added
						exports
41	206	192	238	112	82	total (S$ million)
50	69	53	50	40	34	as a percentage of sales
2.0	4.3	1.5	1.2	0.5	0.3	as a percentage of manu-factured exports

1973 and 1978 are turning points in employment trend. Employment rose slightly in 1979 and has declined every year since. 1980 was the peak for output and the number of firms; 1985 was an output trough.

Source: *Report on the Census of Industrial Production* (various years) and *Economic Survey of Singapore* (1987)

Until the mid-1970s, textile output exceeded that of garments. Since then, however, garment firms have grown much faster than textile firms. In 1986 the output of garment firms was more than four times that of textile firms. Their share of total manufacturing exports has hovered around 3% since the mid-1970s while that of textiles has fallen steadily from around 2% in the mid-1970s to 0.3% in 1986. In 1980–86, textile exports fell absolutely, but garment exports rose, though at a much slower pace than in the 1970s. This suggests garment firms are still holding their own in export markets whereas textile firms have lost much of their competitive edge.

Two factors contributed to the swift decline of the textile industry from the late 1970s. The first factor is the inability of the industry to compete in major markets against not only other developing country producers but also developed country producers. Many textile firms in Singapore were too small to enjoy scale economies. Others could not employ enough local workers at the going wage rate or were not allowed to bring in enough foreign workers to operate a third shift, which is

Table 5.8. Garment Industry, 1970–86

1970	1973	1975	1979	1983	1986	
162	205	252	364	391	447	number of firms
86	289	286	736	939	1316	output (S$ million)
24	82	92	230	333	385	value added (S$ million)
						employment
10.0	20.9	18.0	29.3	27.2	26.3	total (thousands)
62	102	71	80	70	59	per firm
						per worker (S$ thousand)
1.6	2.3	2.9	4.6	7.8	8.9	remuneration
2.4	3.9	5.1	7.9	12.2	14.6	value added
						exports
56	227	198	528	649	994	total (S$ million)
65	79	69	72	70	80	as a percentage of sales
2.7	4.7	2.6	3.1	2.8	4.1	as a percentage of manu- factured exports

1973 was a peak year for employment and output. Output and value added fell in 1974 and have risen every year since, except 1985. 1975 was an employment trough. 1979 was the peak for employment; the decline since has not been steady.

Source: Report on the Census of Industrial Production (various years) and *Economic Survey of Singapore* (1987)

essential for operating efficiency. They could have raised wages but did not for fear of setting off a competitive wage spiral with other employers, such as those in the electronics and service industries, which were also short of female workers. The second factor was the rapid increase in domestic operating costs, including government charges and mandatory add-on labor costs, which hurt the industry's competitiveness.

The textile and garment industry is a major employer of labor, particularly female operators. Employment in the industry rose rapidly from 1,300 in 1960 to a peak of 39,300 in 1979, the year the government introduced policies to encourage employers to use less labor and more machinery. As an established industry, textiles and garments has a much higher proportion of workers over 30 years old than other labor-intensive industries like disk drives (which is the largest employer of female labor in the manufacturing sector). Because of this, mean wages in textiles and garments are higher than those in other industries, even though starting wages are lower.

From 1979 to 1985, employment in textile and garment firms shrank by nearly a third to 27,500. Most of the shrinkage took place in textiles, where employment plunged from 10,100 in 1979 to 3,100 in 1985. This shrinkage took place smoothly. Local workers who left or were laid off found jobs easily in other sectors. Laid-off foreign workers were repatriated. There was consequently no demand by workers to preserve employment. Saving specific types of jobs was also not a priority concern of unions, which have a close relationship with the ruling party and support the government's restructuring strategy. Firms did not ask for government protection because their problems arose from weak external demand, not import competition.

With economic recovery since 1986, employment in the textile and garment industry has risen to around 30,000—still far below the peak in 1979. About a third of the workers laid off after 1979 were foreigners who had to leave Singapore when their employment contracts were terminated. Of the rest, most found new jobs in other manufacturing industries, especially electronics, and the commerce sector. In 1985, some of the 2,000 workers laid off by textile and garment firms became unemployed but only for a short period because of the speedy recovery of the economy from the recession. Laid off workers were paid compensation by their employers according to their length of service, but they received no unemployment payment from the government.

Except in 1985, the industry, although shedding labor overall, has been chronically short of local labor and highly dependent on foreign labor. In 1987 the industry reportedly had over 3,000 vacancies. Foreigners, mostly from Malaysia, make up 45% of the 30,000 workers in the industry (*Business Times*, 1988 November 28). The industry cannot recruit many more foreign workers because the government does not permit any firm to have a work force that is more than 50% foreign.

There are three reasons for the persistent labor shortage in the textile and garment industry. First, the industry is widely perceived to be a sunset industry whose days are numbered in an economy emphasizing high value-added activities. This perception has affected the industry's ability to attract and retain new workers. Second, because of the slow rate of labor force growth, there has been a general shortage of unskilled local labor. Textile and garment firms offer less attractive starting wages and working conditions than other industries such as electronics that also require large numbers of female operators. In consequence, they face more severe labor shortages. They cannot raise wages to attract local workers from other sectors because that would only increase production costs and make them less competitive internationally. Profit margins are already slim, averaging 2–3% of sales. (There are no published profit data on the industry. This estimate was provided by Paul Ho, manager of the Textile and Garment Manufacturers' Association of Singapore Training Center in an interview on 1988 November 15.)

Third, the industry has been unable to recruit enough foreign workers because of the government's policy to reduce Singapore's dependence on unskilled foreign labor. In November 1988 the government, in an effort to dampen the growing demand for foreign workers, reduced the maximum permitted proportion of foreign workers in a firm's work force from 50% to 40%. It also announced increases in the levy employers must pay the government for importing foreign workers from S$170 in 1988 to S$220 from January 1989, and S$250 from June 1989. This levy, first introduced in 1986, is designed to ensure that the total cost to the employer of hiring foreign labor is similar to that of hiring local workers. The two policy changes will raise the cost of foreign labor and exacerbate the labor problems of textile and garment firms.

Adjustment Mechanisms and Their Effectiveness

The textile and garment industry has adjusted to the chronic labor shortage and rising domestic costs in a number of ways. It has invested in new machinery and equipment, both to save labor and to increase productivity. But productivity growth was not fast enough to offset the significant rise in labor costs in 1980–84. As a result, unit labor costs rose by over 5% a year, blunting the industry's competitive edge and causing many marginal firms to leave the industry. Some textile firms that left the industry sold their machinery and equipment to other developing countries including China and Sri Lanka. Other failed firms had their assets disposed of by official receivers. There is no evidence to suggest owners of exiting textile and garment firms enter other industries in Singapore.

A second way textile and garment firms have adjusted is to move into new and higher value-added product lines. They also attempted market diversification but this strategy was less than successful in the first half of the 1980s because of their growing dependence on the North American market. Since 1986, exports to Japan and EEC have risen greatly, in part because of the sharp depreciation of the Singapore dollar against the Japanese yen and major European currencies.

A third adjustment mechanism is relocation. Since the late 1970s, more than thirty, mostly large, firms have relocated all or part of their operations to neighboring countries, especially Malaysia. The larger ones have integrated their operations regionally, farming out to subsidiaries in lower-cost countries highly labor-intensive activities while retaining high value-added work for their Singapore plants. A few garment firms moved most of their production to Johore, the Malaysian state closest to Singapore, but handled marketing, finance, and administration out of Singapore.

The government encourages regional integration by textile and garment firms (as well as other labor-intensive firms), but three factors have slowed the process. First, neighboring countries may not have sufficient quotas, particularly for the "hot" profitable items exported to the important EEC and US markets, and so the amount of production that can be transferred to them is limited. Second, if some processes are carried out in other countries and the semi-finished products imported into Singapore to be finished, there may be problems satisfying "label of origin" requirements. Finally, the process is easier for garment firms than for textile firms, which are more capital-intensive and cannot relocate without incurring huge costs.

Impact of Government Policies

Two types of government policies have influenced the adjustment of the textile and garment industry to changing domestic and international conditions. The first are general policies such as tax incentives, investment allowances, manpower training grants, financial assistance for small firms, interest-free grants for mechanization and computerization, and the phasing out of unskilled foreign labor. In other words, policies aimed at quickening restructuring in all industries. Of these general policies, the foreign labor policy and investment incentives have had the greatest influence on adjustments by textile and garment firms.

The foreign labor policy exacerbated the staffing problems of textile and garment firms. While it forced them to upgrade and mechanize, it also increased their operational problems and affected their viability. Because they are only marginally profitable and cannot raise wages sharply to recruit the local labor they need, textile firms cannot operate a third shift and so cannot fully utilize the costly machinery and equipment they had bought to become more efficient. Some garment firms cannot use up their quota allocations for highly demanded items because they cannot hire enough workers at the going wage rate. They could raise entry wages to attract enough workers but this increase would have to be extended to other workers. Since their profit margins are thin, the resulting increase in their total wage bill would likely exceed the additional income generated by expanding employment.

Generous investment incentives (which are given to all industries) have encouraged textile and garment firms, especially the larger ones, to invest heavily in machinery and equipment. The increased capital spending raised productivity, but it also led to unexpected results. Many garment firms discovered that automation and mechanization were cost-effective only for standardized, large-volume products. They could not adapt the machines easily to produce high-value fashion items that require much hand work. As a result, many firms were stuck with expensive, underutilized machines when they began to concentrate on the production of high value-added items.

Of the specific policies aimed at the textile and garment industry, the most important is the system of quota allocation, which the government employs as its major policy instrument to upgrade the industry. The Trade Development Board, a state agency, administers the quotas allocated to Singapore under various bilateral agreements negotiated under the Multi-Fiber Arrangement (MFA). Its Quota Allocation Committee decides on the amount of quotas to be given to each manufacturer. Not all quota allocations are taken up every year. There is excess demand for some categories of garments (eg, shirts) but not enough demand for other categories (eg, underwear). The quota system is very complicated. Certain items have specific, absolute limits. These tend to be things that producers want to make. Other quota limits are more flexible.

Up to 1987, the Committee decided on the basic and supplementary quotas for each manufacturer. Basic quotas were allocated according to the manufacturer's past performance, a system favoring existing firms, especially the large ones. Supplementary quotas were given firms that had diversified their markets or had low unit prices. Only about 10% of the supplementary quotas were allocated to newcomers. Quotas were not auctioned, as they are in Hong Kong and South Korea. Unutilized quotas had to be surrendered to the Board. The quota allocation system was effective in inducing many firms to upgrade, but its precise impact is hard to assess because other factors, including the availability of investment incentives and labor, also influenced the restructuring decisions of firms.

In any case, it became clear in early 1987 that the Board was not completely satisfied with the quota allocation system. In June 1987 it proposed to replace the system of allocating quotas according to the past performance of firms with a tender system. Its objective was to increase competition and efficiency in the industry by enabling new firms to compete away the rents enjoyed by established firms (*Straits Times,* 1987 September 1). After lengthy discussions with manufacturers fearing a full-fledged tender system would cause uncertainty, fuel speculation, and raise production costs, the Board agreed to a partial auction system, effective from 1988, in which only 25% of the quotas would be tendered (*Business Times,* 1987 December 31). The remaining 75% would continue to be allocated, but a levy of 0.5% would be imposed on the average export price of each quota category allocated according to past performance. Receipts from the levy will be used to promote the industry and finance anti-protectionist lobbying activities.

Whether the new system will facilitate the adjustment of the textile and garment industry to new market conditions is unclear. In the first quota auction in 1988, many producers made high bids to ensure they retained their quota allocations. This suggests they have been enjoying rents and the government has now appropriated part of these rents. The bid system has raised costs and made some firms less competitive compared with firms in other countries.

Other measures directed specifically at the textile and garment industry include financial support for training and trade promotion activities. The industry's training center benefits from government skill-training grants. Government agencies have also provided support to the Textile and Garment Manufacturers' Association of Singapore and its members to organize trade missions and take part in overseas exhibitions, both to secure export orders and to improve the industry's international image.

The evidence is strong that state policies from 1979 to 1984 damaged the competitiveness of the textile and garment industry. Had these policies been pursued more flexibly, the adjustment process of textile and garment firms to growing trade restrictions and competition from other countries would probably have been less painful. As it happened, it took a recession for the government to realize its restructuring strategy had raised costs too sharply and quickly, making it difficult for firms to adjust smoothly.

The costs of adjustment in the industry have been borne mainly by unsuccessful firms and their stockholders and creditors. Laid-off local workers have been able to find new jobs in expanding sectors while laid-off foreign workers have returned home. The cost to taxpayers of capital subsidies and other financial support for the industry has been very small.

For textile firms, despite their improving competitiveness since 1986, the long-term outlook is bleak. Many countries, including the large industrial countries, can produce yarns—the main output of textile mills in Singapore—more cheaply than Singapore. For garment firms that have shown themselves to be more flexible and responsive to emerging market trends, the outlook is not as gloomy. So long as the bilateral MFA system operates, Singapore will be assured of access to major industrial-country markets, even if these markets do not grow much because of rising protectionism. This is because the existing system favors early entrants. If global quotas were introduced to replace the present MFA system, Singapore's textile and garment industry would likely shrink. In a less quota-constrained world market, many Singapore firms, which have shown a capacity to innovate and adjust to global competition, will survive, but others, especially textile firms, will shrink and fold.

In the medium term, if Singapore's currency does not appreciate strongly against major currencies, the garment industry through various adjustments—restructuring, relocation, market and product diversification, capital investments, and skill training—will remain viable. In the long term, however, all its adjustments may not be enough to prevent its decline if the labor problems it faces continue to worsen. As the industry attracts fewer new entrants and access to foreign labor is further restricted by government policy, the industry will find itself burdened with an aging and less productive work force, with adverse consequences on its international competitiveness.

SHIPBUILDING AND REPAIRING

Though it began in the last century, shipbuilding and repairing did not develop into a major international industry until the early 1960s. It is an industry that owes much of its expansion to government direction and participation. Four yards account for 90% of total ship repair capacity in Singapore; three are largely or partly government-owned. In 1965 the government formed a joint venture, Jurong Shipyard, with a Japanese shipyard, Ishikawajima-Harima Heavy Industries. It did so to accelerate the industrialization process and because the local private sector did not then have the capital or expertise. In 1967 the government transferred the activities of the Dockyard Department of the Port of Singapore Authority to a new company, Keppel Shipyard. A year later, it transformed the former British Naval Dockyard in Sembawang to a new commercial yard, Sembawang Shipyard.

Thus in three years, it created three of the largest yards operating in Singapore today. When the government created these three yards, it decided to retain majority ownership of them because it had developed the expertise and experience to run them. It also believed the yards did not need to be in private hands to be run efficiently. Ever since they were established, all three yards (which are listed on the Singapore Stock Exchange) have been operated as profit-making enterprises.

The industry consists of three sectors: repair, building, and oil rig construction (Table 5.9). Ship repair forms the backbone of the industry, accounting for just under half of output in the 1970s and over 80% in the mid-1980s. In the 1960s and '70s, the repair sector expanded rapidly, achieving its peak turnover of S$2.4 billion in 1981. Several factors contributed to its phenomenal growth. The most important was the strong expansion in regional and world seaborne trade, which greatly increased the demand for ship repair. Singapore was able to capitalize on this increase because of its excellent infrastructure, low labor cost and, most important, its strategic location.

Because of the offshore search for oil in the region, foreign rig builders

Table 5.9. Revenue Earned by the Ship Repair, Shipbuilding, and Oil Rig Construction Sectors, 1975–87 (in S$ million)

1975	1977	1979	1981	1983	1985	1986	1987	
460	537	725	1088	673	457	591	688	ship repair
270	530	387	540	430	142	113	337	shipbuilding
248	158	281	790	392	52	20	84	oil rigs
978	1225	1393	2418	1495	651	724	1109	total

Source: Singapore Association of Shipbuilders and Repairers (SASAR), Annual Report (various years)

were attracted to Singapore, and in 1979–81, this sector enjoyed an unprecedented boom along with the other two sectors. But in 1982–85, fortunes changed dramatically with the collapse of oil prices, which led to a sharp fall in tanker trade and oil exploration activities. The industry's turnover declined by over 70% in four years to S$651 million in 1985, below the level in 1973. Ship repair and shipbuilding brought in over 90% of the industry's revenue. Oil rig building, which at its peak in 1981 accounted for about a third of the industry's output, generated only S$52 million. The number of firms in the industry, which had exceeded 200 in 1981, fell by 25%. There were massive layoffs, and many yards provided financial incentives to induce workers to leave. The demand for contract workers, which the industry depends on heavily in good and bad times, collapsed.

Between 1980 and 1985, employment in the industry fell steeply, from around 22,000 (excluding 5,000 contract foreign workers from Malaysia and other neighboring countries) to less than 15,000 (Table 5.10). The industry's share of manufacturing employment fell from 7.8% to 6.1%. Most of the laid-off local workers were able to find alternative jobs in 1982–84 because other sectors of the economy, especially construction, were still growing and short of workers. But in 1985, many laid-off workers had to join the ranks of the unemployed, although not for long because of the economy's rapid recovery. A large number of them did not return to work for the shipyards in the 1986–87 recovery because they had found jobs in other industries, especially manufacturing and construction. Like textile and garment workers, laid-off shipyard workers were given compensation by their employers, the amount varying with length of service.

The severe downturn in the industry was not only the result of cyclical factors. Structural factors—the reduction in world consumption and

Table 5.10. Shipbuilding and Repairing Industry, 1975–86

1975	1979	1980	1984	1985	1986	
122	172	201	196	167	147	number of firms
1202	1533	1657	1346	1012	1012	output (S$ million)
9.5	5.8	5.2	3.3	2.6	2.7	as a percentage of manufacturing output
574	726	860	580	464	410	value added (S$ million)
						employment
28	24	22	18	15	11	total (thousands)
14.7	8.8	7.8	6.7	6.1	4.4	as a percentage of manufacturing employment
						per worker (S$ thousand)
8.5	11.8	13.5	19.0	19.5	19.5	remuneration
20.2	30.2	38.1	31.5	29.9	37.5	value added
						exports
64	67	53	41	54	51	as a percentage of sales

Includes tankers, ships, barges, lighters, boats & oil rigs, and marine engines & ship parts. Through 1979 these are SIC 38411–13; from 1980 onwards they are codes 38411–14.

Source: Report on the Census of Industrial Production (various years)

demand for oil (and hence for oil tankers), the growing volume of oil transported overland, and the establishment of oil refineries at home by oil producers (which reduced the need for tankers to carry oil to Singapore for refining)—were also at work. These factors affected Singapore more than other countries because of its large concentration of ship repair docks. The deepening slump in the industry led to severe price cutting. In 1985 almost all yards reported losses, one major yard closed, and average dock occupancy fell below 56% (from full capacity in 1981).

Adjustment Mechanisms and Their Effectiveness

As the decline steepened in the early 1980s, firms in the industry took a number of steps to improve their competitive position. They cut direct costs and overhead, but because of the high Central Provident Fund contribution rates (25% by employers in 1984), high statutory charges, and the tight labor market, their efforts did not reduce unit labor costs significantly. They also trimmed their own workforce requirements, used less contract labor, retrained workers, invested in new machinery and equipment, and moved into new activities including structural engineering and civil construction work. One shipyard even used part of its land for prawn-breeding. Some of the measures shipyards took improved efficiency and productivity while others, such as the redirection of resources to industrial engineering and construction work, provided revenues from new sources. But they could not arrest the swift and painful contraction in the size of the industry.

In 1985 there were no new rig orders, leading to the folding of three of the five rig builders (all foreign-owned); the other two transformed themselves into builders of small vessels. In the same year, four of the largest local yards—Hitachi Sosen Robin (the one non-government yard), Jurong, Keppel, and Sembawang—agreed to use their docks for only 24 days a month. The agreement, which came as a result of a suggestion made by Singapore's prime minister, Lee Kuan Yew, was swiftly implemented. The government provided no incentives or concessional loans to encourage this 20% reduction in capacity. In 1986 total dock capacity was down to 2.4 million deadweight from about 3 million in 1981, the peak year. But this reduction was much less than the decline in demand.

In addition to suggesting the joint reduction in capacity, the government also suggested Keppel and Sembawang look into the possibility of a merger as a way of cutting costs and improving competitiveness. In 1986 a consulting firm appointed to investigate ways to rationalize the industry proposed such a merger, but the idea was dropped when the management of both yards did not support it.

In 1986 the repair sector recovered strongly, expanding by 29% (SASAR 1986). But shipbuilding and rig construction continued to shrink because of a lack of new orders. Since late 1986, a combination of cost and demand factors—political unrest in the Middle East which diverted tanker traffic and maintenance work to Singapore; the government's cost-cutting measures; and the depreciation of the Singapore dollar against other currencies, especially the yen, which improved the competitiveness of Singapore shipyards—have strengthened the recovery of the shipbuilding and repairing industry. In 1987 the major ship repair firms returned to profitability and suspended their capacity-reduction agreement.

In 1987 shipbuilding and repairing firms, benefiting from cost-cutting measures (including a cut in the employer's contribution rate for CPF from 25% to 10%, reductions in public utility charges, property taxes, etc) and rationalization, which had made them extremely competitive, performed much better than in 1986. Revenue for the industry rose from S$724 million in 1986 to S$1,109 million in 1987, an increase of 53% (SASAR 1987).

The upturn in repairing was due to two main factors—the appreciation of the yen and won, and the growth in seaborne trade. The first factor resulted in yards in Singapore quoting prices 20% lower than South Korea, and more than 50% less than Japan (*Business Times,* 1987 December 30). This price advantage has partly come about because of the efficiency-improving measures taken during the recession years, coupled with Singapore's favorable geographical location, and has enabled Singapore yards to increase market share at the expense of Japanese and Korean yards. The improvement in the industry occurred in all three sectors. Shipbuilders tripled turnover (from S$113 million in 1986 to S$337 in 1987), and rig builders increased revenue from S$20 million in 1986 to S$84 million in 1987. The industry continued to perform well in 1988, with major firms in the industry reporting large profits (*Straits Times,* 1988 December 9).

The experience of government-backed Keppel Corporation, a diversified ship repair, engineering, and property group, illustrates the adjustments the large firms made in the mid-1980s. In 1984–85 Keppel lost S$300 million. A large part of this was sustained as a result of the ill-timed and costly acquisition of Straits Trading, a property group subsequently badly hurt by the collapse of the property market. In 1986 Keppel, which has 35% of the market share in the industry, reported a small profit. The turnaround was due to company cost-cutting programs, including staff reductions (from over 3,000 in 1984 to 1,800 in 1986), and government measures for industry generally, especially the cut in the employer's contribution rate to the CPF from 25% to 10%, and the disposal of loss-making assets, including assets of Straits Trading (*Business Times,* 1987 April 23). Since 1985, Keppel has also diversified into new areas including the export of engineering design capability and technical expertise to other developing countries, and is pursuing new investment opportunities in China, Australia, and ASEAN.

In comparison with Keppel and other large shipyards, shipbuilders and rig builders have had a hard time surviving. For example, Southern Ocean Shipbuilding, a small firm founded in 1979, survived only because its creditors agreed to restructure its debt of more than S$10 million (*Straits Times,* 1987 February 21). Its future, like that of the other small firms in the industry, however, remains precarious.

Impact of Government Policies

General government policies—such as wage correction, foreign labor, capital incentives, and exchange rate—have been important in influencing the adjustment of the shipbuilding and repairing industry in the 1980s. Several of these policies, in particular, the wage correction policy and foreign labor policy, intensified the difficulties the industry had in adjusting to depressed conditions in 1980–84. But they also left the firms that survived the painful adjustment in a strong position to benefit from subsequent cost-cutting measures and improvement in market conditions.

Government programs directed specifically at the industry are few and have not been as influential as general policies in their impact on the industry's adjustment to changing demand conditions. The Ship Financing Scheme, introduced in 1978 to enable buyers to obtain financing at concessional rates for a period of 8½ to 10 years, has not been widely used as the financing rates offered have not been sufficiently attractive. Government-supported training programs have increased the supply of skilled workers in the industry, but government efforts to encourage the merger of small firms have met with little success.

The painful adjustment of 1982–86 together with the appreciation of the Japanese yen and Korean won have made Singapore a highly competitive ship repair center. In 1986 repair costs at Japanese yards were reported to be over 50% higher than Singapore's. Korea's costs were similar to Singapore's but Korea is not strategically located to benefit from the tanker trade, which accounts for 60% of the repair business in Singapore (*Business Times,* 1987 March 25). Since 1986, Singapore's competitive position in ship repairing and building has improved further as Korean costs have risen faster than Singapore's.

Large firms will continue to adjust by improving productivity and moving into new and higher value-added and technically more demanding activities such as ship conversion, ship upgrading, and repair of shipboard communications and control systems. They will also try to sell technical consultancy packages overseas and have begun to invest in Asian countries like India and the Philippines, which have the land and labor to be low-cost ship repairers (Balakrishnan 1989, p 44).

Given its structural problems, the mature but competitive shipbuilding and repairing industry in Singapore is unlikely to sustain the kind of performance it enjoyed in the 1970s or in 1988. Its labor problems will likely intensify as foreign labor becomes more costly and harder to obtain because of government policy to reduce Singapore's dependence on foreign labor. But it will survive because of its proven capacity to overcome difficult challenges and because of Singapore's strategic location, excellent infrastructure, and social and political stability.

OIL REFINING

The rapid growth of the oil refining industry in the 1960s and '70s was due to two factors—government policies and incentives which attracted multinational oil firms to locate themselves in Singapore to serve the fast-growing South East Asian region, and the development of large tankers which reduced greatly the cost of transporting oil from the Middle East to Singapore. After the first oil crisis, the local industry underwent structural changes. It moved into a range of oil-related activities from engineering, exploration, and geophysical services to trading, financing and terminaling (storing and trans-shipping) services. In 1975, as part of a general strategy to broaden the base of Singapore's industrial structure, the Singapore government and a Japanese consortium led by Sumitomo agreed to form a joint venture to build a huge petrochemical complex to satisfy the expected large demand for petrochemical products in the Asian-Pacific region. Because of excess capacity in the world petrochemical industry, the project, which became operational in 1984, suffered heavy losses until 1987.

In 1988 the government sold part of its equity in the project to Shell. Sumitomo was not interested in increasing additional equity and the government felt the project would benefit from the experience and expertise of a multinational oil company such as Shell. The two major companies in the complex are Polyolefin Company (70% owned by Nihon Singapore Polyolefin and, until 1988, 30% by the Singapore government) and the Petrochemical Corporation of Singapore, the main upstream plant. They became profitable in 1987 because of rising demand and lower expenditure for feedstock (*Business Times*, 1988 June 20).

In the late 1970s, the oil industry, which is dominated by five large refineries—British Petroleum, Esso, Mobil, Shell, and the largely government-owned Singapore Refining Company—linked with regional firms to reduce dependence on Middle East oil and to sell refining services to oil producers in the region, particularly Indonesia and Malaysia.

In the early 1980s, Singapore refineries were using as much as 40% of their capacity to process crudes for Indonesia and Malaysia. But third-party processing declined as Indonesian refineries came on stream after 1984. By 1986, Singapore refineries were no longer processing crude on term contracts for Indonesia. This loss was partly offset by term processing for China, which has limited refining capacity. Processing of Malaysian crudes has continued, but it is expected to fall off rapidly when the 100,000 barrels per day (bpd) Malacca refinery comes on stream in the early 1990s.

The decline in third-party processing together with the fall in oil demand in the Asian-Pacific region, especially Japan, caused a slump in the industry. Government policy was not a major factor in the rapid decline of the industry—unlike textiles and garments and shipbuilding and repairing. In 1980–85, the industry barely grew, and in 1986—the worst year—output plunged 36% to S$7 billion from S$11 billion in the previous year. The decline in value-added was, however, much less steep because of improved efficiency and the concentration on higher value products. Export of petroleum products fell to S$10.0 billion in 1986 from S$13.4 billion in 1985. In 1987–88, both output and exports continued to shrink as oil markets remained weak (Table 5.11).

Adjustment Mechanisms and Their Effectiveness

The oil refining industry has adjusted to the fall in oil demand in several ways. First, it has reduced crude-distillation capacity, which at its peak was over 1 million bpd, to effectively 850,000 bpd (which still makes Singapore the world's third-largest refining center, after the US Gulf Coast and Rotterdam). Competitive factors rather than government policy induced this reduction. Second, firms made new investments to take advantage of the changing structure of demand for oil products, and to strengthen Singapore's position as a "swing" producer that can respond flexibly to the specific product deficits of Asian-Pacific countries. In 1980–86, the industry invested S$1.7 billion in energy-saving equipment, computer systems and secondary processing facilities to meet the shift in demand away from heavy fuel oil towards lighter oil products.

Table 5.11. Oil Refining Industry, 1975–87

1975	1979	1980	1984	1985	1987	
11	10	10	12	12	12	number of firms
4753	9471	11520	12449	11031	7287	output (S$ million)
38	36	36	30	29	17	as a percentage of manu-facturing output
605	1206	1470	956	874	779	value added (S$ million)
						employment
3.3	3.2	3.3	3.6	3.5	3.2	total (thousands)
1.7	1.2	1.2	1.3	1.4	1.4	as a percentage of manu-facturing employment
						per worker (S$ thousand)
19.8	27.1	29.8	42.0	44.2	49.9	remuneration
182	376	440	265	250	241	value added
						exports
66	73	67	65	64	61[a]	as a percentage of sales

a. Data are for 1986
Source: *Report on the Census of Industrial Production* (various years) through 1985, then *Economic Survey of Singapore* (1986 and '87)

In 1987–88 oil refining companies announced plans for substantial investments in secondary processing plants—hydrocrackers, reformers, and catalytic crackers—to obtain higher value-added oil products (*Straits Times,* 1987 July 30). Esso was investing S$150 million in a visbreaker that will enable it to produce more jet fuel, diesel, and naphtha (*Straits Times,* 1987 September 21). Mobil was spending S$170 million to increase its capacity to process lighter oil products, while Shell announced plans to invest S$480 million in a catalytic-cracker complex. The availability of generous tax write-offs for manufacturing investments was an important factor in the decision of oil companies to upgrade their facilities.

Third, the industry has continued to diversify from oil refining into oil-related services. It expanded Singapore's earlier role as a regional oil trading center and moved strongly into various oil-related services including terminaling. The government played a catalytic part in enlarging Singapore's role as a provider of terminaling services. It did so for purely pragmatic reasons—to accelerate the diversification of Singapore as an oil refining and trading center. It formed, in the early 1980s, joint ventures with two separate Dutch companies—Van Ommeren and Paktank—to build two oil terminals with a total storage capacity of 800,000 cubic meters (5 million barrels). Both business and security factors may have influenced its decision to participate in these ventures.

Fourth, the industry has moved into new activities including offshore support operations for countries that are exploring for oil. For example, a Singapore consortium, led by Intraco, the government-backed trading company, won a contract in 1983 to build and operate a supply base in China.

Fifth, oil refiners have reduced their staff by not replacing workers who leave, and by offering financial incentives to older workers to retire. However, their staff cutbacks have been small compared to those in the textile and garment industry or the shipbuilding and repairing industry. Between 1982 (the peak year, when the industry employed 3,784 workers) and 1987, oil refining shed 500 workers—a small number compared to the employment reduction in the two industries discussed earlier. Most of the reduction took place in 1986–87, when over 400 workers left the industry.

Sixth, the slump encouraged oil refiners to be more marketing-oriented and entrepreneurial in satisfying the specific and varied needs of their customers. Esso, for instance, developed an operational capacity to process over thirty different crudes from Asian, Pacific, and Middle East oil producers. Oil refiners have also become more flexible in establishing new sources of crudes and in developing new marketing and processing arrangements for their clients. Crudes used to come to Singapore from the Middle East (mainly Saudi Arabia), Indonesia, and Malaysia; now they also flow in from China, India, and other Asian-Pacific countries. The markets for Singapore's refined oil products have expanded beyond the East Asian region, the west coast of the United States, and the Middle East to other regions including the South Pacific, Europe, and West Africa.

In addition to these adjustments, several developments on the demand side helped the industry in 1986–88. The first was the phased deregulation of the Japanese oil industry begun in 1986, which has created a new market for refined oil products for Singapore companies and resulted in a sharp increase in the export of petroleum exports to Japan. In 1987 about 30% of Singapore's export of refined petroleum products went to Japan. Had the Japanese market not been liberalized, oil refiners would have fared much worse in 1987–88.

The second development is the firming of oil prices after the wild fluctuations of the early to mid-1980s. This development has increased the willingness of oil traders to risk buying crudes for processing. The third is the improvement in the economic performance of many Asian-Pacific countries, which has increased demand. As a swing producer with an ability to meet diverse needs quickly, Singapore's oil refining industry in 1986–87 gained from this growth in demand. The industry has also benefited from China's modernization. Even with planned new refineries, China is unlikely to meet its own domestic demand for another decade. This means a steady number of third-party processing contracts for Singapore refineries (Doshi 1988).

All these favorable developments will likely continue in the next few years. The industry, with its heavy investments and experience in adjusting to adverse market conditions, will be able to capitalize on these developments. It may not rank high in terms of value added—S$728 million in 1987, compared with S$6.5 billion for machinery and appliances, and S$1.1 billion for transport equipment. But it is important because of its huge capital investments and its multiplier effects (eg, it has facilitated Singapore's development into an oil trading center). As in the past, the industry will receive priority attention from the government and will continue to benefit from Singapore's pro-business policy environment, excellent infrastructure, and strategic location—assets critical to its operational efficiency but which many resource-rich countries in the region do not possess.

COMPARISON OF ADJUSTMENT EXPERIENCES

The sources of the serious problems faced in the 1980s by the three industries studied here—textiles and garments, shipbuilding and repairing, and oil refining—are different. Both market factors and government policies contributed to the declining competitiveness of textiles and garments and shipbuilding and repairing in 1980–84. For these two industries, the key market factors were competition from other producers and slow growth in demand. A strong Singapore dollar also hurt their competitiveness, as did government restructuring policies, which sharply raised their operating costs while limiting their access to foreign labor. In the case of oil refining, its problems stemmed from the large world surplus in capacity as a result of completion of new refineries and slow growth in demand.

The three industries have adjusted to their problems in different ways. Labor shedding has been much more important for textiles and garments and for shipbuilding and repairing than for oil refining. Relocation and investments abroad have been practical only for textile and garment firms. All three industries have moved into new activities and markets, but not with the same success. The oil refining industry has branched out into new services and found new customers for its underutilized refineries. In contrast, the textile and garment industry, which has upgraded to produce higher value-added items, became increasingly dependent on the US market, a trend reversed only in 1987 when its exports to Europe expanded significantly. Shipbuilding and repairing diversified into industrial engineering and construction work. Several large shipyards acquired firms in related fields such as shipping and also went into unrelated activities including trading and property development.

In all three industries, there have been capacity reductions. In textiles, a competitive industry characterized by easy entry and exit of firms, capacity shrank through the death of firms, the elimination of third shifts (because of a shortage of workers), and the idling of plant and machinery in surviving firms. In garments, similar adjustments also occurred, but less drastically, during the 1985–86 recession. In fact, the capacity of the industry has increased since 1986 with the entry of many new firms.

In shipbuilding and repairing, an industry dominated by a few large firms with heavy government participation, many firms collapsed, but capacity was only greatly reduced following an agreement (terminated in 1987) among the four leading firms. In oil refining, oligopolistic and largely foreign-owned, capacity reduction has taken the form of mothballing dated primary refining facilities and delaying completion of planned facilities. Except for its role in prompting the four major shipyards to reach an agreement on capacity reduction, the government played no direct role in the capacity shrinkage of the three industries. Nor does it have any long-term plan to ensure that each industry reaches an optimum size.

Government economic policies in 1979–84 were based on the belief low value-added activities dependent on abundant labor in Singapore would eventually lose their comparative advantage, and that state interventions were crucial to the more efficient use of the economy's limited land and labor resources. Policy impact on textiles and garments and on shipbuilding and repairing was different from expectation.

While policy induced new investments in plant and equipment and promoted the shift of scarce labor and land resources out of these two industries, it also affected international competitiveness by raising operating costs, especially labor costs, sharply. Had the government not quickened the restructuring process, adjustments to deteriorating external conditions would probably have been less wrenching. This is not to suggest that the government's restructuring strategy was a mistake, rather that its execution was ill-timed, occurring as it did during a period of falling oil prices and weakening external demand. Cost-cutting measures together with a more favorable external environment have helped to revive both the textiles and garments, and shipbuilding and repairing industries.

PROSPECTS AND TRADE POLICY IMPLICATIONS

Singapore's restructuring strategy, adopted in 1979 and revised after the recession of 1985–86, seeks to move the economy away from activities in which it was losing comparative advantage and into activities that capitalize on Singapore's stability, skills, and location. While its execution was ill-timed, its objective was a positive one—to quicken the economy's adjustment to changing internal and external conditions. Protecting local industries against foreign competition was never an important policy issue, as it is in countries with large domestic markets, because of Singapore's commitments to and practice of free trade, and the high export orientation of its manufacturing sector.

The adjustment measures taken by the three industries in response to state policies as well as market forces have altered Singapore's trade patterns. Product diversification has brought textile and garment firms into increased competition with up-market producers like Hong Kong. Relocation has created new competitors in lower value-added items for other countries producing for the low end of the textile and garment market. Market diversification will continue, especially into the Japanese market, which still takes only a small share of Singapore's garment exports.

Although the performance of the textile and garment industry improved in 1986–87, partly because of strong EEC demand and the opening up of the Japanese market, protectionism in industrial countries against textile and garment imports has not faded away. A weakening of the Singapore currency against the Japanese yen and the major European currencies also helped exports. In 1988 the industry's expansion slowed to 8% (from 40% in 1987) mainly because of weaker US demand and the appreciation of the Singapore dollar against the US dollar (*Business Times*, 1988 November 28). The rise in wages in 1988, following three years of wage stability, also eroded the competitiveness of the industry.

Domestically, government policy will be, as in the past, to induce the industry to upgrade itself further and reduce its labor requirements through retraining and mechanization. Internationally, it will concentrate on ways to expand Singapore's access to major industrial-country markets under the present MFA system.

Shipbuilding and repairing underwent rapid and painful adjustments in the 1980s, and emerged from them in reasonably good shape. Recovery since late 1986 owes much to the strengthening of currencies of its major competitors, Japan and South Korea. Unlike textiles and garments, where comparative advantage rests in part on international protection, shipbuilding and repairing is an industry where competitiveness is built on Singapore's strategic location, a proven track record for efficiency and flexibility, excellent infrastructural support, and human skills. So long as it keeps costs down and the Singapore dollar does not appreciate strongly against currencies of countries with large shipbuilding and repair capacity like Japan and South Korea, the industry will retain its comparative advantage. Indeed, it is likely to increase its world market share in ship repair and in the construction of small and medium vessels. (Without a fully integrated steel industry, Singapore cannot compete with Japan or South Korea in building large tankers.)

Government policy will continue to support diversification as part of a strategy to transform Singapore into a total maritime center offering a wide range of services. The main constraint on expansion is labor, which the industry has much difficulty recruiting because of the widespread perception it is only a sunset industry but also one where work is physically demanding and dangerous.

Oil refining's future will continue to be strongly influenced by external forces. Foreign government involvement is one such force. In the Asian-Pacific region, state ownership of oil refining capacity has increased from 22% in 1977 to 36% in 1985 (Hilten 1986). Producing countries' national oil companies are moving further into downstream activities to secure captive markets for their crudes and oil producers, a trend that will reduce Singapore's role as an oil refiner and trader. Already, Indonesian crude is going to that country's refineries, when once it came to Singapore.

In the early 1990s the world surplus in refining capacity will continue as more refineries come on stream. This means Singapore refiners will continue to operate below capacity. They will continue to compete for third-party and spot processing contracts. But these provide only temporary work at low profit margins. Their diversification into oil-related services including trading will also continue. In the longer term, refiners recognize the only viable strategy is to invest in additional secondary processing facilities so they can expand their role as a balancing producer and better satisfy the growing demand for lighter oil products. Government policy, by offering generous tax write-offs, has been to support fully this strategy, which will lead to both product and market diversification.

Long-Term Prospects

The long-term prospects for the three industries are different. For textiles and garments, the adjustment problems are likely to become more severe for two reasons. First, its labor problems will worsen because of reduced access to foreign labor and increased difficulty of attracting new workers into the industry. Second, with rising wage costs, quota rents are likely to diminish, probably disappearing for textiles because it faces much more severe external competition than garments. Employment will contract, especially rapidly for textiles, but the burden will be borne mostly by the foreign workers who comprise 40% of the work force. If Singapore's economy grows by 4–6% a year, as projected, in the 1990s, the employment contraction in textiles and garments will not cause serious economic and social problems because alternative employment opportunities will be available.

The outlook for shipbuilding and repair is brighter. This is an industry in which Singapore, with its strategic location and superb infrastructure, is likely to maintain a competitive edge. Moreover, the industry has in recent years become much more competitive as a result of various efficiency-improving adjustments it has had to make. But its performance in the 1990s will be adversely affected by two factors, even if world demand is strong, First, the industry, like textiles and garments, will encounter more difficulty in recruiting both local and foreign labor

Table 5.12. Textile Exports by Importing Region, 1971–86 (in $S thousands and percents)

1971		1981		1985		1986		
$S	%	$S	%	$S	%	$S	%	
0.4	*	16.2	6	10.2	10	10.9	8	Japan
8.8	4	19.5	8	5.5	6	9.4	7	EEC
15.2	7	48.0	19	11.3	11	9.8	8	North America
10.8	5	27.6	11	16.8	17	12.8	10	other DME
35.2	16	111.3	45	43.9	44	42.9	33	total DME
0.9	*	13.2	5	11.8	12	8.6	7	socialist countries
182.0	83	124.1	50	45.4	45	77.2	60	developing countries
217.9		248.6		101.2		128.7		total

Exports include re-exports. There is even more variation in the distribution of trade than suggested by this Table. For example, the EEC's share in 1984 was just over 2%.
DME = developed market economies
* less than 0.6%
Source: Singapore External Trade Statistics, various issues

Table 5.13. Garment Exports by Importing Region, 1971–86 (in $S thousands and percents)

1971		1981		1985		1986		
$S	%	$S	%	$S	%	$S	%	
2.3	2	2.3	*	2.1	*	4.0	*	Japan
22.6	16	284.7	36	94.7	11	136.6	13	EEC
55.9	40	332.8	42	683.6	78	832.0	78	North America
9.1	7	63.1	8	26.5	3	37.4	4	other DME
89.9	65	682.9	87	806.9	92	1009.9	94	total DME
3.2	2	1.8	*	4.3	*	2.2	*	socialist countries
45.5	33	103.6	13	65.8	8	60.2	6	developing countries
138.6		788.3		877.0		1072.3		total

Exports include re-exports. There is even more variation in the distribution of trade than suggested by this table.
DME = developed market economies
* less than 0.6%
Source: Singapore External Trade Statistics, various issues

Table 5.14. Petroleum and Petroleum Product Exports by Importing Region, 1971–86 (in S$ millions and percents)

1971		1981		1985		1986		
S$	%	S$	%	S$	%	S$	%	
243	21	3111	23	2715	20	2013	21	Japan
4	*	104	1	273	2	78	1	EEC
19	2	321	2	1068	8	552	6	North America
118	10	1477	11	1105	8	656	7	other DME
385	34	5012	37	5159	38	3298	34	total DME
—	—	31	*	236	2	398	4	socialist countries
753	66	8596	63	8067	60	5968	62	developing countries
1138		13639		13463		9665		total

Exports include re-exports. There is even more variation in the distribution of trade than suggested by this Table.
DME = developed market economies
*less than 0.6%
Source: *Singapore External Trade Statistics,* various issues

Table 5.15. Shipbuilding and Repairing Exports by Importing Region, 1971–86 (in S$ millions and percents)

1971		1981		1985		1986		
S$	%	S$	%	S$	%	S$	%	
0.1	*	—	—	0.5	*	—	—	Japan
2.7	8	14.4	2	1.0	*	3.2	3	EEC
6.7	20	611.0	63	27.7	7	26.9	25	North America
.2	1	1.5	*	3.5	1	2.9	3	other DME
9.7	28	626.9	65	32.7	8	32.9	30	total DME
—	—	19.0	2	2.1	*	9.3	8	socialist countries
24.4	72	319.8	33	391.6	92	66.9	61	developing countries
34.1		965.7		426.4		109.0		total

Exports include re-exports. There is even more variation in the distribution of trade than suggested by this Table.
DME = developed market economies
*less than 0.6%
Source: *Singapore External Trade Statistics,* various issues

—local labor because of the diminishing supply of new labor force entrants, and foreign labor because of increased restrictions on access to foreign labor. Second, the Singapore dollar is likely to appreciate against major currencies if Singapore's late 1980s economic performance and balance of payments surpluses continue. This appreciation will hurt the industry's competitiveness.

Oil refining has made significant and positive adjustments in the late 1980s, adjustments which have improved its competitive edge. It will face more competition from regional refineries, but because it is investing heavily in new plant and equipment to increase its value added and flexibility, the industry will retain its competitive edge for many years to come.

In the future, government policy on all three industries, as well as others, whatever their performance, will likely be similar to what it is today. It will be directed at facilitating market-oriented adjustments, not at protecting them from job loss or external competition. The government realizes that its strong commitment to free trade and competition has given Singapore tangible economic benefits. It is therefore most unlikely to abandon this commitment in an attempt (which it knows will be costly and ineffective) to arrest the decline of industries that have lost their competitive edge in world markets.

BIBLIOGRAPHY

Balakrishnan, N. 1989. "Springing a Leak." *Far Eastern Economic Review*, Feb 16.

Business Times (Singapore).
　　1987 Mar 25. "Singapore ship repairing in fine shape again."
　　1987 Apr 23. "Keppel looks forward to a better year."
　　1987 Dec 30. "Sailing out of stormy waters."
　　1987 Dec 31. "Textile manufacturers cry foul."
　　1988 Jun 20. "Bullish outlook oiling wheels of petrochem investment."
　　1988 Nov 28. "Growth tapering off in textile, garment sector."

Department of Statistics, Singapore. Various years. *Census of Industrial Production.*

Doshi, Tilak. 1988. "Singapore: Optimism for the Houston of Asia?" *Far Eastern Economic Review*, May 26, p 86–88.

Hilten, Dick Van. 1986. "Refining: Today's Changing Patterns and Tomorrow's Prospects." Paper presented at the Financial Times' Conference on Pacific Basin Oil and Gas—Prices, Investment and the Business Outlook," Hong Kong, Sep 26.

Krause, Lawrence B. 1987a. "Thinking about Singapore." In Lawrence B. Krause,

Koh Ai Tee, and Lee (Tsao) Yuan, editors, *The Singapore Economy Reconsidered,* p 1–20. Singapore: Institute of Southeast Asian Studies.

——. 1987b. "The Government as an Entrepreneur." In Lawrence B. Krause, Koh Ai Tee, and Lee (Tsao) Yuan, editors, *The Singapore Economy Reconsidered.* Singapore: Institute of Southeast Asian Studies.

Lee (Tsao) Yuan. 1987a. "The Government in Macroeconomic Management." In Lawrence B. Krause, Koh Ai Tee and Lee (Tsao) Yuan, editors, *The Singapore Economy Reconsidered.* Singapore: Institute of Southeast Asian Studies.

——. 1987b. "The Government in the Labor Market." In Lawrence B. Krause, Koh Ai Tee and Lee (Tsao) Yuan, editors, *The Singapore Economy Reconsidered.* Singapore: Institute of Southeast Asian Studies.

Lim, Chong Yah and Associates. 1987. *Policy Options for the Singapore Economy.* Singapore: McGraw Hill.

Lim, Linda YC. 1983. "Singapore's Success: The Myth of the Free Market Economy." *Asian Survey* 23(6): 752–64 (Jun).

Lim, Linda and Pang Eng Fong. 1986. *Trade, Employment and Industrialisation in Singapore.* Geneva: ILO.

MAS = Monetary Authority of Singapore. 1982. *Annual Report, 1981/82.*

Ministry of Trade and Industry, Singapore. Various years. *Economic Survey of Singapore.*

——. 1986 Feb. *The Singapore Economy: New Directions* (Report of the Economic Committee).

Pang, Eng Fong. 1986. "Trade, Protectionism and Industrial Adjustment: The Case of the Textile and Garment Industry in Singapore." Paper presented at the Conference on Trade, Protectionism and Industrial Adjustment organized by the Institute of Southeast Asian Studies and North South Institute, Singapore, Aug 29–31.

——. 1988. "Development Strategies and Labor Market Changes in Singapore." In Eng Fong Pang, editor, *Labor Market Developments and Structural Change: The Experience of ASEAN and Australia,* p 195–242. Singapore University Press.

SASAR = Singapore Association of Shipbuilders and Repairers. Various years. *Annual Report.*

Straits Times (Singapore).
    1987 Feb 21. "Creditors back firm's debt restructure plan."
    1987 Jul 30. "Oil refiners get set to take on overseas rivals."
    1987 Sep 1. "Garment firms concerned over quota review plan."
    1987 Sep 21. "Esso invests $150m more."
    1988 Nov 25. "Govt cannot have total hands-off policy on wages."
    1988 Dec 9. "Singapore shipyards calm about move to raise workers' levy."

Tay, Boon Nga. 1986. "The Structure and Causes of Manufacturing Sector Protection in Singapore." In Christopher Findlay and Ross Garnaut, editors, *The Political Economy of Manufacturing Protection: Experiences of ASEAN and Australia,* p 135–58. London: Allen and Unwin.

6

HONG KONG
Structural Adjustment in a Free-Trade, Free Market Economy

Yin-Ping Ho and Tzong-Biau Lin

Since its inception as a British enclave in 1843, the most important characteristic of the Hong Kong economy has been its almost total dependence on international trade. This is hardly surprising. How else could a tiny settlement with no mineral resources and limited farmland manage to provide viable means of livelihood for its growing millions of humanity?[1]

Starting with an excellent harbor and a geographic location along the major East-West routes, Hong Kong engaged in trade. The pattern of trade and industrial development that emerged is intriguing because it occurred in a free-enterprise environment. Indeed, in a world where the

Thanks are due to Hugh Patrick, Alan Bollard, H. Edward English, J. Hong Kim, Michael Young, and Larry Meissner for helpful comments and valuable suggestions on earlier drafts. Helpful comments were also received from the participants in the two successive workshops on this project. Naturally the authors are solely responsible for any remaining errors, shortcomings, and obscurities.

1. Hong Kong's entire land area—consisting of Hong Kong Island proper, Kowloon Peninsula, Stonecutters Island, the New Territories (comprising the area north of Kowloon up to the Shenzhen River) and 235 outlying tiny islands—totals 1,071 square kilometers. Of this, about 17% is built up, and less than 9% is suitable for crop and fish farming, while scrub and grasslands, badlands, and afforested areas claim the remaining 75%. Most of the 5.6 million people cram into an area of about 105 square kilometers.

merits of economic growth and development in a free-trade and free-market environment have, by and large, been selling at a discount, Hong Kong's development experience presents a picture of multiple paradoxes for advocates of a statist approach. It represents perhaps the world's nearest contemporary equivalent to the 19th century ideal of laissez-faire industrial capitalism. (For some lucid description of Hong Kong's laissez-faire capitalism see Owen 1971; Riedel 1974; Rabushka 1979; Woronoff 1980; Lin, Mok, and Ho 1980; Youngson 1982; and Sung 1986.)

Hong Kong has been fortunate in that it started its export-oriented industrialism in light manufactures about a decade earlier than most of its contemporary competitors, particularly South Korea and Taiwan, which were heavily preoccupied with political and military quandaries in the late 1940s and early '50s. The development strategy pursued in almost all developing economies during the period was largely one of import substitution under a regime of high rates of protection. Hong Kong embraced export-oriented manufacturing fairly quickly in large part because of the well-established commercial infrastructure of an entrepôt. Hong Kong was the first developing territory to successfully break into the vast consumer markets of North America and Western Europe and sell light manufactures. By the early 1960s, it had managed to become the leading exporter of manufactured goods among the developing world (Lary 1968; Rahman 1973; Lydall 1975).

Overall Economic Performance

The export-led growth achieved by Hong Kong during the past three decades or so has been justly regarded as exemplary among the less developed countries (LDCs). As shown in Table 6.1, which presents an overview of Hong Kong's growth record during the period 1961–87, gross domestic product (GDP) at constant market prices grew at a compound annual average rate of over 10%. On a per capita basis, the corresponding rate was about 7.7%. By 1987, GDP per capita had reached HK$64,174 (about US$8,227), placing it, in East and South East Asia, behind only Japan and (probably) Singapore.

This exemplary development was initiated and has been sustained by a rapid and continual expansion in export industrialism. During the same period, domestically produced exports grew at an average rate of 11% in real terms. In consequence, Hong Kong has developed into one of the world's leading trading emporia. In terms of merchandise goods alone, it is now the 12th largest exporting entity in the world. One may be amazed to note that Hong Kong's total export amount is at present still greater than its giant neighbor—China. In per capita terms, Hong

Table 6.1. Major Growth Indicators

Real Growth Rates (Percents Per Annum)				1987 Level (HK$ Billion Except as Noted)	
1961 –71	1971 –81	1981 –87	1961 –87		
11.3	10.8	7.2	10.1	360	GDP at market prices
8.6	8.0	5.8	7.7	64	GDP per capita (thousands)
					gross capital formation
10.7	14.2	3.4	10.3	91	total domestic (GDFC)
7.5	11.1	0.8	7.3	30	building and construction
11.7	12.1	5.4	10.4	40	plant and machinery
					international trade
13.3	11.0	14.0	12.6	378	total exports
11.0	17.1	20.3	15.4	183	re-exports
13.9	8.9	10.0	11.0	195	domestic exports
14.7	8.9	9.8	11.3	187	manufactured exports
11.3	10.3	11.8	11.1	378	total imports
					(in millions, at mid year)
2.5	2.4	1.4	2.2	5.6	population
3.2	4.2	1.7	3.2	2.8	total labor force
3.6	2.9	–0.6	2.4	0.9	manufacturing employment
6.5	3.7	4.2	4.9	119	manufacturing wages (HK$/day)

All growth rates are compound annual rates.
Sources: Hong Kong Census and Statistics Department: Estimates of Gross Domestic Product; Hong Kong Review of Overseas Trade; Hong Kong Monthly Digest of Statistics; Report of the 1961 Census.

Kong's position is even more remarkable. For instance, per capita exports in 1986 stood at US$6,411, about 3.4 times the British level, 3.7 times the Japanese, and over 7 times the United States.

The growth of manufacturing production, together with the development of other economic activities, brought about an increased demand for labor large enough to absorb the increase in supply. Consequently, for manufacturing workers as a group, real average daily wages have increased at a compound annual rate of approximately 5% over the period. As has been well documented, Hong Kong's economic and institutional setting provides a fine example of the classical wage model, which predicts the change in wage rates is positively related to the excess demand for labor (see Turner et al 1980; Chen 1984; Deyo 1987; Chau 1988). Stated alternatively, under a tight labor market situation, people are responding to higher-wage opportunities, so it is a market pull rather than push mechanism that is at work. Of course, over time, such a substantial increase in real wages could not have been sustained without a corresponding rise in labor productivity.

This booming economic activity is also seen in the rapid increase in real gross domestic capital formation, at an average rate of over 10% compounded annually over the period. This figure is indicative of both the economy's rapid industrial expansion and of its construction effort. It is worth noting all the entire-period growth figures discussed so far tend to conceal fluctuations from one year or sub-period to another. The sub-period growth rates outlined in Table 6.1 show that the growth of GDP, capital formation, and manufacturing employment have had a downward trend. Despite this slowing, the evidence of sustained growth during the past quarter century can hardly be disputed.

Macroeconomic Policy

Hong Kong is perhaps the economy with the least government intervention. There are no central planning commissions, no central bank, no general tariffs, no industry and export subsidies, no tax holidays, no minimum wage legislation (with the exception of wages paid to Filipina maids), no restrictions on the entry and repatriation of capital or on the conversion and remittance of profits and dividends, and the like. The Hong Kong government firmly believes that entrepreneurs in an open market know best how and what to produce and which market to sell in. Therefore, their business acumen should be allowed to thrive without interference by the government. It does not see its role as providing direct subsidies to any particular sector of industry, but as creating the conditions under which legitimate business may prosper and grow (Bremridge 1981; Haddon-Cave 1982; Howe 1983).

Despite the fact the Hong Kong government has never retreated from its stance of free enterprise and minimal interference, it does not adhere dogmatically to a "do-nothing" approach, ignoring all social needs. Instead, it exercises, through a process of ad hoc consultation, its power to intervene in economic processes when market or social and political situations dictate it should do so. It is interesting to note that the Hong Kong community at large, through a network of some 435 advisory boards and committees, all set up by the government on an ad hoc basis, participate in such decision-making processes.

The Hong Kong government takes the view that, because of the external orientation of the economy, it is normally futile and even damaging to the performance of the economy for the government to attempt to plan the allocation of competing resources or to frustrate the operations of market forces. This implies that no industry-specific intervention will be undertaken except where it is clearly in the long-run interests of the economy.

Degree of External Orientation

Hong Kong has always been an outward-looking economy. The extent of Hong Kong's external orientation can be gauged from the ratios of its imports and exports to total GDP (Tables 6.2 and 6.3). Imports averaged over 84% during the period 1961–87, with an upward trend since the late 1970s. Exports have ranged between 60 and 105% of GDP, with a strong upward trend since the mid 1970s. Taken together, the total value of Hong Kong's two-way trade rose to about 2.1 times GDP in 1987 from a range of 1.4 to 1.6 during most of the 1960s, '70s, and early '80s. Such a high and increasing degree of openness is rarely seen, even among the family of small, open economic entities.

Continual export-oriented growth over the post-Korean War years has graduated the Hong Kong economy from the developing world to the ranks of the newly industrialized economies (NIEs) (see Corbo et al 1985; James et al 1987). But it has also made Hong Kong vulnerable to the vagaries and vicissitudes of a rapidly changing external environment. Given the fact that over 90% of its manufacturing output is eventually exported, creeping protectionism in Hong Kong's major overseas markets is beyond doubt a nagging development, particularly for textiles and clothing.

Table 6.2. Trade Levels, 1961–87 (current HK$ billion)

1961	1967	1971	1975	1979	1983	1985	1987	
9.9	19.2	37	63	162	336	467	756	total trade (X + M)
−2.0	−1.7	−3.1	−3.6	−9.9	−14.7	3.7	0.1	trade balance (X − M)
								exports
3.9	8.8	17	30	76	161	235	378	total (X)
2.9	6.7	14	23	56	104	130	195	domestic (DX)
1.0	2.1	3	7	20	56	105	183	re-exports (RX)
2.6	6.4	13	22	54	100	124	187	manufactured (MX)[3]
								imports
6.0	10.4	20	33	86	175	231	378	total (M)
5.0	8.4	17	26	66	119	126	195	retained (RM)[1]

See Table 6.3 for notes and sources

Table 6.3. Indicators of External Orientation, 1961–87 (percents)

1961	1967	1971	1975	1979	1983	1985	1987	
83	80	83	79	77	68	55	52	RM / M[1]
75	76	80	77	74	65	55	52	DX / X[2]
90	95	96	97	96	96	95	96	MX / DX[3]
								trade balance as a
−52	−19	−18	−12	−13	−9	2	0	percentage of exports
								percentage of GDP
65	60	68	64	71	77	89	105	exports
99	71	80	72	80	85	88	105	imports
164	131	149	136	151	162	177	210	total trade (X + M)

Components may not add to 100 due to rounding. There are no trends in any of Table 6.3's series. The value series in Table 6.2 have all increased steadily, except for the trade balance.

1. Retained Imports (RM) are total imports net of those destined for re-export. RM/M is the percentage of retained imports in total imports.

2. DX/X is the percentage of domestic exports in total exports. 100 minus DX/X is the percentage of re-exports.

3. Manufactured Exports (MX) covers SITC 512–899 (United Nations Commodity Indexes for Standard International Trade Classification). MX/DX is the percentage of manufactured exports in domestic exports.

Sources: Hong Kong Census and Statistics Department: various issues of Hong Kong Trade Statistics and of Estimates of Gross Domestic Product.

After mercantilist forces abroad, changes in comparative advantage have a major impact on Hong Kong. Since the mid-1970s the cost of labor and the price of land in Hong Kong have been rising quite inexorably relative to LDCs. The main concern of this paper is to identify some specific sources of relative decline in Hong Kong's traditional manufacturing industries, with particular emphasis on the problems, mechanisms, and policy options related to structural adjustment.

TOWARDS DE-INDUSTRIALIZATION OR RE-SERVICIZATION?

As is well documented in the literature on economic growth, the course of economic progress is accompanied by continual structural changes involving intersectoral shifts of resources. The changing structure of Hong Kong's economy as reflected by the relative shares of major sectors in GDP for the past quarter century is shown in Table 6.4.

Given Hong Kong's geographic structure and factor endowment, it is not unexpected to observe that not only has the primary sector never been important, its contribution dwindled steadily over the past decades.

Table 6.4. Distribution of GDP by Industrial Sector, 1961–86 (percents)

1961	1971	1975	1979	1983	1986	
						sectors
4	2	1.5	1.1	0.8	0.6	primary[1]
32	35	34	36	32	29	secondary[2]
64	63	64	63	68	70	tertiary[3]
						subsectors
24	28	27	28	23	22	manufacturing
6	5	6	7	6	5	construction
11	18	17	21	18	17	financial services[4]

GDP is at factor cost.
Sector distribution may not add to 100% due to rounding.
1. Agriculture, fishing, mining, and quarrying.
2. Manufacturing, construction, and utilities.
3. Services, including ownership of premises.
4. Finance, insurance, real estate ("FIRE"), and business services.
Sources: Chang 1969 and Hong Kong Census and Statistics Department: various issues of *Estimates of Gross Domestic Product.*

The most significant change in Hong Kong's industrial structure in the 1960s was a marked increase in the contribution of manufacturing. Its share in GDP was less than 24% in 1961 and went up to nearly 31% in 1970, reflecting the rapid pace of Hong Kong's export industrialism.

A Shift Toward De-industrialization?

Starting from the early 1970s, the pace of manufacturing growth has been less consistent. Its share of GDP declined from about 31% in 1970 to less than 21% in 1982. Though it increased some 3 percentage points during the two subsequent years, it fell back to about 22% in the mid-1980s. This reflects a de-industrialization process.

In terms of employment by sectors, such a de-industrialization process is also clearly reflected in a steady decline in the share of manufacturing employment (Table 6.5). From 1971 to 1987 the employment share of manufacturing dropped well over 12 percentage points, which is even more pronounced than the decline in its contribution to GDP over the period. As a matter of fact, in the 1980s manufacturing employment has seen a significant decline in absolute terms.

Of course de-industrialization can occur in a variety of ways, and thus has many different meanings. (Rowthorn and Wells 1987 present a detailed account of the theory of de-industrialization, its chemistry of occurrence, and its possible explanations. Also see Cairncross 1978.)

Table 6.5. Working Population by Industry and Other Characteristics

1961	1971	1976	1981	1983	1987	
						total (in millions)
1.19	1.55	1.85	2.40	2.46	2.71	working population
1.21	1.62	1.92	2.50	2.57	2.76	labor force
1.8	4.4	3.6	3.9	3.8	1.8	unemployment rate (%)
Labor Force Participation Rates (%)[1]						
90	85	80	82	81	80	males
37	43	44	49	48	49	females
64	64	62	66	65	65	overall
Employment Distribution by Sector (%)						
8	4	2.7	2.0	1.2	1.5	primary[2]
49	53	51	50	46	44	secondary[3]
43	43	46	48	53	55	tertiary[4]
						subsectors
43	47	45	41	37	35	manufacturing
5	5	6	8	8	8	construction
1.6	2.7	3.4	4.7	6	6	financial services[5]

1. The labor force participation rate is the proportion of the population age 15 and over who are in the labor force, including unemployed.
2. Agriculture, fishing, mining, and quarrying.
3. Manufacturing, construction, and utilities.
4. Services, including ownership of premises.
5. Finance, insurance, real estate ("FIRE"), and business services.
Sources: Hong Kong Census and Statistics Department: various issues of the General Household Survey: Labor Force Characteristics; and various Census reports.

Rowthorn and Wells, by observing the behavior of per capita income and unemployment through the course of time, rightly point out two kinds: positive and negative. Positive de-industrialization is associated with full employment, rising real incomes, and movement into areas of new comparative advantage, while the negative form is associated with stagnant real incomes and rising unemployment. In practice, of course, intermediate cases are possible, and an economy may sometimes experience both at the same time. Following the criteria of rising real income with full employment, we may safely conclude the de-industrialization that has occurred in Hong Kong since the early 1970s is by and large the positive sort.

Towards a Service Economy Anew?

In the decade of the 1970s, the most notable structural change was the re-emergence of Hong Kong as a fast-growing regional service center. In terms of contribution to the economy's aggregate output, the service sector rose from less than 61% in 1970 to 70% in 1987. In addition to Hong Kong's rapid development as a financial center, this upsurge has been assisted by the opening of China, which has not only led to a revival of Hong Kong's traditional role as an entrepôt for trade with China, but also induced a demand for financing and other business services.

Similar to merchandise trade, the pattern and evolution of Hong Kong's service trade can be explained in terms of a comparative advantage that arises mainly from the unique features of the capitalistic enclave (Sung 1988). The strategic geographic and time-zone location of the territory and its natural deep water harbor are what can be termed its natural advantages. More important, there are man-made conditions — its free exchange regime, the free movement of money, a simple and low taxation policy, and the well-known policy stance of "positive nonintervention." Also among these are effective law enforcement and a sound infrastructure of complementary services such as efficient transportation and telecommunications networks, accounting and specialized legal services. Taken together, they have created a favorable environment necessary for Hong Kong to become a servicing center in the region. This is best exemplified by the successful evolution of the economy into a regional financial center in the 1970s.

Given its comparative advantage in entrepôt trade and provision of tourist, financial, and shipping services, Hong Kong has traditionally had a large service sector when compared with other economies at a similar stage of development. In the late 1980s, with its service sector accounting for 70% of output, Hong Kong is undoubtedly one of the most service-oriented economies in the world. Conceivably, as China's gateway to overseas markets, the output and employment shares of Hong Kong's service sector will see further rises in the years to come.

Based on the longitudinal trends discussed above, one may argue that de-industrialization in Hong Kong is not necessarily a pathological phenomenon. The process was, to a very considerable extent, the consequence of improvements in Hong Kong's non-manufacturing activities. Under these circumstances, with the exception of the world recession of 1974–75, Hong Kong has experienced no serious unemployment.

Despite its relative decline over the period, manufacturing has remained the single most important sector in both absolute and relative terms, and the main impetus to Hong Kong's economic growth and employment creation. It needs little elaboration that the significance of export-oriented manufacturing in Hong Kong is not confined to its role as a leading employer or a major foreign exchange earner for the territory; it has other valuable characteristics. In particular, there are direct and indirect linkage effects, such as the demand for both immediate and secondary supporting services including banking, insurance, legal services, advertising, transportation, and the like. The importance of manufacturing thus goes far beyond the official relative GDP contribution and employment statistics. As far as the future is concerned, manufacturing will certainly continue to create job opportunities for a significant number of workers, particularly those who cannot adapt to service industries.

The relative decline of Hong Kong's manufacturing sector since the mid-1970s no doubt has a cyclical component, but many hold that the origins of the slowdown are also rooted in a number of basic structural maladies, posed by an increasingly integrated world economy. The world economy has been going through a period of turbulence and structural shifts since the early 1970s. Energy crises, rapid international transfers of technology, mass emergence of competition in labor-intensive manufacturers, creeping neo-mercantilism in Western industrial countries, and the traditional protectionism of Japan and most of the developing economies have put increasing pressure on export-oriented manufacturing industries throughout the world. This calls for an attentive look at bottlenecks and policy measures relating to Hong Kong's industrial restructuring.

The drive for industrial restructuring has now almost become a common development strategy for most national economies, export-oriented or otherwise. In fact, there is nothing fundamentally new about this progression. It is a natural process associated with economic growth and change. But as pointed out by two World Bank economists: "What is new is the magnitude, suddenness, rapidity, and complexity of the industrial restructuring necessitated by a much changed global economic environment over the past decade. The intensified pressure for change and its economic and social implications have increasingly led governments of all economic persuasions to play a more active role in inducing and facilitating effective restructuring so that international competitiveness can be improved or regained" (Sood and Kohli 1985, p 46).

In a trade-dependent economy such as Hong Kong, exposed to nearly all economic infections abroad, the government authority, not unlike governments elsewhere, sees itself as having an important role in working with industry to develop and support the implementation of desirable restructuring strategies (Ho 1986; Chen 1987).

Before scrutinizing the longer-term economic and industrial policies the Hong Kong government will take, we first make a general examination of Hong Kong's domestic export structure and its change, and of those major industries that have been in trouble or relative decline during the 1970s or '80s. Such examinations, along with a broad review of the extent of actual adjustment that has taken place during the period, will enable us to know more clearly the achievements and limitations of Hong Kong's manufacturing industries. This in turn will enable us to map out some appropriate strategies for Hong Kong's future course of industrial restructuring.

CHANGING EXPORT STRUCTURE

A conspicuous feature of the development of manufacturing industry in Hong Kong has been the high degree of export orientation: with about 90% of its final output being sold overseas, "manufactured exports" can almost be used synonymously with "manufacturing output."

Export Commodity Structure

Table 6.6 shows the commodity structure of Hong Kong's domestic exports in manufactures during the period 1961–87. Except for a few years during the late 1960s and early '70s, well over half of total domestic exports between 1961 and 1976 was accounted for by textiles and clothing. Undoubtedly, this ratio is high by world standards, but in the context of Hong Kong's economic setting, it is not unexpected. Their decline to less than half since 1977 is by and large due to increasing import restrictions imposed on Hong Kong's textile and clothing products by its major trading partners on the one hand, and the result of growing competition from other NIEs and LDCs on the other.

Hong Kong's domestic exports reflect the change occurring in the structure of manufacturing industries—a definite move away from the production of simple textiles and such products as footwear and plastic flowers towards the higher stages of the textile production chain and towards greater amounts of other types of manufactured goods such as plastic toys, watches, and electronics. Accordingly, the relative decline of the textile industry since the early 1960s and that of the clothing industry since the mid-1970s have been counterpoised by the rapid growth of these newer industries. Still, it is worth noting that among the

Table 6.6. Exports of Domestically Manufactured Products

1961	1967	1971	1975	1979	1983	1987	
2.9	6.7	14	23	56	104	195	total domestic exports (in HK$ billions)

Percentage Distribution by Industry

23	14	10	9	7	7	8	textiles
29	35	40	45	36	33	34	clothing
4	3	3	1	1	1	1	footwear
*	3	9	10	10	18	13	electronics[1]
2	6	2	4	6	3	6	electrical goods
*	1	1	3	8	8	7	watches and clocks
1	1	1	1	1	1	1	precision instruments[2]
5	8	9	6	8	8	6	toys and dolls[3]
7	5	3	2	2	2	2	plastic products
4	3	2	3	3	2	2	sundry metal manufactures
1	1	2	2	2	2	1	handbags and travel goods
25	21	18	14	16	16	17	all other exports

1. Electronics includes all telecommunications, sound recording and reproducing, and automatic data processing apparatus and equipment.

2. Precision instruments includes all professional, scientific, and controlling instruments and apparatus, plus photographic and optical goods. Watches and clocks are listed separately, so are excluded here.

3. Plastic products excludes plastic toys and dolls.

* Less than 0.5%.

Sources: Hong Kong Census and Statistics Department: various December issues of Hong Kong Trade Statistics, and various annual issues of Hong Kong Review of Overseas Trade.

other manufacturing industries included in "all others" in the table, none (with the notable exception of wigs) had been of significance in Hong Kong.

In terms of commodity concentration, in spite of efforts to broaden its industrial base, Hong Kong's domestic exports were apparently becoming more concentrated on a handful of light manufacturers. While the five leading product groups accounted for about 68% in 1961, the corresponding figure rose to 77% from the mid-1970s onwards. This situation is a basis of the oft-repeated call for industrial diversification.

Export Market Structure

Aside from commodity concentration, another conspicuous feature characterizing Hong Kong's export trade is its direction, with an increasing trend towards the developed country (DC) markets. By far, the countries of the Organization for Economic Cooperation and Development (OECD), taken as a group, have been Hong Kong's most important export market. As shown in Table 6.7, their combined share went up to more than four-fifths by the late 1960s from about two-thirds in the early 1960s. Despite the relative decline since the mid 1980s, this group of the world's major DCs still absorbed about three-fourths of Hong Kong's domestic exports in 1987.

Country-wise, the three most industrially advanced DCs—the United States, the United Kingdom, and West Germany—have constituted Hong Kong's leading markets over the period, but their relative shares have changed quite considerably. Most notably, at least from the time of separate listing of Hong Kong's domestic exports and re-exports from its total export statistics in 1959, the United States has replaced the United Kingdom as the principal market. For most of the postwar years, Japan has been Hong Kong's 4th largest export market. However, its

Table 6.7 Distribution of Domestic Exports by Principal Markets (percents)

1961	1967	1971	1975	1979	1983	1987	
							region
25	41	45	36	37	46	40	North America
29	30	31	36	35	26	26	Western Europe
27	14	11	12	14	18	27	Asia
19	15	13	17	15	11	8	rest of the world
							country
23	37	42	32	34	42	37	United States
20	17	14	12	11	8	7	United Kingdom
4	6	8	12	11	8	8	West Germany
4	3	4	4	5	4	5	Japan
*	*	*	*	1	6	14	China
49	37	32	39	38	32	29	all others
							organization
45	33	28	28	23	19	16	British Commonwealth
61	78	83	81	80	78	73	OECD

* less than 0.4%. (0.1% in most years 1967–78).
See Table 6.6, which includes HK$ amounts of total domestic exports, for sources.

relative intake saw no improvement over the years. Given Japan's complex import procedures and its distribution system, Hong Kong's poor market penetration is not unexpected.

Adding to a booming re-export trade, Hong Kong's domestic exports to China have witnessed a dramatic increase over the last decade. In 1977, China absorbed less than 1% of the territory's domestic exports. By 1987 its share had shot over 14%. China has become the second largest domestic export market. Of course, much of this upsurge consists of intermediate goods being processed in China before being returned to Hong Kong for final processing, packaging, and export.

By any comparative measure, the degree of Hong Kong's market concentration is no less than its commodity counterpart. The message from this situation is: the development of Hong Kong's export-oriented manufacturing in the near future will be still closely linked with economic conditions and trade policies in its main overseas markets.

Export Demand-Generated Employment Structure

Through its direct and indirect effects on final demand, Hong Kong's export trade tends to determine the level of its domestic output, income, and employment. As can be expected, the data on manufacturing employment in Table 6.8 reveal much the same pattern as the domestic export data in Table 6.6: there is a high degree of correlation between employment and domestic export structures in Hong Kong's manufacturing sector. This means there is high employment concentration.

While the five leading manufacturing industries employed about 73% of the working population in manufacturing in 1961, the figure went up to nearly 80% in the mid 1970s. In 1987 the proportion stood at about 74%. This points to a rather serious problem for the economy as a sudden and drastic fall in overseas demand for the output of one of its major industries would certainly be detrimental to the overall production activity and hence the stability of employment growth in Hong Kong. (For a quantitative study on this problem, see Lin and Ho 1979.) How to broaden or restructure Hong Kong's industrial base to reduce its vulnerability to external shocks and changes is therefore of vital importance to Hong Kong.

In this respect, neglect of time perspective seems to us to underlie much of the popular discussion of "industrial diversification" in Hong Kong. What is not often appreciated is the fact industrial diversification has been going on for decades in Hong Kong without people consciously noticing it. In retrospect, in response to changing political and economic conditions abroad, a great deal of restructuring has taken place in both

Table 6.8. Distribution of Manufacturing Labor Force (percents)

1961	1967	1971	1975	1979	1983	1987	
29	26	22	17	12	13	14	textiles
19	18	23	35	32	29	30	clothing
4	3	3	2	1	1	1	footwear & rubber products
*	5	7	8	11	11	10	electronics[1]
2	4	2	2	3	4	3	electrical goods
3	5	6	5	5	5	5	plastic toys and dolls
5	7	6	4	5	5	5	other plastic products
1	2	1	2	4	5	4	precision instruments[2]
12	9	8	8	10	8	7	sundry metal manufactures
5	5	4	4	4	5	6	paper and printing
20	16	16	13	13	14	15	other

Data are percentages of total manufacturing labor force. See Table 6.5 for the absolute size of the labor force. Excludes out-workers, part-time and casual employes, and unpaid family workers who worked less than 3 hours during the reference period. Prior to 1973, the coverage of employment statistics was limited to manufacturing establishments registered with or recorded by the Labor Department.

* Less than 0.5%.

1. See Table 6.6 for definition.

2. Includes workers in clocks and watches. See Table 6.6 for definition.

Sources: various issues of Hong Kong Commissioner of Labor: Annual Departmental Report; and of Hong Kong Census and Statistics Department: Hong Kong Monthly Digest of Statistics.

manufacturing and non-manufacturing. Within manufacturing, the clothing industry has long replaced textiles as the largest industry in terms of output, employment, and export earnings. In the meantime, industries such as toys, watches, and light consumer electronics have emerged and grown. On the other hand, there are also quite a number of industries, such as footwear, wigs, enamelware, matches, and toothbrushes, that, in the course of industrial development, have boomed then declined, either relatively or absolutely.

DECLINING INDUSTRIES

Broadly speaking, we can distinguish between "truly declining" and "structurally depressed" or "troubled" industries. The first category faces the loss of long-run competitiveness, either as a result of eclipsed comparative advantage or a secular decline in world demand. Such industries are further characterized by excess productive capacity and redundant labor resources. The second category basically is competitive but is suffering from cyclical and non-cyclical downswings in world demand or other supply-side constraints, particularly those structural bottlenecks arising from rapid changes in technology.

Like all other places, Hong Kong has witnessed many a "truly declining" industry. Enamelware, wigs, and plastic flowers come readily to mind. But unlike most other places, as a predominantly free market economy, Hong Kong has no space for any "truly declining" industries. Business enterprises, large and small alike, are completely free to choose their lines of production, forms of ownership, and technology, but there have never been any protective tariffs and quotas or subsidies to protect inefficient and dying industries (Rabushka 1979; Friedman and Friedman 1979; Youngson 1982). The incompetent and simply unlucky fall by the wayside. Accordingly, Hong Kong's exporting firms and industries must always produce what the world demands, according to comparative advantage. Thus, when confronted with a long-term decline in world demand or loss in comparative advantage, Hong Kong can do nothing about such changes but give the industry up.

For the Hong Kong economy, what is of vital concern to its industrial development over time is how to restructure. This includes dealing with "structurally depressed" industries and those looking ahead to higher production efficiency and external competitiveness. For the Hong Kong economy, the problem of such restructuring efforts is of special significance with respect to its textiles and clothing industries. These two together still occupy the lion's share of the manufacturing sector. Many lines of textile and clothing production in Hong Kong are still rather labor-intensive and its competitive edge in these lines has been lost as its wage levels and industrial rentals have risen much faster than those elsewhere. The deterioration in relative competitiveness was amply reflected in the displacement of Hong Kong's textile and clothing products by those of other Asian NIEs and LDCs in the major importing countries (Lin and Ho 1984).

To prevent the continuation of such a withering, it is often argued Hong Kong has to be more engaged in "manufacturing up"—moving on to more highly technological, perhaps more capital and human capital-intensive industries. The consensus of local industrialists and the government elite is that such a shifting to higher value-added production will be more challenging for private enterprises than previous restructuring and, thus, government support will be called for. The role of the government in the industrial restructuring of Hong Kong will be looked at later. The next section presents a general survey of Hong Kong's declining industries, either real or seemingly apparent, with reference to their adjustment experiences. Much that can be applied to the future can be learned from both the successes and setbacks of past efforts to restructure Hong Kong's industrial base.

Textiles

Since Great Britain in the 18th century, the first step towards a country's industrialization is very often the establishment of a spinning mill or a weaving factory. This was how Hong Kong began in the early 1950s. Although the textile industry did exist in the territory before World War II, it was confined to cottage-type operations. After the Communist takeover of China in 1949, many textile industrialists in Shanghai moved to Hong Kong. There, using new machinery and equipment which, by chance, were still in warehouses awaiting transshipment, they laid the foundation of Hong Kong's modern textile industry. Apart from the infusion of capital and entrepreneurial skills from China, the rapid expansion of textiles owed a lot to the Commonwealth Preference Scheme, which gave Hong Kong's exporters preferential access into Commonwealth countries, notably the United Kingdom. The textile industry manufactures yarn, fabrics, piecegoods, and made-up articles through spinning, weaving, and various finishing processes. Its relative growth, and slowdown, can best be examined by reference to these components.

Spinning. The foundations of Hong Kong's spinning sector were laid by industrialists from Shanghai in the troubled years between 1947 and 1951 when 12 mills with about 180,000 spindles were established (see *Textiles Hong Kong* 1965, p 3). Between the mid 1960s and 1976, the sector experienced rapid growth in terms of spindles, employment, and output. During this period, output grew at a much faster rate than that of employment or the number of spindles. This was largely attributable to the introduction and increasing use of open-end spindles, which require less labor to operate.

However, since the late 1970s, the sector witnessed a continual fall in the number of spindles installed and the size of the employed work force. This was due to slackened overseas demand, particularly for denims, on the one hand, and rising costs of production and growing LDC competition on the other. In terms of product composition, despite the increase in production of synthetic fiber-blended yarns, cotton yarn remains the dominant product.

In addition, since the mid-1970s, owing to the coming back into fashion of cotton apparel, the output of spinning mills in general and that of cotton yarn in particular has increasingly treated the domestic market as a substitution for overseas markets. Most of the cotton yarn produced is used locally for the manufacture of clothing.

Weaving. The development of this sector is similar to that of spinning in a number of respects. The sector witnessed a steady increase in looms, employment, and output during 1955–75 and saw a sharp increase in its output around the mid-1970s, mainly because of a surge in world demand for denims. Second, improved productivity over the same period was due largely to the increased installation of high-speed looms and shuttleless looms. Third, the bulk of the production was of cotton, and increasingly so. In 1987 cotton accounted for 96% of total output of about 885 million square meters of woven fabrics (*Hong Kong* 1988, p 68). As in the case of spinning, a major proportion of the locally woven and finished fabrics was used by local clothing manufacturers (Chen 1987).

During the 1960s and '70s, the weaving sector experienced a marked trend from the production of mainly the heavier and coarser types of fabric such as drills, twills, and ducks towards greater production of the finer count and lighter weight constructions such as poplins and sateens. These fabrics were required in increasing quantities by the local cotton garment industry, whose rapid expansion during the 1960s also stimulated product research by the local weavers into the production of specialty fabrics such as dobby weaves and fancy poplins.

However, like open-end spinning, Hong Kong's weaving sector and those denim items in particular went through a period of reckless expansion and over-production since the mid-1970s. Not unexpectedly, as a result of the slowdown in the sales of denims, a large number of latecomers, who established their factories in the latter part of 1975, have been weeded out in less than no time. It is estimated that in the first half of 1977, about two-thirds of Hong Kong's 300 denim weavers had either gone out of business or sharply cut production.

Finishing. Compared with the spinning and weaving sectors, the finishing sector, vital to the textile industry as a whole, is relatively new. ("Finishing" is the bleaching, dyeing, printing, stenciling, etc of grey fabric—that is, fabric as it comes off the loom, thus also called "loom-state" fabric.) Much of the grey fabric produced between the late 1940s and the mid-1950s was exported without being processed, while during the same period much of the apparel exported from Hong Kong was made from fabrics woven and finished in Japan. In other words, the development of a modern finishing sector capable of delivering substantial quantities of processed fabrics and yarns of acceptable qualities at competitive prices had not kept pace with the development of spinning, weaving, and garment manufacturing at that time.

In the mid-1950s, the situation started to change and a growing number of modernized finishing mills have since been brought into operation. By the late 1970s, some 300 finishing factories employing about 12,000 workers were registered with the Labor Department. In addition to serving the local weavers and garment manufacturers, the finishing sector, particularly the dyeing section, has also attracted considerable overseas orders.

However, in the 1980s, because the industry is a heavy user of water and electricity as well as being land-intensive, it has been hard pressed by the high costs of these three factors, as well as by rising wages and increasing competition from low-cost LDCs. Full capacity of existing plant has not been utilized for a number of years. This is by and large a reflection of firms' inability to pay higher wages because of declining competitiveness.

Prospects for Hong Kong's textile industry are uncertain as the industry continues to be exposed to change after change in fashion and competition. A number of Hong Kong's spinning, weaving, and finishing companies have already relocated in China and other nearby countries such as Indonesia, Malaysia, and the Philippines for the sake of cheaper land and labor. Some have become property developers, transforming their factory sites into commercial complexes or investing in real estate abroad. By all indications, Hong Kong's textile industry has entered a period of consolidation.

Apparel

Almost from its start in the early 1950s, Hong Kong's clothing industry has played a dominant role in the economy. To meet ever-changing overseas demands, its rapid expansion during the 1960s and '70s was accompanied by a steady move towards product diversification and sophistication. Quality-wise, although products in the high price range are at present still less competitive than Italian or French counterparts, Hong Kong replaced Italy as the world's leading exporter of clothing in terms of both quantity and value in 1975.

Looking back, owing to the GATT formulation of the Short Term and then the Long Term Arrangement Regarding International Trade in Cotton Textiles (STA and LTA) in the 1960s, there was a marked trend of diversification within clothing exports from cotton items into synthetic fibers. But with the introduction of the Multi-Fiber Arrangement

(MFA) in the mid-1970s, this trend has reversed. This reversal was also partly due to the coming back into fashion of cotton clothing. By kind of wear, not only has "outergarment" been the major export category of Hong Kong, its relative importance has also increased from about two-thirds of total clothing exports in the late 1960s to almost three-quarters since the early 1980s. As can be expected, in outerwear, since the mid-1970s, there has been a clear trend of increasing importance in the export of non-knitted products made of cotton.

The development and maturing of the clothing industry in Hong Kong has been in part the natural result of growth, and in part a response to mounting Western trade restrictions on clothing exports. Compared with the textile industry, which has come a long way in recent years in modernizing its production capacity, clothing manufacture at present still involves rather labor-intensive processes. Also, unlike textiles, a large proportion of which goes to the local garment sector, the overwhelming bulk of apparel output is for overseas sales. But, not unlike the situation confronted by the textile industry in recent years, full capacity of clothing production has not been reached as a result of wage pressure caused by the persistent strong demand for labor by almost all sectors of economic activity in Hong Kong.

The availability of abundant low-wage labor in earlier years was undoubtedly one major supply-side factor contributing to the spectacular growth of clothing manufacturing in Hong Kong. This favorable factor has gradually eroded. A comparative analysis of the value added and cost structure by industrial groups, as outlined in Table 6.9, reveals that in the mid-1980s, labor cost in the clothing industry accounts for a much higher percentage of gross output than in the other industrial groups. Not surprisingly, as against gross output, the percentage of operating surplus was only about 7% for clothing during 1984–86, as compared to about 10 to 11% for other industrial groups.

Of course, aside from the high labor cost, increased payments for other operating expenses have also cut into profit margins. To reduce their costs, many garment manufacturers have either set up their own factories in China or farmed out the more labor-intensive parts to subcontractors there. And with each property boom, quite a number of them have diversified into real estate in the hope of making a quick buck.

In respect of demand-side restraints, it is conceivable that due to a multiplicity of restrictive trade arrangements now in force, expansion in terms of volume will inevitably proceed more slowly in the future than in the past. But in view of the fact import quotas are set in terms of quantity rather than value, one of the most natural ways to maximize

Table 6.9. Gross Output, Value Added, and Cost Structure of Major Industries

	Textiles			Clothing			Electricals[1]		
Year	Gross Output[2]	Value Added %[3]	Surplus %[4]	Gross Output[2]	Value Added %[3]	Surplus %[4]	Gross Output[2]	Value Added %[3]	Surplus %[4]
1977	10.7	24	6.5	13.7	32	6.4	7.6	27	10.1
1980	18.1	24	7.4	26.9	30	6.3	18.2	22	7.7
1983	26.5	24	9.9	34.8	33	8.6	28.9	25	11.8
1986	40.7	27	11.7	47.4	32	7.0	38.7	23	9.7

	Plastic Products			Sundry Metal Manufactures		
	Gross Output[2]	Value Added %[3]	Surplus %[4]	Gross Output[2]	Value Added %[3]	Surplus %[4]
1977	3.9	36	9.1	3.2	36	9.9
1980	7.6	32	9.0	8.5	33	9.5
1983	11.2	29	9.3	10.0	32	10.7
1986	21.1	29	11.6	13.3	32	12.3

1. Includes electronics and electrical goods.
2. In HK$ billions
3. Value added as a percentage of gross output
4. Operating surplus as a percentage of gross output. Operating surplus is the value attributed to non-labor factors of production inclusive of the provision for consumption of fixed capital. For comparison, although substantially larger companies, operating margins (which are similar to operating surplus) for 10 textile firms publicly traded in the United States were 9.4% in 1983 and 9.2% in 1986 (*Value Line* 1987 Jun 05, p 1621).

Employe compensation is value added minus operating surplus.

Source: various issues of Hong Kong Census and Statistics Department: Estimates of Gross Domestic Products.

returns under the quotas is to diversify laterally and upgrade product quality.

Looking ahead, the prospects for the clothing industry are rather mixed. Some are even skeptical of its near-term outlook in view of high labor and material costs, soaring factory rentals, and growing protectionism in its major overseas market. But thus far Hong Kong still maintains a competitive edge over many of its rivals. Above all, because of its comparatively longer history of development, Hong Kong possesses larger export quotas than Taiwan and South Korea, and especially other LDCs. Thus, one sensible strategy for Hong Kong is to maintain its present quota positions in the principal markets and, at the same time, try to cultivate greener markets.

Plastic Industry

This industry has humble origins in the late 1940s producing mainly artificial flowers and foliage and simple housewares. In the 1960s the export of plastic flowers and foliage was an important foreign exchange earner for the territory. Since the late 1970s, the industry has been capable of producing a large variety of products including toys and dolls, household utensils, travel goods and handbags, packaging products, and polypropylene and fiberglass reinforced plastic furniture.

The growth of the industry is evidenced by the rapid increase in the number of establishments and workers. With three factories employing fewer than 40 workers when it started in 1947, by 1981 there were over 5,000 establishments employing a total of 89,000 workers—about 10% of the total manufacturing work force. However, entering the 1980s, like textiles and clothing, one major constraint on its continual expansion has been labor, which the industry has much difficulty in recruiting because of full employment virtually every year. In 1987, although the employment of its 5,717 establishments still accounted for about 10% of the manufacturing total, the total number of employed workers, when compared to the 1981 level, saw a decline of over 3,000.

In terms of product composition, since the mid-1960s the toys sector has replaced plastic flowers as the major category, with its share in total plastic products rising from about 56% in 1965 to well over 80% in the early 1980s. Accordingly, the growth performance of the industry can be inferred by reference to its toys sector. In more recent years, toy manufacturing has embraced an increasing proportion of electronic and TV games which, though not reckoned as plastic toys, are often made with plastic cases and parts. Taken together, toys remains the fourth largest exporting sector, after clothing, electronics, and textiles.

After supplanting West Germany in 1964 and Japan in 1972 in export sales, Hong Kong was able to maintain its position as the world's largest exporter of toys during the years 1972 to 1985. Despite a relative decline in recent years, Hong Kong continues to be one of the world's leading suppliers. Market-wise, the export of toys has been highly concentrated. In 1987 some 58% was taken by the United States, and the next five largest buyers absorbed 20%. Clearly, in order to lessen the adverse effects of any cyclical market downturns in the future, Hong Kong needs to strive for further market diversification.

Notwithstanding the fact that Hong Kong's toys industry has successfully developed an international image of being versatile and efficient, in the past decade it has lost numerous trading opportunities because of accusations regarding safety standards. As a basic requirement of market acceptance, there is little doubt more attention needs to be paid to toy safety. No less important, to preserve Hong Kong's external competitiveness, greater attention must be paid to production techniques, market research, product design, and packaging.

As regards production techniques, despite the fact there are a number of well-established toy factories where operations have already achieved a high level of automation, especially in processes such as injection molding and die casting, most of the factories have remained too small in size to adopt capital-intensive modes of production. Well over three-quarters of toys manufacturers employed fewer than 20 workers, while small to medium concerns (between 20 and 199 workers) accounted for about 23% of production in 1986. In other words, Hong Kong's toys industry remains basically labor intensive, and like other labor-intensive industries, many toys manufacturers have opened plants in China. To a considerable extent, the accessibility of China's abundant and cheaper labor supply for the more labor-intensive and lower-skilled production processes has assisted Hong Kong's toys manufacturers in staying competitive in increasingly difficult world markets.

Wigs

The dramatic rise and fall of the wigs industry exemplifies the versatility and volatility of Hong Kong manufacturing. The industry was established in 1963, but until 1965 exported little. However, during the latter half of the decade and the early 1970s when the swing of world fashion turned to wigs and other hairpieces, the industry had its glory days in Hong Kong. The rapid growth of wigs exports from 1965 to 1970 attests to Hong Kong's ability to adapt to changing market conditions.

Wigs export value, as indicated in Table 6.10, topped HK$937 million in 1970, amounting to almost 8% of Hong Kong's total domestic exports. At the industry's height in September 1970, there were 478 factories with a work force of 39,000, about 7.3% of total manufacturing employment (England and Rear 1981, p 42). One major factor accounting for Hong Kong's competitiveness in wigs was the close proximity of the essential raw material—human hair. Over 80% of Hong Kong's hair imports came from China (Holgate 1966, p 697).

During the late 1960s and early '70s world fashion took another swing, this time away from wigs of human hair towards those of synthetic fibers. In 1971 about 85% of all exports of wigs were made of synthetic materials. The sharp decline in demand for human-hair wigs had a disastrous impact on the industry. In 1973 exports of wigs regis-

Table 6.10. Wigs: Exports and Employment, 1964–74

1964	1966	1968	1970	1972	1973	1974	
9	71	318	937	224	104	44	exports (HK$ million)
0.5	1.6	12.1	28.9	15.0	7.8	1.5	workers (thousands)

As a Percentage of Overall Manufacturing

| 0.2 | 1.3 | 4.0 | 7.9 | 1.5 | 0.6 | 0.2 | exports |
| 0.2 | 0.5 | 2.8 | 5.4 | 2.7 | 1.4 | 0.2 | workers |

Includes false beards. SITC codes 899.940–.959; International Standard Industrial Classification (ISIC) code 390.9.

Sources: various December issues of Hong Kong Census and Statistics Department: Hong Kong Trade Statistics; various issues of Hong Kong Commissioner of Labor: Annual Departmental Report.

tered only HK$104 million, a decline of almost 90% from the height of 1970. Not surprisingly, by 1976 there remained a mere 29 factories with a work force of fewer than 800 (England and Rear 1981).

The absolute decline of the wigs industry in Hong Kong can be attributed to two factors. One was a shortage of synthetic fiber suitable for meeting the changing demand, further aggravated by strong competition from South Korea, Taiwan, and other low-wage LDCs generally. But this factor was only short-lived. More fundamentally, the decline was due to secular changes in market demand and consumer tastes. As long as this is the case, there is nothing Hong Kong's wigs manufacturers can do about it. Fortunately, the overall growth of the economy was fast enough to absorb the redundant workers.

Electronics

This industry started off on a very limited scale in 1959, engaged solely in the assembly of transistor radios almost wholly from parts imported from Japan. Since then, its expansion has been phenomenal. From the mid-1970s onwards, it has replaced textiles as the second largest foreign exchange earner in Hong Kong. Distinct from other industries, although it was originally developed by a couple of local industrialists, its development since the early 1960s has relied heavily on direct foreign capital participation, particularly from the United States.

After continual development during the 1960s and '70s, since entering the 1980s electronics has been confronted with a number of structural problems. The industry comprises only a few large firms surrounded by a large number of small concerns. The larger ones are mostly foreign-owned or joint-venture types, and have been responsible for the intro-duction of new technologies into Hong Kong. But, since the mid 1980s, the high wage rates and high cost of land prevailing in Hong Kong have led to the growth rates of direct foreign investment slowing considerably. A number of large electronics concerns have reportedly either suspended plans for expansion in Hong Kong or even moved their plants elsewhere.

What is more worrying is that, after some 20 years of unremitting efforts, Hong Kong's electronics industry has remained basically a labor-intensive processing industry relying heavily on a supply of young women with good eyesight and on a substantial supply of imported parts, com-ponents, and semi-manufactures. As shown in Table 6.11, which pre-sents a comparative picture of the production (or export) structure of the electronics industry in some selected economies, Hong Kong's export

Table 6.11. Comparative Structure of Electronics Industries (percents)

	Distribution of Exports				*Distribution of Production*		
Year	*Consumer*[1]	*Parts*[2]	*Profes-sional*[3]	*Year*	*Consumer*[1]	*Parts*[2]	*Profes-sional*[3]
Hong Kong				United States			
1974	52	48	0	1979	12	23	65
1976	64	36	0				
1978	69	30	1	Singapore			
1980	71	29	0				
1986	74	26	1	1980	40	57	3
Taiwan				Japan			
1979	50	47	3	1960	49	29	22
1981	47	49	4	1970	43	20	30
				1979	33	29	38
South Korea							
1980	49	45	6				
1986	40	43	17				

1. Consumer electronics includes radios, cassette recorders, televisions, TV games, calculators, digital clocks and watches, etc.
2. Parts includes components.
3. Professional electronics includes finished items or systems mainly used in businesses, such as computers, printers, and copiers.
Sources: Hong Kong Productivity Center: Study on the Hong Kong Electronics Indus-try (1984, figure 7) except 1986 Hong Kong data are the authors' estimates and Korean data are from Korea Development Bank Report 12 (1988 Apr).

share of consumer electronics grew from 52% in 1974 to 74% in 1986, while "parts and components" declined from 48% to less than 26% over the same period and professional (or industrial) electronics remained virtually absent from the scene. In other words, the direction of Hong Kong's development course is the opposite of that of its competing NIEs, notably South Korea and Taiwan, let alone the trend experienced by advanced economies.

The delineation above implies Hong Kong's electronics industry is, on the whole, still assembly-oriented. An ironic fact arising from this state is that, in spite of its early-bird status among its NIE peers, Hong Kong has at present depended, to a very considerable extent, on Taiwan and South Korea for parts, components, and semi-manufactures. Seen in this light, Hong Kong's electronics industry may face the danger of being edged out of the world market if its manufacturers fail to keep abreast with world trends and continue to rely heavily on competitors for parts and components.

However, the production of standard parts and components usually requires large investment, highly automated processes, proprietary technologies, persistent engineering effort, and long-term management commitment. Hong Kong currently does not have enough incentives, nor possess the comparative advantage, to produce such electronics basics. As pointed out in an official study (Hong Kong Productivity Center 1984), with the incessant failure and growth of small concerns each year (approximately 10% of electronics companies fail and are replaced by new enterprises each year), the weakness of the Hong Kong electronics industry is mainly related to its inability to accumulate sufficient experience, knowledge, and larger capital funds at both the enterprise and industry levels.

All these challenges notwithstanding, much confidence is still placed in electronics. As far as future development is concerned, electronics is an industry of almost unlimited product variation, and Hong Kong's efforts to diversify are unlikely to be limited by trade constraints. If a development strategy for the industry to diversify into higher value-added lines is actively pursued, the industry is generally expected to have the potential to become Hong Kong's leading foreign exchange earner in the 1990s.

Other Manufacturing

In common with the textiles, clothing, plastics, and electronics industries, most other manufacturing enterprises in Hong Kong operate on a small scale in terms of both employment and capital resources and are largely of a labor-intensive nature. These industries, which cover a diverse range of production activities, have had a rather mixed performance, usually characterized by rapid growth of those producing newly launched fad products, and by the relative or even absolute decline of those that, in the course of development, have lost their comparative advantage vis-à-vis other low-cost LDC suppliers.

The assembly of fad products does not usually require high technology, large capital, or a long development period, and thus is well-suited for Hong Kong's small factories, which can react very quickly. On the other hand, fads cannot be relied on as a stable base for sustained growth. Since fad products have short product-life cycles, as the initial consumer enthusiasm subsides, supply immediately exceeds demand, causing price and profits margins to fall.

All in all, mostly in response to market forces rather than government policy, a great deal of restructuring effort, both inter- and intra-industrially, has been made by local industrialists over the past three decades. Inter-industrially, apart from the shift from simple textiles to high-fashion clothing manufacturing, the most prominent sectors are plastics, consumer electronics, and watches and clocks, which started in the early 1950s, the early 1960s, and the early 1970s, respectively. Intra-industrially, the early textile industry has diversified both vertically and horizontally—vertically from cotton spinning and weaving to bleaching, dyeing, stencilling, and printing; and horizontally from cotton to wool, synthetic fibers, leather, fur, and silk, from low-count to high-count spinning, from coarse to high-quality printed fabrics, from grey piecegoods to carpets and rugs, etc. In the same manner, the electronics industry (watch manufacturing in particular) has also developed backward linkages from mere assembling to the manufacturing of parts and components.

An open, export-oriented economy like Hong Kong's has to live with developments beyond its borders. Thus, the most important thing is the ability to keep abreast of changing comparative advantage via continual technological improvement and adjustment to changing market conditions. This means more restructuring in the years to come.

THE INHERENT MARKET MECHANISM AND POLICY OPTIONS FOR STRUCTURAL ADJUSTMENT

Since 1843 Hong Kong has been a free-trading and free-enterprise economy. Although industrial growth was a major objective, no industry-specific measures were taken to shape development into a desired pattern. Assistance was only directed towards providing favorable physical infrastructural conditions, and the market was relied on to work out all the rest.

Congenital Adjustment Mechanism: Some Basic Features

Unfettered Market Selection. In Hong Kong's free-enterprise economy, industrial entrepreneurs will engage in a production activity when it meets their expectations: failure of the venture to meet those expectations will be followed by retrenchment and departure from the business. But this will by no means prevent them from coming back in the next round.

A common occurrence in Hong Kong has been for a new industry — plastic flowers, wigs, toys, transistor radios, electronic watches — to be introduced by one or two firms and then to multiply in a manner reminiscent of cell division. A partner in a firm breaks away to set up a factory of his own, frequently taking a number of skilled workers with him; after some time, some of his smarter employees, seeing that opportunities for profits are still promising, may quit and set up their own business. A report by the Economic Intelligence Unit (1962, p 1) has rightly commented that "time and again its industrial history shows the same pattern of more and more firms rushing headlong into a rising market, flooding it with goods and precipitating a collapse in prices and contraction or stagnation in the volume of trade." What often surprises outside observers is that this unfettered, natural selection process has created a continuous pool of entrepreneurs generally able to survive in Hong Kong's economic setting.

Quick Adaptability to Adverse Market Shifts. An immediate corollary is that entrepreneurs should have the ability to get out of a declining sector. To survive, Hong Kong firms, large and small alike, must be ready to move into new lines, to vary their production plans, and even to switch technologies at short notice. In this respect, the very small scale of firm size in Hong Kong may be viewed as a vehicle for flexible adjustment (see Hsia and Chau 1978).

Hong Kong entrepreneurs as a group have been able to get out of a sector, such as wigs, that is dying, by bringing new machinery into the old premise, retraining existing personnel, recruiting some new workers, and starting production of something else — such as toys. Such flexibility makes it possible for small concerns to cut losses when moving out and to reap considerable windfalls when moving into new growth sectors.

Vast Subcontracting Potential. Another distinctive industrial feature in Hong Kong is that many small enterprises subcontract orders from larger concerns. These dependent subcontractors, together with many other small traditional factories, are a buffer against market forces for the large, well-established enterprises. They add resilience to the entire economy in that they are easy to set up and close down.

But this is not all. The potential for subcontracting activity in Hong Kong ranges far beyond the simple relationship between bigger and smaller firms. By virtue of tremendous potential for subcontracting in Hong Kong, a small concern also has opportunities in every direction. For example, it can seek a huge order on its own, then ask similar firms to produce what exceeds its own capacity. If it has to handle a range of heterogeneous products, say, skirts, blouses, and slacks, but is capable of only producing one well with its existing equipment, it can farm out the others to specialized plants. Or, if it can only do part of a given process, it can have the other operations handled by firms upstream and downstream. In fact, there are quite a number of Hong Kong entrepreneurs with no factory at all. Working out of their offices, they have the whole manufacturing operation subcontracted.

The Quick Payback Expectation. The competitive pressures in Hong Kong's "crude capitalism" encourage the taking of high profits whenever possible. More recently, this disposition of the Hong Kong entrepreneur is further aggravated by a desire to make as much, and more importantly, as quickly as possible as the political risks of 1997 loom ahead. Indeed, the "get-rich-quick mentality" is always close to the surface in Hong Kong. Most investors here have a very short-term planning horizon. England and Rear (1975, p 34) observed: "Most of those who invest in Hong Kong do not plan beyond five years—at the end of that time they expect to have received back two or three times the value of their investment."

Not surprisingly, in a world of incessant market fluctuations, the mortality rate among Hong Kong's small factories, particularly with respect to those with a short-term business vision, is one of the highest in the world. However, what is perhaps surprising is that the number of new attempts has consistently outweighed the failures and the total keeps on rising over time.

Changing Policy Stances Towards Industrial Development

There can be no doubt Hong Kong has come a long way from the days when it produced mainly low-priced shoddies and other traditional textiles. One frequent criticism of its products is that they still lack original ideas and design and are mostly made to order, if not adapting or imitating overseas styles. By and large we think Hong Kong must accept such criticism. Up to now, the overall level of production technology is low by most industrial world standards, and the typical firm here spends little, if at all, on research and development.

However, with changed circumstances, what is effectively workable yesterday may not be equally workable today or tomorrow. In the early stage of export industrialism in the territory, besides entrepreneurship, only capital, relatively unskilled labor, and simple technology were needed. They were amply available because of external inflows. Under these conditions, the free working of "crude capitalism" provides local entrepreneurs with a Darwinian test of their ability to survive. But, since the worldwide economic recession of the mid-1970s, what with the surging protectionist practices on the one hand, and rapid technological diffusion and hence accelerating competition from lower-cost LDCs on the other, the outlook for Hong Kong's traditional labor-intensive industries is far from rosy, if not bleak.

Against this general background the Hong Kong government set up an Advisory Committee on Diversification (ACD) in late 1977 to study prospects for the economy and subsequently to advise "whether the process of diversification of the economy, with particular reference to the manufacturing sector, can be facilitated by the modification of existing policies or the introduction of new policies" (Hong Kong Government Secretariat 1979, p 2).

The ACD report covers a long list of recommendations on such topics as labor force training, industrial land utilization and development, industrial support facilities and technical backup services, trade and industrial investment promotions, financial services developments, conduct of external commercial relations, and Hong Kong's economic relationship with China. To say the least, the ACD report may be viewed as a watershed in the history of Hong Kong's economic development. Never before had the government taken up the role of an active overseer of the economy. (For a general evaluation of the ACD recommendations, see Lin and Ho 1981 and 1982.)

Industry Development Board. The formation of the Industrial Development Board (IDB) in November 1980, which was to plan, monitor, and advise on various programs in the field of industrial development, is undoubtedly the single most important result of the ACD's recommendation. The IDB was merged with the Industry Advisory Board of the Industry Department to form the Industry Development Board (also abbreviated IDB) in October 1983 to provide greater impetus to the Board's work and to rationalize the government consultative machinery.

The IDB, chaired by the Financial Secretary, comprises representatives from trade and industry, academic institutions, and government officials.

It has three committees—General Development, Science and Technology Support, and Infrastructure and Support Services—to assist its work, which covers almost all industry-related matters. The Science and Technology Support Committee advises on a range of topics including the long-term potential of technologies such as biotechnology, laser, and information technology. It has two subcommittees to advise on the development of electronics technology and computer-aided design and manufacture (CAD and CAM).

Also, on the advice of the IDB, the government has:

1. Funded semiconductor research and development since 1983 at the two universities
2. Assisted the set up of a Plastics Technology Center on the campus of Hong Kong Polytechnic
3. Paid for local engineers to study application-specific integrated circuit (ASIC) technology overseas
4. Allocated funds for various consultancy studies, notably including the study on technology transfer and quite a number of techno-economic and marketing research studies on electronics, plastics, textile and clothing, and metal and light engineering industries.

Apart from disseminating the findings of this research to industry, those studies in particular that identify weaknesses and strengths of the industries concerned and assess future demands and development trends are used by the authority to pinpoint the direction and extent of assistance for these industries. The studies play a key role in government's overall thinking and policy on restructuring of industries. In addition to these specific initiatives, consultants commissioned by the IDB are working on a feasibility plan for a Technology Center in Hong Kong.

Evolving Policy Measures and Options for Structural Adjustment

The global economic environment is a given for a small economic entity such as Hong Kong. The ability to benefit from a favorable world environment or to compensate for an unfavorable one hinges very much on the existence of a sound economic and industrial policy package in the domestic economy. Seen in this perspective, to ensure the future success of Hong Kong's industrial development, the emphasis should be on careful articulation and analysis of policy options and, in particular, making the right choice. This section briefly delineates the essential policy measures now in existence as well as some broad comments on perceivable trends in the policies the Hong Kong government will include in a long-term development strategy.

Industrial Support and Physical Infrastructure. One major characteristic of Hong Kong's industrial structure is that each industry includes few large firms and a large number of small concerns whose activities are largely responsive to buyers' orders from abroad or to subcontracting orders from either their peers or larger counterparts.

According to the findings of a 1986 industrial survey, there were well over 33,000 manufacturing establishments (accounting for about two-thirds of the total) employing fewer than 10 persons, compared to only 42 factories employing 1,000 or more (see Table 6.12). If we define those establishments employing fewer than 50 persons as small enterprises, over 92% of all industrial concerns in Hong Kong are small; together they employ 41% of the manufacturing labor force.

The proportion of small-scale enterprises has tended to increase over time. As shown in Table 6.13, in the mid-1970s, the average number of workers per factory was about 22; by the mid-1980s, the number had dwindled to less than 18. Many of these small concerns lack the capability to find and absorb new technology and resources for investment in product and process improvement activities because of the high cost involved. Simply put, Hong Kong's ability to continue product and

Table 6.12. Distribution of Employment and Value Added in Manufacturing Establishments, 1986

Number of Plants	Persons Engaged		Value Added			Plant Size (Employees Per Plant)
	Number[1]	%[2]	Amount[3]	%[4]	Per Employee[5]	
33,337	127.4	13.5	6.0	9.5	46.7	1–9
7,459	98.0	10.4	5.4	8.7	55.5	10–19
5,467	162.2	17.2	9.9	15.8	61.2	20–49
2,314	156.8	16.7	9.7	15.5	62.1	50–99
931	127.6	13.5	9.3	14.9	73.3	100–199
442	130.1	13.8	9.8	15.7	75.7	200–499
107	74.1	7.9	7.0	11.2	94.5	500–999
42	66.5	7.0	5.5	8.8	83.1	1000–
50,099	942.7		62.8		66.6	total

1. In thousands
2. Percentage of total persons engaged in manufacturing
3. In HK$ billions
4. Percentage of total value added in manufacturing
5. In HK$ thousands
Source: Hong Kong Census and Statistics Department: 1986 Survey of Industrial Production

Table 6.13. Characteristics of Manufacturing Establishments in Selected Industries (in thousands, except average employment)

1975	1979	1983	1987	
				all manufacturing
31.0	42.2	46.8	50.4	establishments
679	880	865	875	persons employed
21.9	20.8	18.5	17.4	average employment
				textiles
3.4	4.7	4.9	5.3	establishments
113	128	112	123	persons employed
33.1	27.4	22.8	23.1	average employment
				clothing
8.6	8.6	9.1	9.4	establishments
239	255	256	258	persons employed
27.7	29.6	28.1	27.5	average employment
				plastic products
3.4	4.6	5.1	5.7	establishments
64	92	83	86	persons employed
18.5	19.8	16.1	15.0	average employment
				sundry metal manufacturers
5.0	7.4	6.5	6.9	establishments
57	84	66	63	persons employed
11.5	11.4	10.3	9.2	average employment

Source: various issues of *Hong Kong* (Annual Report)

process improvements is greatly inhibited by the lack of industrial support facilities and technical backup services.

The significance of such facilities and services is evident from the fact that, as Hong Kong moves up-market, its products will be increasingly subject to higher standards of quality, consumer safety, and environmental protection. Other East Asian NIEs have already begun to face these issues and Hong Kong obviously cannot afford to be left behind. However, in the absence of government support, the provision of an adequate range of support may involve too large an investment for any one company or even group of companies.

With formation of the IDB in the early 1980s, Hong Kong began to place genuine emphasis on providing technical support services to assist industries to improve productivity and competitiveness via the manufacture of products with better design, quality, and safety standards. Some notable examples are the establishments of the Standards and Calibration Laboratory in 1984, the Laboratory Accreditation Scheme in 1985, and the Design Innovation Company in 1987. In addition, the Hong Kong Productivity Center (HKPC)—the government's executive arm in terms of technical and technological support for industry—has also formulated a wide range of additional services designed to enhance the productivity of Hong Kong's exporting industries.

Other than these, to redress Hong Kong's technological deficiencies better, a number of policy options are also being studied or planned. For instance, the two universities and the two polytechnics are being given more funds to do research on possible industrial applications for the latest electronics and CAD and CAM technologies. The decision to appoint a Committee on Science and Technology is also a positive step. The major task of this Committee will be to seek out and develop new scientific ideas of relevance to Hong Kong and to advise government departments on how they might best be applied (see *Address by the Governor* 1987/88, p 16).

Turning to physical infrastructure development, particularly important are the improvements being made to ease the movement of goods and people to and from China. Apart from Hong Kong's own vigorous efforts, a Chinese team has also investigated the feasibility of a six-lane highway to Shenzhen and a railway from Guangdong (Canton) to Hong Kong's Kwai Chung Container Terminal. Kwai Chung, seabed in the late 1960s, in 1987 replaced Rotterdam as the world's largest container port in terms of tonnage.

More importantly, to sustain and promote Hong Kong's export-led growth, it is essential for its airport and port facilities to continue to be expanded. The government has engaged consultants to study the options for a new international airport and other port development projects. (See Jacobs 1987 for further details.) It is envisaged that the results of these studies, which are expected to be completed during 1989, will then enable the policy makers to decide on the best way to develop sufficient port and airport capacity to meet demands in the next century.

Industrial Land. Of all factor inputs, land has been and is likely to remain the scarcest resource in Hong Kong. The economic burden of high land prices has posed a serious deterrent to the development of high-technology manufacturing that requires heavy or extensive capital equipment or is otherwise not suitable for operation in multistory factory buildings. This has led to an outflow of investment to neighboring economies with much cheaper land and more attractive lease terms as well as the draining of financial resources from manufacturing to real estate speculation. It is therefore widely felt that the government, as the ultimate landlord and the single largest producer of land in Hong Kong, has an obligation to prevent these unhealthy developments via, in particular, the use of land policy as an active tool in encouraging the establishment of new industries of long-term importance to Hong Kong's industrial development.

It was not until the mid-1970s that the government, in recognition of the need to broaden the industrial base and upgrade the technological level of industry, decided some industrial estates designed specifically for relatively land-intensive and heavier industries should be established. To meet this purpose, the Hong Kong Industrial Estates Corporation (HKIEC), a nonprofit autonomous body funded by government loans, was created by statute in 1977.

HKIEC was first charged with the task of developing a 66–hectare industrial estate at Taipo. In 1978 an additional 67 hectares at Yuen Long was added. As expected, the development of these two estates has been progressing well. Leases are offered to industrial users selected in accordance with two primary criteria (see HKIEC's *Annual Report 1978– 1979*, p 12):

1. The manufacturing processes of industries established on the estate must be of a requirement or nature rendering them unsuitable to be carried on in an ordinary multi-story industrial building.
2. Priority is given to industrial processes, which, compared with existing manufacturing industry: (a) are significantly new or produce significantly new products; (b) involve a higher level of technology; (c) provide employment at a higher level of skill; (d) produce for sale on the local market products that are required by existing industries; (e) produce a significant proportion of products for export; and (f) produce products with a high added value from local contents.

Besides providing sites to industrialists for the construction of their own specifically built factory buildings, the HKIEC also builds factory premises meeting the requirements of a wide range of manufacturing operations. These are available for immediate occupancy through sale or rental at prices representing the actual development cost to the HKIEC.

As a further measure to assist the development of those industries unable to operate within the two industrial estates, the government has also instituted a "Special Industries Policy"—that is, it sells leases in certain areas by tender or by private treaty on special terms. As can be expected, because of stringent lease conditions, which generally stipulate a higher capital investment and restrict the use of the site to the industrial concern to which it is sold, only a small number of grants have been made under the Policy since its institution in the mid-1970s.

However, while attempts are being made to attract investment with a higher technological basis by making available industrial land, many a local critic points out the government seems to neglect the importance of small enterprises that do not qualify for such applications. Such enterprises, taken together, have been and will continue to be the backbone of Hong Kong's industrial structure in the foreseeable future. The government can, therefore, ill afford to stay aloof to the appeals of small industrialists for industrial land.

To enable small concerns to acquire their own factory premises, the government can consider, as suggested by some critics, the idea of allocating land to establish new industrial estates—perhaps through an expanded Industrial Estates Corporation. On the financial front, it is envisaged that a policy similar to Hong Kong's "home ownership scheme" can be carried out to assist them in the purchase of their own factories.

In this context, it is announced in the *Address by the Governor* (1988/89) that, to ensure sufficient industrial land is available in the 1990s and beyond, the government is studying a number of options and measures, including the construction of a third industrial estate on reclaimed land at Junk Bay in the immediate future.

Industrial Finance. Conceivably, modernizing existing production facilities and developing new industries with a higher capital intensity require the financing of large outlays with longer payback periods. However, a common behavioral factor affecting the pace of such industrial restructuring in Hong Kong is commercial bank lending policy towards long-term industrial loans. Most bank loans made to manufacturing in Hong Kong are short term and on a self-liquidating basis. Long-term loans at fixed rate are usually not available to manufacturers. Moreover, only large and well-established firms have access to even these facilities. Smaller concerns generally are self-financed or rely on small non-bank money lenders for financial support (see Jao 1974; Sit, Wong, and Kiang 1979). A thesis study found that about 85% of the start-up capital of small manufacturing concerns (those employing fewer than 200 persons, which means almost 99% of total industrial units) came from the owner's own savings, 10% was borrowed from relatives and friends, about 3% was financed by major customers and other sources, and only 2% came from banks and finance houses (Kwok 1977, table 7.3).

Hong Kong has reached a stage of development where long-term industrial finance is more than ever necessary for maintaining its growth momentum. Taiwan, South Korea, and Singapore have long supported their industries in this way. Thus, the proposal to establish an "industrial development bank," which was turned down by the authority concerned in the late 1950s and again in the late 1970s, has to receive careful reconsideration.[2]

Equity financing through a public stock market has only a meager role in financing manufacturing industries (Lin and Siu 1986, p 13; Hong Kong Productivity Center 1984, p 72). In 1986 no more than a handful of electronics firms and about 10 textile and garment concerns were listed on the Stock Exchange of Hong Kong (SEHK), accounting for somewhat over 2% of the market's total capitalization. Hong Kong's stock market comprises mainly property, shipping, banking, and public utilities companies. The property sector alone accounts for some 75% of total market capitalization.

As regards other alternatives for industrial finance, the idea of "venture capital" has become a topic of ongoing discussion. Some of the notable developments are:

1. In late 1986, the Hong Kong Association of Banks (HKAB) set up a working party to examine the possibility of venture capital funding in Hong Kong.
2. Subsequently, the Stock Exchange proposed a second market for securities, to provide an intermediate step between venture capital and full listing.

Since the formation of Hong Kong's Unified Stock Exchange in April 1986, the local investment climate has become more conducive to establishment of a secondary market for the realization of venture capital equity. The government could build on such developments and encourage the creation of this market.

Direct Foreign Investment Promotion. The choice between more or less direct foreign investment (DFI) is a dilemma for many LDCs. In Hong Kong, the authority does not question the judgment of local or overseas investors. It has never dangled any special inducements in front of overseas investors. Equally, it has never put any barriers in their way. In short, Hong Kong is open to overseas investment, with no discrimination in favor or against local investment.

2. An Industrial Bank Committee was appointed by the government in 1959 "to advise whether there was a need for an industrial bank for the financing of industry in Hong Kong and, if so, whether government should take steps to set up such an institution." The proposal was turned down by the Committee as unnecessary, but it did not "exclude the possibility that an industrial bank may become necessary, or at least desirable, at future stage of development" (see "No Industrial Bank for Hong Kong?") However, after some 20 years of industrial development, the 1979 ACD Report on this issue came to the same conclusion as that reached in the late 1950s.

Although the initiation of Hong Kong's export industrialism was mainly based on local efforts, DFI has played an important part in its growth process, particularly the diversification of industries. At present, overseas firms with controlling interest (over 50% ownership) constitute fewer than 1% of Hong Kong's manufacturing establishments. However, the number of firms per se is not a good measure of the relative importance of overseas firms because, in general, they are much larger than the local ones. According to the 1986 Survey of Industrial Production, the average number of employees in a foreign establishment (as defined above) is about 180, compared with an overall average of less than 19. Thus, taken together, they employ over 8% of the total manufacturing labor force. In terms of value added in manufacturing, their contribution is even bigger—about 13%. Table 6.14 provides an overview of foreign involvement.

The continued inflows of capital and technology, notably from the United States, Japan, the United Kingdom, and West Germany, have made a substantial contribution to employment generation and industrial upgrading in Hong Kong. More importantly, this DFI represents some of the most advanced sectors of Hong Kong's industry. In a sense,

Table 6.14. Distribution of Employment and Value Added in Manufacturing Establishments by Percentage of Overseas Interest, 1986

Number of Plants	Persons Engaged		Value Added		Overseas Interest (Percentage Ownership)
	Number[1]	%[2]	Amount[3]	%[4]	
49,311	836.0	88.7	52.5	83.6	nil
67	4.8	0.5	0.7	1.1	1–24
276	22.3	2.4	1.6	2.6	25–49
71	8.1	0.9	0.6	1.0	50–74
37	8.6	0.9	1.0	1.6	75–99
337	63.0	6.7	6.4	10.1	100
50,099	942.7		62.8		total

1. In thousands
2. Percentage of total persons engaged in manufacturing
3. In HK$ billions
4. Percentage of total value added in manufacturing
5. In HK$ thousands
Source: Hong Kong Census and Statistics Department: 1986 Survey of Industrial Production

foreign firms have played the role of a tutor to local firms (Lin and Mok 1985).

Organized promotion work overseas, that is to say the process of actively making known the attractions of Hong Kong as an unconstrained manufacturing base, is a comparatively recent effort and is still on a modest scale compared with what is done by many LDCs. A so-called "One Stop Unit" within Hong Kong's Industry Department was set up at the instigation of the Industrial Development Board in 1982. The Unit was established to:

1. Provide introductions for overseas investors interested in establishing manufacturing operations in Hong Kong in joint ventures, subcontracting or licensing arrangements;
2. Organize missions to advanced industrialized countries to seek sellers of new technologies or improved methods;
3. Provide comprehensive information to overseas investors on the establishment of factory operations in Hong Kong.

But at all events, the increased DFI promotion activity marks no change of basic free-trading and non-discrimination policy. Rather it is a reflection of the government's view that the time is right to give a positive boost to the ongoing process of upgrading technology and spreading the base of industrial structure.

Labor Market Adjustment. In most other labor markets, the market forces of supply and demand are constrained by strong unions, oligopolistic industries, and government regulation—including labor legislation, unemployment benefits, and the like. All these impediments to market forces are practically absent in Hong Kong. Therefore, analogous to entrepreneurial and firm flexibility in entry and exit, change of product mix, etc, Hong Kong's labor force in general, and its unskilled and semi-skilled work force in particular, has moved flexibly from one firm to another, and one line of production activity to another. Being an extremely small city-economy means there are no problems of regional specialization and relocation.

In general, the adjustment has involved the positive pull of new jobs rather than sudden, sharp losses of demand. There has been full employment since the early 1960s—in fact, a tight labor market except for cyclical downturns of short duration. Indeed, most workers since the late 1950s have seen expanding job opportunities and rising real wages. Accordingly, adjustment has had relatively little cost to workers. Mobility for them is more often a step up rather than a step sideways.

Apparently the adjustment cost has been borne by firms, particularly small concerns unable to pay the going rate to retain their workers. However, given the laissez-faire policy of the government, it costs very little for a small firm to start or to liquidate a business. In 1988 the annual license fee for a private company was HK$650, less than a week's pay for an unskilled worker.

The flexibility in Hong Kong's labor force is best exemplified by spinning and weaving, where employment declined by 63% from its mid-1970s peak of 62,000 to 23,000 in 1986. During this period, jobs were added in finishing activities, so for textiles as a whole, employment did not decrease. Employment in wigs peaked at 39,000 in September 1970, when it was over 7% of total manufacturing employment. It was only 1,500 three years later. The displaced workers were apparently quickly absorbed in expanding industries.

All said, the Hong Kong labor market quite readily can handle substantial short-term fluctuations in specific industry employment. The flexibility of a competitive labor market to a very considerable extent contributes to the renowned ability of Hong Kong industrialists, large and small alike, to seize new opportunities and to rebound quickly from recessions.

Hong Kong workers have improved their know-how and upgraded their skills on the job. They are ready to learn new techniques and new skills, and to put in the longest working week of city dwellers in the region. The labor force is credited with a strong work ethic, high adaptability, and motivation. However, the challenge of restructuring the territory's industrial base will require substantial investment in human resource training and the expansion of educational capacities. To further upgrade the skill of workers, the government has to place new emphasis on tertiary, technical, and vocational training.

Education and Manpower Training. For Hong Kong's future, the need for social investment is not limited to capital and physical infrastructure. With shortage of skills a major bottleneck to development, the improvement of labor through education and training is at least as important as the accumulation of physical capital (Liu 1980). Not unlike developments elsewhere, Hong Kong has also come a long way in the postwar years in meeting the rising expectations of its people for more and better education.

In Hong Kong, free general education for all was introduced at the primary level in 1971 and extended to junior secondary level in 1978. Since then, all children in Hong Kong could look forward to at least nine years of compulsory, tuition-free education. As shown in Table

6.15, efforts made in the 1970s are beginning to bear fruit. In the first place, the proportion of the population with no schooling dropped from over 28% in 1971 to about 20% in 1986. Further, the proportion with secondary education increased from less than 22% in 1971 to nearly 42% in 1986. Over the same period, the group with only a primary education has dropped over 10 percentage points. One may be amazed to note that by the early 1980s Hong Kong had more students per capita doing higher secondary education than Britain (Jenkins 1982, p 3). In particular, results of the 1981 Census revealed that in the 16–17 age group, Hong Kong had 61% in full-time education compared with Britain's 46% (Jenkins 1982, p 13).

However, these comparative figures can in no way imply the educational attainment or talent pyramid of Hong Kong's population and hence its labor force is anywhere close to that of countries like Britain, Japan, or the United Sates. We can safely say the distribution of educational attainment of Hong Kong's population protrudes at the lower middle, if not upper bottom, with the largest proportion having primary

Table 6.15. Educational Characteristics of Hong Kong's Population, 1961–86 (percents)

1961	1966	1971	1976	1981	1986	
						distribution by educational attainment
38	35	28	26	22	20	no schooling
45	46	48	43	37	33	primary
15	18	22	29	37	42	secondary[1]
–	–	–	0.6	1.8	2.2	tertiary, non-degree course[2]
1.4	1.7	1.7	2.2	2.5	3.3	tertiary, degree course
						student population ratios by age group
		92	96	98	99	5–9
		90	91	94	99	10–14
		45	50	51	62	15–19
		8	8	6	9	20–24

1. Secondary includes matriculation in ordinary diploma or certificate courses in polytechnics and technical institutes.

2. Tertiary non-degree includes higher diploma or endorsement, associateship, and other non-degree courses in polytechnics and other post-secondary colleges; diploma or certificate courses in education and technical-teacher colleges, and nurse training courses.

Sources: Hong Kong Census and Statistics Department: various Census Reports

and secondary education. By contrast, the talent pyramids of Britain, Japan, the United States and the like bulge at the upper middle, each having the largest proportion of their work force with secondary or tertiary educations. As revealed in the *Address by the Governor* (1988/ 89), Hong Kong has 36,000 full-time equivalent places in its tertiary institutions. These provide first-degree courses for about 6.5% of young people in the relevant age group, and non-degree studies for another 4%. These figures are low by developed-country standards.

As Hong Kong moves up-market, it requires an increasing number of graduate students, particularly those proficient in product design and development, marketing, and management. In this regard, two major policy options recently endorsed or planned are:

1. As enacted by the Legislative Council in July 1987, Hong Kong is now in the process of establishing a third university—The Hong Kong University of Science and Technology, at a site near Clearwater Bay. This new university, with emphasis on electronics engineering and that type of higher technology, is expected to accept its initial batch of first-year first-degree students in 1991;

2. To meet the needs of those who have not previously benefited from higher education, as well as those who have but who need to update or renew their skills, the government has also set up an ad hoc planning committee for the establishment of an Open Learning Institute. This institute, Hong Kong's 6th degree-awarding institution, will substantially increase the opportunities for tertiary education.

Taken together, Hong Kong's plans for tertiary education expansion during the 1990s seems quite impressive. They amount to a doubling of degree opportunities for those who wish to take advantage of them. It aims to provide over 62,000 full-time equivalent places in higher education by the turn of the century. In other words, by the year 2000, more than 14% of young people in the relevant age group will be able to pursue first-degree courses and 6% to pursue studies at the non-degree level (*Address by the Governor* 1988/89, p 78). Even so, the proportion of Hong Kong's teenagers able to receive tertiary education will remain small by developed-country standards. This is reflected in the fact more than 25,000 Hong Kong students are estimated to be studying at tertiary institutions overseas. This situation implies there is still considerable room for further expansion in this area.

Tertiary education is only one important aspect of investment in human capital. Equally important is the provision of technical manpower training. Notwithstanding the characteristics of Hong Kong's labor force, particularly its peaceful and hard-working attitudes, and dexterity and quick adaptability to changing working conditions, one frequent comment is that its average technical attainment is still low compared to other industrialized countries. On the basis of an all-industry survey in the early 1970s, operatives and general workers accounted for 75% of total employment, whereas craftsmen were 19% and technicians less than 6% (Hetherington et al 1971, Appendix F). The 1976 by-Census reported 96% of the employed population in the manufacturing sector did not have formal technical or vocational training.

Seen in this connection, establishment of the statutory Vocational Training Council (VTC) in 1982 to oversee technical education and industrial training is certainly a step forward. On the VTC's recommendation, the government formed 19 training boards and 7 general committees. The general committees are responsible for training areas common to all or several sectors of the economy, while the training boards are responsible for determining manpower needs and designing more specialized training programs. By 1988 the VTC had launched 16 industrial training centers.

The VTC also operates 8 technical institutes with 62,000 full-time and part-time places at both craftsman and technician levels. It has planned to provide another 3,000 full-time and part-time places in 1990. In short, significant strides have been made by the VTC in technical and vocational training.

After all, in a world of rapidly advancing technology and keen competition, education and manpower training policy must be subject to a continuous process of review and be receptive to new ideas. On the other hand, indiscriminate expansion of all types of education, especially if subsidized, can lead to a misallocation of scarce resources. To ensure efficient allocation of resources, education planning at large will have to take into account the growth and distribution of the school-age population. As regards technical education and industrial training, care must be taken to ensure that expansion is in the right direction. In a nutshell, the aim must be to match the know-how and skills taught at the technical institutes and training centers to the needs of the economy.

Exchange Rates. After a period of much instability in the foreign exchange market, a "linked exchange rate system" was introduced in Hong Kong in October 1983. Since then, the market rate has stayed close to the linked rate of HK$7.8 to US$1. Under this system, the exchange value of the Hong Kong dollar against other currencies is dependent on the performance of the US dollar. Since 1985, the depreciation of the US dollar, and hence the Hong Kong dollar, against most other major currencies has contributed to the external competitiveness of its products. However, one should be reminded that the single most important aim of the linked rate system is to provide stability rather than to enhance competitiveness. When the US dollar was showing great strength in 1984 and early 1985, Hong Kong's competitiveness suffered and its domestic exports declined. Hong Kong has thus taken the rough with the smooth.

Stability is not a godsend. In 1988, with the US dollar sinking to new lows, Hong Kong could not help but confront a number of problems. On the external commercial relations front, Hong Kong faces growing pressure for revaluation not only from the United States, but also from EEC countries. On the home front, the slide of the US dollar has on several occasions sparked widespread speculation of a change in the link. In an effort to curb speculative buying of the Hong Kong dollar, the Hong Kong Association of Banks, after some frantic discussions during the second week of January 1988, painfully endorsed imposing punitive charges on large deposits of Hong Kong dollars.

As can be expected, all along, bankers, officials and academic economists here have been debating with great vigor the merits and demerits of the linked rate system. Quite a number of academic economists are of the opinion that, with changed market conditions, floating or repegging the local currency to a trade-weighted basket of currencies may be a better policy option. With respect to unpegging, officials have expressed concern about an uncontrollable depreciation before 1997. Critics of this defense say the link would not be an effective safeguard against a major flight from the Hong Kong dollar. As regards basket pegging, officials are also of the opinion that such a composite system will give rise to great complication and market confusion.

Clearly, Hong Kong is now at a crossroad as concerns the choice of exchange rate policy. The dilemma is that sticking to the present system may not be good, but switching to other options may be no better, if not worse. Indeed, in the quest for an ideal monetary system, there is no such thing as a perfect exchange rate regime; all systems have merits and drawbacks. The most important criterion is whether the benefits outweigh the costs of managing the system. Stated differently, a monetary system must be judged on the basis of its effects on the price levels and especially transaction costs of business activities.

After all, the key objective of the pegging is to maintain local confidence in Hong Kong's future—this was the single most important reason for introducing the link system in October 1983. Seen in this light, the probability of a change in the existing arrangement, either in the form of a repeg or de-link is very slim. Hence as a matter of fact, Piers Jacobs, the Financial Secretary of Hong Kong, has on many occasions stressed that because of political reasons the link will remain until 1997 when sovereignty reverts to China.

The China Factor

With the signing of the Sino-British Joint Declaration of the Future of Hong Kong on 19 December 1984, Hong Kong entered a period of transition. This Declaration is a historic agreement which will govern the future of Hong Kong for more than half a century to come. According to the agreement, China pledges to adopt an innovative "one country two systems" policy in its relationship with Hong Kong after resumption of sovereignty on 1 July 1997. From that date onwards, under the provisions of Article 31 of the Chinese Constitution, Hong Kong will become a Special Administrative Region (SAR) of China.

Under the agreement, except in the area of foreign policy and military defense, which will be China's responsibility, the future Hong Kong SAR will enjoy a high degree of autonomy. In brief, the institutional framework that has accounted for Hong Kong's success appears to have been fully endorsed and enshrined in the agreement. But despite all this, there is still considerable controversy about Hong Kong's political and economic viability after 1997. After all, the Sino-British agreement, like any other international treaty, is successful only as long as it is faithfully observed and implemented. And, on top of this, for the agreement to work properly, international recognition and acceptance of Hong Kong as an independent economic entity after 1997 are vitally necessary conditions.

Indeed, the Sino-British agreement is important not only for Hong Kong but also because it is an indication to the people of the Chinese mainland in general, and of Taiwan in particular, that China intends to persist with an open-door policy and with domestic economic reforms. Not surprisingly, the agreement has also been welcomed by most of Hong Kong's major trading partners—the United States, the countries of the EEC, Japan, Canada, Australia, and the ASEAN countries.

Hong Kong's existence has depended very much on its usefulness to China. For a long time, Hong Kong has been China's largest export market and China has been the largest or second largest supplier (after Japan) of goods to Hong Kong. Following China's adoption of an open door policy in 1978, trading activities between the two have developed even more rapidly. Since the early 1980s, China has been involved in nearly 80% of Hong Kong's re-exports, either as a market or as a source of supply. And starting in 1984 it replaced the United States as Hong Kong's largest trading partner.

Clearly, further opening of China offers tremendous opportunities to Hong Kong. With the opening of four mainland Special Economic Zones (SEZs) in 1980 and, in 1984, authorization of 14 coastal cities to pursue flexible policies similar to those of the SEZs, Hong Kong has been given a good opportunity to move land- and labor-intensive industries to the other side of the border (Jao and Leung 1986). "In Guangdong Province alone, there are between 1.5 and 2 million people employed directly or indirectly by Hong Kong businesses. This is more than (in fact, about twice as large as) the total number employed in the manufacturing sector in Hong Kong" (*Address by the Governor* 1988/89, p 6).

It needs little elaboration that the factor endowments of China and Hong Kong are largely complementary: the former has plentiful land, labor, natural resources, and raw materials, whereas the latter excels in skills in light manufactures production, marketing and managerial know-how, legal and financial expertise, shipping facilities, and above all, an efficient, flexible economic system (see Sung 1985). The recent surge of domestic exports to China, consisting mainly of semi-manufactures, is an obvious reflection of the significance of the compensation trade and outward processing arrangements between the two places.[3]

It is estimated that between 1979 and 1987 some two-thirds of all pledged external investment in China came from Hong Kong. In particular, it is officially accepted that well over 80% of direct foreign investment in Guangdong's SEZs originated from Hong Kong residents. Despite these developments, an important weakness of Hong Kong's industrial policy is that, from the viewpoint of a long-term development strategy, the "China factor" has still not been fully integrated into the government's industrial policy package.

Looking ahead, some commentators have predicted that as SEZs and the Pearl River Delta region expanded industrially, parts of Hong Kong's manufacturing sector are likely to come under pressure. Critics of this concern argue Hong Kong will not mark time as China develops. Instead, it can take advantage of the complementary factors to upgrade

3. Compensation trade is a form of technical cooperation whereby foreign firms supply plant or equipment and technical services to Chinese enterprises, which pay with the goods produced. Outward processing is a simpler form of cooperation in which foreign firms provide samples and the necessary raw materials or semi-manufactures for Chinese enterprises to produce goods of the required quality and specifications; Chinese enterprises receive processing fees in return for their service input.

and restructure towards high-quality and technology-intensive manufactures. In other words, as long as Hong Kong can maintain the lead, the China factor will provide profitable opportunities in the short run as well as the long run (see Sung 1985).

In this respect, an important factor so far neglected by most commentators is that, although China is relatively underdeveloped in the production of light consumer manufactures, it has a large industrial system and heavy industries base, and relatively advanced basic research in industrial electronics. The potential of introducing such technologies into Hong Kong has been largely untapped. Seen in this connection, a policy option for better coordinating industrial relations and identifying opportunities for profitable cooperation between the two places, is to set up a special office within the government secretariat in Hong Kong to oversee the "China factor" in the context of Hong Kong's industrial restructuring process.

It is clear the economic relationship between China and Hong Kong has been founded on mutual benefits. Throughout the postwar years, China has been able to supply Hong Kong with ample basic foodstuffs, consumer necessities, and raw materials at competitive prices, and Hong Kong, in turn, has been China's single most important source of foreign exchange earnings. Undoubtedly, Hong Kong's ability to sustain the value of its international convertible currency and hence to provide regularly about 30 to 40% of China's total foreign exchange earnings for its modernization needs are the major criteria in the definition of "usefulness to China." (See Youngson 1983 and Chai 1988.)

This natural reliance will probably prevail despite any political disturbances in China. While the events of summer 1989 make projections less easy and clear-cut, in our judgment China will persist over the longer run on a path of economic reconstruction requiring all sorts of international cooperation, and Hong Kong will play a multiple role.

Not only is Hong Kong's present position unique, the arrangement for its future is also unique. "One country two systems" is an innovative but uncharted concept. It has never been tried elsewhere. Understandably, its very uniqueness leads many to wonder if it can work. In this regard, it is gratifying to note that, since the ratification of the Sino-British Joint Declaration in mid-1985, the Sino-British Joint Liaison Group, through almost continuous discussions on implementation of the Joint Declaration, has a successful record so far. Most notably, from the Joint Liaison Group's suggestion and subsequent moves taken by both the Chinese and British authorities, Hong Kong became the 91st contracting party to the GATT on 23 April 1986, ending uncertainty over

Hong Kong's international trading position when the British umbrella is removed.[4]

Needless to say, in the run up to 1997 a lot of changes will take place, and many changes will have an impact on Hong Kong's economic and industrial policies. Political changes will likely move economic policy in a more interventionist direction. In particular, the drive for democratization may lead to the rise of special interest groups that can lobby for their own specific interests at the expense of the general public (Sung 1985; Olson 1965). Hong Kong's laissez-faire economic creed may, to a greater or lesser extent, be attenuated if an elected legislative framework eventually proposes an over-interventionist industrial policy for Hong Kong. Change carries risks, especially if economically unenlightened people take charge. But Hong Kong should not resist change when change means progress.

In order to minimize the risk of change, we have to realize the origins of Hong Kong's success. In formulating new policy options, wherever possible all the favorable factors that have nurtured Hong Kong's economic growth should be retained. Any policies and practices that might be suitable elsewhere but that would increase rigidity and reduce flexibility would be highly inappropriate. These include minimum wage regulations, foreign exchange control, and the like. Last but not least, in considering the implementation of any policy option, a proper balance should be struck between what is socially desirable and what is economically affordable.

TRADE POLICY IMPLICATIONS

Over the postwar years there have been, on balance, very significant reductions in barriers to international trade, largely as a result of the seven rounds of multilateral trade negotiations conducted since the late 1940s under the auspices of GATT. Import tariffs on light manufactures in almost all OECD countries have, for the most part, been reduced to low levels. However, following the heyday of rapid expansion in the 1960s and early '70s, the world economy has been going through rougher

4. Previously, Hong Kong's tie to GATT derived from the United Kingdom's accession to the GATT on behalf of its dependent territories including Hong Kong. Under GATT rules, Hong Kong, being a separate customs territory, had rights and obligations as if it were a contracting party in its own right. Hong Kong trade officials participated as members of the UK delegation, but expressed views using the formula "UK speaking on behalf of Hong Kong." Hong Kong officials were at liberty to take positions to safeguard the interest of Hong Kong, even though at times such positions were not necessarily in congruence with those of the United Kingdom.

waters and this has led to a resurgence of protectionism. This has notoriously been the case with textile and clothing manufactures. In Hong Kong these two industries still account for some 42% of domestic exports and about 44% of the manufacturing work force.

Because of its extreme dependence on overseas markets, Hong Kong's ability to diversify must ultimately depend on whether its products will be allowed adequate access to such markets. Seen in this connection, protectionism appears as a greater threat to Hong Kong's economic future than competition from low-cost LDCs. This implies a matter of vital importance to the continued growth of the economy is the successful conduct of international commercial relations so as to safeguard Hong Kong's access to overseas markets. (For more on this, see Lin and Mok 1980.)

In Hong Kong, responsibility for developing and implementing external commercial relations is vested in the Trade Department within the framework of a basically free trade policy. Functionally put, commercial relations activities can be segregated into three broad areas—gathering information, making representations, and conducting negotiations. More recently, it has also become common for exporting economies to engage professional lobbyists to further their interests in major importing countries, notably the United States. With regard to the conduct of trade negotiations, particularly those relating to textiles and clothing, the competence of Hong Kong's negotiators is widely recognized by both its NIE and LDC colleagues as well as its DC counterparts. However, the Trade Department's information gathering and representational roles are still rather underdeveloped.

In the past, many a time, just when Hong Kong became aware of its negotiating partners' intention to impose more-restrictive schemes, that intention had become firm policy. This experience implies Hong Kong should try to collect on-the-spot information and try to influence attitudes as quickly and effectively as possible. To meet this purpose, one immediate measure the Trade Department can take is to increase the strength of its existing overseas offices and the number of such offices, particularly in countries where a vast number of bilateral trade negotiations are likely.

More importantly, Hong Kong should continue to uphold the principle of free trade, despite the fact the global trading environment has become increasingly protectionist. Admittedly, as an extremely small, trade-dependent territory, Hong Kong carries little weight, either politically or economically, in most international trade councils. Indeed, Hong Kong does not have the ability to engage in retaliatory measures even if it wanted to. Hong Kong's full adherence to GATT principles is such that it is often quoted as a paradigm of free trade (Balassa and Williamson 1987). Unlike all other economies, Hong Kong has no trade liberalization policy, as it has no trade restrictions to liberalize. In a nutshell, the single most important course of Hong Kong's trade policy is to safeguard its rights and to discharge its obligations in the pursuit of free trade.

In this regard, the later months of 1986 saw the start of a new round of multilateral trade negotiations under the auspices of GATT, the 8th such round since the agreement became effective in 1947. The main task of the Uruguay Round of multilateral trade negotiations will be to stem, and hopefully push back, the protectionist forces that have been growing stronger in more recent years. Hong Kong is, for the first time, participating fully in its own right in these negotiations and, given the overwhelming importance of international trade for the territory, its overall aim must, by all manner of means, be to support the forces working towards a further freeing of the conduits of world trade.

BIBLIOGRAPHY

Address by the Governor (Sir David Wilson). 1987/88 and 1988/89. Hong Kong Governor's Office.

Balassa, Bela, and John Williamson. 1987. *Adjusting to Success: Balance of Payments Policy in the East Asian NICs.* Washington DC: Institute for International Economics.

Bremridge, Sir John. 1981. "Government's Role in the Economy—Past, Present and Future." Speech presented at the Annual Seminar of Hong Kong Management Association on Nov 9. Processed.

Cairncross, Alec. 1978. "What is De-industrialisation?" In Frank Blackaby, editor, *De-industrialisation.* National Institute of Economic and Social Research, Economic Policy Papers 2. London: Heinemann Educational Books.

Chai, Joseph C. H. 1988. "Economic Relations with China." In H. C. Y. Ho and L. C. Chau, editors, *The Economic System of Hong Kong.* Hong Kong: Asian Research Service.

Chang, E. R. 1969. *Report on the National Income Survey of Hong Kong.* Hong Kong: Government Printer.

Chau, L. C. 1988. "Labor and Labor Market." In H. C. Y. Ho and L. C. Chau, editors, *The Economic System of Hong Kong.* Hong Kong: Asian Research Service.

Chen, Edward K. Y. 1984. "The Economic Setting." In David Lethbridge, editor, *The Business Environment in Hong Kong,* 2d ed. Hong Kong: Oxford University Press.

———. 1987. "Foreign Trade and Economic Growth in Hong Kong: Experience and Prospects." In Colin I. Bradford, Jr and William H. Branson, editors, *Trade and Structural Change in Pacific Asia*. A National Bureau of Economic Research Conference Report. University of Chicago Press.

Corbo, Vittorio, Anne O. Krueger, and Fernando Ossa, editors. 1985. *Export-Oriented Development Strategies: The Success of Five Newly Industrializing Countries*. Westview Special Studies in Social, Political, and Economic Development. Boulder CO: Westview Press.

Deyo, Frederic C. 1987. "State and Labor: Models of Political Exclusion in East Asian Development." In Frederic C. Deyo, editor, *The Political Economy of the New Asian Industrialism*. Cornell Studies in Political Economy. Cornell University Press.

Economic Intelligence Unit. 1962. *Industry in Hong Kong*. A report commissioned for the Federation of Hong Kong Industry. Hong Kong: South China Morning Post Press.

England, Joe, and John Rear. 1975. *Chinese Labor Under British Rule*. Hong Kong: Oxford University Press.

———. 1981. *Industrial Relations and Law in Hong Kong*. Hong Kong: Oxford University Press.

Friedman, Milton, and Rose D. Friedman. 1979. *Free to Choose: A Personal Statement*. New York: Harcourt Brace Jovanovich.

Haddon-Cave, Sir Philip. 1982. "Public Policy and Economic Success." Speech presented at the Annual Banquet of the Overseas Bankers' Club at Guildhall in the City of London on Feb 1. Processed.

Hetherington, R. M. et al. 1971. *The Final Report of the Industrial Training Advisory Committee*. Hong Kong: Government Printer.

Ho, Yin-Ping. 1986. "Hong Kong's Trade and Industry: Changing Patterns and Prospects." In Joseph Y. S. Cheng, editor, *Hong Kong in Transition*. Hong Kong: Oxford University Press.

Holgate, Christine. 1966. "Fair Hair." *Far Eastern Economic Review* 54: 697–99 (Dec 29).

Hong Kong (Annual Report). Various years 1981 to 1988. Hong Kong Government Information Services.

Hong Kong Government Secretariat. 1979. *Report of the Advisory Committee on Diversification*.

———. 1988. *1988 Economic Prospects*.

Hong Kong Productivity Center. 1984. *Study on the Hong Kong Electronics Industry*. A report commissioned for Industry Development Board. Hong Kong: Government Printer.

Howe, Christopher. 1983. "Growth, Public Policy and Hong Kong's Economic Relationship with China." *The China Quarterly* # 95 p 512–33 (Sep).

Hsia, Ronald, and Laurence Chau. 1978. *Industrialization, Employment and Income Distribution: A Case Study of Hong Kong*. London: Croom Helm.

Jacobs, Piers. 1987. "The Mid-year Review, 1987." Speech delivered to the Hong Kong Economic Association on Sep 21. Processed.

James, William E., Seiji Naya, and Gerald M. Meier. 1987. *Asian Development: Economic Success and Policy Lessons.* University of Wisconsin Press, for the International Center for Economic Growth.

Jao, Y. C. 1974. *Banking and Currency in Hong Kong: A Study of Postwar Financial Development.* London: Macmillan.

—— and C. K. Leung, editors. 1986. *China's Special Economic Zones: Policies, Problems and Prospects.* Hong Kong: Oxford University Press.

Jenkins, Graham. 1982. "People—Hong Kong's Greatest Asset." In *Hong Kong 1982.* Hong Kong Government Information Services.

Kwok, P. V. 1977. "Small Manufacturing Businesses in Hong Kong: An Analysis of Their Economic Significance, Performance, and Management Characteristics." Master's thesis, University of Hong Kong.

Lary, Hal B. 1968. *Imports of Manufactures from Less Developed Countries.* Columbia University Press.

Lin, Tzong-Biau and Yin-Ping Ho. 1979. "Export Instabilities and Employment Fluctuations in Hong Kong's Manufacturing Industries." *Developing Economies* 17: 182–202 (Jun).

——. 1981. "Export-Oriented Growth and Industrial Diversification in Hong Kong." In Wontack Hong and Lawrence B. Krause, editors, *Trade and Growth of the Advanced Developing Countries in the Pacific Basin.* Papers and Proceedings of the Eleventh Pacific Trade and Development Conference. Seoul: Korea Development Institute.

——. 1982. "The Past Experience, Present Constraints, and Future Course of Industrial Diversification in Hong Kong." In Joseph Y. S. Cheng, editor, *Hong Kong in the 1980s.* Hong Kong: Summerson Eastern.

——. 1984. *Industrial Restructuring in Hong Kong.* Asian Employment Programme Working Papers. Bangkok: ILO-ARTEP (International Labor Office —Asian Regional Team for Employment Promotion).

Lin, Tzong-Biau and Victor Mok. 1980. *Trade Barriers and the Promotion of Hong Kong Exports.* Hong Kong: Chinese University Press.

——. 1985. "Trade, Foreign Investment, and Development in Hong Kong." In Walter Galenson, editor, *Foreign Trade and Investment: Economic Development in the Newly Industrializing Countries.* University of Wisconsin Press.

Lin, Tzong-Biau, Victor Mok, and Yin-Ping Ho. 1980. *Manufactured Exports and Employment in Hong Kong.* Hong Kong: Chinese University Press.

Lin, Tzong-Biau and Alan K. Siu. 1986. "The Garment Industry in Hong Kong." Processed.

Liu, Pak-Wai. 1980. "Investment in Human Capital and Economic Growth in Hong Kong." In Chi-Keung Leung, J. W. Cushman, and Gungwu Wang, editors, *Hong Kong: Dilemmas of Growth.* Canberra: Research School of Pacific Studies, Australian National University and the Center of Asian Studies, University of Hong Kong.

Lydall, H. F. 1975. *Trade and Employment: A Study of the Effects of Trade*

Expansion on Employment in Developing and Developed Countries. Geneva: International Labor Office.

"No Industrial Bank for Hong Kong?" 1960. *Far Eastern Economic Review* 29: 226–31 (Aug 4).

Olson, Mancur. 1965. *The Logic of Collective Action: Public Goods and the Theory of Groups.* Harvard University Press.

Owen, Nicholas. 1971. "Economic Policy." In Keith Hopkins, editor, *Hong Kong: The Industrial Colony, A Political, Social and Economic Survey.* Hong Kong: Oxford University Press.

Rabushka, Alvin. 1979. *Hong Kong: A Study of Economic Freedom.* The 1976–77 William H. Abbott Lectures in International Business and Economics. Graduate School of Business, University of Chicago.

Rahman, A. H. M. Mahfuzur. 1973. *Exports of Manufactures from Developing Countries: A Study of Comparative Advantage.* Rotterdam [Netherlands] University Press.

Riedel, James. 1974. *The Industrialization of Hong Kong.* Kieler Studien 124. Tubingen: JCB Mohr.

Rowthorn, R. E., and J. R. Wells. 1987. *De-Industrialization and Foreign Trade.* Cambridge University Press.

Sit, Victor Fung-Shuen, Siu-Lun Wong, and Tsin-Sing Kiang. 1979. *Small Scale Industry in a Laissez-faire Economy: A Hong Kong Case Study.* Hong Kong: Center of Asian Studies, University of Hong Kong.

Sood, Anil, and Harinder Kohli. 1985. "Industrial Restructuring in Developing Countries." *Finance & Development,* Dec p 46–49.

Sung, Yun-Wing. 1985. "The Role of the Government in the Future Industrial Development of Hong Kong." In Y. C. Jao, Chi-Keung Leung, Peter Wesley-Smith, and Siu-Lun Wong, editors, *Hong Kong and 1997: Strategies for the Future.* Hong Kong: Center of Asian Studies, University of Hong Kong.

——. 1986. "The Hong Kong Development Model and Its Future Evolution: Neoclassical Economics in a Chinese Society." Paper presented at the Symposium on Economic Development in Chinese Societies held in Hong Kong by the Hong Kong Economic Association and Hong Kong Institute for Promotion of Chinese Culture. Processed.

——. 1988. "A Theoretical and Empirical Analysis of Entrepot Trade: Hong Kong and Singapore and Their Roles in China's Trade." In Leslie V. Castle and Christopher Findlay, editors, *Pacific Trade in Services.* Proceedings of the 16th Conference on Pacific Trade and Development held at Wellington, New Zealand, Jan 1987. Boston: Allen and Unwin.

Textiles Hong Kong. 1965. Hong Kong Government Information Services.

Turner, H. A. et al. 1980. *The Last Colony: But Whose?—A Study of the Labor Movement, Labor Market and Labor Relations in Hong Kong.* Cambridge University Press.

Woronoff, Jon. 1980. *Hong Kong: Capitalist Paradise.* Hong Kong: Heinemann Asia.

Youngson, A. J. 1982. *Hong Kong Economic Growth and Policy*. Hong Kong: Oxford University Press.

——, editor. 1983. *China and Hong Kong: The Economic Nexus*. Hong Kong: Oxford University Press.

Note: Hong Kong government agency documents are published by the Government Printer unless noted otherwise.

7

TAIWAN
Adjustment in an Export-Oriented Economy

Rong-I Wu

Although Taiwan is considered an archetypal example of development by a natural resources-poor, export-oriented economy, many of its first exports were agricultural. Other exports were processed imported primary-sector products such as plywood. Taiwan has moved on to other things, and this essay examines the canned food and plywood industries in Taiwan as examples of declining industries on the island. The automobile industry is also discussed as an example of a heavily protected and government-promoted industry that faces major adjustment as protection is removed. Together these three serve as illustrations of how Taiwan has coped with the adjustments required by the rapid structural transformation its economy has undergone in the 40 years since the Republic of China government was established on Taiwan and how it might cope with the increasing openness of its domestic markets.

The essay begins with a brief outline of the economy's rapid growth, including the trade policies used in promoting that growth. The second section provides an overview of declining industries in Taiwan. This is followed by the three case studies. A concluding section assesses Taiwan's movement toward less-protected markets.

Table 7.1. Indicators of Macroeconomic Performance, 1951–87
(compound annual rate of growth from beginning to end of period shown)

Period	GNP	GNP per Capita	GDP by Sector of Origin				Trade	
			Agri-culture	Industry	Manu-facturing	Service	Exports	Imports
1951–60	8.0	4.5	—	—	—	—	8.3	8.9
1961–70	9.6	6.8	3.9	14.6	16.4	9.8	22.2	17.3
1971–80	9.7	7.7	1.8	12.8	13.2	9.5	16.3	14.2
1981–87	7.8	6.5	1.2	8.6	9.6	7.7	13.2	8.8
1951–87	8.9	6.4	—	—	—	—	15.1	12.6
1961–87	9.2	7.3	2.4	12.3	13.3	9.1	17.7	13.9

Sources: *Taiwan Statistical Data Book* 1989 (table 3–3a), *National Income* 1988 (p 17 table 6 and p 66–69 table 2), and *Industry of Free China* (1988 May, table 3).

GROWTH AND CHANGE IN ECONOMIC STRUCTURE

Taiwan's GNP growth has been among the world's fastest.[1] Between 1952 and 1987, GNP grew at an average annual rate of 8.9%, which translates to 6.4% per capita. Despite some cyclical slowdowns, growth was never below 8% over each decade. From US$145 in 1951, GNP per person surpassed the $1,000 mark in 1976 and topped $6,000 in 1988, close to the levels of Hong Kong and Singapore. This rapid development has meant the economic structure underwent very obvious changes. Using the broad divisions of agriculture, industry, and service sectors, while services' share of GDP has remained in the 44–46% range during the 1951–87 period, industry has steadily replaced agriculture—going from 21 to 48%. Taiwan's growth record is shown in Table 7.1. Table 7.2 outlines the changes in industrial structure.

Despite its declining share, agriculture has had positive growth. This characteristic of Taiwan's development is quite significant, owing to the fact the aims of rapid industrialization in many developing countries have led them to neglect development of the agricultural sector. Indeed, although food was partly imported, the sector consistently has provided export items, including sugar and the processed foods discussed later, thereby playing an important role in earning foreign exchange. Still, agricultural products (including processed ones) going from 91% of

1. Among monographs on Taiwan's early development, Kuo, Ranis, and Fei (1981) is the most compact, covering the period 1952–79; others include Ho (1978) for the colonial and early industrialization period (through 1970), Galenson (1979) for the postwar period through 1975, Lin (1973), and Li (1988) for a government minister's overview.

Table 7.2. Distribution of GDP (at current prices), 1951–87
(annual average for each period, in percents, except total GDP is in NT$ billion)

1951–55	'56–60	'61–65	'66–70	'71–75	'76–80	'81–85	1987	
								total GDP
160.6	230.8	339.7	548.3	902.4	1,417	1,994	2,796	1981 constant prices
21.5	46.8	89.8	173.1	425.9	1,043	2,083	3,098	current prices
								sectors
31.2	27.3	24.8	18.7	12.5	9.5	6.9	5.3	agriculture
47.3	47.0	46.2	47.0	46.5	45.8	47.8	46.8	services
21.5	25.7	29.1	34.3	41.0	44.7	45.3	47.9	industry
								industry
1.8	2.4	2.0	1.6	1.2	1.1	0.7	0.5	mining
1.0	1.4	2.0	2.2	2.2	2.4	3.7	3.7	utilities[1]
4.4	4.0	3.9	4.1	4.3	6.1	4.8	4.1	construction
14.3	17.9	21.2	26.5	33.2	35.1	36.1	39.6	manufacturing
								manufacturing
3.8	5.2	5.4	4.4	3.1	2.8	2.2	2.1	food
								beverages and
2.2	2.7	2.7	2.8	3.6	2.3	2.4	2.1	tobacco
2.7	2.3	2.9	2.8	3.7	3.5	2.5	3.4	textiles
0.3	0.5	0.7	0.8	0.5	1.8	2.5	2.2	garments
*	*	*	0.1	0.3	0.5	0.6	0.7	leather
0.6	0.8	1.0	1.1	1.5	1.1	0.9	0.9	wood and furniture
0.9	1.2	1.2	1.2	1.4	1.5	1.5	1.7	paper and printing
1.4	1.1	2.0	2.8	4.0	4.1	4.6	2.9	chemicals[2]
							2.4	plastics[2]
0.5	0.5	1.3	2.7	2.9	2.3	2.4	3.1	petroleum[3]
0.2	0.2	0.2	0.2	0.4	0.5	0.5	0.5	rubber
0.6	1.1	1.2	1.4	1.3	1.6	1.4	1.2	non-metallic[4]
0.2	0.7	0.7	0.6	1.5	1.9	2.1	2.2	base metals
0.1	0.2	0.3	0.6	0.7	1.2	1.4	1.6	metal products
0.2	0.2	0.5	0.8	1.1	1.1	1.1	1.6	machinery
0.2	0.3	0.6	2.1	3.8	4.0	4.2	5.5	electrical equipment
0.3	0.4	0.6	1.4	1.7	2.0	2.4	2.7	transport equipment
0.4	0.4	0.3	0.6	1.7	2.9	2.2	2.8	other[5]

1. Utilities includes electricity, gas, and water
2. Chemicals includes plastics until 1987
3. Includes oil refining and coal products
4. Non-metallic minerals (mostly cement)
5. Other includes precision instruments, which reached 0.3% in 1987
* 0.06 or less
Annual NT$ data for selected years are in Table 7.8
Source: National Income 1988 (p 58–69 tables 1 and 2)

Table 7.3. Export Structure (percents, except total exports)

1952–55	'61–65	'71–75	'81–83	'86–87	Product Category
19.3	15.8	6.5	2.0	1.3	crude agricultural
14.8	5.8	0.1	0.3	0.1	rice
3.5	6.1	0.7	0.1	0.1	bananas
1.0	3.9	5.7	1.6	1.1	other
71.3	40.0	10.1	5.4	5.0	processed agricultural
59.1	24.0	3.9	0.4	0.0	sugar
6.1	2.5	0.4	0.1	0.1	tea
2.6	8.0	3.2	0.8	0.3	canned food
3.5	5.5	2.6	4.1	4.6	other
9.4	44.2	83.4	92.6	93.7	industrial
1.7	15.6	28.0	21.2	17.4	textiles and apparel
0.0	1.8	3.7	3.6	3.7	wood (including furniture)
0.0	5.2	3.7	1.6	0.6	plywood
0.0	0.0	5.1	7.0	8.8	plastic articles
0.0	0.9	2.3	4.9	6.0	metal articles
0.0	0.9	3.3	3.9	4.2	machinery
0.0	1.5	15.3	18.5	24.0	electrical equipment
					total exports[1]
1.7	130	158	900	1,606	NT $ (billion)
115	326	4,096	23,312	46,731	US $ (million)

1. Average annual exports during period shown
Source: Taiwan Statistical Data Book 1989 (p 208, 213, and 227, being tables 11–4, 11–8, and 11–12a)

exports in 1951 to 6% in 1987. Table 7.3 shows other changes in export structure.

Per capita GNP growth has been characterized by significant productivity increases, on the order of 6% a year in the 1952–87 period (measured as 8.9% GNP growth minus 2.9% employment growth). This represents both a shift from low productivity areas to higher ones and increased efficiency within industries—reflecting capital investment and increasing labor force skills.

Taiwan has used both import-substitution and export-promotion trade policies. Import substitution predates export promotion. Both policies, and export promotion in particular, relate to a quest for foreign exchange—or, more specifically, a drive to have enough to pay for the imports needed to protect the security and promote the growth of Taiwan. Consumer goods were the principal initial target of import substitution. The policy reached its limits in the late 1950s when capacity utilization in many industries had fallen to very low levels and economic inefficiencies were becoming apparent. The domestic market was saturated, though more from limited buying power than from any surfeit of consumption. This was the background against which development strategy switched to export promotion beginning in the late 1950s.

Taiwan was very much in the vanguard in shifting emphasis to exports, and it has been an increasingly trade-oriented economy—in 1987 exports were over half of GNP, and total trade equaled almost 89% of GNP. As export growth has waxed and waned, so has GNP growth. Also, raw material imports have followed the pattern of exports. Exports having continually increased faster than imports, Taiwan moved into a trade surplus in the early 1970s. In the late 1980s, the sheer size of the surplus and accumulated reserves have posed serious economic and political problems, which are discussed later. Table 7.4 provides an overview of Taiwan's trade and balance of payments.

Import Substitution

Although export-oriented, Taiwan has also maintained import-substitution policies. As with many developing countries, these initially were to preserve scarce foreign exchange and promote industrialization. There have been two periods of import substitution. The first was in the 1950s, when labor-intensive consumer goods (so-called light manufactures) were the target and the policy was the conventional wisdom in developmental economics. The second was the 1970s, when the government (again along with many other developing economies at the time) began actively to promote capital-intensive heavy and chemical industries and, later, technology-oriented ones—termed "second-stage import substitution." In both periods, the policies used by Taiwan included low-interest loans, tax relief, high tariffs, and import controls on specific items.

Requiring local content was not done until 1965, and as of 1989 it applied only to the automobile industry. For various periods, requirements affected parts of such industries as machinery (for example, tractors), electrical equipment (televisions, VCRs, refrigerators), and transport equipment (motorcycles and bicycles), to the extent the goods were sold in the domestic market. This had an impact on the development of local parts industries, including the maintenance of higher prices and lower quality relative to imports.

Import Controls. Import controls were probably the most important measure for promoting import substitution in the early period, particu-

Table 7.4. Trade Indicators (in US$ million except as noted)

Year	(Commodity Trade Only) Exports X	Imports M	Surplus	Percent of GNP X	M	Per Capita Trade[1]	Balance on Current Account	(At Year end) Foreign Exchange Reserves	Exchange Rate NT$/US$
1952	116	187	(71)	8.5	14.7	38	—	—	15.60
1962	218	304	(86)	11.3	15.8	46	(51)	71	40.05
1972	2,988	2,514	474	37.8	31.9	364	513	952	40.05
1975	5,309	5,952	(643)	34.7	38.6	704	(588)	1,074	38.00
1981	22,611	21,200	1,411	47.0	44.1	2438	630	7,235	37.84
1982	22,204	18,888	3,316	45.8	39.0	2246	2,347	8,532	39.91
1983	25,123	20,287	4,836	48.5	39.2	2442	4,412	11,859	40.27
1984	30,456	21,959	8,497	52.1	37.7	2777	6,976	15,664	39.47
1985	30,726	20,102	10,624	50.2	32.9	2656	9,195	22,556	39.85
1986	39,849	24,165	15,684	53.5	32.6	3307	16,217	46,310	35.50
1987	53,612	34,957*	18,655	53.9	35.2	4527	17,925	76,748	28.55
1988	60,585	49,656*	10,929	50.3	41.6	5571	10,167	73,897	28.17

1. Imports and exports per capita in US$

* Includes gold purchase from United States of US$379 million in 1987 and US$2.879 billion in 1988.

Sources: Taiwan Statistical Data Book 1989; Central Bank of China Financial Statistics (1989 Aug, p 2, for 1982–88 data; various other issues for earlier data).

larly before 1972. In July 1958 Taiwan adopted "Criteria for Import Control" that, in order to preserve foreign exchange, explicitly provided for import controls when an item was produced locally and there was a satisfactory domestic supply. The use of controls was greatest in the 1960s, when upwards of 45% of the entries on a list of some 950 items were either prohibited outright or controlled (required an import license, which was obtainable only if there was no domestic substitute readily available).

In the early 1970s, the number of items on the list exploded, but a much smaller percentage were controlled, as emphasis shifted to tariffs as the main instrument of protection. Only 297 of 13,236 items were controlled after a major rewriting of the list in February 1974, but the number edged up to 763 of 26,610 at the time of the June 1984 rewriting. Since the mid-1970s controlled items are almost all agricultural (seen as being in relative decline), automotive (vehicles and parts, as part of the policy to promote these industries), or military-related. In 1988 there were 158 agricultural products, 125 industrial items, and 117 military items on the list. Efforts are again under way to simplify what one may correctly infer is a source of significant red tape. (For more details, see Wu 1989.)

Tariffs. Nominal tariff rates were maintained at extremely high levels until well into the 1980s. Table 7.5 shows nominal rates and tariff revenues as a percentage of imports. Comparing the two shows that,

Table 7.5. Average Tariff Rates

Year	Nominal Tariff (percent)		Tariff Revenue as a Percentage of Imports
	A	B	
1972	55.7		12.1
1974	52.7		11.7
1975	49.1		9.9
1976	46.2		11.4
1977	43.6		10.4
1978	39.1		11.3
1979			11.6
1980	36.0	31.2	9.0
1981	36.0	31.2	7.5
1982	36.0	31.0	7.6
1983	36.0	31.0	7.6
1984	36.0	26.5	7.7
1985	32.8	22.8	7.9
1986	31.8	20.1	7.7
1987	25.8	9.1	7.5
1988		5.3	

Nominal tariff rates are simple arithmetic averages of all tariff rates. Rates in column A apply to imports in general, those in column B apply to imports from countries or areas that have reciprocal treatment with the Republic of China, including the United States and Japan.
Source: Department of Customs, Ministry of Finance.

For comparison, tariff revenue as a percentage of imports in

1972	1983	1985	
5.9	8.6	5.8	Korea
5.7	1.8	na	Singapore

(As computed by Chen et al and printed in Hou 1988, v 1 p 38)

although average rates (simply the sum of tariff rates divided by the number of rates being averaged) declined, because of the composition of trade the tariff barrier was not really lowered in the 1970s. After 1979, when the tariff schedule was split to give preferential rates to those giving Taiwan reciprocal treatment, there was a one-time drop in this measure of "real" tariffs. Tariff barriers remained virtually unchanged from 1980 to 1986.

Significant tariff reductions date only from 1987. Levels have come down quickly in the two years since, with many rates being halved in February 1988. Further cuts brought the average in early 1989 down to about 12%—an average of 10% for industrial products and 24% for agricultural ones. Automobiles and some agricultural products (raw and processed) still have tariffs in the 40–50% range. Textile and apparel are mostly duty free or have very low rates. Announcements of more or faster-than-scheduled decreases were an almost routine news item in 1988–89.

Export Orientation

In the 1960s, Taiwan increasingly turned to exports to fuel growth. The reason is very simple: it was perceived as the way to earn foreign exchange, accelerate industrialization, and pursue a rapid and more efficient development path. Export promotion in Taiwan has involved the use of three measures: tax rebates on exports, low-interest loans for exporters, and the establishment of export processing zones (EPZs). These policies definitely contributed to the rapid expansion of the economy; each is discussed below.

The policies were directed at all industries, not targeted at specific sectors. Entrepreneurs were left pretty much alone to develop what they could sell profitably in foreign markets within the system of general export promotion. Initially, these were primarily agriculture-related or labor-intensive consumer goods. Thus, in 1952, sugar and rice were the leading exports. By 1966, the textile products group was first, but bananas, canned food, and sugar were just behind. In 1976 textiles continued to be the leading export, followed by electrical machinery and apparatus, and plastic articles. Textiles fell behind electricals in 1984.

Tax Rebates. With scarce natural relative to abundant human resources, Taiwan's exports mainly relied on raw materials imported and processed for export. Particularly in the early days of industrialization— the 1960s and '70s—Taiwan has had high import tariffs and domestic transaction taxes both to raise revenue and discourage consumption generally and imports in particular. To make exports competitive, these imposts were rebated.

Rebates were first utilized in 1951 to encourage export of straw hats to Japan using a specific fiber imported from Japan. Other fibers used in hatmaking were added in 1952. In 1954 all exported items became eligible for rebates on custom tariffs. In 1955 commodity and defense taxes were also rebated, and in 1958 harbor dues were added to the rebate list (Lin 1973, p 100–04).

The amount of the rebates increased as the items covered expanded and exports grew. Rebates apply to customs duties, the defense surtax on customs duties, harbor construction dues, commodity taxes, and the salt tax. They equaled just 1.2% of total relevant tax receipts in 1955, 30% in 1964, and 62% in 1972. As part of trade liberalization, in 1983 the government announced a five-year program to abolish tax rebates. As a result, their level had dropped to 21% in 1986. However, in the face of exporter opposition, the phase-out had not been completely implemented in mid-1989.

Exporters have also received investment incentives in the form of tax exemptions. These include corporate income taxes, business taxes, and stamp taxes. In the 1982–86 period, exemptions to exporters totaled NT$51.7 billion, which is equal to 1% of the value of exports in that period. Although the amount is small, particularly relative to rebates, the program is felt to have been an effective incentive to export expansion.

Low-Interest Loans. Credit has generally been of the revolving, short-term variety: for example, for three months covering the period between receipt of a letter-of-credit (LC) and shipping. The LCs were discounted by the central bank at a lower rate than a commercial bank would charge, if a bank would advance money at all. This provided firms, especially small and medium size ones, needed working capital to fill orders without resorting to the high-cost black market, and thus promoted smaller enterprises as well as exports (Lin 1973, p 105–07). In the 1980s the interest differential between these advances and normal bank loans has decreased, and with the supply of capital generally increasing, in 1989 the government was making plans to end the program.

Export-Processing Zones (EPZ). The opening of the first EPZ in Kaohsiung in 1966 was a direct response to the unattractive investment environment in Taiwan. The unfavorable elements included difficulties obtaining land plus general red tape in procuring the many permits needed to build, open, and operate a factory.

Firms establishing themselves in an EPZ received a variety of preferential treatments in exchange for adding at least 20% domestic value (mainly in the form of labor) to imports that then became exports. Access to a single authority, which expedited forms processing as a liaison to other agencies, was one of them. Besides simplifying the investment process, the EPZ Authority also assisted in export-import applications and foreign exchange needs. In addition to the tax rebates available to all exporters, firms in an EPZ could import machinery duty free and taxes on domestic purchases were rebated. (An early evaluation of the zones is Scott [1979, p. 336]; also see *Industry of Free China* [1967 Jan, p 2–30] and Li [1988].)

Three EPZs were established. Besides Kaohsiung (Taiwan's second largest city) there are zones in Nantzu (just north of Kaohsiung) and Taichung, both opened in 1969. Employment in EPZs had risen to over 71,000 in 1974, then declined in the wake of the oil crisis. The previous peak was regained in 1976, and a new high of 79,000 was reached in 1980 (representing 1.2% of total employment). At their height, in 1987, the zones employed about 91,000; by 1988 the number had declined to 84,000. By 1979 cumulative investment had reached US$282 million, more than five times the initial expectation and almost 15% of private foreign and Overseas Chinese investment in Taiwan for the period 1956–78. The number of firms reached 272 in 1979, and in 1988 there were 244 firms operating in the EPZs. (Data are from the 1989 Aug. issue of *EPZ Concentrates.*)

In 1971–80 the zones accounted for almost three-quarters of Taiwan's trade surplus. In the 1980s their contribution has been dwarfed by the rest of the economy. Through 1987, the zones had exported US$3.174 billion.

The most significant contributions of EPZs have probably been the creation of employment opportunities and the earning of foreign exchange. But, as Taiwan has liberalized and simplified investment and expanded incentives for exporting to those not in zones, the need for and role of EPZs has diminished. Initial plans to build more EPZs were shelved in the early 1970s and in the late 1970s emphasis shifted to creation of the Hsin Chu Science Park. The EPZs, with their inherent emphasis on exports, have in some ways become a problem now that Taiwan has such large trade surpluses. There has been some talk of disbanding the EPZs, but while there has been disinvestment and firms leaving, there are no plans to close them.

Foreign Exchange

The inflow and outflow of foreign exchange was tightly controlled until July 1987. All earnings from exports had to be sold to the Central Bank or other approved institution, which meant these were the source of foreign exchange to pay for imports. (Taiwan's currency is the New Taiwan dollar, written NT$ and usually read simply as NT, as in "this cost 50 NT.")

Continuous trade surpluses since the early 1970s have caused Taiwan's foreign exchange reserves to mount steadily: year-end 1981, US$6.5 billion; 1985, $22.6 billion; 1988, $74 billion, which is 1.5 times the year's total of merchandise imports. During 1988 Taiwan achieved the second highest level of foreign exchange reserves, after Japan and ahead of West Germany, and continued in that position in 1989.

The sharp rise in the current account surplus and foreign exchange reserves from 1985 was not completely sterilized, so the money supply grew very rapidly. Most of the monetary growth spilled over into asset (stock and land) markets. It also generated fears of inflationary pressures —fears reinforced by policy makers' remembrance of China's hyperinflation in the 1940s. This was one factor in the government decision to accelerate tariff cuts.

Growing reserves have also contributed to appreciation of the New Taiwan dollar against the US dollar: from a 40.5 NT peak in September 1985 to 28.6 at year-end 1987, 28.2 in 1988, and 25.9 on 30 June 1989. The 1985 peak to 1987 year-end move meant an almost 44% increase in US dollar-denominated export prices. This shook export industries, particularly because competitors such as Korea, Hong Kong, and Singapore had much smaller currency appreciations. Still, the impact was mitigated by the strength of the currencies of Taiwan's other trading partners—particularly Japan. As the principal source of imports, the yen's even greater appreciation made components less expensive in the domestic market. And, since Taiwan's fuels are mostly priced in US dollars, there was a saving in input costs there as well. Thus, on a trade-weighted basis the NT advanced about 20% in 1986–87, with most of the increase coming in 1987, as is shown in Table 7.6.

It is not clear just how much effect further appreciation of the NT would have on Taiwan's trade balance with the United States. A report in early 1989 from the US General Accounting Office suggests it "may modestly reduce" the bilateral deficit. The report also discusses changes in Taiwan's exchange rate system that took effect in April 1989.

Table 7.6. Nominal Effective Exchange Rates, 1985–88 (trade-weighted, end of month data; 1979 = 100)

	1985	1986	1987	1988
Jan	106.08	96.99	101.95	118.46
Feb	107.34	96.69	102.47	118.42
Mar	104.70	97.66	103.13	117.33
Apr	104.50	96.21	106.01	117.25
May	104.53	98.70	111.98	117.32
Jun	103.22	97.89	113.97	118.19
Jul	99.84	97.37	115.30	119.51
Aug	100.26	99.94	116.79	119.22
Sep	98.15	100.39	117.34	118.91
Oct	97.54	101.65	116.72	118.06
Nov	97.19	102.25	117.49	118.01
Dec	96.98	103.96	118.47	118.84

"Real effective exchange rates on exports, 1979–87" are presented in Liang and Liang (1988, v 2 p 322 table 8). For the nominal exchange rate against the US$ for 1952–76, see Scott (1979, p 326 table 5.3).
Source: Foreign Exchange Trading Center

Government Response to Economic Imbalances

The government has taken a number of steps to address the macroeconomic disequilibrium in Taiwan's economy created by its relatively large foreign exchange reserves. Tariff cuts have been discussed already. The most important step was the July 1987 cessation of requiring that foreign exchange be bought and sold only through authorized institutions. At the same time, restrictions were removed on remittances to and from Taiwan in the course of normal business. However, individuals are still subject to some controls: US$5 million out, $200,000 in, per adult per year.

Fears that rapid appreciation of the NT will hurt small and medium enterprises have prompted the Central Bank to adopt measures to inhibit the NT's rise. Still, in anticipation of further strengthening, there have been flows of "hot money" onto the island—perhaps as much as US$12.5 billion in 1987 (calculated as the difference between the actual increase in foreign exchange reserves during the year of $30.4 billion and the current account surplus of $17.9 billion). Although the NT was volatile against the US dollar in 1988, it moved basically sideways. Political pressure from the United States strengthened the NT over 9% in the first half of 1989, for an overall increase of over 50% for US-dollar denominated export prices from the US dollar's peak in 1985 to mid 1989. Imports have become more attractive and have grown; export growth has continued, though at a somewhat less rapid rate.

DECLINING INDUSTRIES

Some half million people (over 25% of the sector's peak employment in the early 1960s) left agriculture in the 1960s and '70s for higher productivity and income jobs. This means agriculture could be called a declining sector, but most people consider this a positive effect of economic development. In terms of physical output, agriculture generally has had absolute increases. From that standpoint it has been an increasingly productive sector rather than a declining one, although it is substantially less efficient than other sectors. Output per farmer has persisted at about one-third that of workers in non-agriculture. Because the total labor force roughly doubled in the same period, new jobs were created outside agriculture for almost four million workers. (Hou 1978 discusses the labor force.)

It is hard to think of decline in the face of that kind of growth, but there was. Over the 1951–88 period, significant absolute declines in employment occurred in agriculture and in mining (from peaks in the early 1960s), textiles (peak in the late 1970s), and wood (1980s), though the latter two have been volatile. The unemployment rate has been relatively low—under 2% in 1987—so it is easy to see laid-off workers being absorbed by expanding industries. Employment data are in Table 7.7.

Even though there are laws and regulations to protect workers, in practice firms usually have had a free hand to lay off workers if business is not good. Generally layoffs have been without compensation, although some larger firms do make nominal payments. Martial law, in effect from the late 1940s until July 1987, prohibited the right to use strikes or collective bargaining as a way for labor unions to negotiate wage increases or working conditions with employers. Although there is now a right to strike, the procedure to obtain it is so complicated there had been no legal strikes by the end of 1989. However, several labor disputes have resulted in a similar effect: workers have collectively asked for leave. A labor standards law was enacted in 1984, but enforcement only began in 1987. This law has had little effect on cannery workers.

Besides agriculture, mining and several secondary-sector industries have had declining shares of both output and employment during the 1980s. Only for agriculture have the relative declines been steady throughout the period since 1951; the others had rising or at least steady

Table 7.7. Employment, 1951–88 (in thousands)

1951–55	'56–60	'61–65	'66–70	'71–75	'76–80	'81–85	1988	
2984	3323	3612	4219	5204	6170	7058	8272	total
1651	1707	1768	1718	1660	1490	1288	1052	agriculture
816	964	1072	1428	1825	2236	2830	3691	services
518	652	772	1074	1720	2445	2939	3530	industry
								industry
57	75	82	81	62	60	45	26	mining
7	10	14	17	21	25	32	36	utilities
74	99	118	186	300	457	541	624	construction
380	467	558	790	1337	1904	2320	2844	manufacturing
								manufacturing
58	66	74	86	104	120	116	133	food
7	8	8	8	14	15	18	17	beverages and tobacco
53	67	84	144	265	295	254	253	textiles
37	38	36	43	102	127	193	234	garments
29	32	35	41	46	57	85	67	leather
38	50	65	86	126	153	152	135	wood and furniture
32	35	36	45	61	83	103	143	paper and printing
17	25	35	60	120	197	256	340	chemicals
2	2	3	4	8	12	14	14	petroleum[1]
5	6	6	7	17	29	48	76	rubber
18	22	26	34	54	83	94	86	non-metallic[2]
9	12	15	21	29	49	54	71	base metals
11	23	38	58	87	155	224	294	metal products
27	28	29	39	72	110	123	139	machinery
5	10	17	41	119	221	317	491	electrical equipment
27	28	27	31	51	73	85	105	transport equipment
8	15	24	42	69	125	183	246	other

Average annual employment during each five-year period shown
1. Includes oil refining and coal products
2. Non-metallic minerals (mostly cement)
Source: Based on unpublished data from DGBAS (Directorate-General of Budgets, Accounts, and Statistics, except 1988 data, which are from the *Monthly Bulletin of Manpower Statistics* (1989 Jan, p 16–17 table 9).

shares at various times. Mining, food processing, tobacco, textiles, non-metallic minerals (cement, mostly), and wood fall into this latter category. This is what one expects over a four-decade period, particularly for a rapidly growing economy. Table 7.8 provides data on GDP by industry.

Table 7.8. GDP by Industry (in billion current NT$)

1969	1973	1980	1985	1987	
197	410	1,491	2,393	3,098	total GDP
31	49	115	139	165	agriculture
93	181	694	1,152	1,450	services
73	180	682	1,102	1,483	industry
					industry
3	4	14	14	15	mining
4	8	38	99	114	utilities[1]
8	17	93	102	126	construction
57	151	537	887	1,228	manufacturing
					manufacturing
9	10	35	55	66	food
5	10	31	56	65	beverages and tobacco
6	19	50	79	106	textiles
2	8	29	61	67	garments
*	1	9	18	22	leather and fur
3	8	16	19	28	wood and furniture
2	7	25	38	54	paper and printing
6	19	69	67	91	chemicals[2]
			52	73	plastics[2]
6	12	37	54	97	petroleum[3]
*	2	7	13	15	rubber
3	4	25	31	37	non-metallic[4]
1	9	35	52	69	base metals
1	4	21	36	49	metal products
2	4	16	30	49	machinery
5	20	65	108	170	electrical equipment
3	7	32	53	83	transport equipment
				9	11	precision equipment[5]
2	7	37	56	77	other[5]

1. Utilities include electricity, gas, and water
2. Chemicals includes plastics prior to 1985
3. Includes oil refining and coal products
4. Non-metallic minerals (mostly cement)
5. Other includes precision equipment prior to 1985
Distribution of GDP is in Table 7.2
Source: National Income 1988 (p 62–65 table 1)

Mining, though its share in GDP is small to begin with, shrank from 2.5% in 1956–60 to 0.7% in 1981–85. Most mining in Taiwan involves quarrying marble and limestone (used in cement) although there is also some coal. It has also had an absolute decline in the number of workers, and thus (at a fairly aggregate level) can be considered a truly declining industry.

Tobacco has been another steady decliner since the late 1950s. Still, throughout the 1950s and '60s, 0.5% or more of cropland was planted to tobacco—7,700–8,700 hectares each year, jumping to over 11,000 in 1968 (Ho 1978, p 356). The crop is used for cigarette making and in the late 1960s the industry had the third highest value-added per employe of any major industry category, primarily by virtue of having the second highest level of assets per worker. Production peaked in 1984 at 32 billion cigarettes and has declined since, to 28 billion in 1987. Imports of cigarettes have been significantly liberalized, so foreign, primarily US, brands have gained market share. Further trade liberalization and health consciousness mean the industry and the crop will probably continue to decline.

Textiles and garments have been a mainstay of Taiwan's industrialization, and together were the largest industrial sector until 1983 (when they were supplanted by electronics). In 1956–60 they represented 31% of manufacturing output and employed over 22% of manufacturing labor. In 1981–85, these shares were 15% and 19%. Despite relative decline, absolute output has continued to grow. Employment peaked in the late 1970s for textiles, but continued to increase for garments until the mid-1980s, when it leveled off. Even in textiles, the employment reduction has been modest and the workers have been readily absorbed elsewhere. These no doubt will be declining industries in the 1990s, and indeed that process was under way in the late 1980s—thus, the government expects them to be only the third or fourth largest export category by 1990. But so far the adjustment process has been modest.

Several industries would probably have declining relative, if not absolute, employment and output if they were not protected from import competition. Behind barriers, they are, rather, growing. The auto industry is the typical example and is discussed later.

Wages have increased about 10% annually since 1985. Combined with the NT's appreciation, Taiwan has been losing competitiveness in labor-intensive industry. Many firms (foreign and domestic) making such products have moved out of Taiwan, or stopped expanding, as a result. This will lead to changes in the industrial structure, and, more so than in the past, this probably means the absolute decline of some industries in Taiwan.

Because Taiwan's economy involves many family-owned small and medium-sized businesses, adjustment at the firm level has operated in a way not unlike the labor market: the family moves into another industry, or another niche, if business gets bad. Often, capital investment was limited or the equipment has been fairly fully depreciated, so any losses have not been devastating. As firms grow in size and capital intensity, shifting will become more difficult. The same is true for wage earners, as skills become more industry- and firm-specific. (The role of family businesses is discussed by Liu and San [1988, p 263–67] and Hou [1988 p 44].)

The economy has been sufficiently flexible and dynamic—and growth sufficiently strong—that there have not been employment or output losses in one segment so severe that the government has felt the need to intervene to prop up an industry. (Automobile assembly comes close to being an exception, but even if it is allowed to decline, employment and output are small relative to the total economy.) My own view is that this situation will continue.

Thus, in the 1990s many firms will adjust to the stronger NT, higher wages, and lower import tariffs by failing or moving to mainland China or ASEAN countries. Textiles and apparel will decline absolutely. Most firms will, as in the past, fairly successfully adjust to new circumstances.

PLYWOOD

Taiwan's plywood industry has gone from selling over 90% of its production on the domestic market (in 1953–56) to exporting over 90% (in the 1960s) back toward increased reliance on the domestic market (46% of 1986 production). The industry maintained a respectable growth rate, and earned a good deal of foreign exchange as one of the island's principal exports, until the early 1970s. In 1974 production fell sharply, while exports dropped 23% in each of 1974 and 1975 (measured in NT$). Production recovered spectacularly in 1978, and production and exports reached all-time highs in 1979. The industry can be said to have been declining since then. Substantial declines during 1984–86 brought the industry to less than two-thirds its peak production, while exports were about three-fifths of their high. Quite a roller coaster, as shown by the data in Table 7.9.

This volatility is in part because of the cyclic nature of foreign housing markets and also because of limited domestic timber supplies, which necessitates importing most logs. Taiwan's mills have been designed to process a type of tree called lauan, which has been obtained from South East Asian countries.[2]

2. The name lauan is applied to a wide variety of hardwood species of the genus *Shorea*. Lauan is the Philippine name; the trees are known as meranti in Malaysia and

Table 7.9. Plywood Industry Overview, 1960–87 (production and trade in million NT$)

Year	Production Total	Imports of Logs	Imports of Plywood	Exports	Export Ratio[1]	Number of Mills	Employment (000)
1960				87		15	
1965				1,056		18	
1970		1,882		3,116		35	
1971		2,763		3,810		38	
1972		4,205	2	5,464		42	
1973		6,916	2	8,621		64	
1974		8,246	1	6,569		75	
1975		5,662	4	5,067		79	25
1976	8,933	8,360	13	7,227	81	81	26
1977	10,890	12,312	11	8,983	82	80	28
1978	19,338	14,220	13	12,017	62	78	29
1979	25,272	22,699	22	15,139	60	80	29
1980	25,964	22,578	63	13,395	52	72	27
1981	26,411	21,644	153	14,656	55	73	27
1982	22,384	17,520	208	12,994	58	71	24
1983	24,196	17,719	437	14,489	60	69	26
1984	23,930	16,025	1,326	11,091	46	68	24
1985	19,632	11,557	1,144	9,815	50	72	19
1986	23,901	11,076	2,330	9,052	38	76	17
1987	26,117	12,619	3,626	9,711	37	82	17
1988	23,499	14,817	3,173	9,011	38	86	16

1. Value of exports as a percentage of value of production
Sources: Plywood Industry in Taiwan (1989 Mar issue), *The Trade of China* (various annual issues), *Industry of Free China* (various annual issues), and *Yearbook of Earnings and Productivity Statistics* (1988)

The main product, referred to here as "common" plywood, is a 3–ply sheet 4 mm thick and 91 x 182 cm (that is, not a 4 x 8–foot sheet like the US standard). The principal use of the sheets are as door skins, wall paneling, and underlay (subfloors) in housing construction.

Indonesia and as seraya in Sabah. The wood is pale pink to dark red, and is used in a wide range of light structural work as well as in making plywood. Because of the similarity in color, it is not uncommon for lauan to be sold under the name "Philippine mahogany" although it is not a mahogany. Some species reach 70 meters in height and 1.5 meters in diameter. Large diameter is of course important in making plywood. Lauan logs entering international trade are typically 6 meters or more in length and 60 cm or more in diameter.

In volume terms, during the period 1972–80 Indonesia was the principal log supplier, replacing the Philippines (whose log exports to Taiwan have generally declined since a 1972 peak). Indonesian exports peaked in 1978. Malaysia provided a growing share of logs beginning in the mid-1970s and became the principal supplier in 1980. The changing source is because the timber producers have successively developed their own plywood industries, enhancing their direct access to logs with cheap labor and imposing strict controls or outright bans on log exports. The supply situation is expected to worsen, as the Philippines and Malaysia have plans to ban log exports.

In 1983 Indonesia decided to market its plywood aggressively, with Taiwan, Korea, and Japan identified as prime targets. The Indonesian government has offered subsidies to plywood exporters, partly because of severe overcapacity in its domestic industry. This has been mainly low-grade plywood, and Taiwanese firms have imported it to reprocess for export, which accounts for the rapid rise in plywood imports and overlaid exports after 1983 shown in Table 7.10. (Import duties are rebated in such cases.) Reprocessing is not as profitable as starting from a log, but it has helped cushion the absence of logs.

After 1985 the product mix shifted toward processed items with lower prices than had been the case earlier. Under pressure from the United States, in 1985 the tariff on plywood imports was reduced from 30 to 15% for non-coniferous species and to 7.5% for coniferous (as grown in North America). The United States has been the principal export market (44% of total plywood export value in 1987). With the appreciation of the NT against the US dollar since 1985, Taiwanese plywood has become less competitive.

The Government's Role

Taiwanese producers had asked for anti-dumping duties against the imports, but the government limited itself to requesting the Indonesian government stop subsidizing plywood exports. That government had not, as of the summer of 1989, acceded to the request. Indonesian plywood thus continued to sell for around 60% of the price of local plywood in Taiwanese markets.

The government has not directly assisted the industry in any specific ways. As part of a more general program, plywood producers are eligible for assistance being made available to firms investing overseas to secure raw materials. The Ministry of Economic Affairs (MOEA) in May 1987 promulgated the "Scheme for the Promotion of Investments in South East Asia." Under the plan, the government will conduct a comprehen-

Table 7.10. Plywood Production and Prices, 1960–87

Year	Production				Imports		Exports		Prices US$	
	Total¹	Index²	YOY³ %	% Processed	Total¹	% Processed	Total¹	% Processed	Logs	Plywood
1970	750	100		15			682		37.2	103.1
1971	878	117	17	16			781		38.0	81.8
1972	1323	176	59	13		16	1115	0	37.6	95.4
1973	1342	179	3	16		0	1116	1	65.6	188.8
1974	1101	147	−32	22		14	804	1	78.6	152.7
1975	1042	139	−8	22	*	50	768	4	59.3	121.6
1976	1227	164	25	23	9	89	869	9	79.6	147.8
1977	1272	170	6	27	*	4	950	10	89.8	165.1
1978	1607	214	44	20	*	0	1258	14	91.8	189.5
1979	1451	193	−21	26	2	9	1091	15	160.2	262.5
1980	1300	173	−20	28	3	12	868	11	192.9	273.8
1981	1370	183	10	35	13	62	951	7	144.6	244.7
1982	1240	165	−18	34	20	60	822	25	145.5	232.5
1983	1250	167	2	40	39	9	867	26	135.2	229.8
1984	1000	133	−34	54	126	3	601	42	151.0	227.0
1985	850	113	−20	66	129	1	556	54	132.0	210.9
1986	900	120	7	70	275	1	504	62	na	273.7
1987	950	127	7	68	372	2	544	62	na	na

1. In thousand square meters
2. 1970 physical production is 100
3. Year over year change in physical production
* less than 1,000 m²
na not available

Processed percentages are the quantity of processed plywood as a percentage of the quantity of total production, imports, and exports.
Prices are the World Bank's yearly average series for Philippine lauan logs and for 3–ply 4mm lauan sheets 81 × 192 cm in the product's Tokyo wholesale market and thus are not necessarily the prices paid or received in Taiwan. See source for additional details.

Sources: Plywood Industry in Taiwan (1989 Mar issue, p 11 table 5) for production data; *The Trade of China 1970–87* (table 5) for trade data; and, for prices, *World Bank Commodity Trade and Price Trends 1982/83* (p 99 for logs, p 101 for plywood) through 1981 and 1987/88 for the years since

sive search in 60 countries for timber, rattan, rubber, minerals, and other essential raw materials. The Export-Import Bank will expand operations to include financing overseas investment aimed at securing supplies of these materials. The program, which began in 1988, is authorized initially to advance up to US$100 million.

Adjustments

Taiwan's plywood mills have had to contend with increased competition and restricted supplies of raw materials, as well as progressively higher wage rates relative to their new ASEAN competitors. They have reacted in two major ways: turning to the domestic market and upgrading products. There have also been efforts to establish Africa, New Guinea, and North America as log sources, but transport costs are much higher and lauan is not available in these places.

At the industry's peak in Taiwan in 1978 (in terms of physical volume of production and exports) there were 78 mills employing 29,000. As prospects dimmed, firms making common plywood have closed, so that by 1984 there were fewer than 70. Since 1982, when former log suppliers started to become serious competitors in plywood markets, Taiwan has shifted away from producing "common" plywood toward processed products involving fancy veneers, paper overlays, etc. Some firms invested in mills in Indonesia and other log growing countries to produce common plywood, with part of the output being shipped to Taiwan for further processing. Processed plywoods generally are less capital-intensive than turning logs into common plywood, a fact that contributed to a slight increase in the number of Taiwanese mills in the last half of the 1980s. Nevertheless, employment dropped by 45% (some 13,000 workers) in the 1979–88 period.

The ASEAN late-entrants have also been moving into more processed products. In the 1984–88 period Indonesia acquired three Finnish-made special presses used for producing phenolic overlaid panel (panels include fiber and particle board as well as plywood). Phenolic-film is among the fastest growing types of panel, as new uses have been developed for it. Basically, the process increases wear resistance, so it has found its way into construction site uses (including re-usable forms for concrete work), shipping containers, and (most ubiquitously) highway signs. The process can increase the value of basic plywood as much as 50%. The niche has been dominated by a Finnish and a US company (Massey 1989).

Even though much new technology is embedded in machinery that can be imported, without its own source of logs it is doubtful Taiwanese producers can compete with ASEAN, North American, and Scandinavian countries. Many surviving firms have diversified, mostly into furniture making, and this has contributed to the jump in exports of wood furniture from US$389 million in 1982 to $934 million in 1987, suggesting at least superficially that transition was quick, if not smooth.[3]

Taiwan's plywood industry has lost its comparative advantage. The principal proximate causes have been the restrictions on raw material exports by former suppliers, and the fact these countries have developed their own plywood industries. It is difficult to say if the industry would have remained competitive if its access to logs was not restricted. Composites, made from wood chips or logs not suitable for lumber, have taken market share from plywood in the global market, and will continue to do so as logs suitable for plywood making disappear from North American and tropical forests.

But only a few Taiwanese firms have moved from plywood to composites, again because of limited access to the inputs. Nor have they become a local distributor for foreign panel, reflecting the export-production orientation of most mills and the resulting absence of strong local marketing ties. Instead, firms have ceased to exist or reduced their dependence on plywood by moving into other activities, usually furniture making. This has been done as the firms' responses to market forces. Workers have been absorbed into other activities through the normal operation of the labor market. The government has not implemented any policies for the industry, nor has there been any special government assistance to displaced workers.

CANNED FOOD

Because Taiwan's economy was primarily agricultural in the 1950s and '60s, the emergence of a canned food industry to process local crops for export provided both employment and foreign exchange (exports took some 90% of production). Thus, the industry occupies an important role in Taiwan's early development, but it has been in relative decline for several decades and is now in absolute decline. Although food processing continues to be an important industry in Taiwan, canned food production peaked in 1978 (in value terms), exports in 1980.

---

3. Much of the wood used in the furniture is imported composite panel—MDF (medium-density fiberboard) and particle board. The difficulty in processing tropical species, small scale, and high resin costs have kept Taiwan and most other western Pacific nations out of the composite panel arena. (Japan imports chips and thus supplies some of its panel needs from local production.) Most panel exported to Taiwan from the United States returns to the US as furniture (Pease 1988).

Employment has fluctuated significantly, falling less than production over the period from the mid-1970s to 1987, but more quickly following the particularly high level of employment in 1984. Data are in Table 7.11.

Taiwan cans a wide range of food products. Pineapple, citrus fruits (mandarin oranges), bamboo shoots, asparagus, and mushrooms are considered the "traditional" canned goods, the last two being the most important. Except for bamboo shoots, Taiwan's traditional major canned exports are commonly used in a variety of cuisines and are not particularly "Chinese."

Increased preferences for, and availability of, fresh or frozen vegetables and fruits in North America and Europe have reduced demand growth for canned varieties—a phenomenon affecting the worldwide canned goods industry, not just Taiwan's. For Taiwan, slow or negative

Table 7.11. Taiwan's Canned Food Industry, Overview, 1954–87

Year	Production NT$[1]	Exports NT$[1]	Exports US$[1]	Export Ratio %[2]	Number of Firms	Employment[3]
1954			4		61	
1964			28		128	
1975			154		217	
1976	9,720	10,478	276	108		25
1977	13,735	12,510	329	91		26
1978	14,761	14,487	390	98	249	27
1979	15,188	14,572	405	96		26
1980	18,138	17,416	484	96		27
1981	17,416	14,343	390	82	235	26
1982	14,633	13,890	355	95	229	24
1983	15,377	13,234	330	86	222	25
1984	15,649	13,458	340	86	218	31
1985	14,694	11,387	286	78	190	29
1986	13,972	12,460	330	89	188	25
1987	11,906	9,338	294	78	168	21
1988	11,117	6,645	232	60	151	17

1. In millions.
2. The ratio is the value of exports as a percentage of total production.
3. In thousands.
Sources: Industrial Production Statistics Monthly (1984 Dec, p 158 table D-3; and 1989 Jun, p 175 table D-3); *Yearbook of Earnings and Productivity Statistics* 1989 (p 12 table 4); and various issues of the *Monthly Statistics of Trade.*

growth in most of its product areas has been exacerbated by increased production costs, combined with the appreciation of the NT against the US dollar since 1985. Thus, except for pineapples, all of the traditional canned goods have had generally downward trends in the 1980s, and during that time pineapple canners have seen Thailand become the main exporter to the US. Tomato products, meats, and fish have had rising production since the mid-1970s, and it is their growth that led the recovery in overall canned food production in 1984–85. Data are in Table 7.12.

Table 7.12. Canned Food Industry Production, 1976–87 (in thousand standard cases

Year	Aspara- gus[2]	Mush- rooms	Bamboo Shoots	Tomato Products	Other Vegetables	Fruits[3]	Meats[4]	Fisher Produc
1976	3,596	3,011	3,197	1,747	1,749	3,064	100	83
1977	3,629	4,611	3,604	1,655	3,122	2,535	128	1,25
1978	3,423	4,368	5,055	2,606	3,039	3,392	188	1,27
1979	3,834	3,377	5,119	2,385	2,584	3,652	153	1,31
1980	4,529	2,890	2,709	2,491	3,441	4,526	213	1,64
1981	2,896	2,291	4,383	1,956	2,360	3,789	282	1,25
1982	1,517	2,429	4,545	2,344	2,358	2,565	318	96
1983	1,420	2,305	4,448	2,016	2,389	3,064	285	1,15
1984	2,237	2,486	3,217	2,838	2,726	991	256	1,77
1985	1,927	2,545	3,366	1,956	3,014	801	198	1,87
1986	1,209	2,246	2,906	2,939	2,357	2,154	284	2,20
1987	798	1,649	3,102	2,810	2,277	1,644	272	2,08

1. A standard case is 45 pounds (24 cans)
2. Asparagus became a major crop in the mid 1960s, going from 270 to 10,877 hectares plan in just two years, 1965–66. The peak harvest was in 1971; the 1987 harvest was just one-thir the peak.
3. Includes pineapples, citrus fruits, lychees, and others. The large numbers for canned fruit 1978–80 represent exceptionally high pineapple packing. From 1980 to 1981 the pineapple p dropped 87%, from a record 1,949 cases to just 257. The pack fell another 27% in 1982 and t began to rise again, reaching 978 in 1987. Citrus fruits peaked in 1978. The drop in pineapple p was due mainly to strong competition from Thailand. Because most canned pineapple is expor the drop in exports was quickly reflected in a drop in canning. Pineapple's peak production wa 1971. The largest area planted to pineapples was in 1967, after which it steadily lost ground.
4. Meat includes pork, beef, and snails, most of it supplied domestically.
5. Fish includes tuna, bonito, mackerel, and sardines from deep sea fisheries; and crab, lobs eel, and shrimp from inshore or fish farming sources.
Sources: Industrial Production Statistics Monthly (1989 Aug, p 78–81; and 1985 Jan, p 61– Data on production and other items, including yields and area planted, can be found in the Tai Statistical Data Book.

Production and Marketing Agreements

Like a number of Taiwanese industries, canned food has production and marketing agreements established under government auspices. This means all output of an item has been sold under a single brand name. In the past, when the industry had no close rivals in world markets, the inefficiencies caused by the agreements were not particularly glaring, but under the competitive conditions of the late 1980s, they are obvious. Quite simply, Taiwanese producers have not been as efficient as they might have become in a less-protected environment.

Mushrooms, asparagus, and bamboo shoots were canned and marketed under separate schemes adopted in 1963, 1965, and 1970, respectively. Farmers had supply agreements with the factories. A "joint business export company" (owned by the canned food producers) handled marketing, pricing, assignment of shares in the import quotas imposed by some European countries, and loans. The rationale was to overcome the weakness of small-scale production. When Taiwan was a major supplier of these three products in world markets, the export companies probably were able to garner higher prices than would otherwise have prevailed. As a minimum, foreign buyers were prevented from coming in and bidding prices down by going to new entrants or playing one firm off against another. In a sense, it was the functional equivalent of an optimal tariff on these exports, with the rents going to the producers.

Even before the joint companies were established, before 1960 in fact, entry of new firms was restricted. In 1955 the Goods and Materials Bureau of the Taiwan provincial government was designated the sole legal importer of tin plate. Close control was also imposed on makers of tin cans. In this way, the government was able to control entry into the canning industry.

Production Costs

Table 7.13 shows the distribution of production costs for four of the principal products. Raw materials and tin cans together make up 65–75% of costs. Raw material prices have risen more quickly than packaging prices since the table was computed, but the data provide a benchmark of relative importance. Raw material prices reflect rising agricultural wages and decreased productivity, as many farmers have chosen not to update equipment.

Between 1978 and 1981 the percentage price increases for asparagus and for mushrooms (at the farm gate, in NT per kilogram) were much more than for the export prices of these products canned (in US dollars).

Table 7.13. Distribution of Production Costs of Principal Canned Products, 1981 (in percents)

Pineapple	Mushrooms	Asparagus	Bamboo Shoots	
32.3	51.2	52.9	32.9	the raw food
7.5	4.7	8.1	11.6	labor
33.1	23.3	20.1	36.7	tin cans
6.4	4.0	3.2	8.8	indirect costs
9.0	9.1	9.1	8.7	fixed costs
6.1	4.8	4.4	8.1	packing
5.6	2.9	2.2	3.2	other

Source: Council on Economic Planning and Development 1983

In the 1981–85 period, mushroom prices were more or less flat, while asparagus increased 12%. Over the 1978–85 period, canned asparagus had essentially no change in price, while the raw crop price increased 35%; canned mushrooms rose 11% in price, while raw mushrooms were up 26%. All this meant narrowing margins for the canners. It also meant declining incentives for growers, as crop prices failed to keep pace with inflation.

Tin plate is the main component of tin cans. Although Taiwan has set up its own production of plate, most is imported, primarily from Japan, because the local industry is not competitive in price or quality. The appreciation of the yen against the NT has thus boosted canning costs.

Trade

The United States has been the principal market, so the appreciation of the NT against the US dollar has hurt cost competitiveness. Still, Taiwan provided almost half of US imports of canned mushrooms in 1988, and about 6% of all canned food imports that year. Mushrooms made up about two-thirds of canned exports to the United States. With only small increases in the US dollar price, Taiwanese canners have seen a drop in revenue measured in local currency.

Exports began declining even before the NT started rising—1980 was the peak year for exports, and by 1985 they had already declined almost to the level of 1973.

In physical volume, world trade in canned mushrooms increased from 21.5 to 27 million standard cases, or almost 26%, in the 1981–86 period (4.6% annually). Taiwan's share fell from 15 to 13% in this period. Those gaining share include mainland China and the Netherlands. Mainland China used its low labor costs to increase production and actively promoted mushroom exports. The Netherlands vigorously expanded mushroom culture in the early 1980s. In 1978 the European Community ceased issuing import permits for Taiwanese canned mushrooms. When issuance was resumed in 1979, a quota of 1,000 tonnes was imposed. The quota has since risen, reaching 2,628 tonnes in 1987. The United States imposed a 20% duty in 1979, but in 1980–83 reduced the rate by 5 points each year, thus canceling the increase.

Asparagus shipments worldwide fell from 9 to 6 million cases in the 1981–86 period. Taiwan's share has been volatile but basically declining —close to 79% in 1980, just over 61% in 1986. Again, mainland China has been a major gainer in market share, going from only 47,000 cases in 1980 to 978,000 in 1986.

Adjustment

Canned food workers are primarily semi-skilled and live in rural areas. The jobs are not as seasonal as in some countries because of the variety of crops and growing conditions that allow multiple harvests during a year. But Taiwan is compact enough that even rural residents can commute to jobs in non-agricultural activities fairly easily, and the ongoing wage increases in other areas has put pressure on both agriculture's and canning's labor costs. Even without the problems of demand, canning would thus face a less robust future.

Squeezed on both the demand and supply sides, by 1987 canning output had decreased by 23% from its 1984 peak, employment by 32% (some 10,000 workers). The workers have apparently been bid away, so adjustment problems for them have been minimal.

Most canners are family-run businesses. The industry's decline has been marked by bankruptcies and attempts to remain competitive. The latter includes upgrading product quality and production technology, developing new products, and investing overseas. The joint business operation schemes are also being re-evaluated. There has been no explicit, specific government plan to help the industry, although the government has offered preferential financing and tax breaks for overseas investment.

Although the government sets standards for exported canned foods, there is a wide range of product quality, as well as of production efficiency. Because each item is sold under a single brand name at the same price, some canners felt they would be better off if they could differentiate their products. The first agreement to go was for pineapples: in 1987 the Joint Canned Pineapple Factory was abolished. The United Canned Asparagus Producers Export Company and the Canned

Food Producers Association also laid off a large percentage of their staff. The government has adopted stricter hygiene and sanitation standards now that the Associations no longer provide such policing. Firms are now being encouraged to develop their own brand image, and are allowed to use flexible pricing.

Canned Chinese food in the United States—although using some Taiwanese ingredients—has been sold primarily under the labels of American companies: La Choy (half the market) and Chung King (which was bought by a Singapore-based group in 1989). This category has had steadily declining sales since the mid-1980s. It is unclear the extent to which new and innovative "Chinese cuisine" canned food products will catch on, though certainly worldwide acceptance of Chinese dishes continues to grow.

While canned foods are declining, food processing continues to provide opportunities. Although the techniques and equipment are significantly different between freezing and canning, some canners have moved into frozen foods—generally into prepared foodstuffs rather than simply frozen versions of the basic items they had canned. (For more on frozen foods in Taiwan, see Pierce 1985, Branstetter 1986, and QFFI 1986. For historical background on food processing in Taiwan, see Chen 1978 and Lee 1980.)

Taiwan's frozen food industry has extensively revamped product lines (including adding Chinese foods) and modernized plant, helping it grow in both domestic and foreign markets (see Saulnier 1987). Sales reached US$1 billion in 1986. Frozen pea pods (classed as "peas" in trade data) have become a Taiwan export to the United States. Although worth less than $7 million in 1988, that was 61% of frozen peas and 5% of all frozen foods imported into the US. Aquaculture has grown to feed the frozen seafood industry (much of which goes to Japan). In 1986 there were 1700 mainly family-run shrimp farmer-processors and 116 full-scale factories to freeze their output.

VEHICLES AND AUTO PARTS

The automobile industry, including auto parts, has had an increasing share of industrial production, and employment has risen. It is thus, strictly speaking, not a declining industry. But this has been because of highly protective measures adopted by the government rather than the industry's competitiveness. In the late 1980s and early '90s, that protection is being dismantled. With the abolition of most import controls, the gradual reduction of tariff rates, and the resulting increase in competition from imported cars, the assembly industry must adjust. Table 7.14 provides an overview of the industry.

The government in the past has provided strong incentives specifically to promote the industry in Taiwan. The two principal ones have been limits on imports and domestic content requirements for local production. The latter was intended to create backward linkages to stimulate development of the components industry. However, in 1985 plans were announced to liberalize imports of automobiles, albeit slowly. That year is used to divide much of the discussion in this essay. After examining the structure of the assembly industry and the protectionist regime before 1986, the government's plan for the industry's adjustment is outlined. What has happened since is then discussed, including what may be the local industry's integration into the global strategies of the major international firms.

Table 7.14. Motor Vehicle Production

| | Production | | | |
| | | Trucks | | Output in |
Year	Cars	& Buses	Employment	Million NT$
1966	3,641	883		557
1969	11,327	586		1,153
1972	21,997	105		2,274
1975	31,158	120	5,911	6,328
1976	30,908	105	6,453	6,277
1977	44,141	131	7,053	8,946
1978	76,634	543	9,230	15,926
1979	115,462	641	11,455	23,925
1980	132,116	464	12,443	40,238
1981	129,863	303	11,586	33,944
1982	125,897	538	10,984	34,687
1983	148,295	957	11,212	42,268
1984	162,274	3,381	12,583	47,190
1985	149,150	3,125	12,710	40,568
1986	170,923	3,731	13,107	52,639
1987	247,267	5,849	14,157	76,046
1988	268,531	7,194	14,904	83,205

Capacity in 1987 and 1988 was 551,000. Capacity utilization was 61% in 1986, 46% in 1987, and 50% in 1988.

Sources: *Industrial Production Statistics Monthly* (1977 Feb, p 77 table 7; 1981 Jul, p 80 table 12; and 1987 Jun, p 160 table C-2) and *Yearbook of Productivity Statistics 1989* (p 52–55 table 4).

Structure of the Industry Before 1986

Yue Loong, established in 1953, was Taiwan's first automobile company. Under a technical cooperation agreement with Willys of the United States, the company began producing Jeeps in August 1957. In 1960 the company first produced passenger cars, assembling Nissan's Blue Bird.

When San Fu, Taiwan's second assembler, was established in 1966, it had a technical agreement with Fuji Heavy Industries. The next two assemblers, started in 1967, also had agreements with Japanese companies: San Yang with Honda, and Lio Ho with Toyota. China Motors, a subsidiary of Yue Loong, became the fifth producer (mainly trucks) in 1974 with technical support from Mitsubishi Motor.

In 1977 a sixth firm, Yue Tyan, was allowed to enter the market to produce passenger cars in cooperation with Peugeot. At that time the government announced no more applications would be approved except for those exporting over half of their output. This in effect precluded any further entry.

Protection Before 1986

Contained in the government's April 1961 "Measures to Develop the Local Car Industry" was the provision that locally assembled automobiles must contain 60% locally made parts. In 1977 the ratio was raised to 70%.

Protection has been afforded assemblers since local production of passenger cars began in 1960. Imports of fully assembled new cars by private citizens were prohibited in the 1960s. At the same time, the government wanted competition, so it encouraged entry. By 1971 there were four assemblers, none with a capacity over 20,000 units. Quality was very poor and prices much higher than on international markets. Realizing this, the government liberalized imports in December 1971. Cars were subject to the 75% tariff; light trucks, vans, and buses had a 65% rate. Less than 2½ years later (in May 1974), import controls were reimposed—even with the tariffs, the local industry was not competitive with imports, which had captured 35% of the market in 1973.

With Taiwan running a large trade surplus with the United States, pressure was applied to open Taiwan's markets. Consequently, in November 1977, the government allocated a quota for importation of US cars, and in 1978 also allowed imports of European cars. This left Japanese firms, the strongest competitors in the world market, excluded from imports. The United States was not satisfied, and in April 1979 Taiwan abolished quotas on US cars but left them subject to a 75%

tariff. In August 1980, quotas on European cars with a displacement of less than 3000cc were lifted. Tariffs on 2000cc cars were reduced to 65%. This was the situation until 1986.

Behind these barriers, cars were expensive. In 1985, before taxes (which also applied to locally made cars and which added another third or more, depending on the car's size) a subcompact such as the San Yang Civic 1500cc cost US$7,655. With taxes, this is roughly equal to six months' income for a middle-level manager. John Fei calculated that in 1986 locally made cars were $1,600 more expensive than comparable Japanese ones, costing consumers $250 million. He added the local economy would be better off if an earthquake destroyed the vehicle producers.

The Automobile Industry Development Plan of 1985

Despite adoption of passenger car import controls in 1960, and the high level of protection accorded since then, the industry has been unable to produce an automobile acceptable by international standards. As a result, consumers have been quite dissatisfied. The industry has relied on government protection for its very survival, but several firms have been dissatisfied with the government for having changed protection policies several times just as they have invested to conform to the old ones. They feel this has impeded adjustment and complicated long-term planning.

Against this backdrop, and under pressure from the United States and local public opinion, in 1985 the government adopted a development plan for the industry that reduces protection over the six-year period 1986–91.

The plan lowers tariffs on small passenger cars (defined as those weighing 3.5 tons or less) from 65 to 60% in February 1986, and calls for further cuts, to 30% by 1991. Tariffs on auto parts, including completely knocked down kits, are maintained at 35% until 1989, and then are reduced, reaching 25% in 1991. The local content requirement of 70% was reduced to 50% in 1989. Cutting tariffs on parts and in local content helps local automakers by reducing their costs. Imports from Korea are subject to a quota that is being liberalized 30% a year— 6,760 cars in 1990, 11,424 in 1992. Korea is not importing Taiwanese-made vehicles, but did agree to take other items, including Chinese liquor. Japanese imports remain prohibited (except for some trucks), but because of their investment and licensing arrangements with the local industry, Japanese firms participate in the local market.

With the announcement that tariffs would be lowered, sales of domestically made cars dropped 9% in 1985. Many in the local industry expected most of any increase in domestic sales to go to imports, but this decidedly has not been the case. Other ramifications of the plan are discussed below.

One of the government's key intentions is to develop Taiwan as a source of auto parts. Having failed in almost 30 years of protecting an integrated industry to see it develop into a world-class competitor, the decision was decided to narrow the focus. The idea became showing the multinationals that Taiwanese firms could meet world standards in parts. But, not quite prepared to give up on a domestic assembly industry, the way to do this was seen as showing those parts off in complete cars. This time, however, the multinationals would be encouraged to become even more involved in building them. A welcome was extended to foreign automakers to go beyond technical cooperation and invest in the local assembly industry (Radley 1986, Gawronski 1986).

The government recognized the importance of these alliances to the viability of the industry, and sought to make sure the multinationals included Taiwanese firms—assemblers and parts makers—in their worldwide strategies. In other words, the government was conscious of a need to be part of an international division of labor, whatever the consequences to development of a fully integrated domestic industry.

"Will Taiwan be Asia's Next Automotive Powerhouse?"

That question was the subhead on a 1986 article in *Automotive News;* and *Forbes* had, the previous summer, raised the question of Taiwan becoming "another player on the stage" of automobile exporters (Tanzer 1985, Tank 1986a). The volume of automobile exports from Taiwan until then had been very limited; only some 4,500 units were shipped overseas before 1986, primarily by Ford Lio Ho. But twice before Taiwan has had major expectations for exports. Each time it did not happen, although in the wake of the second attempt the parts industry may be integrated into the worldwide sourcing systems being developed by the major international players and each of the assemblers became associated with one of these multinational firms.

The first attempt came in 1982 when there were discussions between Toyota and the China Steel Corporation, which is owned by the government, to build an export-oriented auto plant capable of producing 300,000 vehicles a year. An agreement was initialed in December of that year, but after some 21 months of dickering over local content and export ratios, in September 1984 the proposal collapsed.

Yue Loong's chair, Vivian Yen, who has a master's degree from

Columbia University in international relations, has been outward looking in her expectations and ambitions for the company she has run since
1976. In the mid 1980s she was negotiating with both Nissan (to help
Yue Loong sell older models in Asian countries and new cars in the
United States) and Chrysler. This, along with Ford's decision to include
Taiwan in its emerging strategy of worldwide sourcing, represents the
second attempt. In the summer of 1986 a government spokesman felt
"By 1990 US$1 billion of auto exports would be a reasonable estimate"
including motorcycle and auto parts—already $426 million in 1985,
mostly for the after market (quoted in Tank 1986b, p 29).

Under plans developed in 1985, Ford Lio Ho, 70% owned by Ford,
was to export the Laser, a 1500cc car designed by Ford's Japan affiliate,
Mazda. Ford invested about US$36 million to expand and automate its
local plant in expectation of shipping 30,000 cars a year from Taiwan
beginning in 1986. At the time, Taiwanese assembly workers earned
about US$3 an hour, including fringe benefits, which was similar to
Korea's level and only some 25% of Japan's. Still, the Laser would cost
more to make in Taiwan than Mazda's cost to make the same model in
Japan. Ford felt increasing volume would narrow the gap. Cars made
for export are not subject to local content rules, so the plan included
extensive use of parts imported duty free. (The exemption is an admission the local content requirement was not able to achieve its desired
objective of developing a competitive parts industry.)

Fuji Heavy Industries (Subaru) spent US$11.4 million for a 45% stake
in a joint venture with Taiwan Vespa (which put up $19.5 million) in
September 1986. The new company, Ta Ching, planned to start produc-

Table 7.15. Motor Vehicle Exports, 1981–88

Year	Total Value	Sedans	Trucks & Buses
1981	1.3	3	551
1982	1.0	2	448
1983	1.2	0	504
1984	1.3	40	462
1985	2.5	16	45
1986	25.2	4562	129
1987	49.5	7759	115
1988	19.8	2499	0

Total exports are in US$ million; other data are units
Source: Monthly Statistics of Trade (Dec issue of each year).

tion in 1988 with 6,000 vehicles, rising to 36,000 in 1989 and 48,000 cars plus 12,000 trucks in 1990. At least half was to be exported.

In July 1986 Ford Lio Ho started to export what was then designated the Mercury Tracer to Canada. This helped boost total industry exports to almost 4,700 units in 1986 and 7,900 in 1987. However, Tracer exports were discontinued in 1988 because they were not cost-competitive. The strong yen had made the parts imported from Japan expensive, and the strong NT had made assembly labor less competitive. Ford also builds the car in Mexico.

In 1987 San Fu began making UBS-Troopers for Isuzu to export to General Motors in the United States, but fairly quickly only around the

Table 7.16. Relationships between Taiwanese and Foreign Automakers, 1989

Local Firm, Percentage of Equity Held by and Name of Foreign Partner with Year Investment Was First Made	Notes
China Motors 25 Mitsubishi (1985)	Had been a wholly-owned subsidiary of Yue Loong making trucks; Mitsubishi, 22% owned by Chrysler, has been a technical collaborator since 1986
Ford Lio Ho 70 Ford (1972)	Builds cars designed by Mazda, which is 25% owned by Ford. Local models are the Ford Laser and TX-3 (Mazda 323-based) and Telstar and TX-5 (626-based). Imports Ford Sierra and Scorpio from Europe, Sable from US. In 1972, Toyota ended a technical relationship with Ho Tai, Lio Ho's predecessor, to bet on the mainland market.
Kuo Tzui 22 Toyota (1985) 25 Hino (1984) (Hino is a Toyota affiliate making diesel trucks and buses, pickups, and some cars)	Was a truck and bus maker—produced only 2,600 vehicles in 1985. Restructured in October 1987 as a joint venture. Local partner is a distributor, Ho Tai Motors. Began making Zace utility vehicle in September 1988; Corona (a compact with 1800 or 2000cc engine) from completely knocked down kits in Spring 1989; some imports from NUMMI (GM-Toyota joint venture in the US).

Local Firm, Percentage of Equity Held by and Name of Foreign Partner with Year Investment Was First Made	Notes
San Fu	Technical cooperation with Renault since 1981 (assembles R9, R11, R12 under license) and Fuji Heavy Industries (vans and trucks). Under November 1986 agreement, assembles Isuzu Trooper II sports/utility vehicle for export to US; Isuzu is 40% owned by General Motors. There was discussion in 1986 of GM taking a 25% equity stake, primarily to develop relationships with local parts suppliers, according to speculation at the time.
San Yang 13 American Honda (1974)	Technical tie-up since 1967. Also makes Honda-designed motorcycles and scooters (some exported). The 1500cc Civic is the best-selling small car in Taiwan. Imports Accord from US, and Legend from UK (where it is made by Austin Rover).
Ta Ching 45 Fuji Heavy [Subaru] (1986 Sep)	Partner is Taiwan Vespa, 100% owned by Italy's Piaggio. Assembly of Subaru Justy begun in 1989.
Yue Loong 25 Nissan (1985)	Technical ties with Nissan since 1960. Discussions with Chrysler in mid-1980s came to nothing, as did talks in 1988 with GM about assembling the Opel.
Yue Tyan	Technical cooperation with Peugeot since 1977, Daihatsu (a Toyota affiliate mainly in subcompacts) since 1982, and Subaru (1986). Began as a motor scooter producer in collaboration with Italy's Piaggio.

See Tank 1986a for additional comments on the companies.

Other firms include Chinese Automobile Co Ltd, originally the exclusive distributor (until March 1988) for Yue Loong, now one of three GM import distributors, and a manufacturer of medium and heavy-duty commercial vehicles. Prince Motors, loosely affiliated with Yue Loong, makes an extended passenger and cargo van called the Super Homer and a 6.4 ton truck. Chin Hsian Industrial producers specialty trucks and commercial trailers. (Snyder 1988a, p 30)

It takes time to obtain government approval and then implement a foreign investment or joint venture, so one sees various dates in different sources. The dates here are when the application was approved by the government, which can be considered something of a median between announcement of the intention and the beginning of operations.

minimum-contracted 200 a month were being shipped. There is no longer much optimism in the industry about developing export markets, particularly in North America, because of the inability to achieve scale economies in assembly and the appreciation of the NT. Export data are in Table 7.15.

Changing Market Shares and Relationships Since 1985

The two leading local assemblers, Yue Loong and Ford Lio Ho, felt the 1985 adjustment policy was something of a double cross. Yue Loong had invested heavily in 1981 in an engineering center and in a greenfield plant on a 350–hectare site that included space for suppliers to build. The plant, with a capacity of 70,000 cars, could easily have supplied all the automobiles being purchased in Taiwan at the time. Both Yue Loong and Ford had plans to become exporters under the old rules—Yue Loong with a car it had designed primarily itself—and they felt the new policy would make that more difficult, or at least less profitable. This may have been a factor in Yue Loong's decision to sell a 25% equity position to Nissan for US$50 million in September 1985.

Although Yue Loong and Ford did not become exporters in the mid 1980s as they had planned, the period 1985–86 is a watershed for the industry because of the strategic alliances forged then and subsequently. Nissan, Ford, and Honda all had ties with local assemblers prior to 1985, and they were strengthened with additional investment. Toyota and Mitsubishi Motor took equity positions in local firms in 1985, while Fuji Heavy Industries (Subaru) entered a joint venture in 1986. This increased the number of local assemblers to seven.

There were eight assemblers in 1989, with a combined capacity of 551,000 units and over 14,000 workers. One of these, Kuo Tzui Motors, began producing cars only in 1988, until then having been only a heavy truck producer. Ta Ching Motors completed its plant in 1989. Table 7.16 shows the relationships between Taiwanese and foreign firms, and Table 7.17 gives additional information on each assembler.

The ventures have probably not worked out as expected. For the most part, they appear to have been motivated primarily by the desire to use Taiwan as an export base—including to mainland China (for more on this, see Snyder [1988a, p 34]). Also, Japanese firms were looking for a source of low-end cars with which to counter Korean inroads in that market. The United States was alert to this as a possible attempt to circumvent US voluntary export restraints on Japanese cars, and publicly warned against it (Radley 1986).

In part because it was then the largest firm, with far and away the

Table 7.17. Assemblers at 1988 Yearend

Firm	Estab- lished	Open[1]	Employ- ment	Capacity	Output	Capacity Utilization
China Motors	1969	1974	1000	60,000	35,665	59
Ford Lio Ho[2]	1972	1973	1900	90,000	79,595	88
Kuo Tzui	1984	1984	600	60,000	2,448	4
San Fu	1966	1968	1657	45,000	25,166	56
San Yang	1967	1969	4184	48,000	36,771	77
Ta Ching	1986			20,000		
Yue Loong	1953	1957	3419	168,000	62,727	37
Yue Tyan	1977	1979	1487	60,000	32,572	54

1. Date first produced a vehicle
2. Ford Lio Ho succeeded Ho Tai Motors in 1972.
Prince Motors and Chinese Automobile Co have been approved to assemble cars and will begin to do so in the 1990s.
Source: Taiwan Transportation Vehicle Manufacturers Assoc, unpublished data

biggest investment, Yue Loong has felt the impact of the new import rules and the changed currency relationships more than the other firms. The company would almost definitely have preferred to remain independent, but it is not clear it would survive without being affiliated with a major multinational firm. Nissan was planning to supply Australian-built engines in 1987 as part of an up-grading of the quality of Yue Loong cars, but this had not been implemented by the end of 1989.[4]

Almost all the parts in Ford Lio Ho's export model came in a CKD (completely knocked down) kit from Japan. On the other hand, the company's Taiwan plant was shipping some 13,000 Mazda B-series engines to Ford Australia in 1986. As a reward for this exporting, Ford was allowed to reduce the local content of cars marketed in Taiwan by as much as 20 percentage points.

In 1986 the government reduced the 50% export commitment required of joint ventures (adopted in 1977) to a percentage equal to half the share the foreign firm had in the joint venture plus a percentage of

4. In the early 1980s, with government encouragement, Yue Loong designed and, in October 1986, put on the market Taiwan's first indigenous car, the Feeling (the Chinese characters mean Flying Antelope). The Nissan Stanza was used as a starting point, but different driving conditions in Taiwan than in Japan led to Yue Loong's reworking first the suspension and then, ultimately, almost everything except the engine. At the time, Chrysler was said to be considering distributing it in the United States, Nissan in Japan. Instead, the car was not exported, and flopped in the domestic market. It quickly acquired a bad reputation for quality and in August 1988, production was discontinued. For more on Yue Loong's problems and the Feeling, see Snyder (1988a; 1988b, p 36).

subsequent production increases, and later completely dropped any export requirement. Importation of Japanese-designed cars built in Europe or the United States was also allowed beginning in 1986. Direct imports from Japan remain banned.

Because of continued large trade surpluses, in 1987 the tariff reduction timetable was speeded up, with the 1988 level set at 42.5% rather than the originally scheduled 55%. (This was part of a broad reduction in tariffs; most of the reductions were significantly larger than that for automobiles.)

The tariff reductions and appreciation of the NT helped imports achieve 32% market penetration in 1988, with sales of 127,000 units. This compares to 48,000 units and less than 17% penetration in 1987. Sales of all cars benefit in this period from the rapid rise in incomes during the mid 1980s—by 1988 a subcompact such as the San Yang Civic cost less than a year's pay of one of the firm's assembly line workers. Sales data are in Table 7.18.

In 1988 imported cars sold at an average 30% premium to comparable domestically produced models. Sales of US-made cars skyrocketed in 1988—including some US-built Honda Accords. Until then Germany had the largest share on a value basis, with Mercedes and BMW leading the high end and Opel doing well in the mid range. Although European styling is much admired, as one *Automotive News* headline put it, "American land yachts [have been] snapped up as true 'family' cars"— their extra width allows an extended family to travel together (Snyder 1988b, p 30).

Table 7.18. Auto Sales, 1984–88

Year	In Thousand Units			In Billion NT$			Import Share (of Value)	Tariff Rate
	Domestic	Import	Total	Domestic	Import	Total		
1984	162	12	174	42	3	46	7.4	65
1985	148	16	164	36	4	40	11.0	65
1986	164	24	189	45	7	52	13.7	60
1987	240	48	288	65	13	79	17.1	55
1988	263	132	390	72	35	107	32.9	42.5

Excise taxes of 25% are collected on cars under 2000 cc. For 2000–3000 cc cars, the rate is 35%, and over 3000 cc it is 60%.

Source: *Monthly Statistics of Trade* (1984–88 Dec issues, table 6), *Industrial Production Statistics Monthly* (1989 Jun, p 160 table C-2 and p 182 table D-3); and unpublished data from the Taiwan Transportation Vehicle Manufacturers Assoc.

Auto Parts Industry

There are over 2,000 firms in the auto parts industry, but only about 300 had the capacity to supply the local assembly industry in 1989. There are many small parts makers producing for the after market—domestic and foreign—rather than OEM (original equipment) market. Many of the companies have attained competitiveness in international markets: the level of exports skyrocketed in the mid 1980s, as shown in Table 7.19.

Taiwan's auto parts industry is quite heterogeneous. Broadly, it has three segments: large plants producing for domestic or foreign assembly, as with Ford Lio Ho's engine plant; smaller firms producing less competitively for domestic assembly under local content requirements; and a myriad of quite small firms that make add-ons and components—including crash parts—for older American and Japanese cars for the US after market.

Table 7.19. Auto Parts Overview, 1983–88 (US$ millions, except as noted)

1983	1984	1985	1986	1987	1988	*Exports of*
93	117	133	140	213	235	vehicle accessories
200	210	219	261	361	451	auto parts
52	50	75	92	138	112	motorcycle parts
42	58	64	75	77	72	wiring harnesses
78	117	130	186	247	261	other auto products
465	553	618	754	823	1131	total parts and accessories
10	15	21	8	16	48	motorcycles
1	1	3	25	50	20	cars, trucks, and buses
476	568	642	787	889	1199	total industry exports
968	1173	1094	1300	2029	2515	total production of parts and accessories
48	47	56	58	41	45	exports as a percentage of parts and accessories production
25	28	28	29	32	33	employment in auto parts (in thousands)

Source: Monthly Statistics of Trade (1983–85 Dec issues, table 6); *Industrial Production Statistics Monthly* (1989 Jun, p 160 table C-2 and p 182 table D-3); *Yearbook of Earnings and Productivity Statistics* (1989, p 52–55 table 4); and unpublished data from the China External Trade Development Council.

The ambition to promote OEM auto parts as an export item was a key element in the 1985 automobile industry adjustment plan. When Toyota became part of the Kuo Tzui joint venture, a number of affiliated parts producers, including Nippondenso, also made plans to open in Taiwan. An estimated 35 had done so by the time production began in 1988. Toyota also bought 80% of Fung Yung, one of the island's major parts makers. Ford Lio Ho, spurred by the increasing cost of parts from Japan, has also worked to develop local suppliers. In 1986 Ford was already importing into the United States wiring harnesses made by Taiwan Yamazaki—an affiliate of a Japanese firm and the only significant exporter of OEM auto parts from Taiwan.

As with the assemblers, the government has sought to encourage local firms to establish technical collaboration with foreign companies. As US firms continue to shift toward the Japanese system of having a limited number of closely related suppliers, most Taiwanese firms will be looking for places on the second or third tier. Joint ventures or direct investment by first-tier firms is also being encouraged. As in assembly, how Taiwan fares in the global restructuring of the components industry is a very open question.

Metamorphosis Rather Than Decline?

Taiwan has benefited from a general (if bureaucratically cumbersome) openness to foreign investment and the resulting integration into world markets. The automobile industry, or at least auto parts, may yet be another example. Things may not have worked out as the foreign firms, particularly the Japanese, originally expected. Taiwan no longer seems to be a competitive locale to make subcompact CBU (completely built up) vehicles for markets in developed countries. In 1989 there was overcapacity in this category worldwide and in Taiwan. But at the time of their investments, they said they were in for the long term.

Moreover, firms recognized they had to upgrade production efficiency before they could export built up autos, and that this involved increasing the level and sophistication of the island's auto parts industry. In other words, they at least publicly accepted what the government wished to encourage. And in the longer term the plants could be profitable. Few expected the major realignment of exchange rates after 1985, or the upheavals on the mainland, that so upset the assumptions behind the investments.

In any case, the completely independent assembler in Taiwan no longer exists. Moreover, with a domestic market of about 400,000 vehicles, there is general agreement not all the existing players will survive. But it may take some time to know who will. (For speculation, see Vines 1988 and Snyder 1988a and 1988b.) Whatever the fate of individual companies, Taiwan is now betting the multinationals' integration of the domestic industry into their worldwide strategies will provide the local industry—parts makers if not also assemblers—the overall survival and success that protection did not.

CONCLUSION

Taiwan has simultaneously used both import-substitution and export-promotion policies. Both initially were intended to alleviate foreign exchange shortages and accelerate industrialization. They succeeded. By 1971, Taiwan had both rapidly growing trade and a trade surplus, implying it had products competitive on world markets. However, rather than proceeding to adjust trade policy by lowering tariffs to increase competition in domestic markets and allowing consumers to enjoy lower prices, the government continued protectionist policies. The result has been a rising trade surplus, rising foreign currency reserves, pressure on the currency to appreciate, and the enmity of several of Taiwan's major trading partners.

The economy's high growth rate in the past is attributable directly to the proper use of export-promotion policy (and a world, particularly a United States, willing and even eager to purchase those exports). Export-promotion measures were adopted, beginning in the late 1950s, more to facilitate any exporting at all than to target any specific industry or subsidize exporters. Therefore, the ability of local producers to export is attributable to the increase in the international competitiveness of their products, and in the past this has reflected the use of cheap labor producing labor-intensive products.

Exporters have received tax rebates, but this is not strictly speaking an export incentive. With the steady reduction of tariffs, the rebating of import taxes to exporters has become less important and there is some talk of abolishing the practice. Taiwan has made only limited numbers of low-interest loans available, and in an economy that is awash in liquidity, finding low-cost credit is no longer a major problem for the credit-worthy, though the problems of a conservative and inefficient banking system persist. Establishment of the EPZs can be considered a special response to a past inability of the government to normalize and simplify its financial and economic system.

The government has not implemented measures to assist industries that have lost comparative advantage, such as plywood and canned food. Even textiles, which has seen an employment loss even greater than these two, has not received specific help. Quite simply, the fast pace of growth in the economy has provided increasing employment opportunities, absorbing those released from firms in declining industries as well as new labor force entrants. Indeed, the loss of competitiveness and eventual decline of some industries is accepted as a natural process in which the government should not intervene.

This market-oriented approach to structural adjustment for declining industries has, however, focused mainly on export industries. On a broader front, much depends on the willingness of policy makers to forsake the carryover of an earlier, protectionist way of thinking. For legitimate strategic reasons, in light of Taiwan's geopolitical location and history, it is not surprising policy makers have long stressed considerable self-sufficiency for key sectors. Thus the policy and practices of import protection have persisted past their economic justification, and just as that has been increasingly realized, interest groups opposing import liberalization have had the opportunity to articulate their position in the more open domestic political environment that has emerged in the late 1980s. Agriculture, as it shifts from having been highly export competitive to facing stiff import competition, partly as a consequence of Taiwan's remarkably successful economic development, is a prime example.

When and how to terminate, and even reverse, an earlier successful import-substitution policy for a particular industry is not easy to determine. In this regard, automobiles are an important, and perhaps still relatively optimistic, case. The automobile industry, even after some 30 years of infant industry protection, has barely achieved adolescence. And now it has been married off to foreign firms. The industry's experience seems to indicate import-substitution policies do not achieve the objective of industrial development if an appropriate protection policy is not designed and implemented, and indeed that there may not be any such appropriate policy. In the first place, there actually needs to be a domestic market for the product relative to production economies of scale. When the government began protecting the auto industry in 1960, and probably for 25 years thereafter, there simply were not enough people who could afford automobiles to allow development of an industry at the scale necessary to be competitive. The protected companies were profitable, but only because domestic prices were so high.

The government has changed its policy toward protection of the auto industry several times. One reason is the failure to attain the objective of international competitiveness in domestic production, which led to consumer complaints about quality and cost. Changes have also been made because of pressure from the United States in the face of its large trade deficit with Taiwan. It is somewhat ironic that because of the export success of industries that received only general support, an industry the government specifically promoted and strongly protected has been forced open to avoid trade friction.

It is never too late to liberalize trade. Although the strains will be heavy, there is a definite consensus within the government and among consumers for accelerated liberalization. Low wages and abundant labor resources were the basic reasons entrepreneurs adopted labor-intensive technologies in the past, but with improving levels of education and technical skills, rising wages, abundant capital, low interest rates, and the appreciation of the NT, there are now incentives to shift to industries that are more technically advanced, use more skilled labor, and are more capital intensive. Taiwanese industry has demonstrated an ability to adapt, and should be able to continue to do so.

Taiwan's export-oriented successful economic development has made it a model for developing countries. Especially noteworthy is the fact Taiwan, following American foreign aid in the 1950s, has never relied on large net infusions of foreign borrowing. Indeed, from the early 1970s it ran a small current account surplus. These burgeoned in the mid and late 1980s and contributed to the pressures, domestic and especially foreign (particularly from the United States), to engage in significant import liberalization. Taiwan in the late 1980s has taken a new policy stance by materially reducing tariffs and ending many import quotas, while having the currency appreciate substantially. Certainly these policy positions, and the realities of Taiwan's trade position, mean the government is very unlikely to help declining industries in the future through new import barriers, or even move significantly away from its current market-oriented approach to adjustment.

Taiwan is actively seeking to broaden and deepen its relations with other nations: only 5% of the island's trade is with the 24 countries that recognize the Republic of China diplomatically. It is a push-pull thing, with the private sector pulling the government and the government pushing the private sector, and there is no clear idea where this is going in the next 10 years. The government has taken a more assertive approach since the summer of 1989. One result was, by October, the re-establishment of diplomatic relations with three countries (Grenada, Belize, and Liberia). And Foreign Minister Lien Chan has indicated Taiwan's rejoining the United Nations is a personal, if not official, aim.

Clearly the relationship with the United States is of vital importance. Taiwan has expressed interest in a free trade agreement with the United States, which could alleviate part of the trade imbalance and bring other benefits to the two economies. As regards Asia-Pacific cooperation, Taiwan has participated actively in the tripartite Pacific Economic Cooperation Conference (PECC) and the businessmen's Pacific Basin Economic Council (PBEC).

The government is examining its trade policy with a view toward aligning it with GATT rules, and although not formally a party to the Uruguay Round of negotiations, Taiwan has monitored them closely. It is Taiwan's intention to apply for admission to GATT. As it moves to comply with the GATT, the government is indicating its policy is to encourage Taiwan to be more active and to take more responsibility in the world economy.

BIBLIOGRAPHY

Bennet, Dirk. 1986. "And Now, Ford of Taiwan." *Business Week,* Aug 11 p 44.

Branstetter, Henry. 1986. "Frozen Shrimp Outlook: 1988 and Beyond; Aquaculture Impact Is the Vanguard of A Virtual Market Revolution." *Quick Frozen Foods International,* v 27: Jan p 110.

Chen, Hsi-huang. 1978. "Taiwan's Food Processing Industry." *Economic Review* (of the International Bank of China) # 181 p 5 (Jan).

Council for Economic Development and Planning. 1983. *Development Plan for the Canned Food Industry.*

——. 1988. *Survey and Study on the Current Situation of Food Industry in Taiwan.* Taipei.

Galenson, Walter, editor. 1979. *Economic Growth and Structural Change in Taiwan, The Postwar Experience of the Republic of China.* Cornell University Press.

Gawronski, Frank. 1986. "Taiwan Bids Welcome to Foreign Car Makers." *Automotive News,* Jun 2 p 6.

Ho, Samuel P. S. 1978. *Economic Development of Taiwan, 1860–1970.* Yale University Press.

Hou, Chi-ming. 1978. "Manpower Development in Taiwan." *Industry of Free China,* Aug p 2–18 and Sep p 8–22.

——. 1988. "Strategy for Economic Development in Taiwan and Lessons for Developing Economies (1)." In *Conference on Economic Development Experiences of Taiwan and Its New Role in an Emerging Asia-Pacific Area,* v 1 p 31–58. Taipei: Institute of Economics, Academia Sinica.

Hung, Li-chun. 1988 Dec. "A Study on the Real Effective Exchange Rate Index." *Proceedings of the Chinese Economic Association.* In Chinese.

Kuo, Shirley W. Y., Gustav Ranis, and John C. H. Fei. 1981. *The Taiwan Success Story: Rapid Growth with Improved Distribution in the Republic of China, 1952–1979.* Boulder CO: Westview Press.

Lee, Robert CT. 1980. "A Review and Outlook of Taiwan's Agribusiness."

Economic Review (of the International Bank of China) # 194 p 1 (Mar).

Li, Kuo-ting. 1988. *The Evolution of Policy Behind Taiwan's Development Success*. Yale University Press.

Liang, Kuo-shu and Ching-ing Hou Liang. 1988. "Taiwan's New International Role in Light of Changes in Comparative Advantage, Trade Patterns and the Balance of Payments." In *Conference on Economic Development Experiences of Taiwan and Its New Role in an Emerging Asia-Pacific Area*, v 2 p 305–43. Taipei: Institute of Economics, Academia Sinica.

Lin, Chin-yuan. 1973. *Industrialization in Taiwan, 1946–72: Trade and Import-Substitution Policies for Developing Countries*. New York: Praeger.

Liu, Paul KC and Gee San. 1988. "Social and Institutional Basis for Economic Development in Taiwan." In *Conference on Economic Development Experiences of Taiwan and Its New Role in an Emerging Asia-Pacific Area*, v 1 p 257–75. Taipei: Institute of Economics, Academia Sinica.

Massey, Rick. 1989. "Overlaid Plywood Faces Worldwide Market Gain." *Forest Industries*, v 116: Apr p 32.

Pease, David A. 1988. "Global Panel Markets Show Excellent Promise." *Forest Industries*, v115: May p 40.

Pierce, John J. 1985. "Southeast Asia a Growing Force in International FF Trade," includes related articles on industry and food service transportation. *Quick Frozen Foods International*, v 27: Oct p 61.

QFFI. 1986. "Meat Takes Lead in FF Production as Taiwan Export Giant Beefs Up," (Luxe Enterprises Ltd, I-Mei Frozen Foods Co). *Quick Frozen Foods International*, v 28: Oct p 175.

Radley, Kevin. 1986. "Taiwan: Another Asian Outpost Has Its Sights Set on Exports, Beginning with a Foray into Canada." *Ward's Auto World*, v 22: May p 64.

Saulnier, John M. 1987. "Push into Value-Added Ethnic Imports Marks Evolution of Taiwan FF Industry." *Quick Frozen Foods International*, v 29: Oct p 141.

Scott, Maurice. 1979. "Foreign Trade." In Walter Galenson, editor, *Economic Growth and Structural Change in Taiwan*. Cornell University Press.

Snyder, Jesse. 1988a. "Danger Lurks in Taiwan's Auto Boom: Market Too Small to Feed All Players." *Automotive News*, Sep 12 p 1.

———. 1988b. "American Land Yachts Snapped Up as True 'Family' Cars." *Automotive News*, Sep 12 p 30.

Tank, Andrew. 1986a. "Made in Taiwan: Will Taiwan be Asia's Next Automotive Powerhouse?" *Automotive News*, Sep 29 p 29.

———. 1986b. "Taiwan Flying High with New Car Intro." *Automotive News*, Dec 22 p 1.

Tanzer, Andrew. 1985. "Another Player on the Stage? Will Taiwan Join the Ranks of the World's Automobile Exporters?" *Forbes*, Jun 17 p 38.

———. 1987. "End Run" (Japanese automakers in Taiwan). *Forbes*, May 4 p 87.

TIER = Taiwan Institute of Economic Research. Taipei.

——. 1987 May. *Survey on Important Industries: Plywood Industry.* Processed. In Chinese.

——. 1988a. *Plywood* (Special issue of *Taiwan Economic Research Monthly*). (Sep). In Chinese.

——. 1988b Jun. *Study of the Development Strategies of the Automobile Industry.* Processed. In Chinese.

US General Accounting Office. 1989. *US Trade Deficit: Impact of Currency Appreciations in Taiwan, South Korea, and Hong Kong.* GAO/NSIAD 89 130.

Vines, Stephen. 1987. "Taiwan's Automakers Emphasize Home Market; First Half Up 30%." *Automotive News,* Aug 24 p 26.

——. 1988. "Import Sales Strong in Taiwan: But Opel Is Only Foreign Make to Exhibit at Nation's Auto Show." *Automotive News,* Jun 20 p 22.

Wu, Rong-I. 1985. "Taiwan's Success in Industrialization." *Industry of Free China,* Nov p 7–22.

——. 1989. "Economic development strategies and the role of direct foreign investment in Taiwan." In *Advances in Financial Planning and Forecasting,* Supplement I: *Taiwan's Foreign Investment, Exports and Financial Analysis,* p 65–89. JAI Press.

8

KOREA
Market Adjustment in Declining Industries, Government Assistance in Troubled Industries

Ji-Hong Kim

Korean planners expected declining sectors eventually, and in a sense even helped create them by promoting new sectors for development. But the early five-year plans and industry-promotion laws did not adequately consider what might be involved, particularly because "decline" was more or less assumed to be relatively slow or no growth rather than an actual contraction of output—at least at the level of aggregation the planners considered. As production methods changed and labor costs rose, making an industry declining as regards employment, displaced workers were expected to find new jobs in the growing sectors. To date, most of the labor force adjustment from structural change has in fact occurred as expected, with relatively little direct government involvement.

Dealing with declining or troubled firms has been another matter. Until the mid 1980s, government involvement with adjustment assistance tended to be firm specific. The reasons are complex, tied up with the way development occurred in the 1970s, how the economy was jolted by the oil shocks, and other elements. Even had the government developed more detailed plans for the industries it expected to decline, events would probably have overwhelmed them. And many of the declining and troubled industries of the 1980s are not the ones expected. For these reasons, it is no wonder there was a certain ad-hocness to the government's response, and because it was generally firms that presented problems, it seemed reasonable to address the problems at the firm level.

Korea appears to have reached a new stage of economic development. Some of the problems faced by certain industries are systemic or involve a significant number of the firms. This has led to a shift to industry-specific policies. Declining industries confront the Korean government with a dilemma—the conflicting policies of withdrawing or adding resources.

In several declining industries, government policy is needed to aid the withdrawal of resources. It is a fundamental principle that the optimum allocation of resources, especially scarce resources, should be pursued through the market mechanism. When rational decision making by the private sector alone cannot achieve the optimal solution easily, government policy can be very significant, as policies can actually promote use of the market mechanism. Government intervention can be vital in the presence of market imperfections (particularly exit barriers), economies of scale, externalities, and the incentive-distorting effects of government policies. In most withdrawal cases, the overriding concern prodding intervention is what happens to workers released from a declining industry.

In other cases, government intervention is needed to add resources to restructure a declining industry, in order to shape the desired industrial structure. Restructuring involves turning a declining industry into a competitive one. When restructuring is in fact possible, it requires an infusion of new resources—capital, labor, technology, and the like. It can take various forms, some working within the market mechanism, and others not. Thus governments help train workers (human capital), offer tax credits, provide subsidized loans, consent to organization of cartels to raise prices, and erect trade barriers to help revive (or create) an industry. In some cases, however, the possibility of a government restructuring plan may in itself serve to delay adjustment, as potential declining industries have added incentive to wait for a government rescue. Arguments in favor of additional investment are sometimes excuses to continue the process of bailing out troubled companies.

The objective of this paper is to promote understanding of industrial policy towards the declining industries and the mechanisms of industry structural adjustment in Korea. The first section, by way of background, reviews structural changes in the Korean economy, while the second summarizes adjustment assistance policy. Three industries, each representing a different type of decline, have been selected as cases in which Korea has lost or is losing competitiveness. These are coal mining, in absolute decline; shipbuilding, in cyclical decline; and textiles and clothing, in relative decline.

The reverberations in Korea of the second oil shock were stronger than the first. With the glut of oil tankers, the slowdown in shipbuilding was especially dramatic, as new foreign orders plummeted over 40% from 1983 to 1984, and another 68% from 1984 to 1985 (measured in gross tons; declines were even steeper in US dollars because of falling prices). Coal—anthracite coal—faces hard times. But as the country's principal indigenous primary energy source, and of great importance to mining regions, the industry's decline is as much a political as an economic issue. Textiles and clothing continue to be Korea's major foreign exchange earner, but this area faces protectionist pressure in its markets and increased competition from other developing countries with even lower labor costs. Restructuring is going on to move "up market"—to higher value-added products—but this is also what competitors in Taiwan, Hong Kong, and Singapore are doing. Following the case studies, conclusions and some lessons from Korea's experiences are presented.

THE INDUSTRIAL STRUCTURE IN TRANSITION

The Korean economy has experienced very rapid changes in the 1980s.[1] Real GNP has increased at around 8% annually, and although consumption has not increased as quickly, it has also made impressive gains. The government adopted an export-promotion policy fairly early in the course of economic development, in order to overcome the country's small domestic market size and to earn foreign currency. Exports have increased from $17 billion (1980) to $61 billion (1988), and a sizable surplus of $3 billion in the trade balance in 1986 marked a turn in the Korean macroeconomic environment. The trade surplus continued to rise, reaching $9 billion for 1988, substantially larger than the government predicted. However, beset by labor strife and other problems, economic growth slowed somewhat in 1989 and the trade and current account surplus declined sharply. Nonetheless, long-run growth prospects remain good.

Because the domestic saving rate was on average lower than gross investment until the mid 1980s, the amount saved did not meet invest-

1. Among useful overviews of Korea and its development, including the period before the 1980s, are Leipziger (1987), which is a World Bank country study made in 1985; Bartz (1972), worthwhile for its discussions of geography and the 1960s; KDI (1975), for a well-illustrated and at times candid discussion; and KOIS (1978 and 1987).

ment requirements. Consequently, the gap was financed by foreign borrowing, which peaked at a cumulative gross of $47 billion in 1985. Due to the saving and trade surpluses since then, total foreign debt had decreased to $36 billion by the end of 1987 and declined further in 1988.

Because of the favorable turn in the balance of payments, the Korean won appreciated rapidly beginning in 1985, and this trend may well continue in the longer term, depending on domestic economic performance. The won was 792 to the US dollar at the end of 1987, 680 at the end of 1988, and 665 in June 1989 (even as the dollar strengthened against the yen and European currencies). The real effective exchange rate adjusted for relative price movements has appreciated since 1987.

Moreover, while the gross investment rate has been stable in the 1980s (32% in 1980, 30% in 1986), domestic savings continued to rise, going from 21% (1980) to 33% (1986), so it has surpassed gross investment. Table 8.1 summarizes Korea's growth in the 1970s and '80s.

Structural Change

The structure of production in Korea shifted continuously from agriculture to manufacturing throughout the 1970–85 period, regardless of

Table 8.1. Macroeconomic Indicators

1970	1974	1978	1982	1984	1986	1988	
18.6	24.2	36.0	41.2	50.0	59.2	na	GNP in trillions of 1980 won
				96.1	121.9	165.5	manufacturing production index (1985 = 100)
Merchandise Trade (US$ billion)							
0.8	4.5	12.7	21.9	29.2	34.7	60.7	exports (FOB)
2.0	6.9	15.0	24.3	30.6	31.6	51.8	imports (CIF)
na	5.9	27.2	37.1	43.1	45.1	31.2	foreign debt
na	484	484	749	827	861	684	won per US dollar at end of year

In the mid-1980s the Bank of Korea adopted a new system of national accounts (SNA). A convenient summary of the differences, including GNP comparisons under the old and new SNA for 1980–84 is Leipziger 1987 (1:133).

Source: Various issues of the Bank of Korea *National Account,* but a more convenient source of national account and trade data is the *Korean Statistical Yearbook,* which typically will have preliminary data for the prior year plus revised data for the 5 years before that.

Table 8.2. Distribution of Domestic Gross Output, 1975–86, with a Comparison to Taiwan (percents)

the means of measurement (output, value added, or employment). In terms of total output, for example, the share of agriculture declined drastically, from 17% in 1970 to less than 8% in 1985. By contrast, the share of manufacturing, 40% in 1970, was over 50% by 1975 and remained at around that level through 1985. The variation in the size of sectoral shares differs considerably for each of the three measurements. In 1985 agriculture accounted for 25% of employment and 12% of value added, while its share of output was less than 8%. By contrast, manufacturing provided 23% of employment, 30% of value added, and 50% of output.

Trends in Manufacturing

Among manufacturing sectors, the share of light industry in total output fell considerably between 1975 (30%) and 1985 (22%), though total output increased. For example, food and beverages; textiles, apparel, and leather; as well as lumber and wood products provided progressively smaller shares. Heavy industry, on the other hand, expanded significantly. Table 8.2 shows the distribution of gross output by manufacturing sector.

As a result of the "picking winners" approach, which includes the HCI (heavy and chemical industry) drive during the second half of the 1970s, heavy industry output had surpassed that of light industry by 1980. Two goals of the HCI drive were to promote import substitution in intermediate materials and to make capital goods a source of exports. Although the shares of all three HCI sectors (chemicals, primary metals, and machinery) increased between 1970 and 1985, there are some differences in their development in the pre- and post-1980 periods. After recording substantial gains before 1980, chemicals and primary metals lost ground slightly in the 1980s, while machinery (including metal products) continued expanding share even after 1980.

A detailed examination of developments in the metal products and machinery sector during 1980–85 shows the increase was particularly substantial in general machinery and transportation equipment. These industries have also provided a significant number of new jobs since 1980, and are expected to be among the faster-growing industries for future labor absorption.

Employment

Because the economically active population increased by 8% in the 1980–85 period, employment has been a serious concern to Korean

Table 8.2. Distribution of Domestic Gross Output, 1975–86, with a
Comparison to Taiwan (percents)

Korea		Taiwan	Korea		
1975	1980	1984	1985	1986	
12.8	8.3	5.5	7.7	7.1	agriculture, forestry & fishery
0.9	0.8	0.7	0.7	0.7	mining
1.5	2.2	2.7	2.3	2.2	utilities
6.2	8.0	4.7	8.1	7.1	construction
50.5	51.0	59.3	50.0	51.5	manufacturing
28.1	29.7	27.1	31.2	31.4	services
					manufacturing
29.8	24.7	24.2	21.7	22.2	light
20.7	26.3	35.1	28.3	29.3	heavy
					light manufacturing
14.7	10.7	7.5	9.1	9.0	food, beverage
9.9	8.4	8.8	7.3	7.7	textiles, apparel, leather
1.1	1.1	1.5	0.7	0.7	lumber and wood products
1.4	1.6	2.0	1.8	1.8	paper, printing, publishing
1.5	1.9	1.9	1.8	1.8	non-metallic minerals
1.2	1.0	2.5	1.0	1.2	other
					heavy manufacturing
10.7	12.6	15.1	11.4	10.5	chemicals & chemical products
3.4	5.1	5.0	4.9	4.9	primary metal manufacturing
6.6	8.6	15.0	12.0	13.9	metal products and machinery
					services
8.3	7.1	6.7	6.6	6.9	wholesale and retail trade
1.2	1.1	0.6	0.9	0.9	restaurants, hotels
5.1	5.9	3.9	5.9	5.7	transportation, warehousing, and communication
3.7	5.6	6.1	6.9	7.1	finance, insurance, real estate
3.5	3.6	5.3	3.3	3.5	public administration and defense
4.2	4.6	3.7	5.8	5.6	other services
2.1	1.8	0.8	1.8	1.7	not elsewhere classified

Because this table covers gross output, it shows a higher percentage for manufacturing activities than does a distribution of GNP or GDP. Thus, eg, manufacturing was 30% of 1980 GDP and 32% of 1982 GDP (both in 1980 won at market prices).

Source: Bank of Korea *Input Output Tables*

policy makers. Moreover, employment issues are widely expected to become even more prominent for several reasons. (1) The employment elasticity with respect to output has fallen from an estimated 0.45–0.50 in the 1970s to about 0.25 in the 1980s, and it is expected to remain at that level. (2) There will be significant labor displacement from agriculture. (3) Skill mix requirements will change substantially as employment opportunities shift from low- to high-skill jobs as a consequence of industrial change.

Total employment increased 7.5% from 1980 to 1985, rising from 12.2 to 13.1 million. There has been a shift from the primary sector to services and heavy industry. Light industry has lost workers, although textiles and apparel continue to be a major source of employment. The metals and machinery industry has exhibited the fastest employment growth since 1970. These changes reflect the deepening of the industrial structure. Changes in employment distribution are shown in Table 8.3.

With respect to overall job creation, increases in employment will occur in skilled areas and in the service sector. Investments in human capital will take on greater importance as the overall technology level of the economy increases. With respect to the labor mix, the three industries projected to grow fastest from 1987 to 1996 are electronics, machinery, and autos. In general, they require higher skill levels than does light manufacturing. This increases the importance of retraining, in which public sector initiatives would be helpful.

Real Wages and Labor Productivity

Before 1975, real wages rose at a slower rate than labor productivity, because of the large surplus in labor supply, especially from rural areas. However, during the period 1976–78, the boom in labor demand associated with rapid economic growth and the HCI drive, together with the government's policy to raise the minimum wage, pushed both nominal and real wages higher. Several economists call the 1976–78 period the Lewisian turning point in the sense that the supply of labor became much less elastic. After the second oil shock, the government introduced strong measures for price stability. Real wages declined in 1980 and 1981 due to the sharp recession (the inflation rate was high and GNP growth was actually negative for the first time). While growth in nominal wages has been slower than before, real wages doubled between 1981 and 1988, and may be expected to rise further. Labor productivity also has increased rapidly due to the introduction of higher-quality capital equipment and modern management techniques such as computer systems.

Table 8.3. Distribution of Employment, 1975–86 (percents, except as noted)

1975	1980	1985	1986	
11.7	13.7	15.0	16.9	total employment, in millions
41.3	31.9	25.5	24.3	agriculture, forestry & fishery
1.1	1.1	1.1	1.1	mining
0.2	0.3	0.3	0.3	utilities
4.1	5.4	6.1	5.8	construction
19.2	21.7	22.9	24.0	manufacturing
34.1	39.5	44.1	44.4	services
				manufacturing
13.5	13.8	12.7	13.1	light
5.7	7.9	10.1	10.9	heavy
				light manufacturing
2.8	2.9	2.7	2.6	food, beverage
7.9	7.4	6.4	6.6	textiles, apparel, leather
0.6	0.7	0.5	0.5	lumber and wood products
0.8	0.9	1.0	1.0	paper, printing, publishing
0.7	0.9	0.9	0.9	non-metallic minerals
0.7	1.1	1.1	1.4	other
				heavy manufacturing
1.9	2.5	3.0	3.3	chemicals and chemical products
0.5	0.7	0.9	0.9	primary metal manufacturing
3.3	4.7	6.2	6.8	metal products and machinery
				services
13.0	14.9	15.9	15.5	wholesale and retail trade
3.5	3.7	4.8	4.9	restaurants, hotels
4.1	4.2	4.7	4.7	transportation, warehousing, and communication
3.3	4.5	4.9	5.0	finance, insurance, real estate
3.4	3.7	3.6	3.7	public administration and defense
6.7	8.5	10.1	10.5	other services

Since 1986 the economy has experienced particularly sharp increases in real wages. There are several reasons. (1) In the wake of political liberalization, demands for a more equal income distribution have become stronger. (2) Labor unions have become more widespread. (3) The disequilibrium of labor supply and demand between growing and declining industries has deepened. Growing industries have experienced considerable difficulty in employing qualified workers, while there remains a large pool of under-qualified labor. As wages in growing industries have risen, unions have also used their bargaining power to change working conditions.

Export Growth and Structural Change

Although not as dependent on trade as Taiwan, since Korea began pursuing an export-promotion policy the role of exports has increased continuously. Exports grew over 23% a year in the 1970s, even faster than the economy as a whole. Thus, 21% of final demand was exports in 1975, 23% in 1980, and 26% in 1985.

The composition of exports has changed significantly. While textiles and apparel are still the major source of foreign exchange, some light industrial manufactures, such as wigs and plywood, have contracted compared to 1970, while capital-intensive products such as ships and steel became more important. This does not mean light manufactured exports have become uncompetitive, as shown by the continued resiliency of clothing, footwear, luggage, and cutlery. Table 8.4 lists the top ten exports in several years since 1970.

At the same time, during the 1980s, Korea's comparative advantage clearly emerged in shipbuilding, electrical equipment, metal products, and iron and steel. Thanks to the HCI promotion, by 1980 the share of HCI in exports (38% in 1987) had surpassed that of light industry (35%). Although costly to establish, the competitiveness of the HCI industries may legitimately be described as the successful development of infant industries requiring middle-level technology and skilled labor. In some industries, most prominently in chemicals and machinery, Korea has yet to establish itself in international markets.

Korea appears to have made significant progress in shifting its export structure from labor-intensive to capital-intensive and moderately skill-intensive products. The initial transition to capital-intensive exports owes its success and speed to the government involvement of the 1970s, which helped establish industries of sufficient scale to be internationally competitive. As is evident in the case studies, however, some of these interventions have come to pose a significant moral hazard and have made restructuring more complicated in the 1980s.

Emergence of Declining Industries

After the second oil shock in 1979, financial difficulties in large industries posed a new challenge to Korean policy makers. Shipbuilding is dealt with as one of this essay's case studies. Another industry in

Table 8.4. Top Ten Exports, 1970–87

1970	1975	1981	1987
textiles and apparel	textiles and apparel	textiles and apparel	textiles and apparel
plywood	electronic products	electronic products	electronic and communication equipment
wigs	steel products	steel products	transportation equipment (automobiles)
minerals	plywood	footwear	footwear
electronics products	footwear	ships	metal products
fruits and vegetables	deep-sea fish	machinery	iron and steel products
footwear	ships	synthetic resin products	electrical equipment
tobacco	metal products	auto tires	fiber yarns
steel products	petroleum products	metal products	petrochemical products
metal products	synthetic resin products	plywood	ships

Source: Korea Traders Association (*The Trend of Foreign Trade*) and Bank of Korea (*Monthly Statistical Bulletin*, various issues)

considerable difficulty has been overseas construction, which was mostly in oil-producing countries.

In addition to these exogenously precipitated declines, the rapid growth of the Korean economy has required a massive shift of resources from less efficient sectors into more efficient sectors. In the transition, some industries have declined. The issue of structural adjustment in Korea became particularly significant in the 1980s, and its rise to salience was the result of several factors: higher costs of labor and raw materials, competition from other industrializing economies, the appreciation of the won, and changes in domestic demand structure due to higher incomes. These factors sent negative reverberations through many sectors of Korean industry, contributing to the decline of several lower value-added and export-oriented industries, including textiles and plywood.

ADJUSTMENT ASSISTANCE POLICY

The government has sought to design policies to help declining industries settle into gradual rather than convulsive decline. Its efforts have been based on a package of policies tailored to assist the industries as well as to ameliorate the pain of factor relocation for depressed companies and displaced workers. This section explains the government's policies towards declining industries, including pre- and post-1986 policies, as well as comments on issues to be addressed by future policies. (Also see Leipziger 1988.)

Pre-1986 Policy: Firm-Specific Intervention

Certain features unique to Korea complicate the standard arguments regarding government involvement in troubled industries. The government helped create several of them, including shipbuilding, shipping, and overseas construction. In the second half of the 1970s, the government intervened aggressively by providing fiscal incentives and subsidized credit, and by encouraging new entrants. This promotion policy was successful in cushioning Korea's trade balance after the first oil shocks (the bill for crude oil imports rose from 2.2% of GNP in 1972 to 9.2% in 1980). But it put the government in the position of an implicit risk partner and created the expectation that the government would provide a soft landing for individual firms in these large-scale, capital-intensive industries, should the situation deteriorate. The direct promotional role of the government has made market-determined adjustment more difficult.

In shipping, for example, the Shipping Promotion Act (1962) brought about a rapid increase in the number of firms (from 19 in 1970 to 64 in 1980) in the liner and bulker trade, as shipowners enjoyed easy access to bank credit as a favored industry. When low world trade volume led to a severe worldwide recession and a series of insolvencies, the government intervened with the Shipping Rationalization Program (1983–85)— merging firms, ordering cutbacks in capacity, and providing credit to the survivors.

Similarly, overseas construction was actively promoted by the government during the economic boom in oil-producing countries during the 1970s. The Construction Industry Promotion Law (1975) and other incentives led to an explosion of firms authorized to do overseas construction business. The builders generated large foreign currency earnings and sent close to 200,000 Korean workers abroad. Then, new orders dropped precipitously: from over $13 billion in each of 1981 and 1982 to half that in 1984 and less than $5 billion in 1985. Employment

fell by 70,000 between 1982 and 1985, exacerbating an emerging unemployment problem.

As the oil-country market softened, the industry's highly leveraged
firms engaged in sharp price cutting and under-bidding to secure jobs
and thus obtain advanced payments, generally lowering the profitability
of construction exports. The government, however, made no attempt to
rescue the industry as a whole. Small firms were allowed to go bankrupt,
while large firms were forced to merge with stronger ones in return for
help in rolling over their massive debts. The industry is not likely to
recover soon, although the ending of the Iran-Iraq war offers some hope.

There are striking similarities in the experiences of shipbuilding and
overseas construction. Both over-expanded, due largely to explicit government promotion policies, and once markets began to weaken, financially strapped firms engaged in destructive competition and widespread
distress financing. Moreover, because the distress of these key industries
in the early 1980s was so severe, and the then-only-recently (in 1980)
privatized banks had neither the experience nor the capital to manage
them, there was a palpable fear the collapse of under-capitalized firms
could cause a catastrophic chain reaction in financial markets.

Ultimately both industries were bailed out by government rationalization programs. Such programs typically reduce the number of firms
according to plans orchestrated by the government. Troubled, and in
some cases, even bankrupt firms were "placed" with financially healthier
ones and, as inducement, the government facilitated the rescheduling of
debts as well as infusing new credit.

As part of the Shipping Rationalization Program (1983–85), the
government reorganized the shipping industry, determining the number
of survivors (17 of 63 firms) and setting capacity reduction targets. As
several firms refused to accept these measures, the government threatened to withhold financial incentives from firms that refused to coop-
erate. The government accepted part of the losses of the troubled enterprises, in large measure to prevent undue injury to the domestic banking
system and capital market. (For more on shipping, see Leipziger 1987, v
2 p 131–47).

The short-term benefits of Korean restructuring operations are clear.
Dislocations in labor markets as well as disruptions in financial markets
are reduced. Confidence in the Korean industrial and financial environment is maintained. The former is important in the domestic political
context, the latter in preserving Korea's access to international financial
markets.

On the other hand, Korea's rationalization programs often fail to
impose the discipline on restructuring that is brought to bear by market
solutions. First, financial sectors are generally excluded from the sub-

stantive aspects of the restructuring process: with respect to past loans, their losses are to some extent assumed by the government; with respect to new loans, they are not assigned a central role either in shaping or in monitoring the restructuring program. Second, rationalization programs were firm-specific and thus inconsistent across industries and within industries. Often the firms with many employes were bailed out while small firms were neglected even when they were in better financial condition or otherwise better-equipped to compete.

Third, the government did not have clearly defined objectives and procedures to limit its role. Once a bailout begins, it can easily lead to hemorrhaging of resources to ensure its success. In the case of the Shipping Rationalization Program (1983–85), a second round of refinancing was needed in 1987, and the amount of debt rescheduled (3.2 trillion won for the six major firms) was even higher than in 1983. Fourth, the surviving firms have received mixed signals about the environment in which they must operate. On the one hand, they have had an opportunity to take necessary measures to reduce capacity and improve long-run profitability, but on the other, they have had some ill-defined commitment from the government for continuing support. After a restructuring plan is adopted, firms are reluctant to reduce capacity if they believe they may outlast other firms, and in any case they will be rescued again if they falter.

In general, the government's willingness to manage restructuring creates a significant moral hazard. Given the prospect of government rescue in the event of adverse business conditions, firms are more willing to undertake risky strategies. Banks may finance such strategies partly because their own exposure is limited by the prospect of government rescue. Once adverse conditions materialize, firms and lenders may postpone adjustment in anticipation of government intervention, engaging in what is sometimes termed "distress finance." The Korean experience of the early and mid 1980s tells us that, before bailout efforts are made, the government should make sure the objectives, conditions, and rules are clear. Interventions should be time-limited and conditional, and great care should be taken to avoid repeated bailouts.

Post-1986 Policy: Industry Specific

With the increasing sophistication of the economy, the continuing pressure of international competition, and the crisis generated by structurally declining industries, the Korean government recognized a new framework was needed to streamline industrial policy. The resulting Industrial Development Law (IDL), approved by the National Assembly in December 1985, was conceived in part to replace the existing promotional laws governing seven industries: machinery, electronics, textiles, iron and steel, non-ferrous metals, petrochemicals, and shipbuilding. These seven laws, which played a promotional role for 15 years, were abolished.

The new framework adopted an industry-specific approach, and focuses primarily on the improvement of industrial technology and productivity. The primary objective of the IDL is to compensate for market failure in two areas. One area comprises sectors in which it would be difficult, through the independent efforts of the private sector, to attain international competitiveness, despite a prospective comparative advantage for the Korean economy. Therefore, the government encourages investment and specialization in those sectors through indirect incentives aimed at promoting technological development and securing international competitiveness.

The other area is structurally inefficient declining industries, those in which Korea is gradually losing competitiveness because of changes in industrial structure or economic conditions. Concern that unfavorable scale or methods of production will continue for a prolonged period means government intervention is justified for sound industrial development.

In these two special areas, the government's role is two-fold: first, to rationalize growing industries until they become internationally competitive and, second, gradually to phase out declining industries, where possibly by encouraging firms to switch to another industry. This phasing-out process is intended to upgrade production facilities or assist the market mechanism of exit. The policy could contribute to international industrial cooperation by encouraging the migration of a more advanced economy's declining industries to someplace with an emerging comparative advantage.

One difference of the IDL from pre-1986 rationalization programs is that the period of rationalization is strictly limited to three years. Further, to minimize the scope of government intervention, the industries included are strictly limited to those in a declining sector or a sector deemed able to achieve international competitiveness.

Another improvement is the restatement of procedures to deal with industrial restructuring. To avoid unilateral government intervention, a consensus-building process was adopted that promotes the exchange of a wide range of opinions from various economic circles. To qualify for government assistance, an industry has to apply for the designation as an "industry for rationalization," demonstrating it has lost competitiveness and that most firms in the industry have severe surplus capacity. After consultation with the Industrial Development Deliberative Council and the Deliberation Committee on Industrial Policy (both created by IDL), the Ministry of Trade and Industry (MTI) drafts a rationalization plan, which can involve special loans, mergers, cooperative behavior, capacity reduction, import restrictions, and entry deterrence.

The Council includes experts on industrial policy from the private sector (professors, research economists, and entrepreneurs) while the Committee coordinates views on rationalization policy among concerned government organizations. The procedures involved in the IDL are still geared to publicly led restructurings, however, so the government will continue to have a central role, at least for the time being, in financial workouts. Moreover, the legislation provides MTI with a great deal of latitude with respect to intervention measures. When an industry is designated for rationalization, management of the firms involved are, in principle, expected voluntarily to exert efforts to ensure the effective implementation of the plan.

Between July 1986 and December 1987, eight industrial categories were designated for rationalization with specific time limits of two or three years. (All but the fertilizer program were to end by the summer of 1989.) Automobiles, diesel engines, heavy electrical equipment, and heavy construction equipment are categorized as emerging. Textiles, non-ferrous metals, dyeing, and fertilizer are categorized as declining. Textiles is one of the case studies, and it and dyeing are discussed later.

The ferro-alloy and non-ferrous metals industries originally were promoted to avoid total dependence on foreign sources, despite the high cost of electricity (55 won per kwh compared to 49 in Taiwan and 18 in Canada). This ill-fated promotion ended up with a low operating ratio. To improve the ratio, under a plan initiated in July 1986 for a three-year period, new entry was banned. Two firms were merged to monopolize copper smelting. Three firms were designated to specialize in manganese steel, and a long-term supply contract with Pohang Steel (POSCO) was arranged for them by MTI.

Because the IDL provides MTI with a great deal of latitude, applying it in the real world raises a host of questions. One of the most critical, and controversial, issues is how to identify the two categories of industry. The two consulting groups (the Industrial Development Deliberative Council and the Deliberation Committee on Industrial Policy) are commissioned to identify which industries to subject to the IDL, but the IDL does not provide definitions. Another issue is that the intervention measures are not specified. This can lead to over-support or overkill. Measures such as mergers or bans on entry can contribute to an increase in economic concentration and conflict with the antitrust laws.

Future Policy: A Functional Approach

Public intervention in declining industries has been necessitated in part by the general weakness of financial institutions and by the absence of strong private mechanisms for industrial restructuring. Korea's continuing industrial transformation will necessitate the withdrawal of resources from certain industries. Thus, exit policy procedures that work more smoothly than at present are needed.

The government therefore has clear priorities if it is to avoid continual involvement. It must (1) strengthen financial markets, (2) allow industrial decisions to follow market signals as much as possible, and (3) identify the few cases where involvement is justified.

Financial Markets. Because of its direct involvement in industry-level restructuring, the government has exercised strong influence over the resulting structure of industry. In some cases, the government dictated the ultimate number of surviving firms and designated merger partners — essentially financially strong firms absorbing troubled ones in return for subsidized loans from banks. Much of the government's dominant role as an industrial organizer stems from its role in industrial finance and the inefficiency (weakness) of the financial sector. (The reform and liberalization of Korean financial markets is a major policy issue. For further reading, see Edwards 1988, p 185–94.)

A basic shift in financial markets must take place if the burden of restructuring declining firms is to be shifted from the public to the private sector. In an attempt to promote such a change, the government enacted legislation in 1985 that includes incentives for highly leveraged firms or banks involved in the rationalization process to sell subsidiaries or fixed assets. The aim of these incentives is to induce firms to sell peripheral assets, such as real estate, and refinance themselves or help banks dispose of collateral they currently hold. Ultimately, these procedures can promote greater corporate self-reliance. And the role of the banking sector, as the prime creditor, will need to be strengthened. This argues for greater bank autonomy, which can only be established on the basis of stronger bank finances and managerial autonomy from both the government and major borrowers. There should be greater differentiation in lending rates and strict leveraging limits, particularly for conglomerates (*chaebol*). To achieve this, greater financial transparency is needed.

Market Signals. While the government has begun the process of altering industrial expectations, it must be willing to let market prices determine the ultimate viability of industries and refrain as much as possible from arbitrary intervention. In several instances, intervention with implicit protection, as practiced for several declining industries, can be shown to have been costly for the Korean economy in terms of both efficiency and trade diplomacy. The longer market signals are ignored, the costlier the ultimate adjustments turn out to be.

The issue of trade liberalization merits examination in the context of declining-industry policy. Many economists argue that international prices provide the best signal for both competitiveness and the domestic viability of an industry. Import prices are thus valuable industrial guidelines. Faced with pressure to liberalize imports, Korea can utilize this opportunity to deepen its industrial structure. By taking a proactive rather than a reactive stance toward declining industries, trade friction with Korea's major trading partners may be alleviated.

Limited Involvement. Essentially, the government has no advantage over the market mechanism in determining industrial structure, so any imputed market failures must be pervasive enough to warrant intervention. In the future, as financial markets mature, government intervention should be limited to industry-wide restructuring efforts in exceptional situations, as where competitors cannot agree on capacity reductions in declining industries with large capital investments and scale economies, or in industries that are competing in oligopolistic international markets.

Insofar as Korea's industrial structure will be subject to many more jolts in the future, as a consequence of changes in comparative advantage, corporate miscalculations, and basically exogenous factors (such as protectionism and oil shocks), there is merit in avoiding ad hoc policy measures and establishing more explicit and consistent guidelines for intervention. These would cover circumstances and procedures under which intervention occurs and the maximum time and cost of that intervention.

COAL MINING: ABSOLUTE DECLINE

Coal is Korea's only indigenous fossil fuel.[2] Unfortunately, it is low-grade anthracite, having a low heat value, tending to powderiness (which

2. Coal, technically a rock rather than a mineral, includes three broad types: anthracite (hard coal, which has little volatile matter), bituminous (soft coal, which is the source of bitumen, coke, and coal tar), and lignite (brown coal). Peat is a precursor of coal. Anthracite usually is more clean-burning than bituminous, and has more heat value, but this is less true of Korean deposits. Most coal mined and traded internationally is bituminous, and data (except for production data) only sometimes distinguish between anthracite

Table 8.5. Primary Energy Consumption: Distribution by Source (in percents)

1961	1966	1971	1975	1980	1986	1987	Projections		
							1991	2001	
32.1ᵃ	45.7	28.7ᵃ	27.4	22.5	21.0	18.4	15.6	6.1	anthracite
	0.5		1.9	7.6	16.5	15.8	16.2	27.3	bituminous
8.1	16.6	50.6	56.8	61.1	46.7	44.3	46.5	46.9	petroleum
					0.1	3.1	3.1	2.1	LNG
				2.0	11.6	14.4	15.3	14.9	nuclear
1.7	1.8	1.5	1.5	1.1	1.7	2.0	1.5	1.3	hydroelectric
58.1	35.4	19.2	12.4	5.7	2.4	2.0	1.9	1.3	firewood, etc

ᵃ Includes both anthracite and bituminous. All bituminous is imported.

Projections are by the Korea Energy Economic Institute (as reported in the *Business Korea Yearbook* 1988/89, p III-12)

Sources: Ministry of Energy and Resources, *Yearbook of Energy Statistics* (1987), except 1961 and 1971 are from KOIS (1978, p 566 table 34); and 1987 is from the *Korean Business Review* (1988 Feb, p 50)

makes transportation difficult), and occurring mostly in deep, fairly narrow veins in rugged terrain (which makes mining relatively expensive). The residential and commercial sectors consume 90% of the mines' output, primarily in the form of briquettes (*yontan*) for space heating, but cleaner fuels have become cost-competitive. Together, these characteristics describe an industry with a limited future. This is acknowledged in the government's 1987 whitepaper "Long-term Energy Policies and Prospects toward the 2000s": anthracite production will decline due to rising mining costs and a shift in demand to cleaner household fuels.

In some ways, this is ironic. In the past, the government has promoted the industry, and now must face the consequences of its success. As a result of past involvement, a government corporation is the principal producer of coal, and government regulation is involved in every aspect of the industry, including setting anthracite and briquette prices, subsidizing production, and limiting new entry and imports. The effects of one government intervention have invited another intervention, making the situation more and more complex. Table 8.5 summarizes anthracite's place in Korea's energy picture. Table 8.6 gives the sources and uses of anthracite, while Table 8.7 provides an overview of the industry.

---

and bituminous. Coal is sometimes referred to as steam or metallurgical. These describe usage. Although virtually all metallurgical coal is bituminous, any coal burned to produce steam (as in a thermal power plant) can be called steam coal. Coking coal is bituminous coal processed to produce coke, used in making steel, and is a subset of metallurgical coal. Note that much US data use short tons (2,000 pounds) which are about 91% of a tonne. A longer account of the Korean coal industry is Kim 1988.

Table 8.6. Anthracite Sources and Use (thousand tonnes and percents)

1966	1975	1980	1986	1987	Projections		Use
					1991	2001	
8,466	13,615	18,037	24,250	23,587	25,097	14,094	residential
72	85	87	90	90	93	91	& commercial
970	643	708	277	206	217	174	industrial
8	4	3	1	1	1	1	
1,346	1,349	1,865	2,285	2,444	1,530	1,124	electric
12	9	9	8	9	6	7	
987	340	220	116	90	109	109	other
8	2	1	1	—	—	1	
11,769	15,945	20,830	26,928	26,327	26,953	15,501	consumption total
11,614	17,593	21,215	28,168	27,055	new supply total[1]		
11,614	17,593	18,524	24,253	24,273	domestic production		
0	0	2,691	3,915	2,782	imports		
0	0	13	15	11	imports as a percentage of consumption		

1. New supply is the sum of production and imports, and thus ignores inventories, which have varied significantly from year to year.

For 1988 the Korea Coal Association preliminary estimate for consumption was 25,597,000 tonnes; production, 24,237,000; and imports, 1,670,000. The distribution by use did not change.

Anthracite-fueled power plants provided 5% of installed electrical generating capacity in 1988. This is expected to shrink to 2% in 2001.

Sources: Ministry of Energy and Resources, *Yearbook of Energy Statistics* (1987), for all except 1987, which is from the *Business Korea Yearbook* 1988/89 (p III-12).

In the immediate postwar years, coal was promoted to preserve both scarce foreign exchange and the remaining forests (as recently as 1962, wood provided over half of Korea's energy consumption). To meet increased energy demand from industrialization under its five-year development plans, the government included measures to promote coal production. The First Plan (1962–66) included extensive geological surveying of coal mining areas, and government-owned Daehan (Korea Coal Corporation) was directed to support exploration and development of private mines. From the mid 1950s to early '60s, production tripled, and by 1967 had almost doubled again. That year, the government adopted a fuel modernization policy. Coal was obviously going to be unable to

Table 8.7. Coal Mining: Overview

Year	Output (thousand tonnes)	Government Support (million won)	Support per Tonne	Private Mines' Output Share (%)	Number of Mines	Labor Productivity[1]	Employment
1960					131[a]		24,66▮
1962	7,444[b]	268[c]		52.5[d]			
1964	9,622			51.8	177[a]		37,04▮
1967	12,436			62.1			
1968	10,242			58.4			
1970	12,393	2,684	21	64.1			36,02▮
1972	12,403	4,447	359	69.3			37,40▮
1975	17,593	19,386	1,102	74.0	239	1.10[e]	45,64▮
1977	17,268	21,353	1,237	73.9	145	1.13[g]	48.77▮
1980	18,624	111,413	5,982	74.3[f]	196	1.20	56,17▮
1982	20,116	132,027	6,563	75.1	349	1.15	62,31▮
1985	22,543	121,493	5,389	77.6	361	1.22	64,74▮
1986	24,253	104,424	4,306	78.5[h]	361	1.26	68,86▮
1987	24,274	78,064	3,216	78.7	363	1.26	68,49▮
1988	24,237	75,488	3,107	78.5	347	1.35	62,25▮

Government support includes subsidies under the 1969 Extraordinary Law for Coal Minir▮ Promotion and financial loan funds administered by the Korean Mining Promotion Corporation ▮ program that goes back to 1961 but which was not large until 1970). Excluded are loans made ▮ finance stockpiling to avoid seasonal fluctuations in production; these reached 4.5 billion won in t▮ early 1970s. Government-owned mines also received support.

1. Labor productivity is measured in tonnes per miner per shift, often called OMS (output p▮ man-shift).

Sources: Ministry of Energy and Resources, Yearbook of Energy Statistics (1987), except 198▮ data are from the Korea Coal Association Magazine # 21 and as follows:
[a] KOIS 1987, p 398–99
[b] 1962–68 from KOIS 1978, p 568 table 36
[c] from KDI 1975, p 208
[d] 1962–75 from KOIS 1978, p 568 table 36
[e] Hasan and Rao 1979, p 281
[f] 1980–85 from KOIS 1987, p 399 table 29
[g] Coal Miners Association Magazine, # 19 (1987)
[h] 1986–87 from Business Korean Yearbook 1988/89, p III-11

meet the ever-increasing demands for energy: it was tying up too much space on the railroads (which were being converted to diesel engines), it was more expensive than oil, and domestic refining capacity had been created. In general, the policy became to use oil (plus, to a lesser extent, nuclear and hydroelectric power) to meet most of the growing energy need. Coal output dropped sharply in 1968.

Fairly quickly the government backtracked on its de-emphasis of coal. Various kinds of financial assistance were made available, and a 10% tax was levied on bunker-C oil (used in power plants), with the proceeds earmarked for coal mine development and marketing. (The tax has since been reduced to 6%.) Anthracite-fired electric power plants were built near the mines; however, coal consumption by thermal power plants in 1973 was still below that of 1966. Production jumped almost 21% from 1969 to 1970, though the contribution to energy consumption (which had peaked at 46% in 1966) continued to fall. By 1971 coal output had reached a new high of 12.8 million tonnes. The Third Five-Year Plan (1972–76) called for expansion of output to 17 million tonnes. In the wake of the oil crisis of late 1973 came plans intended to reduce dependence on imported energy sources. Coal was on another upswing in its roller-coaster ride: the 17–million-tonne output level was surpassed in 1975, and exceeded demand. Nonetheless, in the face of uncertain oil markets, Korea suspended coal exports that year. This proved wise, as supply was soon outstripped, and in 1978 anthracite was imported for the first time.

The Fourth Five-Year Plan (1977–81) projected 6% annual increases in residential use of domestic coal. New thermal power plants capable of using Korean coal were planned, and financial assistance was extended to miners both directly and in the form of infrastructure development such as timbering mines shafts. The second oil shock hit Korea even harder than the first, and in 1980 consumption of petroleum products decreased. Once again government policy became one of maximizing production, primarily by offering subsidies.

Output projections were not met: tonnage grew an average of 3.8% a year in the 1977–86 period, with some down years and some spurts. Anthracite has been imported throughout the 1980s to fill the gap. But it was fortunate that mines did not expand more than they did, as the external environment of the industry has changed again, dramatically.

Production probably peaked at 24.3 million tonnes in 1987, barely above the 1986 level; 1988 output was 24.2 million tonnes. The decline has begun, and—by 1991 at the latest—it is expected to become rapid. If just because there are only some 30 years of reserves at current output levels, decline has been inevitable, but it is being hastened by lower demand (which peaked in 1986).

Production costs will increase as labor costs rise and remaining deposits become harder to mine, which means lower productivity. Mining companies have avoided investment in the face of inability and uncertainty, while equipment has become worn and obsolete. Domestic coal has—and will continue to—become progressively less price competitive relative to other fuels and imported coal.

More fundamentally, as consumer incomes have risen, cleaner fuels have replaced coal for space heating. In 1987, three-fourths of households still depended on briquettes for heating, but the fuel has a bad image both on the micro level of how messy it is to handle in the home and on the macro level of concern over air pollution. The Coal Industry Promotion Board feels this has created conditions for a decline in coal consumption regardless of price factors (*Business Korea* 1989 Mar, p 66). The Economic Planning Board has predicted an average annual decline in anthracite consumption of 2.6% over the three years 1989–91.

Protection of coal mining has become too expensive. But producers, labor unions, and regional governments and politicians oppose quick adjustment for fear of adverse employment and other economic effects. Most of the coal is mined from the Chongson and Samchok fields. Located in Kangwon, the province in Korea's northeast corner, they have some 60% of the country's reserves. Before the first coal boom, Kangwon was "a rugged, mountainous hinterland, traditionally regarded as poverty-stricken and remote" (Bartz 1972, p 141). Although the value of coal output is less than 1% the value of gross manufacturing output, and the industry had only 68,800 direct workers (out of a labor force of 16 million) in 1986, it will not be politically easy to reverse the long-standing policy of maximizing domestic production regardless of cost because of its local (regional) implications.

Structure of the Industry

The industry is very fragmented. Government subsidies made it very profitable for small firms to remain independent, despite attempts beinning with the 1961 Coal Development Law to unify small private mines. Daehan (the Korea Coal Corporation), which is controlled by the Ministry of Energy and Resources, is the single largest mining comany. Daehan's share of output has declined steadily since the late 1960s, to just over 20% in 1988; its production has fluctuated around 5 million tonnes during the 1980s. Most of the mines are owned by individuals or small private companies, but one corporation is traded on the Seoul stock exchange, Daesung Consolidated Coal, established in 1965. Although domestic coal mining accounted for 81% of Daesung's 1987 sales, it has been diversifying into construction and coal importing.

Between 1976 and 1986, the number of mines increased sharply, from

222 to 361. Almost all of the increase was in relatively inefficient small mines (of less than 100,000 tonnes annual production). Only 10 mines had more than 500,000 tonnes capacity, but they produced over 46% of output in 1984. In contrast, the 303 mines having less than 60,000 tonnes capacity produced only 22%. Most small mines are owned by individuals. The 20 mines with more than 500 workers produced over 65% of output, and employed almost 67% of workers.

In 1969 industry employment was about 35,000, Daehan operated 8 mines, CCM (Consolidated Coal) had 5, and there were some 200 other small private mines. During the 1970s the number of mines fluctuated around that level, even as production rose, with most output coming from mines with capacity under 70,000 tonnes. The broadening of subsidies in the wake of the second oil crisis caused the number of mines to rise quickly. Virtually all the mines opened in the 1970s and '80s produce under 100,000 tonnes per year, and cannot be considered efficient.

Small mines cannot afford extensive machinery, and thus rely on labor-intensive mining methods. According to the Korea Coal Association, in 1986 only 36% of mines employed digging machines (up from 8% in 1980, but well below the level of developed countries). The result is productivity significantly below other countries with deep mines. Thus the output per miner per shift in Korea of just under 1.3 tonnes in 1987 compares to 3.7 in Japan and 3.5 in England. (US data are not comparable because of the high proportion of coal taken from open pits.)

Mines are not safe places, and Korean mines have particularly poor records. In the four years 1984–87, 692 people died in coal mine accidents and another 10,000 were seriously injured. In 1987 there were 7 deaths per million tonnes mined; in England, the figure was just 0.3. Small operations have a disproportionate share of the accidents: mines producing 100,000 tonnes or less accounted for 26% of production but 40% of the accidents in 1986.

Cost-Push Pressure

As mines become deeper (in the early 1990s most coal is coming from shafts 260–500 meters underground), the huge investment in structures and safety equipment, combined with increasing labor costs, have steadily increased the cost of domestic coal production. Labor accounted for 33–45% of production costs until the economy-wide explosion of wages from mid 1987 pushed them to 50–55%. Nominal wages increased 10% annually during 1980–85, but jumped 15% in 1987 and '88. Wages in the industry have been higher than in manufacturing because of the high accident risk and difficult working environment. Thus, in 1987 the average monthly wage in mining was 414,000 won, compared to 329,000 for manufacturing and 387,000 for all industry.

Young people have tended to seek easier jobs, even with lower salaries, rather than work in the mines. This is fine with the government, which seeks to reduce the number of miners in the long run. But in the short and medium run, because the government has wanted to keep the industry alive, as recently as 1987 it offered incentives such as special treatment regarding military service and support of miner welfare facilities in order to attract experienced miners.

Foreign Supply

Anthracite has fallen in price on world markets since the mid 1980s, and because the won has been appreciating, this price decline has been even more pronounced for Korea. Since the mid 1980s, Korea has had a surplus on its current account. These two facts undermine one of the historical justifications for supporting the domestic industry: the need to preserve foreign exchange through exploitation of local coal. This was a powerful argument in the 1970s, particularly after the oil crises. It no longer is.

Bituminous coal is already a major import, primarily by KEPCO (Korean Electric Power), POSCO (Pohang Steel), and the cement industry, and demand is expected to continue to rise. Korea's bituminous coal trade is a political as much as an economic matter, and in any case is beyond the scope of this essay.

The government controls anthracite imports for household and commercial heating use through Daehan, although it is no longer the only importer. Import levels and market share have fluctuated for a variety of reasons in the 1980s. Because demand for anthracite is expected to decline, peak import tonnage may well prove to be 1986 for some years. This is true even though the strong won has helped make imported anthracite cheaper than domestic since late 1986. How much of the market will be satisfied by imports is more a political than an economic question. One complication is that the government has set a minimum standard for the heat value of yontan, and because so much domestic coal no longer meets the standard, it is necessary to mix in imported coal when making briquettes. Because mild weather reduced demand, imports dropped 61% in the first quarter of 1989 compared to the same period of 1988. This suggests imports probably will absorb or provide for short-term fluctuations in demand, but will not displace much domestic production on a sustained basis at least until the domestic mining has been rationalized.

Table 8.8 summarizes domestic and imported anthracite costs and pricing. Briquette prices have been kept low to help low-income families. This has led to demand for coal beyond what there would otherwise be, and it meant the government lost money on imports until 1987.

Shifting Demand

The long fall of oil prices has reduced the competitiveness of anthracite. Even if oil begins to increase again in real terms, it is unlikely coal will regain an edge. This is especially true as environmental pollution costs become more important. Gas has been increasingly preferred for cooking, although yontan actually gained market share for household space heating between 1985 and 1987. In part because of a warm winter, overall anthracite consumption declined over 13% in the first quarter of 1989 compared to the same period in 1988. Oil, bituminous

Table 8.8. Domestic and Imported Anthracite Prices
(won per tonne, except as indicated)

1982	1983	1984	1985	1986	1987	
						domestic
39,380	39,710	40,975	45,994	48,952	51,330	selling price[1]
45,943	45,726	46,745	51,383	53,258	54,546	cost with subsidies[2]
						imports
65,246	59,394	59,466	56,994	51,690	45,103	won cost[3]
66.13	63.07	55.32	50.31	48.42	43.55	US$ cost[3]
35,508	36,639	38,130	42,966	45,080	49,220	selling price[4]
2,292	813	804	2,333	3,915	2,782	thousand tonnes
11.0	3.8	3.3	9.2	13.9	10.6	supply share in percents
1.42	1.30	1.27	1.11	0.97	0.83	ratio of import to domestic cost

1. The domestic selling price has been adjusted (raised) to reflect its lower heat value relative to imported coal. The heat value of imports in 1982–84 is taken as 5,500 kcal/kg; in 1985–87, 5,800.
2. Domestic cost includes both direct and indirect subsidies; see Table 8.7.
3. Import cost is CIF. The won cost also includes incidental landing costs.
4. The import selling price is what the government, as the sole importer, sold the coal for.

Source: Ministry of Energy and Resources

coal, and nuclear are preferred alternatives for expansion of electric power generation.

Samchully, one of the leading distributors of yontan and part owner of Samchuck Coal, is an example of a company diversifying away from anthracite. The company has the capacity to produce about 4 million tonnes of yontan annually, and this accounted for 74% of its 1987 revenue. Samchully has diversified into coke and activated carbon for industrial customers, and city gas—a direct replacement of yontan. The company expects to benefit from the government's gas-substitution policy.

Government Policies

Since the 1950s, the government has generally promoted the coal mining industry, first because it was the only indigenous source of fuel (other than firewood and capital-intensive hydroelectric) then, later, also because the support had helped create an industry politically strong enough to demand special attention. Thus, an attempt to shift away from coal in 1967 instead resulted in a significant increase in subsidies and a 10% tax (later reduced to 6%) on bunker-C oil (the kind generally burned in Korea's electric power plants).[3]

The oil crises of the 1970s strengthened the industry's role as *the* domestic fuel source, and thus a preserver of scarce foreign exchange. Trusting demand elasticity was such that it could both help the industry and promote conservation, the government raised the price of coal to consumers 51% in 1974 and another 25% in 1975. Further substantial price hikes came during 1977 (78%) and 1979–81 (159%), so that after the last 1981 hike, the price was almost 10 times the 1973 level (compared to an approximate 5–fold increase in prices generally).

During the latter 1970s the government made grants of 70% of the cost of getting a mine into production and loaned 15% on concessionary terms. A would-be mine operator needed to provide only 15% from his own funds. These subsidies were given without regard to the quality of the coal produced. The subsidies, administered by KMPC (the Korea Mining Promotion Board), came from general government revenue and the tax on bunker-C oil.

Circumstances have changed yet again, but the industry remains re-

3. Loans are offered through the government's Korea Mining Promotion Corporation. Other assistance has included loans for stockpiling during the off-season, freight rebates for rail transportation, support for mine exploration activities, and preferential treatment in transmission and distribution facilities.

Early government policies toward the industry are described more fully by KDI (1975, p 203–08) and KOIS (1978, p 566–69).

luctant to face its inevitable decline. Maintenance of current production levels requires either an increase in anthracite's price or an increase in production subsidies. However, neither of these is a solution for the Korean coal mining industry, as both prevent firms from exiting or restructuring. Moreover, both reduce the efficiency of the economy and distort the allocation of resources.

The cost of continuing to subsidize the industry has mounted to the point where the government has become somewhat more willing to confront the issue. Production costs continue to rise and there is less need to keep briquette prices artificially low. Moreover, imports have become cheaper than domestic production. In short, virtually every market force points to coal being a declining industry. After two years of study, in December 1988 the government established the Rationalization Project of the Coal Industry.

The project seeks to close 237 mines (out of 354) by 1993, all of which have been producing less than an average of 53,750 tonnes annually. This will reduce employment by over half, to 26,000 from 53,000. It also plans for a doubling of average production per (remaining) mine, which means overall output will fall only slightly over a third. Output per man per shift is expected to improve to 1.9 tonnes, still much below Japan or Great Britain, but almost half-again the 1988 level.

The government is providing severance assistance equivalent to 10–13 months wages to laid-off miners. In addition, subsidized loans (6% annual interest, due in five years with a five-year grace period) of up to 5 million won are provided those who want to start their own businesses. For the owners of closed mines, a subsidy of 8,100 won per tonne of output (annual average over the period 1985–87) is provided to compensate for unrecoverable underground assets. The cost of the project is estimated at 174 billion won, to be paid from the bunker-C oil tax. The plan has gotten off to a shaky start because of disagreements between government agencies on technical aspects of implementation. There is also concern about where future funding for injured miners will come from—money currently is from a tax on coal, but the rate assumes payments of about one-tenth the actual award (*Business Korea* 1989 Jul).

Once the smallest, inherently inefficient, mines have been closed under this plan, further rationalization of the industry is to be effected by lowering the domestic price gradually until it approaches the world price. By using price as a guideline for the survival of mines, firm-specific intervention by the government can be minimized. The present import quota system will need to be maintained during this process, but in the long run must be abolished.

Lee Bong-suh became energy minister in early 1988 after helping negotiate an agreement to import significant amounts of LPG from Indonesia—LPG intended to replace anthracite briquettes. In a speech titled "Energy Policy in the Age of the Open Economy" (20 May 1988), Lee made an almost-explicit declaration the government would no longer support the mining industry regardless of cost. Even more than the fuel modernization policy of 1967, this attempt has market forces on its side.

But the government must contend with politics, so to help offset falling demand by households, the energy plan was revised to include a 200-megawatt anthracite-fired power plant "for the purpose of national resource utilization and mining industry rationalization" (*Korea Business World* 1989 Feb, p 42).

SHIPBUILDING: CYCLICAL DECLINE

The Korean shipbuilding industry is a valuable case study of industrial targeting with mixed results. In the early 1970s, as part of the Heavy and Chemical Industry drive (HCI), the government pinpointed shipbuilding as a key industry and provided many incentives, including subsidized loans, tax incentives, and import protection. The industry has gone on to become a significant force in the international market and a vital part of the Korean economy. But the early and mid 1980s were a rough time for shipbuilders worldwide, as the industry suffered from the recession in shipping. Orders and prices both fell dramatically. In Korea, new orders peaked in 1983; completions, in 1986. From a major contributor of foreign exchange (around 16% of exports in 1983–85), the industry became a burden to the Korean economy.[4]

Many observers, and not just self-interested ones, think the difficulties experienced by Korean shipyards during the 1980s are cyclical rather than secular, and thus can be overcome. Indeed, at the end of 1987, Korea had the largest order book in the world (based on tonnage), and in 1988 backlog reached a new high—over 6.2 million gross tons, or two years' work. In the summer of 1988, the industry was talking

4. Discussions of shipbuilding can become confusing for two reasons related to the data. First, there are several ways to measure capacity, and there is no simple relationship among them. These are explained in the notes to Table 8.10. Second, ship construction has long lead times, so there are three series of importance in looking at the industry's ongoing situation: new orders, completions, and order backlog. Even after new orders start to drop, building on-order ships can keep actual production rising. To know where the industry is and has been, one also needs to know the work in progress—a ship 99% built in a year will not show in that year's completions, so completions are not a proxy for actual activity in a yard. Be aware that "production" is sometimes used incorrectly as a synonym for "completions."

confidently of overtaking Japan as the number one shipbuilder in the early 1990s, and otherwise painting a rosy picture—in sharp contrast to only a short time earlier. Worldwide orders increased in early 1989, and industry and government officials felt supply and demand finally were getting into better balance as shipowners moved to upgrade their fleets with more-efficient ships, as well as to hedge against further price increases.

But 1989 also saw significant labor unrest, particularly at the country's largest yard, which caused cancellations and lost orders, even as appreciation of the won has also reduced the industry's competitiveness. Moreover, the weight of debt and past losses have made many companies financially precarious. Together, these could scuttle recovery, perhaps even parts of the industry. Thus, in the summer of 1989, while optimism remained about worldwide demand, Korean firms and government policy makers have been chastened.

This section looks at the rise of the industry, the changed environment of the late 1980s, diversification of the companies away from shipbuilding, the troubles of the major firms, and government policy.

Shipbuilding's Development

Certain characteristics of shipbuilding have made it a particularly appropriate industry for Korea. First, it is labor intensive and therefore can employ Korea's abundant supply of workers. Second, it uses materials and goods from more than 50 other industries, including machinery, iron and steel, electronics, chemicals, and furniture, and thus stimulates widespread industrial development through linkage effects. Third, Korea has suitable ports. Additionally, the industry is related to national security, uses comparatively little energy, and produces little pollution.

In 1962 the Shipbuilding Industry Encouragement Act subsidized the domestic industry, making up for the unfavorable margin between the price of locally and foreign made ships. This helped establish a base for improvement of the industry. Also, through the Shipbuilding Promotion Act in 1967 and the Machinery Promotion Act in 1969, the government provided institutional arrangements to extend subsidized financial support from both government and banking sources to shipbuilding, its parts suppliers, and its customers. (Additional background on the industry's early years is found in KDI 1975, p 76–80, Hasan 1976, p 187–93, and Korea Development Bank 1988.)

During the 1970s, shipbuilding's development was particularly notable. The government, encouraged by the potential for export and the great tanker boom, designated it a key export industry within the HCI drive and provided financial support for its take-off. The industry achieved remarkable growth, soon making Korea the world's number two shipbuilder, after Japan. The rapid expansion is attributable to Korea's comparative advantages in labor and government support, as Korean shipbuilders displaced less competitive European yards. This export-oriented growth contrasts with how Japan's industry developed. There, in its early days shipbuilding grew initially from the country's own needs and demand. Tables 8.9 and 8.10 provide an overview of international and Korean shipbuilding.

Beginning in 1973, the government actively promoted construction of large shipyards. One of the structural characteristics of the industry thus has been the dependence on huge shipyards, designed for production of large ships (100,000 dwt and above) in general, and tankers in particular. From the opening of Hyundai's Mipo yard in 1974 until 1981, the expansion of Mipo and other facilities increased Korea's shipbuilding capacity steadily, despite two oil shock-induced recessions. Completion of the Daewoo Shipbuilding and Heavy Machinery (DSHM) Okpo Yard in 1981 brought total production capacity to over 4.5 GT in terms of normal capacity. Registered shipbuilding companies total 252 (1988 yearend), but the 4 major companies (Hyundai, Daewoo, Samsung, and KSEC) account for over 90% of total capacity; Hyundai alone accounts for half. Mipo, in Ulsan, run by Hyundai Heavy Industry, is the largest yard in the world; Korea's next biggest is Okpo, on Koje Island. Other large yards are those of KSEC (Korea Shipbuilding and Engineering) in Pusan and Samsung's on Koje Island. Table 8.11 gives data on the major shipyards.

Korea acquired a good deal of technological help from Japanese companies—at least until the early 1980s, when the Japanese cut back sharply, having realized they were helping build up strong competitors in what was becoming a shrinking market.

Japanese sources also supply a substantial percentage of parts. The government has encouraged the development of local sources, and estimates of the domestic-content ratio of exported ships have trended upwards, from less than half in 1980 to over three-fourths in 1988. The goal is 95% by 1995. Official domestic-content ratio series understate this reliance because if a component is assembled in Korea, it generally is counted as entirely domestic even if many of its parts are imported. Companies are expected to contribute 1% of revenues for joint research to help increase local content and domestic technological capability. All told, some 300 billion won of private and government money are expected to be spent in the 1988–95 period (*Business Korea* 1989 Jul, p 78).

The industry has rarely achieved profits, primarily because of interest charges on the debt taken on to pay for rapid expansion as the industry sought to grow and gain market share in the 1970s. Indeed, expansion was so rapid in the 1970s that yards apparently worked far below capacity, though there may be some data problems because of the timing of completions.

In 1981 and '82, meager profits were earned, but then, just as expansion of the Samsung and Daewoo yards was completed, the world shipbuilding industry experienced severe difficulties due to the slump in shipping resulting from stagnant trade volume, with resulting surplus

Table 8.9. Summary of World Shipbuilding Industry
(in 1,000 gross tons and percents)

Year	Korea		Japan		AWES[1]		World Total
New Ship Orders Received							
1975	511	3.7	6786	49.2	2780	20.2	13,793
1976	323	2.5	7245	56.0	2785	21.5	12,937
1977	632	5.7	5778	52.1	2957	26.7	11,091
1978	297	3.7	3475	43.3	2102	26.2	8,026
1979	1060	6.3	8337	49.5	4177	24.8	16,843
1980	1706	9.0	9997	52.7	4472	23.6	18,969
1981	1372	8.1	8303	49.2	4130	24.5	16,877
1982	1075	9.6	5570	49.8	2096	18.7	11,187
1983	3733	19.2	10982	56.5	2069	10.7	19,423
1984	2289	14.7	8844	56.8	2095	13.4	15,581
1985	1339	10.4	6358	49.3	2040	15.8	12,906
1986	3056	24.1	5518	43.6	1667	13.2	12,664
1987	4160	30.2	4771	34.7	2573	18.7	13,763
Completions							
1975	410	1.2	16991	49.7	13070	38.2	34,203
1976	814	2.4	15868	46.8	12714	37.5	33,922
1977	562	2.0	11707	42.5	10731	39.0	27,532
1978	604	3.3	6307	34.7	6625	36.4	18,194
1979	495	3.5	4697	32.9	4686	32.8	14,289
1980	522	4.0	6094	46.5	2965	22.6	13,101
1981	929	5.5	8400	49.6	4129	24.4	16,932
1982	1401	8.3	8163	48.5	3784	22.5	16,820
1983	1539	9.7	6670	41.9	4417	27.8	15,911
1984	1473	8.0	9711	53.0	3497	19.3	18,334
1985	2620	14.4	9503	52.3	9221	16.1	18,157
1986	3642	21.6	8178	48.5	2037	12.1	16,864
1987	2077	17.3	5633	46.9	1924	16.0	12,015

Table 8.9. Summary of World Shipbuilding Industry *(Continued)*
(in 1,000 gross tons and percents)

Year	Korea		Japan		AWES[1]		World Total
Order Book							
1975	1630	2.0	31359	38.1	na		82,346
1976	1060	1.9	18215	32.9	22227	40.1	55,373
1977	1102	3.0	9910	27.0	13907	37.9	36,725
1978	736	2.8	6533	25.3	8902	34.4	25,859
1979	1271	4.5	9331	33.0	8370	29.6	28,302
1980	2489	7.2	13072	37.7	9741	28.1	34,628
1981	2977	8.4	12655	35.8	9803	27.8	35,311
1982	2551	8.7	10067	34.5	7956	27.3	29,172
1983	4618	14.2	14027	43.0	5671	17.4	32,619
1984	5798	18.9	13072	42.6	4642	15.1	30,688
1985	4667	18.0	9729	37.6	3984	15.4	25,862
1986	4223	19.8	6568	30.7	3546	16.6	21,364
1987	6021	26.7	5038	22.3	4510	20.0	22,542
1988	10782	28.6	9981	26.5	na		37,670

1. AWES is the Association of Western European Shipbuilders

New ships minus completions does not equal change in order book because of cancellations.

As of 1988 Jan 1, the world's merchant fleet included just over 23,300 oceangoing ships of 1,000 gross tons or more, totaling about 589,000 GT. Because of their favorable laws, some 28% of these were registered in Liberia or Panama. Korea ranked 13th in both tonnage and number of ships.

Source: Lloyds' Register of Shipping, except 1988 order book is from Fairplay Information Systems and the size of the fleet is as reported in *Sea Power* (1990 Jan, p 231–32).

shipping tonnage. The Korean industry, dependent on overseas demand for 70 to 90% of its orders, had a serious problem. New orders evaporated. Moreover, delivery delays of ships ordered at higher prices aggravated the financial difficulties of shipbuilders.

The Late 1980s Environment

Even though Korean yards worked at 70–85% of capacity in 1986 and 1987, and worldwide demand was recovering in the late 1980s, the industry was facing difficulties, the result of several unfavorable changes in its environment. Pricing and the level and structure of demand will probably be less of a problem in the 1990s than they were in most of the 1980s. But ongoing problems include maintaining price competitiveness in the face of the rapid appreciation of the won and increased labor

Table 8.10. Shipbuilding in Korea, an Overview, 1976–88

1976	1979	1982	1985	1986	1987	
35	42	65	72	62	57	employment[1]
2.8	3.0	2.1	2.0	1.6	1.3	employment as a percentage of total manufacturing labor force
82	182	327	391	406	438	average monthly wage[2]
na	na	167	255	265	252	number of yards[3]
						new ship production[4]
302	221	574	329	456	601	domestic
551	314	1216	2467	2259	1340	export
298	519	2831	5040	1815	1138	exports in million US$[5]
3.9	3.5	13.1	16.6	5.2	2.4	exports as a percentage of total exports

1. Employment is in thousand full-time-worker equivalents, for the 12 largest companies (ranked by sales). Source: Ministry of Trade and Industry
2. In thousand won. Source: Economic Planning Board
3. Includes repair yards (one prior to 1981, two since). During the 1980s the four major builders have had over 90% of capacity, the "medium six" firms have had about 6%, and the small yards shared the rest.
4. In thousand GT.
5. Exports include new ships, floating structures, yachts, and repairs (SITC 7353–59).

Source: Korea Shipbuilding Association, *Shipbuilding Data Bank*, 1988, except as listed in notes

Measurements in the shipping and shipbuilding industries

Ship, and thus shipbuilding, capacity can be measured in a number of ways. Deadweight tons (dwt) is the weight in metric or long tons required to bring a vessel to its water line. Dwt can be used to measure any kind of ship, including tankers and dry cargo. Dry cargo ships typically are measured in gross tons (GT), a measure of the ship's interior space (1 GT = 100 cubic feet).

Tankers are rated by tonnes (metric tons) of crude oil they can carry. A VLCC carries 200,000+ tonnes of crude (about 1.47 million barrels). (The density of crude varies, but a standard conversion factor is 7.33 barrels per tonne. A barrel contains 42 US gallons.)

Container ships are often rated in TEUs (twenty-foot equivalent unit). This refers to a container (also called a "box") that is 20 feet long. But not all 20–foot containers have the same interior capacity, and 40–foot containers are generally more than twice the volume of 20–foot ones even though they are counted as only 2 TEUs. Modern container-ships stack the boxes on the deck, so the GT is not a meaningful measure of their size.

There is no precise relationship between dwt and GT. Tankers, bulk carriers, and larger ships generally, have higher ratios of dwt to GT. This is because the horsepower and crew size needed do not increase as fast as ship size, reducing the proportion of space and weight needed for engines, fuel, and crew.

Table 8.11. Major Shipyards

Hyundai	Daewoo	Samsung	KSEC	
Ulsan	Koje-do	Koje-do	Pusan	location[1]
Mipo	Okpo	Koje		name
1974	1981	1974	1937	first built
1,560	740	280	200	capacity, 1988[2]
1,000	1,000	250	150	maximum vessel size[3]
7	3*	2	3*	drydocks
2	2	2	4	berths
20,781	13,342	3,578	2,264	employment, yearend 1988
24,998	28,196	6,530	4,388	employment, yearend 1984[4]
1,781	672	462	0	new order, 1988[2]
88	84	84	0	export ratio, 1988[5]
97	93	99	76	export ratio at peak in 1983[5]

* Includes one floating dock
1. Koje-do is an island southwest of Pusan. Okpo and Koje are towns on the island.
2. In thousand GT
3. In thousand dwt
4. 1984 was the peak year for employment for all yards except Hyundai. Its peak was in 1985, at 30,184 workers.
5. New export orders as a percentage of total new orders (in thousand GT)
Source: Korean Investors Service, [Shipbuilding] Industry Report 1988

costs, as well as continued dependence on Japanese technology and intermediate goods. The most visible concern in the late 1980s has been the controversy over the government's bailout efforts for two major shipbuilders (Daewoo and KSEC), which have been suffering from huge debts and accumulating losses.

Due to worldwide overcapacity, prices for new ships dropped after the 1981–82 recession by as much as half for many types of ships, including oil tankers. Prices began to show signs of recovery in 1986, and by mid 1989 they were surpassing 1981 levels for tankers and some other ship types. This is in part the result of informal agreement between Korean and Japanese firms (see, eg, the Far Eastern Economic Review 1989 May 25, p 70). With the high level of worldwide capacity, it is not certain how much stronger the increases can be. But Korean firms realize they only exacerbated their problems when they made aggressively low bids in the mid 1980s in order to keep the cash flowing.

For most of the 1980s, the demand pattern changed away from the kinds of ships Korean yards are designed to build. Worldwide trade in petrochemical products decreased while trade in bulk commodities, including coal and grains, increased. This meant demand for tankers was stagnant and demand for specialized ships (LPG carriers, container ships, etc) increased. Historically, low value-added vessels, including tankers and large bulk carriers, accounted for the majority of ships constructed in Korean yards, and the yards were designed to build primarily these types of vessels. In 1982 the proportion of such ships reached 85%. High value-added, and generally smaller, ships such as container and chemical carriers accounted for just 15% of tonnage built in 1987. In the late 1980s there has been a revival in tanker building, to replace aging fleets (about 60% of the VLCC fleet operating in 1989 was built in 1974–76). Moreover, Korean yards have been able to expand the repertoire of ships types they build.

Although the domestic industry has made efforts on its own to improve technology, in the past it has relied primarily on the acknowledged world leader, Japan, whose companies are much more reluctant to share their advances than they were in the 1970s.

Labor disputes have been a big blow to the industry, resulting in unexpected wage increases and delivery delays. In 1987 an estimated 20% of sales (including repairs) was lost as a result of shutdowns from labor disputes. Wage hikes and the appreciation of the won have created cost-push pressures, and the industry's competitiveness with Japan has eroded somewhat. Materials constitute over 70% of a ship's cost (it varies depending on ship type), and there is still a high dependence on Japan for parts and components. The strengthening of the won against the yen in 1988–89 worsened shipyard profitability.

Trade friction with OECD countries has increased. Since 1987 Japan and the EC countries have pressured the Korean industry to reduce capacity and pressured the government to limit its subsidization of new shipbuilding. Thus, the terms and conditions of deferred export financing granted by Korea were decided in accordance with guidelines set by the OECD. Meanwhile, Japanese builders can borrow from private Japanese financial institutions at lower interest rates because interest rates in Japan are low.

The various problems, particularly those of accumulated losses and heavy debt burdens, are taken seriously by the government and the companies. Thus, in the autumn of 1987, a senior official at each of Hyundai and Daewoo moved to take hands-on control of their shipbuilding affiliates. The government and companies are confronting the issue is a variety of ways. Diversification, which has been going on since the 1970s, is receiving greater emphasis. It has become part of a general restructuring of the industry that will involve government bailouts of one sort or another. New markets are also being opened: in 1989

Hyundai won a $162 million order for six bulk carriers for the Soviet Union, which will be financed by the Korean Export Import Bank.

Diversification

To avoid overdependence on the export ship market and better utilize space and dock facilities, Korean shipyards have, since 1977, looked for refit work and for work constructing floating structures (oil rigs and special equipment). Exports of these categories have risen reasonably steadily, apart from 1979, and in 1983 reached $1,908 million, almost half the industry's export earnings, including $1,543 million for refits (double the 1982 level) and $365 million for floating structures (triple the 1981 level). Refit requires special training and skills, together with advanced technology and marketing arrangements.

By 1987, Hyundai had become the fifth largest builder of offshore platforms in the world. In 1985 Hyundai won a $120 million contract from Exxon for two offshore exploration facilities, including a 29,000 tonne one that Exxon says is the biggest in the world. Both were completed in 1989 and installed off the California coast. With a shipbuilding-dependency of 60%, Hyundai's goal is 50% in the early 1990s. Besides oil-related projects, which provided revenues of 170 billion won in 1987, the company is looking to build iron and steel mills and petrochemical plants (140 billion won in 1987 revenue). Hyundai has been, until the strike that began in December 1988, the financially healthiest of the major builders. Indeed, it booked profits every year until 1988, although in many years they were slim.

Samsung Heavy is already the most diversified of the majors, partly because it is a much smaller shipbuilder than Daewoo and Hyundai. The company expects to reduce shipbuilding to 20% of 1990 sales (versus 25% of 1987 revenues). Besides expanding its existing heavy equipment (including excavators, bulldozers, etc) and machinery businesses, the firm is looking at tidal power projects, and, with the Iran-Iraq war in abeyance, plant construction.

Daewoo has the highest (over 90% in 1985, 80% in 1987) dependence on the shipbuilding market. In the late 1980s, the goal was to reduce dependence to 50% by the mid 1990s. As part of attempts to resolve the firm's financial difficulties, discussed later, the ratio was set at 30% by 1992, but later 36% by 1993 has been projected. DSHM's initial diversification plans involved moving into domestic offshore oil rigs, sewage disposal facilities, general construction in Korea, and plant construction in South East Asia. More recently, automobiles and aircraft have been targeted. A three-year technical collaboration agreement was made with Suzuki, Japan's premier subcompact maker, under which DSHM will make a "people's car" at a plant in the Chang Won industrial complex. Whatever the diversifications, however, much of the reduction will be achieved simply by merging other Daewoo Group subsidiaries into DSHM.

Korean shipbuilding firms derive a much higher proportion of their revenue from that activity than their Japanese counterparts. For example, the seven major Japanese shipbuilding firms derived only around 24% of their 1985 revenue from shipbuilding, which makes them "shipbuilding" companies in name only. In 1987, Korean companies got 70% of their revenues from shipbuilding, compared to 20% in Japan. The government's goal is 40% by the year 2000.

Troubled Companies

Korean shipbuilders are debt-ridden from past expansions and losses. The four major firms had combined debts of 3.7 trillion won at the end of 1987. In the four years 1985–88 the big four lost some 765 billion won, including 342 billion in 1987 and another 311 billion in 1988 on sales of 2,290 billion. All but Hyundai Heavy Industry registered snowballing losses after the collapse of earnings began in 1985, and in 1988 even Hyundai lost money. Interest on debt is the major reason for overall losses—major firms actually had operating profits in 1987. The situation poses serious problems for the firms and the economy.

A bitter strike at Hyundai, which began in December 1988, had by April 1989 led to the cancellation of 3 ships (worth $110 million) and ending of negotiations on 9 others (worth $400 million). The company, which accounted for 15% of total world shipbuilding in 1988, reopened with about half its labor force in mid February, but partly because the strike became as much a confrontation within the union as between the workers and the company, full resolution was complicated. The strike was finally ended by an amphibious raid by police. Hyundai Heavy has about 24,000 employees, some 11% of Ulsan's work force, as well as 115 closely affiliated companies and around 600 subcontractors.

Samsung Group is the only large chaebol (conglomerate) with no independent unions and it intends to stay that way. After 16–19% wage increases in April 1989, Samsung shipyard workers had the highest wages (an average of around 600,000 won monthly) of any major shipbuilder. Nonetheless, in June they struck, seeking 25% wage hikes (to narrow differentials with white-collar workers) and four-month bonuses. The strike lasted about two weeks, with the workers more or less backing down. Samsung Heavy Industries has a negative net worth.

KSEC (Korea Shipbuilding and Engineering), smallest of the big four, has been fighting for its life since 1983. The company's financial position was worsened by the delay of acceptance of six ships ordered by a Norwegian owner. (It was not uncommon in the mid 1980s for buyers to walk away even after ships were completed and certified for delivery. In September 1985, 22 ships worth $567 million had not been accepted from Korean yards essentially because the buyer did not want them or no longer could pay for them.)

In April 1987 a court placed KSEC's finances under the control of the Bank of Seoul, its major creditor, and the Export-Import Bank of Korea. KSEC has not received any new orders since, but continued (in spring 1989) to employ about 3500, finishing orders previously booked. Initially, it was expected KSEC would be absorbed by another company by the spring of 1988, but those involved were unable to reach any agreement on disposition of the troubled firm. In the end, the company was "auctioned"—although what was involved was more negotiations over how much capital a buyer and the government would each put up to save the firm. Hanjin, a major Korean shipping company that also controls Korean Air, tendered the best bid at the May 1989 sale. Hanjin expects to use KSEC for repairing and building its own ships.

Daewoo Shipbuilding and Heavy Machinery (DSHM), the second largest builder, recorded a loss of 213 billion won in 1988, following losses of 88 billion won in 1987. A 1987 strike was settled with hefty wage increases (on average, 15% in 1987, 20% in 1988). In 1988 DSHM asked the government for financial support, saying it could not function with its accumulated debts (which reached 1.3 trillion won at yearend 1988) coupled with wage increases and reduced orders. The government response in March 1989 took the company, and many outside observers, aback with its severity. Among other things, the government wanted Daewoo Group chairman Kim Woo-Choong personally to contribute capital. The situation is complicated because it is seen as a major test of the Sixth Republic's willingness to control the chaebol. Although upwards of 13,000 jobs are at stake directly, as well as the economy of the area around the yard, the public does not seem disposed to bail out what is seen as a badly managed chaebol subsidiary.

That DSHM should be a test is perhaps unfair because Daewoo took over the company in 1978 at the request of the government. At that time, Daewoo claims, the government promised that the Korean Development Bank (KDB) would maintain a 49% ownership share. But KDB put in only 100 billion won of additional capital, compared to 300 billion from Daewoo, dropping KDB's share to 33%. Daewoo subsequently has wanted the KDB to pay up. In turn, Daewoo Group proposed it would then merge several of its other subsidiaries into DSHM as well as contribute more capital. Kim Woo-Choong, Daewoo Group chairman, assumed personal direction of DSHM in 1987, a move seen as part of fulfilling a pledge that summer to striking shipbuilding workers that the company would be revived. He is reported in the press as seeing reviving the company as a challenge and an opportunity to show his management skills yet again.

In May 1989 it looked as though the bailout would be much closer to the government's proposal than to Daewoo's. Then came a further twist: workers, whose union had agreed not to demand "high" rates of pay increases until the company was profitable, asked for a 53% wage hike and a 44–hour week. (DSHM has the lowest wages of the four majors, an average of 561,000 won monthly.) After the company said no, a worker set himself afire and jumped to his death from a company dormitory. The next day, workers walked out. The government threatened to scrap the bailout plan if they did not return to work or if the company acceded to the workers' demands. In June, when the walkout spread to white-collar staff, Daewoo announced it would shut down if matters were not settled quickly. The workers agreed to a deferred wage increase.

DSHM had about $1 billion in orders on its books in mid 1989, so there is some confidence the company can survive if its debt load is restructured successfully. However, some of these backorders were booked in 1986 and '87 at low prices simply to attract business, so the company does not expect to be able to achieve profits until 1991.

Government Policy and Prospects

Most shipbuilding employees, as well as numerous creditors, expected bailouts in the late 1980s. Those in favor of government intervention paint a rosy picture for Korean yards, given the upbeat mood in the global industry. Worldwide, orders are on the rise as outdated ships near retirement. Those opposing intervention argue bailouts will lead to calls for similar help from other financially distressed industries. Action was continually deferred, mainly because of the failure of interested parties to reach agreements, but in late August 1989 debt restructuring and additional loan packages were approved by the government for three yards (DSHM, KSEC, and Inchon, the fifth largest builder).[5]

5. Events undoubtedly will outrun the publishing schedule of this book. I will not attempt to predict how long the labor peace of the summer of 1989 lasts, how any bailouts are actually finally implemented, or what becomes of DSHM. In the wake of the bailout announcement, *Business Korea* made the shipbuilding industry a cover story (1989 Aug, p 20–29). More complete discussions of the situation at DSHM include *Korea Business World* (1989 May, p 46), *Korea Newsreview* (1989 Apr 8, p 21; and 1989 Jun 3, p 20), and *Business Korea* (1989 Mar, p 60). KSEC is discussed in *Korea Business World* (1988

Even if the firms' financial problems are worked out, the industry faces a much more difficult environment than it did in its early years, though perhaps not as rough as in the mid 1980s. Korean firms no longer have the cost edge they once did. On one side, builders in LDCs, including the People's Republic of China, have built up their ability to construct smaller and low-value-added ships that once might have come from Korean yards. On the other side, Japan has significantly stronger firms, with better technology that offsets much of what labor-cost edge Korea has. Kim (1987, p 13 table 6) shows the distribution of costs for different kinds of ships for both Korea and Japan in 1984 and 1986. For bulk carriers, Japan was less expensive, while Korea had an edge of 3–6% for container ships and tankers.

Labor is 20–30% of a ship's costs, so Korea's wage increases, particularly if combined with increased productivity, will not eliminate the difference. Shipbuilding labor productivity has no clear measure. Because the data are available, probably the most common is simply dividing gross tons by the number of workers. By this measure, Korean yards are far behind the Japanese (44 versus 188 GT per worker in 1988). If labor peace is maintained, this gap should close. On the other hand, some shippers will pay as much as 10% more for a Japanese ship, reflecting perceptions in quality, reliability, and resale value. A buyer may send just 2 inspectors to monitor a Japanese yard, but 15 to Korea. (*Far Eastern Economic Review* 1989 May 25, p 74.)

Korea has advantages, and is adding to them. POSCO is one of the most efficient steel producers in the world, and steel is an important part of a ship's cost. Backward linkages continue to increase the quality and quantity of domesticly procured components—a process helped by a specific government policy initiative. Moreover, the firms have moved beyond building primarily tankers—a point driven home when Samsung captured a West German firm's $400 million order for five container carriers, which will help keep the yard in full operation into 1991. Overall, the worldwide industry is on an upswing, and Korean firms can reasonably expect to ride it.

TEXTILES AND APPAREL: RELATIVE DECLINE

From the early stages of Korea's economic growth, textiles and apparel have been strategic exports—stimulated by strong overseas demand and the export drive policy of the government. In the early 1980s,

---

Aug, p 54). An overview of the revival of the shipbuilding industry in Korea and Japan is in *Far Eastern Economic Review* (1989 May 25, p 70–74).

however, these industries experienced a slowdown because of rising import barriers in advanced countries and stiffening competition in world markets. Declining labor productivity growth from rapidly increasing wages also hampered performance. However in 1985–86 the economy was aided by the "three lows"—low oil prices, low interest rates, low US dollar. These factors sharpened price competitiveness, raising both exports and profitability until 1987. Then profitability began to deteriorate, due to the "three highs": won appreciation, rising wages, and higher raw material prices. In less than a year, costs jumped some 30%, according to a Korean Export Association of Textiles report to the government in late 1987. Still, 1987 exports were substantially above both advanced estimates and the 1986 actual level, and continued to increase in 1988.

Protectionism in Korea's traditional overseas markets and the changed cost structure indicate these industries are in relative decline. But this has been expected (and happening) since at least the mid 1970s, so that by the early 1980s textiles and apparel were routinely thought of as sunset industries. It is true that even if the three highs are again replaced by three lows, the original comparative advantage Korea had, based primarily on low wages, has been lost. But the groups have not lost all competitiveness, and they are changing to act on the opportunities open to them.[6]

This section begins with an overview of the composition and history of these industries. Factors affecting their ongoing evolution are then taken up. These include protectionism, the age of production equipment, competition from developing economies, and rising wages. Next, how firms have dealt with changing circumstances is looked at. Changing product mix, product diversification (including out of textiles), and offshore production, as well as modernization of facilities, are being used. The section concludes with an analysis of the government's role in adjustment (past and future) and of the industries' prospects.

6. Korean, and other, sources often use "textiles" as a blanket term for what, in US SIC classification are the textile mill products (22) and apparel (23) major groups, plus the synthetic fiber industry group (282, from the chemicals major group). "Textiles and apparel" is used in this essay for these industries collectively. "Textiles" and "textiles group" generally includes synthetic fibers, but otherwise covers only textile mill products (eg, spinning and weaving).

It should also be remembered that the apparel group covers principally the "cut up and needle" trades. Knit goods that are essentially made directly from yarn into garments are actually textile mill products (industry group 225). Hosiery and certain types of underwear comprise the bulk of such knit goods, although some night and outerwear (gloves, sweaters) are also covered. Korean and other sources sometimes include knit wear when referring to apparel. Here "clothing" and "garments" refer to apparel plus knit wear.

Overview

It can be said "the textile industry earned the investment funds spent to develop Korea's heavy and chemical industries." And it was, by Park Young-Dae, director of the textile and consumer goods industry bureau at the Ministry of Trade and Industry (*Business Korea* 1987 Aug, p 41). In the 25 years 1962–86, textiles and apparel accounted for over 41% of Korea's total foreign exchange earnings. And a majority of Korea's major conglomerates (chaebol) are literally rags to riches stories, having started in some aspect of these businesses. But that is the past. Since the mid 1970s, these industries have declined relative to other manufacturing. Between 1976 and 1987, their share of manufacturing value added dropped from 19 to 12%; of employment, from 24 to 18%. In total exports, share slipped from 38 to 25% in the same period.

These were not, however, absolute declines—indeed, all three indicators show absolute growth—and the industries remain an important force in Korean manufacturing and exports. In 1987, they provided employment for 784,000 out of a manufacturing work force of 4.4 million, making them the largest major groups for nonagricultural employment. There are also significant linkages with other sectors, especially machinery and chemicals.

These industries can be classified into sectors by output and by process: spinning (yarns), weaving (fabrics), and knitting (fabrics and garments) and by material (cotton, wool, synthetics). Because of the considerable heterogeneity of product and process among and even within each of these, each has evolved differently and faces different prospects. For example, apparel, which has greater employment than textiles, is characterized by a large number of small, often family-owned, firms that work as subcontractors for large general trading companies and operate with relatively simple, labor-intensive technology and limited capital. Textiles tend to be at the other extreme—spinning, weaving, and knitting mills can be very large-scale and capital-intensive. The average Korean cotton spinning mill, with about 150,000 spindles and over 2,000 workers, is larger than the average US or European mill. And Cheil Wool's Taegu plant is the largest integrated worsted factory in the world.

All the sectors grew rapidly during the 1970s (the aggregate annual rate was almost 20% in real value-added terms between 1970 and 1978) and virtually all have experienced a sharp slowdown since (about 7.5% during 1979–87) even as the rest of the economy was doing well. This could portend a loss of competitiveness that will make this a true declining industry in the 1990s, but the industries and their firms can be expected to resist declines vigorously. The extent of variations in recent growth performance among sectors can be seen in the output and employment data, which are given in Tables 8.12 and 8.13. Export data by item are given in Table 8.14.[7]

Cotton Yarns. Cotton spinning had been particularly hard hit by the recession of the early 1980s and gyrations in the price of cotton (which

Table 8.12. Textiles and Apparel: Overview, 1971–87 (at 1980 prices)

1971	1976	1982	1985	1987	*Textile, Apparel, and Synthetic Fibers*
					value added
458	1,304	1,899	2,297	2,835	in billion won
2.4	4.4	4.5	4.4	4.3	as a percentage of GNP
15.7	18.7	15.9	13.7	12.3	as a percentage of manufacturing sector
					exports
452	2,740	5,925	7,004	11,718	in million US$
42.3	33.8	27.4	23.1	24.8	as a percentage of total exports
					employment
163	641	746	725	784	in thousands
1.6	5.1	5.2	4.8	4.8	as a percentage of total employment
12.2	24.0	24.5	20.7	17.8	as a percentage of manufacturing employment

Source: Bank of Korea and Korea Federation of Textile Industries

Table 8.13. Textile and Apparel Employment by Sector (in thousands)

1980	1982	1984	1985	1986	1987	
732	742	721	725	768	783	total
368	383	384	394	397	393	apparel
119	112	109	104	106	109	spinning
98	95	81	74	100	116	weaving
60	52	60	71	77	79	knitting
20	19	20	20	21	23	synthetic fibers
67	85	68	63	67	64	other[1]

1. Other includes fish nets, canvas, towels, dyeing, twisting, and others
Source: Korea Federation of Textile Industries (*Statistics on Textile Industry* 1988)

7. Further details on these industries can be found in Jung (1986). This section supersedes parts of the discussion of textiles (covering through 1984) found in Leipziger (1987, v 2 p 148–88).

Table 8.14. Textile and Apparel Exports by Item (in millions of US$)

1970	1975	1980	1985	1987	Item
389	1870	5014	7004	11718	total exports
60	154	690	694	809	yarns (total)
6	60	333	223	258	cotton
7	70	236	355	375	synthetics
45	22	65	20	28	silk
2	2	56	96	148	wool
111	433	1396	1855	3266	fabrics (total)
42	111	286	339	583	cotton
6	128	723	1094	1889	synthetics
1	42	107	101	178	silk
6	21	76	84	122	wool
3	35	89	83	107	embroidered
35	84	88	116	207	shibori
219	1283	2927	4457	7644	made-up goods (total)
16	123	76	202	453	other
7	30	112	79	111	fishing nets and ropes
6	52	103	102	187	hosiery
190	1078	2636	4074	6893	clothing

Yarn and fabric totals include items not listed separately.
Natural fibers include blends.
Shibori are silk-based woven textiles.
Other includes miscellaneous fabrics (including linen, lamie, and jute) and cotton products (such as bags, table covers, and handkerchiefs).
Clothing includes leather and fur garments; the two largest clothing items are shirts and sweaters.
Source: Korean Federation of Textile Industries, Statistics on Textile Industry, various annual issues.

accounts for something under a third of production costs). But the 1985–86 boom brought idle spindles back into production and went at least part-way toward restoring the industry's finances. Nearly 62% of the industry's output went overseas in 1987. Economies of scale help make this sector one of fairly large companies—there were 23 in 1989.

The largest, Choongnam Spinning, accounts for one-sixth of domestically produced cotton yarn (down from one-fifth in the mid 1980s). It is also in weaving, dyeing, and fabric printing. Choongnam has over 13,000 workers, up from 10,500 in the mid '80s partly from diversification into such disparate fields as auto parts and hotels. The company was on the verge of being placed in receivership in 1985, because of a staggering debt load, when the three lows (low interest rates, oil prices, and exchange rate) rescued it.

Cotton Fabrics. The cotton weaving sector has been slower growing than spinning, primarily because of slumping export markets—exports took 86% of 1987 production—in the face of keen competition from new exporting countries. Korea's comparative advantage had been chiefly in mass produced low-priced products, but since the early 1980s this market has been eroded by the emergence of producers in China and Pakistan, which have price advantages given their abundance of local raw materials and low wages. Both of these countries significantly increased raw cotton production in the 1980s, and have developed spinning industries to process it locally for a domestic fabric industry. Competitive pressure has caused firms to install shuttleless looms to enhance labor productivity. Such looms increased from 3.6% of total looms in 1983 to 8.5% in 1987. However, this is still low compared to Taiwan and Hong Kong.

Japan and Hong Kong have been the major customers for cotton fabric, taking 35% of such exports in 1987, followed by Europe (14%) and the US (11%). Japan and Hong Kong have taken an increasing share —the ratio was 26% in 1983—as Korea has tried to penetrate non-quota markets.

Wool Yarns and Fabrics. The wool sector shows concentrated market structure, with Cheil Wool (a member of the Samsung Group) commanding 40% of the domestic market and Kyung Nam Wool 25% in 1987. The two firms had 7,500 workers that year. Spinners have steadily installed capacity to meet increased export demand from countries such as Hong Kong and Japan. At the same time, an estimated 41% of the industry's spindles were considered obsolete in 1986. Worsted weaving facilities have shrunk since 1983, as equipment has been retired, but higher capacity utilization has meant output increases. The other wool subsectors (non-worsteds, blends, and other) have actively modernized by installing shuttleless looms, including water jet and rapier looms. Such new looms provided 21% of capacity in 1987, compared to 9% in 1983. Still, the industry estimated 28% of wool weaving facilities were obsolete in 1986.

In 1987 exports amounted to 58% of total wool fabric production. That compares to 50% in 1983. The US was the biggest customer, taking 25% of total wool fabric exports, mostly pure worsted and blends. Hong Kong took 21% of exports, mostly pure worsted, and Japan took 20%.

Synthetics. The chemical (synthetic) fiber industry is divided into petroleum-based fibers (including polyester, acrylic, and nylon) and cellulose-based (including acetate and rayon; sometimes called regenerated fibers, they are made from wood pulp, etc). The industry has grown steadily during the 1970s and '80s in Korea, with capacity expansion and product-line broadening in line with the growth of the country's spinning industry. The Korean chemical fiber industry was seventh largest in the world, based on capacity, at the end of 1987.

This is a concentrated industry as far as specific products are concerned. Thus (1987 data), Hanil Synthetic (17,500 workers) provides almost 60% of domestically produced acrylic yarn, and 70% of acrylic fiber. Tongyang, the largest nylon filament and cord maker in the world, provides 51% of Korea's output of these items, while Kolon makes 30% and Kohap makes 25% of the nylon fiber (a different niche).

Since the early 1980s, the industry's shares of total manufacturing value added and of production have been declining gradually. Among the factors inhibiting more rapid growth have been protectionism in advanced countries and the emergence of competitors such as China and other Asian economies. A shift in consumption patterns from synthetics to natural fibers was another factor. Between 1980 and 1986, the share of synthetic fiber consumption in total fiber consumption decreased from 58 to 50%.

Major fiber producers are concentrating on the renovation of their facilities rather than expansion, as they seek to increase productivity and improve quality. The companies also have actively pursued product differentiation and new material development using heavy R&D investment. Reflecting consumer preference for natural fibers, new materials such as silk-like and cotton-like synthetics have been developed.

As a medium-term strategy, the industry is shifting from consumer-oriented to industrial-oriented synthetics. This started with such areas as aramid pulp, carbon fiber, artificial lawns, and polyester tire cord; more recently it has included antistatic yarn, conductive fiber, and ultra-fine denier filament.

Kolon, one of the largest firms in the industry, is an example of this sort of diversification. Indeed, the company is evolving into a general chemical producer, and even has entered a joint venture with Japan's Fanuc to make robots for the Korean automobile industry. Tongyang Nylon, another major company and about the same size as Kolon, has diversified even further afield, so that in 1986 non-textile products provided 16% of revenue.

Garments. Apparel and knit garments have contributed greatly to the nation's exports and employment during the 1970s and '80s. Apparel is characterized by its labor intensiveness and both it and knit wear are export industries. The apparel industry includes some 3,270 companies, employing 417,000 people (1986). Its share of gross output in manufacturing has fallen from 5.5% in 1981 to 3.7% in 1986 because it has grown less fast than manufacturing as a whole. As competitors in China and ASEAN countries have emerged in the 1980s, apparel has come to be viewed as a declining industry.

Because exports account for about 70% of production, the industry is sensitive to fluctuations in overseas markets and to global business conditions. Sweaters and shirts have been the two largest product categories, over 40% of exports in the mid 1980s. The US took over half of exports in 1985, but there has been a move to diversify away from such heavy dependence on a single, potentially even more protectionist market. As a result, Korean firms have penetrated non-quota areas such as Africa, South East Asia, and the Middle East.

Apparel production facilities comprise sewing machines and incidental equipment such as cutting devices and dyeing machines. While technological change has been relatively rapid in cutting and pressing, it has been slow in sewing, the labor-intensive nucleus of garment making. Knit wear, however, is not labor intensive; knitting garments is more like spinning yarn and weaving fabric, which is one reason it is included in the same major industrial group as these activities, rather than in the apparel group. Computer-controlled knitting machines for socks, gloves, and sweaters have been actively introduced, as have computer-aided design systems (particularly for socks and jacquards).

Despite technological upgrading during the 1980s, garment making still relies heavily on obsolete facilities, which causes production bottlenecks. The Korean Federation of Textile Industries estimated in 1987 that more than half the industries' equipment needed replacing. Further modernization of production facilities is required as the best way to improve productivity and thus to mitigate rising wages.

Factors Affecting Prospects

Competitiveness and protectionism in export markets confront the Korean textile and apparel industries. It is concern over how successfully these problems can be dealt with that has led to the "declining" label being applied to textiles and apparel. Competitiveness is a two-front issue: wage-based competition from developing countries and technology-based competition from advanced countries. Labor productivity is a factor in both, and that relates to wages, which rose with a vengeance in Korea in the late 1980s. Shaky finances also pose a threat to many firms.

Rising wages. The impact of rising wages depends on the share of labor costs in total costs and the extent to which real wages rise faster than productivity. Knitting and production of yarns and fabrics have become very capital-intensive processes. Apparel as a whole is more labor-intensive than textiles, but there is wide variation within it. Thus, a lined dress requires more labor than, for example, a man's shirt.

Monthly earnings in the textile and apparel industries have been lower than in other manufacturing. This is true in most countries and reflects the age, gender, and the skill of the labor force. From 1976 through 1987, wages increased at about the same rate in apparel and in manufacturing, but grew more slowly in textiles. However, in 1986 and '87, textile wages were the fastest growing of the three. For most of the 1976–87 period, wages grew faster than productivity for textiles. The same is true of apparel for the years 1976–85, but productivity growth exceeded wage increases during 1985–87. (Data are from the Korea Productivity Center and, for wages, the Economic Planning Board.) However, in 1988 nominal wages exploded in all sectors, so that by September 1988 wages had risen some 50% over 1987 levels in manufacturing and in textiles and apparel.

Shaky Finances. Textiles and apparel grew in the 1960s and early '70s on access to easy credit from the government-run banking system: the Bank of Korea estimates that in 1970 textile firms' overall financing costs were more than 5 percentage points less than for manufacturing as a whole. Both industries were favored not only in receiving loans for plant, equipment, and working capital, but also at the marketing stage with export-promotion loans. In the mid 1970s, however, government priorities shifted to heavy and chemical industries (HCI), so that in 1978 textiles' costs were 3 points above manufacturing's. (The Bank's series on apparel firms is so volatile it is difficult to interpret.) Since 1980 financing costs have been on the order of 14–18% for both manufacturing and textiles, with no clear or consistent advantage to either.

Reduced access to credit is considered a reason textiles has not been able to acquire new equipment. This is true only in the narrow sense that the more money one can borrow, and the more cheaply one can borrow it, the bigger and more profitable one can become (if the money is used wisely). Initially, higher interest rates did not deter overall investment in textile machinery: it totaled 717 billion won in 1977–79, 62% of it for expansion. In 1980–82, spending on expansion dropped over 69% compared to the previous 3-year period, but funds for replacement and modernization fell only 4%, and this probably had more to do with the fact the industry lost money in these years than with the level of interest rates. Both categories rebounded smartly in the 1983–85 period —with updating more than doubling, to 558 billion won. For 1988, the Korea Development Bank estimates industry investment was 875 billion won, over 12% of which was for replacement and 63% for expansion, and 25% for automation, energy savings, etc.

Although precise data are hard to come by, some chaebol, involved with the government in HCI projects, diverted their cash flow into these new areas from their textile and apparel operations. This, combined with declining profitability since the late 1970s, has many firms claiming they have insufficient internally generated funds to pay for the level of retooling needed to stay competitive (at current or greater output levels) in the 1990s. Bank of Korea data suggest textile firms as a group recorded 3.7% gross profit margins on sales, and 2.8% net in 1988; this compares with 3.2% after-tax margins posted by major publicly traded US firms. Variation among sectors and firms was of course significant, but most firms made at least modest profits.

Many Korean firms are highly leveraged, and the resulting interest and loan amortization payments can be a major burden—often turning operating profits into overall losses. In the early 1980s, the government restricted dividend payments by textile firms to strengthen equity, but in the mid 1980s equity comprised only about 20% of the industry's capital, although this was up from the 14–16% range of the 1970s (Jung 1986, p 11 table 6). Extensive use of credit to expand in the 1970s may, in the late 1980s, have left the textile industry too leveraged to buy the equipment it needs to compete in the 1990s, at least at the scale it has in the 1980s.

Aging Machinery, Changing Technology. Significant technical innovation continues to take place in textile machinery. The new technologies have been intended primarily to offset the advantage of cheap labor, combining precision machinery with computerized controls to achieve speeds not thought possible even 10 years ago. And the new equipment often does more than just enhance labor productivity: for example, computerized knitting machines can make many garments in final shape or fewer pieces. This method uses less than 90% of the fabric required for conventional cutting and sewing. A Korean firm that has installed such machines at its plant in South Carolina can produce a cotton sweater for 5% less (FOB) than a sweater from Hong Kong or Taiwan made on older knitters (*Korea Business World* 1989 Jan).

The new technologies have been implemented primarily in the advanced countries, so Korea's cost advantage in textile mill products is no longer as great as it once was. Firms in these countries can make yarn and fabric at home, then ship it overseas to be made up as garments. Germany and Italy are the largest textile makers in the world and, not coincidentally, Germany is the leading textile machine maker.

At one time, Korea stayed abreast of new technologies by buying them embodied in new machines. But Korea began to fall behind as the pace of expansion slowed with the industries' changing situation in the late 1970s and early '80s. This has been termed the "machine vintage" problem and it has been a concern since at least the mid 1980s when a large and rising part of Korea's machinery stock started becoming older than its life for tax purposes (typically 6–9 years). Thus, a survey in late 1988 suggested 80% of Korea's cotton industry machinery was super-annuated (*Korea Business World* 1989 Jan, p 41).

It is difficult to judge the reality of the vintage problem, as properly maintained machines can produce for decades—as demonstrated by the history of British textiles. Given technological change, that history may well be what Korean firms have in mind. Firms' taxable incomes have increased as their depreciation expenses have decreased, which reduces their cash flow from operations and thus their ability to invest in new equipment.

Although it is not surprising that firms seek government support to replace older machines, the key issue is whether it makes economic sense for them to do so (and if it does, government support is not necessary). If industry segments and specific firms will indeed lose competitiveness and decline, then the process of divesting and transferring cash flow elsewhere should be encouraged, not discouraged.

Protectionism. Restrictions on apparel and textile trade are based on the MFA (Multi-Fiber Arrangement), signed for the first time in 1974 under the auspices of GATT, with its goal being the orderly conduct of world trade in textiles and apparel. The MFA has been used primarily to protect the textile and apparel industries of importing countries at the expense of those countries' consumers and of exporters. In particular, restraints under the MFA have been applied almost exclusively to NIEs and developing countries. On the other hand, the establishment of country-specific import quotas favoring LDCs has accelerated the development of lower-cost clothing industries in such countries. (For more on MFA and the global textiles and apparel industries, see Cline 1987.)

MFA 4 started on 1 August 1986, and has generally more extensive and restrictive restraints than MFA 3 did. The product coverage of the bilateral agreements associated with MFA 4 tend to be more comprehensive, and growth and flexibility provisions have been applied more restrictively. Under the new agreement, ramie, linen, and silk—previously non-quota items—became subject to quotas.

Korean exports were hit severely, as major customers (the US, the European Community, and Canada) immediately moved to further restrict their imports under MFA 4. The US put the brakes on Korea's growing shipments of textiles and apparel by limiting imports into the US to an average annual growth rate of 0.825% for 1986–89 (compared to over 2% under earlier agreements). The EC agreement limits Korean exports to 2.5% annual growth for 1987–91. A further blow came when the EC announced removal in 1988 of a number of Korean products from its GSP (generalized system of preferences, which are special tariff concessions to LDCs).

The trade situation continued to deteriorate during 1988 because of advanced country protectionism. In November the EC authorized four members to ban "temporarily" a range of NIE textiles. But Japan provided the biggest shock when, in October, the government filed a claim against Korean knit wear, claiming imports were damaging local industries and threatening jobs. Korean companies agreed to "voluntary export restraints" (de facto quotas).

Competition from Developing Countries. ASEAN countries and China are posing a strong challenge to Korea, especially in apparel, and this has eroded Korea's share of world markets. China, exploiting low wages and abundant cotton, is the world's largest textile producer and has begun to make its presence felt in world trade. It also has moved up steadily as a garment exporter. The developing countries have much lower wages and, as new participants, have been subjected to the developed countries' very restrictive quotas only in the late 1980s. Up to a point, lower wages generally also indicate lower productivity and lower quality (or at least less-complex products), but the wage differentials are sufficiently great that developing countries can oust Korea from markets for low-quality and simple items.

Raw Materials. Cotton and wool are entirely imported, and in 1988 about 60% of materials such as chemical pulp and acetate flake for synthetics came from overseas. And of course the petroleum used to make such chemicals in Korea is all imported. Because about half the cotton is from the US, the industry is quite vulnerable to US yields. Australia provides about 80% of the wool, with the rest coming from New Zealand and Great Britain. Some 80% of raw silk comes from China, and when the Chinese restricted exports in 1988, Korean silk companies were able to operate at only about half capacity.

Synthetic fiber imports have been restricted to help development of the local industry, but shortages in 1987 led to liberalization. At the same time, fiber producers were encouraged to limit exports.

Private-Sector Adjustment Strategy

Growth of textiles and apparel is expected to be slow due to unfavorable circumstances. But even slow growth can be profitable, and industry trade associations and individual firms have taken steps to adjust. The main thrust has been to improve profit margins through factory automation and moving to higher value products. Elements of the strategy include changing the product mix, the markets sold into, the technology, and the cost structure. There has also been a move by some firms to produce offshore and to sell more apparel in the domestic market.

Product Mix. "Up market" is the catch phrase of many industries in many countries. It is the consensus direction in which to move, and thus the road is as crowded and pushy as the low-wage path of the past. But shifting to higher value-added, higher quality items has so far been a successful strategy for maximizing the value of quotas placed on Korean exports to the US and EC, and it has thus softened the consequences of increasing competition from Asian textile producers at the low end of the market. Moving up market requires investment in new machinery, in design facilities, and in marketing arrangements.

Up-market demand is fickle, with frequent shifts. This has reduced the size of the average order in many product segments, which can work to the advantage of a small firm. But, particularly in fabrics, buyers have tried to protect themselves by shifting more design responsibility onto producers. Part of this is an expectation that sellers will come to them. This is a break from the past, when buyers of standardized basic textiles scouted for the Sears and K-Marts of the world. Not until the late 1980s did Korean firms need to have sophisticated marketing skills or the ability to handle design changes on their own. Small producers have blamed a lack of capital for their remaining dependent on buyer-provided instructions or on standard or traditional designs.

Technology. Product differentiation in even such seemingly mundane markets as men's and women's briefs (the number of colors and shapes has proliferated as brands jostle for retail shelf space) has meant more reliance on small, flexible production technology as opposed to simply high-volume machines. Because so much of Korean firms' present equipment is of the basic high-volume kind, to some extent this puts them at a disadvantage across a broad spectrum of spinning, weaving, and knitting.

The high demand for labor outside of textiles and apparel, as well as the relatively poor working conditions within the industry, have raised labor costs and encouraged the industry to substitute capital for labor. The bulk of this substitution has been in spinning and weaving—having already been highly capital-intensive.

The chemical fiber area is one that has greatly increased its R&D expenditures in the latter half of the 1980s. Over 20 new textile materials have been developed, most of them types of polyester. In 1987 only 1 of the 23 major non-synthetic spinners had a technical research lab, Choongnam, the largest cotton spinner. Its lab, with 20 researchers, has worked on dyeing and fabric-finishing techniques, as both of these are important in increasing value added.

Geographical Diversification. The US sucked in Korean textile and apparel products in increasing amounts through most of the 1960s and early '70s, and most of the rest of exports went to Japan. In a typical year these two countries absorbed as much as two-thirds of total exports. Protectionism—in the form of the MFAs and bilateral quota agreements—changed that. During the 1970s, Korea diversified, selling into the EC, Middle East, Hong Kong, and even Africa and Latin America. By 1980 the individual shares of the US and Japan had dropped considerably (to 22 and 18%, respectively). After 1980 the US share rose, then fell again. Korea's vulnerability to demand fluctuations in the two countries remains high. Table 8.15 shows the geographical distribution of exports.

There are not many new places left for Korean firms to sell, although

Table 8.15. Textile and Apparel Exports by Destination (in millions of US$ and percentages)

1975		1980		1985		1986		1987		Destination
495	26	1113	22	2560	37	2964	34	3573	30	United States
465	25	885	18	966	14	1132	15	2197	19	Japan
288	15	1041	21	903	13	1360	16	1986	17	EC
		107	2	61	1	70	1	97	1	ASEAN
1870		5014		7004		8734		11718		total

Total includes destinations not listed separately

Source: Korean Federation of Textile Industries, *Statistics on Textile Industry,* various annual issues.

geographical diversification will continue in the form of shifting shares among importing countries. Despite rising barriers to its products in OECD countries, Korea generally managed to increase the value of its exports to these countries until MFA 4, and even to the United States and some others since then. But this growth is explicitly constrained by various trade agreements. As a supplier of yarn and fabric to ASEAN and LDCs, Korea faces impressive competition from other NIEs and the OECD, and these countries' domestic markets often are not much more open than those of the OECD (or Korea itself, for that matter). Korean firms have made tentative steps to market in communist countries: to this end, Daewoo held a trade fair in East Berlin in 1988.

The domestic market also offers opportunities. Rising incomes, increasing leisure time, and a desire, particularly among the young, to express individuality, all contribute to people becoming more fashion conscious. This is happening in Korea, and foreigners have been among those who have noticed. Benetton opened a store in Seoul in October 1987. At the end of 1988 there were 27 Benetton outlets in Korea, with plans to have 150 by the end of 1990, operated by a Korean franchisee. Many of the garments Benetton sells are at least partially made in Korea, and a joint venture to increase local production of what is sold locally is a possibility.

Cheil Wool Textile, the oldest wool maker in Korea, is a local company that has expanded in the local market. In 1983 Cheil contracted with an Italian firm for assistance building a highly automated men's suit factory. The company had garnered 15% of the market by 1987. The market is not large, because many men have their suits tailor-made (an activity classed as retail trade in the SIC) but it is expected to grow.

Offshore Production. Faced with mounting protectionism in advanced countries and rising labor costs at home, several Korean apparel companies (and a smaller number of textile firms) have established factories outside Korea. As the 1980s came to an end, they were speeding up investment abroad and cutting back on domestic expansion. The government has cooperated with the shift offshore, even sending a research team to Latin America in 1987 to look at investment possibilities.

The companies initially focused on countries such as the Dominican Republic and Costa Rica, which offered a way to end-run US import restrictions because they have tariff preferences under the Caribbean Basin Initiative. They also have free-trade zones, which means reduced or waived taxes and other concessions. More than 32 Korean companies had plants in the region at the end of 1988. Some of these plants are joint ventures with US firms, with the American partner handling marketing. (*Business Korea* 1987 Sep, p 90, lists Korean textile plants in the Americas as of the end of August 1987.)

The second wave of investment has been in South East and South West Asia. Some firms have built in the US. In 1987 the Korean Federation of Textile Industries and a group of Korean apparel and textile companies, proposed a large-scale integrated facility in the US in a joint venture with The Limited, a US apparel firm. In September 1988 there were 66 cases of Korean overseas investment in apparel and textile facilities, involving over US $38 million, a 50% increase in just nine months.

The Government's Role

The government showered textile and apparel with cheap credit and bestowed preferential tax and depreciation treatment in the 1960s and early '70s, successfully following an established path of economic development whereby these groups became important foreign exchange earners and industrial employers. The second stage of that path is less kind to what are sometimes called, often derisively, light or traditional industries such as these. Thus, in the mid 1970s, the government began an HCI (heavy and chemical industry) development plan. The assumptions were that Korea would lose competitiveness in labor-intensive industries soon, that consumer goods (which is most of what is usually meant by light industry) including textiles are inherently labor-intensive, and that such industries did not have enough steam left in them to power the country's future growth needs.

The government was thus attempting to anticipate the need for structural change and the inevitability of dislocations for some industries. And the emphasis on HCI profoundly affected textile and apparel. As noted, financing costs and wages rose sharply in the latter 1970s. Firms were at times brutally weaned from subsidized credit, having instead to quench much of their thirst for funds in the curb (informal) market. General worldwide inflation was amplified by the HCI drive, and wages were bid up throughout the economy. Things did not work out as expected for either the heavy and chemical industries or textiles and apparel, although the story is much more complex than a simple failure of government policy. In fact, as is so often the case, the policy's successes have been part of the reason for the problems of the 1980s.

In any event, by the early 1980s the HCI drive was being scaled back as high technology became the next turnpike. Textiles and apparel have again been accepted as an important sector, and government officials in 1987 confidently predicted dry goods would continue to be Korea's biggest foreign exchange earner well into the 1990s, even suggesting that, in the '90s, Seoul would become an international fashion center (*Korean Business Review* 1988 Feb, p 46).

The government's renewed interest has several aspects. These include a textile modernization fund, support of a domestic textile machinery industry, capacity controls, and import protection, each of which, along with miscellaneous programs, are discussed below.

Textile Modernization Fund. In 1981 the government set up the Textile Modernization Fund (TMF) to provide low-interest loans (6–8% per annum at a time the market rate was over 15%) with medium-term maturity (5–8 years) to modernize factories. The main beneficiaries were intended to be the small and medium size companies, which, although they provide less than half of output and value added, do employ more than half of workers.

The government and the industry were each supposed to put up 60 billion won, but it was not forthcoming. By mid 1985 only about 27 billion had been collected and loaned. At almost the same time the TMF was established, the government adopted a tight fiscal policy and also began to realize the benefits of backing off from a too-micro industrial policy.

Thus the Fund was one of many programs considered less important than the macroeconomic stability the tight fiscal policy sought to achieve. For its part, the industry's low profits discouraged contributions.

In 1986 the Industrial Development Law (IDL) was enacted, replacing industry-specific promotion laws. The textile and dyeing industries are among the industries included for rationalization under the IDL. One part of this was 180 billion won in 5% loans so that equipment over 9 years old could be scrapped, and mills could shift to higher value-added items. In the first year of the loan program, some 86 billion won was spent, virtually all by the weaving industry, to replace over 14,000 machines with new, automated ones.

Machinery. Imports provide most textile and apparel equipment. (In 1986 the industry imported $271 million worth of equipment, 60% of it from Japan.) But a local industry has developed, and in 1987 the Ministry of Trade and Industry put together a policy package to boost it. The plan calls for an increase in self-sufficiency from 36% in 1986 to 55% by 1991. This will allow part of the money made available to the industry for new machines to be spent locally. Some Korean firms have exhibited at international trade fairs and their offerings—which are generally aimed at the small-scale-operator niche—have gotten the attention of competitors.

Modernization of equipment will be geared toward the ability to manufacture diverse products in small quantities, which contrasts with past emphasis on basic volume expansion.

Capacity Control. Under the Textile Modernization Law enacted in 1979, the government adopted a permit (licensing) system to control investment in all segments of the textile industry, though not in apparel. Capacity control can be exercised in a way that promotes orderly expansion of capacity to take advantage of scale economies or allows inefficient firms to exit with as little disruption as possible. Control under the 1979 law did not achieve this potential, and it was abolished by the enactment of the IDL.

Under the IDL, new entrants into textiles and dyeing were prohibited for the three years of the rationalization period (1986–89). This was intended to promote capacity reduction and encourage incumbent firms to upgrade their production facilities. As a downstream industry, dyeing was operating at 62% of capacity in 1985. The government believes the industry is essential for the production of high-priced textiles. Encouraged by subsidized loans of 3 billion won, old equipment was scrapped and new machines brought in. With the increase in textile exports, the operating ratio had increased to 76% in 1987.

Import Protection. Domestic producers have been protected by tariffs, quotas, and non-tariff barriers. But there has been significant liberalization. In the early 1980s there were 1,089 textile and apparel-related items on the restricted import list. By the end of 1984 the number was down to 105, and by 1987 there were just 18 textile items still on the list. In 1988, 98% of product imports in these industries were free of quotas or restrictions, though tariff protection persists. Tariffs on textile inputs tend to be lower (and have been reduced more during the 1980s) than tariffs on finished goods. Thus fibers face a 10% duty; yarns, 15–20%. For fabrics, the range is 30–35%; and for clothing and made-up articles, it is 35–50%.

Other Programs. The government pursues an active R&D policy at a general level, through support for the budget of the Korea Advanced Institute for Science and Technology (KAIST), and a firm-specific level, with loans and tax credits for R&D expenses. The government has also aggressively helped companies import advanced dyeing technologies and equipment. A Textile Technology Promotion Center was established in

Taegu, Korea's textile heartland, with a 1 billion won fund. The Center's purpose is to provide the training needed to operate newer, more-automated equipment. Support is also provided the Korea Federation of Textile Industries, the principal trade organization.

To upgrade the quality of garments, the development of design has been emphasized. A Textile Week, including an International Designer's Fair, was held in Seoul under the sponsorship of the government in October 1987.

Prospects. Korea's textile and apparel industries have experienced dramatic expansions of both production facilities and export volumes during the 1980s. Thus they have contributed significantly to the nation's economic development through large foreign exchange earnings and job creation. However, it is anticipated the problems surrounding the industries will be aggravated in the foreseeable future, and their relative share of GNP will decline. But this is an expected and accepted part of Korea's economic development. In many ways, what is remarkable is how much longer than expected the textile and apparel industries have remained so relatively important.

Firms will almost definitely shed labor as they shift offshore and to more technology-, capital-, and design-intensive means of production and products. In this way, Korean firms will remain important players in world markets, just as Benetton and many US firms have. Textiles and apparel will in due course become eclipsed industries, but not sunset ones.

TRADE POLICY

Korea's trade policy has long been one of active export promotion combined with import restrictions aimed at promoting import substitution, as well as protecting the agricultural sector and conserving foreign exchange. High tariffs have been part of this, as have restrictive licensing requirements, and a generally complex set of import rules.

Reforms began in the mid 1960s, particularly as regards simplifying the system. Thus, in place of an approved list of imports, a "negative list" approach was adopted: all commodities not listed were automatically approved for import (AA items). AA items were mostly raw materials and intermediate goods not domestically available. The negative list covered "non-essential" and "luxury" goods as well as import-competing items. The list and quotas were determined twice a year by the government, on the basis of import needs, the balance of payments situation, and the protection requirements of domestic industries.

There were three reforms of the tariff system in the 1970s (1973, '76, and '78) but all were limited in scope. Thus, although the average level of tariffs was lowered, selected ones were raised—such as those on heavy-industry products in 1978. The average of tariffs in the 1960s was around 40%; in the '70s, around 30% until the 1978 reform, which dropped the average to about 25%.

In the 1980s, tariff cuts have come more quickly and broadly, and the list of imports needing approval has been pared. In 1983 the government announced a five-year reform aimed at compressing the tariff structure by reducing the highest rates, rationalizing the structure by giving similar treatment to similar items, and reducing the average nominal tariff from 25% to 13% by January 1989. The cuts took the rate for manufactured goods to just over 11%, and it is set to be 6.2% in 1993. That will be comparable to 1988 rates in the United States (6.1%), Canada (7.3%), and the EEC (6.7%).

Although prohibitively high tariffs have been and are in effect for many AA items, quantitative restrictions have been more important than tariffs in controlling imports, although this has become less true in the 1980s. Remaining restrictions apply primarily to textiles, miscellaneous manufactured goods, agricultural and fishery products, and domestically available raw materials. Thus, in 1989, of 8278 items on Korea's manufactured-goods tariff schedule, only 41 were not automatic-approval. However, 506 of 1963 primary-sector items continued to be on the negative list. Almost half of these have been targeted for liberalization.

Several developments have occurred that have had a profound impact on trade policy making in Korea. First, Korea has begun to lose autonomy in its decision making. Second, the adjustment costs of further opening appear large. There is also a political problem.

The early liberalizations were unilateral on Korea's part, although the government certainly expected its measures to weigh positively in the US government's review of its Generalized System of Preferences (GSP) in 1986, though without success. With the trade surplus of 1986, Korea could no longer claim entitlement to the GATT IV waiver of reciprocity by invoking balance of payment problems. In this way, and particularly because of the size of the trade imbalance with the United States, Korea is much more exposed to the demands and wishes of its trading partners than in the past.

Korea's market opening has progressed to the stage where further or faster opening may impose adjustment costs that are viewed as unnecessarily large by many. These costs include damaging infant sectors and compromising important noneconomic national policy objectives. Not surprisingly, they also reflect the demands of existing interest groups in

Korea's political democratization process. These various arguments are loudest in the areas of services and agriculture, where there has not yet been much opening. While undoubtedly the concerns are exaggerated and misused, they do have a foundation in reality.

Many of the reforms of the late 1980s came in response to US pressure, and the pressure is likely to continue. This creates a problem. The policy reforms implemented in response to US pressure have fostered the impression among the Korean electorate that reform is intended to benefit the US economy at the expense, in many cases, of the Korean economy. In short, it is a power game the US always wins. This is exacerbated by the fact Koreans tend to be more mercantalist than free-trade oriented. It is generally easier to see (or be someone experiencing) the costs of trade reform than it is to see the offsetting benefits. With the executive and legislative branches of the US government in the hands of different political groups, the politicians have been willing to use the heat of trade issues for their own short-term advantage.

CONCLUSIONS

The Korean shipbuilding and coal mining industries were developed with government initiative and heavy protection. As the market environment has changed, the protection became too expensive. The government faces two dilemmas: the withdrawal or addition of resources, and the acceleration or deceleration of the adjustment process.

Market-displacing policies may invite distortions one after another. Thus, subsidies can improve the situation in the short run, if the goal is to keep firms and workers in the industry. But precisely because they prevent firms and workers from exiting, subsidies reduce the efficiency of the economy and distort the allocation of resources in the longer term. Moreover, as the subsidized sectors increase in scale, they are inclined to protect their own interests, and it becomes more costly to adjust for the distortion. For this reason, the maximum duration and the conditions of the intervention should be specified.

Market-conforming policies seek to modify market outcomes by compensating for distortions caused by the inefficiency of the market mechanism. The Korean industries discussed in this essay tell us that government policy towards declining industries should be market conforming.

BIBLIOGRAPHY

Bartz, Patricia. 1972. *South Korea*. London: Oxford University Press.
Cline, William R. 1987. *The Future of World Trade in Textiles and Apparel*. Washington DC: Institute for International Economics.

Edwards, Sebastian. 1988. "Financial Deregulatin and Segmented Capital Markets: The Case of Korea." *World Development* 16(1): 185–94.

Hasan, Parvez. 1976. *Korea: Problems and Issues in a Rapidly Growing Economy.* A World Bank country economic report. Johns Hopkins University Press.

——, and DC Rao. 1979. *Korea: Policy Issues for Long-term Development.* A World Bank country economic report, looking back and ahead 15 years. Based on a 1976 mission to Korea. Johns Hopkins University Press.

Jung, Soon-Dong. 1986. "Textile Industry in Korea." *Korea Exchange Bank Monthly Review,* v 20: Oct p 3.

KDI = Korea Development Institute. 1975. *Korea's Economy: Past and Present.* Seoul: KDI.

Kim, Joong-Hyun. 1987. "The Shipbuilding Industry in Korea." *Korea Exchange Bank Monthly Review,* v 21: Nov p 9.

——. 1988. "Korean Coal Mining Industry." *The Korea Development Review* 10(2): 91–115 (Summer).

KOIS = Korean Overseas Information Service. 1978 and 1987. *A Handbook of Korea.* Seoul: KOIS, Ministry of Culture and Information. 1978 is the 1st ed; 1987, the 6th.

Korea Development Bank. 1988. "International Competitiveness of Korean Shipbuilding Industry." [The Bank's] *Monthly Economic Review,* v 392: Jul.

Korea Exchange Bank. 1984. *The Korean Economy: Review and Prospects.* 6th ed.

Korea Federation of Textile Industries. 1988. *Statistics of Textile Industry* #19.

Krugman, Paul. 1983. "Targeted Industrial Policies: Theory and Evidence." In *Industrial Change and Public Policy,* A symposium sponsored by the Federal Reserve Bank of Kansas City, p 123–55. Kansas City MO: Public Affairs Dept, Federal Reserve Bank of Kansas City.

——. 1984. "The US Response to Foreign Industrial Targeting." *Brookings Papers on Economic Activities* 1:77–131.

Lapan, Harvey E. 1976. "International Trade, Factor Market Distortion, and the Optimal Dynamic Subsidy." *American Economic Review* 66(3): 335–46 (Jun).

Leipziger, Danny M. 1987. *Korea: Managing the Industrial Transition.* A World Bank country study. 2 v. Covers through 1984.

——. 1988. "Industrial Restructuring in Korea." *World Development,* v 16: Jan p 121–35.

Sakong, Il, and Leroy Jones. 1980. *Government, Business, and Entrepreneurship in Economic Development: The Korean Case.* Harvard University Press.

Sekiguchi, Sueo, and Toshihiro Horiuchi. 1984 (English translation 1988). "Trade and Adjustment Assistance." In Ryutaro Komiya, Masahiro Okuno, and Kotaro Suzumura, editors, *Industrial Policy of Japan,* ch 14. San Diego: Academic Press.

World Bank. 1984. *Korea: Development in Global Context.* A World Bank country study, based on a 1983 mission.

9

JAPAN
A Plethora of Programs

Sueo Sekiguchi

Japanese industrial policy is best known for its supposed success in promoting the economy's postwar growth. But Japan has also had declining industries and regions heavily dependent on those industries. So of course there have been policies to address these problems, and they are the topic of this paper.

Adjustment assistance policies were ad hoc and sector-specific before the 1970s because only a few manufacturing sectors declined in the 1950s and '60s. Sectors receiving assistance were coal mining, sulfur mining, and textiles. Coal mining had to shrink because of substitution by petroleum products; sulfur mining because of cheap sulfur from oil refining; and textiles because of catching up by developing countries and import restriction by advanced countries. The economy's real growth rate in the 1970s, while still a respectable 5% per annum, was substantially slower than in the preceding decade. Indeed, after 1973 when

I am grateful to Harumi Takahashi, Shin Yasunobu and Shin-ichi Motegi of MITI, Yutaka Aoki of the Ministry of Labor, Hideki Kono of the Agency for Small and Medium Enterprises, and Yoshiro Sekine of the Fair Trade Commission for their kind collaboration in data collection. I am also indebted to Professors Hugh T. Patrick, Edward H. English, Michael Young, Ji-Hong Kim, Pang Eng Fong, and other participants of the workshops, as well as Lawrence B. Krause, for their comments on earlier drafts. I would also like to thank Sadako Okuyama for her assistance. Needless to say, views expressed in this paper are my own and should not be attributed to those who collaborated and commented, and I am solely responsible for whatever deficiency may remain.

major currencies were floated and the yen appreciated dramatically, a growing number of manufacturing sectors started a rapid decline. Macro indicators are presented in Table 9.1.

This essay investigates adjustment problems and policy responses in Japan for both long-run and short-run declining industries. After the following overview section, intra-industry adjustment (for cyclicly trou-

Table 9.1. Gross National Product and Expenditure, 1970–87
(at 1980 market prices in trillion yen)

1970	1974	1978	1982	1985	1987	
87.5	110.2	130.8	149.0	162.3	174.4	consumer expenditure
14.8	17.8	21.9	25.1	27.0	28.5	government expenditure
53.7	63.0	72.1	78.9	87.4	102.0	gross fixed asset formation
4.9	4.6	0.9	1.3	2.7	1.0	change in stocks
161.0	195.6	225.7	254.3	279.4	305.8	national expenditure
13.8	22.4	28.6	42.8	55.3	54.4	exports
22.7	34.7	35.8	40.7	42.8	47.9	imports
152.1	183.3	218.5	256.4	291.8	312.4	gross national product

Components of Fixed Asset Formation

11.8	14.6	17.2	14.8	14.0	18.5	residential
28.6	31.1	31.3	40.6	52.4	59.9	private non-residential
13.3	17.2	23.5	23.4	21.0	23.6	public

Other Indicators

359	292	210	249	239	145	yen per dollar (average of daily rates)
	65	89	108	115	115	consumer price index (1980 = 100)

Data are for calendar years. A trillion has 12 zeros. Export and import data are for goods and services only; factor income is not included. Change in stocks were particularly high in 1970 and '74 compared to all other years in the 1970s and '80s.

Distribution of GNP at current prices in 1988 was 57% personal consumption, 9% government consumption, 31% gross fixed capital formation, 13% exports, and 10% imports.

Sources: The exchange rate and CPI are from the IMF's 1988 *International Financial Statistics Yearbook*. All else is from the Economic Planning Agency's *Annual Report on National Accounts 1989* (March), which contains significantly more detail; however the descriptions are only in Japanese. The *OECD Economic Surveys* series for Japan uses the same source for a table in its Statistical Annex that is essentially the same as the one here; however there is usually a one-year lag in its reflecting revisions in the EPA series.

bled industries) is discussed, not only from a purely economic viewpoint, but from a political one as well. Two cases, paper (where Japan is a small importing country) and shipbuilding (where Japan is the world's dominant producer and exporter), are then reviewed. Adjustment processes and policy responses in long-run declining industries are investigated generally in the third section, while specific policies under the laws of 1978 and 1983 are the focus of the fourth and fifth sections. I then discuss the adjustment processes and policies, as well as future prospects, under the assistance laws of 1987 and 1988. Finally, I explore implications of those policies for international trade and trade policies.[1]

Overview

Employment in several manufacturing sectors has declined year by year since 1970, aggravated by the first oil crisis. Thus, higher oil prices shrank energy-intensive and petroleum-intensive sectors, such as aluminum smelting and petrochemicals. Shipbuilding faced serious excess capacity due to a drastic decline in demand for tankers and the request by other ship-exporting countries that Japan reduce its exports. The rise of wage rates in dollar terms added to the difficulties.

Table 9.2 gives a breakdown of employment adjustment. In terms of regular employment (that is, full-time "permanent" workers at firms with 30 + employees), overall manufacturing continued to absorb labor during 1977–86, but there was significant shuffling. In the period 1977–86, textiles reduced employment by 25%, lumber and wood products by 42%. Earlier growth sectors such as iron and steel, chemicals, and transport equipment contracted employment by 19, 9, and 4%. In contrast, electrical machinery expanded employment 47% (493,000), accounting for more than the total increase of manufacturing employment in this period.

Table 9.3 focuses on selected declining or stagnant industries. Textiles, particularly spinning and woven-fabric mills, reduced employment more drastically than apparel and some downstream sectors. Iron smelting accounted for almost all the employment reduction in iron and steel, and (because other subsectors added workers) more than all of the overall decline before 1982. The shipbuilding subsector of transport

1. This paper extends into the 1980s the discussion of adjustment assistance in Sekiguchi and Horiuchi (1984). For the definition of long-run and short-run declines, readers should refer to the Introduction to this volume. Here long-run decline means the industry in question has lost international competitiveness under normal conditions, while a short-run decline means the industry is in "trouble" due to temporary causes and is expected to be competitive again, when normal conditions prevail.

Table 9.2. Employment by Sector (in thousands)

1977	1982	Change '77–82	1986	Change '82–86	Industry
17,766	19,707	1,942	20,235	528	all industry covered
72	62	– 10	54	– 8	mining
1,224	1,390	166	1,310	– 80	construction
7,211	7,368	157	7,615	247	manufacturing
2,477	2,875	398	2,992	117	wholesale & retail trade[1]
951	1,043	92	1,046	3	finance & insurance
78	81	3	85	4	real estate
2,227	2,306	79	2,136	– 170	transport & communications
218	247	29	230	– 17	public utilities
3,308	4,336	1,028	4,767	431	services

Manufacturing Industries

648	720	72	767	47	foods & tobacco
455	384	– 71	343	– 41	textiles
298	299	1	293	– 6	apparel
145	105	– 40	84	– 21	lumber & wood products
119	113	– 6	106	– 7	furniture & fixture
194	177	– 17	180	3	pulp and paper
273	276	3	289	13	printing & publishing
480	444	– 36	439	– 5	chemical products
49	47	– 2	41	– 6	petroleum & coal products
126	126	0	124	– 2	rubber products
32	33	1	26	– 7	leather products
323	307	– 16	289	– 18	ceramic & clay products
419	376	– 43	338	– 38	iron & steel
154	151	– 3	155	4	non-ferrous metals
401	418	17	413	– 5	fabricated metals
668	708	40	721	13	machinery
1,059	1,282	223	1,552	270	electric machinery
889	859	– 30	854	– 5	transportation equipment
206	242	36	271	29	precision machinery
262	303	41	328	25	miscellaneous

Data are thousands of regular (ie, full-time, permanent) employees on December 31 at establishments with 30 or more employees. Sum may not equal total due to rounding.
    1. Wholesale and retail trade in 1986 includes restaurants and bars.
Source: Rodo-sho 1977, 1982, 1987

Table 9.3. Employment in Selected Declining Industries (in thousands)

1977	1982	Change '77–82	1986	Change '82–86	Industry
					textiles
122	98	−24	81	−17	spinning
85	71	−14	62	−9	woven fabric
96	98	2	91	−7	knitting
72	69	−3	63	−6	dyeing & finishing
80	48	−32	46	−2	other
					chemical products
114	107	−7	107	0	industrial organic chemicals
64	50	−14	45	−5	chemical fibers
302	287	−15	287	0	other
					others
58	51	−7	43	−8	millwork & plywood
90	80	−10	76	−4	pulp & paper mills
114	114	0	105	−9	cement & hydraulic
210	161	−49	139	−22	iron smelting
54	55	1	62	7	electric wire & cable
229	156	−73	110	−46	shipbuilding & repairing
1,308	1,110	−198	984	−126	total
		−15		−11	change as a percentage of prior period employment

Number of regular (ie, full-time, permanent) employes on December 31 at establishments with 30 or more employes.
Source: Rodo-sho 1977, 1982, 1987.

equipment shrank employment by 119,000 in the 1977–86 period, indicating other subsectors (motor vehicles, mostly) expanded. All this suggests industry composition underwent a significant change because of the appreciation of the yen, increases in wage rates, and other factors such as the hike of petroleum prices.

To confront the changing circumstances, the Japanese government enacted a set of adjustment assistance laws in 1978. Assistance for large corporations was assigned to MITI (the Ministry of International Trade and Industry); that for labor (through assistance to depressed industries and to depressed regions) to the Ministry of Labor; and assistance to small-scale firms in depressed regions, to the Agency for Small and Medium Enterprises (ASME) under MITI. As it was assumed adjustment should be completed in several years, most of the 1978 laws were time limited, effective for just five years.

By industry, the law for assistance to large corporations covered 14 sectors including aluminum smelting, shipbuilding, and textiles. Because small firms faced crises not only because of the difficulties of large corporations (for which they often were subcontractors) but also through such arrangements as 200–mile ocean economic zones, assistance through ASME covered a broader spectrum of industries and regions. So did the assistance to workers.

By 1983, when the old laws expired, new declining sectors had emerged in addition to those specified by the preceding laws. These included petrochemicals, which the second oil crisis had caused to lose competitiveness. The yen remained relatively undervalued until 1985, partly because of an overvalued US dollar, and this helped many industries survive, if not prosper, by exporting to the United States and places with currencies pegged to the dollar, such as Hong Kong. However, in late 1985 the yen started appreciating, reaching a new peak in the 120s in 1987. Thus, several new sectors became eligible to receive adjustment assistance. Besides petrochemicals, these included cement, sugar refining, and various non-ferrous metals. Most of the industries that had received assistance under the 1978 law remained eligible. Assistance to workers, including through employers, as well as aid to depressed regions, was further increased.

One characteristic of the new laws was that assistance became anticipatory and preventive of crises—encouraging R&D investment and business mergers (to avoid defaults on bank loans) and the like. On the labor front, training workers before they were displaced was more generously subsidized, and new employers of those displaced also received a generous subsidy. Job conversion, the movement of workers out of declining into growing industries, was also subsidized. Aid to small companies was geared to encouraging those in declining industries to enter new businesses, and incentives for firms to invest in depressed regions were also provided.

As the 1983 laws were again time limited, mostly to five years, they were to be revised in 1988. MITI drafted a new law, enacted in December 1987, which specified equipment that should be scrapped. Equipment in the steel industry was thus targeted, as were things used in industries that previously had not received assistance, including electric wire and mining machinery. Many of the sectors that had been receiving adjustment assistance did not have items on the list, which implies some survived without assistance and some faded away.

The foregoing description of adjustment assistance only refers to long-run declining sectors—more precisely, to sectors predicted to fade away in the long run. There is also assistance to industries felt to be facing a temporary decline for such reasons as an overshooting of the yen's exchange rate or temporary restrictions on exports at an importing country's request. Under such circumstances, domestic supply often exceeds domestic demand plus export demand, and producers try to survive by shifting resources to other uses temporarily. It is presumed that supply capacity is not excessive under normal conditions.

Calling such adjustment "intra-industry" adjustment, the Japanese government actively intervened in investment allocation and control of production in the 1950s and '60s. Obviously such interventions were not always effective. When the domestic market was separated from the international market, intervention worked if the government held some leverage—such as allocation of financial resources and import quotas. Cut-throat competition among domestic producers was often called "excessive competition" (*kato kyoso*) by some industrialists and bureaucrats and was used for justifying intervention.

While no pecuniary incentive was given directly to producers who accepted production cuts and other elements of intra-industry adjustment, the Japanese government granted exemption from the antitrust law's general prohibition of cartel formation. These were called "recession cartels" and have been legal since 1953. Although the institutional circumstances changed significantly, particularly as trade liberalization received more emphasis, many industries resorted to recession cartels during periods when "excess" supply led to price falls. Thus, many were formed after the second oil crisis. The number of recession cartels has declined in the late 1980s. The cartels allocated production cuts among cartel members, usually for three to nine months, hoping product prices would recover in that time.

INTRA-INDUSTRY ADJUSTMENT AND RECESSION CARTELS

Until the mid 1980s, recession cartels were considered a way to reduce the cost of adjustment within an industry where existing capacity was expected to be fully used under normal conditions. They were introduced in 1953 as an exception to the general prohibition of cartel actions in the Antitrust Law of Japan.[2]

Two conditions are required for a recession cartel to be allowed: a

2. Article 24–3 of the Antitrust Law permits certain joint actions by producers for overcoming a recession. At the same time, "rationalization cartels" are allowed under certain conditions to help joint actions to reduce production costs and for technological innovation (Article 24–4). There are also "designated cartels," discussed later, that provide for reduction of industry-wide capacity. They are created under adjustment assistance laws.

large number of producers face a crisis of default on their debts because product prices persist below average costs, and the immediate difficulty cannot be overcome by each individual firm's efforts at cost reduction. When the Fair Trade Commission (FTC) acknowledges the conditions exist, producers can take such joint actions as restricting the level of production or sales and the use of productive equipment or, when production control is difficult because of technical reasons, in effect collude to raise prices.

When the FTC permits joint action, the cartel must (1) not go beyond the target, (2) not unduly hurt the interests of consumers and other enterprises, (3) not unduly discriminate against some producers, and (4) not unduly restrict participation in and exit from the cartel. If there is an objection by consumers to the FTC's decision to approve a cartel or a request by producers to form a cartel, the FTC must hold a hearing, which is open to the public. The FTC also must consult with the Minister in charge (normally MITI's), although the FTC retains the final authority to disapprove a cartel.

While this description may be adequate from a legal point of view, there are a number of ambiguities from an economic one. For instance, if entry and exit are unrestricted, the effectiveness of joint action is limited and the cartel therefore will not achieve the goal stated in the law. If there are factors that implicitly force the majority of producers to participate, the cartel works. As there were high tariffs and non-tariff barriers in the 1960s, a joint action cutting production used to lead to a recovery of price for the producers. However, in the wake of the reduction of official barriers beginning in the 1970s, anti-recession cartels generally are much less effective.

Actually, MITI tried in the 1950s and '60s to control fixed investment as well as production levels when domestic supply exceeded demand so significantly as to trigger defaults on loans. A recession cartel was considered a short-run rescue. One school of economists criticized MITI's intervention in investment allocation, arguing that "excessive competition," which MITI used to justify intervention, was in fact an *effect* of interventions. An influential, representative example of this school is Ryutaro Komiya (1975), who actively criticized MITI's intervention policies in the 1960s. They argued as follows:

1. Because of investment allocation by MITI, manufacturers rushed to invest when allowed, which, in turn, led to building excess capacity.
2. Firms could expect a rescue through joint-action when excess capacity appeared, which encouraged their capacity expansion.
3. Since investment used to be allocated under MITI guidance, based on

existing market share or the like, it was advantageous for manufacturers to expand capacity to obtain a larger share of the investment allocation.

The effectiveness of such interventions depended on various conditions, however. Leader manufacturers tended to follow the guidance, but aggressive followers often successfully refused. Many examples are found in the steel industry in the 1960s. The steel industry formed a cartel in the late 1950s and early '60s to resist price declines during recession periods. Miwa (1984) considers this was de facto administrative guidance by MITI and concludes that, because MITI did not have effective leverage, the guidance was ineffective. (Also see Krause and Sekiguchi 1976.)

Ito, Kiyono, Okuno, and Suzumura (1984) evaluated cartel actions in an attempt to find ways to reduce the social cost of "excessive competition." Using game theory, they found situations where exit by any individual firm was unlikely to be in the exiting firm's interest, but exit by some firm was in society's interest. They thus argue that government intervention or joint action leading to exit, with compensation from those staying in the industry, can be desirable from a societal standpoint. But they are skeptical that in practice intervention will in fact achieve such a result. In industries with only a very few manufacturers, such as aircraft, their model probably applies. There is some question as to the relevance of their assertion to other actual cases, however.

Even in situations where Ito et al's illustration is relevant, two problems arise. One is allocative efficiency and the other is distributive equity. If temporary overcapacity exists, less efficient producers should exit first (temporary exit in this case) on efficiency grounds. When such an action is against the will of the player, the cost of temporary exit should be shared with the other players on equity grounds. In the following case studies, I focus on these two aspects. Ito et al ignored the foreign sector when they showed a case for government interventions and cartel actions. So I seek to clarify the external environment's impact on the effectiveness of cartel actions.

Table 9.4 shows recession cartels formed during the 1981–82 recession. They tend to be short-lived—three to nine months—but sometimes they were repeatedly established and dissolved, which suggests the ineffectiveness of such responses. (Also, because the FTC's published data are generally only for fiscal yearend, cartels were sometimes dissolved only to be re-established in the new year.) In any case, cartel actions, although considered exceptional, tended to last longer than MITI and the participants originally expected.

Recession cartel use has declined significantly from the 1950s to the

Table 9.4. Recession Cartels During the 1981–82 Recession

Industry	Number of Firms	Joint Action	Period of Existence (all begin in 1981)	Total Duration (in months)
yarn[1]	79	S	May 01–Jun 30	
	79	S	Jul 01–Sep 30	5
kraft paper	8	S	Jun 06–Aug 31	
	9	S	Sep 06–Sep 31	
	9	S	Nov 08–Dec 31	7
coated paper	11	O	Jun 21–Aug 31	
	11	S	Sep 06–Nov 30	
	11	S	Dec 15–1982 Feb 15	8
high-quality paper	13	same as coated paper		8
polyethylene	13	P	Aug 01–Oct 31	
	13	P	Nov 08–1982 Jan 31	
	13	P	1982 Feb 11–Mar 31	7
vinyl chloride	20	P S	May 01–Aug 31	
	20	P S	Sep 01–Oct 31	
	20	P S	Nov 28–1982 Feb 28	9
fibers[1]	9	P	Dec 25–1982 Mar 31	3
ethylene	12	P	1982 Oct 16– 1983 Mar 31	6
glass board[1]	11	P	Aug 15–Oct 31	3
asbestine slate	26	P	1982 Nov 01– 1983 Jan 31	3

Joint actions: P = production cut; O = reduction in operating days per month; S = machines sealed. Under P, firms agree to specific production levels, which they can achieve as they see fit; this makes it the least efficiency-distorting joint action and also the most stringent. O and S limit capacity use, but do not directly limit the amount the firm can produce. O does this by setting a specific number of days the firm can operate, S by sealing specific machines. See the case study in the text on kraft paper for an example of how these actions were implemented.

1. Made of discontinuous fibers. Used by textile industry.

Source: Kosei Torihiki Iinkai 1982

'80s. Whether they were effective or not actually depended on market conditions. Joint-reduction of production is not effective in raising prices if foreign supply is elastic. In this regard, the institutional setting since the 1970s differs from that in the 1950s and '60s. If entry and exit are unrestricted, as the Law requires, when foreign supply is inelastic, performance also depends on how large a market share the participants occupy.

Let us look in more detail at two cartels: kraft paper and shipbuilding. (The following summarizes a larger study, Sekiguchi 1985.) The kraft paper industry was competing against less expensive foreign products, and Japan's import share in the world market was less than 4% in 1981. Shipbuilding had a recession cartel for 20 months from August 1979 through March 1981. Japan's shipbuilding industry in 1978 held a 48% market share in world trade, and thus represents a "large country" exporting case.

Recession Cartel in Kraft Paper

This industry faced a demand decline not only from foreign competition but also because plastic bags (made from ethylene) were emerging as a strong substitute, and new modes of grain transportation, not using bags, were spreading. The 10 largest producers, with 98% of total domestic production, formed a recession cartel covering November 1978 through April 1979. Then, from June to December 1981, they established three recession cartels almost consecutively for roughly seven months in total. For convenience, let us call the 1978–79 one the "first cartel" and the 1981 ones the "second cartel." The first cartel included 10 companies. At the outset of the second, 8 joined; a 9th joined later.

The joint action of the first cartel was to reduce output by restricting operating days to 17–21 per month. The range reflected the capacity of machines, those with higher capacity being assigned a larger reduction in operating days. Allocation of production cuts was managed by a working committee of cartel members. The committee sealed machines to ensure the reductions.

The number of participants in the second cartel fell to eight at the outset because one producer had gone bankrupt (thus exiting the industry) and another refused to join, though it joined later. The method for reducing output was similar to that under the first cartel, though the reductions were more stringent (operating days per month were set at 11.5 to 16). Because two other categories of paper products were also subject to production cuts this time, it became easier to prevent diversion of machine use for secretly breaking the agreements.

When we compare price behavior before and after formation of the first cartel, however, it is unclear whether the cartel was effective. It is true production was reduced substantially, and domestic prices hit bottom after the cartel was formed. But it is also true that import prices had started rising before implementation of the cartel. While the domestic price had been some 25% higher than CIF plus distribution costs in 1977 and 1978, the gap disappeared from December 1978 through April 1980. Thus, despite the cartel, the domestic price was determined primarily by the international price. This was a natural result, if imports of foreign kraft paper were not restricted. By April 1980 prices had recovered to the level at the end of 1977, but this was largely attributable to the rise in international prices and the depreciation of the yen taking place from the autumn of 1978 till the end of the period under discussion.

From April 1980 till January 1981, the domestic price remained high, some 13% above CIF plus distribution costs. As imports increased and domestic prices dropped in early 1981, the second cartel was formed. Domestic prices rose while import prices continued to decline. Even after the cartel was dissolved, domestic prices enjoyed a large margin over CIF plus distribution costs, at least until the start of 1984, though both domestic and import prices came down steadily. Thus, the price behavior of kraft paper through and after the second cartel is a puzzle. The rise in domestic prices against a decline of import prices suggests implicit import restriction, but imports increased two-fold during the cartel period. The gap between the two prices may reflect difference in product categories.

There is a Japanese Association of Paper Importers in which distributors, as well as almost all large manufacturers (including foreign joint ventures), participate. Such close connections among producers and distributors might have meant pressure on the latter not to increase imports at the time of cartel implementation (see Sekiguchi and Matsumura 1985).

Recession Cartel in the Shipbuilding Industry

As world demand for large ships shrank drastically after the first oil crisis and OECD countries requested Japan reduce its market share, most shipbuilders faced substantial excess capacity. This, in turn, led producers to cut prices. Large shipbuilding companies had significantly diversified their activities before the oil crisis, which was fortunate, because among the 60 biggest shipbuilding companies, the number with a net loss from shipbuilding increased to 25 in 1977 and to 43 in 1978. The number of firms exiting the industry reached 24 in 1977 and was 10 in 1978, mostly small companies. In the face of such distress, shipbuilding was a specified industry in the 1978 law. However, while it accepted assistance under the new law, it did not resort to a "designated cartel" (discussed later). Instead, a recession cartel was the principal means of reducing capacity and curtailing production.

The shipbuilding industry is supervised by the Ministry of Transportation (MOT), not by MITI, and had repeatedly curtailed production under administrative guidance by MOT. The price effect had been significant as the industry was a strong exporter, and had no competitive foreign supply coming into the domestic market. Because the FTC publicly suspected such administrative guidance had violated the Antitrust Law, MOT's guidance was switched to creating a recession cartel in August 1979 to solve the problems of excess capacity.

This made the situation of capacity reduction in shipbuilding a little confusing. Shipbuilders formed a recession cartel for 20 months covering August 1979 through March 1981. Larger manufacturers bore a larger share of reductions in both operating ratios and capacity. Using the peak of 1973–75 as the base, the 7 largest firms' operating rates were set at 34%; the middle 17's at 45%, and the smaller 16's at 49%. The smallest firms did not join the cartel. Targeted and actual capacity scrapping are shown in Table 9.5.

While producers could in principle opt to stay out, all manufacturers above a certain size participated. This cartel had clear sanctions: a company that refused monitoring had to pay a penalty of up to ¥10

Table 9.5. Shipbuilding Industry: Capacity Reductions, 1978 through March 1980

Firm-size Category:					
Largest	*Middle*	*Smaller*	*Other*	*Total*	
7	17	16	21	61	number of firms
5,690	2,890	790	400	9,770	capacity[1]
Percent of Category's Capacity to be Scrapped					
40	30	27	15	35	target
39	36	32	13	37	achieved

1. In thousand "compensated gross registered tons."
Among firms equipped to build vessels over 10,000 gross tons, large firms are those producing over 1 million gross tons annually; medium produce over 100 thousand; small produce less. Other firms are those not included elsewhere that can produce a 5,000 GT vessel.
Source: Compiled from Yonezawa (1984 p 441, table 4), which is based on data in the Un'yu Hakusho [Transport White Paper] for 1980. The source provides absolute numbers plus the number of yards before and after closures (50 of 138 yards were closed).

million; a firm producing more than allowed had to pay up to ¥100 thousand per gross ton of standard quality freighter for the portion exceeding allocated production.

Because there are many subcontractors in this industry supplying parts to large firms, production reductions by large builders reduces demand for the products of subcontractors. Therefore, the smallest firms, although exempted from the cartel's reduction in production, generally also had to reduce production. To assist these subcontractors, the government extended assistance to small firms in specified depressed regions, a topic examined later.

Production curtailment led to a dramatic recovery in the order prices of ships. Prices had fallen some 30% during 1976–78 before the recession cartel was formed, but rose some 55% from the bottom in 1978 to the end of 1981, based on orders received by 33 major shipbuilders. As Japan was and still is a large country in the shipbuilding industry, production reduction through a recession cartel had a significant impact on world prices as well.

There are several reasons why larger firms bore proportionately more of the adjustment than smaller firms. For one, demand for larger ships declined most. A more significant factor affecting burden sharing seems to have been the principle that larger companies should shoulder more of the burden for social and political reasons. The industry consists of large corporations that have diversified their activities and many small firms that are specialized. The larger enterprises could accept a larger reduction in shipbuilding and still be viable companies overall, which was less true of the smaller firms.

Another reason larger companies undertook a disproportionate reduction in production through joint actions seems to relate to their role in industry associations. The individuals heading the associations generally are from the larger firms. To garner support from smaller firms for the association's lobbying efforts, larger firms took a greater share of the cuts.

Summary of the Case Studies

These two case studies clearly show that, when the domestic market is integrated into the international market, joint reduction of production is of minimal use for recovery, especially when the industry is a small, import-competing sector in the international market. Recession cartels can be of some use in the case of a large exporting sector such as Japanese shipbuilding. When the industry declines in the long run, however, a short-run rescue is of limited use. A side effect of such joint actions may be creation of a climate where producers and distributors easily collude for reducing imports.

The actual performance of recession cartels seems to be counter to efficiency improvement if larger manufacturers are more efficient. A recession cartel has never played the role of letting the costly producers exit while the more efficient stay. The arrangement instead protected the weaker at a cost to the stronger at the expense of consumers. Thus it played an income redistribution role.

Even though a recession cartel is non-effective medicine under most circumstances, it may be good politics. As long as the government escapes any fiscal burden, it is less costly to the government. It is consumers who must pay the cost of protection when a recession cartel is effective.

LONG-RUN DECLINE AND ADJUSTMENT ASSISTANCE

In principle, at least from the criterion of economic efficiency, it is better for a nation to move quickly to a new production mix if it is certain an industry is to disappear in the long run because of comparative disadvantage. The only problem is that some factors of production may be unemployed, creating foregone income in the present. Rapid changes in industrial composition can be preferred even in such cases if the time discount rate for the nation is low, so that it highly values future income relative to present income. But in practice the costs of rapid change are often perceived as being greater than the benefits.[3]

What the government can do under such circumstances includes (1) removing barriers hindering factor reallocation among industries by such means as providing economic units with information to stimulate reallocation, providing workers with training for new jobs, and so on; (2) when the need for adjustment results from the availability of less-expensive imports, slowing domestic price changes by means of import restrictions, under the rubric of "safeguards," or giving subsidies to producers in order to maintain employment of production factors; and (3) giving subsidies to growing sectors to absorb those factors displaced in the declining sector.

As the best policy response is to remove the causes for adjustment difficulty directly, removing barriers is the best policy. Subsidies to industries separate the relative prices the producers face from those the consumers face. In this context, distortion is generated in production,

3. Optimal reallocation of resources when there are adjustment costs has been investigated by Lapan (1976), Neary (1982), Mussa (1982), and others. The correspondence between theory and policy implementation is discussed by Sekiguchi and Horiuchi (1984).

but consumption is free from distortion. The effects on the adjustment processes of subsidies under (2) and (3) are the opposite of each other. The former delays, and the latter promotes, adjustment. "Positive adjustment assistance policies," to use OECD terminology, largely fall into categories (1) and (3) in this interpretation of policy objectives and instruments.

In reality, most governments try to facilitate adjustment using all three options. The removing barriers (best) policy is undertaken by many governments, but its effectiveness is limited: partly because of the rigidity of wage rates, unemployment becomes large scale, which works against the policy's sustained implementation. Stimulation of industrial adjustment by means of subsidies to growing industries is in line with changing comparative advantage structure, but again its effectiveness seems limited, and in practice frictional unemployment has actually grown in many countries.

Safeguard mechanisms against imports distorts consumption as well as production, and is inferior to the two other policy options. As far as policy implementation is concerned, however, it is simpler to manage. Ideally, such a safeguard mechanism is put in place for only a specified and fairly short time. If producers judge that within this limited period they will be unable to reduce costs and remain competitive in their existing activities, they will take it as a signal for switching activities. Thus it is the producers themselves who decide whether to stay in or exit from the industry; the government is free from allocating subsidies among producers.

In the dimension of policy implementation, there are many problems. Who can and how does one predict an industry will decline in the long run? The information required to decide the size of subsidies is not available in the real world. Thus, actual policy implementation largely depends on the judgment of bureaucrats, though they may have some means of consulting with industrialists.

Regional allocation of resources is a very important issue. When an industry is a significant aspect of a region's economy, the decline of the industry creates a serious problem for the community. Workers often cannot afford to move away to new jobs, or they often resist doing so. As the budget of the local government depends heavily on activities of specific industries, a drastic shrinkage of an industry often destroys its fiscal base. This, in turn, weakens the local government's capability to assist adjustment.

Japanese policy since the early 1970s has been more oriented to subsidization than overt import restrictions, so it has been characterized as "positive adjustment assistance policy" in OECD terms. Emphasis has been on promoting new industries—option (3) above. This argument is inadequate, however.

Looking into the details of policy instruments, many subsidies, even those to facilitate shifting of employment, might actually have protected declining sectors. Thus, there is little evidence those displaced in declining sectors are employed in growing sectors, so subsidized shifting of employment might have resulted in a mere shuffling among firms within declining sectors. In such cases, policy slows adjustment. When the foreign supply of goods is inelastic, various joint actions among domestic producers through cartels might reduce imports of competing foreign products. Collusion among domestic producers and distributors might thereby play the role of an implicit safeguard mechanism (category 2) even though it was not a public policy.

Generally speaking, the adjustment assistance policy of the Japanese government has been both extremely detailed and subsidy-oriented. At the same time, in some aspects the policy instruments have been bewilderingly complex and even duplicating. Adjustment assistance was sector-specific and ad hoc before 1977, limited essentially to coal mining and textiles. Then, in 1978, adjustment policy became more general as a number of industrial sectors were deemed to have entered a long-run declining phase.[4]

Complication in the policy system is introduced by competition among various government departments, so it is useful to review the general framework and division of labor among ministries before moving to specific policies.

Government organizations involved in adjustment assistance and the division of authority since 1978 are as follows:

Assistance to:	Ministry involved:
large enterprises	MITI
small enterprises	ASME (under MITI)
workers by industry	Ministry of Labor
workers by region	Ministry of Labor

MITI had overseen the growth of manufacturing in earlier periods, as well as supervised and regulated the conduct of enterprises in this sector. Most laws concerning industrial policies have been prepared by MITI

4. For policies before 1977, see Sekiguchi (1976 and 1984, p. 372–76 of English edition). Although declining industries and regions were specified either by laws or by Ministry Ordinances under the laws of 1978, this seems to be for the convenience of policy implementation, because a general description of eligibility might not appeal to potential applicants.

itself. In the sphere of adjustment assistance, MITI focused on assisting larger enterprises. ASME, created specifically to deal with small and medium firms, is an independent agency under the broader umbrella of MITI. These two institutions have promoted industries and assisted adjustment in most manufacturing sectors. As small firms of specific industries sometimes are concentrated in specific regions, ASME tends to promote regional development under the heading of support to small firms.

As for the Ministry of Labor, there is nothing unique to Japan. It has functioned as a supervisor to maintain fair practices in employment, including health and safety standards. It is also engaged in job placement and payment of unemployment insurance benefits. In some cases, other ministries such as Agriculture and Fishery, and Transportation are also involved in adjustment assistance. The former, for example, covers the cocoon and silk industries, and sugar refining; the latter is in charge of shipbuilding.

Mention also should be made of the role of the Fair Trade Commission (FTC). Because the FTC regulates unfair competition and private monopoly, it supervises the conduct of government organizations as well as private firms. When the FTC judges certain administrative guidance violates the Antitrust Law, it often confronts other ministries. Merger and cartel actions recommended by MITI sometimes have provoked objection by the FTC.

The next two sections review policy instruments and the performance of industrial adjustment in the periods 1978–82 and 1983–87. The 1978 laws expired in 1982 and revised laws were enacted in 1983.[5]

ADJUSTMENT ASSISTANCE, 1978–82

As adjustment problems arose in many manufacturing sectors after the first oil crisis, centering around energy-intensive and petroleum-intensive industries, MITI prepared a law for adjustment assistance policy in general. However, it was difficult for the various ministries to coordinate among themselves on an overall law. So in the end, MITI, ASME, and the Ministry of Labor each prepared laws to cover their own bailiwicks—although MITI's Industry Stabilization Law served as the base for the other two. The three laws were enacted in 1978.

5. Many of the laws have the word "temporary" in their full titles; this has been illusory, as is shown by the discussion. Sekiguchi and Horiuchi (1984, p 378 table 2, and p 384 table 5 of the English edition) list details of the 1978 laws. Full titles of the other laws mentioned can be obtained from the author.

Large Firm Assistance

The 1978 Industry Stabilization Law provided MITI with four policy instruments.

1. Either the law or a ministry ordinance specified the industries qualified to receive assistance.
2. MITI's minister could ask manufacturers who needed assistance to submit a "Basic Stabilization Plan" under which producers had to scrap capacity.
3. A Trust Fund for specified depressed industries was created, which guaranteed credit from private financial institutions to firms scrapping capacity.
4. When the Minister recognized it was difficult for producers to achieve targets by themselves, he could recommend producers form a "designated cartel" (*shiji karuteru*) for joint-action capacity reduction, provided the FTC agreed.[6]

There were 14 industrial sectors specified as eligible to receive assistance. The largest single designated industry was shipbuilding, but there were 6 categories of fibers (synthetic and nonsynthetic) which together made textiles the largest overall industry involved. Some of the 14 resorted to cartel actions to scrap capacity, but others did not. Some made use of the Trust Fund for credit guarantees, but others did not. Target and achieved capacity reductions and employment changes are summarized in Table 9.6.

There is no significant difference in the achievement of scrapping goals between those industries where cartel actions were taken and those where they were not. If there is a difference, it is that all industries recommended for (and actually taking) cartel actions made use of the Trust Fund, whereas only shipbuilding resorted to the Fund among those that did not form a designated cartel. Those industries not using the Fund achieved scrapping comparable to that of those using the Fund.

Credit guarantees probably did not appeal to the manufacturers in question, as they used only ¥23.2 billion worth despite the fact the Fund was authorized to ¥100 billion. At ¥14.2 billion, shipbuilding was by far the largest user of the Fund. One reason for the unattractive-

6. Later, Peck et al (1987) called them "indicative cartels." The essence is that the Minister could recommend cartel formation for the purpose of capacity reduction, but producers could refuse. As a matter of fact, however, all industries receiving a recommendation to form a cartel followed it. Because it is politically undesirable to refuse the Minister's recommendation, prior informal consultation probably occurred to secure arrangements before formal steps were taken.

Table 9.6. Industries Designated Under the 1978 Industry Stabilization Law

Employment[1] 1977–81 Decrease			Capacity Reductions[2] (in percent of capacity before scrapping)		Industry (in US SIC sequence)
As a Percent of 1977	Total[3]	At End of 1981[3]	Planned	Achieved by End of 1981	
Eight Industries with Cartel Recommendation[4]					
34	18	15	10	10	worsted yarn
a	a	6	15	14	cardboard
13	16	39	17	22	discontinuous acrylic fiber
16	12	59	19	20	continuous nylon fiber
15	12	69	11	11	continuous polyester fiber
16	10	56	17	18	discontinuous polyester fiber
25	*	*	26	26	ammonia
28	*	*	45	42	urea
16	48	246			total of 8 with cartel
Six Industries Without Cartel Recommendation					
15	11	61	6	4	cotton spinning
10	*	*	20	19	hydrous phosphoric acid
33	*	1	21	21	ferro-silicon
14	5	31	14	13	steel (open hearth and electric furnace only)
43	3	4	32	55	aluminum smelting
30	50	114	35	37	shipbuilding
25	70	212			total of 6 without cartel
20	118	459			total of all 14 industries

Data are for fiscal years ending March 31 of the following year.

1. Employment is in thousands of regular employes, which means full-time, permanent workers at establishments with 30 or more employes.

2. Capacity is in thousand tonnes per year for all industries except shipbuilding, which is in thousand gross tons (at yards with a capacity of more than 5,000 GT per year).

3. In thousands.

4. Joint actions were carried out in all industries where they were recommended. Synthetic fiber industries implemented cartelization under the initial plan, but such action was not recommended under the second plan.

* Less than 1,000. In 1981, employment in urea was 300; in ammonia, 790. In ferro-silicon, employment declined 514, to 1,022. In hydrous phosphoric acid, employment declined 45, to 422.

a. Employment in cardboard increased 2% to 5,960.

Source: Derived from absolute numbers in Sekiguchi and Horiuchi (1984, p 380–82 (tables 3 and 4) of the English edition) which are from data in Kosei Torihiki Jiho #538 (1982 Nov 12) and Kosei Torihiki Kyokai (1982).

ness of credit guarantees under this system might be that the interest-lowering effect of the guarantee was not significant enough to compensate for the unfavorable announcement effects of being a "declining industry" or a "declining enterprise." As commercial banks provided actual financing, it was beyond MITI's ability to arrange low interest loans.

The fiscal cost of adjustment assistance under the 1978 law was only credit guarantees, and many industries did not rely on them, so it is difficult to measure the effects of policy on adjustment performance. However, it seems market forces, not policy, promoted adjustment. The adjustment performance of these 14 industries is detailed in Sekiguchi and Horiuchi (1984, p 380–81 table 3 of the English edition).

Aluminum smelting shrank drastically both in terms of production and employment, with imports more than doubling between 1978 and '81 and production declining by roughly half. Nonetheless, operating ratios remained as low as 59%. In shipbuilding, production recovered in 1981 and a higher operating ratio was achieved, but employment had declined by 50,000 (a 31% decrease) in the same period.

While imports as a percentage of apparent consumption rose for various synthetic fibers, textiles, ferro-silicon, and cardboard, the changes were more modest. Yamazawa (1984) says that in the case of textiles, there may have been informal harassment of importers. Bureaucrats overseeing the textile industry in MITI warned major textile importers to refrain from importation to avoid excess supply. In general, however, other than normal tariffs, there was no acknowledged use of import restrictions as part of adjustment assistance at this time.

Tariffs

To explain the Japanese tariff system, basic rates are described in the Law of Tariffs (1910), which has seldom been revised. Rates for actual application are decided almost every year by the Council on Tariffs. The tariff thus set is called the "temporary" rate. When the Japanese government unilaterally accelerated tariff reductions, it lowered such temporary rates. Since the government has been committed to tariff reductions under GATT, tariffs registered at GATT are called GATT rates and they are applied to GATT member countries if they are lower than the temporary rates. But imports from a non-GATT country will pay the temporary rates even if they are higher than the GATT rates. GSP (General Scheme of Tariff Preference) rates are applied to less developed countries.

Between 1979 and 1983 GATT rates were lowered on most products of the designated industries, but increased for most kinds of yarn and wrought aluminum. Temporary rates were newly instituted or jumped substantially on many products. The result was that rates actually paid by GATT members were higher in 1983 than in 1979 on man-made-fiber yarns and unwrought aluminum, lower or the same on the other items. For non-GATT members, tariffs were higher except for unwrought aluminum. Overall tariff policy became slightly more protective for declining industries. GSP rates were 0% on most of these items in both years.

Worker Assistance

Workers displaced in specified depressed industries and regions received help from the Ministry of Labor. Depressed industries were mostly those listed in the Industry Stabilization Law, with assistance going to workers either directly or through employers. An ordinance of the Ministry of Labor (MOL) enumerated both industries and regions. Among industries MOL included that were not designated by the stabilization law were fishery and fish processing (fish-related industries faced difficulty because of application of a 200–mile economic zone by many coastal nations), plywood, and silk. Thus 40 industrial sectors were covered. As for regions, 44, mostly municipalities, were specified.

By Industry. When a company in a stipulated industry planned to displace more than a specified number of employees (100 or more in total, or 30 or more per month) it had to submit a plan of re-employment to MOL. Actually the plan was received by the head of the Public Employment Stabilization Bureau under the ministry. Once the plan was approved, those about to be displaced were given "Job-Seeker Certificates" (hereafter, job-seeker card). The following assistance was provided card holders.

Workers received a basic subsidy and a training subsidy. Each person got ¥101,000 per month (roughly comparable to the starting salary of a college graduate). Additional subsidies were given for long-distance job seeking activities and for moving to obtain a new job. Thus, assistance to workers was fairly generous. A holder of a job-seeker card was eligible to receive such subsidies directly.

New employers of card holders qualified to receive a subsidy worth ¥16,000 per person per month for training. When the workers were age 45 to 65, new employers were eligible to receive a wage subsidy equivalent to one-fourth of the yearly wage bill. If the employer belonged to the category of small- and medium firms, this subsidy was expanded to one-third of the wage bill. There was also a special wage subsidy for handicapped workers.

By Region. Assistance for regions consisted of four elements. First, those displaced in the specified regions were eligible for extended payment of employment insurance benefits, with additional preferential treatment of aged workers. Second and third, the regions received priority allocation of public works, with job-seeker card holders having preference for the jobs. Fourth, the Public Employment Stabilization Bureau increased its job placement activities. (The Bureau has information on both job seekers and job vacancies, and endeavors to match them. The term "job mediation" is used by the Bureau to describe a placement.)

Assistance to employment adjustment in depressed regions was not assistance to re-employment in manufacturing; rather, it was merely income support to the unemployed and public works to offset unemployment. The budget for employment assistance amounted to ¥10.4 billion for fiscal year 1982. As it was all direct subsidy, the assistance to re-employment was much more significant in money terms than assistance to large firms (which received only a credit guarantee). By industry, workers in the textile and shipbuilding sectors received the largest share of the assistance. The government reported a cumulative 103,200 workers received job-seeker cards from the enactment of the laws through November 1982. Overall unemployment at any one time during the period 1978–82 was just under 1.4 million.

The public works allocated to the depressed regions with priority were reported to have employed a cumulative 2.58 million workdays by the end of November 1982. Considering the average number of unemployed, the contribution of public works to the reduction of unemployment was not significant, however. The law stated at least 40% of the workers employed should be those displaced in the specified regions. Thus, employment effects of public works on those displaced might be 2.58 x 0.4 = 1.02 million workdays—not even one workday per unemployed person.

Small Enterprise Assistance. Generally speaking, policy for small-scale enterprises was much more complicated, as there was and has been constant assistance to such firms independent of declines. This discussion is confined to policies under the 1978 laws.

Many sectors listed in Table 9.6 had many subcontractors, especially in the textile and shipbuilding industries. Besides the overlap from industries designated by the Industry Stabilization Law, fishery and fish processing and plywood manufacturing were covered by the small-industry assistance law. In all, small firms in 7 sectors and 32 regions were selected as eligible for assistance and they received the following assistance.

1. Small firms in the sectors and regions thus specified received a cumulative ¥42.7 billion in emergency loans at an interest rate of 6.1 to 6.6% per annum (market rates were 6.0 to 8.3% at this time) by the end of fiscal 1981. Also, special loans worth ¥1.7 billion for business conversion was extended in the same period. A governmental financial institution which provided credit guarantees for small firms expanded the ceiling of guarantees, with the total reaching ¥18.6 billion.
2. Special reductions of corporate and personal income taxes under this law amounted to ¥2.4 billion in the same period. Subsidies given to invite investment by outside companies in the specified regions amounted to ¥1.5 billion.
3. Repayment of past loans used for modernization of equipment was postponed.

Summary of Policies Under the Laws of 1978

As the pecuniary incentives were small in MITI's policy instruments, the effects of policy appears minimal. Furthermore, there was no significant difference in adjustment performance between cases with and without cartels. The effects of policy on reallocation of workers are unclear because data relevant to measuring the effects have not been published. Nonetheless, the impact appears to have been quite modest.

One point that is clear is that assistance to workers favored those who worked for a large company because job-seeker cards were given only to those displaced as part of a large group. This violates a principle of equal treatment of the unemployed. Although there is no reason why they should receive preferential treatment compared to those displaced from small firms, those laid off by large firms received prior allocation of jobs in public works and were given generous subsidies for various activities.

As regards assistance to small firms in depressed regions, tax relief and emergency loans were provided, though it is impossible to measure the effects, since no data have been published yet. It appears that such adjustment assistance was largely adjustment decelerating rather than accelerating, as it protected small firms damaged by demand decline. Assistance to small firms might have stabilized the economy, but the various emergency measures maintained continued production by inefficient firms. At the same time, stability might have reduced protectionist pressure for import restrictions, but it might also have postponed the replacement of local production by foreign imports.

Adjustment problems reached a peak in 1978–79 as the yen's appreciation was drastic in 1977–78, but problems might have been alleviated thereafter because of the currency's depreciation. Nonetheless, aluminum smelting, textiles, and shipbuilding continued to contract rapidly. The second oil crisis put petrochemicals into difficulty after 1980. Thus, adjustment tasks entered a second phase.

ADJUSTMENT ASSISTANCE, 1983–87

To replace the Industry Stabilization Law, which expired in April 1983, MITI prepared the Structural Improvement Law, emphasizing the importance of anticipating and preventing crises. This law was also to be effective for five years. The most significant policy changes were encouragement of mergers and business cooperation, and subsidization of R&D. The former most directly addressed petrochemicals, which faced serious difficulty after the second oil crisis. The latter was intended to accelerate shifting firms in difficulty into growing industries. The new law also changed the name of the credit guarantee program, because it was recognized the announcement effect of guaranteeing credit for "Specified Depressed Industries" made it more difficult for these enterprises to raise funds to finance programs to change their lines of business.

The offering of incentives for exploring new businesses involved tax breaks (including special treatment of loss carryovers, a special depreciation allowance for newly built equipment, and tax reductions for newly established firms), energy-related subsidies (¥2.2 billion in fiscal 1983 for conversion from oil to coal as an energy source and ¥2.3 billion for R&D for new energy technology), and a small (¥0.46 billion) subsidy for R&D for the "revitalization of industries" (that is, diversification into a growing industry). Investment in new business joined scrapping of facilities in being eligible for preferential finance.

The industries covered by the law were designated either by the law explicitly or by Ministry ordinance in the same way as the 1978 law. The latter procedure can be summarized as follows: On an ongoing basis, committees (organized by industry under the Council on Industrial Structure) consisting of industry, labor union, consumer, and presumably neutral scholar representatives discussed problems facing their industry. When a committee considered the difficulties were serious, it recommended some policy responses. Such industries became candidates for assistance.

As MITI has sections overseeing and monitoring the performance of various industries, communication between MITI and industry associations has always been intense, and this probably helped consensus mak-

Table 9.7. Industries Designated by the 1983 Structural Improvement Law as Eligible to Receive Assistance

Period of Designated Cartel	Other Joint Actions	Industry (in US SIC sequence)
no	DL JP	sugar refining
84 Jun–88 Mar	DL	cardboard
83 Nov–86 Sep	M JR	paper
83 Sep–87 Sep	JS	polyolefin
83 Sep–87 Sep	DL	polyvinylchloride resin
no	DL	styrene
no	DL	viscous fiber
83 Sep–86 Mar	DL	ethylene
no	DL	ethylene oxide
no	DL	ammonia
no	DL	urea
83 Sep–88 Mar	M	chemical fertilizer
no	DL	soluble phosphoric fertilizer
no	DL	wet phosphoric fertilizer
no	DL	hard PVC tube
85 Jan–88 Mar	DL JS	cement
no	JR	high carbonate ferro-chromium
no	none	ferro-nickel
no	none	ferro-silicon
no	none	aluminum
no	none	electric furnace steel
no	JI	electric wire

"No" means a designated cartel was not established. The law expired in March 1988 (the end of fiscal 1987).

Joint actions: DL (division of labor) involves each firm narrowing its product line and then exchanging with other producers in order to provide its customers the firm's original range of products. JI, joint investment; JP, firms allocated production among themselves; JR, joint R&D; JS, joint sales companies established by producers; M, mergers.

Source: Dates and joint actions are as provided the author by Kosei Torihiki Iinkai (Fair Trade Commission) from unpublished data; other data are from MITI (1988).

ing. Under the new law, the Minister of MITI specified 21 industrial sectors (11 continued from the 1978 specification, 10 newly specified) as eligible to receive assistance. Sugar refining was also designated as eligible, under the supervision of the Ministry of Agriculture. Thus, 22 industries were specified in total. The dropping of shipbuilding and the addition of petrochemicals were the major changes in which industries were covered. Designated cartels were formed in 7 of the 22 industries.

Table 9.7 shows their dates and the specific joint actions each of the industries took for adjustment.

Nature of Adjustments

Table 9.8 gives target capacity reductions, capacity actually scrapped by September 1987, and capacity operating ratios in 1982 and 1986. Operating ratios recovered in all but two cases, although the ratio remained low (particularly relative to break-even) in such long-run stagnating industries as electric furnace steel, fertilizer, and cement. The most dramatic adjustment took place in aluminum smelting. While this industry had reduced capacity substantially under the 1978 law, it targeted a further 78% capacity reduction, and actually cut 86%. Nonetheless, the operating ratio continued to decline, going from 40 to 35% in the same period. Firms did not take any joint action to achieve reductions. Aluminum became a single-firm industry in 1987, with its own captive source of cheap hydroelectric power.

Petrochemicals, which were newly specified, took joint actions following MITI guidance, as the FTC retreated substantially from regulating actions that reduced competition. Some 20 to 36% of capacity was targeted for scrapping. Actual performance varied, however. Some sectors achieved their targets, and others did not. Most petrochemical subsectors recovered rapidly in the mid-1980s, due partly to a recovery of demand and partly to an appreciation of the yen, which reduced the cost of imported oil. As operating ratios recovered, reaching to the high 90%s in some cases, firms abandoned plans for reducing capacity.

As for joint actions, most of these petrochemical sectors narrowed their product lines, becoming more specialized in specific goods, and exchanged products. In the case of polyolefins, firms established joint-selling companies. (The principal polyolefins are polyethylene and polypropylene, which are basic intermediates in an extremely wide range of products, including thermoplastics—food-wrap type films, molding, pipes, etc—and synthetic fibers—mainly for fish nets, carpets, and upholstery. See British Petroleum 1977, p 380–83, 399–400, 416.)

These joint-selling arrangements, including product exchanges, were in general made within business groups. Because there are quite a number of business groups in Japan, it follows that joint-selling might not have changed the situation significantly regarding either competition reduction or cost reduction. In other words, the arrangements typically involved product lines that were more complementary than overlapping, as different firms within a business group only occasionally compete directly. One purpose was thus to cut marketing costs. Another, pro-

Table 9.8. Capacity Reduction under the 1983 Structural Improvement Law
(in thousand tonnes per year and percents)

Capacity Reduction				Operating Ratio[3]		
'88 Jun Target		Actual '87 Sep				Industry
%[1]	absolute	absolute	%[2]	'82	'86	(in US SIC sequence)
26	1000	630	63	57	65	sugar refining
20	1540	850	55	62	86	cardboard
11	950	890	94	72	91	paper
22	900	850	94	65	98	polyolefin
21	490	450	92	64	92	polyvinylchloride resin
26	470	340	73	70	98	styrene
15	8	32	66	79	84	viscous fiber
36	2290	2020	88	56	93	ethylene
27	200	120	61	64	80	ethylene oxide
20	660	1120	170	60	80	ammonia
36	830	860	103	47	58	urea
13	810	880	109	64	71	chemical fertilizer
32	240	210	88	47	54	soluble phosphoric fertilizer
17	130	150	112	65	74	wet phosphoric fertilizer
19	116	116	100	62	77	hard PVC tube
23	30,000	31,000	103	62	69	cement
10	57	138	242	47	50	high carbonate ferro-chromium
12	51	48	94	56	68	ferro-nickel
14	50	57	114	53	40	ferro-silicon
14	3800	2380	63	75	80	electric furnace steel
78	1290	1420	110	40	35	aluminum
14	86	86	100	68	85	electric wire

1. Percentage of 1983 capacity targeted to be scrapped by 1988 Jun.
2. Percentage of targeted capacity scrapped by 1987 Sep. Thus, a number over 100 indicates more than the targeted capacity was scrapped.
3. Operating ratios are for the fiscal years shown (ends March of following year).
Source: MITI 1988

moted by MITI, was to strengthen ties within business groups, which reduce opportunities for foreign suppliers to sell in Japan. Detailed information about the performance of joint-selling is not available, however; the foregoing is based on discussions I have had with MITI officials.

Changes in production and trade levels between 1982 and 1986 are shown in Table 9.9. It appears there is no significant difference in performance between industries that did and those that did not form cartels. Although the cartelized industries are toward the top of the list ranked by recovery of physical output, this is more likely due to demand recovery, as imports increased even faster than output in 5 of the 7 cases.

As far as import penetration is concerned, no strong patterns emerge. In some sectors, penetration was nil—generally areas where costs are easily passed on to the ultimate consumer, for example because they are related to agriculture. Industry associations may have created barriers to foreign products trying to penetrate the domestic market of the seven industries with negligible or no imports. For whatever reasons, industries choosing designated cartels typically were facing little import competition—in 1982 imports provided less than 5% of domestic demand, except for ethylene, where import share was 10%. Although industries choosing not to form such cartels included several that faced no imports, those that did have import competition generally faced more competition from imports than did cartelized industries.

Designated cartels did not prevent imports from rising significantly: the market share of imports increased by about half in 3 industries and (because of the small initial share) astronomically for cement. On the other hand, in 2 of the 6 cases that had imports, imports lost market share, although it is not clear this is attributable to the existence of the cartels. For the 10 non-cartelized industries that had any import competition, by 1987 imports had gained market share in 8 of them. The other 2 saw import share end about where it began—though in one case (ferro-nickel) share was declining after rising during the period.

Factors such as the closeness of producer-distributor networks undoubtedly had more to do with how well imports did than presence or absence of a cartel. Also important was the strength of the production base. Where the output was a commodity input to other firms and Japan had a conspicuously uncompetitive base, users were able to lobby policy makers for more imports. Aluminum and some other metals are examples of this—although aluminum imports actually had lower market share during most of the period than at the end.

The fact the yen's exchange rate was relatively undervalued against the US dollar until the autumn of 1985, might have reduced import pressure, though the economy grew relatively fast during 1982–85. Import tariffs were generally lower in 1988 than in 1983. For GATT countries, the only exception among the industries being discussed was corrugated paper and paperboard, where the rate more than doubled (to 9.6%). For non-members of GATT, unwrought aluminum also had a

Table 9.9. Output, Trade, and Employment in Industries Designated under the 1983 Law

1986's Physical Volume as a Percentage of 1982's			1987 Nov Number of		Industry (in US SIC sequence)
Output	Imports	Exports	Firms	Workers (thousands)	
94	—	54	24	2.4	sugar refining
138	100	279	64	13.1	cardboard *
121	211	107	50	38.1	paper *
129	185	115	20	2.5	polyolefin *
123	164	662	15	2.0	PVC resin *
137	262	226	8	0.3	styrene
83	183	60	8	1.3	viscous fibers
123	163	160	11	1.0	ethylene *
103	164	220	6	0.3	ethylene oxide
93	—	—	10	0.5	ammonia
66	23	20	5	0.1	urea
94	—	76	48	1.9	chemical fertilizers *
83	105	—	8	0.2	soluble phosphoric fertilizers
92	89	0	10	0.3	wet phosphoric fertilizers
101	—	50		1.715	hard PVC tubing
88	nm	41	23	14.5	cement *
85	172	100	7	0.6	high carbonate ferro-chromium
99	119	47	4	0.6	ferro-nickel
51	133	100	7	0.3	ferro-silicon
38	88	60	1	1.6	aluminum
110	—	44	53	21.2	electric furnace steel
93	—	27	47	8.5	electric wire

* Industry forming a designated cartel

nm Not meaningful (large increase from a very small base)

There were negligible imports of refined sugar, and no imports of chemical fertilizers (as narrowly defined), ammonia, hard PVC tubing, electric furnace steel, and electric wire. There were no ammonia or soluble phosphoric fertilizer exports, and no wet phosphoric fertilizer exports after 1983.

tariff rate increase (from 0 to 1%). The Japanese government declared in 1986 and 1987 that restructuring the economy to import more was a major policy goal, so tariff increases were not an option for the government.

Worker Assistance

Elements of the two 1978 laws for worker assistance were integrated into one law—the Employment Assistance Law of 1983—in July 1983. Help for small firms and communities became more anticipatory, by providing subsidies for diversification into other industries and for promotion of R&D for new businesses. Other types of help were essentially the same as under the 1978 laws, but subsidy levels were increased.

A generous subsidy was provided employers who retrained those who were to be displaced: two-thirds of the wage bill was subsidized for six months (three-fourths in the case of small firms undertaking the same job). Furthermore, when new employers recruited workers receiving such assistance, they were eligible for a wage subsidy of one-fourth of the wage bill for a year; one-third when the new employer was a small firm. The amounts of direct assistance paid to individual workers who received training, sought new jobs, or moved to new working places was also increased.

Table 9.10 shows the number of workers receiving job-seeker cards by industry. During fiscal 1983 through the end of November 1987, the total number of workers who received cards was 63,738, with most coming from shipbuilding and textiles. The number of recipients drastically increased beginning in fiscal 1986 when a rapid appreciation of the yen took place.

As far as shifting employment to growing industries was concerned, the government placed greater importance on assistance through enterprises. This applies to both industry-based and region-based assistance, although the nature of assistance was different between the two. Because there are regions where the main industrial activities have been declining, assistance to regions tended to continue for a longer period than aid to industries. It was not a temporary phenomenon that a specific region stagnated. In such a region, what was needed was not assistance to adjustment but policies for regional development, which should be another matter. In fact, in the 1987–92 period, assistance to employment promotion in specified regions has become a policy independent of adjustment assistance.

Although the law was integrated into one, adjustment assistance was provided under two headings—depressed industries and depressed re-

Table 9.10. Employment Assistance by Industry, 1983–87

Programs[1]					Job-Seeker Cards Issued[2]					Industry
1983	'84	'85	'86	'87*	1983	'84	'85	'86	'87*	
10	2	1	—	—	106	24	24	—	—	sugar refining
0	6	2	3	1	0	47	22	0	35	processing of fishery products
8	8	11	8	6	57	234	166	159	217	silk
179	119	74	113	27	1945	760	1027	1616	370	other textiles
62	12	8	8	4	492	136	38	44	15	dyeing
100	79	43	54	15	996	1549	878	912	229	timber & plywood
2	4	3	2	—	202	28	30	28	—	cardboard
0	0	—	—	—	0	1	—	—	—	petrochemical
—	—	0	8	4	—	—	0	158	6	rayon & acetate
4	0	—	—	—	82	79	—	—	—	synthetic fibers
1	2	2	4	—	3	0	18	13	—	fertilizer
1	6	1	2	1	20	64	13	1	12	oil refining
33	3	0	27	15	851	196	11	466	514	cement & bricks
5	2	—	12	4	132	4	—	437	15	non-ferrous metal
48	13	11	40	77	1446	426	230	1248	1497	steel
0	2	0	17	1	54	3	29	119	157	aluminum
—	1	—	—	—	—	1	—	—	—	electric wires
96	56	294	759	173	869	1501	3334	17472	6394	shipbuilding
42	98	35	176	169	902	1857	423	4273	6021	others
591	413	485	1,233	497	8,157	6,910	6,243	26,946	15,482	total

1. Number of programs in effect at some time during the fiscal year.
2. Number of cards issued during fiscal year.
* To end of 1987 Nov.
Source: Ministry of Labor, unpublished data.

gions. Generally speaking, data on implementation are fragmentary and not well prepared for evaluation of the policies in the case of the Employment Assistance Programs under the Ministry of Labor. Moreover, most of the data have not been published, so it is difficult to evaluate policy effects. This also applies to assistance to small enterprises in depressed regions. The Ministry has made some data available to me; they are in Tables 9.11 through 9.14.

Comparing Tables 9.11 and 9.12, subsidies through employers were

Table 9.11. Assistance to Workers in Specified Depressed Industries, Fiscal 1983–87

1983	1984	1985	1986	1987[1]	Cumulative[2]	
Number of Programs Accepted						
434	413	485	1,234	394	2,960	
Job-seeker Cards Issued (including to handicapped workers)						
5,686	6,833	6,191	26,741	11,749	58,200	
Number of People With Cards Who Got Jobs						
4,829	5,779	3,423	9,826	8,088	31,945	
Job-seeker Cardholders Age 45–65						
1,381	2,004	1,723	1,247	1,090	7,445	number
378	556	497	381	458	2,270	payments[3]
Re-employment[4]						
1,208	1,518	1,065	203	1,734	5,728	recipients
114	140	98	18	169	539	payments[3]
Extended Insurance Employment Benefits[5]						
2,553	2,105	1,164	2,695	3,731	12,248	recipients
839	834	436	912	1,258	4,279	payments[3]

1. Through 1987 September.
2. For the period 1983 April through 1987 September.
3. Total payments in million yen.
4. The Ministry of Labor refers to its training and job preparation program as "re-employment." Includes per diems for those in training, as well as several other programs.
5. Extensions of up to 90 days for those 40 or older; 60 days if younger.
Source: Ministry of Labor, unpublished data

Table 9.12. Subsidies for Firms Employing Workers from Specified Depressed Industries, Fiscal 1983–87 (in million yen except as noted)`

1983	1984	1985	1986	1987[1]	Cumulative[2]	
Total Subsidies						
1,881	2,054	2,035	4,585	3,702	14,257	
For Payments by Previous Employer to Laid-off Workers						
852	955	773	1,877	1,256	5,713	
Training[3]						
938	427	641	1,653	1,147	4,806	subsidy
172	76	106	261	157	772	days (thousands)
Leasing Workers to Others (shuko)[4]						
68	142	176	720	686	1793	subsidy
313	496	448	2,054	2,164	5,475	persons
Job Placement[5]						
15	524	441	323	606	1,909	subsidy
40	1,485	1,043	706	1,082	4,356	persons eligible

1. Through 1987 September.
2. For the period 1983 April through 1987 September.
3. Paid to either current or new employer. New employers received up to ¥18,700 per worker per month for up to six months. Current employer receives two-thirds (three-fourths if a small firm) of wage bill plus ¥1,500 per day. If the training by the current employer is for job conversion, the subsidy is three-fourths (four-fifths if a small firm).
4. Two-thirds (three-fourths if a small firm) of wage bill.
5. Several programs subsidizing wages of new hires, as well as a payment of about one month's wage for each new hire.
Source: Ministry of Labor, unpublished data

significantly larger than direct assistance to workers in depressed industries. As the total assistance to firms in depressed industries was ¥14.3 billion during the period April 1984 through September 1987, subsidies through employers were more industry-based than region-based. In contrast, direct assistance to workers in depressed industries, at ¥7.1 billion, was much smaller than subsidies of ¥27.1 billion to workers in the depressed regions. This appears simply to reflect the fact there were fewer enterprises in depressed regions through which to implement assistance, and therefore, the government had to provide income support

Table 9.13. Subsidies for Firms Employing Workers from Specified Depressed Regions, Fiscal 1983–86 (in million yen except as noted)

1983	1984	1985	1986	Cumulative[1]	
Total Subsidies					
1,747	1,973	1,954	3,803	9,477	
For Payments by Previous Employer to Laid-off Workers					
709	598	590	1,368	3,265	
Training[2]					
931	1,299	1,277	2,194	5,701	subsidy
170	233	211	344	958	days (thousands)
Leasing Workers to Others (shuko)[3]					
107	76	87	242	512	subsidy
373	240	203	884	1,700	persons

1. For the period 1983 Apr though 1987 Mar, when the program ended.
2. See table 9.12, note 3.
3. See table 9.12, note 4.
Source: Ministry of Labor, unpublished data

directly to workers. Because the extended payment of employment insurance benefits played a much greater role in depressed regions, aid to workers in depressed regions was not adjustment assistance but income support.

Small Firm Assistance

New elements such as subsidies for worker training and for developing new markets and new technology were introduced. As each region generally had a Small and Medium Enterprise Cooperative, these associations were what qualified to receive subsidies. If a revitalization program submitted to the governor of a prefecture was approved, a subsidy of up to ¥10 million was given, with the central and local governments each providing half. Those small firms designated as eligible also qualified to receive low interest loans through the Small Business Finance Corporation (Chusho Kigyo Kinyu Koko), a governmental financial institution. The fund earmarked for this program was expanded from ¥210 million to ¥300 million in fiscal 1983 and the interest rate was

Table 9.14. Subsidies for Workers in Specified Depressed Regions, Fiscal
1983–87

1983	1984	1985	1986	Cumulative[1]	
Extended Employment Benefits					
5,411	6,950	6,195	6,031	24,587	payments[2]
6,654	6,192	5,516	5,234	23,593	recipients[3]
Unemployed Aged 45–65					
344	533	341	236	1,454	payments[2]
1,193	1,884	1,273	916	5,266	recipients
Re-employment[4]					
6	355	425	254	1,040	payments[2]
61	3,467	4,139	2,371	10,038	recipients

1. For the period 1983 Apr through 1987 Mar, when the program ended.
2. In million yen. Monthly payments per person were ¥70–100 thousand.
3. Average number per month.
4. The Ministry of Labor refers to its training and job preparation program as "re-employment."
Source: Ministry of Labor, unpublished data

set at 7.1% per annum compared with an ordinary rate of 8.1%. The rate was to be raised to 7.8% from the fourth year of the program.

Other policy instruments were similar to those under the previous law. While 30 regions (coterminous with the same number of municipalities) were eligible under the 1978 law, ASME this time specified 53 regions (covering 57 municipalities). Quantitative data suitable for policy evaluation have not been published yet.

A serious defect with adjustment assistance to small firms is that the law does not obligate the government to review policy implementation and effects. Moreover, the government has enacted laws that might duplicate each other. Thus, there is a law (dating from 1976) that also deals with assistance to small and medium-scale enterprises for business conversion. It was revised on its initial expiration in 1986 to run another seven years.

There is also another adjustment assistance law under ASME small and medium firms in regions where producers are specialized in specific products, such as tableware manufacturers in the Tsubame area in Niigata prefecture. The "temporary" law was enacted in July 1979 to be effective for seven years. Under this law the government specified 198 regions eligible to receive special assistance. When the law expired in

July 1986, the program was integrated into the 1983 law covering small and medium-scale enterprises. The most important purpose of the law was assisting small firms seriously injured by the yen's appreciation.

Evaluation of 1983 Policies

Assistance to workers consisted of extended payment of employment insurance benefits and relatively small amounts of subsidy for seeking employment in a growing industry. In this sense it functioned as income support, not adjustment promotion. While per capita assistance for changing jobs was fairly generous, the total amount of the subsidy for it was relatively small. This implies either the number of workers involved in large-scale displacement was small or screening for assistance was strict. However, it is unclear on what criteria such screening was done.

Significantly generous subsidies were given employers who trained, recruited, or even just leased workers. Generous wage subsidies to employers might have made other producers in the same sector absorb the displaced workers, as a study by the Ministry of Labor (1983) reported that most textile workers who changed jobs moved to other enterprises in the same industry. In such a case, employment assistance only shuffled employment within the declining industry, thus protecting the declining sector, even though it promoted intra-industry adjustment. But with such assistance lasting for over a decade, the overall result is "counter-positive adjustment" as far as moving resources out of a declining sector is concerned.

The subsidies to workers through employers might reflect the Japanese business and social climate. Traditionally, workers enjoyed lifetime employment with a seniority wage system. This contributed to group loyalty on the part of the employees. Representatives of company unions and executives of the enterprises thus played a cooperative game, as Aoki (1984, 1987) has pointed out. It was, therefore, an important job of the personnel department of a company to maintain employment and to find new jobs for displaced employees. Under such circumstances, it was not workers but enterprises that had the information collection capability to find new jobs and to train workers. Therefore, it may be more effective to assist enterprises to reduce frictional unemployment. After all, such a policy resulted in subsidizing all firms that recruited these workers.

Although it is important to support business activities in local communities to maintain their economic base, political pressure through Diet members has complicated assistance policies. It is appealing to constituents for their political representatives to obtain subsidies for them from the government, so politicians easily agree to such programs. But this has created a situation where there are many programs to help small firms, and nothing has been done to examine the costs and benefits of them, or even to coordinate them when they overlap.

First, there is assistance to small firms in general, which is not temporary in nature. Second, there is assistance to regional development, also not temporary. Third, there is assistance to declining industries. Thus, the government policy in this field is a mixture of various elements, and they are not necessarily adjustment promoting. It might be more important for the government to give signals to assist than actually to provide systematic assistance. This is so even though the actual spending on these programs is quite low.

Whether small firms should be subsidized or not has been a controversial issue. The size of firms often reflects the nature of technology, and small firms have advantages on their own account, so there is in general no a priori justification for protecting small firms just for being small. Patrick and Rohlen (1987) discuss the political power of small firms and various protections provided them.

The encouragement of mergers and business cooperation was among the new elements of 1983 policy. However, the effects of most joint actions are ambiguous. And, in fact, there does not appear to be any significant difference in the adjustment performance between industries that formed designated cartels and those that did not. To the extent there were mergers, it is unclear if they can be attributed to government policy. One reason the government moved to rescue firms in troubled industries appears to be that the commercial banks that had lent heavily to these firms urged the government to extend assistance. Aid to the firms was thus aid to the banks.

To look at the policies from three criteria—efficiency, equity and stability—it seems government policy was more oriented to stability. Efficiency was often sacrificed for stability, as is seen in the protection of small firms and generous subsidies to individual workers. Equity was ignored when the government gave the preferential job-seeker certificates only to workers displaced on a large scale at one time, as they had usually worked for a large company. It is surprising society accepted such a program. A compensation for such inequity might have contributed to the complicated assistance available to small firms.

Efficiency, though the government officially made it a stated objective of various policy instruments, has not been pursued consistently. Cartel actions tend merely to allocate capacity reductions on a limited equity basis, in that the participants shared the cost equally, ignoring the consumers' burden. Various subsidies resulted in assisting declining sectors to hang on rather than the stated goal of shrinking. Substitution of domestic products with cheaper imports has proceeded only slowly, with import penetration remaining minimal in some sectors.

It was against such a background that Japan avoided large-scale frictional unemployment in the decade 1978–87. However, it was continued domestic demand growth and the resulting creation of new job opportunities, not specific declining industry policies, that made this possible.

THE LATE 1980S AND BEYOND

A rapid appreciation of the yen from the autumn of 1985 through 1987 accelerated foreign direct investment by Japanese enterprises and the importation of manufactured goods. Domestic production stagnated in 1986, before growing again in 1987 and '88. With the government declaring a policy of improving access to Japanese markets for foreign goods, following the Maekawa Reports (1986, 1987), the need for adjustment assistance policies was strengthened, for the longer run if not so much the shorter.

In 1988 MITI revised the 1983 law, which expired in 1987, enacting the Adjustment Facilitation Law. The Employment Assistance Law of 1983 was divided into two laws in March 1987: the Revised Employment Assistance Law for Depressed Industries and the Law for Promotion of Regional Employment. The first is time-limited and the latter is to be permanently effective. ASME revised, in December 1986, the Law for Adjustment Assistance to Small Firms and enacted a Law on Assistance to Business Conversion of Specified Small Firms.

The new laws were enacted only recently, so it is too early to evaluate their effects. In what follows, I confine myself to making a brief review of major changes in policy approach.

The Adjustment Facilitation Law of 1988

A significant change in policy approach is that with the new law the government has abolished the system of designated cartels. Instead, voluntary business cooperation among firms is encouraged, with some preferential financing. According to the Fair Trade Commission (FTC), as mergers and business cooperation per se are not illegal, conduct is to be regulated on a case by case basis. Thus, whether joint actions increase or decrease largely depends on the policy stance of the FTC.

In addition, the law specifies types of equipment to be scrapped, and provides more pecuniary incentives than before. Although the government explains the provisions for scrapping are intended to avoid assisting and protecting specific industries, it seems there is virtually no difference in effects, because the machinery is fairly specific to an industry.

The law strengthens pecuniary incentives to promote (1) business conversion (that is, moving into a growing industry), (2) business partnerships for overcoming difficulty, and (3) new investment in specified depressed regions. The main policy instruments consist of (1) low interest loans by the Japan Development Bank (at a 5% rate) in addition to the credit guarantee already provided, and (2) a reduction of taxes on land purchases and business registration, as well as accelerated depreciation allowances and more generous carryover of losses attributable to capacity scrapping.

Emphasis is placed on investment promotion in depressed regions, the employment effect of which has been significant. Thus, MITI has expanded its involvement into employment, an area previously reserved for the Ministry of Labor.

The list of equipment to be scrapped covers 198 types, including blast, electric, and revolving furnaces for steel; textile machines; various machines for non-ferrous metal mining; as well as those for cement, oxygen extraction, and silk processing (under the supervision of the Ministry of Agriculture).

Employment Assistance Laws of 1987 and 1988

Although the two laws of 1978 were merged in 1983, they were separated again in March 1987 into assistance by industry and by region. The latter was designated the Law on Promotion of Regional Employment and became permanent, while the former is to be effective only until 1995. The reason for this revision was that employment promotion in specific regions was considered a task beyond adjustment assistance. In other words, issues involving regional promotion are felt to be ongoing and to transcend employment adjustment.

As rapidly expanding foreign direct investment by Japanese firms is considered to have reduced employment opportunities in Japan, the law on employment assistance by industry was revised, in July 1988, to cover those displaced by increased overseas investment. The menu of policy instruments remained almost the same as before, however. Thus, the same criticism applies to the revised assistance law: why should those displaced by increased foreign direct investment receive preferential treatment?

Assistance to Small Firms Under the Law of 1986

Assistance for business conversion was provided by the revised law of 1986, which is to be effective for seven years. The policy instruments used are the same as in the preceding laws. According to ASME, industries to be assisted have been divided into two categories: structurally troubled sectors and those that face difficulty only because of the yen's appreciation. The former covers 201 sectors and the latter, 151. The number of sectors is probably overstated as industrial subsectors are counted. Textiles, for instance, is divided into some ten subsectors. To roughly characterize, assistance is provided traditional labor-intensive sectors.

ASME has extended assistance to small firms in 51 regions, which include 216 municipalities. Against the criticism that the government has only diffused subsidies to various regions for political reasons, ASME responded that a strict application of the criteria for selection resulted in picking appropriate regions. In fact, the regions where shipbuilding and textiles are concentrated are designated as eligible, and these are definitely declining industries. The list of specified regions and industries remained similar to those covered by preceding laws.

Major policy changes in the 1988 revision can be summarized as follows:

1. Emphasis was shifted from short-run assistance to declining industries to longer-run assistance to depressed regions. This applies not only to assistance to employment and to small firms, which already were targets of programs, but also to MITI's policy toward large corporations. A most striking change is that MITI has created for itself the task of assisting investment that generates employment opportunities in depressed regions. This suggests the policy framework is not formulated for proper policy goals but is dominated by the interest of the government organizations. As the ministries and agencies try to expand their power, or at least protect their own interests, the probability of policy duplication and complication becomes enormous. A restructuring of the tasks of the government is badly needed.

2. Pecuniary incentives for large corporations were enhanced further. This includes low interest financing and tax reduction for investment in depressed regions. MITI may finally have accepted that administrative guidance and cartel actions are ineffective without pecuniary incentives. The institutional legacy of the 1950s and '60s, such as the Japan Development Bank and the Small Business Finance Corporation, together with the Postal Saving System, which provides financial sources for these governmental financial institutions, supports such a policy approach.

Since these institutions also try to survive and grow, the menu of policy instruments has expanded.

3. A new factor being used for justification of assistance is overseas investment by Japanese firms, as it is considered to have reduced domestic employment. Apart from the equity issue mentioned earlier, there is an identification problem. How can the government identify displacement of workers triggered by overseas investment? Should assistance be limited to those directly damaged by such investment? Why not to the indirectly damaged? When, then, do we have to specify those displaced by overseas investment to receive special treatment vis-à-vis other unemployed?

The patchwork approach by individual ministries and agencies creates a new problem: Suppose a company displaces workers on a large scale due to overseas investment. The company can receive subsidies for retraining and job placement activities for those workers. If the company invests in a specified region with certain employment effects, it is also eligible for preferential financing and tax relief. When the company recruits those who hold job-seeker cards, it benefits from a fairly generous wage subsidy. In short, present policies include a range of subsidies to a company that triggers unemployment!

4. While the system of designated cartels was abolished, government encouragement of business cooperation among domestic producers and distributors remains and poses a danger. Although FTC policy formally determines whether or not concentration actually proceeds, the result is likely to make import penetration more difficult. There will be fewer domestic producers, and they will have well-established distribution systems. Import has been nil or negligible in several declining sectors, regardless of whether or not there have been designated cartels or other admitted joint actions.

It seems the industrial associations in the traditional manufacturing sectors have established strong bonds among domestic producers and distributors. Fertilizer, cement, electric furnace steel, and electrical wire are such examples. Nil or slow import penetration may have alleviated adjustment difficulties for producers, but it was at the expense of users. Before encouraging business cooperation, a thorough examination of the factors that have limited imports should be undertaken.

Future Prospects

A most important factor affecting the future of industrial adjustment in Japan is the exchange rate. Changes in relative prices of natural resources, including oil, are also important, but the scope of influence is limited. In fact, adjustment problems after 1986 have been triggered mostly by the drastic appreciation of the yen. If the value of the yen continues to rise in the 1990s, Japanese industry will have to shift more and more to non-traded sectors. Such a change has actually been taking place. Imports of manufactured goods from NIEs (newly industrialized economies) are taking over the domestic market in a broader category of goods, though the trend is only beginning to appear in trade statistics because of time-lags.

When the Japanese government tried in the 1950s to promote new manufacturing industries such as synthetic fibers and petrochemicals, in addition to steel and automobiles, it took roughly two decades for these sectors to become competitive. Then decline started in the so-called heavy industries including steel, aluminum, and petrochemicals, as well as the traditional labor-intensive manufacturing industries. It is now sensed that standardized manufacturing sectors such as electrical appliances and automobiles have entered a transitional phase to stagnation, if not decline, as far as Japanese onshore production is concerned. Major Japanese companies in these industries are of course now transnational.

While it is dangerous to generalize, promoting new industries can be justified for reducing monopolist or oligopolist rents when the number of participants is limited in international markets. Importation and diffusion of new technology are also pursued through industry-building policies. Thus, industrial policies to promote new industries have some relevance. In these respects, the Japanese government was successful in the 1950s and '60s.

It was easier for the Japanese government and business sectors to pick promising industries when they had the experience of predecessors to go by. This condition has changed since the late 1970s. It has become more difficult to reach a consensus in picking future winners, as industrialists themselves now have to take real risks in exploring promising but uncharted areas. Slower growth after the catch-up process has decreased the growth rate of new job opportunities for those displaced in declining sectors.

Product innovation and introduction of new industries expand the areas where domestic factors of production can be absorbed. Then, the adjustment process goes more smoothly. It seems for this reason MITI now heavily emphasizes the importance of R&D. In the dimension of policy implementation, however, it is difficult to encourage R&D investment in general. MOF has a generic distaste for tax credits, and to avoid abuse of tax incentives the government (MITI) feels it has to identify specific types of R&D, which may lead nowhere. Certainly a general R&D tax credit has had mixed reviews in the United States and elsewhere (see Mansfield 1986, Crawford 1988, and GAO 1989). Consensus policy making approaches have become less and less effective in this sphere.

There is a big contrast between the role MITI played in the 1950s and '60s and what it will be playing in the 1990s. The role of MITI seems to have changed from one of leadership to that of a follower of the private sector, its part increasingly being to take care of troubled industries (often its former growth clients) and regions. Symptoms of change are the growing budgets for employment assistance, for aid to small firms in various forms, and expanded pecuniary incentives for adjustment by large corporations. Politicians seem to play a more important role in such a trend. Dispersion of subsidies, both direct and indirect, to depressed regions and to small firms expands incessantly, as politicians use them for buying votes.

One point of interest is whether the close ties within business groups and parent firm-subcontractor relations will intensify or weaken. In the 1980s, business groups (*keiretsu* and less formal associations) contributed to reducing frictional unemployment through such arrangements as leasing of workers. Firms within trade associations were considered to be willing to maintain markets even at the cost of short-run losses. By maintaining customers relations, refraining from making a more profitable spot transaction, they are viewed as sharing risks among association members. Nakatani (1987) drew such a conclusion from his empirical analyses of the performance of firms that belonged to associations but were otherwise independent. Parent firm-subcontractor relations have a similar aspect.

To the extent such relations among domestic producers and distributors are reduced, the social environment that has facilitated employment reallocation within business groups will change. Then, reallocation of employment will be done in a more individualistic manner with the help of public mediation only. In these circumstances, assistance to employment adjustment in Japan will be more directly aimed at workers and regions, bypassing enterprises.

IMPLICATIONS FOR TRADE

Among the elements of demand for the Japanese yen, that for settlement of trade in goods will continue to expand, whereas that for asset portfolios may not grow so fast because of limited use of yen-denominated assets. Nonetheless, growing demand for the yen through the cumulative current accounts surplus in the balance of payments will lead to a further appreciation, which will be a source of pressure for a further shuffling of industrial composition. Such events as drastic price increases for petroleum and other raw materials, and military conflicts in some regions, have tended to depreciate the yen and these factors may devalue the yen occasionally.

Those policies that result in aiding declining sectors will eventually hurt exporting sectors through an appreciation of the yen. Declining sectors in traded goods will therefore demand further assistance, and a vicious circle will ensue. Finally, growing and exporting sectors will enter into a stagnant phase earlier than otherwise.

Another factor making exporting sectors stagnant earlier is import restrictions imposed by importing countries. In many NIEs, adjustment assistance tasks have been triggered by import restrictions imposed by industrial countries. Many countries try to maintain domestic production of specific goods for political reasons such as national security. While the economic cost of such policies is enormous, the reality seems that politics dominates economics in these areas. So-called managed trade may spread.

Despite such circumstances, the Japanese government has avoided resorting to any overt trade restraints to assist domestic industries. This is the government's response to foreign pressure to make the Japanese market more open, and most Japanese, except farmers, seem to support such a policy. Part of the cost of that support has been the wide variety of adjustment assistance offered by the government.

A controversial issue concerning safeguard mechanisms is selectivity that violates GATT article 19. Against an argument made by some European countries that selective (that is, country-specific) safeguards are allowed, the Japanese government has insisted the article should be strictly construed. As long as adjustment assistance is available, there is no reason to introduce a selective safeguard mechanism, because it is enough to slow down import increases no matter where they come from. Selectivity will only distort trade flows by switching source countries. Thus bilateral restrictions on imports is not consistent with the policy objective of adjustment assistance. If there is unfairness on the side of exporting countries, it can be dealt with under GATT article 6 on anti-dumping, and by other measures.

A factor that makes article 19 not effective may be the obligation on the country in question that it offer compensation to its trading partners. Politically, this seems extremely difficult because the interest groups involved have no reason to accept the burden of compensation for the actions of another industrial sector. As far as adjustment assistance is concerned, it seems there is no need for such compensation, though it may create a problem of abuse. On this point, the stance of the Japanese government is unclear, probably being more faithful to the present article 19.

As long as Japan continues to accumulate a large current account surplus, the government is constrained from resorting to import-restrictive measures, even though sectoral problems differ from overall balance issues. On the domestic front, a large government with a relaxed budget constraint permits the government to maintain the present wide range of assistance.

In more specific terms, the implications of Japanese adjustment assistance for international trade policy can be summarized as follows

First, the government has been proud of not having resorted to safeguards against imports and has officially announced it is against such bilateral arrangements as voluntary export restraints (VERs). Although MITI in fact played an active role in persuading Japanese exporters to accept VERs on the export of color TVs and automobiles to the United States, its official stance has been against VERs.

Responding to criticism that the Japanese market is effectively closed to imports, MITI has argued it is not a result of government policy, but rather, the private sector is responsible for such behavior. This argument is not persuasive, however, because MITI's strategy that domestic producers and distributors promote mergers and business cooperation is likely to strengthen closer ties among domestic units. While the system of designated cartels was abolished, recession cartels and other joint actions may contribute to reducing imports in a climate where the members easily collude with each other. Import monitoring and early warning by each industry division within MITI may also restrain aggressive importing under the rubric of orderly importation.

Although the Japanese government has refrained from taking safeguard measures against imports in general, actually it did resort to a selective safeguard mechanism by requesting voluntary export restraint by Korea and China on silk products. The request was accepted by the two countries.

Moreover, the situation seems to be changing rapidly. The Association of Knitting Industries of Japan in October 1988 brought a dumping lawsuit against imports from Korea. While the case attracted a good deal of attention because the government has not applied counter-dumping measures since 1945, the Korean Association of Textile Export declared on 1 February 1989 that it would implement a VER on members' exports of knitted products to Japan. At the same time, the Japanese party announced dropping of the lawsuit. The minister of MITI commented that MITI welcomed this private agreement between Korea and Japan.

Assistance to employment adjustment might have worked to subsidize declining sectors as many workers with wage subsidies are actually recruited by other firms in the same industry. Since domestic production is larger than otherwise, this results in decreased imports of competing products. Thus, an apparent promotion of industrial adjustment only ends in protecting declining sectors. It is time for the Japanese government to make an overall review of adjustment assistance policies to simplify them and to make policy instruments consistent with policy goals.

Second, increased importation of manufactured goods due to the appreciated yen has given rise to serious concern about unemployment. Indeed, it is not only foreign exporters but Japanese manufacturers that promote importation of these goods. Overseas investment and OEM arrangements (goods produced to specification and sold with the importer's brand name) accelerate importing by Japanese manufacturers.

The government seems to have some contradictory objectives. To recycle the huge overseas surplus and to promote international economic cooperation, it counts on overseas investment in manufacturing; to promote domestic investment, especially in depressed regions, it subsidizes investment in such regions. Whether overseas investment promotes aggressive importing into Japan seems to depend on circumstances. If distributors, and manufacturers with distributing activities, make it a long-run strategy to sell foreign products in the domestic market, they will be a strong interest group to introduce innovation in marketing in the domestic market. However, as some sole import agents also produce close substitutes domestically, they are unlikely to be aggressive importers. So the overall trend is yet to be seen.

Small manufacturers and workers will request safeguard mechanisms against drastic increases of imports. Thus, importers must take into consideration the reaction of these groups, especially when they maintain customers relations with small manufacturers. To make things transparent in the view of foreign exporters, it seems better for the government to make a clear-cut and simple rule for explicit safeguard schemes.

Finally, if the Japanese government pursues a small-government strategy, as former Prime Minister Nakasone did in the face of growing budget deficits, the basic policy approach will have to be re-examined. As the administrative cost of comprehensive assistance programs, especially for small businesses, is enormous, and government failure is unavoidable, it may become more acceptable to slow price changes through time-limited tariffs on imports that displace domestic products, thereby keeping the adjustment subsidy minimal. Then, adjustment assistance will be much simpler, using a safeguard scheme for short-run relief for adjustment.

An important principle in the management of the safeguard mechanism is to assure that imports do in fact grow steadily, following market forces. More specifically, import quotas, if used, should be increased steadily so domestic producers take such increased competition into consideration in their production planning.

The implications of the foregoing for Japan as a trader are as follows. It is abnormal that Japan has no imports in such declining sectors as electric furnace steel, chemical fertilizers, electrical wire, and other products as evidenced in this paper. If there is an implicit safeguard mechanism to restrict imports, it should be changed into an official scheme so that foreign exporters can understand it. Having no import penetration is worse than implementation of safeguard mechanisms.

It should be noted that Japanese government assistance to troubled and (at least partially) to declining industries has been, on the whole, to allow market forces to operate. Until now, essentially no new import restrictions have been imposed by the government, unlike the behavior of most other industrialized nations. For large firms in concentrated industries, the government has been quite successful in arranging, in cooperation with firms, an orderly scrapping of equipment and capacity. For smaller firms, in depressed industries and regions, the efforts have been more ameliorative, encouraging stability and, in more recent years, technological innovation, upgrading of products, and even moving into new businesses. Workers have benefited through job retraining and new job opportunities, as well as supplemental income support.

On the whole these programs have not been expensive. In particular the programs for small businesses and their workers seem surprisingly limited in the amount of money expended and in their impact. It suggests they may have been done more for political reasons of trying to give the appearance of doing something, while in fact doing very little. The major cost may be that of supporting a bureaucracy to administer an increasingly complex and often inconsistent welter of small business programs. Certainly Japan and its trading partners would benefit from a more consistent and transparent approach to the problems of structural adjustment.

Rapid domestic growth in the late 1980s based on sound macroeconomic policies has made the inevitable adjustments to change in comparative advantage and to yen appreciation through the market much easier. The question for the 1990s is whether structural adjustment problems will become severe if manufactured imports continue to grow rapidly; and if that occurs, whether the government will pour substantially more resources into existing programs, or instead will develop new approaches to structural adjustment.

BIBLIOGRAPHY

Aoki, Masahiko. 1984. *The Cooperative Game Theory of the Japanese Firms.* Oxford University Press.

——. 1987. "The Japanese Firm in Transition." In Kozo Yamamura and Yasukichi Yasuba, editors, *The Political Economy of Japan: The Domestic Transformation,* p 263–88. Stanford University Press.

Bhagwati, Jagdish, ed. 1982. *Import Competition and Response.* University of Chicago Press.

British Petroleum. 1977. *Our Industry: Petroleum.* London.

Crawford, Mark. 1988. "Industries Lobby Hard for R&D Tax Credit." *Science* 239: 858 (Feb 19).

GAO = US General Accounting Office. 1989. *Tax Policy and Administration: The Research Tax Credit Has Stimulated Some Additional Research Spending.* GAO/GGD 89 114 (Sep 5).

IMF (International Monetary Fund). *International Financial Statistics Yearbook.* June 1987 and 1988 issues.

Ito, Motoshige, Kazuharu Kiyono, Masahiro Okuno, and Kotaro Suzumura. 1984. "Economic Theory of Industrial Policy." Part 3 of Ryutaro Komiya et al, editors, which see.

Komiya, Ryutaro. 1975. *Gendai Nihon keizai kenkyu* (Studies in contemporary Japanese economy). Tokyo Daigaku Shuppankai (University of Tokyo Press).

——, Masahiro Okuno, and Kotaro Suzumura, editors. 1984. *Nihon no sangyo seisaku.* Tokyo Daigaku Shuppan Kai (University of Tokyo Press). English translation: 1988 as *Industrial Policy of Japan.* San Diego: Academic Press.

Kosei Torihiki Iinkai (Fair Trade Commission of Japan). 1986. *Nenji hokoku* (White Paper of 1986).

——, Keizai Chosa Kenkyukai (Economic Research Group). 1982 Nov. "Teiseicho Keizaika no sangyo chosei to kyoso seisaku" (Industrial adjustment and competition policy under low economic growth). Processed.

Kosei Torihiki Kyokai (Fair Trade Association), ed. 1982. "Keiza chosakai hokoku: teiseicho keizaika no sangyochosei to kyoso seisaku, tokuni iwayuru kozo fukyo sangyomondai ni tsute" (Economic research group report: industrial adjustment and competition policy under low economic growth, especially in connection with so-called structurally depressed industries). Processed.

Krause, Lawrence B. and Sueo Sekiguchi. 1976. "Japan and the World." In Hugh Patrick and Henry Rosovsky, editors, *Asia's New Giant: How the Japanese Economy Works,* p 383–458. Washington DC: The Brookings Institution.

Lapan, Harvey. 1976. "International Trade, Factor Market Distortions, and the Optimal Dynamic Subsidy." *American Economic Review* 66(3): 335–46 (Jun).

Maekawa Report, 1986. Formal English title: "The Report of the Advisory Group on Economic Structural Adjustment for International Harmony Submitted to the Prime Minister on April 7." Tokyo. Processed.

———, 1987. Formal English title: "The Report of the Advisory Group on Economic Restructuring Submitted to the Prime Minister on April 23." Tokyo. Processed.

Mansfield, Edwin. 1986. "The R&D Tax Credit and Other Technology Policy Issues." *American Economic Review* 76(2): 190 (May).

Ministry of Labor, see Rodo-sho.

MITI, see Tsushyo Sangyo-sho.

Miwa, Yoshiaki. 1984. "Sangyonai chosei" (Intra-industry adjustment). In Ryutaro Komiya et al, editors, which see. In the English translation, this is chapter 18: "Coordination Within Industry."

Mussa, Michael. 1982. "Government Policy and the Adjustment Process." In Jagdish Bhagwati, editor, *Import Competition and Response*, p 73–120. University of Chicago Press.

Nakatani, Iwao. 1987. "The Economic Role of Financial Corporate Grouping." In Masahiko Aoki, editor, *The Economic Analysis of the Japanese Firms*, p 227–58. Amsterdam: North-Holland.

Neary, J. P. 1982. "Intersectoral Capital Mobility, Wage Stickiness, and the Case for Adjustment Assistance." In Jagdish Bhagwati, editor, *Import Competition and Response*, p 39–67. University of Chicago Press.

Nihon Kanzei Kyokai (Japan Tariff Association). *Jikko kanzeiritsu hyo* (Customs Tariff Schedule of Japan). 1979, 1983, and 1988 issues. Tokyo: Japan Tariff Association.

Patrick, Hugh T. and Thomas P. Rohlen. 1987. "Small-Scale Family Enterprises." In Kozo Yamamura and Yasukichi Yasuba, editors, *The Political Economy of Japan: The Domestic Transformation*, p 331–84. Stanford University Press.

Peck, Merton J., Richard C. Levin, and Akira Goto. 1987. "Picking Losers: Public Policy toward Declining Industries in Japan." *Journal of Japanese Studies* 13(1): 79–123 (Jan).

Rodo-sho (Ministry of Labor). *Rodo tokei nenkan* (Yearbook of Labor Statistics). 1977, 1982, and 1987 issues.

———. 1983. "Tokutei hukyo gyoshu rishokusya no saishushokuto no jittai" (A trace of re-employment of those who were displaced in the specified depressed industries). *Shokugyo antei koho* (Bulletin of employment stabilization) v 34 # 18. Koyo seisakuka, Rodo-sho (Employment Policy Section, Ministry of Labor).

Sekiguchi, Sueo. 1976. "Industrial Adjustment Policies in Japan." In Organization for Economic Cooperation and Development (OECD), *Adjustment for Trade: Studies in Industrial Adjustment Problems and Policies*. Paris: OECD.

———. 1985. "Hukyo karutero no keizai bunseki" (Economic analysis of recession cartels). The Institute of Social and Economic Research, Osaka University, Discussion Paper 132.

—— and Toshihiro Horiuchi. 1984. "Trade and Adjustment Assistance." In Ryutaro Komiya et al, editors, which see.

—— and Atsuko Matsumura. 1985. "Yushutunyu niokeru kyodo koi" (Joint actions in export and import: Conducts of Associations of Import and Export). The Institute of Social and Economic Research, Osaka University, Discussion Paper 134.

Tsushyo Sangyo-sho, Sangyo Seisaku-kyoku (MITI, Bureau of Industrial Policy). 1988 Mar. "Tokutei sangyo kozo kaizen rinjisoti-ho shiko jyokyo" (Policy implementation under the Structural Improvement Law). Processed.

Yamazawa, Ippei. 1984. "The Textile Industry." In Ryutaro Komiya et al editors, which see.

Yonezawa, Yoshie. 1984. "The Shipbuilding Industry." In Ryutaro Komiya et al, editors, which see.

INDEX

This index is organized around industrial topics, thus the Pacific Basin countries do not appear as main entries but only as sub and sub-sub entries.

The case study industries are listed on page 4 table 2.

All statistical tables are indexed being indicated by the "t" after the page number.

STUDIES OF THE EAST ASIAN INSTITUTE

The Ladder of Success in Imperial China, by Ping-ti Ho. New York: Columbia University Press, 1962.

The Chinese Inflation, 1937–1949, by Shun-hsin Chou. New York: Columbia University Press, 1963.

Reformer in Modern China: Chang Chien, 1853–1926, by Samuel Chu. New York: Columbia University Press, 1965.

Research in Japanese Sources: A Guide, by Herschel Webb with the assistance of Marleigh Ryan. New York: Columbia University Press, 1965.

Society and Education in Japan, by Herbert Passin. New York: Teachers College Press, 1965.

Agricultural Production and Economic Developments in Japan, 1873–1922, by James I. Nakamura. Princeton: Princeton University Press, 1967.

Japan's First Modern Novel: Ukigumo Of Futabatei Shimei, by Marleigh Ryan. New York: Columbia University Press, 1967.

The Korean Communist Movement, 1918–1948, by Dae-Sook Suh. Princeton: Princeton University Press, 1967.

The First Vietnam Crisis, by Melvin Gurtov. New York: Columbia University Press, 1967.

Cadres, Bureaucracy, and Political Power in Communist China, by A. Doak Barnett. New York: Columbia University Press, 1968.

The Japanese Imperial Institution in the Tokugawa Period, by Herschel Webb. New York: Columbia University Press, 1968.

Higher Education and Business Recruitment in Japan, by Koya Azumi. New York: Teachers College Press, 1969.

The Communists and Peasant Rebellions: A Study in the Rewriting Of Chinese History, by James P. Harrison, Jr. New York: Atheneum, 1969.

How the Conservatives Rule Japan, by Nathaniel B. Thayer. Princeton: Princeton University Press, 1969.

Aspects of Chinese Education, edited by C. T. Hu. New York: Teachers College Press, 1970.

Documents of Korean Communism, 1918–1948, by Dae-Sook Suh. Princeton: Princeton University Press, 1970.

Japanese Education: A Bibliography of Materials in the English Language, by Herbert Passin. New York: Teachers College Press, 1970.

Economic Development and the Labor Market in Japan, by Koji Taira. New York: Columbia University Press, 1970.

The Japanese Oligarchy and the Russo-Japanese War, by Shumpei Okamoto. New York: Columbia University Press, 1970.

Imperial Restoration in Medieval Japan, by H. Paul Varley. New York: Columbia University Press, 1971.

Japan's Postwar Defense Policy, 1947–1968, by Martin E. Weinstein. New York: Columbia University Press, 1971.

Election Campaigning Japanese Style, by Gerald L. Curtis. New York: Columbia University Press, 1971.

China and Russia: The "Great Game," by O. Edmund Clubb. New York: Columbia University Press, 1971.

Money and Monetary Policy in Communist China, by Katharine Huang Hsiao. New York: Columbia University Press, 1971.

The District Magistrate in Late Imperial China, by John R. Watt. New York: Columbia University Press, 1972.

Law And Policy in China's Foreign Relations: A Study of Attitude and Practice, by James C. Hsiung. New York: Columbia University Press, 1972.

Pearl Harbor as History: Japanese-American Relations, 1931–1941, edited by Dorothy Borg and Shumpei Okamoto, with the assistance of Dale K. A. Finlayson. New York: Columbia University Press, 1973.

Japanese Culture: A Short History, by H. Paul Varley. New York: Praeger, 1973.

Doctors in Politics: The Political Life of the Japan Medical Association, by William E. Steslicke. New York: Praeger, 1973.

The Japan Teachers Union: A Radical Interest Group in Japanese Politics, by Donald Ray Thurston. Princeton: Princeton University Press, 1973.

Japan's Foreign Policy, 1868–1941: A Research Guide, edited by James William Morley. New York: Columbia University Press, 1974.

Palace and Politics in Prewar Japan, by David Anson Titus. New York: Columbia University Press, 1974.

The Idea of China: Essays in Geographic Myth and Theory, by Andrew March. Devon, England: David and Charles, 1974.

Origins of the Cultural Revolution, by Roderick MacFarquhar. New York: Columbia University Press, 1974.

Shiba Kokan: Artist, Innovator, and Pioneer in the Westernization of Japan, by Calvin L. French. Tokyo: Weatherhill, 1974.

Insei: Abdicated Sovereigns in the Politics of Late Heian Japan, by G. Cameron Hurst. New York: Columbia University Press, 1975.

Embassy at War, by Harold Joyce Noble. Edited with an introduction by Frank Baldwin, Jr. Seattle: University of Washington Press, 1975.

Rebels and Bureaucrats: China's December 9ers, by John Israel and Donald W. Klein. Berkeley: University of California Press, 1975.

Deterrent Diplomacy, edited by James William Morley. New York: Columbia University Press, 1976.

House United, House Divided: the Chinese Family in Taiwan, by Myron L. Cohen. New York: Columbia University Press, 1976.

Escape from Predicament: Neo-Confucianism and China's Evolving Political Culture, by Thomas A. Metzger. New York: Columbia University Press, 1976.

Cadres, Commanders, and Commissars: the Training of the Chinese Communist Leadership, 1920–45, by Jane L. Price. Boulder, Colo.: Westview Press, 1976.

Sun Yat-Sen: Frustrated Patriot, by C. Martin Wilbur. New York: Columbia University Press, 1977.

Japanese International Negotiating Style, by Michael Blaker. New York: Columbia University Press, 1977.

Contemporary Japanese Budget Politics, by John Creighton Campbell. Berkeley: University of California Press, 1977.

The Medieval Chinese Oligarchy, by David Johnson. Boulder, Colo.: Westview Press, 1977.

The Arms of Kiangnan: Modernization in the Chinese Ordnance Industry, 1860–1895, by Thomas L. Kennedy. Boulder, Colo.: Westview Press, 1978.

Patterns of Japanese Policymaking: Experiences from Higher Education, by T. J. Pempel. Boulder, Colo.: Westview Press, 1978.

The Chinese Connection: Roger S. Greene, Thomas W. Lamont, George E. Sokolsky, and American-East Asian Relations, by Warren I. Cohen. New York: Columbia University Press, 1978.

Militarism in Modern China: The Career of Wu P'ei-Fu, 1916–1939, by Odoric Y. K. Wou. Folkestone, England: Dawson, 1978.

A Chinese Pioneer Family: The Lins of Wu-Feng, by Johanna Meskill. Princeton: Princeton University Press, 1979.

Perspectives On a Changing China, edited by Joshua A. Fogel and William T. Rowe. Boulder, Colo.: Westview Press, 1979.

The Memoirs of Li Tsung-Jen, by T. K. Tong and Li Tsung-jen. Boulder, Colo.: Westview Press, 1979.

Unwelcome Muse: Chinese Literature in Shanghai and Peking, 1937–1945, by Edward Gunn. New York: Columbia University Press, 1979.

Yenan and the Great Powers: The Origins of Chinese Communist Foreign Policy, by James Reardon-Anderson. New York: Columbia University Press, 1980.

Uncertain Years: Chinese-American Relations, 1947–1950, edited by Dorothy Borg and Waldo Heinrichs. New York: Columbia University Press, 1980.

The Fateful Choice: Japan's Advance into Southeast Asia, edited by James William Morley. New York: Columbia University Press, 1980.

Tanaka Giichi and Japan's China Policy, by William F. Morton. Folkestone, England: Dawson, 1980; New York: St. Martin's Press, 1980.

The Origins of the Korean War: Liberation and the Emergence of Separate Regimes, 1945–1947, by Bruce Cumings. Princeton: Princeton University Press, 1981.

Class Conflict in Chinese Socialism, by Richard Curt Kraus. New York: Columbia University Press, 1981.

Education Under Mao: Class and Competition in Canton Schools, by Jonathan Unger. New York: Columbia University Press, 1982.

Private Academies of Tokugawa Japan, by Richard Rubinger. Princeton: Princeton University Press, 1982.

Japan and the San Francisco Peace Settlement, by Michael M. Yoshitsu. New York: Columbia University Press, 1982.

New Frontiers in American-East Asian Relations: Essays Presented to Dorothy Borg, edited by Warren I. Cohen. New York; Columbia University Press, 1983.

The Origins of the Cultural Revolution: II, The Great Leap Forward, 1958–1960, by Roderick MacFarquhar. New York: Columbia University Press, 1983.

The China Quagmire: Japan's Expansion of the Asian Continent, 1933–1941, edited by James William Morley. New York: Columbia University Press, 1983.

Fragments of Rainbows: The Life and Poetry of Saito Mokichi, 1882–1953, by Amy Vladeck Heinrich. New York: Columbia University Press, 1983.

The U.S.-South Korean Alliance: Evolving Patterns of Security Relations, edited by Gerald L. Curtis and Sung-joo Han. Lexington, Mass.: Lexington Books, 1983.

Discovering History in China: American Historical Writing on the Recent Chinese Past, by Paul A. Cohen. New York: Columbia University Press, 1984.

The Foreign Policy of the Republic of Korea, edited by Youngnok Koo and Sungjoo Han. New York: Columbia University Press, 1984.

State and Diplomacy in Early Modern Japan, by Ronald Toby. Princeton: Princeton University Press, 1983.

Japan and the Asian Development Bank, by Dennis Yasutomo. New York: Praeger Publishers, 1983.

Japan Erupts: The London Naval Conference and the Manchurian Incident, edited by James W. Morley. New York: Columbia University Press, 1984.

Japanese Culture, third edition, revised, by Paul Varley. Honolulu: University of Hawaii Press, 1984.

Japan's Modern Myths: Ideology in the Late Meiji Period, by Carol Gluck. Princeton: Princeton University Press, 1985.

Shamans, Housewives, and other Restless Spirits: Women in Korean Ritual Life, by Laurel Kendell. Honolulu: University of Hawaii Press, 1985.

Human Rights in Contemporary China, by R. Randle Edwards, Louis Henkin, and Andrew J. Nathan. New York: Columbia University Press, 1986.

The Pacific Basin: New Challenges for the United States, edited by James W. Morley. New York: Academy of Political Science, 1986.

The Manner of Giving: Strategic Aid and Japanese Foreign Policy, by Dennis T. Yasutomo. Lexington, Mass.: Lexington Books, 1986.

Security Interdependence in the Asia Pacific Region, James W. Morley, Ed., Lexington, MA-DC: Heath and Co, 1986.

China's Political Economy: The Quest for Development Since 1949, by Carl Riskin. Oxford: Oxford University Press, 1987.

Anvil of Victory: The Communist Revolution in Manchuria, by Steven I. Levine. New York: Columbia University Press, 1987.

Single Sparks: China's Rural Revolutions, edited by Kathleen Hartford and Steven M. Goldstein. Armonk, N.Y.: M. E. Sharpe, 1987.

Urban Japanese Housewives: At Home and in the Community, by Anne E. Imamura. Honolulu: University of Hawaii Press, 1987.

China's Satellite Parties, by James D. Seymour. Armonk, N.Y.: M. E. Sharpe, 1987.

The Japanese Way of Politics, by Gerald. L. Curtis. New York: Columbia University Press, 1988.

Border Crossings: Studies in International History, by Christopher Thorne. Oxford & New York: Basil Blackwell, 1988.

The Indochina Tangle: China's Vietnam Policy, 1975–1979, by Robert S. Ross. New York: Columbia University Press, 1988.

Remaking Japan: The American Occupation as New Deal, by Theodore Cohen, Herbert Passin, ed. New York: The Free Press, 1987.

Kim Il Sung: The North Korean Leader, by Dae-Sook Suh. New York: Columbia University Press, 1988.

Japan And The World, 1853–1952: A Bibliographic Guide to Recent Scholarship in Japanese Foreign Relations, by Sadao Asada. New York: Columbia University Press, 1988.

Contending Approaches to the Political Economy of Taiwan, edited by Edwin A. Winckler and Susan Greenhalgh. Armonk, NY: M. E. Sharpe, 1988.

Aftermath of War: Americans and the Remaking of Japan, 1945–1952, by Howard B. Schonberger. Kent: Kent State University Press, 1989.

Suicidal Narrative in Modern Japan: The Case of Dazai Osamu, by Alan Wolfe. Princeton: Princeton University Press, 1990.

Neighborhood Tokyo, by Theodore C. Bestor. Stanford: Stanford University Press, 1989.

Missionaries of the Revolution: Soviet Advisers and Chinese Nationalism, by C. Martin Wilbur Julie Lien-ying How. Cambridge, MA: Harvard University Press, 1989.

Education in Japan, by Richard Rubinger and Beauchamp. Honolulu: University of Hawaii, 1989.

Financial Politics in Contemporary Japan, by Frances Rosenbluth. Ithaca: Cornell University Press, 1989.

Thailand and the United States: Development, Security and Foreign Aid by Robert Muscat. New York: Columbia University Press, 1990.

State Power, Finance and Industrialization of Korea, by Jung-Eun Woo. New York: Columbia University Press, 1990.

Anarchism and Chinese Political Culture, by Peter Zarrow. New York: Columbia University Press, 1990.

Competitive Ties: Subcontracting in the Japanese Automotive Industry, by Michael Smitka. New York: Columbia University Press, 1990.

China's Crisis: Dilemmas of Reform and Prospects for Democracy, by Andrew J. Nathan. Columbia University Press, 1990.

The Study of Change: Chemistry in China 1840–1949, by James Reardon-Anderson. New York: Cambridge University Press, 1991.

Explaining Economic Policy Failure: Japan and the 1969–1971 International Monetary Crisis, by Robert Angel. New York: Columbia University Press, 1991.

Pacific Basin Industries in Distress: Structural Adjustment and Trade Policy in the Nine Industrialized Economies, edited by Hugh T. Patrick with Larry Meissner. New York: Columbia University Press, 1991.

From Bureaucratic Polity to Liberal Corporatism: Business Associations and the New Political Economy of Thailand, by Anek Laothamatas. Boulder, Co.: Westview Press, 1991.